WORLD OF
IDEAS

————❦————

*ESSENTIAL READINGS
FOR COLLEGE WRITERS*

ALSO WRITTEN OR EDITED BY LEE A. JACOBUS

Improving College Reading, Fifth Edition, 1988

Aesthetics and the Arts, 1968

Issues and Response, 1968, 1972

Developing College Reading, Fourth Edition, 1990

Seventeen from Everywhere: Short Stories from around the World, 1971

Poems in Context (with William Moynihan), 1974

John Cleveland: A Critical Study, 1975

The Humanities through the Arts (with F. David Martin), Fourth Edition, 1990

The Sentence Book, Third Edition, 1989

The Paragraph and Essay Book, 1977

Sudden Apprehension: Aspects of Knowledge in Paradise Lost, 1976

Longman Anthology of American Drama, 1982

Humanities: The Evolution of Values, 1986

Writing as Thinking, 1989

The Bedford Introduction to Drama, 1989

Third Edition

A
WORLD OF
IDEAS

———❦———

ESSENTIAL READINGS
FOR COLLEGE WRITERS

EDITED BY
LEE A. JACOBUS
University of Connecticut

Bedford Books of St. Martin's Press
BOSTON

For Bedford Books
Publisher: Charles H. Christensen
Associate Publisher: Joan E. Feinberg
Managing Editor: Elizabeth M. Schaaf
Developmental Editor: Stephen A. Scipione
Production Editor: Mary Lou Wilshaw
Copyeditor: Kathryn Blatt
Text Design: Anna Post George
Portraits: Anatoly Dverin, Lyrl C. Ahern, and Bill Ogden, PC & F,
  Incorporated
Cover Design: Hannus Design Associates
Cover: François Bonvin, *Still Life,* 1876. National Gallery, London

Library of Congress Catalog Card Number: 88–63093
Copyright © 1990 by Bedford Books of St. Martin's Press

Manufactured in the United States of America.
4 3 2 1 0
f e d c b

For information, write: St. Martin's Press, Inc.
175 Fifth Avenue, New York, NY 10010

Editorial Offices: Bedford Books of St. Martin's Press
29 Winchester Street, Boston, MA 02116

ISBN: 0–312–02011–2

Acknowledgments

Aristotle. "Tragedy and the Emotions of Pity and Fear." From *Poetics,* translated by Gerald F.
  Else. Copyright © 1967 by the University of Michigan. Used by permission of the University of Michigan Press.
St. Augustine. "Memory and the Happy Life." Selection is reprinted from *The Confessions of
  St. Augustine,* translated and edited by J. G. Pilkington. Copyright 1927 by Boni & Liver-
  ight; copyright renewed 1955.
Marcus Aurelius. "Stoicism and Self-Discipline." From *Meditations* by Marcus Aurelius, translated by Maxwell Staniforth (Penguin Classics, 1964). Copyright © 1964 by Maxwell Staniforth. Reproduced by permission of Penguin Books Ltd.

*Acknowledgments and copyrights are continued at the back of the book on pages 751–752,
which constitute an extension of the copyright page.*

PREFACE

When I describe this book to friends, I often say that it includes selections from Plato, Aristotle, Darwin, Wollstonecraft, Douglass, Freud, and no one less important. Although that is a mild exaggeration, it is very close to the truth. When the first edition of *A World of Ideas* was published, the notion that students in first-year composition courses ought to be able to read and write about challenging works by great thinkers was a radical one. I expected that the choice of selections in this book would appeal to a small minority of people who, like me, regard the first college composition course as a chance (for too many students, alas, the only chance) to introduce some of the significant ideas of our culture. To my delight, there were more of us than I had thought, and each year our ranks appear to be swelling.

All of the selections in this volume are of the highest quality. Each was chosen for its importance, range of thought, and capacity to sustain discussion and stimulate good writing. Unlike most composition anthologies that include such figures, this one does not offer two pages of Bacon, four pages of Kuhn, and a page-and-a-half of Aristotle. Instead, every writer is represented by as complete a selection as is practicable, averaging about fifteen pages in length. The selections are not edited to fit, but instead all of the arguments are developed completely as the authors wrote them. Developing a serious idea takes time. Most students respect the fact that the further you read in the work of an important thinker, the better is your grasp of its ideas.

New in This Edition

All of the more than one hundred instructors who responded to questionnaires about the second edition wanted the book improved—but no one wanted it changed. This presented me with a pleasant dilemma. Those instructors who had written to tell me that they were still successfully teaching selections from the first edition will be pleased that some of those favorites have returned. Many users of the book wrote to suggest that more women writers be included, an intention of mine already. With the addition of four new selections to this edition, there are more women represented than ever before. The inclusion of selections from Asian thinkers also makes the book more truly representative of the "world" of ideas.

The third edition now contains thirty-six readings, with twelve of them new and two restored from the first edition. The new authors include Loren Eiseley, Charlotte Perkins Gilman, Mary Daly, Lao-Tzu, José Ortega y Gasset, Lucretius, Marcus Aurelius, St. Augustine, Simone de Beauvoir, and Siddhārtha Gautama, the Buddha. New selections were chosen to represent John Maynard Keynes and Carl Jung. Restored authors include Friedrich Nietzsche and Mary Wollstonecraft.

The readings in each part of the book now focus on broad questions of timeless importance, such as Part One's "Must the need for a stable social order conflict with the need for individual liberty?" These questions, which in some form or other we have all put to ourselves, provide an interrogative context from which students can approach the selections and understand areas of connection among them. The universality of these questions reflects and emphasizes the enduring significance of the selections themselves. Finally, the coverage of critical reading has been expanded by two sections on evaluating ideas and writing about ideas.

A Text for Readers and Writers

Introductions to Evaluating and Writing About Ideas. "Evaluating Ideas: An Introduction to Critical Reading" concentrates on techniques that students can use to make the ideas of great thinkers meaningful. Because this is, and always has been, a reader for writers, I try to emphasize ways in which the text can be read in order to develop ideas for writing. The best method for developing such ideas is annotating the text carefully—establishing both a dialogue with the text as well as a system for retrieving ideas formulated during that dialogue. In this section, I offer an example of a portion of Machiavelli's essay on "The Qualities of the Prince" in an annotated form. The annotations are discussed for their own usefulness and for techniques by which similar annotations can be developed while reading other essays in the book. Annotation is the key to critical reading.

At the back of the book, "Writing About Ideas: An Introduction to Rhetoric" explains how a reader can apply the procedures of annotation in order to perform the critical thinking that results in a good written response to the ideas in any of the selections in the book. This section relies on the annotations of the Machiavelli selection expounded in "Evaluating Ideas: An Introduction to Critical Reading." A sample essay on Machiavelli, using all of the techniques taught in the context of reading and writing, gives students an idea of how they might write their own material. In addition, this section helps students understand how they can put to work some of the basic rhetorical principles discussed throughout the book.

Introductions for Each Selection. Each selection is preceded by a detailed introduction to the life and work of the author, as well as comments about the selection's primary ideas. The most interesting rhetorical achievements of the selection are also identified and discussed, with an eye toward helping the student discover how rhetorical techniques can achieve specific effects. These essays all offer useful models for writing: Douglass and Eiseley representing narrative; Machiavelli and Darwin, example; Bacon and Daly, enumeration; Kuhn, cause and effect. They are the kinds of models that beginning writers find useful: models of thought and models of structure—in other words, the materials of invention and arrangement.

Suggestions for Discussion and Writing. At the end of each essay is a group of discussion questions designed for use inside or outside the classroom. While they focus on key issues and ideas, they are also designed to stimulate a general discussion. Suggestions for writing that help the student practice some of the rhetorical strategies employed by the author follow. These suggestions range from personal responses to complete essays that involve research and comparison or contrast with other essays in the anthology.

Instructor's Manual. I have also prepared an extensive manual, *Resources for Teaching A World of Ideas*, that contains further background on the selections, examples from my own classroom responses to the authors, and more suggestions for classroom discussion as well as student writing assignments. A sentence outline for each selection has been carefully prepared by Carol Verburg and Ellen Troutman and can be photocopied and handed out to students. The idea came from Darwin's own phrase outlines preceding each chapter of *On the Origin of Species.* These outlines may be used to go over the more difficult selections. A sentence outline offers guidance for the cautious student. At the end of the manual, I have provided brief bibliographies for all thirty-six authors. These bibliographies can be photocopied and distributed to those students who wish to explore the primary selections in more depth.

Acknowledgments

One of the most helpful suggestions for revising this edition came from Michael Bybee at the University of Oregon. He was so concerned that I include Asian thinkers in this edition that he sent me many fascinating pieces to read, all of which he had taught to his own students in conjunction with the second edition. As a result of our mutual concern, the third edition contains two important selections, one by Lao-Tzu, and another by Siddhārtha Gautama, the Buddha, as interpreted by Buddhist monks.

An Asian-American student had also written to encourage me to include such pieces. One of my student contacts from the People's Republic of China spent a year at the University of Connecticut, using the second edition in his work with American students. He is now translating the book into Chinese for publication in China and plans to use it to teach university classes in Shanghai.

This edition, like its predecessors, is especially indebted to those at Bedford Books of St. Martin's Press who lavished a great deal of care and attention on every detail: Charles H. Christensen, Joan E. Feinberg, Elizabeth M. Schaaf, my editor Steve Scipione, Mary Lou Wilshaw, Kathryn Blatt, Jane Betz, Sarah Royston, Constance Mayer, and Paula Spencer. I want to thank Anatoly Dverin, Lyrl Ahem, and Bill Ogden of PC & F, Incorporated, for their wonderful portraits, which have added a special human touch to the book. I also want to thank the students—quite a few of them—who wrote me directly about their experience reading the first two editions. I have paid attention to all that they said and I am warmed by their regard for the high quality of the material in this book.

Among the professors who respect quality and who were immensely generous with their criticism and praise, the following provided me with detailed recommendations for improving this and the second edition. A good number of them have spoken with me personally about their experiences with the book. I only hope they feel that their efforts were worthwhile. These people are Victoria Aarons, Trinity University; E. Abdon, Community College of Allegheny County; Susan Albertine, St. Olaf College; Stephen E. Alford, Nova College; Le Roy E. Annis, University of Puget Sound; Vern Bailey, Carleton College; Craig Barrow, University of Tennessee, Chattanooga; John Batty-Sylvan, City College of San Francisco; Stephen Bauer, College of New Rochelle; Adrian Beaudoin, Florida Junior College; L. Bensel-Meyers, University of Tennessee; Helle Bering-Jensen, Tufts University; Boyd U. Berry, Virginia Commonwealth University; Thomas N. Biuso, Colby-Sawyer College; C. S. Blinderman, Clark University; Don Blount, University of Southern Carolina, Aiken; Carol A. Bock, University of Minnesota, Duluth; Thomas F. Bonnell, Saint Mary's College; Jennifer Bradley, University of California at Los Angeles; William Brevda, Central Michigan University; William K. Buckley, Indiana University Northwest; Neal H. Burns, University of Massachusetts; Margaret N. Butler, Millersville University; Phil Carman, School of the Ozarks; William K. Carpenter, Fort Hays State University; Michael Cass, Mercer University; Gregory Castle, University of California, Los Angeles; Dennis Chaldecott, California State University, San Jose; Dr. M. G. Chaney, Weber State College; Dr. Miriam Cheiken, Nassau Community College; Donna R. Cheney, Weber State College; Wilma Clark, University of Wisconsin, Eau Claire; Michael Clarke, Loyola University; Robert W. Cochran, University of Vermont, Burlington; Alfred Cohn, New College of Hofstra; Camille Colatosti, University of Michigan; David D. Cooper, University of California, Santa Barbara; William Cooper, Allan Hancock College; Steffie Corcoran, Oklahoma State University; Taylor Corse, University of Tennessee at Martin; Raymond Craig, University of California, Davis; Eileen Crawford, University of the District of Columbia; Douglas E. Crowell, Texas Tech University; Nancy Daggett, Aims Community College; Carole Kiler Dareski, Keene State College; Harold E. Davis, Angelo State University; Elmore J. DeGrange, Southern University, New Orleans; L. Dessner, University of Toledo; Robert Di Chiara, Nassau Community College; John A. R. Dick, University of Texas, El Paso; Grace Donovan, Stonehill College; Nan Dougherty, University of Wisconsin, Eau Claire; Crystal Downing, University of California, Santa Barbara; Marya M. Dubose, Augusta College; Maurice DuQuesnay, University of Southwestern Louisiana; Robert R. Edwards, State University of New York at Buffalo; James M. Eldred, University of Illinois, Champaign-Urbana; Judith H. Elmusa, Suffolk University; Audrey Ellwood, Merritt College; Edward Eriksson, Suffolk Community College; Richard Fabrizio, Pace University; Mark Fachnitz, James Madison University; J. M. Fenwick, Anne Arundel Community College; Dr. Susan French Ferguson, Mountain View College; Norman Finkelstein, Xavier University; Richard J. Finneran, Tulane University; Elinor C. Flewellen, Santa Barbara City College; Arend Flick, University of California, Santa Barbara; Jane Follis, Indiana State University, Evansville; Milton P. Foster, Eastern Michigan University; Reinhard Friederich, University of Hawaii at Manoa; Robert H. Garner, Southern University, New Orleans; Jonathan A. Glenn, Holy Cross Junior College; Arthur Wayne Glowka, Georgia College; Janet E. Goebel, Indiana University of Pennsylvania; Robert Golden, Rochester Institute of Technology; Myrna Goldenberg, Montgomery College; Ellen Goldner, Brandeis University; George Goodin, Southern Illinois University; Douglas E. Grohne, Western Illinois University; L. M. Grow, Broward Community College; Rachel Hadas, Rutgers University; James Hafley, St. John's University; Virginia S. Hale, University of Hartford; Michael L. Hall, Centenary College; Evelyn Haller, Doane College; V. B. Halpert, Fairleigh Dickinson University; Judith Hayn, Washburn University; M. Hefferon, Marist College; Donald Heidt, College of the Canyons; Gary Heinzel, Austin Community College; Jack Hibbard, St. Cloud State University; James E. Hicks, St. Louis University; Angela Hogne, Middle Tennessee State University; Gail Houston, University of California at Los Angeles; D. Howard, Mesa College; John Hulsman, Rider College; Ann Hurley, Skidmore College; Vernon Hyles, University of Arkansas; David Ihrman, State University of New York, Binghamton; Bob Isaacson, Allan Hancock College; Greg Jacob, Pacific University; Carol Jamieson, Niagara County Community College; Ellwood Johnson, Western Washington University; Howard P. Jones, Allan Hancock College; James H. Jones, Northern Michigan University; Michael Karman, University of Redlands; James Kastely, University of Hawaii, Manoa; Peter Katopes, Adelphi University; Dr. Norm Katz, Harvard University; Jane Kaufman, University of Akron; Cletus Keating, University of Denver; Jill Averil Keen, University of Wisconsin, Plattesville; Elizabeth Keyser, University of California, Santa Barbara;

Kathleen E. Kier, Queens College; James R. Kinzey, Virginia Commonwealth University; Earl D. Kirk, Baker University; Marcelline Krafchick, California State University; Michael P. Kramer, University of California, Davis; Jeanne Krochalis, Pennsylvania State University; Dr. Philip Krummrich, Drury College; John Lamb, Lewis University; Dale Larson, Grays Harbor College; William Lenehan, University of Wisconsin; Steve Levinson, City College of San Francisco; Madelon Lief, Lawrence University; Howard Lord, New College of Hofstra University; Carmine Luisi, Brooklyn College; Richard Lunt, State University of New York, Potsdam; Rosemary Lyons-Chase, Columbia-Greene Community College; Patricia MacDonald, Palomar College; Raymond MacKenzie, Mankato State University; Loralee MacPike, California State University, San Bernardino; Phillip Mahaffey, Texas Tech University; William T. Maraldo, Texas Lutheran College; Dr. Ann Marlowe, Missouri Southern State College; Charles Marr, Edinboro University; Nathalie Marshall-Nadel, Nova University; Steven J. Masello, Aurora University; Stephen Mattson, University of California, Santa Barbara; Clark Mayo, California State University, San Bernardino; Paul McBrearty, St. Louis Community College; Mary McCord, University of Texas, San Antonio; Jessie McCune, Indiana State; W. McMahon, West Kentucky University; Robin McNallie, James Madison University; Stephen Meats, Pittsburg State University; Collin Meissner, University of Notre Dame; Daniel C. Melnick, Cleveland State University; Kathleen Meyer, North Dakota State University; Terry L. Meyers, College of William and Mary; Lloyd Michaels, Allegheny College; Dennis Moore, University of Iowa, Iowa City; Susan Morris, Creighton University; Michael Morrison, University of California at Los Angeles; G. F. Morely Mower, James Madison University; William J. Murphy, Boston University; Peter Neumeyer, San Diego State University; Elizabeth Nist, Utah Valley Community College; Jerome J. Notkin, Hofstra University; Patricia A. Okker, University of Illinois; Leslie Palmer, North Texas State University; James Robert Payne, New Mexico State University; Kathy Phillips, University of Hawaii, Honolulu; James Plath, University of Wisconsin, Milwaukee; Henriette Lazaridis Power, University of Pennsylvania; Cheryl E. Pridgeon, Florida Atlantic University and College of Boca Raton; Richard K. Priebe, Virginia Commonwealth University; Richard J. Prywstowsky, Irvine Valley College; Richard Publow, Illinois Valley Community College; Sura P. Rath, Louisiana State University, Shreveport; Marc L. Ratner, California State University, Hayward;

Richard Reid, Grand Rapids Junior College; Keith Reierstad, Aims Community College; Hugh Remash, Seattle Community College; J. A. W. Rembert, The Citadel; Jack W. Rhodes, The Citadel; Dr. Stanley Rich, University of South Carolina; Gerald Richman, Suffolk University; David E. Robinson, Winona State University; Robert D. Robinson, Ohio Northern University; Anne B. Rogers, Centenary College; Dale H. Ross, Iowa State University; John Rothfork, New Mexico Institute of Mining and Technology; Shirley Samuels, University of California, Berkeley; Marilyn Saveson, Otterbein College; Keith W. Schlegel, Frostburg State College; Judith Schnee, Bentley College; James E. Schonewise, University of Notre Dame; Phillip A. Schreffler, St. Louis Community College, Meramec; Linda G. Schulze, Rutgers University; Elizabeth S. Scott, University of Richmond; Robert Selinski, San Jose State University; Steven R. Serafin, Long Island University; Joan Sevick, Nassau Community College; Kathleen Shaw, Modesto Junior College; Peter Shillingsburg, Mississippi State University; Ronald C. Shumaker, Clarion University, Paul Shuttleworth, Northeast Technical Community College; Gay Sibley, University of Hawaii, Manoa; Dr. Donald J. Silberman, Jersey City State College; Lantz Simpson, Santa Monica College; Carl Singleton, Fort Hays State University; Hassell B. Sledd, Slippery Rock University; Robert A. Smart, Bradford College; Susan Sutton Smith, State University College at Oneonta; Harvey Solganick, Eastfield College; Frank L. Stallings, Northern Kentucky University; Dorothy Sterpka, University of Connecticut, Hartford; Bruce R. Stevenson, MiraCosta College; Matthew R. Stewart, Virginia Polytechnic Institute and State University; J. Michael Stitt, University of Nevada, Las Vegas; Christina C. Stough, California State University; Richard Stracke, Augusta College; Nina Straus, State University of New York, Purchase; Joyce Suellentrop, Kansas Newman College; Andrew Tadie, Seattle University; Tom T. Tashiro, City College of the City University of New York; Samuel J. Tindall, Duquesne University; William N. Tingle, University of California, Santa Barbara; Charles P. R. Tisdale, University of North Carolina; Patricia Tobin, Rutgers University; Patrick Tompkins, Iowa State University; Hector A. Torres, University of New Mexico; Samuel J. Umland, University of Nebraska, Lincoln; John R. Valone, Sacramento City College; Luise van Keuren, Juniata College; Carolyn J. Wall, Holy Cross College; Jane R. Walpole, Piedmont Virginia Community College; Stephen Warner, State University of New York, Fredonia; Lynn Waterhouse, Trenton State College; Philip West, Skidmore College; Lynn K. Whitby, Southern Illinois University; Laurie Calu White, University of North Carolina, Greensboro; Barbara M. Williams, Slippery Rock University; John

S. Williams, University of the Pacific, Stockton; Allison Wilson, Jackson State University; Burton Wilson, University of Miami; William A. Wilson, San Jose State University; William C. Woods, Longwood College; Nancy Yacher, Washburn University; Dr. J. W. Yarbrough, South Dakota State University; Sally B. Young, University of Tennessee at Chattanooga; Todd R. Zeiss, James Madison University; Dr. Edward J. Zimmerman, Canisius College; M. S. Zuckerman, Los Angeles Valley College; Robert Zweig, Queens College.

CONTENTS

PART FOUR
IDEAS IN THE
WORLD OF SCIENCE
CAN WE KNOW THE SECRETS OF NATURE?
HOW CAN WE *KNOW* THAT WE KNOW?

–377–

P A R T   S I X

**IDEAS IN THE
WORLD OF THE ARTS**

SHOULD OUR PROPER RESPONSE TO ART
BE EMOTIONAL OR INTELLECTUAL?

–631–

A
WORLD OF
IDEAS

ESSENTIAL READINGS
FOR COLLEGE WRITERS

EVALUATING IDEAS

---∙∞∙---

An Introduction
to Critical Reading

THE SELECTIONS in this book demand a careful and attentive reading. The authors whose works have changed the way we view our world, our institutions, and ourselves make every effort to communicate their views with clarity and style. But their views are complex and subtle, and as a result, we must train ourselves to read sensitively, responsively, and critically. Critical reading is basic for approaching the readings in this book. Indeed, it is basic for approaching any reading material that deserves serious attention.

Reading critically means reading actively: questioning the premises of the argument, speculating on the ways in which evidence is used, comparing the statements of one writer with those of another, and holding an inner dialogue with the author. These differ completely from the passive reception we employ when we watch television or read lightweight materials. Being an active, participating reader makes it possible to derive the most out of good books.

Critical reading involves most of the processes in the following list:

1. *Prereading:* Developing a sense of what the piece is about and what its general purposes seem to be.

2. *Annotating:* Using a pencil or a pen to mark those passages that seem important enough to return to later. Annotations establish a dialogue between you and the author.
3. *Questioning:* Raising issues that you feel need to be taken into consideration. These may be issues that you feel the author has treated well, or that the author has treated badly. They are issues that you feel are important. Questioning can be done as part of the annotation process.
4. *Reviewing:* Rereading your annotations and underlinings in order to grasp the entire "picture" of what you've just read. Sometimes writing a summary of the piece as you review will make the meaning even clearer.
5. *Forming your own ideas:* The final step consists of reviewing what you have read, developing your own views on the issues, and evaluating the way that the writer presents the issues.

THE PROCESS OF CRITICAL READING

Prereading

Before you read a particular selection, you may find it useful to turn to the beginning of the part in which it appears. There you will find an introduction that discusses the broader issues and questions central to all the selections in the part that may help you to focus your thoughts and formulate your opinions, as you read the essays themselves.

Begin any selection in this book by reading its headnote. Each headnote supplies historical background on the writer, sets the intellectual stage for the ideas that are discussed in the essay, and comments on the main ideas in the essay. The headnotes also introduce the main rhetorical or stylistic methods that the writers use to communicate their thoughts. In the process of reading the headnotes, you will develop an overview that helps prepare you for reading the essays.

This kind of preparation is typical of critical reading. It makes the task of reading more delightful, useful, and much easier. In order to illustrate the usefulness of such preparation, we will use the headnote to Niccolò Machiavelli and part of his essay "The Qualities of the Prince." This essay appears in the part on politics, so we already expect the content to be political. The introduction to Machiavelli provides the following points, each point is followed by the number of the paragraph in which it appears.

1. Machiavelli was an Italian aristocrat in Renaissance Italy. (1)
2. Machiavelli describes the qualities necessary for a prince—that is, any ruler, to maintain power. (2)
3. A weak Italy was prey to the much stronger France at this time. (2)
4. Machiavelli recommends securing power by whatever means necessary and maintaining it. (3)
5. His concern for moralizing or acting out of high moral principle is not great. (3)
6. He supports questionable means of becoming and remaining prince. (3)
7. Machiavelli does not fret over the means used to achieve his ends and sometimes advocates repression, imprisonment, and torture. (3)
8. Machiavelli has been said to have a cynical view of human nature. (4)
9. His rhetorical method is to discuss both sides of an issue: cruelty and mercy; liberality and stinginess. (6)
10. He uses aphorisms to make it seem that he is saying something wise and true. (7)

With these observations in mind, the reader knows that the discussion following will be concerned with politics in Renaissance Italy. The question of ends versus means is central to Machiavelli's discussion, and he does not display the highest ideals regarding the general goodness of people. Yet, because of Machiavelli's rhetorical methods, particularly his use of aphorism, the reader can expect that Machiavelli's argument will be exceptionally persuasive.

Thus, as a critical reader, you will be well advised to keep track of these basic statements from the headnote. You need not accept everything that the headnote expresses, but you should certainly be alert to the issues that will probably be central to your experience of the essay. Remember: it is just as reasonable to question the headnote as it is to question the essay itself.

Before reading the essay in detail, you might develop an overview of its meaning by scanning it quickly. In the case of "The Qualities of the Prince," note the subheadings, such as "On Those Things for Which Men, and Particularly Princes, Are Praised or Blamed." Checking each of the subheadings before you read the entire piece might provide you with a map or guide to the essay.

Annotating and Questioning

The annotations you make as you read a text establish a dialogue between you and the author. You can underline or highlight important statements that you feel help clarify the author's position. They may be statements to which you will want to refer later. Think of them as serving one overriding purpose: to make it possible for you to review the piece and understand its key points without having to reread it entirely.

Your dialogue with the author will be most visible in the margins of the essay, which is one reason the margins in this book are so generous. Take issue with key points or note your assent—the more you annotate, the more you free your imagination to develop your own ideas. My own personal methods involve both notations of agreement and of disagreement. I annotate thoroughly so that after a quick glance I know what the author is saying as well as what I thought of the essay when I read it closely. My annotations help me keep the major points fresh in my mind.

Annotation keeps track both of what the author says and of what our responses are. No one can reduce annotation to a formula—we all do it differently—but it is not a passive act. Reading with a pencil or a pen in hand should become second nature. Without annotations, you often have to reread entire sections of an essay in order to remember the gist of an argument that may once have been clear and understandable but that, after a time lapse, has become part of the fabric of the prose and thus is "invisible." Annotation is the conquest of the invisible; it provides a quick view of the main points that are there.

When you annotate:

Read with a pen or a pencil.

Underline key sentences—for example, definitions and statements of purpose.

Underline key words that appear often.

Note the topic of paragraphs in the margins.

Ask questions in the margins.

Make notes in the margins to remind you to work up ideas later.

Mark passages you might want to quote in your essay.

Keep track of points with which you disagree.

Some sample annotations follow, using the second essay in the book, Niccolò Machiavelli's "The Qualities of the Prince." A sixteenth-century text in translation, *The Prince* is challenging to work with. My annotations appear in the form of underlinings and marginal comments and questions. Only the first few paragraphs appear here, but the entire essay is annotated in my copy of the book.

A Prince's Duty Concerning Military Matters

The prince's profession should be war.

A prince, therefore, must not have any other object nor any other thought, nor must he take anything as his profession but war, its institutions, and its discipline; because that is the only profession which befits one who commands; and it is of such importance that not only does it maintain those who were born princes, but many times it enables men of private station to rise to that position; and, on the other hand, it is evident that when princes have given more thought to personal luxuries than to arms, they have lost their state. And the first way to lose it is to neglect this art; and the way to acquire it is to be well versed in this art.

Examples

Francesco Sforza became Duke of Milan from being a private citizen because he was armed; his sons, since they avoided the inconveniences of arms, became private citizens after having been dukes. For, among the other bad effects it causes, being disarmed

Being disarmed makes you despised. Is this true?

makes you despised; this is one of those infamies a prince should guard himself against, as will be treated below: for between an armed and an unarmed man there is no comparison whatsoever, and it is not reasonable for an armed man to obey an unarmed man willingly, nor that an unarmed man should be safe among armed servants; since, when the former is suspicious and the latter are contemptuous, it is impossible for them to work well together. And therefore, a prince who does not understand military matters, besides the other misfortunes already noted, cannot be esteemed by his own soldiers, nor can he trust them.

He must, therefore, never raise his thought from this exercise of war, and in peacetime he must train himself more than in time of war; this can be done in

*Training
action/mind*

*Knowledge of
terrain*

Two benefits

two ways: one by action, the other by the mind. And as far as actions are concerned, besides keeping his soldiers well disciplined and trained, he must always be out hunting, and must accustom his body to hardships in this manner; and he must also learn the nature of the terrain, and know how mountains slope, how valleys open, how plains lie, and understand the nature of rivers and swamps; and he should devote much attention to such activities. Such knowledge is useful in two ways: first, one learns to know one's own country and can better understand how to defend it; second, with the knowledge and experience of the terrain, one can easily comprehend the characteristics of any other terrain that it is necessary to explore for the first time; for the hills, valleys, plains, rivers, and swamps of Tuscany, for instance, have certain similarities to those of other provinces; so that by knowing the lay of the land in one province one can easily understand it in others. And a prince who lacks this ability lacks the most important quality in a leader; because this skill teaches you to find the enemy, choose a campsite, lead troops, organize them for battle, and besiege towns to your own advantage.

[There follow the examples of Philopoemon, who was always observing terrain for its military usefulness, and a recommendation that princes read histories and learn from them. Three paragraphs are omitted.]

On Those Things for Which Men, and Particularly Princes, Are Praised or Blamed

Now there remains to be examined what should be the methods and procedures of a prince in dealing with his subjects and friends. And because I know that many have written about this, I am afraid that by writing about it again I shall be thought of as presumptuous, since in discussing this material I depart radically from the procedures of others. But since my intention is to write something useful for anyone who understands it, it seemed more suitable to me to search after the effectual truth of the matter rather than its imagined one. And many writers have imagined for themselves republics and principalities that have never been seen nor known to exist in reality; for there is such a gap between how one lives and how one ought to live that anyone who abandons what is done for what ought to be done learns his ruin rather than his preservation: for <u>a man who wishes to make</u> <u>a vocation of being good at all times will come to ruin</u> <u>among so many who are not good.</u> Hence it is necessary for a <u>prince</u> who wishes to maintain his position <u>to learn how not to be good,</u> and to use this knowledge or not to use it according to necessity.

Leaving aside, therefore, the imagined things concerning a prince, and taking into account those that are true, I say that all men, when they are spoken of, and particularly princes, since they are placed on a higher level, are judged by some of these qualities which bring them either <u>blame or praise.</u> And this is why one is considered generous, another miserly (to use a Tuscan word, since "avaricious" in our language is still used to mean one who wishes to acquire by means of theft; we call "miserly" one who excessively avoids using what he has); one is considered a giver, the other rapacious; one cruel, another merciful; one treacherous, another faithful; one effeminate and cowardly, another bold and courageous; one humane, another haughty; one trustworthy, another cunning; one harsh, another lenient; one serious, another frivolous; one religious, another unbelieving; and the like. And I know that everyone will admit that it would be a very praiseworthy thing to find in a prince, of the qualities mentioned above, those that are held to be good, but since it is neither possible to have them nor to observe them all completely, because human nature does not permit it, <u>a prince must be prudent enough to know</u> <u>how to escape the bad reputation of those vices that</u> <u>would lose the state for him, and must protect himself</u> <u>from those that will not lose it for him, if this is pos-</u> <u>sible; but if he cannot, he need not concern himself</u> <u>unduly if he ignores these less serious vices. And,</u> <u>moreover, he need not worry about incurring the bad</u>

Those who are good at all times come to ruin among those who are not good.

Prince must learn not to be good.

Note the prince's reputation

Prince must avoid reputation for the worst vices.

Some vices may be needed to hold the state. True?

Some virtues may end in destruction.

reputation of those vices without which it would be difficult to hold his state; since, carefully taking everything into account, one will discover that something which appears to be a virtue, if pursued, will end in his destruction; while some other thing which seems to be a vice, if pursued, will result in his safety and his well-being.

Reviewing

The process of review, which takes place after a careful reading, is much more useful if you have annotated and underlined the text well. To a large extent, the review process can be devoted to accounting for the primary ideas that have been uncovered by your annotations and underlinings. For example, reviewing the Machiavelli annotations shows that the following ideas are crucial to Machiavelli's thinking:

> The prince's profession should be war, so the most successful princes are probably experienced in the military.
>
> If they do not pay attention to military matters, princes will lose their power.
>
> Being disarmed makes the prince despised.
>
> The prince should be in constant training.
>
> The prince needs a sound knowledge of terrain.
>
> Machiavelli says he tells us what is true, not what ought to be true.
>
> Those who are always good will come to ruin among those who are not good.
>
> To remain in power, the prince must learn how not to be good.
>
> The prince should avoid the worst vices in order not to harm his reputation.
>
> To maintain power, some vices may be necessary.
>
> Some virtues may end in destruction.

Putting Machiavelli's ideas in this raw form does an injustice to his skill as a writer, but annotation is designed to result in such summary statements. We can see that there are some constant themes, such as the insistence that the prince be a military person. As the headnote tells us, in Machiavelli's day Italy was a group of rival city-states and France, a larger, united nation, was invading these states one by one. Machiavelli dreamed that one powerful prince, such as his favorite, Cesare Borgia, could fight the French and save Italy. He emphasized the importance of the military because he lived in an age in which war was a constant and real threat.

Machiavelli anticipates the complaints of pacifists—those who argue against war—by telling us that those who remain unarmed are despised. To demonstrate his point, he gives us examples of those who lost their position as princes because they avoided being armed. He clearly expects these examples to be persuasive.

A second important theme pervading Machiavelli's essay is his view on moral behavior. For Machiavelli, being in power is much more important than being virtuous. He is quick to admit that vice is not desirable and that the worst vices will do harm to the prince's reputation. But he also says that the prince need not worry about the "less serious" vices. Moreover, he need not worry about incurring the bad reputation of those vices without which it would be difficult to hold his state. In the same spirit, he tells us that there are some virtues that might lead to the destruction of the prince.

Forming Your Own Ideas

One of the most important reasons for critically reading texts of the kind that appear in this book is to enable you to develop your own critical positions on issues that writers raise. Identifying and clarifying the main ideas is only the first step; the next step in critical reading is evaluating those ideas.

For example, you might ask whether, as most people have suggested, Machiavelli's ideas have any relevance for today. After all, he wrote four hundred years ago and times have changed. You might feel that Machiavelli is relevant strictly to the Italian Renaissance, or, alternately, that his principles are timeless and that every age can learn from them. Most people treat Machiavelli as if he were a political philosopher whose views are useful anytime and anywhere.

If you agree with the majority, then you may want to examine his ideas to see if you can accept them. Consider just two of those ideas and their implications:

Should rulers always be members of the military? Should they always be armed?

Should rulers ignore virtue and practice vice when it is convenient?

Should the ruler of a nation first demonstrate competence as a military leader? In his commentary on government, Lao-Tzu offers different advice because his assumptions are that the ruler ought to respect the rights of individuals. For Lao-Tzu the waging of war is an annoying, essentially wasteful activity. On the other hand, Machiavelli never once questions the usefulness of war: to him, it is basic to government. As a critical reader, you can take issue with such an assumption, and in doing so you will deepen your understanding of Machiavelli.

If we were to follow Machiavelli's advice, then we would choose presidents on the basis of whether or not they had been good military leaders. Among those we would not have chosen from our country's history might be Thomas Jefferson, Abraham Lincoln, and Franklin Delano Roosevelt. Those who were high-ranking military men include George Washington, Ulysses S. Grant, and Dwight D. Eisenhower. If you followed Machiavelli's rhetorical technique of using examples to convince your audience, you could choose from either group in order to prove your case.

Of course, there are examples from other nations. It has been common since the 1930s to see leaders of certain nations always dressed in their military uniforms: Benito Mussolini (Italy); Adolf Hitler (Germany); Joseph Stalin (Russia); Idi Amin (Uganda); Moammar Khadaffi (Libya). These are all tyrants who tormented their citizens and their neighbors. That gives us something to think about. Should a president dress in full military regalia all the time? Is that a good image for the ruler of a free nation?

Do you want a ruler, then, who is usually virtuous, but embraces vice when it is necessary? This is a very difficult question to answer. When Jimmy Carter swore to the American people that he would never lie to them, many Americans were skeptical. They thought that politics was essentially a game of careful and judicious lying—at least at times. In other words, these Americans were already committed to Machiavelli's position.

These are only a few of the questions that are raised by my annotations in the few pages from Machiavelli that we have examined. There are many other issues that could be uncovered by these annotations and many more from subsequent pages of the essay. Critical reading can be a powerful means by which to open what you read to discovery and discussion.

Once you begin a line of questioning, the ways in which you think about a passage begin expanding. You find yourself with more ideas of your own that have grown in response to those you have been reading about. Reading critically, in other words, gives you an enormous return on your investment of time. If you have the chance to investigate your responses to the assumptions and underlying premises of passages, such as Machiavelli's, you will be able to refine your thinking even further. For example, if you agree with Machiavelli that rulers should be successful military leaders for whom small vices may be useful at times, and you find yourself in a position to argue with someone who feels Machiavelli is mistaken in this view, then you will have a good opportunity to evaluate the soundness of your thinking. You will have a chance to see your own assumptions and arguments tested.

In many ways, this entire book is about such opportunities. The essays that follow offer you powerful ideas from great thinkers. They invite you to participate in their thoughts, exercise your own knowledge and assumptions, and arrive at your own conclusions. Basically, that is the meaning of education.

PART ONE

IDEAS IN THE WORLD OF POLITICS

MUST THE NEED FOR A STABLE SOCIAL ORDER CONFLICT WITH THE NEED FOR INDIVIDUAL LIBERTY?

Lao-Tzu
Niccolò Machiavelli
Jean Jacques Rousseau
Thomas Jefferson
Mary Wollstonecraft
Frederick Douglass
Henry David Thoreau
Martin Luther King, Jr.

INTRODUCTION

THE EIGHT SELECTIONS in this part cover a range of political ideas that extend from ancient China to the modern United States. The issues that concern writers on politics are multitudinous, but at their root are questions that relate to the balance between individual freedoms and the exercise of power by the state.

Power and its effects upon the individual have always been topics of first interest to politicians. The delicate balance between the needs of individuals to assert their rights and the needs of a strong government to maintain the order and stability that make individual freedom meaningful has never been easy to achieve—in any culture or in any age.

Lao-Tzu, the founder of Taoism, one of the three major Chinese religions, advocated a complex form of inactivity. His writings, *Tao Te Ching*, loosely translated as "The Way of Power," concern questions of governance and the role of the individual. His ideas, because they are centered in a mysticism that is intensely antimaterialistic, are not easy for the Western mind to grasp. Yet they have been influential in China for almost twenty-five hundred years.

Niccolò Machiavelli was a practical man of the Renaissance, with very little that could be called mystical in his concerns for power and its effect on the individual. His name has become a synonym for political cunning. Yet his motives in recommending a ruthless wielding of power on the part of his prince derived largely from his fear that a weak ruler would lose his state to France or to another powerful plundering nation. Therefore, to a large extent, Machiavelli ignores questions of independence and liberty. However, underlying his discussion is the conviction that a strong prince will, in the long run, guarantee the peace and happiness of the citizen for whom independence is, otherwise, irrelevant.

Jean Jacques Rousseau, in "The Origin of Civil Society," takes a highly theoretical approach to governance when he searches for the model of the contemporary state. He finds his model in the family, and, assuming that the family is fundamental, natural, and inevitable, he examines it to see exactly what a citizen's proper place should be in a modern government. Rousseau, from a traditional point of view that angered Mary Wollstonecraft among others, saw the power in the head of the family, the father. From such origins flows a coherent theory of responsibility and independence. Rousseau is in certain ways typical of mid-eighteenth-century thinkers when he searches for first principles. If you agree with his method, you will then find yourself agreeing with his conclusions.

In an important way, Thomas Jefferson declares his independence from the Rousseauian view of government. The paternalism of England was too much for him, and his response was to break from the family entirely. Jefferson piles offense upon offense, indignity upon indignity, to make us feel the weight of British paternalism. Jefferson had one reason to reject the Rousseauian view, while Mary Wollstonecraft, defending a feminist view, had her own reasons. One of the first and still among the most influential and eloquent writers in favor of women's independence, Mary Wollstonecraft shows how the structure of a society—both governmental and cultural—can oppress a large proportion of its population and deny them freedom. And it can do so while praising freedom.

Some of that irony is painfully present in Frederick Douglass's careful discussion of his escape from slavery and his efforts to enjoy the privileges of freedom in New England before the American Civil War. Here we have a clear case of a government that enforced slave laws—both in the North and in the South—while advocating independence.

The question of how the individual should react in the face of a government whose laws are vicious is taken up by Henry David Thoreau. His refusal to pay taxes that he knew would be used in a war against Mexico—a war he felt was immoral and dishonorable— brought him into conflict with the law. He realized that he would have to pay a penalty for his views, and he was willing to do so. The problem he faced in 1849 has arisen in governments around the world and is still an issue today.

The laws in the United States have often resulted in conflicts with individual conscience. Not only by supporting slavery did the laws collude to harm the individual but also by refusing to grant women the vote, by upholding Jim Crow laws that enforced second-class citizenship for blacks, and by extending the Vietnam War, which was the subject of a nationwide protest based on the kinds of questions of conscience raised by Thoreau.

For fighting against the Jim Crow laws, Martin Luther King, Jr., went to jail. While there, he wrote a letter to clergymen who he felt should be firmly on his side, on the side of equality and freedom. His letter was in the tradition of many other such letters from prison, and its effect is still powerful.

The writers in this part of the book share striking qualities of endurance in their work. They have been and will be read for centuries both because their causes are important and because their way of presenting their beliefs is effective. Each of these writers is a capable rhetorician, using fundamental techniques to express his or her ideas in ways that affect our thoughts and our feelings.

Further, none of the central ideas presented in these selections can be said to be totally original with the writer. And each writer was well aware of this fact. The power that inheres in these essays comes not so much from the originality of the ideas but from an appropriate and convincing combination of style, energy, and commitment on the part of the writers. These writers convince us that what they are saying is of immense importance and that they feel strongly the emotions that are related to, and aroused by, the ideas they present. It is the depth of their commitment to such ideas, their capacity to involve us in them, and the rhetorical conviction by which they present them that compel us to respond as we do.

LAO-TZU

———— ◆◇◆ ————

Thoughts from the Tao Te Ching

Lao-tzu (604?–531? B.C.) *is a name that means "Master Lao" or "Old Master." The man who bore this title was named Li Erh and is traditionally said to have been born in the state of Ch'u in 604 B.C., making him a contemporary of Confucius. He was employed as librarian and historian in the royal court. However, he was also a metaphysician and thinker who inspired many of his contemporaries. Tradition holds that near the end of his life, when he decided to leave the court of the Chou dynasty, where he lived and worked his entire life, he was persuaded by the keeper of the city gate to write his thoughts down for him—and others—to keep. The keeper of the gate feared that Lao-Tzu was heading into a self-imposed exile and that no one would ever know what he had thought. Fortunately, Lao-Tzu agreed to his request, and after he left Chow he was never seen again.*

Legends have grown up around Lao-Tzu. For example, he was said to have gestated more than fifty years in his mother's womb so that when he was born he was already white-haired and venerable. He was said to have lived as long as two hundred years. He was the founder of Taoism, which began apparently not as a religion but as a

Translated by D. C. Lau.

kind of philosophy. The term Tao *is very difficult to translate into English, but it has been interpreted to mean "the way." Yet the "way" has been interpreted in two senses. One is as a path, since the Chinese written character for* Tao *is related to the concept of path. The second way is as a method—as in "the way to gain enlightenment." Both meanings are clearly implied in the text, and both successfully interpret it.*

Yet the text of the Tao Te Ching *is problematic because of its many ambiguities. Carefully annotated editions of the text are often interrupted by commentary that explains why it is so difficult to be absolutely sure what Lao-Tzu means at a given moment. Sometimes the text seems to be purposely ambiguous—a rhetorical device that promotes examination and careful speculation on the part of the reader. This ambiguity is also often annoying to a Western reader who is used to having ideas clearly spelled out and explained. Lao-Tzu seems to take a view that ideas are like seeds to be planted in the mind of a listener, to take root and grow as the soil will permit.*

To modern American readers, Lao-Tzu's formulations seem "laid-back" rather than anxious and intense. He seems the very opposite of those materialistic and grasping people who sacrifice everything for amassing money and goods. Lao-Tzu takes the view that such things are leaden weights of the soul, that they are meaningless and trivial, and that the truly free and enlightened person will regard them as evil.

Because of its antimaterialist doctrine, the Tao Te Ching *can be baffling to the modern mind—which may indicate the extent to which we, as moderns, are committed to a materialist philosophy. Lao-Tzu's antimaterialism led him to recommend that politicians practice judicious inactivity. Lao-Tzu saw the busy hustling of the politicians and businessmen of his day—most of whom were oppressively materialistic—as a form of destructive and useless activity. They were busy, humming with action, but all to no purpose. Therefore, the logical analysis of the contemporary situation produced the antidote: inactivity.*

For many of us, inactivity is almost impossible to imagine. To do nothing implies laziness, "dropping out." And at times in China the interpretation of Tao did, indeed, degenerate into a kind of slothful reluctance to take any action. But Lao-Tzu did not counsel sloth: instead he was concerned to avoid the useless busy-ness that he felt distracted people from the true course of enlightenment.

What enlightenment is may be difficult to determine. Those who possess it know what it is; those who do not can hardly hope to imag-

ine it. It may be likened to a state of spiritual peacefulness, a sense of fulfillment. But whatever it may be, it is certainly impossible to achieve if spiritual matters are not put first, and if one is enmeshed in the coils of desire for material goods.

The result of Lao-Tzu's political philosophy is to minimize the power of the state—especially the power of the state to oppress the people. The question of the freedom of the individual is taken into account in a very complex way by asserting that the wise leader will provide the people with what they need, but not annoy them with promises of what they do not need. By keeping people "innocent of knowledge and free from desire" the sage ruler will have a population that will not want what it cannot have. Discontent, as Lao-Tzu interprets it, derives from desiring wrong things or from permitting the clever to act. As he says, "Do that which consists in taking no action, and order will prevail." On the surface such a statement seems almost naive; yet, on reflection it can be seen to possess remarkable wisdom.

LAO-TZU'S RHETORIC

To the Western reader, the Tao Te Ching may, at first glance, appear to be poetry. Instead of using thoroughly developed ideas, Lao-Tzu used a traditional Chinese form that resembles the aphorism, a compressed statement that is weighty with meaning. For this reason, one of the jobs of the reader is to mull over what has been said. Virtually every statement requires thought and reflection. Therefore, the act of reading becomes an act of intense cooperation with the text.

The most profitable way to read this text is with other people so you can see how many different ways it can be interpreted. Your own act of analysis should be measured by your patience and your willingness to think a statement through to see what lies beneath the surface. Take, for example, one of the opening statements:

Not to honor men of worth will keep the people from contention; not to value goods which are hard to come by will keep them from theft; not to display what is desirable will keep them from being unsettled of mind.

Therefore in governing the people, the sage empties their minds but fills their bellies, weakens their wills but strengthens their bones.

Not honoring men of worth means not assuming that wealth is the measure of a person's goodness or value. Not valuing goods that are hard to come by will obviously prevent theft, since the thief would hardly steal that which others do not value. And not showing things that are desirable to people who cannot have them will definitely promote their peace of mind. We know all these things, and it is probably easy to agree with Lao-Tzu that his recipe for contentedness in the state would work. On the other hand, it is also probable that most Westerners would not want to try this recipe. The reasons for making that choice are important to examine.

If the text resembles poetry—and it does so very closely in many passages—it may be also true that it should be read like poetry. It should be read for innuendo, subtle interpretation, and possible meaning in every line. Lao-Tzu was very serious in what he had to say. He felt he was contributing to the spiritual enlightenment of the ruling sage, although he had no real hope that his message would be put into action.

Later ages, however, have seen the significance of his thinking, and today Lao-Tzu has far more readers than he could have imagined. People have seen that much of what he said is reasonable and desirable, and that although it may be impossible for entire states to follow his thinking, it may be possible for individuals to heed his philosophy.

----- ◈ -----

Thoughts from the Tao Te Ching

III

Not to honor men of worth will keep the people from contention; not to value goods which are hard to come by will keep them from theft; not to display what is desirable will keep them from being unsettled of mind.

Therefore in governing the people, the sage empties their minds but fills their bellies, weakens their wills but strengthens their bones.

He always keeps them innocent of knowledge and free from desire, and ensures that the clever never dare to act.

Do that which consists in taking no action, and order will prevail. 3

XIII

Favor and disgrace are things that startle; 4
High rank[1] is, like one's body, a source of great trouble.
What is meant by saying that favor and disgrace are things that 5
startle? Favor when it is bestowed on a subject serves to startle as
much as when it is withdrawn. This is what is meant by saying that
favor and disgrace are things that startle. What is meant by saying that
high rank is, like one's body, a source of great trouble? The reason I
have great trouble is that I have a body. When I no longer have a body,
what trouble have I?

Hence he who values his body more than dominion over the 6
empire can be entrusted with the empire. He who loves his body
more than dominion over the empire can be given the custody of the
empire.

XVII

The best of all rulers is but a shadowy presence to his subjects. 7
Next comes the ruler they love and praise;
Next comes one they fear;
Next comes one with whom they take liberties.
When there is not enough faith, there is lack of good faith. 8
Hesitant, he does not utter words lightly. 9
When his task is accomplished and his work done
The people all say, "It happened to us naturally."

---

[1]It is probable that the word *kuei* ("high rank") here has crept in by mistake, since, as it stands, this line has one word more than the first. If this is the case, then the line should be translated: "Great trouble is like one's body." This brings it into line with the explanation that follows where "high rank" is not, in fact, mentioned. [Lau's note]

XVIII

When the great way falls into disuse   10
There are benevolence and rectitude;
When cleverness emerges
There is great hypocrisy;
When the six relations[2] are at variance
There are filial children;
When the state is benighted
There are loyal ministers.

XIX

Exterminate the sage, discard the wise,   11
And the people will benefit a hundredfold;
Exterminate benevolence, discard rectitude,
And the people will again be filial;
Exterminate ingenuity, discard profit,
And there will be no more thieves and bandits.
These three, being false adornments, are not enough   12
And the people must have something to which they can attach
       themselves:
Exhibit the unadorned and embrace the uncarved block,
Have little thought of self and as few desires as possible.

XXVI

The heavy is the root of the light;   13
The still is the lord of the restless.
Therefore the gentleman when traveling all day   14
Never lets the heavily laden carts out of his sight.
It is only when he is safely behind walls and watch-towers
That he rests peacefully and is above worries.
How, then, should a ruler of ten thousand chariots
Make light of his own person in the eyes of the empire?
If light, then the root is lost;   15
If restless, then the lord is lost.

---

[2]The six relations, according to Wang Pi, are father and son, elder and younger brother, husband and wife. [Lau's note]

XXVII

One who excels in traveling leaves no wheel tracks;　　　　16
One who excels in speech makes no slips;
One who excels in reckoning uses no counting rods;
One who excels in shutting uses no bolts yet what he has shut
　　cannot be opened;
One who excels in tying uses no cords yet what he has tied cannot
　　be undone.
Therefore the sage always excels in saving people, and so abandons　17
no one; always excels in saving things, and so abandons nothing.
This is called following one's discernment.　　　　18
Hence the good man is the teacher the bad learns from;　　　19
And the bad man is the material the good works on.
Not to value the teacher
Nor to love the material
Though it seems clever, betrays great bewilderment.
This is called the essential and the secret.　　　　20

XXIX

Whoever takes the empire and wishes to do anything to it I see　21
will have no respite. The empire is a sacred vessel and nothing should
be done to it. Whoever does anything to it will ruin it; whoever lays
hold of it will lose it.
Hence some things lead and some follow;　　　　22
Some breathe gently and some breathe hard;
Some are strong and some are weak;
Some destroy and some are destroyed.
Therefore the sage avoids excess, extravagance, and arrogance.　　23

XXX

One who assists the ruler of men by means of the way does not　24
intimidate the empire by a show of arms.
This is something which is liable to rebound.　　　　25
Where troops have encamped
There will brambles grow;
In the wake of a mighty army

Bad harvests follow without fail.

One who is good aims only at bringing his campaign to a conclu- 26
sion and dare not thereby intimidate. Bring it to a conclusion but do
not boast; bring it to a conclusion but do not brag; bring it to a conclusion but do not be arrogant; bring it to a conclusion but only when
there is no choice; bring it to a conclusion but do not intimidate.

A creature in its prime doing harm to the old   27
Is known as going against the way.
That which goes against the way will come to an early end.

XLVI

When the way prevails in the empire, fleet-footed horses are rele- 28
gated to plowing the fields; when the way does not prevail in the empire, war-horses breed on the border.

There is no crime greater than having too many desires;   29
There is no disaster greater than not being content;
There is no misfortune greater than being covetous.
Hence in being content, one will always have enough.   30

XLIX

The sage has no mind of his own. He takes as his own the mind of 31
the people.

Those who are good I treat as good. Those who are not good I also 32
treat as good. In so doing I gain in goodness. Those who are of good
faith I have faith in. Those who are lacking in good faith I also have
faith in. In so doing I gain in good faith.

The sage in his attempt to distract the mind of the empire seeks 33
urgently to muddle it. The people all have something to occupy their
eyes and ears, and the sage treats them all like children.

LIV

What is firmly rooted cannot be pulled out;   34
What is tightly held in the arms will not slip loose;
Through this the offering of sacrifice by descendants will never
    come to an end.
Cultivate it in your person   35

And its virtue will be genuine;
Cultivate it in the family
And its virtue will be more than sufficient;
Cultivate it in the hamlet
And its virtue will endure;
Cultivate it in the state
And its virtue will abound;
Cultivate it in the empire
And its virtue will be pervasive.

Hence look at the person through the person; look at the family   36
through the family; look at the hamlet through the hamlet; look at
the state through the state; look at the empire through the empire.

How do I know that the empire is like that? By means of this.   37

LVII

Govern the state by being straightforward; wage war by being   38
crafty; but win the empire by not being meddlesome.

How do I know that it is like that? By means of this.   39

The more taboos there are in the empire   40
The poorer the people;
The more sharpened tools the people have
The more benighted the state;
The more skills the people have
The further novelties multiply;
The better known the laws and edicts
The more thieves and robbers there are.

Hence the sage says,   41
I take no action and the people are transformed of themselves;
I prefer stillness and the people are rectified of themselves;
I am not meddlesome and the people prosper of themselves;
I am free from desire and the people of themselves become simple
    like the uncarved block.

LVIII

When the government is muddled   42
The people are simple;
When the government is alert
The people are cunning.

It is on disaster that good fortune perches;   43
It is beneath good fortune that disaster crouches.
Who knows the limit? Does not the straightforward exist? The   44
straightforward changes again into the crafty, and the good changes
again into the monstrous. Indeed, it is long since the people were perplexed.

Therefore the sage is square-edged but does not scrape,   45
Has corners but does not jab,
Extends himself but not at the expense of others,
Shines but does not dazzle.

LX

Governing a large state is like boiling a small fish.[3]   46
When the empire is ruled in accordance with the way,   47
The spirits lose their potencies.
Or rather, it is not that they lose their potencies,
But that, though they have their potencies, they do not harm the
    people,
It is not only they who, having their potencies, do not harm the
    people,
The sage, also, does not harm the people.
As neither does any harm, each attributes the merit to the other.

LXI

A large state is the lower reaches of a river—   48
The place where all the streams of the world unite.
In the union of the world,   49
The female always gets the better of the male by stillness.
Being still, she takes the lower position.   50
Hence the large state, by taking the lower position, annexes the   51
    small state;
The small state, by taking the lower position, affiliates itself to the
    large state.

---

[3]This is because a small fish can be spoiled simply by being handled. [Lau's note]

Thus the one, by taking the lower position, annexes;   52
The other, by taking the lower position, is annexed.
All that the large state wants is to take the other under its wing;
All that the small state wants is to have its services accepted by
    the other.
If each of the two wants to find its proper place,
It is meet that the large should take the lower position.

LXV

    Of old those who excelled in the pursuit of the way did not use it   53
to enlighten the people but to hoodwink them. The reason why the
people are difficult to govern is that they are too clever.
    Hence to rule a state by cleverness   54
Will be to the detriment of the state;
Not to rule a state by cleverness
Will be a boon to the state.
These two are models.
Always to know the models
Is known as mysterious virtue.
Mysterious virtue is profound and far-reaching,
But when things turn back it turns back with them.
Only then is complete conformity realized.   55

LXVI

    The reason why the River and the Sea are able to be king of the   56
hundred valleys is that they excel in taking the lower position. Hence
they are able to be king of the hundred valleys.
    Therefore, desiring to rule over the people,   57
One must in one's words humble oneself before them;
And, desiring to lead the people,
One must, in one's person, follow behind them.
    Therefore the sage takes his place over the people yet is no burden;   58
takes his place ahead of the people yet causes no obstruction. That is
why the empire supports him joyfully and never tires of doing so.
    It is because he does not contend that no one in the empire is in a   59
position to contend with him.

LXVIII

One who excels as a warrior does not appear formidable;   60
One who excels in fighting is never roused in anger;
One who excels in defeating his enemy does not join issue;
One who excels in employing others humbles himself before them.
This is known as the virtue of non-contention;   61
This is known as making use of the efforts of others;
This is known as matching the sublimity of heaven.

LXXV

The people are hungry: 62
It is because those in authority eat up too much in taxes
That the people are hungry.
The people are difficult to govern:
It is because those in authority are too fond of action
That the people are difficult to govern.
The people treat death lightly:
It is because the people set too much store by life
That they treat death lightly.
It is just because one has no use for life that one is wiser than the 63
man who values life.

LXXX

Reduce the size and population of the state. Ensure that even 64
though the people have tools of war for a troop or a battalion they will
not use them; and also that they will be reluctant to move to distant
places because they look on death as no light matter.

Even when they have ships and carts, they will have no use for 65
them; and even when they have armor and weapons, they will have
no occasion to make a show of them.

Bring it about that the people will return to the use of the knotted 66
rope,
    Will find relish in their food
    And beauty in their clothes,
    Will be content in their abode
    And happy in the way they live.

Though adjoining states are within sight of one another, and the 67
sound of dogs barking and cocks crowing in one state can be heard in
another, yet the people of one state will grow old and die without
having had any dealings with those of another.

QUESTIONS

1. What is Lao-Tzu's first concern for the people? What must the ruler provide them with if they are to be happy?
2. To what extent is the happiness of the individual taken into account by
   Lao-Tzu?
3. Does Lao-Tzu regard the people as inferior? Does he seem paternalistic
   toward them?
4. What are Lao-Tzu's views on the empire and its value? Does he feel the
   empire is of great significance or of little significance?
5. Which statements made in this selection do you feel support a materialist
   view of experience? Can they be resolved with Lao-Tzu's overall thinking
   in the selection?
6. Would you describe Lao-Tzu's position as one that recommends following
   a mean, a middle way between excesses?
7. To what extent is Lao-Tzu in favor of military action? What seem to be
   his views about the military?
8. The term "sage" is used frequently in the selection. Does Lao-Tzu use it
   as a form of praise, or is it a form of dispraise? Is the sage good or bad?

WRITING ASSIGNMENTS

1. The term "the way" is used often in this selection. Write a short essay that
   defines what Lao-Tzu seems to mean by the term. If you were a politician
   and had the responsibility for governing a state, how would you follow the
   way that is implied in Lao-Tzu's statements? Is the way restrictive? Difficult? Open to interpretation? How well do you think it would work?
2. Write a brief essay that examines the following statements from the perspective of a young modern person:

   > There is no crime greater than having too many desires;
   > There is no disaster greater than not being content;
   > There is no misfortune greater than being covetous.

   To what extent do you agree with these statements, and to what extent do
   you feel they are statements that have a political importance? Does the
   United States, as you interpret it, seem to agree with these views, or does

it disagree? What are the most visible political consequences of our nation's position regarding these ideas?

3. Some people have asserted that the American political system benefits the people most when the following views of Lao-Tzu are carefully followed:

> Hence the sage says,
> I take no action and the people are transformed of themselves;
> I prefer stillness and the people are rectified of themselves;
> I am not meddlesome and the people prosper of the themselves;
> I am free from desire and the people of themselves become simple like the uncarved block.

In a brief essay decide to what extent it is true that American leaders follow these precepts. Whether you feel they do or not, do you think that these precepts should be followed? What are the likely results of their being put into practice?

4. Some of the statements Lao-Tzu makes are so packed with meaning that it would take pages to explore them. One such is: "It is on disaster that good fortune perches." Take this statement as the basis of a short essay and, in reference to a personal disaster that you know about, explain the significance of this statement.

5. What does Lao-Tzu imply about the obligation of the state to the individual it governs, and about the obligation of the individual to the state? Is one much more important than the other? Using the texts in this selection, establish what you feel is the optimum balance in the relationship between the two.

6. Compare Lao-Tzu's view of government with those of Machiavelli in the next selection. Consider what seem to be the ultimate purposes of government, what seem to be the obligations of the leader to the people being led, and what seems to be the main work of the state.

NICCOLÒ MACHIAVELLI

The Qualities of the Prince

NICCOLÒ MACHIAVELLI (1469–1527) *was an aristocrat whose fortunes wavered according to the shifts in power in Florence. Renaissance Italy was a collection of powerful city-states which were sometimes volatile and unstable. When Florence's famed Medici princes were returned to power in 1512 after eighteen years of banishment, Machiavelli did not fare well. He was suspected of crimes against the state and imprisoned. Even though he was not guilty, he had to learn to support himself as a writer instead of continuing his career in civil service.*

His works often contrast two forces: luck (one's fortune) and character (one's virtues). His own character outlasted his bad luck in regard to the Medicis, and he was returned to a position of responsibility. The Prince *(1513), his most celebrated work, was a general treatise on the qualities the prince (i.e., a ruler) must have to maintain his power. In a more particular way, it was directed at the Medicis to encourage them to save Italy from the predatory incursions of France and Spain, whose troops were nibbling at the crumbling Italian principalities and who would, in time, control much of Italy.*

From *The Prince*. Translated by Peter Bondanella and Mark Musa.

The chapters presented here contain the core of the philosophy Machiavelli became famous for. His instructions to the prince are curiously devoid of any high-sounding moralizing or any encouragement to be good as a matter of principle. Machiavelli recommends a very practical course of action for the prince: secure power; secure it by practical, simple, and effective means. It may be that Machiavelli fully expects that the prince will use his power for good ends—certainly he does not recommend tyranny. But he also supports questionable means that will achieve the final end of becoming and remaining the prince. Machiavelli believes that there is a conflict between the ends and the means used to achieve them, and he certainly does not fret over the possible problems that may accompany the use of "unpleasant" means, such as punishment of upstarts, or the use of repression, imprisonment, and torture.

Machiavelli's view of human nature has come under criticism for its cynicism. He suggests that a perfectly good person would not last long in any high office because that person would have to compete with the mass of people, who, he says, are basically bad. Machiavelli constantly tells us that he is describing the world as it really is, not as it should be. He implies that if the prince operated as if the world were as it ought to be, he would not last very long. Perhaps Machiavelli is correct, but people have long resented the way he approves of cunning, deceit, and outright lying as means of staying in power.

The contrast with Lao-Tzu's opinions in the Tao Te Ching is instructive. Lao-Tzu's advice issues from a detached view of a universal ruler; Machiavelli's advice is very personal, embodying a set of directives for a specific prince. Machiavelli expounds upon a litany of actions that must be taken; Lao-Tzu, on the other hand, demonstrates that judicious inaction will produce the best results.

MACHIAVELLI'S RHETORIC

Machiavelli's approach is less poetic than Lao-Tzu's, and because he is so pragmatic in his approach—he is writing for a limited and temporal audience—he seems less to be dispensing universal wisdom. While Lao-Tzu's tone is almost biblical, Machiavelli's is writing a how-to-book, relevant to a particular time and a particular place. Yet like Lao-Tzu, Machiavelli is brief and to the point. Each segment of the discussion is terse and economical. Nothing is wasted.

Machiavelli announces his primary point clearly; he usually refers to a historical precedent (or several) to support his point; then he explains why his position is the best one by appealing to both common sense and historical experience. In those cases in which he suspects the reader will not share his view wholeheartedly, he suggests an alternate argument, then explains why it is wrong. This is a very forceful way of presenting one's views. It gives the appearance of fairness and thoroughness—and, as we learn from reading Machiavelli, he is very much concerned with appearances. His method also gives his work fullness, a quality that makes us forget how brief it really is.

One of his rhetorical methods is to discuss opposites, including both sides of an issue. From the first he makes a number of oppositions—the art of war and the art of life, liberality and stinginess, cruelty and clemency, the fox and the lion. The method is simplicity itself, but it is important because it employs one of the basic techniques of rhetoric—the strategy of comparison, in which we perform one of the mind's favorite tasks, comparison and contrast. We may not have much to say about a subject, but somehow we can always think of something to say about how it relates to something else.

The aphorism is another of Machiavelli's rhetorical weapons. The aphorism is a saying—or a sentence that sounds like a saying—which has been accepted as true. Familiar examples are "A penny saved is a penny earned" and "There is no fool like an old fool." Machiavelli tells us: To be feared is much safer than to be loved; any man who tries to be good all the time is bound to come to ruin among the great number who are not good.

Such definite statements have several important qualities. One is that they are pithy—they seem to say a great deal in a few words. Another is that they appear to contain a great deal of wisdom, in part because they are delivered with such certainty, and in part because they sound like other aphorisms that we accept as true. Finally, because they sound like aphorisms, we tend to accept them much more readily than perhaps we should. Use of language that has the appearance of truth is much more likely to be accepted as conveying truth than any other use of language. This may be why the speeches of contemporary politicians (modern versions of the prince) are often sprinkled with such expressions. Machiavelli's rhetorical technique is still reliable, still effective, and still worth studying.

The Qualities of the Prince

A Prince's Duty Concerning Military Matters

A prince, therefore, must not have any other object nor any other thought, nor must he take anything as his profession but war, its institutions, and its discipline; because that is the only profession which befits one who commands; and it is of such importance that not only does it maintain those who were born princes, but many times it enables men of private station to rise to that position; and, on the other hand, it is evident that when princes have given more thought to personal luxuries than to arms, they have lost their state. And the first way to lose it is to neglect this art; and the way to acquire it is to be well versed in this art.

Francesco Sforza[1] became Duke of Milan from being a private citizen because he was armed; his sons, since they avoided the inconveniences of arms, became private citizens after having been dukes. For, among the other bad effects it causes, being disarmed makes you despised; this is one of those infamies a prince should guard himself against, as will be treated below: for between an armed and an unarmed man there is no comparison whatsoever, and it is not reasonable for an armed man to obey an unarmed man willingly, nor that an unarmed man should be safe among armed servants; since, when the former is suspicious and the latter are contemptuous, it is impossible for them to work well together. And therefore, a prince who does not understand military matters, besides the other misfortunes already noted, cannot be esteemed by his own soldiers, nor can he trust them.

He must, therefore, never raise his thought from this exercise of war, and in peacetime he must train himself more than in time of war; this can be done in two ways: one by action, the other by the mind. And as far as actions are concerned, besides keeping his soldiers well disciplined and trained, he must always be out hunting, and must accustom his body to hardships in this manner; and he must also learn the nature of the terrain, and know how mountains slope, how valleys open, how plains lie, and understand the nature of rivers and swamps; and he should devote much attention to such activities. Such knowledge is useful in two ways: first, one learns to know one's own country

1

2

3

---

[1] *Francesco Sforza (1401–1466)* Became duke of Milan in 1450. He was, like most of Machiavelli's examples, a skilled diplomat and soldier. His court was a model of Renaissance scholarship and achievement.

and can better understand how to defend it; second, with the knowledge and experience of the terrain, one can easily comprehend the characteristics of any other terrain that it is necessary to explore for the first time; for the hills, valleys, plains, rivers, and swamps of Tuscany,[2] for instance, have certain similarities to those of other provinces; so that by knowing the lay of the land in one province one can easily understand it in others. And a prince who lacks this ability lacks the most important quality in a leader; because this skill teaches you to find the enemy, choose a campsite, lead troops, organize them for battle, and besiege towns to your own advantage.

Philopoemon, Prince of the Achaeans,[3] among the other praises   4
given to him by writers, is praised because in peacetime he thought of nothing except the means of waging war; and when he was out in the country with his friends, he often stopped and reasoned with them: "If the enemy were on that hilltop and we were here with our army, which of the two of us would have the advantage? How could we attack them without breaking formation? If we wanted to retreat, how could we do this? If they were to retreat, how could we pursue them?" And he proposed to them, as they rode along, all the contingencies that can occur in an army; he heard their opinions, expressed his own, and backed it up with arguments; so that, because of these continuous deliberations, when leading his troops no unforeseen incident could arise for which he did not have the remedy.

But as for the exercise of the mind, the prince must read histories   5
and in them study the deeds of great men; he must see how they conducted themselves in wars; he must examine the reasons for their victories and for their defeats in order to avoid the latter and to imitate the former; and above all else he must do as some distinguished man before him has done, who elected to imitate someone who had been praised and honored before him, and always keep in mind his deeds and actions; just as it is reported that Alexander the Great imitated Achilles; Caesar, Alexander; Scipio, Cyrus.[4] And anyone who reads the

---

[2]***Tuscany*** Florence is in the region known as Tuscany.

[3]***Philopoemon (252?–182 B.C.), Prince of the Achaeans*** Philopoemon, from the city-state of Megalopolis, was a Greek general noted for skillful diplomacy. He led the Achaeans, a group of Greek states that formed the Achaean League, in several important expeditions, notably against Sparta. His cruelty in putting down a Spartan uprising caused him to be reprimanded by his superiors.

[4]***Cyrus (585?–529 B.C.)*** Cyrus II (the Great), Persian emperor. Cyrus and the other figures featured in this sentence—Alexander the Great (356–323 B.C.); Achilles, hero of Homer's *Iliad*; Julius Caesar (100–44 B.C.); and Scipio Africanus, legendary Roman general—are all examples of politicians who were also great military geniuses. Xenophon (434?–?355 B.C.) was one of the earliest Greek historians; he chronicled the lives and military exploits of Cyrus and his son-in-law Darius.

life of Cyrus written by Xenophon then realizes how important in the life of Scipio that imitation was to his glory and how much, in purity, goodness, humanity, and generosity, Scipio conformed to those characteristics of Cyrus that Xenophon had written about.

Such methods as these a wise prince must follow, and never in peaceful times must he be idle; but he must turn them diligently to his advantage in order to be able to profit from them in times of adversity, so that, when Fortune changes, she will find him prepared to withstand such times. 6

On Those Things for Which Men, and Particularly Princes, Are Praised or Blamed

Now there remains to be examined what should be the methods and procedures of a prince in dealing with his subjects and friends. And because I know that many have written about this, I am afraid that by writing about it again I shall be thought of as presumptuous, since in discussing this material I depart radically from the procedures of others. But since my intention is to write something useful for anyone who understands it, it seemed more suitable to me to search after the effectual truth of the matter rather than its imagined one. And many writers have imagined for themselves republics and principalities that have never been seen nor known to exist in reality; for there is such a gap between how one lives and how one ought to live that anyone who abandons what is done for what ought to be done learns his ruin rather than his preservation: for a man who wishes to make a vocation of being good at all times will come to ruin among so many who are not good. Hence it is necessary for a prince who wishes to maintain his position to learn how not to be good, and to use this knowledge or not to use it according to necessity. 7

Leaving aside, therefore, the imagined things concerning a prince, and taking into account those that are true, I say that all men, when they are spoken of, and particularly princes, since they are placed on a higher level, are judged by some of these qualities which bring them either blame or praise. And this is why one is considered generous, another miserly (to use a Tuscan word, since "avaricious" in our language is still used to mean one who wishes to acquire by means of theft; we call "miserly" one who excessively avoids using what he has); one is considered a giver, the other rapacious; one cruel, another merciful; one treacherous, another faithful; one effeminate and cow- 8 ardly, another bold and courageous; one humane, another haughty; one lascivious, another chaste; one trustworthy, another cunning; one harsh, another lenient; one serious, another frivolous; one religious, another unbelieving; and the like. And I know that everyone will admit that it would be a very praiseworthy thing to find in a prince, of the qualities mentioned above, those that are held to be good; but since it is neither possible to have them nor to observe them all completely, because human nature does not permit it, a prince must be prudent enough to know how to escape the bad reputation of those vices that would lose the state for him, and must protect himself from those that will not lose it for him, if this is possible; but if he cannot, he need not concern himself unduly if he ignores these less serious vices. And, moreover, he need not worry about incurring the bad reputation of those vices without which it would be difficult to hold his state; since, carefully taking everything into account, one will discover that something which appears to be a virtue, if pursued, will end in his destruction; while some other thing which seems to be a vice, if pursued, will result in his safety and his well-being.

On Generosity and Miserliness

Beginning, therefore, with the first of the above-mentioned quali-   9
ties, I say that it would be good to be considered generous; nevertheless, generosity used in such a manner as to give you a reputation for it will harm you; because if it is employed virtuously and as one should employ it, it will not be recognized and you will not avoid the reproach of its opposite. And so, if a prince wants to maintain his reputation for generosity among men, it is necessary for him not to neglect any possible means of lavish display; in so doing such a prince will always use up all his resources and he will be obliged, eventually, if he wishes to maintain his reputation for generosity, to burden the people with excessive taxes and to do everything possible to raise funds. This will begin to make him hateful to his subjects, and, becoming impoverished, he will not be much esteemed by anyone; so that, as a consequence of his generosity, having offended many and rewarded few, he will feel the effects of any slight unrest and will be ruined at the first sign of danger; recognizing this and wishing to alter his policies, he immediately runs the risk of being reproached as a miser.

A prince, therefore, unable to use this virtue of generosity in a   10
manner which will not harm himself if he is known for it, should, if he is wise, not worry about being called a miser; for with time he will

come to be considered more generous once it is evident that, as a result of his parsimony, his income is sufficient, he can defend himself from anyone who makes war against him, and he can undertake enterprises without overburdening his people, so that he comes to be generous with all those from whom he takes nothing, who are countless, and miserly with all those to whom he gives nothing, who are few. In our times we have not seen great deeds accomplished except by those who were considered miserly; all others were done away with. Pope Julius II,[5] although he made use of his reputation for generosity in order to gain the papacy, then decided not to maintain it in order to be able to wage war; the present King of France[6] has waged many wars without imposing extra taxes on his subjects, only because his habitual parsimony has provided for the additional expenditures; the present King of Spain,[7] if he had been considered generous, would not have engaged in nor won so many campaigns.

Therefore, in order not to have to rob his subjects, to be able to defend himself, not to become poor and contemptible, and not to be forced to become rapacious, a prince must consider it of little importance if he incurs the name of miser, for this is one of those vices that permits him to rule. And if someone were to say: Caesar with his generosity came to rule the empire, and many others, because they were generous and known to be so, achieved very high positions; I reply: you are either already a prince or you are on the way to becoming one; in the first instance such generosity is damaging; in the second it is very necessary to be thought generous. And Caesar was one of those who wanted to gain the principality of Rome; but if, after obtaining this, he had lived and had not moderated his expenditures, he would have destroyed that empire. And if someone were to reply: there have existed many princes who have accomplished great deeds with their armies who have been reputed to be generous; I answer you: a prince either spends his own money and that of his subjects or that of others; in the first case he must be economical; in the second he must not restrain any part of his generosity. And for that prince who goes out with his soldiers and lives by looting, sacking, and ransoms,

11

---

[5]*Pope Julius II (1443–1513)* Giuliano della Rovere, pope from 1503 to 1513. Like many of the popes of the day, Julius II was also a diplomat and a general.

[6]*present King of France* Louis XII (1462–1515). He entered Italy on a successful military campaign in 1494.

[7]*present King of Spain* Ferdinand V (1452–1516). A studied politician; he and Queen Isabella (1451–1504) financed Christopher Columbus's voyage to the New World in 1492

who controls the property of others, such generosity is necessary; otherwise he would not be followed by his troops. And with what does not belong to you or to your subjects you can be a more liberal giver, as were Cyrus, Caesar, and Alexander; for spending the wealth of others does not lessen your reputation but adds to it; only the spending of your own is what harms you. And there is nothing that uses itself up faster than generosity, for as you employ it you lose the means of employing it, and you become either poor or despised or, in order to escape poverty, rapacious and hated. And above all other things a prince must guard himself against being despised and hated; and generosity leads you to both one and the other. So it is wiser to live with the reputation of a miser, which produces reproach without hatred, than to be forced to incur the reputation of rapacity, which produces reproach along with hatred, because you want to be considered as generous.

On Cruelty and Mercy
and Whether It Is Better to be Loved Than to be Feared
or the Contrary

Proceeding to the other qualities mentioned above, I say that every 12 prince must desire to be considered merciful and not cruel; nevertheless, he must take care not to misuse this mercy. Cesare Borgia[8] was considered cruel; nonetheless, his cruelty had brought order to Romagna,[9] united it, restored it to peace and obedience. If we examine this carefully, we shall see that he was more merciful than the Florentine people, who, in order to avoid being considered cruel, allowed the destruction of Pistoia.[10] Therefore, a prince must not worry about the reproach of cruelty when it is a matter of keeping his subjects united and loyal; for with a very few examples of cruelty he will be more compassionate than those who, out of excessive mercy, permit disorders to continue, from which arise murders and plundering; for these usually harm the community at large, while the executions that come

---

[8]*Cesare Borgia (1476–1507)* He was known for his brutality and lack of scruples, not to mention his exceptionally good luck. He was a firm ruler, son of Pope Alexander VI.

[9]*Romagna* Region northeast of Tuscany; includes the towns of Bologna, Ferrara, Ravenna, and Rimini. Borgia united it as his base of power in 1501.

[10]*Pistoia* (also known as Pistoria). A town near Florence, disturbed by a civil war in 1501 that could have been averted by strong repressive measures.

from the prince harm one individual in particular. And the new prince, above all other princes, cannot escape the reputation of being called cruel, since new states are full of dangers. And Virgil, through Dido, states: "My difficult condition and the newness of my rule make me act in such a manner, and to set guards over my land on all sides."[11]

Nevertheless, a prince must be cautious in believing and in acting, 13 nor should he be afraid of his own shadow; and he should proceed in such a manner, tempered by prudence and humanity, so that too much trust may not render him imprudent nor too much distrust render him intolerable.

From this arises an argument: whether it is better to be loved than 14 to be feared, or the contrary. I reply that one should like to be both one and the other; but since it is difficult to join them together, it is much safer to be feared than to be loved when one of the two must be lacking. For one can generally say this about men: that they are ungrateful, fickle, simulators and deceivers, avoiders of danger, greedy for gain; and while you work for their good they are completely yours, offering you their blood, their property, their lives, and their sons, as I said earlier, when danger is far away; but when it comes nearer to you they turn away. And that prince who bases his power entirely on their words, finding himself stripped of other preparations, comes to ruin; for friendships that are acquired by a price and not by greatness and nobility of character are purchased but are not owned, and at the proper moment they cannot be spent. And men are less hesitant about harming someone who makes himself loved than one who makes himself feared because love is held together by a chain of obligation which, since men are a sorry lot, is broken on every occasion in which their own self-interest is concerned; but fear is held together by a dread of punishment which will never abandon you.

A prince must nevertheless make himself feared in such a manner 15 that he will avoid hatred, even if he does not acquire love; since to be feared and not to be hated can very well be combined; and this will always be so when he keeps his hands off the property and the women of his citizens and his subjects. And if he must take someone's life, he should do so when there is proper justification and manifest cause; but, above all, he should avoid the property of others; for men forget more quickly the death of their father than the loss of their patrimony. Moreover, the reasons for seizing their property are never lacking; and

---

[11]The quotation is from the *Aeneid* (II. 563–564), the greatest Latin epic poem, written by Virgil (70–19 B.C.). Dido in the poem is a woman general who rules Carthage.

he who begins to live by stealing always finds a reason for taking what belongs to others; on the contrary, reasons for taking a life are rarer and disappear sooner.

But when the prince is with his armies and has under his command 16 a multitude of troops, then it is absolutely necessary that he not worry about being considered cruel; for without that reputation he will never keep an army united or prepared for any combat. Among the praiseworthy deeds of Hannibal[12] is counted this: that, having a very large army, made up of all kinds of men, which he commanded in foreign lands, there never arose the slightest dissention, neither among themselves nor against their prince, both during his good and his bad fortune. This could not have arisen from anything other than his inhuman cruelty, which, along with his many other abilities, made him always respected and terrifying in the eyes of his soldiers; and without that, to attain the same effect, his other abilities would not have sufficed. And the writers of history, having considered this matter very little, on the one hand admire these deeds of his and on the other condemn the main cause of them.

And that it be true that his other abilities would not have been 17 sufficient can be seen from the example of Scipio, a most extraordinary man not only in his time but in all recorded history, whose armies in Spain rebelled against him; this came about from nothing other than his excessive compassion, which gave to his soldiers more liberty than military discipline allowed. For this he was censured in the senate by Fabius Maximus,[13] who called him the corruptor of the Roman militia. The Locrians,[14] having been ruined by one of Scipio's officers, were not avenged by him, nor was the arrogance of that officer corrected, all because of his tolerant nature; so that someone in the senate who tried to apologize for him said that there were many men who knew how not to err better than they knew how to correct errors. Such a nature would have, in time, damaged Scipio's fame and glory if he had maintained it during the empire; but, living under the control of the senate, this harmful characteristic of his not only concealed itself but brought him fame.

---

[12]***Hannibal (247–183 B.C.)*** An amazingly inventive military tactician who led the Carthaginian armies against Rome for more than fifteen years. He crossed the Alps from Gaul in order to surprise Rome. He was noted for use of the ambush and for "inhuman cruelty."

[13]***Fabius Maximus (?–203 B.C.)*** Roman general who fought Hannibal. He was jealous of the younger Roman general Scipio.

[14]***Locrians*** Inhabitants of Locri, an Italian town settled by the Greeks in 683 B.C.

I conclude, therefore, returning to the problem of being feared and   18
loved, that since men love at their own pleasure and fear at the pleasure of the prince, a wise prince should build his foundation upon that
which belongs to him, not upon that which belongs to others: he must
strive only to avoid hatred, as has been said.

How a Prince Should Keep His Word

How praiseworthy it is for a prince to keep his word and to live by   19
integrity and not by deceit everyone knows; nevertheless, one sees
from the experience of our times that the princes who have accomplished great deeds are those who have cared little for keeping their
promises and who have known how to manipulate the minds of men
by shrewdness; and in the end they have surpassed those who laid
their foundations upon honesty.

You must, therefore, know that there are two means of fighting: 20
one according to the laws, the other with force; the first way is proper
to man, the second to beasts; but because the first, in many cases, is
not sufficient, it becomes necessary to have recourse to the second.
Therefore, a prince must know how to use wisely the natures of the
beast and the man. This policy was taught to princes allegorically by
the ancient writers, who described how Achilles and many other ancient princes were given to Chiron[15] the Centaur to be raised and
taught under his discipline. This can only mean that, having a half-
beast and half-man as a teacher, a prince must know how to employ
the nature of the one and the other; and the one without the other
cannot endure.

Since, then, a prince must know how to make good use of the   21
nature of the beast, he should choose from among the beasts the fox
and the lion; for the lion cannot defend itself from traps and the fox
cannot protect itself from wolves. It is therefore necessary to be a fox
in order to recognize the traps and a lion in order to frighten the
wolves. Those who play only the part of the lion do not understand
matters. A wise ruler, therefore, cannot and should not keep his word
when such an observance of faith would be to his disadvantage and
when the reasons which made him promise are removed. And if men
were all good, this rule would not be good; but since men are a sorry

---

[15]*Chiron*   A mythical figure, a centaur (half man, half horse). Unlike most centaurs,
he was wise and benevolent; he was also a legendary physician.

lot and will not keep their promises to you, you likewise need not keep yours to them. A prince never lacks legitimate reasons to break his promises. Of this one could cite an endless number of modern examples to show how many pacts, how many promises have been made null and void because of the infidelity of princes; and he who has known best how to use the fox has come to a better end. But it is necessary to know how to disguise this nature well and to be a great hypocrite and a liar: and men are so simpleminded and so controlled by their present necessities that one who deceives will always find another who will allow himself to be deceived.

I do not wish to remain silent about one of these recent instances.   22
Alexander VI[16] did nothing else, he thought about nothing else, except to deceive men, and he always found the occasion to do this. And there never was a man who had more forcefulness in his oaths, who affirmed a thing with more promises, and who honored his word less; nevertheless, his tricks always succeeded perfectly since he was well acquainted with this aspect of the world.

Therefore, it is not necessary for a prince to have all of the above-   23
mentioned qualities, but it is very necessary for him to appear to have them. Furthermore, I shall be so bold as to assert this: that having them and practicing them at all times is harmful; and appearing to have them is useful; for instance, to seem merciful, faithful, humane, forthright, religious, and to be so; but his mind should be disposed in such a way that should it become necessary not to be so, he will be able and know how to change to the contrary. And it is essential to understand this: that a prince, and especially a new prince, cannot observe all those things by which men are considered good, for in order to maintain the state he is often obliged to act against his promise, against charity, against humanity, and against religion. And therefore, it is necessary that he have a mind ready to turn itself according to the way the winds of Fortune and the changeability of affairs require him; and, as I said above, as long as it is possible, he should not stray from the good, but he should know how to enter into evil when necessity commands.

A prince, therefore, must be very careful never to let anything slip   24
from his lips which is not full of the five qualities mentioned above: he should appear, upon seeing and hearing him, to be all mercy, all faithfulness, all integrity, all kindness, all religion. And there is noth-

---

[16]*Alexander VI (1431–1503)* Roderigo Borgia, pope from 1492 to 1503. He was Cesare Borgia's father and a corrupt but immensely powerful pope.

ing more necessary than to seem to possess this last quality. And men in general judge more by their eyes than their hands; for everyone can see but few can feel. Everyone sees what you seem to be, few perceive what you are, and those few do not dare to contradict the opinion of the many who have the majesty of the state to defend them; and in the actions of all men, and especially of princes, where there is no impartial arbiter, one must consider the final result.[17] Let a prince therefore act to seize and to maintain the state; his methods will always be judged honorable and will be praised by all; for ordinary people are always deceived by appearances and by the outcome of a thing; and in the world there is nothing but ordinary people; and there is no room for the few, while the many have a place to lean on. A certain prince[18] of the present day, whom I shall refrain from naming, preaches nothing but peace and faith, and to both one and the other he is entirely opposed; and both, if he had put them into practice, would have cost him many times over either his reputation or his state.

On Avoiding Being Despised and Hated

But since, concerning the qualities mentioned above, I have spoken about the most important, I should like to discuss the others briefly in this general manner: that the prince, as was noted above, should think about avoiding those things which make him hated and despised; and when he has avoided this, he will have carried out his duties and will find no danger whatsoever in other vices. As I have said, what makes him hated above all else is being rapacious and a usurper of the property and the women of his subjects; he must refrain from this; and in most cases, so long as you do not deprive them of either their property or their honor, the majority of men live happily; and you have only to deal with the ambition of a few, who can be restrained without difficulty and by many means. What makes him despised is being considered changeable, frivolous, effeminate, cowardly, irresolute; from these qualities a prince must guard himself as if from a reef, and he must strive to make everyone recognize in his actions greatness, spirit, dignity, and strength; and concerning the private affairs of his subjects, he must insist that his decision be irrevocable; and he should maintain

25

---

[17]The Italian original, *si guarda al fine*, has often been mistranslated as "the ends justify the means," something Machiavelli never wrote. [Translators' note]

[18]*A certain prince* Probably King Ferdinand V of Spain (1452–1516).

himself in such a way that no man could imagine that he can deceive or cheat him.

That prince who projects such an opinion of himself is greatly es- 26 teemed; and it is difficult to conspire against a man with such a repu- tation and difficult to attack him, provided that he is understood to be of great merit and revered by his subjects. For a prince must have two fears: one, internal, concerning his subjects; the other, external, con- cerning foreign powers. From the latter he can defend himself by his good troops and friends; and he will always have good friends if he has good troops; and internal affairs will always be stable when external affairs are stable, provided that they are not already disturbed by a conspiracy; and even if external conditions change, if he is properly organized and lives as I have said and does not lose control of himself, he will always be able to withstand every attack, just as I said that Nabis the Spartan[19] did. But concerning his subjects, when external affairs do not change, he has to fear that they may conspire secretly: the prince secures himself from this by avoiding being hated or de- spised and by keeping the people satisfied with him; this is a necessary matter, as was treated above at length. And one of the most powerful remedies a prince has against conspiracies is not to be hated by the masses; for a man who plans a conspiracy always believes that he will satisfy the people by killing the prince; but when he thinks he might anger them, he cannot work up the courage to undertake such a deed; for the problems on the side of the conspirators are countless. And experience demonstrates that conspiracies have been many but few have been concluded successfully; for anyone who conspires cannot be alone, nor can he find companions except from amongst those whom he believes to be dissatisfied; and as soon as you have uncovered your intent to one dissatisfied man, you give him the means to make him- self happy, since he can have everything he desires by uncovering the plot; so much is this so that, seeing a sure gain on the one hand and one doubtful and full of danger on the other, if he is to maintain faith with you he has to be either an unusually good friend or a completely determined enemy of the prince. And to treat the matter briefly, I say that on the part of the conspirator there is nothing but fear, jealousy, and the thought of punishment that terrifies him; but on the part of the prince there is the majesty of the principality, the laws, the defen- ses of friends and the state to protect him; so that, with the good will of the people added to all these things, it is impossible for anyone to

---

[19]***Nabis the Spartan** (fl. 220 B.C.)* Tyrant of Sparta from 207–192 B.C., routed by Philopoemon and the Achaean League.

be so rash as to plot against him. For, where usually a conspirator has to be afraid before he executes his evil deed, in this case he must be afraid, having the people as an enemy, even after the crime is performed, nor can he hope to find any refuge because of this.

One could cite countless examples on this subject; but I want to satisfy myself with only one which occurred during the time of our fathers. Messer Annibale Bentivogli, prince of Bologna and grandfather of the present Messer Annibale, was murdered by the Canneschi[20] family, who conspired against him; he left behind no heir except Messer Giovanni,[21] then only a baby. As soon as this murder occurred, the people rose up and killed all the Canneschi. This came about because of the good will that the house of the Bentivogli enjoyed in those days; this good will was so great that with Annibale dead, and there being no one of that family left in the city who could rule Bologna, the Bolognese people, having heard that in Florence there was one of the Bentivogli blood who was believed until that time to be the son of a blacksmith, went to Florence to find him, and they gave him the control of that city; it was ruled by him until Messer Giovanni became of age to rule.

I conclude, therefore, that a prince must be little concerned with conspiracies when the people are well disposed toward him; but when the populace is hostile and regards him with hatred, he must fear everything and everyone. And well-organized states and wise princes have, with great diligence, taken care not to anger the nobles and to satisfy the common people and keep them contented; for this is one of the most important concerns that a prince has.

27

28

---

[20]*Canneschi*   Prominent family in Bologna.
[21]*Giovanni Bentivoglio (1443–1508)*   Former tyrant of Bologna. In sequence he was a conspirator against, then a conspirator with Cesare Borgia.

QUESTIONS

1. The usual criticism of Machiavelli is that he advises his prince to be unscrupulous. Does this seem to be the case in this excerpt?
2. Is Machiavelli correct when he asserts that the great number of people are not good? Does our government assume that to be true, too?
3. Politicians—especially heads of state—are the contemporary counterparts of the prince. Should successful heads of state show skill in war to the same extent Machiavelli's prince does?

4. Clarify the advice Machiavelli gives concerning liberality and stinginess. Is this still good advice?
5. Are modern politicians likely to succeed by following all or most of Machiavelli's recommendations?

WRITING ASSIGNMENTS

1. In speaking of the prince's military duties, Machiavelli says, "being disarmed makes you despised." Take a stand on this issue. If possible, choose an example or instance to strengthen your argument. Is it possible that in modern society being defenseless is an advantage?
2. One of Machiavelli's most controversial statements is: "A man who wishes to make a vocation of being good at all times will come to ruin among so many who are not good." What would Lao-Tzu say in response to this statement? Do you feel that political life in the current decade would support this statement? Or do you feel that in our time such a statement is irrelevant?
3. Find evidence within this excerpt to demonstrate that Machiavelli's attitude toward human nature is accurate. Remember that the usual criticism of Machiavelli is that he is cynical—that he thinks the worst of people rather than the best. Find quotations from the excerpt that would support either or both of these views; then use them in an essay, with analysis, to clarify just what Machiavelli's views on human nature are.
4. By referring to current events and current leaders—either local, national, or international—decide whether or not Machiavelli's advice to the prince would be useful to the modern politician. Consider the question of whether the advice is completely useless, completely reliable, or whether its value depends upon specific conditions. Establish first exactly what the advice is; show how it is applicable or inapplicable for specific politicians; then critique its general usefulness.
5. Probably the chief ethical issue raised by *The Prince* is the question of whether or not the ends justify the means that need to be used to achieve them. Write an essay in which you take a stand on this question. Begin by defining the issue: What does the phrase "the ends justify the means" actually mean? What are the difficulties in accepting the fact that unworthy means may achieve worthy ends? If possible, use some historical or personal examples that will give your argument substance. Carefully analyze Machiavelli's references to circumstances in which questionable means have been (or should have been) used to achieve worthy ends. Is it possible for politicians to concern themselves only with ends and ignore the means entirely?
6. Read Jean Jacques Rousseau's "The Origin of Civil Society." Write a letter to Rousseau explaining how Machiavelli's views will affect his theories about the organization of society. Use key terms or key quotations from Machiavelli that you feel shed light on Rousseau's theories.

JEAN JACQUES ROUSSEAU

The Origin of Civil Society

JEAN JACQUES ROUSSEAU (1712–1778) was the son of a watchmaker and grew to be a man of letters, with a wide variety of accomplishments. Among other works, he wrote a novel, Émile; an opera, The Village Soothsayer; and an autobiography, The Confessions. The Social Contract, published in 1762, became a bible of the French Revolution. Sixteen years after Rousseau died, his remains were given a place of honor in the Panthéon in Paris.

The Social Contract is notable for the way in which it establishes the relationship among the members of a body politic. By emphasizing the fact that each member of a society forfeits a certain amount of personal freedom for the greater good of the whole, and by emphasizing that the sovereign has immense responsibilities to the people, Rousseau conceived the structure of government in a novel way. Today we think of that way as basically democratic, since Rousseau constantly talks about certain types of equality which he expects to find in a well-ordered society. Equality before the law is probably the most important element of that society.

Equality before the law, a concept which we approve today, was a very revolutionary view for 1762. It implied that people who were

---

From *The Social Contract*. Translated by Gerard Hopkins.

born aristocrats would be equal before the law with those who were born commoners; it implied the same thing for the wealthy property holder and the pauper. Neither of these conditions obtained in any nation of the time, although Rousseau saw some hope for such equality in the achievements of English law. Rousseau is careful not to say more than was possible considering the times, but he implies that the body politic should be a commonwealth in which property would be much more widely distributed than it was in contemporary France.

He takes an interesting stance in proposing a time, which he calls the natural state, when men were not joined in social orders. Eventually they surrendered that natural state for a civil state; because there was a general willingness to subordinate individual rights, government came into being. The novelty of this idea for Rousseau's day was his emphasis on government as a product of the act of the people's will rather than as a product of the force of the sovereign. It introduced, as well, the concept of the responsibility of the sovereign to govern well, a concept the French monarch Louis XV (1710–1774) was not quick to accept or understand.

But with all the force of democracy behind him, there is a dark side to Rousseau. His portrait of the family as the origin of civil society is fundamentally patriarchal. The father is the undisputed force in the family, and women are relegated to unimportant roles. Mary Wollstonecraft, in Vindication of the Rights of Woman, takes Rousseau to task for being sexist and narrow in his thinking. In one of her chapters, she quotes liberally from Rousseau's novel, Émile, in which he paints a disparaging portrait of women and their capacities.

ROUSSEAU'S RHETORIC

Little of what Rousseau says here is original. His way of putting his points and of organizing and clarifying them is what makes the work effective. One important technique he uses is that of analogy. His most impressive use is the analogy of the family to the state. The technique of analogy always implies comparing a very familiar thing—the family—with something less familiar—the state. Then, Rousseau looks for the similarities between the two, such as the children as the people and the father as the sovereign. Such analogies can be enlightening or dangerous, depending on how far one is willing to push them.

The main rhetorical device Rousseau uses is analysis, particularly analysis of a logical type. He proposes a statement which seems, on *the surface, to be reasonable; then he analyzes it part by part until he proves to the reader that it is either to be accepted or rejected. He is conspicuous in this application of logic in his section "Of Slavery," in which he proves that slavery is not defensible on any ground, including the widely held ground that prisoners of war may legitimately be made into slaves because they owe their lives to their captors.*

During his passages of analysis, Rousseau occasionally pauses to provide definitions of terms or circumstances or concepts. It is usually during the process of defining that Rousseau clarifies his argument so that the truth can be recognized. The technique is both simple and effective and is therefore important for us to examine, since we may use it as easily as he does.

The reference to other authorities, the strategy of testimony, is sometimes overdone by writers of this period. But Rousseau depends on only a few authorities, notably Hugo Grotius, the Dutch legal authority, and Thomas Hobbes, the English social philosopher. They are most prominent in the early pages of the selection, and they provide only a few basic points that are indispensable for the argument. Again, this rhetorical technique is easy for most of us to use, and its effectiveness cannot be underestimated.

Finally, it should be pointed out that Rousseau is in the habit of posing a considerable number of rhetorical questions. He says, "Man is born free, and everywhere he is in chains. Many a man believes himself to be the master of others who is, no less than they, a slave. How did this change take place? I do not know. What can make it legitimate?" He tells us that for the second question he may have a few answers. The technique of posing serious questions and then attempting to answer them is effective because the clarity of the question-and-answer structure is immediately apparent to the reader. Naturally, the technique can be overworked, but a careful balancing of question and answer can help provide a clarity that might otherwise be missing.

Paradox, a rhetorical device designed to capture a reader's attention and to provoke serious thought, is one of Rousseau's strengths. Being born free, but being everywhere now in chains is one of the most arresting paradoxes in literature. It is so strong that it provokes us to share Rousseau's seriousness in searching out the reasons—even to the point of examining the birth of society itself.

The Origin of Civil Society

Note

It is my wish to inquire whether it be possible, within the civil 1
order, to discover a legitimate and stable basis of Government. This
I shall do by considering human beings as they are and laws as they
might be. I shall attempt, throughout my investigations, to maintain
a constant connection between what right permits and interest de-
mands, in order that no separation may be made between justice and
utility. I intend to begin without first proving the importance of my
subject. Am I, it will be asked, either prince or legislator that I take
it upon me to write of politics? My answer is—No; and it is for that
very reason that I have chosen politics as the matter of my book.
Were I either the one or the other I should not waste my time in
laying down what has to be done. I should do it, or else hold my
peace.

I was born into a free state and am a member of its sovereign 2
body. My influence on public affairs may be small, but because I
have a right to exercise my vote, it is my duty to learn their nature,
and it has been for me a matter of constant delight, while meditating
on problems of Government in general, to find ever fresh reasons for
regarding with true affection the way in which these things are or-
dered in my native land.

The Subject of the First Book

Man is born free, and everywhere he is in chains. Many a man 3
believes himself to be the master of others who is, no less than they,
a slave. How did this change take place? I do not know. What can
make it legitimate? To this question I hope to be able to furnish an
answer.

Were I considering only force and the effects of force, I should say: 4
"So long as a People is constrained to obey, and does, in fact, obey, it
does well. So soon as it can shake off its yoke, and succeeds in doing
so, it does better. The fact that it has recovered its liberty by virtue of

56

that same right by which it was stolen, means either that it is entitled to resume it, or that its theft by others was, in the first place, without justification." But the social order is a sacred right which serves as a foundation for all other rights. This right, however, since it comes not by nature, must have been built upon conventions. To discover what these conventions are is the matter of our inquiry. But, before proceeding further, I must establish the truth of what I have so far advanced.

Of Primitive Societies

The oldest form of society—and the only natural one—is the fam-   5
ily. Children remain bound to their father for only just so long as they feel the need of him for their self-preservation. Once that need ceases the natural bond is dissolved. From then on, the children, freed from the obedience which they formerly owed, and the father, cleared of his debt of responsibility to them, return to a condition of equal independence. If the bond remain operative it is no longer something imposed by nature, but has become a matter of deliberate choice. The family is a family still, but by reason of convention only.

This shared liberty is a consequence of man's nature. Its first law   6
is that of self-preservation: its first concern is for what it owes itself. As soon as a man attains the age of reason he becomes his own master, because he alone can judge of what will best assure his continued existence.

We may, therefore, if we will, regard the family as the basic model   7
of all political associations. The ruler is the father writ large: the people are, by analogy, his children, and all, ruler and people alike, alienate their freedom only so far as it is to their advantage to do so. The only difference is that, whereas in the family the father's love for his children is sufficient reward to him for the care he has lavished on them, in the State, the pleasure of commanding others takes its place, since the ruler is not in a relation of love to his people.

Grotius[1] denies that political power is ever exercised in the inter-   8
ests of the governed, and quotes the institution of slavery in support of his contention. His invariable method of arguing is to derive Right from Fact. It might be possible to adopt a more logical system of reasoning, but none which would be more favorable to tyrants.

---

[1]***Hugo Grotius (1583–1645)*** Huig de Groot, a Dutch lawyer who spent some time in exile in Paris. His fame as a child prodigy was considerable; his book on the laws of war and peace *(De Jure Belli et Pacis)* was widely known in Europe.

According to Grotius, therefore, it is doubtful whether the term 9
"human race" belongs to only a few hundred men, or whether those
few hundred men belong to the human race. From the evidence of his
book it seems clear that he holds by the first of these alternatives, and
on this point Hobbes[2] is in agreement with him. If this is so, then
humanity is divided into herds of livestock, each with its "guardian"
who watches over his charges only that he may ultimately devour
them.

Just as the shepherd is superior in kind to his sheep, so, too, the 10
shepherds of men, or, in other words, their rulers, are superior in kind
to their peoples. This, according to Philo,[3] was the argument advanced
by Caligula,[4] the Emperor, who drew from the analogy the perfectly
true conclusion that either Kings are Gods or their subjects brute
beasts.

The reasoning of Caligula, of Hobbes, and of Grotius is fundamen- 11
tally the same. Far earlier, Aristotle, too, had maintained that men are
not by nature equal, but that some are born to be slaves, others to be
masters.

Aristotle[5] was right: but he mistook the effect for the cause. Noth- 12
ing is more certain than that a man born into a condition of slavery is
a slave by nature. A slave in fetters loses everything—even the desire
to be freed from them. He grows to love his slavery, as the companions
of Ulysses grew to love their state of brutish transformation.[6]

If some men are by nature slaves, the reason is that they have been 13
made slaves *against* nature. Force made the first slaves: cowardice has
perpetuated the species.

I have made no mention of King Adam or of the Emperor Noah, 14

---

[2]***Thomas Hobbes (1588–1679)*** Known as a materialist philosopher who did not
credit divine influence in politics. An Englishman, he became famous for *Leviathan*, a
study of politics that treated the state as if it were a monster (leviathan) with a life of its
own.

[3]***Philo (fl. c. 10 B.C.)*** A philosopher known as "the Jewish Plato" who had absorbed Greek culture and wrote widely on many subjects. His studies on Mosaic Law
were considered important.

[4]***Caligula (12–41 A.D.)*** Roman emperor of uncertain sanity. He loved his sister
Drusilla so much that he had her deified when she died. A military commander, he was
assassinated by an officer.

[5]***Aristotle (384–322 B.C.)*** A student of Plato; his philosophical method became the
dominant intellectual force in Western thought.

[6]***state of brutish transformation*** This sentence refers to the Circe episode in Homer's *Odyssey* (X–XII). Circe was a sorceress who, by means of drugs, enchanted men
and turned them into swine. Ulysses (Latin name of Odysseus), king of Ithaca, is the
central figure of the *Odyssey*.

the father of three great Monarchs[7] who divided up the universe be
tween them, as did the children of Saturn,[8] whom some have been
tempted to identify with them. I trust that I may be given credit for
my moderation, since, being descended in a direct line from one of
these Princes, and quite possibly belonging to the elder branch, I may,
for all I know, were my claims supported in law, be even now the
legitimate Sovereign of the Human Race.[9] However that may be, all
will concur in the view that Adam was King of the World, as was
Robinson Crusoe of his island, only so long as he was its only inhabitant, and that the great advantage of empire held on such terms was
that the Monarch, firmly seated on his throne, had no need to fear
rebellions, conspiracy, or war.

Of the Right of the Strongest

However strong a man, he is never strong enough to remain master   15
always, unless he transform his Might into Right, and Obedience into
Duty. Hence we have come to speak of the Right of the Strongest, a
right which, seemingly assumed in irony, has, in fact, become established in principle. But the meaning of the phrase has never been adequately explained. Strength is a physical attribute, and I fail to see how
any moral sanction can attach to its effects. To yield to the strong is
an act of necessity, not of will. At most it is the result of a dictate of
prudence. How, then, can it become a duty?

Let us assume for a moment that some such Right does really exist.   16
The only deduction from this premise is inexplicable gibberish. For to
admit that Might makes Right is to reverse the process of effect and
cause. The mighty man who defeats his rival becomes heir to his
Right. So soon as we can disobey with impunity, disobedience becomes legitimate. And, since the Mightiest is always right, it merely
remains for us to become possessed of Might. But what validity can
there be in a Right which ceases to exist when Might changes hands?
If a man be constrained by Might to obey, what need has he to obey

---

[7]***the father of three great Monarchs***   Adam in the Bible (Genesis 1:1–2:4) fathered
Cain, Abel, and Seth. Noah's sons, Shem, Ham, and Japheth, repopulated the world after
the Flood (Genesis 6:11–9:19).

[8]***children of Saturn***   Saturn, a mythical deity associated with the golden age of
Rome, was father of Jupiter and other gods in the Roman pantheon.

[9]***Sovereign of the Human Race***   Rousseau is being ironic; like the rest of us, he is
descended from Adam.

by Duty? And if he is not constrained to obey, there is no further obligation on him to do so. It follows, therefore, that the word Right adds
nothing to the idea of Might. It becomes, in this connection, completely meaningless.

Obey the Powers that be. If that means Yield to Force, the precept 17
is admirable but redundant. My reply to those who advance it is that
no case will ever be found of its violation. All power comes from God.
Certainly, but so do all ailments. Are we to conclude from such an
argument that we are never to call in the doctor? If I am waylaid by a
footpad at the corner of a wood, I am constrained by force to give him
my purse. But if I can manage to keep it from him, is it my duty to
hand it over? His pistol is also a symbol of Power. It must, then, be
admitted that Might does not create Right, and that no man is under
an obligation to obey any but the legitimate powers of the State. And
so I continually come back to the question I first asked.

Of Slavery

Since no man has natural authority over his fellows, and since 18
Might can produce no Right, the only foundation left for legitimate
authority in human societies is Agreement.

If a private citizen, says Grotius, can alienate his liberty and make 19
himself another man's slave, why should not a whole people do the
same, and subject themselves to the will of a King? The argument
contains a number of ambiguous words which stand in need of explanation. But let us confine our attention to one only—*alienate*. To
alienate means to give or to sell. Now a man who becomes the slave
of another does not give himself. He sells himself in return for bare
subsistence, if for nothing more. But why should a whole people sell
themselves? So far from furnishing subsistence to his subjects, a King
draws his own from them, and from them alone. According to Rabelais,[10] it takes a lot to keep a King. Do we, then, maintain that a subject surrenders his person on condition that his property be taken too?
It is difficult to see what he will have left.

It will be said that the despot guarantees civil peace to his subjects. 20
So be it. But how are they the gainers if the wars to which his ambition may expose them, his insatiable greed, and the vexatious demands
of his Ministers cause them more loss than would any outbreak of

---

[10]*François Rabelais (1494?–1553)* French writer, author of *Gargantua and Pan-
tagruel,* a work noted for its ribald humor and satirical treatment of politics and religion.

internal dissension? How do they benefit if that very condition of civil peace be one of the causes of their wretchedness? One can live peacefully enough in a dungeon, but such peace will hardly, of itself, ensure one's happiness. The Greeks imprisoned in the cave of Cyclops[11] lived peacefully while awaiting their turn to be devoured.

To say that a man gives himself for nothing is to commit oneself 21 to an absurd and inconceivable statement. Such an act of surrender is illegitimate, null, and void by the mere fact that he who makes it is not in his right mind. To say the same thing of a whole People is tantamount to admitting that the People in question are a nation of imbeciles. Imbecility does not produce Right.

Even if a man can alienate himself, he cannot alienate his children. 22 They are born free, their liberty belongs to them, and no one but themselves has a right to dispose of it. Before they have attained the age of reason their father may make, on their behalf, certain rules with a view to ensuring their preservation and well-being. But any such limitation of their freedom of choice must be regarded as neither irrevocable nor unconditional, for to alienate another's liberty is contrary to the natural order, and is an abuse of the father's rights. It follows that an arbitrary government can be legitimate only on condition that each successive generation of subjects is free either to accept or to reject it, and if this is so, then the government will no longer be arbitrary.

When a man renounces his liberty he renounces his essential man- 23 hood, his rights, and even his duty as a human being. There is no compensation possible for such complete renunciation. It is incompatible with man's nature, and to deprive him of his free will is to deprive his actions of all moral sanction. The convention, in short, which sets up on one side an absolute authority, and on the other an obligation to obey without question, is vain and meaningless. Is it not obvious that where we can demand everything we owe nothing? Where there is no mutual obligation, no interchange of duties, it must, surely, be clear that the actions of the commanded cease to have any moral value? For how can it be maintained that my slave has any "right" against me when everything that he has is my property? His right being *my* right, it is absurd to speak of it as ever operating to my disadvantage.

Grotius, and those who think like him, have found in the fact of 24 war another justification for the so-called "right" of slavery. They ar-

---

[11]*cave of Cyclops* The cyclops is a one-eyed giant cannibal whose cave is the scene of one of Odysseus's triumphs in Homer's *Odyssey*.

gue that since the victor has a *right* to kill his defeated enemy, the latter may, if he so wish, ransom his life at the expense of his liberty, and that this compact is the more legitimate in that it benefits both parties.

But it is evident that this alleged *right* of a man to kill his enemies   25 is not in any way a derivative of the state of war, if only because men, in their primitive condition of independence, are not bound to one another by any relationship sufficiently stable to produce a state either of war or of peace. They are not *naturally* enemies. It is the link between *things* rather than between *men* that constitutes war, and since a state of war cannot originate in simple personal relations, but only in relations between things, private hostility between man and man cannot obtain either in a state of nature where there is no generally accepted system of private property, or in a state of society where law is the supreme authority.

Single combats, duels, personal encounters are incidents which do   26 not constitute a "state" of anything. As to those private wars which were authorized by the Ordinances of King Louis IX[12] and suspended by the Peace of God, they were merely an abuse of Feudalism—that most absurd of all systems of government, so contrary was it to the principles of Natural Right and of all good polity.

War, therefore, is something that occurs not between man and   27 man, but between States. The individuals who become involved in it are enemies only by accident. They fight not as men or even as citizens, but as soldiers: not as members of this or that national group, but as its defenders. A State can have as its enemies only other States, not men at all, seeing that there can be no true relationship between things of a different nature.

This principle is in harmony with that of all periods, and with the   28 constant practice of every civilized society. A declaration of war is a warning, not so much to Governments as to their subjects. The foreigner—whether king, private person, or nation as a whole—who steals, murders, or holds in durance the subjects of another country without first declaring war on that country's Prince, acts not as an enemy but as a brigand. Even when war has been joined, the just Prince, though he may seize all public property in enemy territory, yet respects the property and possessions of individuals, and, in so doing,

---

[12]*King Louis IX (1214–1270)* King of France, also called St. Louis. He was looked upon as an ideal monarch.

shows his concern for those rights on which his own laws arc based. The object of war being the destruction of the enemy State, a commander has a perfect right to kill its defenders so long as their arms are in their hands: but once they have laid them down and have submitted, they cease to be enemies, or instruments employed by an enemy, and revert to the condition of men, pure and simple, over whose lives no one can any longer exercise a rightful claim. Sometimes it is possible to destroy a State without killing any of its subjects, and nothing in war can be claimed as a right save what may be necessary for the accomplishment of the victor's end. These principles are not those of Grotius, nor are they based on the authority of poets, but derive from the Nature of Things, and are founded upon Reason.

The Right of Conquest finds its sole sanction in the Law of the 29 Strongest. If war does not give to the victor the right to massacre his defeated enemies, he cannot base upon a nonexistent right any claim to the further one of enslaving them. We have the right to kill our enemies only when we cannot enslave them. It follows, therefore, that the right to enslave cannot be deduced from the right to kill, and that we are guilty of enforcing an iniquitous exchange if we make a vanquished foeman purchase with his liberty that life over which we have no right. Is it not obvious that once we begin basing the right of life and death on the right to enslave, and the right to enslave on the right of life and death, we are caught in a vicious circle? Even if we assume the existence of this terrible right to kill all and sundry, I still maintain that a man enslaved, or a People conquered, in war is under no obligation to obey beyond the point at which force ceases to be operative. If the victor spares the life of his defeated opponent in return for an equivalent, he cannot be said to have shown him mercy. In either case he destroys him, but in the latter case he derives value from his act, while in the former he gains nothing. His authority, however, rests on no basis but that of force. There is still a state of war between the two men, and it conditions the whole relationship in which they stand to one another. The enjoyment of the Rights of War presupposes that there has been no treaty of Peace. Conqueror and conquered have, to be sure, entered into a compact, but such a compact, far from liquidating the state of war, assumes its continuance.

Thus, in whatever way we look at the matter, the "Right" to en- 30 slave has no existence, not only because it is without legal validity, but because the very term is absurd and meaningless. The words *Slavery* and *Right* are contradictory and mutually exclusive. Whether we be considering the relation of one man to another man, or of an individual to a whole People, it is equally idiotic to say—"You and I have made a compact which represents nothing but loss to you and gain to me. I shall observe it so long as it pleases me to do so—and so shall you, until I cease to find it convenient."

That We Must Always Go Back to an Original Compact

Even were I to grant all that I have so far refuted, the champions of 31 despotism would not be one whit the better off. There will always be a vast difference between subduing a mob and governing a social group. No matter how many isolated individuals may submit to the enforced control of a single conqueror, the resulting relationship will ever be that of Master and Slave, never of People and Ruler. The body of men so controlled may be an agglomeration; it is not an association. It implies neither public welfare nor a body politic. An individual may conquer half the world, but he is still only an individual. His interests, wholly different from those of his subjects, are private to himself. When he dies his empire is left scattered and disintegrated. He is like an oak which crumbles and collapses in ashes so soon as the fire consumes it.

"A People," says Grotius, "may give themselves to a king." His 32 argument implies that the said People were already a People before this act of surrender. The very act of gift was that of a political group and presupposed public deliberation. Before, therefore, we consider the act by which a People chooses their king, it were well if we considered the act by which a People is constituted as such. For it necessarily precedes the other, and is the true foundation on which all Societies rest.

Had there been no original compact, why, unless the choice were 33 unanimous, should the minority ever have agreed to accept the decision of the majority? What right have the hundred who desire a master to vote for the ten who do not? The institution of the franchise is, in itself, a form of compact, and assumes that, at least once in its operation, complete unanimity existed.

Of the Social Pact

I assume, for the sake of argument, that a point was reached in the 34 history of mankind when the obstacles to continuing in a state of Nature were stronger than the forces which each individual could employ to the end of continuing in it. The original state of Nature, therefore, could no longer endure, and the human race would have perished had it not changed its manner of existence.

Now, since men can by no means engender new powers, but can 35 only unite and control those of which they are already possessed, there is no way in which they can maintain themselves save by coming together and pooling their strength in a way that will enable them to withstand any resistance exerted upon them from without. They must develop some sort of central direction and learn to act in concert.

Such a concentration of powers can be brought about only as the 36 consequence of an agreement reached between individuals. But the self-preservation of each single man derives primarily from his own strength and from his own freedom. How, then, can he limit these without, at the same time, doing himself an injury and neglecting that care which it is his duty to devote to his own concerns? This difficulty, in so far as it is relevant to my subject, can be expressed as follows:

"Some form of association must be found as a result of which the 37 whole strength of the community will be enlisted for the protection of the person and property of each constituent member, in such a way that each, when united to his fellows, renders obedience to his own will, and remains as free as he was before." That is the basic problem of which the Social Contract provides the solution.

The clauses of this Contract are determined by the Act of Associa- 38 tion in such a way that the least modification must render them null and void. Even though they may never have been formally enunciated, they must be everywhere the same, and everywhere tacitly admitted and recognized. So completely must this be the case that, should the social compact be violated, each associated individual would at once resume all the rights which once were his, and regain his natural liberty, by the mere fact of losing the agreed liberty for which he renounced it.

It must be clearly understood that the clauses in question can be 39 reduced, in the last analysis, to one only, to wit, the complete alienation by each associate member to the community of *all his rights*. For, in the first place, since each has made surrender of himself without reservation, the resultant conditions are the same for all: and, because they are the same for all, it is in the interest of none to make them onerous to his fellows.

Furthermore, this alienation having been made unreservedly, the 40 union of individuals is as perfect as it well can be, none of the associated members having any claim against the community. For should there be any rights left to individuals, and no common authority be empowered to pronounce as between them and the public, then each, being in some things his own judge, would soon claim to be so in all. Were that so, a state of Nature would still remain in being, the conditions of association becoming either despotic or ineffective.

In short, whoso gives himself to all gives himself to none. And, 41 since there is no member of the social group over whom we do not acquire precisely the same rights as those over ourselves which we have surrendered to him, it follows that we gain the exact equivalent of what we lose, as well as an added power to conserve what we already have.

If, then, we take from the social pact everything which is not es- 42 sential to it, we shall find it to be reduced to the following terms: "each of us contributes to the group his person and the powers which he wields as a person under the supreme direction of the general will, and we receive into the body politic each individual as forming an indivisible part of the whole."

As soon as the act of association becomes a reality, it substitutes 43 for the person of each of the contracting parties a moral and collective body made up of as many members as the constituting assembly has votes, which body receives from this very act of constitution its unity, its dispersed *self*, and its will. The public person thus formed by the union of individuals was known in the old days as a *City*, but now as the *Republic* or *Body Politic*. This, when it fulfils a passive role, is known by its members as *The State*, when an active one, as *The Sovereign People*, and, in contrast to other similar bodies, as a *Power*. In respect of the constituent associates, it enjoys the collective name of *The People*, the individuals who compose it being known as *Citizens* in so far as they share in the sovereign authority, as *Subjects* in so far as they owe obedience to the laws of the State. But these different terms frequently overlap, and are used indiscriminately one for the other. It is enough that we should realize the difference between them when they are employed in a precise sense.

Of the Sovereign

It is clear from the above formula that the act of association im- 44 plies a mutual undertaking between the body politic and its constituent members. Each individual comprising the former contracts, so to speak, with himself and has a twofold function. As a member of the sovereign people he owes a duty to each of his neighbors, and, as a Citizen, to the sovereign people as a whole. But we cannot here apply that maxim of Civil Law according to which no man can be held to an undertaking entered into with himself, because there is a great difference between a man's duty to himself and to a whole of which he forms a part.

Here it should be pointed out that a public decision which can enjoin obedience on all subjects to their Sovereign, by reason of the double aspect under which each is seen, cannot, on the contrary, bind the sovereign in his dealings with himself. Consequently, it is against the nature of the body politic that the sovereign should impose upon himself a law which he cannot infringe. For, since he can regard himself under one aspect only, he is in the position of an individual entering into a contract with himself. Whence it follows that there is not, nor can be, any fundamental law which is obligatory for the whole body of the People, not even the social contract itself. This does not mean that the body politic is unable to enter into engagements with some other Power, provided always that such engagements do not derogate from the nature of the Contract; for the relation of the body politic to a foreign Power is that of a simple individual.   45

But the body politic, or Sovereign, in that it derives its being simply and solely from the sanctity of the said Contract, can never bind itself, even in its relations with a foreign Power, by any decision which might derogate from the validity of the original act. It may not, for instance, alienate any portion of itself, nor make submission to any other sovereign. To violate the act by reason of which it exists would be tantamount to destroying itself, and that which is nothing can produce nothing.   46

As soon as a mob has become united into a body politic, any attack upon one of its members is an attack upon itself. Still more important is the fact that, should any offense be committed against the body politic as a whole, the effect must be felt by each of its members. Both duty and interest, therefore, oblige the two contracting parties to render one another mutual assistance. The same individuals should seek to unite under this double aspect all the advantages which flow from it.   47

Now, the Sovereign People, having no existence outside that of the individuals who compose it, has, and can have, no interest at variance with theirs. Consequently, the sovereign power need give no guarantee to its subjects, since it is impossible that the body should wish to injure all its members, nor, as we shall see later, can it injure any single individual. The Sovereign, by merely existing, is always what it should be.   48

But the same does not hold true of the relation of subject to sover- 49
eign. In spite of common interest, there can be no guarantee that the
subject will observe his duty to the sovereign unless means are found
to ensure his loyalty.

Each individual, indeed, may, as a man, exercise a will at variance 50
with, or different from, that general will to which, as citizen, he contributes. His personal interest may dictate a line of action quite other
than that demanded by the interest of all. The fact that his own existence as an individual has an absolute value, and that he is, by nature,
an independent being, may lead him to conclude that what he owes to
the common cause is something that he renders of his own free will;
and he may decide that by leaving the debt unpaid he does less harm
to his fellows than he would to himself should he make the necessary
surrender. Regarding the moral entity constituting the State as a rational abstraction because it is not a man, he might enjoy his rights as
a citizen without, at the same time, fulfilling his duties as a subject,
and the resultant injustice might grow until it brought ruin upon the
whole body politic.

In order, then, that the social compact may not be but a vain for- 51
mula, it must contain, though unexpressed, the single undertaking
which can alone give force to the whole, namely, that whoever shall
refuse to obey the general will must be constrained by the whole body
of his fellow citizens to do so: which is no more than to say that it
may be necessary to compel a man to be free—freedom being that condition which, by giving each citizen to his country, guarantees him
from all personal dependence and is the foundation upon which the
whole political machine rests, and supplies the power which works it.
Only the recognition by the individual of the rights of the community
can give legal force to undertakings entered into between citizens,
which, otherwise, would become absurd, tyrannical, and exposed to
vast abuses.

Of the Civil State

The passage from the state of nature to the civil state produces a 52
truly remarkable change in the individual. It substitutes justice for instinct in his behavior, and gives to his actions a moral basis which
formerly was lacking. Only when the voice of duty replaces physical
impulse and when right replaces the cravings of appetite does the man
who, till then, was concerned solely with himself, realize that he is
under compulsion to obey quite different principles, and that he must

now consult his reason and not merely respond to the promptings of desire. Although he may find himself deprived of many advantages which were his in a state of nature, he will recognize that he has gained others which are of far greater value. By dint of being exercised, his faculties will develop, his ideas take on a wider scope, his sentiments become ennobled, and his whole soul be so elevated, that, but for the fact that misuse of the new conditions still, at times, degrades him to a point below that from which he has emerged, he would unceasingly bless the day which freed him for ever from his ancient state, and turned him from a limited and stupid animal into an intelligent being and a Man.

Let us reduce all this to terms which can be easily compared. What 53 a man loses as a result of the Social Contract is his natural liberty and his unqualified right to lay hands on all that tempts him, provided only that he can compass its possession. What he gains is civil liberty and the ownership of what belongs to him. That we may labor under no illusion concerning these compensations, it is well that we distinguish between natural liberty which the individual enjoys so long as he is strong enough to maintain it, and civil liberty which is curtailed by the general will. Between possessions which derive from physical strength and the right of the first-comer, and ownership which can be based only on a positive title.

To the benefits conferred by the status of citizenship might be 54 added that of Moral Freedom, which alone makes a man his own master. For to be subject to appetite is to be a slave, while to obey the laws laid down by society is to be free. But I have already said enough on this point, and am not concerned here with the philosophical meaning of the word *liberty*.

Of Real Property

Each individual member of the Community gives himself to it at 55 the moment of its formation. What he gives is the whole man as he then is, with all his qualities of strength and power, and everything of which he stands possessed. Not that, as a result of this act of gift, such possessions, by changing hands and becoming the property of the Sovereign, change their nature. Just as the resources of strength upon which the City can draw are incomparably greater than those at the disposition of any single individual, so, too, is public possession when backed by a greater power. It is made more irrevocable, though not, so far, at least, as regards foreigners, more legitimate. For the State, by reason of the Social Contract which, within it, is the basis of all Rights, is the master of all its members' goods, though, in its dealings with other Powers, it is so only by virtue of its rights as first occupier, which come to it from the individuals who make it up.

The Right of "first occupancy," though more real than the "Right of the strongest," becomes a genuine right only after the right of property has been established. All men have a natural right to what is necessary to them. But the positive act which establishes a man's claim to any particular item of property limits him to that and excludes him from all others. His share having been determined, he must confine himself to that, and no longer has any claim on the property of the community. That is why the right of "first occupancy," however weak it be in a state of nature, is guaranteed to every man enjoying the status of citizen. In so far as he benefits from this right, he withholds his claim, not so much from what is another's, as from what is not specifically his. 56

In order that the right of "first occupancy" may be legalized, the following conditions must be present. (1) There must be no one already living on the land in question. (2) A man must occupy only so much of it as is necessary for his subsistence. (3) He must take possession of it, not by empty ceremony, but by virtue of his intention to work and to cultivate it, for that, in the absence of legal title, alone constitutes a claim which will be respected by others. 57

In effect, by according the right of "first occupancy" to a man's needs and to his will to work, are we not stretching it as far as it will go? Should not some limits be set to this right? Has a man only to set foot on land belonging to the community to justify his claim to be its master? Just because he is strong enough, at one particular moment, to keep others off, can he demand that they shall never return? How can a man or a People take possession of vast territories, thereby excluding the rest of the world from their enjoyment, save by an act of criminal usurpation, since, as the result of such an act, the rest of humanity is deprived of the amenities of dwelling and subsistence which nature has provided for their common enjoyment? When Nuñez Balboa,[13] landing upon a strip of coast, claimed the Southern Sea and the whole of South America as the property of the crown of Castille, was he thereby justified in dispossessing its former inhabitants, and in excluding from it all the other princes of the earth? Grant that, and there will be no end to such vain ceremonies. It would be open to His 58

---

[13]*Nuñez Balboa (1475–1519)* Vasco Nuñez de Balboa, Spanish explorer who discovered the Pacific Ocean.

Catholic Majesty[14] to claim from his Council Chamber possession of the whole Universe, only excepting those portions of it already in the ownership of other princes.

One can understand how the lands of individuals, separate but con- 59
tiguous, become public territory, and how the right of sovereignty, extending from men to the land they occupy, becomes at one real and personal—a fact which makes their owners more than ever dependent, and turns their very strength into a guarantee of their fidelity. This is an advantage which does not seem to have been considered by the monarchs of the ancient world, who, claiming to be no more than kings of the Persians, the Scythians, the Macedonians, seem to have regarded themselves rather as the rulers of men than as the masters of countries. Those of our day are cleverer, for they style themselves kings of France, of Spain, of England, and so forth. Thus, by controlling the land, they can be very sure of controlling its inhabitants.

The strange thing about this act of alienation is that, far from de- 60
priving its members of their property by accepting its surrender, the Community actually establishes their claim to its legitimate ownership, and changes what was formerly mere usurpation into a right, by virtue of which they may enjoy possession. As owners they are Trustees for the Commonwealth. Their rights are respected by their fellow citizens and are maintained by the united strength of the community against any outside attack. From ceding their property to the State—and thus, to themselves—they derive nothing but advantage, since they have, so to speak, acquired all that they have surrendered. This paradox is easily explained once we realize the distinction between the rights exercised by the Sovereign and by the Owner over the same piece of property, as will be seen later.

It may so happen that a number of men begin to group themselves 61
into a community before ever they own property at all, and that only later, when they have got possession of land sufficient to maintain them all, do they either enjoy it in common or parcel it between themselves in equal lots or in accordance with such scale of proportion as may be established by the sovereign. However this acquisition be made, the right exercised by each individual over his own particular share must always be subordinated to the overriding claim of the Community as such. Otherwise there would be no strength in the social bond, nor any real power in the exercise of sovereignty.

---

[14]*His Catholic Majesty* A reference to the king of Spain, probably Ferdinand II of Aragon (1452–1516), also known as Ferdinand the Catholic and Ferdinand V of Castile.

I will conclude this chapter, and the present Book, with a remark 62
which should serve as basis for every social system: that, so far from
destroying natural equality, the primitive compact substitutes for it a
moral and legal equality which compensates for all those physical inequalities from which men suffer. However unequal they may be in
bodily strength or in intellectual gifts, they become equal in the eyes
of the law, and as a result of the compact into which they have entered.

QUESTIONS

1. Rousseau says that the oldest and only natural form of society is the
   family. Is this true? Are there any other natural forms of society evident
   to you?
2. What is the meaning of the phrase "might makes right"?
3. Is political power ever exercised in the interest of the governed?
4. Rousseau describes a "body politic." What does he mean by the term?
   What does he mean by "Commonwealth" when he describes the social
   order by that term?
5. Rousseau emphasizes natural, moral, and legal equality. What does each
   kind of equality imply?

WRITING ASSIGNMENTS

1. The famous opening lines—"Man is born free, and everywhere he is in
   chains. Many a man believes himself to be the master of others who is, no
   less than they, a slave"—were greeted with extraordinary enthusiasm in
   Rousseau's time. Is it possible to apply these lines to the condition of people you know in your own community? In the nation at large? In what
   senses do people make slaves of themselves today? In what senses are they
   made slaves by others?
2. Define the difference between one's duty to oneself and one's duty to the
   whole of which one forms a part. Assume that the individual is yourself
   and that the "whole" is your social structure (locally, nationally, on campus). Define each kind of duty, referring as much as possible to specific
   acts or responsibilities; then establish the differences and the ways in
   which they may come into conflict with one another.
3. One of the most controversial statements in this extract is: "All men have
   a natural right to what is necessary to them." Examine this statement
   carefully. What things or circumstances are necessary to people? Be specific and inclusive. Does Rousseau indicate what is necessary and what is
   not? Take a stand on whether or not Rousseau is correct in his statement.

If he is correct, who should provide the necessities to those who cannot provide for themselves? Does Rousseau take into account those who cannot provide for themselves? Should the necessities be provided for those who will not (as opposed to cannot) provide for themselves? If society will not provide necessities, does the individual have the right of revolution? What rights does the individual have?

4. Consider in some detail the appropriateness of the analogy between the family and the state. Is Rousseau correct in making the analogy in the first place? To what extent does he feel it is a reasonable comparison? By analyzing the details of the family as you know it, establish what the similarities and the differences are between the family and the government. Which responsibilities in one situation carry over to the other? In what sense may it be said that learning to live in a family is preparation for learning to live in a social state?

5. Rousseau contrasts natural liberty with civil liberty. Natural liberty is possible in a state of nature; civil liberty is possible in a civil state. Define each kind of liberty carefully, using a number of examples. What will the differences be between life in a state of nature and life in a civil state? Which state is preferable? What are the reasons for your views? Point to Rousseau's own arguments (he prefers the civil state) and analyze them carefully to support your views. Look for opportunities to use analogy in treating this issue.

6. In *Vindication of the Rights of Woman*, Mary Wollstonecraft quotes Rousseau from his novel *Émile:* "Women have, or ought to have, but little liberty; they are apt to indulge themselves excessively in what is allowed them. Addicted in everything to extremes, they are even more transported at their diversions than boys." Does anything in Rousseau's essay support the conclusion that he reaches in this quotation from *Émile?* Does the method that he uses to examine the origins of civic society contribute in any way to his subsequent views on women? Do you find his position in *Émile* contradictory to his position in "Origin of Civil Society"? Write a brief essay that clarifies Rousseau's position on the political independence or dependence of women. Does he consider women to be men's equal?

THOMAS JEFFERSON

The Declaration of Independence

THOMAS JEFFERSON (1743–1826), *an exceptionally accomplished and well-educated man, is probably best known for writing the Declaration of Independence, a work composed under the eyes of Benjamin Franklin, John Adams, and the Continental Congress, which spent two and a half days going over every word. The substance of the document was developed in committee, but Jefferson, because of the grace of his style, was chosen to do the actual writing. The result is one of the most memorable statements in American history.*

Jefferson had a long and distinguished career. He received a classical education and went on to become a lawyer. By the time he took a seat in the House of Burgesses, which governed Virginia, that colony was already on a course toward revolution. His "A Summary View of the Rights of British America" (1774) first brought him to the attention of those who were agitating for independence.

Jefferson's services to Virginia were considerable. In addition to serving in the House of Burgesses, he became governor (1779) and founded the University of Virginia (1819). Many details of the design of the university's buildings reflect Jefferson's considerable skill as an architect. His one book, Notes on Virginia *(1782), is sometimes personal, sometimes public, sometimes scientific, sometimes haphazard. He discusses slavery, racial differences, the effects of the envi-*

ronment on people, and some of his own feelings about revolution while describing his home state, its geography and its people.

Jefferson's services to the nation include being the first secretary of state (1790–1793), second vice-president (1797–1801), and third president (1801–1809). During his presidency he negotiated the Louisiana Purchase, buying 828,000 square miles of land west of the Mississippi from France for only $15 million. He was sympathetic to the efforts of the French to throw off their monarchy, but when Napoleon extended French influence into the rest of Europe by waging war, Jefferson was careful to keep the United States neutral.

Jefferson was a well-educated eighteenth-century gentleman. His training in the classics and his wide reading in modern authors helped him become a gifted stylist. His work has balance and eloquence as well as clarity. The Declaration of Independence says little that was not familiar or widely understood at the time, but what it does say, it says in a fashion that is memorable.

JEFFERSON'S RHETORIC

Jefferson is notable for a number of interesting techniques. One is the periodic sentence, which was very typical of the age. The first sentence of the Declaration is periodic, which means that it is long and carefully balanced, and the main point comes at the end. Such sentences are not popular today, although an occasional periodic sentence can be powerful in contemporary prose. That first sentence says (in paraphrase): When one nation must sever its relations with a parent nation . . . and stand as an independent nation itself . . . the causes ought to be explained. The entire paragraph is taken up by this one sentence. Moreover, the main body of the Declaration is devoted to listing the "causes," so we see that the most important element of the sentence comes at the end.

The periodic sentence demands certain qualities of balance and parallelism which all good writers ought to pay attention to. The first sentence in paragraph 2 demonstrates both qualities. The balance is achieved by making each part of the sentence about the same length. The parallelism is achieved by using certain key linking words in repetition (they are in roman type in the analysis below). Note how the "truths" mentioned in the first clause are enumerated in the succession of noun clauses beginning with "that"; "Rights" are enumerated in the final clause.

> *We hold these truths to be self-evident,*
>   *that all men are created equal,*
>   *that they are endowed by their Creator with certain*
>   *unalienable Rights,*
>   *that among these are Life, Liberty and the pursuit of Happiness.*

Parallelism is one of the greatest stylistic techniques available to a writer sensitive to rhetoric. It is a natural technique—many untrained writers and speakers develop it on their own.

One result of using parallelism is that one tends to employ the very useful device of enumeration, or the list. Many writers use this technique very effectively by establishing from the first that: "There are three important issues I wish to address. . . ."; and then numbering them: "First, I want to say. . . . Secondly. . . ," and so on. Naturally, as with any technique, this can become tiresome. Used judiciously, it is exceptionally authoritative and powerful. Jefferson devotes paragraphs 3–29 to enumerating the "causes" he mentioned in paragraph 1. Each one constitutes a separate paragraph; thus, each has separate weight and importance. Each begins with "He" or "For" and is therefore in parallel structure. The technique is called **anaphora,** *repetition of the same words at the beginning of successive lines. Jefferson's use of anaphora here is one of the best-known and most effective in all literature. The "He" referred to is England's King George III (1738–1820), who is never mentioned by name. It is not a personality Congress is opposed to; it is the sovereign of a nation which is oppressing the United States and a tyrant who is not dignified by being named. The "For" introduces grievous acts the king has given his assent for; these are offenses against the colonies.*

None of the causes is developed in any detail. We do not have specific information about what trade was cut off by the British, what taxes were imposed without consent, how King George waged war or abdicated government in the colonies. Presumably, Jefferson's audience knew the details. What he did, in listing in twenty-seven paragraphs all the causes, was to point out how many there were. And all are so serious that one alone could cause a revolution. The effect of this enumeration is to illustrate the patience of the colonies up to this point. Jefferson is telling the world that the colonies have finally lost patience, as a result of the causes he lists. The Declaration of Independence projects the careful meditations and decisions of exceptionally calm, patient, and—above all—reasonable people. The periodicity of the sentences and the balance of their parallelism underscore thoughtfulness, grace, learning, and ultimately wisdom.

The Declaration of Independence

In Congress, July 4, 1776

The Unanimous Declaration of the Thirteen United States of America

When in the Course of human events, it becomes necessary for one 1
people to dissolve the political bands which have connected them with
another, and to assume among the Powers of the earth, the separate
and equal station to which the Laws of Nature and of Nature's God
entitle them, a decent respect to the opinions of mankind requires that
they should declare the causes which impel them to the separation.

We hold these truths to be self-evident, that all men are created 2
equal, that they are endowed by their Creator with certain unalienable
Rights, that among these are Life, Liberty and the pursuit of Happiness. That to secure these rights, Governments are instituted among
Men, deriving their just powers from the consent of the governed. That
whenever any Form of Government becomes destructive of these ends,
it is the Right of the People to alter or to abolish it, and to institute a
new Government, laying its foundation on such principles and organizing its powers in such form, as to them shall seem most likely to
effect their Safety and Happiness. Prudence, indeed, will dictate that
Governments long established should not be changed for light and
transient causes; and accordingly all experience hath shown, that mankind are more disposed to suffer, while evils are sufferable, than to
right themselves by abolishing the forms to which they are accustomed. But when a long train of abuses and usurpations, pursuing invariably the same Object evinces a design to reduce them under absolute Despotism, it is their right, it is their duty, to throw off such
Government, and to provide new Guards for their future security.—
Such has been the patient sufferance of these Colonies; and such is
now the necessity which constrains them to alter their former Systems
of Government. The history of the present King of Great Britain is a
history of repeated injuries and usurpations, all having in direct object
the establishment of an absolute Tyranny over these States. To prove
this, let Facts be submitted to a candid world.

He has refused his Assent to Laws, the most wholesome and nec- 3
essary for the public good.

He has forbidden his Governors to pass Laws of immediate and 4
pressing importance, unless suspended in their operation till his Assent should be obtained; and when so suspended, he has utterly neglected to attend to them.

He has refused to pass other laws for the accommodation of large 5
districts of people, unless those people would relinquish the right of
Representation in the Legislature, a right inestimable to them and formidable to tyrants only.

He has called together legislative bodies at places unusual, uncom- 6
fortable, and distant from the depository of their Public Records, for
the sole purpose of fatiguing them into compliance with his measures.

He has dissolved Representative Houses repeatedly, for opposing 7
with manly firmness his invasions on the rights of the people.

He has refused for a long time, after such dissolutions, to cause 8
others to be elected; whereby the Legislative Powers, incapable of Annihilation, have returned to the People at large for their exercise; the
State remaining in the mean time exposed to all the dangers of invasion from without, and convulsions within.

He has endeavoured to prevent the population of these States;[1] for 9
that purpose obstructing the Laws for Naturalization of Foreigners; refusing to pass others to encourage their migration hither, and raising
the conditions of new Appropriations of Lands.

He has obstructed the Administration of Justice, by refusing his 10
Assent to Laws for establishing Judiciary Powers.

He has made Judges dependent on his Will alone, for the tenure of 11
their offices, and the amount and payment of their salaries.

He has erected a multitude of New Offices, and sent hither swarms 12
of Officers to harass our People, and eat out their substance.

He has kept among us, in times of peace, Standing Armies without 13
the Consent of our legislature.

He has affected to render the Military independent of and superior 14
to the Civil Power.

He has combined with others to subject us to a jurisdiction foreign 15
to our constitution, and unacknowledged by our laws; giving his Assent to their acts of pretended Legislation:

For quartering large bodies of armed troops among us: 16

---

[1]*prevent the population of these States* This meant limiting emigration to the Colonies, thus controlling their growth.

For protecting them, by a mock Trial, from Punishment for any 17
Murders which they should commit on the Inhabitants of these States:

For cutting off our Trade with all parts of the world: 18

For imposing taxes on us without our Consent: 19

For depriving us in many cases, of the benefits of Trial by Jury: 20

For transporting us beyond Seas to be tried for pretended offences: 21

For abolishing the free System of English Laws in a neighbouring 22
Province, establishing therein an Arbitrary government, and enlarging
its Boundaries so as to render it at once an example and fit instrument
for introducing the same absolute rule into these Colonies:

For taking away our Charters, abolishing our most valuable Laws, 23
and altering fundamentally the Forms of our Governments:

For suspending our own Legislatures, and declaring themselves in- 24
vested with Power to legislate for us in all cases whatsoever.

He has abdicated Government here, by declaring us out of his Pro- 25
tection and waging War against us.

He has plundered our seas, ravaged our Coasts, burnt our towns, 26
and destroyed the lives of our people.

He is at this time transporting large armies of foreign mercenaries 27
to compleat the works of death, desolation and tyranny, already begun
with circumstances of Cruelty & perfidy scarcely paralleled in the
most barbarous ages, and totally unworthy the Head of a civilized nation.

He has constrained our fellow Citizens taken Captive on the High 28
Seas to bear Arms against their Country, to become the executioners
of their friends and Brethren, or to fall themselves by their Hands.

He has excited domestic insurrections amongst us, and has endeav- 29
oured to bring on the inhabitants of our frontiers, the merciless Indian
Savages, whose Known rule of warfare, is an undistinguished destruction of all ages, sexes and conditions.

In every stage of these Oppressions We have Petitioned for Redress 30
in the most humble terms: Our repeated Petitions have been answered
only by repeated injury. A Prince, whose character is thus marked by
every act which may define a Tyrant, is unfit to be the ruler of a free
People.

Nor have We been wanting in attention to our British brethren. We 31
have warned them from time to time of attempts by their legislature
to extend an unwarrantable jurisdiction over us. We have reminded
them of the circumstances of our emigration and settlement here. We
have appealed to their native justice and magnanimity, and we have
conjured them by the ties of our common kindred to disavow these
usurpations, which, would inevitably interrupt our connections and

correspondence. They too have been deaf to the voice of justice and of consanguinity. We must, therefore, acquiesce in the necessity, which denounces our Separation, and hold them, as we hold the rest of mankind, Enemies in War, in Peace Friends.

We, therefore, the Representatives of the united States of America, 32 in General Congress, Assembled, appealing to the Supreme Judge of the world for the rectitude of our intentions, do, in the Name, and by Authority of the good People of these Colonies, solemnly publish and declare, That these United Colonies are, and of Right ought to be Free and Independent States, that they are Absolved from all Allegiance to the British Crown, and that all political connection between them and the State of Great Britain, is and ought to be totally dissolved; and that as Free and Independent States, they have full Power to levy War, conclude Peace, contract Alliances, establish Commerce, and to do all other Acts and Things which Independent States may of right do. And for the support of this Declaration, with a firm reliance on the Protection of Divine Providence, we mutually pledge to each other our Lives, our Fortunes and our sacred Honor.

QUESTIONS

1. What are the laws of nature Jefferson refers to in paragraph 1? Is there evidence to indicate he had read Rousseau?
2. What do you think Jefferson feels is the function of government (para. 2)?
3. What does Jefferson have to say about women? Is there any way you can determine his views from reading him here?
4. Find at least one use of parallel structure in the Declaration. What key terms are repeated as a means of guaranteeing that structure?
5. Which of the causes listed in paragraphs 3–29 are the most serious? Is any one of them trivial? Is any one serious enough to cause a revolution?
6. Find the most graceful sentence in the entire Declaration. Where is it placed in the Declaration? Do you think it was put there consciously, as a means of attracting attention?
7. In what ways do the king's desires for a stable government interfere with Jefferson's sense of his own independence? Is he talking about his independence as a citizen?

WRITING ASSIGNMENTS

1. Jefferson states that the unalienable rights of a citizen are "Life, Liberty and the pursuit of Happiness." Do you think these are indeed unalienable

rights? In the course of answering this question—using careful parallelism of any sort you like—be certain that you define what each of these terms really means. Define them for yourself, for our time.

2. Write an essay with at least three periodic sentences (and underline them) in which you discuss what you feel the function of government should be. You may want to establish first what you think Jefferson's conception of the function of government is, then compare or contrast it with your own.

3. Write an essay in which you examine to what extent Jefferson agrees or disagrees with Lao-Tzu in his conception of human nature and the ways in which a government should function. Does Jefferson seem to share Lao-Tzu's commitment to judicious inactivity? Is there any evidence that the king subscribes to it? What, for you, are the most important similarities and differences between Jefferson's views and those of Lao-Tzu?

4. Jefferson envisioned a government that made it possible for its citizens to have the rights of life, liberty, and the pursuit of happiness. Has Jefferson's revolutionary vision been achieved in America? Begin with a definition of your key terms: "life," "liberty," and "the pursuit of happiness." Then, taking each in turn and using any examples available—drawn from current events, your own experience, your general background in American history—take a clear and well-argued stand on whether our nation has achieved Jefferson's goal.

5. Slavery was legal in America in 1776, and Jefferson reluctantly owned slaves. He had a plan to grant gradual emancipation to the slaves, but it was never presented to Congress because he realized that Congress would never approve it. Jefferson and Franklin financed a plan to buy slaves and return them to Africa, where they founded the nation of Liberia. To what degree does the practice of slavery by the people who wrote it invalidate the Declaration of Independence? Does it invalidate it at all? Take a stand on these questions and defend it. You may wish to read the relevant chapters on Jefferson and slavery in Merrill D. Peterson's *Thomas Jefferson and the New Nation* (1970).

6. What kind of government does Jefferson seem to prefer? How different would he make his government from that of the king against whom he is reacting? Is he talking about an entirely different system or about the same system, but with a different kind of "prince" at the head? How would Jefferson protect the individual against the whim of the state, while also protecting the state against the whim of the individual?

MARY WOLLSTONECRAFT

Pernicious Effects Which Arise from the Unnatural Distinctions Established in Society

MARY WOLLSTONECRAFT (1759–1797) was born into relatively simple circumstances, with a father whose heavy drinking and spending eventually ruined the family and left her and her sisters to support themselves. She became a governess, a teacher, and eventually a writer. Her views were among the most enlightened of her day—particularly regarding women and women's rights. She is thought of in our time as a very forward-looking feminist.

Her thinking, however, is comprehensive and is not to be limited to a single issue. She was known to the American patriot Thomas Paine (1737–1809); to Dr. Samuel Johnson (1709–1784); and to the English philosopher William Godwin (1756–1836), whom she eventually married. Her views on marriage were remarkable for her times; among other things, she felt it unnecessary to marry a man in order to live happily with him. Her first liaison, with an American, Gilbert Imlay, gave her the opportunity to travel and learn something about commerce and capitalism at first hand. Her second liaison, with Godwin, brought her into the intellectual circles of her day. She married Godwin when she was pregnant with Mary, who married the

---

From *Vindication of the Rights of Woman.*

poet Percy Bysshe Shelley and wrote the novel **Frankenstein** *(1818).*
Mary Wollstonecraft died giving birth to this daughter.

The excitement generated by the French Revolution (1789–1799)
caused her to react against the very conservative view put forward by
the philosopher Edmund Burke. Her pamphlet, A Vindication of the
Rights of Men *(1790), was well received. She followed it with* Vindication of the Rights of Woman *(1792), which was translated into*
French.

She sees the feminist problem in political terms. The chapter re-
printed here concentrates on questions of property, class, and law.
As a person committed to the revolutionary principles of liberty,
equality, and fraternity, Wollstonecraft links the present condition
of women to the political and social structure of her society. Her aim
is to point up the inequities in treatment of women—which her soci-
ety simply did not perceive—and to attempt to rectify them.

WOLLSTONECRAFT'S RHETORIC

Stylistically, Mary Wollstonecraft is sometimes wordy. She was
writing for an audience that did not necessarily appreciate brief, ex-
act expression. Rather, they appreciated a more luxuriant and lei-
surely style than we do today. However, she is capable of handling
imagery carefully and does so (especially in the first paragraph) with-
out overburdening her prose. She uses an approach which she herself
calls "episodical observations" (para. 12). These are anecdotes—per-
sonal stories—and apparently casual cataloguings of thoughts on a
number of related issues. She was aware that her structure was not
tight, that it did not develop a specific argument, and that it did not
force the reader to accept or reject her position. This was a wise ap-
proach, since it was obvious to her that her audience was completely
prejudiced against her view. To attempt to convince them of her
views was to invite total defeat.

Instead, she simply puts forward several observations which
stand by themselves as examples of the evils she condemns. Even
those who stand against her will see that there is some validity to her
claims; and they will not be so threatened by her argument as to
become defensive before they have learned something new. Her ap-
peal is always to the higher intellectual capacities of both men and
women. Her complaints are directed, as well, against both men and
women. This balance of opinion, coupled with a range of examples—

all of which are thought-provoking—makes her views seem clear and convincing.

The use of metaphor is also distinctive in this passage. A metaphor is an implied comparison, made without using "like" or "as." The second sentence of the first paragraph is particularly heavy with metaphor: "For it is in the most polished society that noisome reptiles and venomous serpents lurk under the rank herbage; and there is voluptuousness pampered by the still sultry air, which relaxes every good disposition before it ripens into virtue." The metaphor presents society as a garden in which the grass is decaying and dangerous serpents are lurking. Good disposition—character—is a plant that might ripen, but—continuing the metaphor—it ripens into virtue, not just a fruit. A favorite source of metaphors for Wollstonecraft is drapery (dressmaking). When she uses one of these methaphors she is usually reminding us that drapery gives a new shape to things, that it sometimes hides the truth, and that it ought not put a false appearance on what it covers.

One interesting technique she uses, and which we can easily use ourselves, is that of literary allusion. By alluding to important literary works and writers—such as William Shakespeare, Jean Jacques Rousseau, Samuel Johnson, and Greek mythology—she is not only demonstrating her learning but is also showing that she respects her audience, which she presumes shares her learning. She does not show off her learning by overquoting or by referring to very obscure writers. She balances it perfectly, even by transforming folk aphorisms into "homely proverbs" such as, "whoever the devil finds idle he will employ."

A very special area of allusion is to the art of dressmaking, something we associate with women. Her experiences with her difficult father gave her the knowledge of unfortunate gambling tables and card games, another source for allusions. She alludes further to personal experience shared by some of her audience when she talks about the degradation felt by a woman of some intelligence forced to act the governess—glorified servant—in a well-to-do family. Wollstonecraft makes excellent uses of these allusions, never overdoing them, always giving them just the right touch.

Pernicious Effects Which
Arise from the
Unnatural Distinctions
Established in Society

From the respect paid to property flow, as from a poisoned foun- 1
tain, most of the evils and vices which render this world such a dreary
scene to the contemplative mind. For it is in the most polished society
that noisome reptiles and venomous serpents lurk under the rank herbage; and there is voluptuousness pampered by the still sultry air,
which relaxes every good disposition before it ripens into virtue.

One class presses on another; for all are aiming to procure respect 2
on account of their property: and property, once gained, will procure
the respect due only to talents and virtue. Men neglect the duties incumbent on man, yet are treated like demi-gods; religion is also separated from morality by a ceremonial veil, yet men wonder that the
world is almost, literally speaking, a den of sharpers or oppressors.

There is a homely proverb, which speaks a shrewd truth, that 3
whoever the devil finds idle he will employ. And what but habitual
idleness can hereditary wealth and titles produce? For man is so constituted that he can only attain a proper use of his faculties by exercising them, and will not exercise them unless necessity of some kind
first set the wheels in motion. Virtue likewise can only be acquired by
the discharge of relative duties; but the importance of these sacred
duties will scarcely be felt by the being who is cajoled out of his humanity by the flattery of sycophants.[1] There must be more equality
established in society, or morality will never gain ground, and this
virtuous equality will not rest firmly even when founded on a rock, if
one half of mankind be chained to its bottom by fate, for they will be
continually undermining it through ignorance or pride.

It is vain to expect virtue from women till they are in some degree 4
independent of men; nay, it is vain to expect that strength of natural
affection which would make them good wives and mothers. Whilst

---

[1]**sycophants** Toadies or false flatterers.

they are absolutely dependent on their husbands they will be cunning, mean, and selfish, and the men who can be gratified by the fawning fondness of spaniel-like affection have not much delicacy, for love is not to be bought, in any sense of the words; its silken wings are instantly shrivelled up when anything beside a return in kind is sought. Yet whilst wealth enervates men, and women live, as it were, by their personal charms, how can we expect them to discharge those ennobling duties which equally require exertion and self-denial? Hereditary property sophisticates[2] the mind, and the unfortunate victims to it, if I may so express myself, swathed from their birth, seldom exert the locomotive faculty of body or mind; and, thus viewing everything through one medium, and that a false one, they are unable to discern in what true merit and happiness consist. False, indeed, must be the light when the drapery of situation hides the man, and makes him stalk in masquerade, dragging from one scene of dissipation to another the nerveless limbs that hang with stupid listlessness, and rolling round the vacant eye which plainly tells us that there is no mind at home.

I mean, therefore, to infer[3] that the society is not properly orga- 5
nized which does not compel men and women to discharge their respective duties, by making it the only way to acquire that countenance from their fellow-creatures which every human being wishes some way to attain. The respect, consequently, which is paid to wealth and mere personal charms, is a true north-east blast that blights the tender blossoms of affection and virtue. Nature has wisely attached affections to duties to sweeten toil, and to give that vigour to the exertions of reason which only the heart can give. But the affection which is put on merely because it is the appropriated insignia of a certain character, when its duties are not fulfilled, is one of the empty compliments which vice and folly are obliged to pay to virtue and the real nature of things.

To illustrate my opinion, I need only observe that when a woman 6
is admired for her beauty, and suffers herself to be so far intoxicated by the admiration she receives as to neglect to discharge the indispensable duty of a mother, she sins against herself by neglecting to cultivate an affection that would equally tend to make her useful and happy. True happiness, I mean all the contentment and virtuous satisfaction that can be snatched in this imperfect state, must arise from

---

[2]***sophisticates*** Ruins or corrupts.
[3]***infer*** Imply.

well regulated affections; and an affection includes a duty. Men are not aware of the misery they cause and the vicious weakness they cherish by only inciting women to render themselves pleasing; they do not consider that they thus make natural and artificial duties clash by sacrificing the comfort and respectability of a woman's life to voluptuous notions of beauty when in nature they all harmonize.

Cold would be the heart of a husband, were he not rendered unnatural by early debauchery, who did not feel more delight at seeing his child suckled by its mother, than the most artful wanton tricks could ever raise; yet this natural way of cementing the matrimonial tie and twisting esteem with fonder recollections, wealth leads women to spurn. To preserve their beauty and wear the flowery crown of the day, which gives them a kind of right to reign for a short time over the sex, they neglect to stamp impressions on their husbands' hearts that would be remembered with more tenderness when the snow on the head began to chill the bosom than even their virgin charms. The maternal solicitude of a reasonable affectionate woman is very interesting, and the chastened dignity with which a mother returns the caresses that she and her child receive from a father who has been fulfilling the serious duties of his station, is not only a respectable but a beautiful sight. So singular indeed are my feelings, and I have endeavoured not to catch factitious ones, that after having been fatigued with the sight of insipid grandeur and the slavish ceremonies that with cumbrous pomp supplied the place of domestic affections, I have turned to some other scene to relieve my eye by resting it on the refreshing green everywhere scattered by nature. I have then viewed with pleasure a woman nursing her children, and discharging the duties of her station with, perhaps, merely a servant maid to take off her hands the servile part of the household business. I have seen her prepare herself and children, with only the luxury of cleanliness, to receive her husband, who returning weary home in the evening found smiling babes and a clean hearth. My heart has loitered in the midst of the group, and has even throbbed with sympathetic emotion, when the scraping of the well known foot has raised a pleasing tumult. 7

Whilst my benevolence has been gratified by contemplating this artless picture, I have thought that a couple of this description, equally necessary and independent of each other, because each fulfilled the respective duties of their station, possessed all that life could give. Raised sufficiently above abject poverty not to be obliged to weigh the consequence of every farthing they spend, and having sufficient to prevent their attending to a frigid system of economy, which narrows 8 both heart and mind, I declare, so vulgar[4] are my conceptions, that I know not what is wanted to render this the happiest as well as the most respectable situation in the world, but a taste for literature, to throw a little variety and interest into social converse, and some superfluous money to give to the needy and to buy books. For it is not pleasant when the heart is opened by compassion and the head active in arranging plans of usefulness, to have a prim urchin continually twitching back the elbow to prevent the hand from drawing out an almost empty purse, whispering at the same time some prudential maxim about the priority of justice.

Destructive, however, as riches and inherited honours are to the human character, women are more debased and cramped, if possible, by them than men, because men may still, in some degree, unfold their faculties by becoming soldiers and statesmen. 9

As soldiers, I grant, they can now only gather, for the most part, vainglorious laurels, whilst they adjust to a hair the European balance, taking especial care that no bleak northern nook or sound incline the beam.[5] But the days of true heroism are over, when a citizen fought for his country like a Fabricius[6] or a Washington, and then returned to his farm to let his virtuous fervour run in a more placid, but not a less salutary, stream. No, our British heroes are oftener sent from the gaming table than from the plough[7] and their passions have been rather inflamed by hanging with dumb suspense on the turn of a die, than sublimated by panting after the adventurous march of virtue in the historic page. 10

The statesman, it is true, might with more propriety quit the faro bank, or card table, to guide the helm, for he has still but to shuffle and trick.[8] The whole system of British politics, if system it may cour- 11

---

[4] ***vulgar*** Common.

[5] ***incline the beam*** The metaphor is of the balance—the scale that representations of blind justice hold up. Wollstonecraft's point is that in her time soldiers fought to prevent the slightest changes in a balance of power that grew ever more delicate, not in heroic wars with heroic consequences.

[6] ***Fabricius (fl. 282 B.C.)*** Gaius Fabricius, a worthy Roman general and statesman known for resistance to corruption.

[7] ***from the plough*** Worthy Roman heroes were humble farmers, not gamblers.

[8] ***shuffle and trick*** The upper class spent much of its time gambling: faro is a high-stakes card game. Wollstonecraft is ironic when she says the statesman has "still but to shuffle and trick," but she connects the "training" of faro with the practice of politics in a deft, sardonic fashion. She is punning on the multiple meanings of *shuffle*—to mix up a deck of cards and to move oneself or one's papers about slowly and aimlessly—and *trick*—to win one turn of a card game and to do a devious deed.

teously be called, consisting in multiplying dependents and contriving taxes which grind the poor to pamper the rich; thus a war, or any wild goose chase, is, as the vulgar use the phrase, a lucky turn-up of patronage for the minister, whose chief merit is the art of keeping himself in place. It is not necessary then that he should have bowels for[9] the poor, so he can secure for his family the odd trick. Or should some show of respect, for what is termed with ignorant ostentation an Englishman's birthright, be expedient to bubble the gruff mastiff[10] that he has to lead by the nose, he can make an empty show very safely by giving his single voice and suffering his light squadron to file off to the other side. And when a question of humanity is agitated he may dip a sop in the milk of human kindness to silence Cerberus,[11] and talk of the interest which his heart takes in an attempt to make the earth no longer cry for vengeance as it sucks in its children's blood, though his cold hand may at the very moment rivet their chains by sanctioning the abominable traffic. A minister is no longer a minister than while he can carry a point which he is determined to carry. Yet it is not necessary that a minister should feel like a man, when a bold push might shake his seat.

But, to have done with these episodical observations, let me return 12 to the more specious slavery which chains the very soul of woman, keeping her for ever under the bondage of ignorance.

The preposterous distinctions of rank, which render civilization a 13 curse by dividing the world between voluptuous tyrants and cunning envious dependents, corrupt, almost equally, every class of people, because respectability is not attached to the discharge of the relative duties of life, but to the station, and when the duties are not fulfilled the affections cannot gain sufficient strength to fortify the virtue of which they are the natural reward. Still there are some loopholes out of which a man may creep, and dare to think and act for himself; but for a woman it is a herculean task, because she has difficulties peculiar to her sex to overcome which require almost superhuman powers.

A truly benevolent legislator always endeavours to make it the in- 14 terest of each individual to be virtuous; and thus private virtue becoming the cement of public happiness, an orderly whole is consolidated by the tendency of all the parts towards a common centre. But, the private or public virtue of woman is very problematical; for Rousseau, and a numerous list of male writers, insist that she should all her life

---

[9]***bowels for*** Feelings for; sense of pity.
[10]***to bubble the gruff mastiff*** This means to fool even a guard dog.
[11]***Cerberus*** The guard dog of Hades, the Greek hell or underworld.

be subjected to a severe restraint, that of propriety. Why subject her to propriety—blind propriety, if she be capable of acting from a nobler spring, if she be an heir of immortality? Is sugar always to be produced by vital blood? Is one half of the human species, like the poor African slaves, to be subject to prejudices that brutalize them, when principles would be a surer guard, only to sweeten the cup of man? Is not this indirectly to deny woman reason? for a gift is a mockery, if it be unfit for use.

Women are, in common with men, rendered weak and luxurious 15 by the relaxing pleasures which wealth procures; but added to this they are made slaves to their persons, and must render them alluring that man may lend them his reason to guide their tottering steps aright. Or should they be ambitious, they must govern their tyrants by sinister tricks, for without rights there cannot be any incumbent duties. The laws respecting woman, which I mean to discuss in a future part, make an absurd unit of a man and his wife;[12] and then, by the easy transition of only considering him as responsible, she is reduced to a mere cypher.

The being who discharges the duties of its station is independent; 16 and, speaking of women at large, their first duty is to themselves as rational creatures, and the next in point of importance, as citizens, is that which includes so many, of a mother. The rank in life which dispenses with their fulfilling this duty necessarily degrades them by making them mere dolls. Or, should they turn to something more important than merely fitting drapery upon a smooth block, their minds are only occupied by some soft platonic attachment; or, the actual management of an intrigue may keep their thoughts in motion; for when they neglect domestic duties, they have it not in their own power to take the field and march and counter-march like soldiers, or wrangle in the senate to keep their faculties from rusting.

I know that, as a proof of the inferiority of the sex, Rousseau has 17 exultingly exclaimed, How can they leave the nursery for the camp![13] And the camp has by some moralists been termed the school of the most heroic virtues; though, I think, it would puzzle a keen casuist[14] to prove the reasonableness of the greater number of wars that have dubbed heroes. I do not mean to consider this question critically; be-

---

[12]*absurd unit of a man and his wife* In English law man and wife were legally one; the man spoke for both.

[13]*leave the nursery for the camp!* Rousseau's Émile complains that women cannot leave a nursery to go to war.

[14]*casuist* One who argues closely, persistently, and sometimes unfairly.

cause, having frequently viewed these freaks of ambition as the first natural mode of civilization, when the ground must be torn up, and the woods cleared by fire and sword, I do not choose to call them pests; but surely the present system of war has little connection with virtue of any denomination, being rather the school of *finesse* and effeminacy than of fortitude.

Yet if defensive war, the only justifiable war, in the present advanced state of society, where virtue can show its face and ripen amidst the rigours which purify the air on the mountain's top, were alone to be adopted as just and glorious, the true heroism of antiquity might again animate female bosoms. But fair and softly, gentle reader, male or female, do not alarm thyself, for though I have compared the character of a modern soldier with that of a civilized woman, I am not going to advise them to turn their distaff[15] into a musket, though I sincerely wish to see the bayonet converted into a pruning-hook. I only recreated an imagination, fatigue by contemplating the vices and follies which all proceed from a feculent[16] stream of wealth that has muddied the pure rills of natural affection, by supposing that society will some time or other be so constituted, that man must necessarily fulfill the duties of a citizen or be despised, and that while he was employed in any of the departments of civil life, his wife, also an active citizen, should be equally intent to manage her family, educate her children, and assist her neighbours. 18

But, to render her really virtuous and useful, she must not, if she discharge her civil duties, want, individually, the protection of civil laws; she must not be dependent on her husband's bounty for her subsistence during his life or support after his death—for how can a being be generous who has nothing of its own? or virtuous, who is not free? 19

The wife, in the present state of things, who is faithful to her husband, and neither suckles nor educates her children, scarcely deserves the name of a wife, and has no right to that of a citizen. But take away natural rights, and duties become null. 20

Women then must be considered as only the wanton solace of men when they become so weak in mind and body that they cannot exert themselves, unless to pursue some frothy pleasure or to invent some frivolous fashion. What can be a more melancholy sight to a thinking mind than to look into the numerous carriages that drive helter-skelter about this metropolis in a morning full of pale-faced creatures who are 21

---

[15]*distaff* Instrument to wind wool in the act of spinning; notoriously a job only "fit for women."

[16]*feculent* Filthy, polluted; related to *feces*.

flying from themselves. I have often wished, with Dr. Johnson,[17] to place some of them in a little shop with half a dozen children looking up to their languid countenances for support. I am much mistaken if some latent vigour would not soon give health and spirit to their eyes, and some lines drawn by the exercise of reason the blank cheeks, which before were only undulated by dimples, might restore lost dignity to the character, or rather enable it to attain the true dignity of its nature. Virtue is not to be acquired even by speculation, much less by the negative supineness that wealth naturally generates.

Besides, when poverty is more disgraceful than even vice, is not morality cut to the quick? Still to avoid misconstruction, though I consider that women in the common walks of life are called to fulfill the duties of wives and mothers, by religion and reason, I cannot help lamenting that women of a superior cast have not a road open by which they can pursue more extensive plans of usefulness and independence. I may excite laughter by dropping a hint which I mean to pursue some future time, for I really think that women ought to have representatives, instead of being arbitrarily governed without having any direct share allowed them in the deliberations of government. 22

But, as the whole system of representation is now in this country only a convenient handle for despotism, they need not complain, for they are as well represented as a numerous class of hard-working mechanics, who pay for the support of royalty when they can scarcely stop their children's mouths with bread. How are they represented whose very sweat supports the splendid stud of an heir apparent, or varnishes the chariot of some female favourite who looks down on shame? Taxes on the very necessaries of life enable an endless tribe of idle princes and princesses to pass with stupid pomp before a gaping crowd, who almost worship the very parade which costs them so dear. This is mere gothic grandeur, something like the barbarous useless parade of having sentinels on horseback at Whitehall,[18] which I could never view without a mixture of contempt and indignation. 23

How strangely must the mind be sophisticated when this sort of state impresses it! But, till these monuments of folly are levelled by virtue, similar follies will leaven the whole mass. For the same char- 24

---

[17]***Dr. Samuel Johnson (1709–1784)*** The greatest lexicographer and one of the most respected authors of England's eighteenth century. He was known to Mary Wollstonecraft and to her sister, Eliza, a teacher. The reference is to an item published in his *Rambler,* essay 85.

[18]***sentinels on horseback at Whitehall*** This is a reference to the expensive piece of showmanship which continues to our day: the changing of the guard at Whitehall.

acter, in some degree, will prevail in the aggregate of society; and the refinements of luxury, or the vicious repinings of envious poverty, will equally banish virtue from society, considered as the characteristic of that society, or only allow it to appear as one of the stripes of the harlequin coat worn by the civilized man.

In the superior ranks of life every duty is done by deputies, as if 25 duties could ever be waived, and the vain pleasures which consequent idleness forces the rich to pursue appear so enticing to the next rank that the numerous scramblers for wealth sacrifice everything to tread on their heels. The most sacred trusts are then considered as sinecures, because they were procured by interest, and only sought to enable a man to keep *good company*. Women in particular, all want to be ladies. Which is simply to have nothing to do, but listlessly to go they scarcely care where, for they cannot tell what.

But what have women to do in society? I may be asked, but to 26 loiter with easy grace; surely you would not condemn them all to suckle fools and chronicle small beer![19] No. Women might certainly study the art of healing, and be physicians as well as nurses. And midwifery, decency seems to allot to them, though I am afraid the word midwife in our dictionaries will soon give place to *accoucheur*,[20] and one proof of the former delicacy of the sex be effaced from the language.

They might also study politics, and settle their benevolence on the 27 broadest basis; for the reading of history will scarcely be more useful than the perusal of romances, if read as mere biography; if the character of the times, the political improvements, arts, &c., be not observed. In short, if it be not considered as the history of man; and not of particular men, who filled a niche in the temple of fame, and dropped into the black rolling stream of time, that silently sweeps all before it, into the shapeless void called—eternity. For shape, can it be called, "that shape hath none"?[21]

Business of various kinds they might likewise pursue, if they were 28 educated in a more orderly manner, which might save many from common and legal prostitution. Women would not then marry for a support, as men accept of places under government, and neglect the

---

[19]*chronicle small beer!* *Othello* (II.i.158). This means to keep the household accounts.

[20]**accoucheur** Male version of the female midwife.

[21]*"that shape hath none"* The reference is to *Paradise Lost* (II.667) by John Milton (1608–1674); it is an allusion to death.

implied duties; nor would an attempt to earn their own subsistence—
a most laudable one!—sink them almost to the level of those poor
abandoned creatures who live by prostitution. For are not milliners
and mantua-makers[22] reckoned the next class? The few employments
open to women, so far from being liberal, are menial; and when a superior education enables them to take charge of the education of children as governesses, they are not treated like the tutors of sons, though
even clerical tutors are not always treated in a manner calculated to
render them respectable in the eyes of their pupils, to say nothing of
the private comfort of the individual. But as women educated like gen-
tlewomen are never designed for the humiliating situation which necessity sometimes forces them to fill, these situations are considered
in the light of a degradation; and they know little of the human heart,
who need to be told that nothing so painfully sharpens sensibility as
such a fall in life.

Some of these women might be restrained from marrying by a 29
proper spirit or delicacy, and others may not have had it in their power
to escape in this pitiful way from servitude; is not that government
then very defective, and very unmindful of the happiness of one half
of its members, that does not provide for honest, independent women,
by encouraging them to fill respectable stations? But in order to render
their private virtue a public benefit, they must have a civil existence
in the state, married or single; else we shall continually see some worthy woman, whose sensibility has been rendered painfully acute by
undeserved contempt, droop like "the lily broken down by a plowshare."

It is a melancholy truth—yet such is the blessed effect of civiliza- 30
tion!—the most respectable women are the most oppressed; and, unless they have understandings far superior to the common run of understandings, taking in both sexes, they must, from being treated like
contemptible beings, become contemptible. How many women thus
waste life away the prey of discontent, who might have practised as
physicians, regulated a farm, managed a shop, and stood erect, supported by their own industry, instead of hanging their heads sur-
charged with the dew of sensibility, that consumes the beauty to
which it at first gave lustre; nay, I doubt whether pity and love are so
near akin as poets feign, for I have seldom seen much compassion ex-

---

[22]*milliners and mantua-makers* Dressmakers, usually women (as tailors were usually men).

cited by the helplessness of females, unless they were fair; then, perhaps pity was the soft handmaid of love, or the harbinger of lust.

How much more respectable is the woman who earns her own 31 bread by fulfilling any duty, than the most accomplished beauty!— beauty did I say?—so sensible am I of the beauty of moral loveliness, or the harmonious propriety that attunes the passions of a well-regulated mind, that I blush at making the comparison; yet I sigh to think how few women aim at attaining this respectability by withdrawing from the giddy whirl of pleasure, or the indolent calm that stupefies the good sort of women it sucks in.

Proud of their weakness, however, they must always be protected, 32 guarded from care, and all the rough toils that dignify the mind. If this be the fiat of fate, if they will make themselves insignificant and contemptible, sweetly to waste "life away," let them not expect to be valued when their beauty fades, for it is the fate of the fairest flowers to be admired and pulled to pieces by the careless hand that plucked them. In how many ways do I wish, from the purest benevolence, to impress this truth on my sex; yet I fear that they will not listen to a truth that dear-bought experience has brought home to many an agitated bosom, nor willingly resign the priveleges of rank and sex for the privileges of humanity, to which those have no claim who do not discharge its duties.

Those writers are particularly useful, in my opinion, who make 33 man feel for man, independent of the station he fills, or the drapery of factitious sentiments. I then would fain[23] convince reasonable men of the importance of some of my remarks; and prevail on them to weigh dispassionately the whole tenor of my observations. I appeal to their understandings; and, as a fellow-creature, claim, in the name of my sex, some interest in their hearts. I entreat them to assist to emancipate their companion, to make her a *help meet* for them!

Would men but generously snap our chains, and be content with 34 rational fellowship instead of slavish obedience, they would find us more observant daughters, more affectionate sisters, more faithful wives, more reasonable mothers—in a word, better citizens. We should then love them with true affection, because we should learn to respect ourselves; and, the peace of mind of a worthy man would not be interrupted by the idle vanity of his wife, nor the babes sent to nestle in a strange bosom, having never found a home in their mother's.

---

[23]*fain* Happily.

QUESTIONS

1. Who is the audience for Wollstonecraft's writing? Is she writing more for men than for women? Is it clear from what she says that there is an explicit audience with specific qualities?
2. Analyze paragraph 1 carefully for the use of imagery and metaphor. What are their actual affects? Are they overdone?
3. Wollstonecraft begins by attacking property, or the respect paid to it. What does she mean? Does she sustain that line of thought throughout the piece?
4. In paragraph 12, Wollstonecraft speaks of the "bondage of ignorance" in which women are held. Clarify what precisely she means by that expression.
5. In paragraph 30, Wollstonecraft says that people who are treated as if they were contemptible will become contemptible. Is this a political or a psychological judgment?
6. What is the substance of Wollstonecraft's complaint concerning women being admired for their beauty?

WRITING ASSIGNMENTS

1. Throughout the chapter Wollstonecraft attacks the unnatural distinctions made between men and women. Establish carefully what those unnatural distinctions are, why they are unnatural, and whether or not such distinctions persist to the present day. By contrast, establish what some natural distinctions between men and women are and whether or not Wollstonecraft has taken them into consideration.
2. References are made throughout the piece to prostitution and to the debaucheries of men. Paragraph 7 is specific in making reference to the "wanton tricks" of prostitutes. What is Wollstonecraft's attitude toward men in regard to sexuality and their attitudes toward women—both the loose women of the brothels and the women with whom they live? Find explicit passages in the piece which you can quote and analyze in an effort to clarify her views.
3. In paragraph 2, Wollstonecraft complains that "the respect due only to talents and virtue" is instead being given to people on account of their property. Further, she says in paragraph 9 that riches are "destructive . . . to the human character." Establish carefully, by means of reference to her passages and to analysis of those passages, just what Wollstonecraft means by such statements. Then, using your own anecdotes or "episodical observations," take a stand on whether these views are views you yourself can hold for our time. Are riches destructive to character? Is too much respect paid to those who possess property? If it is possible to make use of metaphor, or of allusion—literary or personal—do so.

4. In paragraph 4, Wollstonecraft speaks of "men who can be gratified by the fawning fondness of spaniel-like affection" from their women. Search through the essay for other instances of similar views and analyze them carefully. Establish exactly what the men she describes want their women to be like. What do men today want their women to be like? Have today's men changed very much in their expectations? Why? Why not? Use personal observations where possible in answering this question.

5. The question of what roles women ought to have in society is addressed in paragraphs 26, 27, and 28. What are those roles? Why are they defined in terms of work? Do you agree that they are, indeed, the roles that women should assume? Are there more roles that you would include? Has our age improved with respect to giving women access to those roles? Consider the question of what women actually did in Wollstonecraft's time and what they do today.

FREDERICK DOUGLASS

From
The Narrative of the Life of Frederick Douglass, an American Slave

*F*REDERICK DOUGLASS *(1817–1895) was born into slavery in Maryland; he died not only a free man but a man who commanded the respect of his country, his government, and hosts of supporters. His owner's wife, Mrs. Hugh Auld, was a northerner and did not know about the state law forbidding slaves to learn to read and write. This was a lucky accident, indeed: Mrs. Auld taught Douglass enough so that he could begin his own education—and escape to freedom.*

The selection presented here describes how Douglass gained his victory. In his description—the Narrative *was published in 1845— Douglass was careful to avoid mentioning details that would likely have hurt other slaves' chances of gaining their freedom. Douglass used the papers of a freed black sailor to impersonate him, and so he was able to sail from Baltimore to New York, where he gained his freedom. His method was dangerous but simple. He lived first in New York, then settled in New Bedford, Massachusetts.*

The rest of the Narrative *is filled with stories about his growing up as a slave. He had little connection with his family. His mother, Harriet Bailey, was not able to be close with him, nor was he ever to know who his father was. He records not only the beatings he witnessed as a slave but also the conditions under which he lived and the struggles he felt within himself to be a free man. He himself survived brutal beatings and torture by a professional slave "breaker."*

This section of the Narrative *is fascinating for its revelation of the observations of a freed slave concerning the world he entered. His concerns for work, economy, and justice are everywhere apparent in these pages. When they were published—apparently as a result of encouragement by Harvard students who had heard his powerful oratory—these pages made him one of the most sought-after speakers in the North. He became a lecturer for the Massachusetts Antislavery Society. Yet, as a fugitive slave, he lived in constant fear of being kidnapped and returned to slavery.*

The institution of slavery was legal in the South, and in the North police officers were obliged to return runaways. A slave was property. In every sense, Douglass was a person for whom the concept of independence was a kind of imaginative flight of fancy. The entire weight of the government sat on him to make sure he had few if any rights. His description of how he managed to keep his spirits up in this dreadful situation is extraordinary.

After publication of an early version of his life, to avoid capture he spent two years on a speaking tour of Great Britain and Ireland, then returned to the United States and became the editor of the North Star, *an abolitionist paper in Rochester, New York. One of his chief concerns was for the welfare of the slaves who managed to secure their freedom. When John Brown invited him to participate in the raid at Harpers Ferry, Virginia, Douglass was famous throughout the North. He refused Brown's invitation because he believed that such an act would not benefit the antislavery cause. When the Civil War began, Douglass managed to get Lincoln's ear. Originally there were no plans to free the slaves, but Douglass helped convince Lincoln that it would help the war effort to free them, and in 1863 Lincoln delivered the Emancipation Proclamation.*

The years after the war and Lincoln's death were not good for freed slaves. Terrorist groups in both the North and the South worked to keep them from enjoying freedom, and programs which might have been effective in training black ex-slaves were never fully instituted. During this time Douglass worked in various capacities for the government, as U.S. minister to Haiti (1889–91), as assistant secretary of the Santa Domingo Commission, and as an official in Washington, D.C. He was the first black American to become a national figure and to have powerful influence with the government.

DOUGLASS'S RHETORIC

Douglass was essentially a self-taught man. He is said to have been a commanding speaker who could move people to agree with his views. His speeches were often full and somewhat high-flown in the fashion of the day. This excerpt from the Narrative, *however, is remarkable for having none of the characteristics of the overdone rhetoric we find in the writing of the time. Instead, it is surprisingly direct, simple, and clear. The use of the first person is as simple as one could wish it to be, and yet the feelings that are projected are genuine and moving.*

The structure Douglass employs in the Narrative *is one of the most basic in all rhetoric: the chronological narrative. He begins his story at a given point, explaining what happened at that moment. He then progresses to the next sequence of events, always pushing the narrative closer to the present time. He even includes some key dates, so that one can measure the progress of the narrative. The structure is one that we all recognize and feel comfortable with. There are no interruptions such as flashbacks or ruminations on what might have been. Rather, after his introductory two paragraphs, he tells what happened as it happened.*

Douglass's style is a bit formal by modern standards. His sentences are somewhat long, although they are carefully balanced by an occasional very brief sentence. His paragraphs are in general very long, indeed. He tends to take a given subject and work it out thoroughly before dropping it, and to begin a new subject in the next paragraph. Yet even now, almost a century and a half later, the style appears easy and direct. No modern reader will have difficulty responding to what Frederick Douglass has to say. His views on justice, on liberty, and on the relationship between economy and government are as accessible now as they were when they were originally written.

From
The Narrative of the Life of Frederick Douglass, an American Slave

I now come to that part of my life during which I planned, and   1
finally succeeded in making, my escape from slavery. But before nar-
rating any of the peculiar circumstances, I deem it proper to make
known my intention not to state all the facts connected with the
transaction. My reasons for pursuing this course may be understood
from the following: First, were I to give a minute statement of all the
facts, it is not only possible, but quite probable, that others would
thereby be involved in the most embarrassing difficulties. Secondly,
such a statement would most undoubtedly induce greater vigilance on
the part of slaveholders than has existed heretofore among them;
which would, of course be the means of guarding a door whereby some
dear brother bondman might escape his galling chains. I deeply regret
the necessity that impels me to suppress any thing of importance connected with my experience in slavery. It would afford me great pleasure indeed, as well as materially add to the interest of my narrative,
were I at liberty to gratify a curiosity, which I know exists in the
minds of many, by an accurate statement of all the facts pertaining to
my most fortunate escape. But I must deprive myself of this pleasure,
and the curious of the gratification which such a statement would afford. I would allow myself to suffer under the greatest imputations
which evil-minded men might suggest, rather than exculpate myself,[1]
and thereby run the hazard of closing the slightest avenue by which a
brother slave might clear himself of the chains and fetters of slavery.

I have never approved of the very public manner in which some of   2
our western friends have conducted what they call the *underground
railroad*,[2] but which, I think, by their open declarations, has been

---

[1] *exculpate myself*   This is a mild bit of irony; Douglass means that if he revealed his
method of escape he would be innocent of the charge of not telling the whole truth.

[2] *underground railroad*   An organization of "safe houses" to help escaped slaves find
their way to freedom in Canada. The Fugitive Slave Act (1850) made the work of this
abolitionist group a crime.

made most emphatically the *upperground railroad.* I honor those good men and women for their noble daring, and applaud them for willingly subjecting themselves to bloody persecution, by openly avowing their participation in the escape of slaves. I, however, can see very little good resulting from such a course, either to themselves or the slaves escaping; while, upon the other hand, I see and feel assured that those open declarations are a positive evil to the slaves remaining, who are seeking to escape. They do nothing towards enlightening the slave, whilst they do much towards enlightening the master. They stimulate him to greater watchfulness, and enhance his power to capture his slave. We owe something to the slaves south of the line as well as to those north of it; and in aiding the latter on their way to freedom, we should be careful to do nothing which would be likely to hinder the former from escaping from slavery. I would keep the merciless slave-holder profoundly ignorant of the means of flight adopted by the slave. I would leave him to imagine himself surrounded by myriads of invisible tormentors, ever ready to snatch from his infernal grasp his trembling prey. Let him be left to feel his way in the dark; let darkness commensurate with his crime hover over him; and let him feel that at every step he takes, in pursuit of the flying bondman, he is running the frightful risk of having his hot brains dashed out by an invisible agency. Let us render the tyrant no aid; let us not hold the light by which he can trace the footprints of our flying brother. But enough of this. I will now proceed to the statement of those facts, connected with my escape, for which I am alone responsible, and for which no one can be made to suffer but myself.

In the early part of the year 1838, I became quite restless. I could 3 see no reason why I should, at the end of each week, pour the reward of my toil into the purse of my master. When I carried to him my weekly wages, he would, after counting the money, look me in the face with a robber-like fierceness, and ask, "Is this all?" He was satisfied with nothing less than the last cent. He would, however, when I made him six dollars, sometimes give me six cents, to encourage me. It had the opposite effect. I regarded it as a sort of admission of my right to the whole. The fact that he gave me any part of my wages was proof, to my mind, that he believed me entitled to the whole of them. I always felt worse for having received any thing; for I feared that the giving me a few cents would ease his conscience, and make him feel himself to be a pretty honorable sort of robber. My discontent grew upon me. I was ever on the look-out for means of escape; and, finding no direct means, I determined to try to hire my time, with a view of getting money with which to make my escape. In the spring of 1838, when Master Thomas[3] came to Baltimore to purchase his spring goods, I got an opportunity, and applied to him to allow me to hire my time. He unhesitatingly refused my request, and told me this was another stratagem by which to escape.[4] He told me I could go nowhere but that he could get me; and that, in the event of my running away, he should spare no pains in his efforts to catch me. He exhorted me to content myself, and be obedient. He told me, if I would be happy, I must lay out no plans for the future. He said, if I behaved myself properly, he would take care of me. Indeed, he advised me to complete thought-lessness of the future, and taught me to depend solely upon him for happiness. He seemed to see fully the pressing necessity of setting aside my intellectual nature, in order to contentment in slavery. But in spite of him, and even in spite of myself, I continued to think, and to think about the injustice of my enslavement, and the means of escape.

About two months after this, I applied to Master Hugh for the privi- 4 lege of hiring my time. He was not acquainted with the fact that I had applied to Master Thomas, and had been refused. He too, at first, seemed disposed to refuse; but, after some reflection, he granted me the privilege, and proposed the following term: I was to be allowed all my time, make all contracts with those for whom I worked, and find my own employment; and, in return for this liberty, I was to pay him three dollars at the end of each week; find myself in[5] calking tools, and in board and clothing. My board was two dollars and a half per week. This, with the wear and tear of clothing and calking tools, made my regular expenses about six dollars per week. This amount I was compelled to make up, or relinquish the privilege of hiring my time. Rain or shine, work or no work, at the end of each week the money must be forthcoming, or I must give up my privilege. This arrange-ment, it will be perceived, was decidedly in my master's favor. It re-lieved him of all need of looking after me. His money was sure. He received all the benefits of slaveholding without its evils; while I en-dured all the evils of a slave, and suffered all the care and anxiety of a freeman. I found it a hard bargain. But, hard as it was, I thought it

---

[3]***Master Thomas***   Thomas Lloyd, his owner, had lent Douglass to Hugh Auld of Balti-more. Auld's wife, a northerner, taught Douglass to read and write.

[4]***another stratagem by which to escape***   He had escaped once before and was captured by a professional slave "breaker."

[5]***find myself in***   Douglass means to provide himself with the means to equip him-self with his tools and to pay for his board and clothing.

better than the old mode of getting along. It was a step towards free
dom to be allowed to bear the responsibilities of a freeman, and I was
determined to hold on upon it. I bent myself to the work of making
money. I was ready to work at night as well as day, and by the most
untiring perseverance and industry, I made enough to meet my expenses, and lay up a little money every week. I went on thus from
May till August. Master Hugh then refused to allow me to hire my
time longer. The ground for his refusal was a failure on my part, one
Saturday night, to pay him for my week's time. This failure was occasioned by my attending a camp meeting about ten miles from Baltimore. During the week, I had entered into an engagement with a number of young friends to start from Baltimore to the camp ground early
Saturday evening; and being detained by my employer, I was unable to
get down to Master Hugh's without disappointing the company. I
knew that Master Hugh was in no special need of the money that
night. I therefore decided to go to camp meeting, and upon my return
pay him the three dollars. I staid at the camp meeting one day longer
than I intended when I left. But as soon as I returned, I called upon
him to pay him what he considered his due. I found him very angry;
he could scarce restrain his wrath. He said he had a great mind to give
me a severe whipping. He wished to know how I dared go out of the
city without asking his permission. I told him I hired my time, and
while I paid him the price which he asked for it, I did not know that I
was bound to ask him when and where I should go. This reply troubled
him; and, after reflecting a few moments, he turned to me, and said I
should hire my time no longer; that the next thing he should know of,
I would be running away. Upon the same plea, he told me to bring my
tools and clothing home forthwith. I did so; but instead of seeking
work, as I had been accustomed to do previously to hiring my time, I
spent the whole week without the performance of a single stroke of
work. I did this in retaliation. Saturday night, he called upon me as
usual for my week's wages. I told him I had no wages; I had done no
work that week. Here we were upon the point of coming to blows. He
raved, and swore his determination to get hold of me. I did not allow
myself a single word; but was resolved, if he laid the weight of his
hand upon me, it should be blow for blow. He did not strike me, but
told me that he would find me in constant employment in future. I
thought the matter over during the next day, Sunday, and finally resolved upon the third day of September, as the day upon which I would
make a second attempt to secure my freedom. I now had three weeks
during which to prepare for my journey. Early on Monday morning,
before Master Hugh had time to make any engagement for me, I went

out and got employment of Mr. Butler, at his ship-yard near the draw-bridge, upon what is called the City Block, thus making it unnecessary for him to seek employment for me. At the end of the week, I brought him between eight and nine dollars. He seemed very well pleased, and asked me why I did not do the same the week before. He little knew what my plans were. My object in working steadily was to remove any suspicion he might entertain of my intent to run away; and in this I succeeded admirably. I suppose he thought I was never better satisfied with my condition than at the very time during which I was planning my escape. The second week passed, and again I carried him my full wages; and so well pleased was he, that he gave me twenty-five cents (quite a large sum for a slaveholder to give a slave) and bade me to make a good use of it. I told him I would.

Things went on without very smoothly indeed, but within there 5 was trouble. It is impossible for me to describe my feelings as the time of my contemplated start drew near. I had a number of warm-hearted friends in Baltimore—friends that I loved almost as I did my life—and the thought of being separated from them forever was painful beyond expression. It is my opinion that thousands would escape from slavery, who now remain, but for the strong cords of affection that bind them to their friends. The thought of leaving my friends was decidedly the most painful thought with which I had to contend. The love of them was my tender point, and shook my decision more than all things else. Besides the pain of separation, the dread and apprehension of a failure exceeded what I had experienced at my first attempt. The appalling defeat I then sustained returned to torment me. I felt assured that, if I failed in this attempt, my case would be a hopeless one—it would seal my fate as a slave forever. I could not hope to get off with any thing less than the severest punishment, and being placed beyond the means of escape. It required no very vivid imagination to depict the most frightful scenes through which I should have to pass, in case I failed. The wretchedness of slavery, and the blessedness of freedom, were per-petually before me. It was life and death with me. But I remained firm, and, according to my resolution, on the third day of September, 1838, I left my chains, and succeeded in reaching New York without the slightest interruption of any kind. How I did so—what means I adopted—what direction I travelled, and by what mode of convey-ance—I must leave unexplained, for the reasons before mentioned.

I have been frequently asked how I felt when I found myself in a 6 free State. I have never been able to answer the question with any satisfaction to myself. It was a moment of the highest excitement I ever experienced. I suppose I felt as one may imagine the unarmed mariner to feel when he is rescued by a friendly man-of-war from the pursuit of a pirate. In writing to a dear friend, immediately after my arrival at New York, I said I felt like one who had escaped a den of hungry lions. This state of mind, however, very soon subsided; and I was again seized with a feeling of great insecurity and loneliness. I was yet liable to be taken back, and subjected to all the tortures of slavery. This in itself was enough to damp the ardor of my enthusiasm. But the loneliness overcame me. There I was in the midst of thousands, and yet a perfect stranger; without home and without friends, in the midst of thousands of my own brethren—children of a common Father, and yet I dared not to unfold to any one of them my sad condition. I was afraid to speak to any one for fear of speaking to the wrong one, and thereby falling into the hands of money-loving kidnappers, whose business it was to lie in wait for the panting fugitive, as the ferocious beasts of the forest lie in wait for their prey. The motto which I adopted when I started from slavery was this—"Trust no man!" I saw in every white man an enemy, and in almost every colored man cause for distrust. It was a most painful situation; and, to understand it, one must needs experience it, or imagine himself in similar circumstances. Let him be a fugitive slave in a strange land— a land given up to be the hunting-ground for slaveholders—whose inhabitants are legalized kidnappers—where he is every moment subjected to the terrible liability of being seized upon by his fellow-men, as the hideous crocodile seizes upon his prey!—I say, let him place himself in my situation—without home or friends—without money or credit—wanting shelter, and no one to give it—wanting bread, and no money to buy it—and at the same time let him feel that he is pursued by merciless men-hunters, and in total darkness as to what to do, where to go, or where to stay—perfectly helpless both as to the means of defense and means of escape—in the midst of plenty, yet suffering the terrible gnawings of hunger—in the midst of houses, yet having no home—among fellow-men, yet feeling as if in the midst of wild beasts, whose greediness to swallow up the trembling and half-famished fugitive is only equalled by that with which the monsters of the deep swallow up the helpless fish upon which they subsist—I say, let him be placed in this most trying situation—the situation in which I was placed—then, and not till then, will he fully appreciate the hardships of, and know how to sympathize with, the toil-worn and whip-scarred fugitive slave.

Thank Heaven, I remained but a short time in this distressed situation. I was relieved from it by the humane hand of Mr. David Ruggles, whose vigilance, kindness, and perseverance, I shall never forget. I am

7

glad of an opportunity to express, as far as words can, the love and gratitude I bear him. Mr. Ruggles is now afflicted with blindness, and is himself in need of the same kind offices which he was once so forward in the performance of toward others. I had been in New York but a few days, when Mr. Ruggles sought me out, and very kindly took me to his boarding-house at the corner of Church and Lespenard Streets. Mr. Ruggles was then very deeply engaged in the memorable *Darg* case,[6] as well as attending to a number of other fugitive slaves, devising ways and means for their successful escape; and, though watched and hemmed in on almost every side, he seemed to be more than a match for his enemies.

Very soon after I went to Mr. Ruggles, he wished to know of me where I wanted to go; as he deemed it unsafe for me to remain in New York. I told him I was a calker, and should like to go where I could get work. I thought of going to Canada; but he decided against it, and in favor of my going to New Bedford, thinking I should be able to get work there at my trade. At this time, Anna,[7] my intended wife, came on; for I wrote to her immediately after my arrival at New York (notwithstanding my homeless, houseless, and helpless condition) informing her of my successful flight, and wishing her to come on forthwith. In a few days after her arrival, Mr. Ruggles called in the Rev. J. W. C. Pennington, who, in the presence of Mr. Ruggles, Mrs. Michaels, and two or three others, performed the marriage ceremony, and gave us a certificate, of which the following is an exact copy:

8

> THIS may certify, that I joined together in holy matrimony Frederick Johnson[8] and Anna Murray, as man and wife, in the presence of Mr. David Ruggles and Mrs. Michaels.
>
> JAMES W. C. PENNINGTON.
> *New York, Sept. 15, 1838.*

Upon receiving this certificate, and a five-dollar bill from Mr. Ruggles, I shouldered one part of our baggage, and Anna took up the other, and we set out forthwith to take passage on board of the steamboat John W. Richmond for Newport, on our way to New Bedford. Mr. Ruggles gave me a letter to a Mr. Shaw in Newport, and told me, in case my money did not serve me to New Bedford, to stop in Newport and obtain further assistance; but upon our arrival at Newport, we were so anxious to get to a place of safety, that, notwithstanding we lacked the

9

---

[6]**Darg** *case* Mr. Ruggles tried to help a fugitive slave named Darg escape authorities who were compelled to return him to his owners.

[7]She was free. [Douglass's note]

[8]I had changed my name from Frederick *Bailey* to that of *Johnson*. [Douglass's note]

necessary money to pay our fare, we decided to take seats in the stage, and promise to pay when we got to New Bedford. We were encouraged to do this by two excellent gentlemen, residents of New Bedford, whose names I afterward ascertained to be Joseph Ricketson and William C. Taber. They seemed at once to understand our circumstances, and gave us such assurance of their friendliness as put us fully at ease in their presence. It was good indeed to meet with such friends, at such a time. Upon reaching New Bedford, we were directed to the house of Mr. Nathan Johnson, by whom we were kindly received, and hospitably provided for. Both Mr. and Mrs. Johnson took a deep and lively interest in our welfare. They proved themselves quite worthy of the name of abolitionists. When the stage-driver found us unable to pay our fare, he held on upon our baggage as security for the debt. I had but to mention the fact to Mr. Johnson, and he forthwith advanced the money.

We now began to feel a degree of safety, and to prepare ourselves 10 for the duties and responsibilities of a life of freedom. On the morning after our arrival at New Bedford, while at the breakfast-table, the question arose as to what name I should be called by. The name given me by my mother was, "Frederick Augustus Washington Bailey." I, however, had dispensed with the two middle names long before I left Maryland so that I was generally known by the name of "Frederick Bailey." I started from Baltimore bearing the name of "Stanley." When I got to New York, I again changed my name to "Frederick Johnson," and thought that would be the last change. But when I got to New Bedford, I found it necessary again to change my name. The reason of this necessity was, that there were so many Johnsons in New Bedford, it was already quite difficult to distinguish between them. I gave Mr. Johnson the privilege of choosing me a name, but told him he must not take from me the name of "Frederick." I must hold on to that, to preserve a sense of my identity. Mr. Johnson had just been reading the "Lady of the Lake,"[9] and at once suggested that my name be "Douglass." From that time until now I have been called "Frederick Douglass"; and as I am more widely known by that name than by either of the others, I shall continue to use it as my own.

I was quite disappointed at the general appearance of things in New 11 Bedford. The impression which I had received respecting the character and condition of the people of the north, I found to be singularly erro-

---

[9] *"Lady of the Lake"* A long narrative poem by Sir Walter Scott (1771–1832), published in 1810. The fugitive Lord James of Douglas is a primary character.

neous. I had very strangely supposed, while in slavery, that few of the comforts, and scarcely any of the luxuries, of life were enjoyed at the north, compared with what were enjoyed by the slaveholders of the south. I probably came to this conclusion from the fact that northern people owned no slaves. I supposed that they were about upon a level with the non-slaveholding population of the south. I knew *they* were exceedingly poor, and I had been accustomed to regard their poverty as the necessary consequence of their being non-slaveholders. I had somehow imbibed the opinion that, in the absence of slaves, there could be no wealth, and very little refinement. And upon coming to the north, I expected to meet with a rough, hard-handed, and uncultivated population, living in the most Spartan-like simplicity, knowing nothing of the ease, luxury, pomp, and grandeur of southern slaveholders. Such being my conjectures, any one acquainted with the appearance of New Bedford may very readily infer how palpably I must have seen my mistake.

In the afternoon of the day when I reached New Bedford, I visited 12 the wharves, to take a view of the shipping. Here I found myself surrounded with the strongest proofs of wealth. Lying at the wharves, and riding in the stream, I saw many ships of the finest model, in the best order, and of the largest size. Upon the right and left, I was walled in by granite warehouses of the widest dimensions, stowed to their utmost capacity with the necessaries and comforts of life. Added to this, almost every body seemed to be at work, but noiselessly so, compared with what I had been accustomed to in Baltimore. There were no loud songs heard from those engaged in loading and unloading ships. I heard no deep oaths or horrid curses on the laborer. I saw no whipping of men; but all seemed to go smoothly on. Every man appeared to understand his work, and went at it with a sober, yet cheerful earnestness, which betokened the deep interest which he felt in what he was doing, as well as a sense of his own dignity as a man. To me this looked exceedingly strange. From the wharves I strolled around and over the town, gazing with wonder and admiration at the splendid churches, beautiful dwellings, and finely-cultivated gardens; evincing an amount of wealth, comfort, taste, and refinement, such as I had never seen in any part of slaveholding Maryland.

Every thing looked clean, new and beautiful. I saw few or no dilapi- 13 dated houses, with poverty-stricken inmates; no half-naked children and barefooted women, such as I had been accustomed to see in Hillsborough, Easton, St. Michael's, and Baltimore. The people looked more able, stronger, healthier, and happier, than those of Maryland. I was for once made glad by a view of extreme wealth, without being saddened by seeing extreme poverty. But the most astonishing as well as the most interesting thing to me was the condition of the colored people, a great many of whom, like myself, had escaped thither as a refuge from the hunters of men. I found many, who had not been seven years out of their chains, living in finer houses, and evidently enjoying more of the comforts of life, than the average of slaveholders in Maryland. I will venture to assert that my friend Mr. Nathan Johnson (of whom I can say with a grateful heart, "I was hungry, and he gave me meat; I was thirsty, and he gave me drink; I was a stranger, and he took me in") lived in a neater house; dined at a better table; took, paid for, and read, more newspapers; better understood the moral, religious, and political character of the nation—than nine tenths of the slaveholders in Talbot county, Maryland. Yet Mr. Johnson was a working man. His hands were hardened by toil, and not his alone, but those also of Mrs. Johnson. I found the colored people much more spirited than I had supposed they would be. I found among them a determination to protect each other from the blood-thirsty kidnapper, at all hazards. Soon after my arrival, I was told of a circumstance which illustrated their spirit. A colored man and a fugitive slave were on unfriendly terms. The former was heard to threaten the latter with informing his master of his whereabouts. Straightway a meeting was called among the colored people, under the stereotyped[10] notice, "Business of importance!" The betrayer was invited to attend. The people came at the appointed hour, and organized the meeting by appointing a very religious old gentleman as president, who, I believe, made a prayer, after which he addressed the meeting as follows: *"Friends, we have got him here, and I would recommend that you young men just take him outside the door, and kill him!"* With this, a number of them bolted at him; but they were intercepted by some more timid than themselves, and the betrayer escaped their vengeance, and has not been seen in New Bedford since. I believe there have been no more such threats, and should there be hereafter, I doubt not that death would be the consequence.

I found employment, the third day after my arrival, in stowing a sloop with a load of oil. It was new, dirty, and hard work for me; but I went at it with a glad heart and a willing hand. I was now my own master. It was a happy moment, the rapture of which can be understood only by those who have been slaves. It was the first work, the reward of which was to be entirely my own. There was no Master

14

---

[10]*stereotyped* He means printed. Stereotyping is one of several methods of printing and is used to print both newspapers and books.

Hugh standing ready, the moment I earned the money, to rob me of it. I worked that day with a pleasure I had never before experienced. I was at work for myself and newly-married wife. It was to me the starting-point of a new existence. When I got through with that job, I went in pursuit of a job of calking; but such was the strength of prejudice against color, among the white calkers, that they refused to work with me, and of course I could get no employment.[11] Finding my trade of no immediate benefit, I threw off my calking habiliments, and pre-pared myself to do any kind of work I could get to do. Mr. Johnson kindly let me have his wood-horse and saw, and I very soon found myself a plenty of work. There was no work too hard—none too dirty. I was ready to saw wood, shovel coal, carry the hod, sweep the chim-ney, or roll oil casks—all of which I did for nearly three years in New Bedford, before I became known to the anti-slavery world.

In about four months after I went to New Bedford, there came a 15 young man to me, and inquired if I did not wish to take the "Libera-tor."[12] I told him I did; but, just having made my escape from slavery, I remarked that I was unable to pay for it then. I, however, finally became a subscriber to it. The paper came, and I read it from week to week with such feelings as it would be quite idle for me to attempt to describe. The paper became my meat and my drink. My soul was set all on fire. Its sympathy for my brethren in bonds—its scathing de-nunciations of slaveholders—its faithful exposures of slavery—and its powerful attacks upon the upholders of the institution—sent a thrill of joy through my soul, such as I had never felt before!

I had not long been a reader of the "Liberator," before I got a pretty 16 correct idea of the principles, measures and spirit of the anti-slavery reform. I took right hold of the cause. I could do but little; but what I could, I did with a joyful heart, and never felt happier than when in an anti-slavery meeting. I seldom had much to say at the meetings, be-cause what I wanted to say was said so much better by others. But, while attending an anti-slavery convention at Nantucket, on the 11th of August, 1841, I felt strongly moved to speak, and was at the same time much urged to do so by Mr. William C. Coffin, a gentleman who had heard me speak in the colored people's meeting at New Bedford. It was a severe cross, and I took it up reluctantly. The truth was, I felt

---

[11]I am told that colored persons can now get employment at calking in New Bed-ford—a result of anti-slavery effort. [Douglass's note]

[12]*the "Liberator"* The celebrated abolitionist newspaper edited by William Lloyd Garrison (1805–1879).

myself a slave, and the idea of speaking to white people weighed me down. I spoke but a few moments, when I felt a degree of freedom, and said what I desired with considerable ease. From that time until now, I have been engaged in pleading the cause of my brethren—with what success, and with what devotion, I leave those acquainted with my labors to decide.

QUESTIONS

1. If you find Douglass's story engrossing, try to explain what it is about his rhetorical approach to his subject that makes it so. If you find it dull, explain why. What aspects of Douglass's style are effective? What aspects are not effective?
2. What is the significance of Douglass's concerns with the future, as expressed in paragraph 3? Can you see a psychological validity in the slave-owner's insistence on his forgetting the future entirely? Does that idea have implications for your own life?
3. What did it mean for Douglass to hire himself out? Does the practice surprise you?
4. How much freedom did Douglass have as a slave? What was the nature of that freedom?
5. Find three passages that best reveal racial awareness on the part of Douglass or others mentioned in the narrative.
6. Why was Douglass fearful of being kidnapped?

WRITING ASSIGNMENTS

1. Establish what you feel is the real importance of the "six-cents episode" in paragraph 3. Consider its implications for the value of work, the meaning of money, the relationship between slave and slaveowner, and any other related issue you feel it brings into play. How effective is this episode for revealing the most serious issues that concern Douglass?
2. In paragraph 10, Douglass discusses his name changes and alludes to the issue of his own identity. Using that passage as a starting point, take a stand on the issue of whether or not a person's name is closely connected—or connected at all—with that person's sense of his or her identity. What does Douglass reveal about his own sense of identity? Can you detect any changes he reveals in his sense of himself when he was a slave compared with when he was free?
3. Tell a story in the first person of any injustice you feel has been done to you. Use Douglass's technique of chronological narrative; his clear description of scenes; and his reference to, and description of, people and the in-

clusion of their names. As much as possible use his approach to tell your story.

4. In paragraph 6, Douglass says firmly that once he had gained his freedom he was determined to be wary of strangers and careful not to be kidnapped by those who would get a reward for his return. To that end he declares that he will "Trust no man!" Examine this selecion carefully and, by referring to relevant events and useful quotes, decide whether or not he held to this advice. If you feel that he did not do so, why would he include his statement? Do you think that Douglass reveals himself to be a trusting man at heart? If so (or if not), what does that mean? What is Douglass's deepest feeling about the goodness or the badness of mankind?

5. When he goes to New Bedford, Massachusetts, Douglass reveals a considerable degree of surprise. In paragraph 11 and several following paragraphs, he gives us his reaction and his thinking. He actually is giving forth an economic theory regarding slaveholding and the production (or maintenance) of wealth. Establish carefully just what surprises him, what conclusions he had drawn while in the South, and what new conclusions he must draw in New Bedford. What genuine conclusions do you feel must be drawn as a result of his observations? What is the economic consequence of slavery for Southern society (not just for Southern slaveholders)? Use the selection to gather quotations and references that will make your conclusions clearer and more forceful. Consider, too, Douglass's observations on the way blacks and whites lived and worked in New Bedford. At this time, incidentally, New Bedford was a thriving whaling town with a considerable industry and numerous economic opportunities.

6. Examine Douglass's economic situation both while a slave and while free and compare it directly with the ten recommendations with which Karl Marx ends The Communist Manifesto. Which of the recommendations would have most benefited Frederick Douglass, and which would have done him harm? Which social order—Southern slavery or Northern freedom—seems closer to satisfying Karl Marx's demands for change in an economic system?

7. To what extent is it possible to distinguish between the racial and the political issues raised in Douglass's narrative? How does Douglass regard himself politically, and what is his political situation throughout the passages in this excerpt? What seem to be the political ideals that Douglass holds to? Which of the following writers would he most agree with: Lao-Tzu, Machiavelli, Rousseau, Wollstonecraft, or Jefferson? Is his political position essentially shaped by his experience as a slave?

HENRY DAVID THOREAU

Civil Disobedience

HENRY DAVID THOREAU (1817–1862) began keeping a journal when he graduated from Harvard in 1837. The journal was preserved and published, and it shows us the seriousness, determination, and elevation of moral values which is characteristic of all his great work. He is best known for Walden *(1854), a record of his having left the warm congeniality of Concord, Massachusetts, and the home of his close friend, Ralph Waldo Emerson (1803–1882), for the comparative "wilds" of Walden Pond where he built a cabin, planted a garden, and lived simply.* Walden *tells us of the deadening influence of ownership and extols the vitality and spiritual uplift that comes from living close to nature. It also shows us that civilization's comforts sometimes rob a person of his independence, his integrity, and even his conscience.*

Thoreau and Emerson were prominent among the group of writers and thinkers who were styled the Transcendentalists. They believed that there was something which transcended the limits of sensory experience; in other words, something that transcended materialism. Their philosophy was based on the works of Immanuel Kant (1724–1804), the German idealist philosopher; Samuel Taylor Coleridge (1772–1834), the English poet; and Johann Wolfgang von Goethe (1749–1832), the German dramatist and thinker. These writers praised human intuition and the capacity to see beyond the limits of common experience.

Their philosophical idealism carried over into the plainer social concerns of the day, expressing themselves in works such as Walden *and "Civil Disobedience," which was published in 1849 with the title "Resistance to Civil Government," a year after publication of* The Communist Manifesto. *Although Thoreau all but denies his idealism in "Civil Disobedience," it is obvious that after having spent a night in the Concord jail, he had realized he could not quietly accept his government's behavior in regard to slavery. He had begun to feel not only that it was appropriate but that it was imperative to disobey unjust laws.*

In Thoreau's time the most flagrantly unjust laws were those which supported slavery. The Transcendentalists were strongly opposed to slavery and spoke out against it. Abolitionists in Massachusetts actively harbored escaped slaves and helped them move to Canada and freedom. The Fugitive Slave Act, enacted in 1850, a year after "Civil Disobedience" was published, made Thoreau a criminal because he refused to comply with Massachusetts civil authorities when in 1851 they began to return escaped slaves to the South as the law required.

"Civil Disobedience" has been much more influential in the twentieth century than it was in the nineteenth. Mohandas Gandhi (1869–1948) claimed that while he was editor of an Indian newspaper in South Africa, it helped to inspire his theories of nonviolent resistance. Gandhi eventually brought the British Empire to heel by means of these theories and won independence for India. In the 1960s, Martin Luther King, Jr., applied the same theories in the fight for racial equality in the United States. Thoreau's essay was once again of great import during the latter days of the Vietnam War, when many young men avoided being drafted because they believed that the war was unjust.

"Civil Disobedience" was written after the Walden experience, which began on July 4, 1845, and ended September 6, 1847, when Thoreau quietly returned to Emerson's home. He also returned to "civilization" and discovered that his refusal to pay the Massachusetts poll tax—not a tax on voting but a "per head" tax imposed on all citizens to help support the Mexican War—landed him in the Concord jail. He spent just one day and one night there—his aunt paid the tax for him—but the experience was so extraordinary that he began examining it in his journal.

THOREAU'S RHETORIC

Thoreau's habit of writing in his journal lasted throughout his life, and though he intended to become a poet after college, he was soon convinced that one of the few ways he could hope to earn a living was by writing. However, he made more money from lecturing on the lyceum circuit. The lyceum was a New England institution in most towns. It resembled a kind of adult education program featuring important speakers such as the very successful Emerson and foreign lecturers. The fees were very reasonable, and in the absence of other popular entertainment, the lyceum was a popular proving ground for speakers interested in promoting their ideas.

Thus, "Civil Disobedience" went through three stages of development. First, its beginnings were rough-hewn in the journal, where the main ideas appear, and where experiments in phrasing begin. Thoreau was a constant reviser. In February 1848, "Civil Disobedience" was first delivered as a lecture at the Concord Lyceum. It urged people of conscience to actively resist a government that acted badly. When it was finally written down for publication in **Aesthetic Papers**, a proper intellectual journal edited by Elizabeth Peabody (1804– 1894), the sister-in-law of another important New England writer, Nathaniel Hawthorne (1804–1864), it was refined again, and certain important details were added.

"Civil Disobedience" bears many of the hallmarks of the spoken lecture. For one thing, it is written in the first person and addresses an audience that Thoreau expects will share many of his sentiments but certainly not all his conclusions. His message is to some extent anarchistic, virtually denying government any authority or respect. Political conservatives generally take his opening quote, "That government is best which governs least," as a rallying cry to help reduce the interference of government in everyday affairs. Such conservatives usually mean by this a reduction in the government's capacity to tax wealth for unpopular causes. Communists, too, see the essay as offering support for their cause. But, in actuality, Thoreau is quite simply opposed to any government that is not totally just, totally moral, and totally respectful of the individual.

The easiness of the pace of the essay also derives from its original form as a speech. Even such locutions as "But, to speak practically and as a citizen" (para. 3), obviously connect the essay with its origins. We can imagine that Thoreau himself was able to impart emphasis where it was demanded in the speech—although it is *often said that he was certainly not an overwhelming orator. In fact, short and somewhat homely, he was an unprepossessing figure. Therefore, he was careful to be sure that the writing did the work that, for some speakers, might have been done by means of gesture and theatrics.*

Thoreau's language is marked by clarity. He speaks directly to every issue, giving his own position and recommending the position he feels his audience should accept as reasonable and moral people. One impressive achievement in this selection is Thoreau's capacity to shape memorable statements, virtually aphoristic statements, which have become "quotable" generations later, beginning with his own quotation from the words of John L. O'Sullivan: "That government is best which governs least." Thoreau calls it a motto, as if one could put it on the great seal of a government, or as if it should go on a coin. It contains an interesting rhetorical flourish, impressing itself on our memory through the device of repetition: repeating "govern" and almost rhyming "best" with "least."

His most memorable statements show considerable attention to the rhetorical qualities of balance, repetition, and pattern. "The only obligation which I have a right to assume is to do at any time what I think right" (para. 4) uses the word "right" in two senses: first as a matter of personal volition; second, as a matter of moral rectitude. One's rights, in other words, become the opportunity to do right. "For it matters not how small the beginning may seem to be: what is once well done is done forever" (para. 21) also relies on repetition for its effect as well as on the balancing of the concept of a beginning with its capacity to reach out into the future. The use of the rhetorical device of chiasmus, a crisscross relationship between key words, marks "Under a government which imprisons any unjustly, the true place for a just man is also a prison" (para. 22). We see the pattern in:

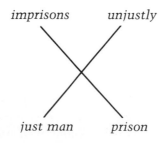

Such attention to phrasing is typical of speakers whose expressions

must catch and retain the attention of listeners. They do not have the advantage of referring to a text, so the spoken words must be forceful.

Thoreau relies also on analogy, comparing men with machines, people with plants, even the citizen with states considering secession from the Union. His analogies are effective and must thus be examined in some detail. He relies, too, on the analysis of circumstance throughout the essay, carefully examining the actions of government to demonstrate their qualities and their results.

His questions include comments on politics (para 1); on the Bible (para. 23); on Confucius (para. 24); and finally on his contemporary, Daniel Webster (1782–1852) (para. 41), demonstrating a wide range of influence but avoiding the pedantic tone that can come from using quotations too liberally or from producing them from obscure sources. Taken all in all, this essay is simple, direct, and uncluttered. Its influence has been in part a result of the clarity and grace which characterize Thoreau's writing at its best.

Civil Disobedience

I heartily accept the motto—"That government is best which governs least",[1] and I should like to see it acted up to more rapidly and systematically. Carried out, it finally amounts to this, which also I believe—"That government is best which governs not at all"; and when men are prepared for it, that will be the kind of government which they will have. Government is at best but an expedient; but most governments are usually, and all governments are sometimes, inexpedient. The objections which have been brought against a standing army, and they are many and weighty, and deserve to prevail, may also at last be brought against a standing government. The standing army is only an arm of the standing government. The government itself, which is only the mode which the people have chosen to execute

---

[1] . . . ***governs least*** John L. O'Sullivan (1813–1895) wrote in the *United States Magazine and Democratic Review* (1837) that "all government is evil, and the parents of evil. . . . The best government is that which governs least." Thomas Jefferson wrote, "That government is best which governs the least, because its people discipline themselves."

their will, is equally liable to be abused and perverted before the people can act through it. Witness the present Mexican war,[2] the work of comparatively a few individuals using the standing government as their tool; for in the outset the people would not have consented to this measure.

This American government—what is it but a tradition, a recent 2 one, endeavoring to transmit itself unimpaired to posterity but each instant losing some of its integrity? It has not the vitality and force of a single living man; for a single man can bend it to his will. It is a sort of wooden gun to the people themselves. But it is not the less necessary for this; for the people must have some complicated machinery or other, and hear its din, to satisfy that idea of government which they have. Governments show thus how successfully men can be imposed on, even impose on themselves, for their own advantage. It is excellent, we must all allow. Yet this government never of itself furthered any enterprise but by the alacrity with which it got out of its way. *It* does not keep the country free. *It* does not settle the West. *It* does not educate. The character inherent in the American people has done all that has been accomplished; and it would have done somewhat more if the government had not sometimes got in its way. For government is an expedient by which men would fain succeed in letting one another alone; and, as has been said, when it is most expedient the governed are most let alone by it. Trade and commerce, if they were not made of India-rubber, would never manage to bounce over the obstacles which legislators are continually putting in their way; and, if one were to judge these men wholly by the effects of their actions and not partly by their intentions, they would deserve to be classed and punished with those mischievous persons who put obstructions on the railroads.

But to speak practically and as a citizen, unlike those who call 3 themselves no-government men, I ask for, not at once no government, but *at once* a better government. Let every man make known what kind of government would command his respect, and that will be one step toward obtaining it.

After all, the practical reason why, when the power is once in the 4 hands of the people, a majority are permitted, and for a long period continue, to rule is not because they are most likely to be in the right,

---

[2] ***The present Mexican War (1846–1848)*** The war was extremely unpopular in New England because it was an act of a bullying government anxious to grab land from a weaker nation. The United States had annexed Texas in 1845, precipitating a welcome retaliation from Mexico.

nor because this seems fairest to the minority but because they are physically the strongest. But a government in which the majority rule in all cases cannot be based on justice, even as far as men understand it. Can there not be a government in which majorities do not virtually decide right and wrong but conscience?—in which majorities decide only those questions to which the rule of expediency is applicable? Must the citizen ever for a moment, or in the least degree, resign his conscience to the legislator? Why has every man a conscience then? I think that we should be men first and subjects afterward. It is not desirable to cultivate a respect for the law, so much as for the right. The only obligation which I have a right to assume is to do at any time what I think right. It is truly enough said that a corporation has no conscience; but a corporation of conscientious men is a corporation *with* a conscience. Law never made men a whit more just; and, by means of their respect for it, even the well-disposed are daily made the agents of injustice. A common and natural result of an undue respect for law is that you may see a file of soldiers, colonel, captain, corporal, privates, powder-monkeys,[3] and all, marching in admirable order over hill and dale to the wars, against their wills, ay, against their common sense and consciences, which makes it very steep marching indeed and produces a palpitation of the heart. They have no doubt that it is a damnable business in which they are concerned; they are all peaceably inclined. Now, what are they? Men at all? or small movable forts and magazines at the service of some unscrupulous man in power? Visit the Navy-Yard,[4] and behold a marine, such a man as an American government can make, or such as it can make a man with its black arts— a mere shadow and reminiscence of humanity, a man laid out alive and standing, and already, as one may say, buried under arms with funeral accompaniments, though it may be—

> Not a drum was heard, not a funeral note,
> As his corse to the rampart we hurried;
> Not a soldier discharged his farewell shot
> O'er the grave where our hero we buried.[5]

The mass of men serve the state thus, not as men mainly, but as machines, with their bodies. They are the standing army, and the mi-   5

---

[3] *powder-monkeys*   The boys who delivered gunpowder to cannons.
[4] *Navy-Yard*   This is apparently the United States Naval yard at Boston.
[5] These lines are from "Burial of Sir John Moore at Corunna" (1817) by the Irish poet Charles Wolfe (1791–1823).

litia, jailers, constables, posse comitatus,[6] &c. In most cases there is no free exercise whatever of the judgment or of the moral sense; but they put themselves on a level with wood and earth and stones; and wooden men can perhaps be manufactured that will serve the purpose as well. Such command no more respect than men of straw or a lump of dirt. They have the same sort of worth only as horses and dogs. Yet such as these even are commonly esteemed good citizens. Others—as most legislators, politicians, lawyers, ministers, and office-holders— serve the state chiefly with their heads; and, as they rarely make any moral distinctions, they are as likely to serve the Devil, without *in-tending* it, as God. A very few, as heroes, patriots, martyrs, reformers in the great sense, and *men*, serve the state with their consciences also and so necessarily resist it for the most part; and they are commonly treated as enemies by it. A wise man will only be useful as a man and will not submit to be "clay" and "stop a hole to keep the wind away," but leave that office to his dust at least:

> I am too high-born to be propertied,
> To be a secondary at control,
> Or useful serving-man and instrument
> To any sovereign state throughout the world.[7]

He who gives himself entirely to his fellow-men appears to them 6 useless and selfish; but he who gives himself partially to them is pronounced a benefactor and philanthropist.

How does it become a man to behave toward this American gov- 7 ernment today? I answer, that he cannot without disgrace be associated with it. I cannot for an instant recognize that political organization as *my* government which is the *slave's* government also.

All men recognize the right of revolution; that is, the right to re- 8 fuse allegiance to, and to resist the government when its tyranny or its inefficiency are great and unendurable. But almost all say that such is not the case now. But such was the case, they think, in the Revolution of '75. If one were to tell me that this was a bad government because it taxed certain foreign commodities brought to its ports, it is most probable that I should not make an ado about it, for I can do without them. All machines have their friction; and possibly this does enough

---

⁶*posse comitatus* Literally, the power of the county; it means a law-enforcement group made up of ordinary citizens.

⁷*"clay," "stop a hole. . . wind away," I am too high born. . . .* These lines are from Shakespeare; the first is from *Hamlet*, V.i.236–7. The verse is from *King John*, V.ii.79–82.

good to counterbalance the evil. At any rate, it is a great evil to make a stir about it. But when the friction comes to have its machine, and oppression and robbery are organized, I say let us not have such a machine any longer. In other words, when a sixth of the population of a nation which has undertaken to be the refuge of liberty are slaves, and a whole country is unjustly overrun and conquered by a foreign army and subjected to military law, I think that it is not too soon for honest men to rebel and revolutionize. What makes this duty the more urgent is the fact that the country so overrun is not our own, but ours is the invading army.

Paley,[8] a common authority with many on moral questions, in his chapter on the "Duty of Submission to Civil Government," resolves all civil obligation into expediency; and he proceeds to say, "that so long as the interest of the whole society requires it, that is, so long as the established government cannot be resisted or charged without public inconveniency, it is the will of God that the established government be obeyed, and no longer. . . . This principle being admitted, the justice of every particular case of resistance is reduced to a computation of the quantity of the danger and grievance on the one side, and of the probability and expense of redressing it on the other." Of this, he says, every man shall judge for himself. But Paley appears never to have contemplated those cases to which the rule of expediency does not apply, in which a people, as well as an individual, must do justice, cost what it may. If I have unjustly wrested a plank from a drowning man, I must restore it to him though I drown myself. This, according to Paley, would be inconvenient. But he that would save his life, in such a case, shall lose it. This people must cease to hold slaves and to make war on Mexico, though it cost them their existence as a people. 9

In their practice, nations agree with Paley; but does anyone think that Massachusetts does exactly what is right at the present crisis? 10

> A drab of state, a cloth-o'-silver slut,
> To have her train borne up, and her soul trail in the dirt.[9]

Practically speaking, the opponents to a reform in Massachusetts are

---

[8]***William Paley (1743–1805)*** An English theologian who lectured widely on moral philosophy. Paley is famous for *A View of the Evidences of Christianity* (1794). "Duty of Submission to Civil Government Explained" is Chapter 3 of Book 6 of *The Principles of Moral and Political Philosophy* (1785).

[9]***A drab.* . . .** From Cyril Tourneur (1575?–1626) *Revenger's Tragedy* (1607), IV.iv.70–72. "Drab" is an obsolete term for a prostitute. Thoreau quotes the lines to imply that Massachusetts is a "painted lady" with a defiled soul.

not a hundred thousand politicians at the South but a hundred thousand merchants and farmers here, who are more interested in commerce and agriculture than they are in humanity, and are not prepared to do justice to the slave and to Mexico, *cost what it may.* I quarrel not with far-off foes but with those who, near at home, co-operate with, and do the bidding of, those far away, and without whom the latter would be harmless. We are accustomed to say that the mass of men are unprepared; but improvement is slow because the few are not materially wiser or better than the many. It is not so important that many should be as good as you as that there be some absolute goodness somewhere; for that will leaven the whole lump. There are thousands who are *in opinion* opposed to slavery and to the war who yet in effect do nothing to put an end to them; who, esteeming themselves children of Washington and Franklin, sit down with their hands in their pockets and say that they know not what to do, and do nothing; who even postpone the question of freedom to the question of free trade, and quietly read the prices-current along with the latest advices from Mexico after dinner and, it may be, fall asleep over them both. What is the price-current of an honest man and patriot today? They hesitate and they regret and sometimes they petition; but they do nothing in earnest and with effect. They will wait, well disposed, for others to remedy the evil, that they may no longer have it to regret. At most, they give only a cheap vote, and a feeble countenance and God-speed, to the right, as it goes by them. There are nine hundred and ninety-nine patrons of virtue to one virtuous man. But it is easier to deal with the real possessor of a thing than with the temporary guardian of it.

All voting is a sort of gaming, like checkers or backgammon, with 11 a slight moral tinge to it, a playing with right and wrong, with moral questions; and betting naturally accompanies it. The character of the voters is not staked. I cast my vote, perchance, as I think right; but I am not vitally concerned that that right should prevail. I am willing to leave it to the majority. Its obligation, therefore, never exceeds that of expediency. Even voting *for the right* is *doing* nothing for it. It is only expressing to men feebly your desire that it should prevail. A wise man will not leave the right to the mercy of chance, nor wish it to prevail through the power of the majority. There is but little virtue in the action of masses of men. When the majority shall at length vote for the abolition of slavery, it will be because they are indifferent to slavery, or because there is but little slavery left to be abolished by their vote. *They* will then be the only slaves. Only *his* vote can hasten the abolition of slavery who asserts his own freedom by his vote.

I hear of a convention to be held at Baltimore,[10] or elsewhere, for   12
the selection of a candidate for the Presidency, made up chiefly of ed-
itors, and men who are politicians by profession; but I think, what is
it to any independent, intelligent, and respectable man what decision
they may come to? Shall we not have the advantage of his wisdom and
honesty nevertheless? Can we not count upon some independent
votes? Are there not many individuals in the country who do not attend conventions? But no: I find that the responsible man, so called,
has immediately drifted from his position, and despairs of his country
when his country has more reason to despair of him. He forthwith
adopts one of the candidates thus selected as the only *available* one,
thus proving that he is himself *available* for any purposes of the dem-
agogue. His vote is of no more worth than that of any unprincipled
foreigner or hireling native who may have been bought. O for a man
who is a *man* and, as my neighbor says has a bone in his back which
you cannot pass your hand through! Our statistics are at fault: the
population has been returned too large. How many *men* are there to a
square thousand miles in this country? Hardly one. Does not America
offer any inducement for men to settle here? The American has dwin-
dled into an Odd Fellow[11]—one who may be known by the development of his organ of gregariousness and a manifest lack of intellect
and cheerful self-reliance; whose first and chief concern, on coming
into the world, is to see that the Almshouses are in good repair; and,
before yet he has lawfully donned the virile garb, to collect a fund for
the support of the widows and orphans that may be; who, in short,
ventures to live only by the aid of the Mutual Insurance Company,
which has promised to bury him decently.

It is not a man's duty, as a matter of course, to devote himself to   13
the eradication of any, even the most enormous wrong; he may still
properly have other concerns to engage him; but it is his duty, at least,
to wash his hands of it and, if he gives it no thought longer, not to
give it practically his support. If I devote myself to other pursuits and
contemplations, I must first see, at least, that I do not pursue them
sitting upon another man's shoulders. I must get off him first, that he
may pursue his contemplations too. See what gross inconsistency is
tolerated. I have heard some of my townsmen say, "I should like to

---

[10]***Baltimore*** In 1848 the political environment was particularly intense; it was a
seedbed for theoreticians of the Confederacy, which was only beginning to be contemplated seriously.

[11]***Odd Fellow*** The Independent Order of Odd Fellows, a fraternal and benevolent
secret society, founded in England in the eighteenth century and first established in the
United States in 1819 in Baltimore.

have them order me out to help put down an insurrection of the slaves, or to march to Mexico—see if I would go"; and yet these very men have each directly by their allegiance and so indirectly, at least, by their money, furnished a substitute. The soldier is applauded who refuses to serve in an unjust war by those who do not refuse to sustain the unjust government which makes the war; is applauded by those whose own act and authority he disregards and sets at naught; as if the State were penitent to that degree that it hired one to scourge it while it sinned, but not to that degree that it left off sinning for a moment. Thus, under the name of Order and Civil Government, we are all made at last to pay homage to and support our own meanness. After the first blush of sin comes its indifference; and from immoral it becomes, as it were, *unmoral*, and not quite unnecessary to that life which we have made.

The broadest and most prevalent error requires the most disinterested virtue to sustain it. The slight reproach to which the virtue of patriotism is commonly liable, the noble are most likely to incur. Those who, while they disapprove of the character and measures of a government, yield to it their allegiance and support, are undoubtedly its most conscientious supporters, and so frequently the most serious obstacles to reform. Some are petitioning the State to dissolve the Union, to disregard the requisitions of the President. Why do they not dissolve it themselves—the union between themselves and the State—and refuse to pay their quota into its treasury? Do not they stand in the same relation to the State that the State does to the Union? And have not the same reasons prevented the State from resisting the Union which have prevented them from resisting the State? 14

How can a man be satisfied to entertain an opinion merely, and enjoy *it*? Is there any enjoyment in it if his opinion is that he is aggrieved? If you are cheated out of a single dollar by your neighbor, you do not rest satisfied with knowing that you are cheated, or with saying that you are cheated, or even with petitioning him to pay you your due; but you take effectual steps at once to obtain the full amount and see that you are never cheated again. Action from principle, the perception and the performance of right, changes things and relations; it is essentially revolutionary and does not consist wholly with anything which was. It not only divides states and churches, it divides families; ay, it divides the *individual*, separating the diabolical in him from the divine. 15

Unjust laws exist: shall we be content to obey them, or shall we endeavor to amend them and obey them until we have succeeded, or shall we transgress them at once? Men generally, under such a govern- 16 ment as this, think that they ought to wait until they have persuaded the majority to alter them. They think that if they should resist the remedy would be worse than the evil. *It* makes it worse. Why is it not more apt to anticipate and provide for reform? Why does it not cherish its wise minority? Why does it cry and resist before it is hurt? Why does it not encourage its citizens to be on the alert to point out its faults and *do* better than it would have them? Why does it always crucify Christ and excommunicate Copernicus and Luther[12] and pronounce Washington and Franklin rebels?

One would think that a deliberate and practical denial of its authority was the only offence never contemplated by government; else why has it not assigned its definite, its suitable and proportionate penalty? If a man who has no property refuses but once to earn nine shillings for the State, he is put in prison for a period unlimited by any law that I know, and determined only by the discretion of those who placed him there; but if he should steal ninety times nine shillings from the State, he is soon permitted to go at large again.

If the injustice is part of the necessary friction of the machine of government, let it go, let it go: perchance it will wear smooth—certainly the machine will wear out. If the injustice has a spring or a pulley or a rope or a crank exclusively for itself, then perhaps you may consider whether the remedy will not be worse than the evil; but if it is of such a nature that it requires you to be the agent of injustice to another, then I say break the law. Let your life be a counter friction to stop the machine. What I have to do is to see, at any rate, that I do not lend myself to the wrong which I condemn.

As for adopting the ways which the State has provided for remedying the evil, I know not of such ways. They take too much time, and a man's life will be gone. I have other affairs to attend to. I came into this world, not chiefly to make this a good place to live in, but to live in it, be it good or bad. A man has not everything to do, but something; and because he cannot do *everything*, it is not necessary that he should do *something* wrong. It is not my business to be petitioning the Governor or the Legislature any more than it is theirs to petition me; and if they should not hear my petition what should I do then? But in this case the State has provided no way: its very Constitution is the evil. This may seem to be harsh and stubborn and unconcilia-

---

[12]**Nicolaus Copernicus (1473–1543) and Martin Luther (1483–1546)** Copernicus revolutionized astronomy and the way humankind perceives the universe; Luther was a religious revolutionary who began the Reformation and created the first Protestant faith.

tory; but it is to treat with the utmost kindness and consideration the only spirit that can appreciate or deserves it. So is all change for the better, like birth and death, which convulse the body.

I do not hesitate to say that those who call themselves Abolition- 20 ists should at once effectually withdraw their support, both in person and property, from the government of Massachusetts, and not wait till they constitute a majority of one before they suffer the right to prevail through them. I think that it is enough if they have God on their side, without waiting for that other one. Moreover, any man more right than his neighbors constitutes a majority of one already.

I meet this American government or its representative, the State 21 government, directly and face to face once a year—no more—in the person of its tax-gatherer; this is the only mode in which a man situated as I am necessarily meets it; and it then says distinctly, Recognize me; and the simplest, the most effectual and, in the present posture of affairs, the indispensablest mode of treating with it on this head, of expressing your little satisfaction with and love for it, is to deny it then. My civil neighbor, the tax-gatherer, is the very man I have to deal with—for it is, after all, with men and not with parchment that I quarrel—and he has voluntarily chosen to be an agent of the government. How shall he ever know well what he is and does as an officer of the government, or as a man, until he is obliged to consider whether he shall treat me, his neighbor, for whom he has respect, as a neighbor and well-disposed man, or as a maniac and disturber of the peace, and see if he can get over this obstruction to his neighborliness without a ruder and more impetuous thought or speech corresponding with his action. I know this well, that if one thousand, if one hundred, if ten men whom I could name—if ten *honest* men only—ay, if *one* HONEST man in this State of Massachusetts, *ceasing to hold slaves*, were actually to withdraw from this copartnership and be locked up in the county jail therefor, it would be the abolition of slavery in America. For it matters not how small the beginning may seem to be: what is once well done is done forever. But we love better to talk about it: that we say is our mission. Reform keeps many scores of newspapers in its service but not one man. If my esteemed neighbor,[13] the State's ambassador, who will devote his days to the settlement of the question of human rights in the Council Chamber, instead of being threatened

---

[13]*esteemed neighbor* Thoreau refers to Samuel Hoar (1778–1856), a Massachusetts congressman, who went to South Carolina to protest that state's practice of seizing black seamen from Massachusetts ships and enslaving them. South Carolina threatened Hoar and drove him out of the state. He did not secure the justice he demanded.

with the prisons of Carolina, were to sit down the prisoner of Massa
chusetts, that State which is so anxious to foist the sin of slavery upon
her sister—though at present she can discover only an act of inhospi-
tality to be the ground of a quarrel with her—the Legislature would
not wholly waive the subject the following winter.

Under a government which imprisons any unjustly, the true place   22
for a just man is also a prison. The proper place today, the only place
which Massachusetts has provided for her freer and less desponding
spirits is in her prisons, to be put out and locked out of the State by
her own act, as they have already put themselves out by their principles. It is there that the fugitive slave and the Mexican prisoner on
parole and the Indian come to plead the wrongs of his race should find
them; on that separate but more free and honorable ground where the
State places those who are not *with* her but *against* her—the only
house in a slave State in which a free man can abide with honor. If
any think that their influence would be lost there, and their voices no
longer afflict the ear of the State, that they would not be as an enemy
within its walls, they do not know by how much truth is stronger than
error, nor how much more eloquently and effectively he can combat
injustice who has experienced a little in his own person. Cast your
whole vote, not a strip of paper merely, but your whole influence. A
minority is powerless while it conforms to the majority; it is not even
a minority then; but it is irresistible when it clogs by its whole weight.
If the alternative is to keep all just men in prison or give up war and
slavery, the State will not hesitate which to choose. If a thousand men
were not to pay their tax-bills this year, that would not be a violent
bloody measure, as it would be to pay them, and enable the State to
commit violence and shed innocent blood. This is, in fact, the definition of a peaceable revolution, if any such is possible. If the tax-gatherer or any other public officer asks me, as one has done, "But what
shall I do?" my answer is, "If you really wish to do anything, resign
your office." When the subject has refused allegiance and the officer
has resigned his office, then the revolution is accomplished. But even
suppose blood should flow. Is there not a sort of blood shed when the
conscience is wounded? Through this wound a man's real manhood
and immortality flow out, and he bleeds to an everlasting death. I see
this blood flowing now.

I have contemplated the imprisonment of the offender rather than   23
the seizure of his goods—though both will serve the same purpose—
because they who assert the purest right, and consequently are most
dangerous to a corrupt State, commonly have not spent much time in
accumulating property. To such the State renders comparatively small

service, and a slight tax is wont to appear exorbitant, particularly if
they are obliged to earn it by special labor with their hands. If there
were one who lived wholly without the use of money, the State itself
would hesitate to demand it of him. But the rich man—not to make
any invidious comparison—is always sold to the institution which
makes him rich. Absolutely speaking, the more money, the less virtue;
for money comes between a man and his objects and obtains them for
him; and it was certainly no great virtue to obtain it. It puts to rest
many questions which he would otherwise be taxed to answer; while
the only new question which it puts is the hard but superfluous one,
how to spend it. Thus his moral ground is taken from under his feet.
The opportunities of living are diminished in proportion as what are
called the "means" are increased. The best thing a man can do for his
culture when he is rich is to endeavor to carry out those schemes
which he entertained when he was poor. Christ answered the
Herodians[14] according to their condition. "Show me the tribute-
money," said he—and one took a penny out of his pocket—if you use
money which has the image of Caesar on it, and which he has made
current and valuable, that is, *if you are men of the State* and gladly
enjoy the advantages of Caesar's government, then pay him back some
of his own when he demands it; "Render therefore to Caesar that
which is Caesar's, and to God those things which are God's"—leaving
them no wiser than before as to which was which; for they did not
wish to know.

When I converse with the freest of my neighbors, I perceive that 24
whatever they may say about the magnitude and seriousness of the
question, and their regard for the public tranquillity, the long and the
short of the matter is that they cannot spare the protection of the existing government, and they dread the consequences to their property
and families of disobedience to it. For my own part, I should not like
to think that I ever rely on the protection of the State. But if I deny
the authority of the State when it presents its tax-bill, it will soon take
and waste all my property and so harass me and my children without
end. This is hard. This makes it impossible for a man to live honestly,
and at the same time comfortably, in outward respects. It will not be
worth the while to accumulate property; that would be sure to go
again. You must hire or squat somewhere and raise but a small crop
and eat that soon. You must live within yourself and depend upon
yourself always tucked up and ready for a start, and not have many

---

[14]***Herodians*** Followers of King Herod who were opposed to Jesus Christ (see Matthew 22:16).

affairs. A man may grow rich in Turkey even, if he will be in all respects a good subject of the Turkish government. Confucius[15] said: "If a state is governed by the principles of reason, poverty and misery are subjects of shame; if a state is not governed by the principles of reason, riches and honors are the subjects of shame." No; until I want the protection of Massachusetts to be extended to me in some distant Southern port, where my liberty is endangered, or until I am bent solely on building up an estate at home by peaceful enterprise, I can afford to refuse allegiance to Massachusetts and her right to my property and life. It costs me less in every sense to incur the penalty of disobedience to the State than it would to obey. I should feel as if I were worth less in that case.

Some years ago the State met me in behalf of the Church and com- 25 manded me to pay a certain sum toward the support of a clergyman whose preaching my father attended, but never I myself. "Pay," it said, "or be locked up in the jail." I declined to pay. But, unfortunately, another man saw fit to pay it. I did not see why the schoolmaster should be taxed to support the priest, and not the priest the schoolmaster; for I was not the State's schoolmaster, but I supported myself by voluntary subscription. I did not see why the lyceum should not present its tax-bill and have the State to back its demand, as well as the Church. However, at the request of the selectmen, I condescended to make some such statement as this in writing:—"Know all men by these presents, that I, Henry Thoreau, do not wish to be regarded as a member of any incorporated society which I have not joined." This I gave to the town clerk; and he has it. The State, having thus learned that I did not wish to be regarded as a member of that church, has never made a like demand on me since; though it said that it must adhere to its original presumption that time. If I had known how to name them, I should then have signed off in detail from all the societies which I never signed on to; but I did not know where to find a complete list.

I have paid no poll-tax[16] for six years. I was put into a jail once on 26 this account, for one night; and, as I stood considering the walls of solid stone, two or three feet thick, the door of wood and iron, a foot thick, and the iron grating which strained the light, I could not help

---

[15]*Confucius (550 or 551–479 B.C.)* The most important Chinese religious leader. His *Analects* (collection) treated not only religious but moral and political matters as well.

[16]*poll-tax* A tax levied on every citizen living in a given area; poll means "head," so it is a tax per head. It was about $2 and was used to support the Mexican war.

being struck with the foolishness of that institution which treated me as if I were mere flesh and blood and bones, to be locked up. I wondered that it should have concluded at length that this was the best use it could put me to and had never thought to avail itself of my services in some way. I saw that if there was a wall of stone between me and my townsmen, there was a still more difficult one to climb or break through before they could get to be as free as I was. I did not for a moment feel confined, and the walls seemed a great waste of stone and mortar. I felt as if I alone of all my townsmen had paid my tax. They plainly did not know how to treat me but behaved like persons who are underbred. In every threat and in every compliment there was a blunder; for they thought that my chief desire was to stand the other side of that stone wall. I could not but smile to see how industriously they locked the door on my meditations, which followed them out again without let or hindrance, and *they* were really all that was dangerous. As they could not reach me, they had resolved to punish my body; just as boys, if they cannot come at some person against whom they have a spite, will abuse his dog. I saw that the State was half-witted, that it was timid as a lone woman with her silver spoons, and that it did not know its friends from its foes, and I lost all my remaining respect for it and pitied it.

Thus the State never intentionally confronts a man's sense, intellectual or moral, but only his body, his senses. It is not armed with superior wit or honesty but with superior physical strength. I was not born to be forced. I will breathe after my own fashion. Let us see who is the strongest. What force has a multitude? They only can force me who obey a higher law than I. They force me to become like themselves. I do not hear of *men* being *forced* to live this way or that by masses of men. What sort of life were that to live? When I meet a government which says to me, "Your money or your life," why should I be in haste to give it my money? It may be in a great strait and not know what to do: I cannot help that. It must help itself; do as I do. It is not worth the while to snivel about it. I am not responsible for the successful working of the machinery of society. I am not the son of the engineer. I perceive that, when an acorn and a chestnut fall side by side, the one does not remain inert to make way for the other, but both obey their own laws and spring and grow and flourish as best they can till one, perchance, overshadows and destroys the other. If a plant cannot live according to its nature, it dies; and so a man. 27

The night in prison was novel and interesting enough. The prisoners in their shirt-sleeves were enjoying a chat and the evening air in 28 the doorway when I entered. But the jailer said, "Come, boys, it is time to lock up"; and so they dispersed, and I heard the sound of their steps returning into the hollow apartments. My room-mate was introduced to me by the jailer as "a first-rate fellow and a clever man." When the door was locked, he showed me where to hang my hat and how he managed matters there. The rooms were whitewashed once a month; and this one, at least, was the whitest, most simply furnished, and probably the neatest apartment in the town. He naturally wanted to know where I came from and what brought me there; and when I had told him, I asked him in my turn how he came there, presuming him to be an honest man, of course; and, as the world goes, I believe he was. "Why," said he, "they accuse me of burning a barn; but I never did it." As near as I could discover, he had probably gone to bed in a barn when drunk and smoked his pipe there; and so a barn burnt. He had the reputation of being a clever man, had been there some three months waiting for his trial to come on, and would have to wait as much longer; but he was quite domesticated and contented, since he got his board for nothing and thought that he was well treated.

He occupied one window, and I the other; and I saw that if one   29 stayed there long, his principal business would be to look out the window. I had soon read all the tracts that were left there and examined where former prisoners had broken out and where a grate had been sawed off and heard the history of the various occupants of that room; for I found that even here there was a history and a gossip which never circulated beyond the walls of the jail. Probably this is the only house in the town where verses are composed, which afterward printed in a circular form but not published. I was shown quite a long list of verses which were composed by some young men who had been detected in an attempt to escape, who avenged themselves by signing them.

I pumped my fellow-prisoner as dry as I could, for fear I should   30 never see him again; but at length he showed me which was my bed and left me to blow out the lamp.

It was like travelling into a far country, such as I had never ex-   31 pected to behold, to lie there for one night. It seemed to me that I never had heard the town-clock strike before, nor the evening sounds of the village; for we slept with the windows open, which were inside the grating. It was to see my native village in the light of the Middle Ages, and our Concord was turned into a Rhine stream, and visions of knights and castles passed before me. They were the voices of old burghers that I heard in the streets. I was an involuntary spectator and auditor of whatever was done and said in the kitchen of the adjacent village-inn—a wholly new and rare experience to me. It was a closer view of my native town. I was fairly inside of it. I never had seen its institutions before. This is one of its peculiar institutions; for it is a shire town.[17] I began to comprehend what its inhabitants were about.

In the morning our breakfasts were put through the hole in the 32 door, in small oblong-square tin pans, made to fit, and holding a pint of chocolate, with brown bread and an iron spoon. When they called for the vessels again, I was green enough to return what bread I had left; but my comrade seized it and said that I should lay that up for lunch or dinner. Soon after he was let out to work at haying in a neighboring field, whither he went every day, and would not be back till noon; so he bade me good-day, saying that he doubted if he should see me again.

When I came out of prison—for someone interfered and paid that 33 tax—I did not perceive that great changes had taken place on the common, such as he observed who went in a youth and emerged a tottering and gray-headed man; and yet a change had to my eyes come over the scene—the town and State and country—greater than any that mere time could effect. I saw yet more distinctly the State in which I lived. I saw to what extent the people among whom I lived could be trusted as good neighbors and friends; that their friendship was for summer weather only; that they did not greatly propose to do right; that they were a distinct race from me by their prejudices and superstitions, as the Chinamen and Malays are; that, in their sacrifices to humanity, they ran no risks, not even to their property; that, after all, they were not so noble but they treated the thief as he had treated them and hoped, by a certain outward observance and a few prayers, and by walking in a particular straight though useless path from time to time, to save their souls. This may be to judge my neighbors harshly; for I believe that many of them are not aware that they have such an institution as the jail in their village.

It was formerly the custom in our village, when a poor debtor came 34 out of jail, for his acquaintances to salute him, looking through their fingers, which were crossed to represent the grating of a jail window, "How do ye do?" My neighbors did not thus salute me but first looked at me and then at one another as if I had returned from a long journey. I was put into jail as I was going to the shoemaker's to get a shoe which was mended. When I was let out the next morning I proceeded to finish my errand, and having put on my mended shoe, joined a

---

[17]***shire town*** A county seat, which means the town would have a court, county offices, and jails.

huckleberry party who were impatient to put themselves under my conduct; and in half an hour—for the horse was soon tackled—was in the midst of a huckleberry field on one of our highest hills two miles off, and then the State was nowhere to be seen.

This is the whole history of "My Prisons." 35

I have never declined paying the highway tax, because I am as de- 36 sirous of being a good neighbor as I am of being a bad subject; and as for supporting schools I am doing my part to educate my fellow countrymen now. It is for no particular item in the tax-bill that I refuse to pay it. I simply wish to refuse allegiance to the State, to withdraw and stand aloof from it effectually. I do not care to trace the course of my dollar, if I could, till it buys a man or a musket to shoot one with— the dollar is innocent—but I am concerned to trace the effects of my allegiance. In fact, I quietly declare war with the State, after my fashion, though I will still make what use and get what advantage of her I can, as is usual in such cases.

If others pay the tax which is demanded of me from a sympathy 37 with the State, they do but what they have already done in their own case, or rather they abet injustice to a greater extent than the State requires. If they pay the tax from a mistaken interest in the individual taxed, to save his property, or prevent his going to jail, it is because they have not considered wisely how far they let their private feelings interfere with the public good.

This, then, is my position at present. But one cannot be too much 38 on his guard in such a case, lest his action be biassed by obstinacy or an undue regard for the opinions of men. Let him see that he does only what belongs to himself and to the hour.

I think sometimes, Why, this people mean well; they are only ig- 39 norant; they would do better if they knew how: why give your neighbors this pain to treat you as they are not inclined to? But I think again, this is no reason why I should do as they do or permit others to suffer much greater pain of a different kind. Again, I sometimes say to myself, When many millions of men, without heat, without ill will, without personal feeling of any kind, demand of you a few shillings only, without the possibility, such is their constitution, of retracting or altering their present demand, and without the possibility, on your side, of appeal to any other millions, why expose yourself to this overwhelming brute force? You do not resist cold and hunger, the winds and the waves, thus obstinately; you quietly submit to a thousand similar necessities. You do not put your head into the fire. But just in proportion as I regard this as not wholly a brute force but partly a human force, and consider that I have relations to those millions as to so many millions of men, and not of mere brute or inanimate things, I see that appeal is possible, first and instantaneously, from them to the Maker of them, and secondly, from them to themselves. But if I put my head deliberately into the fire, there is no appeal to fire or to the Maker of fire, and I have only myself to blame. If I could convince myself that I have any right to be satisfied with men as they are, and to treat them accordingly, and not according, in some respects, to my requisitions and expectations of what they and I ought to be, then, like a good Mussulman[18] and fatalist, I should endeavor to be satisfied with things as they are and say it is the will of God. And, above all, there is this difference between resisting this and a purely brute or natural force, that I can resist this with some effect; but I cannot expect, like Orpheus,[19] to change the nature of the rocks and trees and beasts.

I do not wish to quarrel with any man or nation. I do not wish to   40
split hairs, to make fine distinctions, or set myself up as better than my neighbors. I seek rather, I may say, even an excuse for conforming to the laws of the land. I am but too ready to conform to them. Indeed, I have reason to suspect myself on this head; and each year, as the tax-gatherer comes round, I find myself disposed to review the acts and position of the general and State governments, and the spirit of the people, to discover a pretext for conformity.

> We must affect our country as our par-
> ents;
> And if at any time we alienate
> Our love or industry from doing it honor,
> We must respect effects and teach the
> soul
> Matter of conscience and religion,
> And not desire of rule or benefit.[20]

I believe that the State will soon be able to take all my work of this sort out of my hands, and then I shall be no better a patriot than my fellow-countrymen. Seen from a lower point of view, the Constitution, with all its faults, is very good; the law and the courts are very respect-

---

[18]***Mussulman***   Muslim; a follower of the religion of Islam.

[19]***Orpheus***   In Greek mythology Orpheus was a poet whose songs were so plaintive that they affected animals, trees, and even stones.

[20]***We must affect. . . .***   From George Peele (1558?–1597?), *The Battle of Alcazar* (acted 1588–89; printed 1594), II.ii. Thoreau added these lines in a later printing of the essay. They emphasize the fact that one is disobedient to the state as one is to a parent—with love, affection, and from a cause of conscience. Disobedience is not taken lightly.

able; even this State and this American government are, in many respects, very admirable and rare things, to be thankful for, such as a great many have described them; but seen from a point of view a little higher, they are what I have described them; seen from a higher still, and the highest, who shall say what they are, or that they are worth looking at or thinking of at all?

However, the government does not concern me much, and I shall 41 bestow the fewest possible thoughts on it. It is not many moments that I live under a government, even in this world. If a man is thought-free, fancy-free, imagination-free, that which *is not* never for a long time appearing *to be* to him, unwise rulers or reformers cannot fatally interrupt him.

I know that most men think differently from myself; but those 42 whose lives are by profession devoted to the study of these or kindred subjects content me as little as any. Statesmen and legislators, standing so completely within the institution, never distinctly and nakedly behold it. They speak of moving society but have no resting-place without it. They may be men of a certain experience and discrimination and have no doubt invented ingenious and even useful systems, for which we sincerely thank them; but all their wit and usefulness lie within certain not very wide limits. They are wont to forget that the world is not governed by policy and expediency. Webster[21] never goes behind government and so cannot speak with authority about it. His words are wisdom to those legislators who contemplate no essential reform in the existing government; but for thinkers, and those who legislate for all time, he never once glances at the subject. I know of those whose serene and wise speculations on this theme would soon reveal the limits of his mind's range and hospitality. Yet, compared with the cheap professions of most reformers, and the still cheaper wisdom and eloquence of politicians in general, his are almost the only sensible and valuable words, and we thank Heaven for him. Comparatively, he is always strong, original, and, above all, practical. Still his quality is not wisdom but prudence. The lawyer's truth is not Truth but consistency, or a consistent expediency. Truth is always in harmony with herself and is not concerned chiefly to reveal the justice that may consist with wrong-doing. He well deserves to be called, as he has been called, the Defender of the Constitution. There are really no blows to be given by him but defensive ones. He is not a leader but

---

[21]***Daniel Webster (1782–1852)*** One of the most brilliant orators of his time. He was secretary of state from 1841 to 1843, which is why Thoreau thinks he cannot be a satisfactory critic of government.

a follower. His leaders are the men of '87.[22] "I have never made an effort," he says, "and never propose to make an effort; I have never countenanced an effort, and never mean to countenance an effort, to disturb the arrangement as originally made, by which the various States came into the Union." Still thinking of the sanction which the Constitution gives to slavery, he says, "Because it was a part of the original compact—let it stand." Notwithstanding his special acuteness and ability, he is unable to take a fact out of its merely political relations and behold it as it lies absolutely to be disposed of by the intellect—what, for instance, it behooves a man to do here in America today with regard to slavery but ventures, or is driven, to make some such desperate answer as the following, while professing to speak absolutely, and as a private man—from which what new and singular code of social duties might be inferred? "The manner," says he, "in which the governments of those States where slavery exists are to regulate it, is for their own consideration, under their responsibility to their constituents, to the general laws of propriety, humanity, and justice, and to God. Associations formed elsewhere, springing from a feeling of humanity, or any other cause, have nothing whatever to do with it. They have never received any encouragement from me, and they never will."[23]

They who know of no purer sources of truth, who have traced up   43
its stream no higher, stand, and wisely stand, by the Bible and the Constitution, and drink at it there with reverence and humility; but they who behold where it comes trickling into this lake or that pool gird up their loins once more and continue their pilgrimage toward its fountain-head.

No man with a genius for legislation has appeared in America.   44
They are rare in the history of the world. There are orators, politicians, and eloquent men by the thousand; but the speaker has not yet opened his mouth to speak who is capable of settling the much-vexed questions of the day. We love eloquence for its own sake and not for any truth which it may utter or any heroism it may inspire. Our legislators have not yet learned the comparative value of free-trade and of freedom, of union, and of rectitude, to a nation. They have no genius or talent for comparatively humble questions of taxation and finance, commerce and manufacturers and agriculture. If we were left solely to the wordy wit of legislators in Congress for our guidance, uncorrected by the seasonable experience and the effectual complaints of the peo-

---

[22]**men of '87**   The men who framed the Constitution in 1787.
[23]These extracts have been inserted since the Lecture was read. [Thoreau's note]

ple, America would not long retain her rank among the nations. For eighteen hundred years, though perchance I have no right to say it, the New Testament has been written; yet where is the legislator who has wisdom and practical talent enough to avail himself of the light which it sheds on the science of legislation?

The authority of government, even such as I am willing to submit to—for I will cheerfully obey those who know and can do better than I, and in many things even those who neither know nor can do so well—is still an impure one: to be strictly just, it must have the sanction and consent of the governed. It can have no pure right over my person and property but what I concede to it. The progress from an absolute to a limited monarchy, from a limited monarchy to a democracy, is a progress toward a true respect for the individual. Even the Chinese philosopher[24] was wise enough to regard the individual as the basis of the empire. Is a democracy such as we know it the last improvement possible in government? Is it not possible to take a step further towards recognizing and organizing the rights of man? There will never be a really free and enlightened State until the State comes to recognize the individual as a higher and independent power, from which all its own power and authority are derived, and treats him accordingly. I please myself with imagining a State at last which can afford to be just to all men and to treat the individual with respect as a neighbor; which even would not think it inconsistent with its own repose if a few were to live aloof from it, not meddling with it, nor embraced by it, who fulfilled all the duties of neighbors and fellow-men. A State which bore this kind of fruit and suffered it to drop off as fast as it ripened would prepare the way for a still more perfect and glorious State, which also I have imagined but not yet anywhere seen.

45

---

[24]*Chinese philosopher*   Thoreau probably means Confucius.

QUESTIONS

1. How would you characterize the tone of Thoreau's address? Is he chastising his audience? Is he praising it? What opinion do you think he has of his audience?
2. How well does Thoreau use irony? Choose an example and comment on its effectiveness. (One example is in para. 25.)
3. What do you think Thoreau's views are on the relationship of a majority and a minority in the eyes of government?
4. What kind of person does Thoreau seem to be? Can you tell much about

his personality? Do you think you would have enjoyed knowing him? If you could meet him, what would you talk about with him?

5. Are Thoreau's concepts of justice clear?

6. Is it possible that when Thoreau mentions the Chinese Philosopher he means Lao-Tzu? Would Lao-Tzu agree that the empire is built upon the individual?

7. Do you feel that the government of Thoreau's time was built on the individual or on the individual's best interests? Do you think our current government is based on the individual's best interests?

WRITING ASSIGNMENTS

1. Find the quotations that best describe government. Once you have examined them carefully, write an essay that establishes the kind of government Thoreau seems to be referring to. Be sure to include the values of the government Thoreau refers to, the way it sees its obligations to the governed, and the way it treats matters of justice and moral issues. Describe Thoreau's idea of what the American government of his time was in enough detail so that someone who has not read the essay would have a clear sense of Thoreau's view of its nature.

2. Compare the government of Thoreau's day with that of our own. How much alike are the two governments? What specific qualities do the governments have in common? What qualities differ? Do you believe that the United States government has improved since Thoreau's time? Has it improved enough so that Thoreau might want to retract some of the things he says?

3. According to Thoreau, what should the role of conscience be in government? What do you feel Thoreau means by "conscience"? Is it possible for a government to act out of conscience? If a government did act out of conscience, how would it act? Does our government act out of conscience? Does any government that you know about act out of conscience?

4. Thoreau says: "Unjust laws exist: shall we be content to obey them, or shall we endeavor to amend them and obey them until we have succeeded, or shall we transgress them at once?" (para. 16). Answer Thoreau's question in an essay that focuses on issues that are of significance to you; be as practical and cautious as you feel you should be and provide your own answer to this question, not what you feel Thoreau's answer might be. What forms would Thoreau's disobedience be likely to take? What would the limits of his actions be?

5. Establish clearly what being in jail taught Thoreau. What was life in jail like? Why did it have the effect it had on him? Is it unreasonable for Thoreau to have reacted so strongly to being in a local jail for only a single day?

6. Establish which of the writers in Part One has most in common with Thoreau and which has least in common. Use passages from each, and analyze them in relationship to what Thoreau says in "Civil Disobedience." Ask yourself whether the writer you feel is most like Thoreau would have gone to jail as Thoreau did. Would that writer have disobeyed a law that was perceived as immoral? Would that person be doing the right thing?

MARTIN LUTHER KING, Jr.

―――――⦿―――――

Letter from Birmingham Jail

MARTIN LUTHER KING, JR. *(1929–1968) was the most influential leader for black civil rights in America for a little more than fifteen years. He was an ordained minister with a doctorate in theology from Boston University. He worked primarily in the South, where he worked steadily to overthrow laws that promoted segregation and to increase the number of black voters registered in southern communities.*

The period from 1958 to 1968 was the most active in American history for demonstrations and activities that resulted in opening up opportunities for black Americans. Many laws existed prohibiting blacks from sitting in certain sections of buses, from using facilities such as water fountains in bus stations, and from sitting at luncheon counters with whites. Such laws—patently unfair and insulting, not to mention unconstitutional—were not challenged by local authorities. Martin Luther King, Jr., who had become famous for supporting a program to integrate buses in Montgomery, Alabama, was asked by the Southern Christian Leadership Conference to assist in the fight for civil rights in Birmingham, Alabama, where the SCLC meeting was to be held.

King was arrested as the result of a program of sit-ins at luncheon counters and wrote the letter printed here to a number of Christian ministers who had criticized his position. King had been arrested before and would be arrested again—resembling Thoreau somewhat in his attitude toward laws that did not constitute moral justice.

King, like Thoreau, was willing to endure suffering because of his views, especially when, as in the case of civil rights, he found himself faced with punitive laws. His is a classic case of the officers of the government pleading that they were dedicated to maintaining a stable civil society, even as they inhibited King's individual rights. In 1963, many of the good people to whom King addressed this letter firmly believed that peace and order might be threatened by granting blacks the true independence and freedom that King insisted were their rights and that indeed was their right under the constitution. This is why King's letter, less than thirty years later, seems to have been aimed at an injustice that would have been more appropriate in Douglass's time than in the time of John F. Kennedy.

Eventually, the causes King had promoted were victorious. His efforts helped not only to change attitudes in the South but also to spur legislation that has benefited Americans all over the country. His views concerning nonviolence were spread throughout the world and were the basis of his successful efforts to change the character of life in America. By the early 1960s he had become world-famous, a man who stood for human rights and human dignity virtually everywhere. He won the Nobel Peace Prize in 1964.

King himself was nonviolent, but his program left both King and his followers open to the threat of violence. The sit-ins and voter registration programs spurred countless acts of violence, bombings, threats, and murders on the part of the white community. His life was often threatened, his home bombed, his followers harassed. He was assassinated at the Lorraine Motel in Memphis, Tennessee, on April 4, 1968. But before he died he saw—largely through his own efforts, influence, and example—the face of America change.

KING'S RHETORIC

The most obvious rhetorical tradition King assumes in this important work is that of the books of the Bible which were originally letters, such as Paul's Epistle to the Ephesians and his several letters to the Corinthians. Many of Paul's letters were written while he was in prison in Rome. In each of those instances, Paul was establishing a moral position which was far in advance of that of the citizens who received the letters, and at the same time Paul was doing the most important work of the early Christian Church: spreading the Word to those who wished to be Christians but who needed clarification and encouragement.

It is not clear that the churchmen who received the letter fully understood the rhetorical tradition King assumed—but since they were men who preached from the Bible they certainly should have understood. The general public, which is less acquainted or concerned with the Bible, may have needed some reminding, and the text itself alludes to the mission of Paul and to his communications to his people. King assumes this rhetorical tradition, not only because it is effective, but because it resonates with the deepest aspect of his calling: spreading the gospel of Christ. Brotherhood was his message.

King's tone is one of utmost patience with his critics. He seems bent on winning them over to his point of view, just as he seems confident that—because they are, like him, clergymen—their goodwill should help them see the justice of his views.

His method is that of careful reasoning, centering on the substance of their criticism, particularly focusing on their complaints that his actions were "unwise and untimely." Each of those charges is taken in turn, with a careful analysis of the arguments against his position; then follows a statement, in the clearest possible terms, of his own views and why he feels they are worth adhering to. The "Letter from Birmingham Jail" is a model of careful and reasonable analysis of a very complex situation. It succeeds largely because it remains concrete, treating one issue after another carefully, refusing to be caught up in passion or posturing. King remains grounded in logic. He is convinced that his statement of his views will convince his audience.

Letter from Birmingham Jail

April 16, 1963

MY DEAR FELLOW CLERGYMEN:[1]

While confined here in the Birmingham city jail, I came across your 1
recent statement calling my present activities "unwise and untimely."
Seldom do I pause to answer criticism of my work and ideas. If I
sought to answer all the criticisms that cross my desk, my secretaries
would have little time for anything other than such correspondence in
the course of the day, and I would have no time for constructive work.
But since I feel that you are men of genuine good will and that your
criticisms are sincerely set forth, I want to try to answer your statement in what I hope will be patient and reasonable terms.

I think I should indicate why I am here in Birmingham, since you 2
have been influenced by the view which argues against "outsiders
coming in." I have the honor of serving as president of the Southern
Christian Leadership Conference, an organization operating in every
southern state, with headquarters in Atlanta, Georgia. We have some
eighty-five affiliated organizations across the South, and one of them
is the Alabama Christian Movement for Human Rights. Frequently we
share staff, educational, and financial resources with our affiliates.
Several months ago the affiliate here in Birmingham asked us to be on
call to engage in a nonviolent direct-action program if such were
deemed necessary. We readily consented, and when the hour came we
lived up to our promise. So I, along with several members of my staff,
am here because I was invited here. I am here because I have organi-
zational ties here.

---

[1]This response to a published statement by eight fellow clergymen from Alabama
(Bishop C. C. J. Carpenter, Bishop Joseph A. Durick, Rabbi Hilton L. Grafman, Bishop
Paul Hardin, Bishop Holan B. Harmon, the Reverend George M. Murray, the Reverend
Edward V. Ramage and the Reverend Earl Stallings) was composed under somewhat con-
stricting circumstances. Begun on the margins of the newspaper in which the statement
appeared while I was in jail, the letter was continued on scraps of writing paper supplied
by a friendly Negro trusty, and concluded on a pad my attorneys were eventually permitted to leave me. Although the text remains in substance unaltered, I have indulged in the
author's prerogative of polishing it for publication. [King's note]

But more basically, I am in Birmingham because injustice is here. 3
Just as the prophets of the eighth century B.C. left their villages and
carried their "thus saith the Lord" far beyond the boundaries of their
home towns, and just as the Apostle Paul left his village of Tarsus[2]
and carried the gospel of Jesus Christ to the far corners of the Greco-
Roman world, so am I compelled to carry the gospel of freedom beyond
my own home town. Like Paul, I must constantly respond to the Macedonian call for aid.[3]

Moreover, I am cognizant of the interrelatedness of all communi- 4
ties and states. I cannot sit idly by in Atlanta and not be concerned
about what happens in Birmingham. Injustice anywhere is a threat to
justice everywhere. We are caught in an inescapable network of mutuality, tied in a single garment of destiny. Whatever affects one directly, affects all indirectly. Never again can we afford to live with the
narrow, provincial, "outside agitator" idea. Anyone who lives inside
the United States can never be considered an outsider anywhere
within its bounds.

You deplore the demonstrations taking place in Birmingham. But 5
your statement, I am sorry to say, fails to express a similar concern for
the conditions that brought about the demonstrations. I am sure that
none of you would want to rest content with the superficial kind of
social analysis that deals merely with effects and does not grapple with
underlying causes. It is unfortunate that demonstrations are taking
place in Birmingham, but it is even more unfortunate that the city's
white power structure left the Negro community with no alternative.

In any nonviolent campaign there are four basic steps: collection of 6
the facts to determine whether injustices exist; negotiation; self-purification; and direct action. We have gone through all these steps in
Birmingham. There can be no gainsaying the fact that racial injustice
engulfs this community. Birmingham is probably the most thoroughly
segregated city in the United States. Its ugly record of brutality is
widely known. Negroes have experienced grossly unjust treatment in
the courts. There have been more unsolved bombings of Negro homes
and churches in Birmingham than in any other city in the nation.
These are the hard brutal facts of the case. On the basis of these con-

---

[2]***village of Tarsus*** Birthplace of St. Paul (?–67A.D.), in Asia Minor, present-day Turkey, close to Syria.
[3]***the Macedonian call for aid*** The citizens of Philippi, in Macedonia (northern
Greece) were among the staunchest Christians. Paul went to their aid frequently; he also
had to resolve occasional bitter disputes within the Christian community there (see Philippians 2:2–14).

ditions, Negro leaders sought to negotiate with the city fathers. But the latter consistently refused to engage in good-faith negotiation.

Then, last September, came the opportunity to talk with leaders of   7
Birmingham's economic community. In the course of the negotiations, certain promises were made by the merchants—for example, to remove the stores' humiliating racial signs. On the basis of these promises, the Reverend Fred Shuttlesworth and the leaders of the Alabama Christian Movement for Human Rights agreed to a moratorium on all demonstrations. As the weeks and months went by, we realized that we were the victims of a broken promise. A few signs, briefly removed, returned; the others remained.

As in so many past experiences, our hopes had been blasted, and   8
the shadow of deep disappointment settled upon us. We had no alternative except to prepare for direct action, whereby we would present our very bodies as a means of laying our case before the conscience of the local and the national community. Mindful of the difficulties involved, we decided to undertake a process of self-purification. We began a series of workshops on nonviolence, and we repeatedly asked ourselves: "Are you able to accept blows without retaliating?" "Are you able to endure the ordeal of jail?" We decided to schedule our direct-action program for the Easter season, realizing that except for Christmas, this is the main shopping period of the year. Knowing that a strong economic-withdrawal program would be the by-product of direct action, we felt that this would be the best time to bring pressure to bear on the merchants for the needed change.

Then it occurred to us that Birmingham's mayoral election was   9
coming up in March, and we speedily decided to postpone action until after election day. When we discovered that the Commissioner of Public Safety, Eugene "Bull" Connor, had piled up enough votes to be in the run-off, we decided again to postpone action until the day after the run-off so that the demonstrations could not be used to cloud the issues. Like many others, we waited to see Mr. Connor defeated, and to this end we endured postponement after postponement. Having aided in this community need, we felt that our direct-action program could be delayed no longer.

You may well ask, "Why direct action? Why sit-ins, marches, and   10
so forth? Isn't negotiation a better path?" You are quite right in calling for negotiation. Indeed, this is the very purpose of direct action. Nonviolent direct action seeks to create such a crisis and foster such a tension that a community which has constantly refused to negotiate is forced to confront the issue. It seeks so to dramatize the issue that it can no longer be ignored. My citing the creation of tension as part

of the work of the nonviolent resister may sound rather shocking. But I must confess that I am not afraid of the word "tension." I have earnestly opposed violent tension, but there is a type of constructive, nonviolent tension which is necessary for growth. Just as Socrates[4] felt that it was necessary to create a tension in the mind so that individuals could rise from the bondage of myths and half truths to the unfettered realm of creative analysis and objective appraisal, so must we see the need for nonviolent gadflies to create the kind of tension in society that will help men rise from the dark depths of prejudice and racism to the majestic heights of understanding and brotherhood.

The purpose of our direct-action program is to create a situation so   11 crisis-packed that it will inevitably open the door to negotiation. I therefore concur with you in your call for negotiation. Too long has our beloved Southland been bogged down in a tragic effort to live in monologue rather than dialogue.

One of the basic points in your statement is that the action that I   12 and my associates have taken in Birmingham is untimely. Some have asked: "Why didn't you give the new city administration time to act?" The only answer that I can give to this query is that the new Birmingham administration must be prodded about as much as the outgoing one, before it will act. We are sadly mistaken if we feel that the election of Albert Boutwell as mayor will bring the millennium[5] to Birmingham. While Mr. Boutwell is a much more gentle person than Mr. Connor, they are both segregationists, dedicated to maintenance of the status quo. I have hoped that Mr. Boutwell will be reasonable enough to see the futility of massive resistance to desegregation. But he will not see this without pressure from devotees of civil rights. My friends, I must say to you that we have not made a single gain in civil rights without determined legal and nonviolent pressure. Lamentably, it is an historical fact that privileged groups seldom give up their privileges voluntarily. Individuals may see the moral light and voluntarily give

---

[4]*Socrates (470?–399 B.C.)* The tension in the mind King refers to is created by the question-answer technique known as the Socratic method. By posing questions in the beginning of the paragraph, King shows his willingness to share Socrates' rhetorical techniques. Socrates was imprisoned and killed for his civil disobedience (see paragraph 21). He was the greatest of Greek philosophers.

[5]*the millennium* A reference to Revelation 20, according to which the Second Coming of Christ will be followed by 1,000 years of peace, when the devil will be incapacitated. After this will come a final battle between good and evil, followed by the Last Judgment.

up their unjust posture; but, as Reinhold Niebuhr[6] has reminded us, groups tend to be more immoral than individuals.

We know through painful experience that freedom is never volun- 13 tarily given by the oppressor; it must be demanded by the oppressed. Frankly, I have yet to engage in a direct-action campaign that was "well timed" in the view of those who have not suffered unduly from the disease of segregation. For years now I have heard the word "Wait!" It rings in the ear of every Negro with piercing familiarity. This "Wait" has almost always meant "Never." We must come to see, with one of our distinguished jurists, that "justice too long delayed is justice denied."[7]

We have waited for more than 340 years for our constitutional and 14 God-given rights. The nations of Asia and Africa are moving with jet-like speed toward gaining political independence, but we still creep at horse-and-buggy pace toward gaining a cup of coffee at a lunch counter. Perhaps it is easy for those who have never felt the stinging darts of segregation to say, "Wait." But when you have seen vicious mobs lynch your mothers and fathers at will and drown your sisters and brothers at whim; when you have seen hate-filled policemen curse, kick, and even kill your black brothers and sisters; when you see the vast majority of your twenty million Negro brothers smothering in an airtight cage of poverty in the midst of an affluent society; when you suddenly find your tongue twisted and your speech stammering as you seek to explain to your six-year-old daughter why she can't go to the public amusement park that has just been advertised on television, and see tears welling up in her eyes when she is told that Funtown is closed to colored children, and see ominous clouds of inferiority beginning to form in her little mental sky, and see her beginning to distort her personality by developing an unconscious bitterness toward white people; when you have to concoct an answer for a five-year-old son who is asking, "Daddy, why do white people treat colored people so mean?"; when you take a cross-country drive and find it necessary to sleep night after night in the uncomfortable corners of your automobile because no motel will accept you; when you are humiliated day in and day out by nagging signs reading "white"

---

[6]*Reinhold Niebuhr (1892–1971)* Protestant American philosopher who urged church members to put their beliefs into action against social injustice. He urged Protestantism to develop and practice a code of social ethics, and wrote in *Moral Man and Immoral Society* (1932) of the point King mentions here.

[7]*"justice too long delayed is justice denied"* Chief Justice Earl Warren's expression in 1954 was adapted from English writer Walter Savage Landor's phrase, "Justice delayed is justice denied."

and "colored", when your first name becomes "nigger," your middle name becomes "boy" (however old you are) and your last name becomes "John," and your wife and mother are never given the respected title "Mrs."; when you are harried by day and haunted by night by the fact that you are a Negro, living constantly at tiptoe stance, never quite knowing what to expect next, and are plagued with inner fears and outer resentments; when you are forever fighting a degenerating sense of "nobodiness"—then you will understand why we find it difficult to wait. There comes a time when the cup of endurance runs over, and men are no longer willing to be plunged into the abyss of despair. I hope, sirs, you can understand our legitimate and unavoidable impatience.

You express a great deal of anxiety over our willingness to break 15 laws. This is certainly a legitimate concern. Since we so diligently urge people to obey the Supreme Court's decision of 1954 outlawing segregation in the public schools, at first glance it may seem rather paradoxical for us consciously to break laws. One may well ask: "How can you advocate breaking some laws and obeying others?" The answer lies in the fact that there are two types of laws: just and unjust. I would be the first to advocate obeying just laws. One has not only a legal but a moral responsibility to obey just laws. Conversely, one has a moral responsibility to disobey unjust laws. I would agree with St. Augustine[8] that "an unjust law is no law at all."

Now, what is the difference between the two? How does one deter- 16 mine whether a law is just or unjust? A just law is a man-made code that squares with the moral law or the law of God. An unjust law is a code that is out of harmony with the moral law. To put it in the terms of St. Thomas Aquinas:[9] An unjust law is a human law that is not rooted in eternal law and natural law. Any law that uplifts human personality is just. Any law that degrades human personality is unjust. All segregation statutes are unjust because segregation distorts the soul and damages the personality. It gives the segregator a false sense of superiority and the segregated a false sense of inferiority. Segregation, to use the terminology of the Jewish philosopher Martin Buber,[10]

---

[8]*St. Augustine (354–430)* Early bishop of the Christian church; great church authority who deeply influenced the spirit of Christianity for many centuries.

[9]*St. Thomas Aquinas (1225–1274)* The greatest of the medieval Christian philosophers and one of the greatest church authorities.

[10]*Martin Buber (1878–1965)* Jewish theologian; *I and Thou* (1923) is his most famous book.

substitutes an "I-it" relationship for an "I-thou" relationship and ends up relegating persons to the status of things. Hence segregation is not only politically, economically, and sociologically unsound, it is morally wrong and sinful. Paul Tillich[11] has said that sin is separation. Is not segregation an existential expression of man's tragic separation, his awful estrangement, his terrible sinfulness? Thus it is that I can urge men to obey the 1954 decision of the Supreme Court, for it is morally right; and I can urge them to disobey segregation ordinances, for they are morally wrong.

Let us consider a more concrete example of just and unjust laws. 17 An unjust law is a code that a numerical or power majority group compels a minority group to obey but does not make binding on itself. This is *difference* made legal. By the same token, a just law is a code that a majority compels a minority to follow and that it is willing to follow itself. This is *sameness* made legal.

Let me give another explanation. A law is unjust if it is inflicted 18 on a minority that, as a result of being denied the right to vote, had no part in enacting or devising the law. Who can say that the legislature of Alabama which set up that state's segregation laws was democratically elected? Throughout Alabama all sorts of devious methods are used to prevent Negroes from becoming registered voters, and there are some counties in which, even though Negroes constitute a majority of the population, not a single Negro is registered. Can any law enacted under such circumstances be considered democratically structured?

Sometimes a law is just on its face and unjust in its application. 19 For instance, I have been arrested on a charge of parading without a permit. Now, there is nothing wrong in having an ordinance which requires a permit for a parade. But such an ordinance becomes unjust when it is used to maintain segregation and to deny citizens the First Amendment privilege of peaceful assembly and protest.

I hope you are able to see the distinction I am trying to point out. 20 In no sense do I advocate evading or defying the law, as would the rabid segregationist. That would lead to anarchy. One who breaks an unjust law must do so openly, lovingly, and with a willingness to accept the penalty. I submit that an individual who breaks a law that

---

[11]*Paul Tillich (1886–1965)* An important twentieth-century Protestant theologian who held that Christianity was reasonable and effective in modern life. Tillich saw sin as an expression of man's separation from God, from himself, and from his fellow man. King sees the separation of the races as a further manifestation of man's sinfulness. Tillich, who was himself driven out of Germany by the Nazis, stresses the need for activism and the importance of action in determining moral vitality, just as does King.

conscience tells him is unjust, and who willingly accepts the penalty of imprisonment in order to arouse the conscience of the community over its injustice, is in reality expressing the highest respect for law.

Of course, there is nothing new about this kind of civil disobedi- 21
ence. It was evidenced sublimely in the refusal of Shadrach, Meshach, and Abednego to obey the laws of Nebuchadnezzar,[12] on the ground that a higher moral law was at stake. It was practiced superbly by the early Christians, who were willing to face hungry lions and the excruciating pain of chopping blocks rather than submit to certain unjust laws of the Roman Empire. To a degree, academic freedom is a reality today because Socrates practiced civil disobedience. In our own nation, the Boston Tea Party represented a massive act of civil disobedience.

We should never forget that everything Adolf Hitler did in Ger- 22
many was "legal" and everything the Hungarian freedom fighters[13] did in Hungary was "illegal." It was "illegal" to aid and comfort a Jew in Hitler's Germany. Even so, I am sure that, had I lived in Germany at the time, I would have aided and comforted my Jewish brothers. If today I lived in a Communist country where certain principles dear to the Christian faith are suppressed, I would openly advocate disobeying that country's antireligious laws.

I must make two honest confessions to you, my Christian and Jew- 23
ish brothers. First, I must confess that over the past few years I have been gravely disappointed with the white moderate. I have almost reached the regrettable conclusion that the Negro's great stumbling block in his stride toward freedom is not the White Citizen's Counciler[14] or the Ku Klux Klanner, but the white moderate, who is more devoted to "order" than to justice; who prefers a negative peace which is the absence of tension to a positive peace which is the presence of justice; who constantly says, "I agree with you in the goal you seek, but I cannot agree with your methods of direct action"; who paternalistically believes he can set the timetable for another man's freedom; who lives by a mythical concept of time and who constantly advises the Negro to wait for a "more convenient season." Shallow

---

[12]***Nebuchadnezzar (c. 630–562 B.C.)*** Chaldean king who twice attacked Jerusalem. He ordered Shadrach, Meshach, and Abednego to worship a golden image. They refused, were cast into a roaring furnace, and were saved by God (see Daniel 1:7-3:30).

[13]***Hungarian freedom fighters*** The Hungarians rose in revolt against Soviet rule in 1956. Russian tanks put down the uprising with great force that shocked the world. Many freedom fighters died, and many others escaped to the West.

[14]***White Citizen's Counciler*** White Citizen's Councils organized in Southern states in 1954 to fight school desegregation as ordered by the Supreme Court in May 1954. The councils were not as secret or violent as the Klan; they were also ineffective.

understanding from people of good will is more frustrating than absolute misunderstanding from people of ill will. Lukewarm acceptance is much more bewildering than outright rejection.

I had hoped that the white moderate would understand that law 24 and order exist for the purpose of establishing justice and that when they fail in this purpose they become the dangerously structured dams that block the flow of social progress. I had hoped that the white moderate would understand that the present tension in the South is a necessary phase of the transition from an obnoxious negative peace, in which the Negro passively accepted his unjust plight, to a substantive and positive peace, in which all men will respect the dignity and worth of human personality. Actually, we who engage in nonviolent direct action are not the creators of tension. We merely bring to the surface the hidden tension that is already alive. We bring it out in the open, where it can be seen and dealt with. Like a boil that can never be cured so long as it is covered up but must be opened with all its ugliness to the natural medicines of air and light, injustice must be exposed, with all the tension its exposure creates, to the light of human conscience and the air of national opinion, before it can be cured.

In your statement you assert that our actions, even though peace- 25 ful, must be condemned because they precipitate violence. But is this a logical assertion? Isn't this like condemning a robbed man because his possession of money precipitated the evil act of robbery? Isn't this like condemning Socrates because his unswerving commitment to truth and his philosophical inquiries precipitated the act by the misguided populace in which they made him drink hemlock? Isn't this like condemning Jesus because his unique God-consciousness and never-ceasing devotion to God's will precipitated the evil act of crucifixion? We must come to see that, as the federal courts have consistently affirmed, it is wrong to urge an individual to cease his efforts to gain his basic constitutional rights because the quest may precipitate violence. Society must protect the robbed and punish the robber.

I had also hoped that the white moderate would reject the myth 26 concerning time in relation to the struggle for freedom. I have just received a letter from a white brother in Texas. He writes: "All Christians know that the colored people will receive equal rights eventually, but it is possible that you are in too great a religious hurry. It has taken Christianity almost two thousand years to accomplish what it has. The teachings of Christ take time to come to earth." Such an attitude stems from a tragic misconception of time, from the strangely irrational notion that there is something in the very flow of time that will inevitably cure all ills. Actually, time itself is neutral; it can be used either destructively or constructively. More and more I feel that the people of ill will have used time much more effectively than have the people of good will. We will have to repent in this generation not merely for the hateful words and actions of the bad people, but for the appalling silence of the good people. Human progress never rolls in on wheels of inevitability; it comes through the tireless efforts of men willing to be co-workers with God, and without this hard work, time itself becomes an ally of the forces of social stagnation. We must use time creatively, in the knowledge that the time is always ripe to do right. Now is the time to make real the promise of democracy and transform our pending national elegy into a creative psalm of brotherhood. Now is the time to lift our national policy from the quicksand of racial injustice to the solid rock of human dignity.

You speak of our activity in Birmingham as extreme. At first I was 27
rather disappointed that fellow clergymen would see my nonviolent efforts as those of an extremist. I began thinking about the fact that I stand in the middle of two opposing forces in the Negro community. One is a force of complacency, made up in part of Negroes who, as a result of long years of oppression, are so drained of self-respect and a sense of "somebodiness" that they have adjusted to segregation; and in part of a few middle-class Negroes who, because of a degree of academic and economic security and because in some ways they profit by segregation, have become insensitive to the problems of the masses. The other force is one of bitterness and hatred, and it comes perilously close to advocating violence. It is expressed in the various black nationalist groups that are springing up across the nation, the largest and best known being Elijah Muhammad's Muslim movement.[15] Nourished by the Negro's frustration over the continued existence of racial discrimination, this movement is made up of people who have lost faith in America, who have absolutely repudiated Christianity, and who have concluded that the white man is an incorrigible "devil."

I have tried to stand between these two forces, saying that we need 28
emulate neither the "do-nothingism" of the complacent nor the hatred and despair of the black nationalist. For there is the more excellent way of love and nonviolent protest. I am grateful to God that, through

---

[15]***Elijah Muhammad's Muslim movement***   The Black Muslim movement, which began in the 1920s but flourished in the 1960s under its leader, Elijah Muhammad (1897–1975). Among notable figures who became Black Muslims were the poet Imamu Amiri Baraka (b. 1934), the world championship prizefighter Muhammad Ali (b. 1942), and the controversial reformer and religious leader Malcolm X (1925–1965). King saw their rejection of white society (and consequently brotherhood) as a threat.

the influence of the Negro church, the way of nonviolence became an integral part of our struggle.

If this philosophy had not emerged, by now many streets of the   29
South would, I am convinced, be flowing with blood. And I am further convinced that if our white brothers dismiss as "rabble-rousers" and "outside agitators" those of us who employ nonviolent direct action, and if they refuse to support our nonviolent efforts, millions of Negroes will, out of frustration and despair, seek solace and security in black nationalist ideologies—a development that would inevitably lead to a frightening racial nightmare.[16]

Oppressed people cannot remain oppressed forever. The yearning   30
for freedom eventually manifests itself, and that is what has happened to the American Negro. Something within has reminded him of his birthright of freedom, and something without has reminded him that it can be gained. Consciously or unconsciously, he has been caught up by the *Zeitgeist*,[17] and with his black brothers of Africa and his brown and yellow brothers of Asia, South America, and the Caribbean, the United States Negro is moving with a sense of great urgency toward the promised land of racial justice. If one recognizes this vital urge that has engulfed the Negro community, one should readily understand why public demonstrations are taking place. The Negro has many pent-up resentments and latent frustrations, and he must release them. So let him march; let him make prayer pilgrimages to the city hall; let him go on freedom rides[18]—and try to understand why he must do so. If his repressed emotions are not released in nonviolent ways, they will seek expression through violence; this is not a threat but a fact of history. So I have not said to my people, "Get rid of your discontent." Rather, I have tried to say that this normal and healthy discontent can be channeled into the creative outlet of nonviolent direct action. And now this approach is being termed extremist.

But though I was initially disappointed at being categorized as an   31
extremist, as I continued to think about the matter I gradually gained a measure of satisfaction from the label. Was not Jesus an extremist for love: "Love your enemies, bless them that curse you, do good to

---

[16]*a frightening racial nightmare* The black uprisings of the 1960s in all major American cities, and the conditions that led to them, were indeed a racial nightmare. King's prophecy was quick to come true.

[17]**Zeitgeist** German word for the intellectual, moral, and cultural spirit of the times.

[18]*freedom rides* In 1961 the Congress of Racial Equality (CORE) organized rides of whites and blacks to test segregation in southern buses and bus terminals with interstate passengers. More than 600 federal marshalls were needed to protect the riders, most of whom were arrested.

them that hate you, and pray for them which despitefully use you, and persecute you." Was not Amos an extremist for justice: "Let justice roll down like waters and righteousness like an ever-flowing stream." Was not Paul an extremist for the Christian gospel: "I bear in my body the marks of the Lord Jesus." Was not Martin Luther an extremist: "Here I stand; I cannot do otherwise, so help me God." And John Bunyan: "I will stay in jail to the end of my days before I make a butchery of my conscience." And Abraham Lincoln: "This nation cannot survive half slave and half free." And Thomas Jefferson:[19] "We hold these truths to be self-evident, that all men are created equal. . . ." So the question is not whether we will be extremists, but what kind of extremists we will be. Will we be extremists for hate or for love? Will we be extremists for the preservation of injustice or for the extension of justice? In that dramatic scene on Calvary's hill three men were crucified. We must never forget that all three were crucified for the same crime—the crime of extremism. Two were extremists for immorality, and thus fell below their environment. The other, Jesus Christ, was an extremist for love, truth, and goodness, and thereby rose above his environment. Perhaps the South, the nation, and the world are in dire need of creative extremists.

I had hoped that the white moderate would see this need. Perhaps 32 I was too optimistic; perhaps I expected too much. I suppose I should have realized that few members of the oppressor race can understand the deep groans and passionate yearnings of the oppressed race, and still fewer have the vision to see that injustice must be rooted out by strong, persistent, and determined action. I am thankful, however, that some of our white brothers in the South have grasped the meaning of this social revolution and committed themselves to it. They are still all too few in quantity, but they are big in quality. Some—such as Ralph McGill, Lillian Smith, Harry Golden, James McBride Dabbs, Ann Braden, and Sarah Patton Boyle—have written about our struggle[20] in eloquent and prophetic terms. Others have marched with

---

[19]*Amos, Old Testament prophet (8th century B.C.); Paul (?–67 A.D.); Martin Luther (1483–1546); John Bunyan (1628–1688); Abraham Lincoln (1809–1865); and Thomas Jefferson (1743–1826)* These figures are all noted for religious, moral, or political innovations that changed the world. Amos was a prophet who favored social justice; Paul argued against Roman law; Luther began the Reformation of the Christian Church; Bunyan was imprisoned for preaching the gospel according to his own understanding; Jefferson drafted the Declaration of Independence.

[20]*written about our struggle* These are all prominent southern writers who expressed their feelings regarding segregation in the South. Some of them, like Smith and Golden, wrote very popular books with a wide influence. Some, like McGill and Smith, were severely rebuked by white southerners.

us down nameless streets of the South. They have languished in filthy, roach-infested jails, suffering the abuse and brutality of policemen who view them as "dirty nigger-lovers." Unlike so many of their moderate brothers and sisters, they have recognized the urgency of the moment and sensed the need for powerful "action" antidotes to combat the disease of segregation.

Let me take note of my other major disappointment. I have been 33 so greatly disappointed with the white church and its leadership. Of course, there are some notable exceptions. I am not unmindful of the fact that each of you has taken some significant stands on this issue. I commend you, Reverend Stallings, for your Christian stand on this past Sunday, in welcoming Negroes to your worship service on a non-segregated basis. I commend the Catholic leaders of this state for integrating Spring Hill College several years ago.

But despite these notable exceptions, I must honestly reiterate that 34 I have been disappointed with the church. I do not say this as one of those negative critics who can always find something wrong with the church. I say this as a minister of the gospel, who loves the church; who was nurtured in its bosom; who has been sustained by its spiritual blessings and who will remain true to it as long as the cord of life shall lengthen.

When I was suddenly catapulted into the leadership of the bus pro- 35 test in Montgomery, Alabama, a few years ago, I felt we would be supported by the white church. I felt that the white ministers, priests, and rabbis of the South would be among our strongest allies. Instead, some have been outright opponents, refusing to understand the freedom movement and misrepresenting its leaders; all too many others have been more cautious than courageous and have remained silent behind the anesthetizing security of stained-glass windows.

In spite of my shattered dreams, I came to Birmingham with the 36 hope that the white religious leadership of this community would see the justice of our cause and, with deep moral concern, would serve as the channel through which our just grievances could reach the power structure. I had hoped that each of you would understand. But again I have been disappointed. . . .

There was a time when the church was very powerful—in the time 37 when the early Christians rejoiced at being deemed worthy to suffer for what they believed. In those days the church was not merely a thermometer that recorded the ideas and principles of popular opinion; it was a thermostat that transformed the mores of society. Whenever the early Christians entered a town, the people in power became disturbed and immediately sought to convict the Christians for being "disturbers of the peace" and "outside agitators." But the Christians pressed on, in the conviction that they were "a colony of heaven," called to obey God rather than man. Small in number, they were big in commitment. They were too God intoxicated to be "astronomically intimidated." By their effort and example they brought an end to such ancient evils as infanticide and gladiatorial contests.

Things are different now. So often the contemporary church is a 38 weak, ineffectual voice with an uncertain sound. So often it is an arch-defender of the status quo. Far from being disturbed by the presence of the church, the power structure of the average community is consoled by the church's silent—and often even vocal—sanction of things as they are.

But the judgment of God is upon the church as never before. If 39 today's church does not recapture the sacrificial spirit of the early church, it will lose its authenticity, forfeit the loyalty of millions, and be dismissed as an irrelevant social club with no meaning for the twentieth century. Every day I meet young people whose disappointment with the church has turned into outright disgust.

Perhaps I have once again been too optimistic. Is organized religion 40 too inextricably bound to the status quo to save our nation and the world? Perhaps I must turn my faith to the inner spiritual church, the church within the church, as the true *ekklesia*[21] and the hope of the world. But again I am thankful to God that some noble souls from the ranks of organized religion have broken loose from the paralyzing chains of conformity and joined us as active partners in the struggle for freedom. They have left their secure congregations and walked the streets of Albany, Georgia, with us. They have gone down the highways of the South on torturous rides for freedom. Yes, they have gone to jail with us. Some have been dismissed from their churches, have lost the support of their bishops and fellow ministers. But they have acted in the faith that right defeated is stronger than evil triumphant. Their witness has been the spiritual salt that has preserved the true meaning of the gospel in these troubled times. They have carved a tunnel of hope through the dark mountain of disappointment.

I hope the church as a whole will meet the challenge of this deci- 41 sive hour. But even if the church does not come to the aid of justice, I have no despair about the future. I have no fear about the outcome of

---

[21]**ekklesia** Greek word for church; it means not just the institution but the spirit of the church.

our struggle in Birmingham, even if our motives are at present misunderstood. We will reach the goal of freedom in Birmingham and all over the nation, because the goal of America is freedom. Abused and scorned though we may be, our destiny is tied up with America's destiny. Before the pilgrims landed at Plymouth, we were here. Before the pen of Jefferson etched the majestic words of the Declaration of Independence across the pages of history, we were here. For more than two centuries our forebears labored in this country without wages; they made cotton king; they built the homes of their masters while suffering gross injustice and shameful humiliation—and yet out of a bottomless vitality they continued to thrive and develop. If the inexpressible cruelties of slavery could not stop us, the opposition we now face will surely fail. We will win our freedom because the sacred heritage of our nation and the eternal will of God are embodied in our echoing demands.

Before closing I feel impelled to mention one other point in your 42 statement that has troubled me profoundly. You warmly commended the Birmingham police force for keeping "order" and "preventing violence." I doubt that you would have so warmly commended the police force if you had seen its dogs sinking their teeth into unarmed, nonviolent Negroes. I doubt that you would so quickly commend the policemen if you were to observe their ugly and inhumane treatment of Negroes here in the city jail; if you were to watch them push and curse old Negro women and young Negro girls; if you were to see them slap and kick old Negro men and young boys; if you were to observe them, as they did on two occasions, refuse to give us food because we wanted to sing our grace together. I cannot join you in your praise of the Birmingham police department.

It is true that the police have exercised a degree of discipline in 43 handling the demonstrators. In this sense they have conducted themselves rather "nonviolently" in public. But for what purpose? To preserve the evil system of segregation. Over the past few years I have consistently preached that nonviolence demands that the means we use must be as pure as the ends we seek. I have tried to make clear that it is wrong to use immoral means to attain moral ends. But now I must affirm that it is just as wrong, or perhaps even more so, to use moral means to preserve immoral ends. Perhaps Mr. Connor and his policemen have been rather nonviolent in public, as was Chief Pritchett in Albany, Georgia, but they have used the moral means of nonviolence to maintain the immoral end of racial injustice. As T. S.

Eliot[22] has said, "The last temptation is the greatest treason: To do the right deed for the wrong reason."

I wish you had commended the Negro sit-inners and demonstrators 44
of Birmingham for their sublime courage, their willingness to suffer, and their amazing discipline in the midst of great provocation. One day the South will recognize its real heroes. They will be the James Merediths,[23] with the noble sense of purpose that enables them to face jeering and hostile mobs, and with the agonizing loneliness that characterizes the life of the pioneer. They will be old, oppressed, battered Negro women, symbolized in a seventy-two-year-old woman in Montgomery, Alabama, who rose up with a sense of dignity and with her people decided not to ride segregated buses, and who responded with ungrammatical profundity to one who inquired about her weariness: "My feets is tired, but my soul is at rest." They will be the young high school and college students, the young ministers of the gospel and a host of their elders, courageously and nonviolently sitting in at lunch counters and willingly going to jail for conscience' sake. One day the South will know that when these disinherited children of God sat down at lunch counters, they were in reality standing up for what is best in the American dream and for the most sacred values in our Judaeo-Christian heritage, thereby bringing our nation back to those great wells of democracy which were dug deep by the founding fathers in their formulation of the Constitution and the Declaration of Independence.

Never before have I written so long a letter. I'm afraid it is much 45
too long to take your precious time. I can assure you that it would have been much shorter if I had been writing from a comfortable desk, but what else can one do when he is alone in a narrow jail cell, other than write long letters, think long thoughts, and pray long prayers?

---

[22]***Thomas Stearns Eliot (1888–1965)*** Renowned as one of the twentieth century's major poets, Eliot was born in the United States, but in 1927 became a British citizen and a member of the Church of England. Many of his poems focused on religious and moral themes. These lines are from Eliot's play *Murder in the Cathedral,* about Saint Thomas à Becket (1118–1170), the archbishop of Canterbury, who was martyred for his opposition to King Henry II.

[23]***the James Merediths*** James Meredith (b. 1933) was the first black to become a student at the University of Mississippi. His attempt to register for classes in 1962 created the first important confrontation between federal and state authorities, when Governor Ross Barnett personally blocked Meredith's entry to the university. Meredith graduated in 1963 and went on to study law at Columbia University.

If I have said anything in this letter that overstates the truth and 46
indicates an unreasonable impatience, I beg you to forgive me. If I have
said anything that understates the truth and indicates my having a
patience that allows me to settle for anything less than brotherhood, I
beg God to forgive me.

I hope this letter finds you strong in the faith. I also hope that 47
circumstances will soon make it possible for me to meet each of you,
not as an integrationist or a civil rights leader but as a fellow clergyman and a Christian brother. Let us all hope that the dark clouds of
racial prejudice will soon pass away and the deep fog of misunderstanding will be lifted from our fear-drenched communities, and in
some not too distant tomorrow the radiant stars of love and brotherhood will shine over our great nation with all their scintillating
beauty.

> Yours in the cause of
> Peace and Brotherhood,
> MARTIN LUTHER KING, JR.

QUESTIONS

1. What is the definition of "nonviolent direct action"? In what areas of human life is it best directed? Is politics its best area of application? What
   are the four steps in a nonviolent campaign?
2. Is King optimistic about the future of race relations in America? What
   evidence in the letter points in the direction of optimism or pessimism?
3. Which paragraphs in the letter are the most persuasive? Why? Did any part
   of the letter actually change your thinking on an important issue? Which
   part? Why was your thinking changed?
4. If you had to select the best-written paragraph in the essay, which would
   it be? Why?
5. King cites "tension" in paragraph 10 and elsewhere as a beneficial force. Is
   it beneficial? What kind of tension does he mean?
6. Was King an extremist (paras. 30–31)?
7. In his letter, to what extent does King consider the needs of women?
   Would he feel that issues of women's rights are totally unrelated to issues
   of racial equality?
8. What is King's judgment of how a government should function in relation
   to the needs of the individual? Does he feel like Thoreau's "Chinese philosopher," that the "empire is built on the individual"?

WRITING ASSIGNMENTS

1. In paragraph 43 King says, "I have consistently preached that nonviolence demands that the means we use must be as pure as the ends we seek." What, exactly, does he mean by this? Define the ends he seeks; define the means he approves. Do you agree with him on this point? If you have read the selection from Machiavelli, could you contrast their respective views? Which view seems more reasonable to you?

2. Write a brief letter protesting an injustice that you feel may not be entirely understood by people you respect. Clarify the nature of the injustice, the reasons that people will hold to an unjust view, and the reasons why your views should be accepted. Consult King's letter and consciously use his techniques.

3. The first part of the letter is a defense of King's having come to Birmingham as a Christian to help his fellows gain their rights. He challenges the view that he is an outsider, using such expressions as "network of mutuality" and "garment of destiny." How effective is the argument that he raises? Are you convinced by it? Examine the letter for expressions such as those just quoted that justify King's intervention on behalf of his brothers and sisters. If the logic of his position holds, what other social areas might justify intervention? In what area of life might you endeavor to exert your own views on behalf of mankind? Would you expect your endeavors to be welcomed? Are there any areas in which you might consider it wrong to intervene?

4. In paragraphs 15–22, King discusses two kinds of laws, those which are morally right and those which are morally wrong. Analyze his argument carefully, establishing what you feel his views are. For King, which laws are morally right? Name several such laws that you know about. Which laws are morally wrong, according to King? Name some laws, if possible, that you have personal knowledge of. Take a stand on one or two current laws that you feel are morally wrong. Be sure to be fair in describing the laws. Establish their nature and then explain why they are morally wrong. Would you feel justified in breaking these laws? Would you feel prepared, as King was, to pay the penalties demanded of one who breaks the law?

5. Make a comparison of King's letter with sections of Paul's letters to the faithful in the New Testament. Either choose a single letter, such as the Epistle to the Romans, or select passages from Romans, the two letters to the Corinthians, the Galatians, the Ephesians, the Thessalonians, or the Philippians. What positions have Paul and King held in common or opposition concerning brotherly love, the mission of Christ, the mission of the church, concern for the law, and the duties of the faithful? Inventory the New Testament and the letter carefully for concrete evidence of similar or contrary positions.

6. To what extent might Martin Luther King's views about government coincide with those of Lao-Tzu? Is there a legitimate comparison to be made

between King's policy of nonviolent resistance and Lao-Tzu's judicious inactivity? To what extent would King have agreed with Lao-Tzu's views? Would Lao-Tzu have supported King's position in his letter, or would he have interpreted events differently?

PART TWO

IDEAS IN THE WORLD OF ECONOMICS

SHOULD WE JUDGE A SOCIETY'S ECONOMIC STRUCTURE BY ITS EFFECT ON THE INDIVIDUAL LIBERTY OF ITS MEMBERS?

Karl Marx
Charlotte Perkins Gilman
Thorstein Veblen
John Maynard Keynes
John Kenneth Galbraith

INTRODUCTION

ECONOMIC SYSTEMS ARE to some extent political in nature, but they also extend beyond politics. Each person is affected by the economic circumstances in whatever society he or she is a part. The great disputes in our time have been between various forms of socialism—such as Marxist socialism and fascism—contending with various forms of capitalism. These economic disputes became political, and wars resulted. In the last part of the twentieth century it seems clear that the socialist brands of economics have lost out to the capitalist brands. In the Soviet Union, new moves have been made to make state factories profitable, to encourage small businesses, and to learn from the capitalist societies. In China, capitalism is being embraced widely and enthusiastically. In England, decades of socialism have given way to an age of privatization and new capitalism. Japan has become one of the greatest capitalist powers.

The question of wealth and power interests everyone. And to one extent or another, each of the writers in Part Two is concerned with the effects of an economic system on the lives of individuals in the society. In our time, a period of relative wealth, we are still beset with issues related to poverty, a condition that even an era of wealth and economic growth cannot seem to alleviate.

Karl Marx's *The Communist Manifesto* is a special kind of document that clarifies the relationship between a people's condition and the economic system in which they live. Marx saw that capitalism provided the opportunities that the wealthy and powerful needed in order to take advantage of labor. He argued that because labor cannot efficiently sell its product, management can take advantage of labor and not only maintain control but also keep labor in perpetual economic bondage.

Himself a poor man, Marx knew poverty firsthand. One of his close associates, Friedrich Engels, who collaborated on portions of the Manifesto, was the son of a factory owner and so was able to observe closely how the rich can oppress the poor. For both of them, the economic system of capitalism produced a class struggle between the rich, the bourgeoisie, and the laboring classes, or proletariat.

Although Charlotte Perkins Gilman was not a professional economist, she was one of the earliest and most careful thinkers concerned with the role of women in the economy. She was a lifelong writer, lecturer, and editor fighting for women's rights in the late nineteenth century. Gilman was especially interested in the work of Charles Darwin and applied some of his thinking to feminist issues. For example, she felt that selection depended on the female, not the male, and that the future (as well as the past) development of the human race depended on the woman's discrimination in her choice of a sexual partner. Gilman's views placed her in the forefront of feminist thinkers. Even today we can learn from her because for many women the situation has not changed as much as we might have expected.

Thorstein Veblen, in "Pecuniary Emulation," begins to question the powerful surge of middle-class materialism that manifested itself in enormous wealth and smug self-satisfaction in the late nineteenth and early twentieth centuries. *The Theory of the Leisure Class* (1899) is a careful analysis of nineteenth-century wealth and its power. Immense fortunes were in the possession of relatively few people, and the social order had been distorted by this wealth. Veblen was disturbed by the materialism of the culture and by the sacrifice of intellectual values to business interests and profits. The materialism Veblen condemned contributed to the major European wars of this century, and we still regard such materialism as a social problem because the wealth of the nation is so unevenly distributed.

Veblen portrayed the environment of nineteenth-century America as he knew it. He respected some of the doctrines of Marx although he drew quite a different conclusion. This essay is indebted not only to Marx but also to Darwin in its emphasis on evolutionary changes of capitalism and points to Galbraith in its examination of the antithesis of poverty. Veblen wanted to know why people need to be wealthy—what drives them. In essence, he investigated the motives that shape the lives of those living in a capitalist economy.

John Maynard Keynes is probably the best-known twentieth-century economist. An instructor at Cambridge University in England for many years, his most important early work involved an accurate and farsighted analysis of the economics of recovery after World War I. During the period of the Great Depression of the 1930s, his influence may have been greater in the United States than in Great Britain. President Franklin D. Roosevelt followed his advice to boost public spending, loosen credit restrictions, and promote a freer economic environment that could profit from expansion and growth. Keynes's theories are based on production and consumption and remain important today as the basis of modern capitalism. Keynes held that by permitting ambitious business people to pursue their goals of wealth, the entire community would benefit. His views, despite revisionist trends in recent years, are still central to our economic policies in the West.

The final selection, by John Kenneth Galbraith, dates from the middle of the twentieth century and sounds a note that none of the earlier thinkers treated—the question of poverty. It is not that the earlier writers were unaware that poverty existed; after all, each mentions it in passing. Rather these writers were concerned with the accumulation and preservation of wealth. Galbraith, in his study of the economics of contemporary America, also focuses on wealth; the title of his most famous book is *The Affluent Society* (1958). He is, however, interested in pointing toward something greater than the issue of getting and spending, something more important than affluence per se. His concern is with the wise allocation of the wealth that American society has produced. His fears that selfishness and waste will dominate the affluent society have led him to write about some of the most important social issues related to economics: poverty and its effects. If Keynes was correct in seeing wealth as the appropriate subject matter of economics, then Galbraith pointed to a negative quality, the opposite of wealth, as also being worthy of close examination.

Most of these economic theorists agree that a healthy economy can relieve the misery and suffering of a population. Most agree that wealth and plenty are preferable to impoverishment and want. But some are also concerned with the effects of materialism and greed on the spiritual life of a nation. Veblen sees a society in which spiritual values are withering; Galbraith sees a society with enormous power to bring about positive social change, the capacity to make positive moral decisions. But Galbraith, for all his optimism, reminds us that we have made very little progress in an area of economics that has been a focus of thought and action for a generation.

KARL MARX

The Communist Manifesto

KARL MARX *(1818–1883) was born in Germany to Jewish parents who converted to Lutheranism. A very scholarly man, Marx studied literature and philosophy, ultimately earning a doctorate in philosophy at the University of Jena. He was denied a university position and was forced to begin making a livelihood from journalism.*

Soon after beginning his journalistic career, Marx came into conflict with Prussian authorities because of his radical social views, and after a period of exile in Paris he was forced to live in Brussels. After several more forced moves, Marx found his way to London, where he finally settled in absolute poverty. His friend Friedrich Engels (1820–1895) contributed money to prevent his and his family's starvation, and Marx wrote the books for which he is famous while at the same time writing for and editing newspapers. His contributions to the New York Daily Herald *number over three hundred items between the years 1852 and 1862.*

Marx is best known for his theories of socialism, as expressed in The Communist Manifesto *(1848)—which, like much of his impor-*

Translated by Samuel Moore. Part III of *The Communist Manifesto*, "Socialist and Communist Literature," is omitted here.

tant work, was written with Engels's help—and in the three volume Das Kapital *(Capital), the first volume of which was published in 1867. In his own lifetime he was not well known, nor were his ideas widely debated. Yet he was part of an ongoing movement composed mainly of intellectuals. Vladimir Lenin (1870–1924) was a disciple whose triumph in the Russian Revolution of 1917 catapulted Marx to the forefront of world thought. Since 1917 Marx's thinking has been scrupulously analyzed, debated, and argued. Capitalist thinkers have found him illogical and uninformed, whereas Communist thinkers have found him a prophet and keen analyst of social structures.*

In England, Marx's studies concentrated on economics. His thought centered on the concept of an ongoing class struggle between those who owned property—the bourgeoisie—and those who owned nothing but whose work produced wealth—the proletariat. Marx was concerned with the forces of history, and his view of history was that it is progressive and, to an extent, inevitable. This view is very prominent in The Communist Manifesto, *particularly in his review of the overthrow of feudal forms of government by the bourgeoisie. He thought that it was inevitable that the bourgeoisie and the proletariat would engage in a class struggle from which the proletariat would emerge victorious. In essence, Marx took a materialist position. He denied the providence of God in the affairs of man and defended the view that economic institutions evolve naturally and that, in their evolution, they control the social order. Thus, communism was an inevitable part of the process, and in the* **Manifesto** *he was concerned to clarify the reasons why it was inevitable.*

One of Marx's primary contentions was that capitalism is "not personal, it is a social power." In a sense, he focused on one of the problems of economics in relation to government. If capital is a social power, then using it to oppress the society is a fearful thing. It is true, as Marx says, that the "past dominates the present," since the accumulation of past capital determines how people will live in the present. Capitalist economists see capital as a personal power, but a power that, as John Kenneth Galbraith might say, should be used in a socially responsible way. When John Maynard Keynes discussed the end of laissez-faire economics—the kind that Marx complained of and the kind in which oppression of the poor was possible (perhaps inevitable)—he pointed to a new direction in capitalism. It may be a direction that Marx could not have anticipated.

M A R X ' S R H E T O R I C

The selection included here omits one section, the least important for the modern reader. The first section has a relatively simple rhetorical structure that depends upon comparison. The title, "Bourgeois and Proletarians," tells us right away that the section will clarify the nature of each class and then go on to make some comparisons and contrasts. The concepts as such were by no means as widely discussed or thought about in 1848 as they are today, so Marx is careful to define his terms. At the same time, he establishes his theories regarding history by making further comparisons with class struggles in earlier ages.

Marx's style is simple and direct. He moves steadily from point to point, establishing his views on the nature of classes, on the nature of bourgeois society, on the questions of industrialism and its effects upon modern society. He considers questions of wealth, worth, nationality, production, agriculture, and machinery. Each point is dealt with in turn, usually in its own paragraph.

The organization of the next section, "Proletarians and Communists" (paras. 60–133), is not, despite its title, comparative in nature. Rather, with the proletariat defined as the class of the future, Marx tries to show that the Communist cause is the proletarian cause. In the process, Marx uses a fascinating rhetorical strategy. He assumes that he is addressed by an antagonist—presumably a bourgeois or a proletarian who is in sympathy with the bourgeoisie. He then proceeds to deal with each popular complaint against communism. He shows that it is not a party separate from other workers' parties (para. 61). He clarifies the question of abolition of existing property relations (paras. 68–93). He emphasizes the antagonism of capital and wage labor (para. 76); he discusses the disappearance of culture (para. 94); he clarifies the question of the family (para. 98) and of the exploitation of children (para. 101). The new system of public education is brought up (para. 102). The touchy issue of the "community of women" is raised (paras. 102–110), as well as the charge that Communists want to abolish nations (para. 111). Religion is brushed aside (para. 116), and when he is done with the complaints he gives us a rhetorical signal: "But let us have done with the bourgeois objections to Communism" (para. 126).

The rest of the second section contains a brief summary, and then Marx presents his ten-point program (para. 131). The structure is sim-

ple, direct, and effective. In the process of answering the charges against communism, Marx is able to clarify exactly what it is and what it promises. By contrast with his earlier arguments, the ten points of his Communist program seem clear, easy, and (again by contrast) almost acceptable. While the style is not dashing (despite a few memorable lines), the rhetorical structure is extraordinarily effective for the purposes at hand.

In the last section (paras. 135–146), in which Marx compares the Communists with other reform groups such as those agitating for redistribution of land and other agrarian reforms, he indicates that the Communists are everywhere fighting alongside existing groups for the rights of people who are oppressed by their societies. As Marx says, "In short, the Communists everywhere support every revolutionary movement against the existing social and political order of things." Nothing could be a more plain and direct declaration of sympathies.

The Communist Manifesto

A specter is haunting Europe—the specter of Communism. All the Powers of old Europe have entered into a holy alliance to exorcise this specter; Pope and Czar, Metternich[1] and Guizot,[2] French Radicals[3] and German police-spies.   1

Where is the party in opposition that has not been decried as communistic by its opponents in power? Where the Opposition that has not hurled back the branding reproach of Communism against the more advanced opposition parties, as well as against its reactionary adversaries?   2

Two things result from this fact.   3

I. Communism is already acknowledged by all European Powers to be itself a Power.   4

---

[1]*Prince Klemens von Metternich (1773–1859)* Chancellor of Austria (1809–1848) who had a hand in establishing the peace after the final defeat in 1815 of Napoleon (1769–1821); Metternich was highly influential in the crucial Congress of Vienna (1814–1815).

[2]*François Pierre Guizot (1787–1874)* Conservative French statesman, author, and philosopher. Like Metternich, he was opposed to communism.

[3]*French Radicals* Actually middle-class liberals who wanted a return to a republic in 1848 after the eighteen-year reign of Louis Philippe (1773–1850), the "citizen king."

II. It is high time that Communists should openly, in the face of the whole world, publish their views, their aims, their tendencies, and meet this nursery tale of the specter of Communism with a Manifesto of the party itself.

To this end, Communists of various nationalities have assembled in London and sketched the following Manifesto, to be published in the English, French, German, Italian, Flemish and Danish languages.

Bourgeois and Proletarians[4]

The history of all hitherto existing society is the history of class struggles.

Freeman and slave, patrician and plebeian, lord and serf, guild-master and journeyman, in a word, oppressor and oppressed, stood in constant opposition to one another, carried on uninterrupted, now hidden, now open fight, a fight that each time ended, either in a revolutionary re-constitution of society at large, or in the common ruin of the contending classes.

In the earlier epochs of history we find almost everywhere a complicated arrangement of society into various orders, a manifold gradation of social rank. In ancient Rome we have patricians, knights, plebeians, slaves; in the Middle Ages, feudal lords, vassals, guild-masters, journeymen, apprentices, serfs; in almost all of these classes, again, subordinate gradations.

The modern bourgeois society that has sprouted from the ruins of feudal society, has not done away with class antagonisms. It has but established new classes, new conditions of oppression, new forms of struggle in place of the old ones.

Our epoch, the epoch of the bourgeoisie, possesses, however, this distinctive feature; it has simplified the class antagonisms. Society as a whole is more and more splitting up into two great hostile camps, into two great classes directly facing each other: Bourgeoisie and Proletariat.

From the serfs of the Middle Ages sprang the chartered burghers of the earliest towns. From these burgesses the first elements of the bourgeoisie were developed.

---

[4]By bourgeoisie is meant the class of modern Capitalists, owners of the means of social production and employers of wage labor. By proletariat, the class of modern wage laborers who, having no means of production of their own, are reduced to selling their labor-power in order to live. [Engels's note]

The discovery of America, the rounding of the Cape,[5] opened up   13
fresh ground for the rising bourgeoisie. The East Indian and Chinese
markets, the colonization of America, trade with the colonies, the increase in the means of exchange and in commodities generally, gave
to commerce, to navigation, to industry, an impulse never before
known, and thereby, to the revolutionary element in the tottering feudal society, a rapid development.

The feudal system of industry, under which industrial production   14
was monopolized by closed guilds, now no longer sufficed for the
growing wants of the new market. The manufacturing system took its
place. The guild-masters were pushed on one side by the manufacturing middle-class: division of labor between the different corporate
guilds vanished in the face of division of labor in each single workshop.

Meantime the markets kept ever growing, the demand ever rising.   15
Even manufacture no longer sufficed. Thereupon, steam and machinery revolutionized industrial production. The place of manufacture was taken by the giant, Modern Industry, the place of the industrial middle-class, by industrial millionaires, the leaders of whole
industrial armies, the modern bourgeois.

Modern industry has established the world market, for which the   16
discovery of America paved the way. This market has given an immense development to commerce, to navigation, to communication by
land. This development has, in its turn, reacted on the extension of
industry; and in proportion as industry, commerce, navigation, railways extended, in the same proportion the bourgeoisie developed, increased its capital, and pushed into the background every class handed
down from the Middle Ages.

We see, therefore, how the modern bourgeoisie is itself the product   17
of a long course of development, of a series of revolutions in the modes
of production and of exchange.

Each step in the development of the bourgeoisie was accompanied   18
by a corresponding political advance of that class. An oppressed class
under the sway of the feudal nobility, an armed and self-governing association in the medieval commune,[6] here independent urban republic

---

[5] ***the Cape***   The Cape of Good Hope, at the southern tip of Africa. This was a main sea
route for trade with India and the Orient. Europe profited immensely from the opening
up of these new markets in the sixteenth century.

[6] ***the medieval commune***   Refers to the growth in the eleventh century of towns whose
economy was highly regulated by mutual interest and agreement.

(as in Italy and Germany), there taxable "third estate"[7] of the monarchy (as in France), afterwards, in the period of manufacture proper, serving either the semi-feudal or the absolute monarchy as a counterpoise against nobility, and, in fact, corner stone of the great monarchies in general, the bourgeoisie has at last, since the establishment of Modern Industry and of the world-market, conquered for itself, in the modern representative State, exclusive political sway. The executive of the modern State is but a committee for managing the common affairs of the whole bourgeoisie.

The bourgeoisie, historically, has played a most revolutionary part.   19

The bourgeoisie, wherever it has got the upper hand, has put an   20 end to all feudal, patriarchal, idyllic relations. It has pitilessly torn asunder the motley feudal ties that bound man to his "natural superiors," and has left no other nexus between man and man than naked self-interest, than callous "cash payment." It has drowned the most heavenly ecstasies of religious fervor,[8] of chivalrous enthusiasm, of Philistine sentimentalism, in the icy water of egotistical calculation. It has resolved personal worth into exchange value, and in place of the numberless indefeasible chartered freedoms, has set up that single, unconscionable freedom—Free Trade. In one word, for exploitation, veiled by religious and political illusions, it has substituted naked, shameless, direct, brutal exploitation.

The bourgeoisie has stripped of its halo every occupation hitherto   21 honored and looked up to with reverent awe. It has converted the physician, the lawyer, the priest, the poet, the man of science, into its paid wage laborers.

The bourgeoisie has torn away from the family its sentimental veil,   22 and has reduced the family relation to a mere money relation.

The bourgeoisie has disclosed how it came to pass that the brutal   23 display of vigor in the Middle Ages, which reactionists so much admire, found its fitting complement in the most slothful indolence. It has been the first to show what man's activity can bring about. It has

---

[7]**"third estate"** The clergy was the first estate, the aristocracy the second estate, and the bourgeoisie the third estate.

[8]**religious fervor** This and other terms in this sentence contain a compressed historical observation. "Religious fervor" refers to the Middle Ages; "chivalrous enthusiasm" refers to the rise of the secular state and to the military power of knights; "Philistine sentimentalism" refers to the development of popular arts and literature in the sixteenth, seventeenth, and eighteenth centuries. The word "Philistine" meant those who were generally uncultured, that is, the general public. "Sentimentalism" was a code word for the encouragement of emotional response rather than rational thought.

accomplished wonders far surpassing Egyptian pyramids, Roman aqueducts and Gothic cathedrals; it has conducted expeditions that put in the shade all former Exoduses of nations and crusades.

The bourgeoisie cannot exist without constantly revolutionizing   24
the instruments of production, and thereby the relations of production, and with them the whole relations of society. Conservation of the old modes of production in unaltered form was, on the contrary, the first condition of existence for all earlier industrial classes. Constant revolutionizing of production, uninterrupted disturbance of all social conditions, everlasting uncertainty and agitation distinguish the bourgeois epoch from all earlier ones. All fixed, fast frozen relations, with their train of ancient and venerable prejudices and opinions, are swept away, all new formed ones become antiquated before they can ossify. All that is solid melts into the air, all that is holy is profaned, and man is at last compelled to face with sober senses, his real conditions of life, and his relations with his kind.

The need of a constantly expanding market for its products chases   25
the bourgeoisie over the whole surface of the globe. It must nestle everywhere, settle everywhere, establish connections everywhere.

The bourgeoisie has through its exploitation of the world-market   26
given a cosmopolitan character to production and consumption in every country. To the great chagrin of reactionists, it has drawn from under the feet of industry the national ground on which it stood. All old-established national industries have been destroyed or are daily being destroyed. They are dislodged by new industries, whose introduction becomes a life and death question for all civilized nations, by industries that no longer work up indigenous raw material, but raw material drawn from the remotest zones; industries whose products are consumed, not only at home, but in every quarter of the globe. In place of the old wants, satisfied by the productions of the country, we find new wants, requiring for their satisfaction the products of distant lands and climes. In place of the old local and national seclusion and self-sufficiency, we have intercourse in every direction, universal interdependence of nations. And as in material, so also in intellectual production. The intellectual creations of individual nations become common property. National onesidedness and narrowmindedness become more and more impossible, and from the numerous national and local literatures there arises a world-literature.

The bourgeoisie, by the rapid improvement of all instruments of   27
production, by the immensely facilitated means of communication, draws all, even the most barbarian nations into civilization. The cheap prices of its commodities are the heavy artillery with which it batters

down all Chinese walls, with which it forces the barbarians' intensely obstinate hatred of foreigners to capitulate. It compels all nations, on pain of extinction, to adopt the bourgeois mode of production; it compels them to introduce what it calls civilization into their midst, i.e., to become bourgeois themselves. In a word, it creates a world after its own image.

The bourgeoisie has subjected the country to the rule of the towns. 28 It has created enormous cities, has greatly increased the urban population as compared with the rural and has thus rescued a considerable part of the population from the idiocy of rural life. Just as it has made the country dependent on the towns, so it has made barbarian and semi-barbarian countries dependent on civilized ones, nations of peasants on nations of bourgeois, the East on the West.

The bourgeoisie keeps more and more doing away with the scat- 29 tered state of the population, of the means of production, and of property. It has agglomerated population, centralized means of production, and has concentrated property in a few hands. The necessary consequence of this was political centralization. Independent, or but loosely connected provinces, with separate interests, laws, governments, and systems of taxation, became lumped together in one nation, with one government, one code of laws, one national class interest, one frontier and one customs tariff.

The bourgeoisie, during its rule of scarce one hundred years, has 30 created more massive and more colossal productive forces than have all preceding generations together. Subjection of Nature's forces to man, machinery, application of chemistry to industry and agriculture, steam-navigation, railways, electric telegraphs, clearing of whole continents for cultivation, canalization of rivers, whole populations conjured out of the ground—what earlier century had even a presentiment that such productive forces slumbered in the lap of social labor?

We see then: the means of production and of exchange on whose 31 foundation the bourgeoisie built itself up, were generated in feudal society. At a certain stage in the development of these means of production and of exchange, the conditions under which feudal society produced and exchanged, the feudal organization of agriculture and manufacturing industry, in one word, the feudal relations of property became no longer compatible with the already developed productive forces; they became so many fetters. They had to burst asunder; they were burst asunder.

Into their place stepped free competition, accompanied by a social 32 and political constitution adapted to it, and by the economical and political sway of the bourgeois class.

A similar movement is going on before our own eyes. Modern bour-   33
geois society with its relations of production, of exchange and of property, a society that has conjured up such gigantic means of production
and of exchange, is like the sorcerer, who is no longer able to control
the powers of the nether world whom he has called up by his spells.
For many a decade past, the history of industry and commerce is but
the history of the revolt of modern productive forces against modern
conditions of production, against the property relations that are the
conditions for the existence of the bourgeoisie and of its rule. It is
enough to mention the commercial crises that by their periodical return put on its trial, each time more threateningly, the existence of
the entire bourgeois society. In these crises a great part not only of the
existing products, but also of the previously created productive forces,
are periodically destroyed. In these crises there breaks out an epidemic
that, in all earlier epochs, would have seemed an absurdity—the epidemic of overproduction. Society suddenly finds itself put back into a
state of momentary barbarism; it appears as if a famine, a universal
war of devastation, had cut off the supply of every means of subsistence; industry and commerce seem to be destroyed; and why? Because there is too much civilization, too much means of subsistence,
too much industry, too much commerce. The productive forces at the
disposal of society no longer tend to further the development of the
conditions of the bourgeois property; on the contrary, they have become too powerful for these conditions by which they are fettered, and
as soon as they overcome these fetters they bring disorder into the
whole of bourgeois society, endanger the existence of bourgeois property. The conditions of bourgeois society are too narrow to comprise
the wealth created by them. And how does the bourgeoisie get over
these crises? On the one hand by enforced destruction of a mass of
productive forces; on the other, by the conquest of new markets, and
by the more thorough exploitation of the old ones. That is to say, by
paving the way for more extensive and more destructive crises, and by
diminishing the means whereby crises are prevented.

The weapons with which the bourgeoisie felled feudalism to the   34
ground are now turned against the bourgeoisie itself.

But not only has the bourgeoisie forged the weapons that bring   35
death to itself; it has also called into existence the men who are to
wield those weapons—the modern working class—the proletarians.

In proportion as the bourgeoisie, i.e., capital, is developed, in the   36
same proportion is the proletariat, the modern working class, developed, a class of laborers who live only so long as they find work, and
who find work only so long as their labor increases capital. These la-

borers, who must sell themselves piecemeal, are a commodity, like every other article of commerce, and are consequently exposed to all the vicissitudes of competition, to all the fluctuations of the market.

Owing to the extensive use of machinery and to division of labor, the work of the proletarians has lost all individual character, and, consequently, all charm for the workman. He becomes an appendage of the machine, and it is only the most simple, most monotonous and most easily acquired knack that is required of him. Hence, the cost of production of a workman is restricted almost entirely to the means of subsistence that he requires for his maintenance, and for the propagation of his race. But the price of a commodity, and also of labor, is equal to its cost of production. In proportion, therefore, as the repulsiveness of the work increases the wage decreases. Nay more, in proportion as the use of machinery and division of labor increases, in the same proportion the burden of toil increases, whether by prolongation of the working hours, by increase of the work enacted in a given time, or by increased speed of the machinery, etc. 37

Modern industry has converted the little workshop of the patriarchal master into the great factory of the industrial capitalist. Masses of laborers, crowded into factories, are organized like soldiers. As privates of the industrial army they are placed under the command of a perfect hierarchy of officers and sergeants. Not only are they the slaves of the bourgeois class and of the bourgeois state, they are daily and hourly enslaved by the machine, by the overlooker, and, above all, by the individual bourgeois manufacturer himself. The more openly this despotism proclaims gain to be its end and aim, the more petty, the more hateful and the more embittering it is. 38

The less the skill and exertion or strength implied in manual labor, in other words, the more modern industry becomes developed, the more is the labor of men superseded by that of women. Differences of age and sex have no longer any distinctive social validity for the working class. All are instruments of labor, more or less expensive to use, according to their age and sex. 39

No sooner is the exploitation of the laborer by the manufacturer, so far at an end, that he receives his wages in cash, than he is set upon by the other portions of the bourgeoisie, the landlord, the shopkeeper, the pawnbroker, etc. 40

The lower strata of the middle class—the small trades-people, shopkeepers and retired tradesmen generally, the handicraftsmen and peasants—all these sink gradually into the proletariat, partly because their diminutive capital does not suffice for the scale on which Modern Industry is carried on, and is swamped in the competition with the 41 large capitalists, partly because their specialized skill is rendered worthless by new methods of production. Thus the proletariat is recruited from all classes of the population.

The proletariat goes through various stages of development. With 42
its birth begins its struggle with the bourgeoisie. At first the contest is carried on by individual laborers, then by the workpeople of a factory, then by the operatives of one trade, in one locality, against the individual bourgeois who directly exploits them. They direct their attacks not against the bourgeois conditions of production, but against the instruments of production themselves; they destroy imported wares that compete with their labor, they smash to pieces machinery, they set factories ablaze, they seek to restore by force the vanished status of the workman of the Middle Ages.

At this stage the laborers still form an incoherent mass scattered 43
over the whole country, and broken up by their mutual competition. If anywhere they unite to form more compact bodies, this is not yet the consequence of their own active union, but of the union of the bourgeoisie, which class, in order to attain its own political ends, is compelled to set the whole proletariat in motion, and is moreover yet, for a time, able to do so. At this stage, therefore, the proletarians do not fight their enemies, but the enemies of their enemies, the remnants of absolute monarchy, the landowners, the non-industrial bourgeois, the petty bourgeoisie. Thus the whole historical movement is concentrated in the hands of the bourgeoisie, every victory so obtained is a victory for the bourgeoisie.

But with the development of industry the proletariat not only in- 44
creases in number; it becomes concentrated in greater masses, its strength grows and it feels that strength more. The various interests and conditions of life within the ranks of the proletariat are more and more equalized, in proportion as machinery obliterates all distinctions of labor, and nearly everywhere reduces wages to the same low level. The growing competition among the bourgeois, and the resulting commercial crisis, make the wages of the workers even more fluctuating. The unceasing improvement of machinery, ever more rapidly developing, makes their livelihood more and more precarious; the collisions between individual workmen and individual bourgeois take more and more the character of collisions between two classes. Thereupon the workers begin to form combinations (Trades' Unions)[9] against the

---

[9]*combinations (Trades' Unions)* The labor movement was only beginning in 1848. It consisted of Trades' Unions that started as social clubs but soon began agitating for labor reform. They represented an important step in the growth of socialism in Europe.

bourgeois; they club together in order to keep up the rate of wages; they found permanent associations in order to make provision beforehand for these occasional revolts. Here and there the contest breaks out into riots.

Now and then the workers are victorious, but only for a time. The real fruit of their battle lies not in the immediate result but in the ever-expanding union of workers. This union is helped on by the improved means of communication that are created by modern industry, and that places the workers of different localities in contact with one another. It was just this contact that was needed to centralize the numerous local struggles, all of the same character, into one national struggle between classes. But every class struggle is a political struggle. And that union, to attain which the burghers of the Middle Ages with their miserable highways, required centuries, the modern proletarians, thanks to railways, achieve in a few years.

This organization of the proletarians into a class, and consequently into a political party, is continually being upset again by the competition between the workers themselves. But it ever rises up again, stronger, firmer, mightier. It compels legislative recognition of particular interests of the workers by taking advantage of the divisions among the bourgeoisie itself. Thus the ten hours' bill in England[10] was carried.

Altogether collisions between the classes of the old society further, in many ways, the course of development of the proletariat. The bourgeoisie finds itself involved in a constant battle. At first with the aristocracy; later on, with those portions of the bourgeoisie itself whose interests have become antagonistic to the progress of industry; at all times, with the bourgeoisie of foreign countries. In all these battles it sees itself compelled to appeal to the proletariat, to ask for its help, and thus, to drag it into the political arena. The bourgeoisie itself, therefore, supplies the proletariat with its own elements of political and general education; in other words, it furnishes the proletariat with weapons for fighting the bourgeoisie.

Further, as we have already seen, entire sections of the ruling classes are, by the advance of industry, precipitated into the proletariat, or are at least threatened in their conditions of existence. These

45

46

47

48

---

[10]***the ten hours' bill in England*** This bill (1847) was an important labor reform. It limited the working day for women and children in factories to only ten hours; at the time it was common for some people to work sixteen hours a day. The bill's passage was a result of political division, not of benevolence on the managers' part.

also supply the proletariat with fresh elements of enlightenment and progress.

Finally, in times when the class-struggle nears the decisive hour, 49 the process of dissolution going on within the ruling class—in fact, within the whole range of an old society—assumes such a violent, glaring character that a small section of the ruling class cuts itself adrift and joins the revolutionary class, the class that holds the future in its hands. Just as, therefore, at an earlier period, a section of the nobility went over to the bourgeoisie, so now a portion of the bourgeoisie goes over to the proletariat, and in particular, a portion of the bourgeois ideologists, who have raised themselves to the level of comprehending theoretically the historical movements as a whole.

Of all the classes that stand face to face with the bourgeoisie today 50 the proletariat alone is a really revolutionary class. The other classes decay and finally disappear in the face of modern industry; the proletariat is its special and essential product.

The lower middle class, the small manufacturer, the shopkeeper, 51 the artisan, the peasant, all these fight against the bourgeoisie, to save from extinction their existence as fractions of the middle class. They are therefore not revolutionary, but conservative. Nay, more; they are reactionary, for they try to roll back the wheel of history. If by chance they are revolutionary, they are so only in view of their impending transfer into the proletariat; they thus defend not their present, but their future interests; they desert their own standpoint to place themselves at that of the proletariat.

The "dangerous class," the social scum, that passively rotting mass 52 thrown off by the lowest layers of old society, may, here and there, be swept into the movement by a proletarian revolution; its conditions of life, however, prepare it far more for the part of a bribed tool of reactionary intrigue.

In the conditions of the proletariat, those of the old society at large 53 are already virtually swamped. The proletarian is without property; his relation to his wife and children has no longer anything in common with the bourgeois family relations; modern industrial labor, modern subjection to capital, the same in England as in France, in America as in Germany, has stripped him of every trace of national character. Law, morality, religion, are to him so many bourgeois prejudices, behind which lurk in ambush just as many bourgeois interests.

All the preceding classes that got the upper hand sought to fortify 54 their already acquired status by subjecting society at large to their conditions of appropriation. The proletarians cannot become masters of the productive forces of society, except by abolishing their own previous mode of appropriation, and thereby also every other previous mode of appropriation. They have nothing of their own to secure and to fortify; their mission is to destroy all previous securities for and insurances of individual property.

All previous historical movements were movements of minorities, or in the interest of minorities. The proletarian movement is the self-conscious, independent movement of the immense majority. The proletariat, the lowest stratum of our present society, cannot stir, cannot raise itself up without the whole superincumbent strata of official society being sprung into the air.

Though not in substance, yet in form, the struggle of the proletariat with the bourgeoisie is at first a national struggle. The proletariat of each country must, of course, first of all settle matters with its own bourgeoisie.

In depicting the most general phases of the development of the proletariat, we traced the more or less veiled civil war, raging within existing society, up to the point where that war breaks out into open revolution, and where the violent overthrow of the bourgeoisie, lays the foundations for the sway of the proletariat.

Hitherto every form of society has been based, as we have already seen, on the antagonism of oppressing and oppressed classes. But in order to oppress a class, certain conditions must be assured to it under which it can, at least, continue its slavish existence. The serf, in the period of serfdom, raised himself to membership in the commune, just as the petty bourgeois, under the yoke of feudal absolutism, managed to develop into a bourgeois. The modern laborer, on the contrary, instead of rising with the progress of industry, sinks deeper and deeper below the conditions of existence of his own class. He becomes a pauper, and pauperism develops more rapidly than population and wealth. And here it becomes evident that the bourgeoisie is unfit any longer to be the ruling class in society, and to impose its conditions of existence upon society as an over-riding law. It is unfit to rule, because it is incompetent to assure an existence to its slave within his slavery, because it cannot help letting him sink into such a state that it has to feed him, instead of being fed by him. Society can no longer live under this bourgeoisie; in other words, its existence is no longer compatible with society.

The essential condition for the existence, and for the sway of the bourgeois class, is the formation and augmentation of capital; the condition for capital is wage labor. Wage labor rests exclusively on competition between the laborers. The advance of industry, whose involuntary promoter is the bourgeoisie, replaces the isolation of the laborers, due to competition, by their involuntary combination, due to association. The development of Modern Industry, therefore, cuts from under its feet the very foundation on which the bourgeoisie produces and appropriates products. What the bourgeoisie therefore produces, above all, are its own grave diggers. Its fall and the victory of the proletariat are equally inevitable.

Proletarians and Communists

In what relation do the Communists stand to the proletarians as a whole?   60

The Communists do not form a separate party opposed to other working class parties.   61

They have no interests separate and apart from those of the proletariat as a whole.   62

They do not set up any sectarian principles of their own, by which to shape and mold the proletarian movement.   63

The Communists are distinguished from the other working class parties by this only: 1. In the national struggles of the proletarians of the different countries, they point out and bring to the front the common interests of the entire proletariat, independently of all nationality. 2. In the various stages of development which the struggle of the working class against the bourgeoisie has to pass through, they always and everywhere represent the interests of the movement as a whole.   64

The Communists, therefore, are on the one hand practically the most advanced and resolute section of the working class parties of every country, that section which pushes forward all others; on the other hand, theoretically, they have over the great mass of the proletariat the advantage of clearly understanding the line of march, the conditions, and the ultimate general results of the proletarian movement.   65

The immediate aim of the Communists is the same as that of all the other proletarian parties: formation of the proletariat into a class, overthrow of the bourgeois of supremacy, conquest of political power by the proletariat.   66

The theoretical conclusions of the Communists are in no way based on ideas or principles that have been invented or discovered by this or that would-be universal reformer.   67

They merely express, in general terms, actual relations springing from an existing class struggle, from a historical movement going on   68 under our very eyes. The abolition of existing property relations is not at all a distinctive feature of Communism.

All property relations in the past have continually been subject to historical change consequent upon the change in historical conditions. 69

The French Revolution, for example, abolished feudal property in favor of bourgeois property. 70

The distinguishing feature of Communism is not the abolition of property generally, but the abolition of bourgeois property. But modern bourgeois private property is the final and most complete expression of the system of producing and appropriating products, that is based on class antagonism, on the exploitation of the many by the few. 71

In this sense, the theory of the Communists may be summed up in the single sentence: Abolition of private property. 72

We Communists have been reproached with the desire of abolishing the right of personally acquiring property as the fruit of a man's own labor, which property is alleged to be the groundwork of all personal freedom, activity and independence. 73

Hard won, self-acquired, self-earned property! Do you mean the property of the petty artisan and of the small peasant, a form of property that preceded the bourgeois form? There is no need to abolish that; the development of industry has to a great extent already destroyed it, and is still destroying it daily. 74

Or do you mean modern bourgeois private property? 75

But does wage labor create any property for the laborer? Not a bit. It creates capital, i.e., that kind of property which exploits wage labor, and which cannot increase except upon condition of getting a new supply of wage labor for fresh exploitation. Property, in its present form, is based on the antagonism of capital and wage labor. Let us examine both sides of this antagonism. 76

To be a capitalist is to have not only a purely personal, but a social status in production. Capital is a collective product, and only by the united action of many members, nay, in the last resort, only by the united action of all members of society, can it be set in motion. 77

Capital is therefore not a personal, it is a social power. 78

When, therefore, capital is converted into common property, into the property of all members of society, personal property is not thereby transformed into social property. It is only the social character of the property that is changed. It loses its class character. 79

Let us now take wage labor. 80

The average price of wage labor is the minimum wage, i.e., that quantum of the means of subsistence which is absolutely requisite to 81 keep the laborer in bare existence as a laborer. What, therefore, the wage laborer appropriates by means of his labor, merely suffices to prolong and reproduce a bare existence. We by no means intend to abolish this personal appropriation of the products of labor, an appropriation that is made for the maintenance and reproduction of human life, and that leaves no surplus wherewith to command the labor of others. All that we want to do away with is the miserable character of this appropriation, under which the laborer lives merely to increase capital and is allowed to live only in so far as the interests of the ruling class require it.

In bourgeois society, living labor is but a means to increase accumulated labor. In Communist society accumulated labor is but a means to widen, to enrich, to promote the existence of the laborer. 82

In bourgeois society, therefore, the past dominates the present; in Communist society the present dominates the past. In bourgeois society, capital is independent and has individuality, while the living person is dependent and has no individuality. 83

And the abolition of this state of things is called by the bourgeois abolition of individuality and freedom! And rightly so. The abolition of bourgeois individuality, bourgeois independence and bourgeois freedom is undoubtedly aimed at. 84

By freedom is meant, under the present bourgeois conditions of production, free trade, free selling and buying. 85

But if selling and buying disappears, free selling and buying disappears also. This talk about free selling and buying, and all the other "brave words" of our bourgeoisie about freedom in general have a meaning, if any, only in contrast with restricted selling and buying, with the fettered traders of the Middle Ages, but have no meaning when opposed to the Communistic abolition of buying and selling, of the bourgeois conditions of production, and of the bourgeoisie itself. 86

You are horrified at our intending to do away with private property. But in your existing society private property is already done away with for nine-tenths of the population; its existence for the few is solely due to its non-existence in the hands of those nine-tenths. You reproach us, therefore, with intending to do away with a form of property, the necessary condition for whose existence is the non-existence of any property for the immense majority of society. 87

In one word, you reproach us with intending to do away with your property. Precisely so: that is just what we intend. 88

From the moment when labor can no longer be converted into capi- 89 tal, money, or rent, into a social power capable of being monopolized, i.e., from the moment when individual property can no longer be transformed into bourgeois property, into capital, from that moment, you say, individuality vanishes.

You must, therefore, confess that by "individual" you mean no other person than the bourgeois, than the middle-class owner of property. This person must, indeed, be swept out of the way and made impossible. 90

Communism deprives no man of the power to appropriate the products of society: all that it does is to deprive him of the power to subjugate the labor of others by means of such appropriation. 91

It has been objected that upon the abolition of private property all work will cease and universal laziness will overtake us. 92

According to this, bourgeois society ought long ago to have gone to the dogs through sheer idleness; for those of its members who work acquire nothing, and those who acquire anything do not work. The whole of this objection is but another expression of the tautology: that there can no longer be any wage labor when there is no longer any capital. 93

All objections urged against the Communistic mode of producing and appropriating material products have, in the same way, been urged against the Communistic modes of producing and appropriating intellectual products. Just as, to the bourgeois, the disappearance of class property is the disappearance of production itself, so the disappearance of class culture is to him identical with the disappearance of all culture. 94

That culture, the loss of which he laments, is, for the enormous majority, a mere training to act as a machine. 95

But don't wrangle with us so long as you apply, to our intended abolition of bourgeois property, the standard of your bourgeois notions of freedom, culture, law, etc. Your very ideas are but the outgrowth of the conditions of your bourgeois production and bourgeois property, just as your jurisprudence is but the will of your class made into a law for all, a will whose essential character and direction are determined by the economical conditions of existence of your class. 96

The selfish misconception that induces you to transform into eternal laws of nature and of reason the social forms springing from your present mode of production and form of property—historical relations that rise and disappear in the progress of production—this misconception you share with every ruling class that has preceded you. What you 97 see clearly in the case of ancient property, what you admit in the case of feudal property, you are of course forbidden to admit in the case of your own bourgeois form of property.

Abolition of the family! Even the most radical flare up at this infamous proposal of the Communists. 98

On what foundation is the present family, the bourgeois family, based? On capital, on private gain. In its completely developed form this family exists only among the bourgeoisie. But this state of things finds its complement in the practical absence of the family among the proletarians, and in public prostitution. 99

The bourgeois family will vanish as a matter of course when its complement vanishes, and both will vanish with the vanishing of capital. 100

Do you charge us with wanting to stop the exploitation of children by their parents? To this crime we plead guilty. 101

But, you will say, we destroy the most hallowed of relations when we replace home education by social. 102

And your education! Is not that also social, and determined by the social conditions under which you educate; by the intervention, direct or indirect, of society by means of schools, etc.? The Communists have not invented the intervention of society in education; they do but seek to alter the character of that intervention, and to rescue education from the influence of the ruling class. 103

The bourgeois clap-trap about the family and education, about the hallowed correlation of parent and child, become all the more disgusting, the more, by the action of Modern Industry, all family ties among the proletarians are torn asunder and their children transformed into simple articles of commerce and instruments of labor. 104

But you Communists would introduce community of women, screams the whole bourgeoisie chorus. 105

The bourgeois sees in his wife a mere instrument of production. He hears that the instruments of production are to be exploited in common, and, naturally, can come to no other conclusion, than that the lot of being common to all will likewise fall to the women. 106

He has not even a suspicion that the real point aimed at is to do away with the status of women as mere instruments of production. 107

For the rest, nothing is more ridiculous than the virtuous indignation of our bourgeois at the community of women which, they pretend, is to be openly and officially established by the Communists. The Communists have no need to introduce community of women, it has existed almost from time immemorial. 108

Our bourgeois, not content with having the wives and daughters of 109 their proletarians at their disposal, not to speak of common prostitutes, take the greatest pleasure in seducing each others' wives.

Bourgeois marriage is in reality a system of wives in common, and 110 thus, at the most, what the Communists might possibly be reproached with, is that they desire to introduce, in substitution for a hypocritically concealed, an openly legalized community of women. For the rest, it is self-evident that the abolition of the present system of production must bring with it the abolition of the community of women springing from that system, i.e., of prostitution both public and private.

The Communists are further reproached with desiring to abolish 111 countries and nationalities.

The working men have no country. We cannot take from them 112 what they don't possess. Since the proletariat must first of all acquire political supremacy, must rise to be the leading class of the nation, must constitute itself the nation, it is, so far, itself national, though not in the bourgeois sense of the word.

National differences and antagonisms between peoples are daily 113 more and more vanishing, owing to the development of the bourgeoisie, to freedom of commerce, to the world-market, to uniformity in the mode of production and in the conditions of life corresponding thereto.

The supremacy of the proletariat will cause them to vanish still 114 faster. United action, of the leading civilized countries at least, is one of the first conditions for the emancipation of the proletariat.

In proportion as the exploitation of one individual by another is put 115 an end to, the exploitation of one nation by another will also be put an end to. In proportion as the antagonism between classes within the nation vanishes, the hostility of one nation to another will come to an end.

The charges against Communism made from a religious, a philo- 116 sophical, and generally, from an ideological standpoint, are not deserving of serious examination.

Does it require deep intuition to comprehend that man's ideas, 117 views and conceptions, in one word, man's consciousness, changes with every change in the conditions of his material existence, in his social relations and in his social life?

What else does the history of ideas prove than that intellectual pro- 118 duction changes in character in proportion as material production is changed? The ruling ideas of each age have ever been the ideas of its ruling class.

When people speak of ideas that revolutionize society they do but 119 express the fact that within the old society the elements of a new one have been created, and that the dissolution of the old ideas keeps even pace with the dissolution of the old conditions of existence.

When the ancient world was in its last throes the ancient religions 120 were overcome by Christianity. When Christian ideas succumbed in the 18th century to rationalist ideas, feudal society fought its death-battle with the then revolutionary bourgeoisie. The ideas of religious liberty and freedom of conscience merely gave expression to the sway of free competition within the domain of knowledge.

"Undoubtedly," it will be said, "religious, moral, philosophical and 121 judicial ideas have been modified in the course of historical development. But religion, morality, philosophy, political science, and law, constantly survived this change.

"There are, besides, eternal truths, such as Freedom, Justice, etc., 122 that are common to all states of society. But Communism abolishes eternal truths, it abolishes all religion and all morality, instead of constituting them on a new basis; it therefore acts in contradiction to all past historical experience."

What does this accusation reduce itself to? The history of all past 123 society has consisted in the development of class antagonisms, antagonisms that assumed different forms at different epochs.

But whatever form they may have taken, one fact is common to all 124 past ages, viz., the exploitation of one part of society by the other. No wonder, then, that the social consciousness of past ages, despite all the multiplicity and variety it displays, moves within certain common forms, or general ideas, which cannot completely vanish except with the total disappearance of class antagonisms.

The Communist revolution is the most radical rupture with traditional property relations; no wonder that its development involves the 125 most radical rupture with traditional ideas.

But let us have done with the bourgeois objections to Communism. 126

We have seen above that the first step in the revolution by the 127 working class is to raise the proletariat to the position of ruling class, to win the battle of democracy.

The proletariat will use its political supremacy to wrest, by degrees, all capital from the bourgeoisie, to centralize all instruments of 128 production in the hands of the State, i.e., of the proletariat organized as a ruling class; and to increase the total productive forces as rapidly as possible.

Of course, in the beginning, this cannot be effected except by 129 means of despotic inroads on the rights of property, and on the conditions of bourgeois production; by means of measures, therefore, which appear economically insufficient and untenable, but which in the course of the movement outstrip themselves, necessitate further inroads upon the old social order, and are unavoidable as a means of entirely revolutionizing the mode of production.

These measures will of course be different in different countries. 130

Nevertheless in the most advanced countries the following will be 131 pretty generally applicable:

1. Abolition of property in land and application of all rents of land to 132 public purposes.
2. A heavy progressive or graduated income tax.
3. Abolition of all right of inheritance.
4. Confiscation of the property of all emigrants and rebels.
5. Centralization of credit in the hands of the State, by means of a national bank with State capital and an exclusive monopoly.
6. Centralization of the means of communication and transport in the hands of the State.
7. Extension of factories and instruments of production owned by the State; the bringing into cultivation of waste lands, and the improvement of the soil generally in accordance with a common plan.
8. Equal liability of all to labor. Establishment of industrial armies, especially for agriculture.
9. Combination of agriculture with manufacturing industries; gradual abolition of the distinction between town and country by a more equable distribution of the population over the country.
10. Free education for all children in public schools. Abolition of children's factory labor in its present form. Combination of education with industrial production, etc., etc.

When, in the course of development, class distinctions have disap- 133 peared, and all production has been concentrated in the hands of a vast association of the whole nation, the public power will lose its political character. Political power, properly so called, is merely the organized power of one class for oppressing another. If the proletariat during its contest with the bourgeoisie is compelled, by the force of circumstances, to organize itself as a class, if, by means of a revolution, it makes itself the ruling class, and, as such, sweeps away by force the old conditions of production, then it will, along with these conditions, have swept away the conditions for the existence of class antagonism, and of classes generally, and will thereby have abolished its own supremacy as a class.

In place of the old bourgeois society, with its classes and class an- 134 tagonisms, we shall have an association in which the free development of each is the condition for the free development of all. . . .

Position of the Communists
in Relation to the Various Existing
Opposition Parties

[The preceding section] has made clear the relations of the Com- 135
munists to the existing working class parties, such as the Chartists in England and the Agrarian Reforms[11] in America.

The Communists fight for the attainment of the immediate aims, 136
for the enforcement of the momentary interests of the working class; but in the movement of the present they also represent and take care of the future of that movement. In France the Communists ally themselves with the Social-Democrats[12] against the conservative and radical bourgeoisie, reserving, however, the right to take up a critical position in regard to phrases and illusions traditionally handed down from the great Revolution.

In Switzerland they support the Radicals,[13] without losing sight of 137
the fact that this party consists of antagonistic elements, partly of Democratic Socialists, in the French sense, partly of radical bourgeois.

In Poland they support the party that insists on an agrarian revo- 138
lution, as the prime condition for national emancipation, that party which fomented the insurrection of Cracow in 1846.[14]

In Germany they fight with the bourgeoisie whenever it acts in a 139
revolutionary way, against the absolute monarchy, the feudal squirearchy, and the petty bourgeoisie.

But they never cease for a single instant to instill into the working 140
class the clearest possible recognition of the hostile antagonism be-

---

[11]*Agrarian Reforms* Agrarian reform was a very important issue in America after the Revolution. The Chartists were a radical English group established in 1838; they demanded reforms in land and labor. They were among the more violent revolutionaries of the day. Agrarian reform, redistribution of the land, was slow to come, and the issue often sparked violence between social classes.

[12]*Social-Democrats* In France in the 1840s, a group who proposed the ideal of labor reform through the establishment of workshops supplied with government capital.

[13]*Radicals* By 1848, European Radicals, taking their name from the violent revolutionaries of the French Revolution (1789–1799), were a nonviolent group content to wait for change.

[14]*the insurrection of Cracow in 1846* Cracow was an independent city in 1846. The insurrection was designed to join Cracow with Poland and to further large-scale social reforms.

tween bourgeoisie and proletariat, in order that the German workers may straightway use, as so many weapons against the bourgeoisie, the social and political conditions that the bourgeoisie must necessarily introduce along with its supremacy, and in order that, after the fall of the reactionary classes in Germany, the fight against the bourgeoisie itself may immediately begin.

The Communists turn their attention chiefly to Germany, because that country is on the eve of a bourgeois revolution,[15] that is bound to be carried out under more advanced conditions of European civilization, and with a more developed proletariat, than that of England was in the seventeenth and of France in the eighteenth century, and because the bourgeois revolution in Germany will be but the prelude to an immediately following proletarian revolution. 141

In short, the Communists everywhere support every revolutionary movement against the existing social and political order of things. 142

In all these movements they bring to the front, as the leading question in each, the property question, no matter what its degree of development at the time. 143

Finally, they labor everywhere for the union and agreement of the democratic parties of all countries. 144

The Communists disdain to conceal their views and aims. They openly declare that their ends can be attained only by the forcible overthrow of all existing social conditions. Let the ruling classes tremble at a Communistic revolution. The proletarians have nothing to lose but their chains. They have a world to win. 145

Working men of all countries, unite! 146

QUESTIONS

1. Begin by establishing your understanding of the terms "bourgeois" and "proletarian." Is the distinction Marx makes clear? Are such terms applicable to American society today? Do you feel that you can be properly associated with one or the other of these groups?
2. Marx makes the concept of social class fundamental to his theories. Can "social class" be easily defined? Are there social classes evident in our society? Are they engaged in a struggle of the sort Marx assumes?

---

[15]*on the eve of a bourgeois revolution* Ferdinand Lassalle (1825–1864) developed the German labor movement and was in basic agreement with Marx, who was nevertheless convinced that Lassalle's approach was wrong. The environment in Germany seemed appropriate for revolution, in part because of its fragmented political structure and in part because no major revolutions had yet occurred there.

3. What are Marx's views about the value of work in the society he describes?
4. Marx says that every class struggle is a political struggle. Is this true?
5. Examine the first part and total up the number of paragraphs devoted to the bourgeoisie and to the proletariat. Which class gets more paragraphs? Why?
6. Is the modern proletariat a revolutionary class?
7. Is Marx's analysis of history clear? Try to summarize his views on the progress of history.
8. Is capital a social force, or is it a personal force? Do you think of your savings (either now or in the future) as belonging to you alone or as in some way belonging to your society?
9. What, in Marx's view, is the responsibility of a government that takes the Manifesto seriously enough to consider reshaping its economic system accordingly?

WRITING ASSIGNMENTS

1. Defend or attack Marx's statement: "The executive of the modern State is but a committee for managing the common affairs of the whole bourgeoisie." Is this generally true? Take three "affairs of the whole bourgeoisie" and test each one in turn.
2. Examine Marx's statements regarding women. Refer especially to paragraphs 39, 98, 105, and 110. Does he give evidence that his views are in conflict with his general society? After you have a list of his statements, see if you can establish exactly what he is recommending. Do you approve of his recommendations?
3. Marx's program of ten points is listed in paragraph 132. Using the technique that Marx himself uses—taking each point in its turn, clarifying the problems with the point, and finally deciding for or against the point—evaluate his program. Which points do you feel are most beneficial to society? Which are detrimental to society? What is your overall view of the general worth of the program? Do you think it would be possible to put such a program into effect?
4. All Marx's views are predicated on the present nature of property ownership and the changes that communism will institute. He says such things as a rupture with property relations "involves the most radical rupture with traditional ideas" (para. 125). And he discusses in depth his proposal for the rupture of property relations (paras. 68–93). Clarify the traditional property relations—what can be owned and by whom—and then contrast with that the proposals Marx makes. Establish your own views as you go along, taking issue or expressing agreement (with your reasons) with Marx as you do so. What kinds of property relations do you see around you? What kinds are most desirable for a healthy society? Does Marx get you worried?

5. What is the responsibility of the state toward the individual within the kind of economic circumstances that Marx describes? How can you balance the independence of those individuals who have amassed great wealth and wish to operate freely, against the independence of those who are poor and have no wealth to manipulate? What are the possibilities of abuse in such circumstances, and what are the remedies that a state can achieve through altering the economic system? What specific remedies does Marx suggest? Are they workable?

6. Do you feel that Marx's suggestions are desirable? Are they likely to produce the effects he desires? What do you see as the impediments against the full success of his program? Critics sometimes complain about Marx's misunderstanding of human nature. Do you feel he has an adequate understanding of human nature?

CHARLOTTE PERKINS GILMAN

Women and Economics:
Cupid-in-the-Kitchen

*CHARLOTTE PERKINS GILMAN STETSON (1860–1935) had a long
and distinguished career as a writer and lecturer. She was born in
Hartford, Connecticut, in a community of intellectuals and social
leaders that included her relatives Henry Ward Beecher, an abolitionist clergyman, and Harriet Beecher Stowe, author of the famous antislavery novel* Uncle Tom's Cabin. *The community was active in
antislavery activities before the Civil War and in women's rights
throughout the nineteenth century.*

*Unfortunately, her father abandoned the family, leaving Gil-
man's mother to raise the children. After thirteen years of occasional
visits, minimal support, and little affection, he agreed to a divorce.
Because of her own emotional sufferings, Gilman's mother refused to
show her children much parental affection, fearing it would build in
them the anticipation of tenderness from others. In the years to
come, Gilman herself developed serious emotional problems that
may well have resulted from this unusual treatment.*

Gilman's first marriage was not happy. She attended college at the

---

From *Women and Economics: A Study of the Economic Relation Between Men and
Women as a Factor in Social Evolution.*

Rhode Island School of Design and married a Providence artist, Charles Walter Stetson, but shortly after their child was born, she found household life intolerable and fell into a deep depression that eventually led to a complete nervous collapse. When away from her husband for a time, she recovered and began to realize that her choice was either a healthy separation or a marriage that might lead to insanity.

She took her daughter to California and settled for a time in Pasadena. Because she needed to earn a living, she turned her hand to writing and lecturing, both of which she successfully fulfilled. She eventually divorced Charles Stetson but remained on friendly terms with him, sending her daughter back to be raised by him and his new wife, Grace Ellery Channing, who was an old friend of hers.

Gilman wrote many stories, poems, and essays. Her autobiography, The Living of Charlotte Perkins Gilman, *published after her death in 1935, remains the source for most of what is known about her personal life.*

Women and Economics *was regarded as a pronunciamento of the women's rights movement. It was published first in 1898 and has been reprinted frequently since and translated into seven languages. Her purpose in the book was to explore the consequences of the gender differentiation that she observed in her society, a differentiation that ensured men's employment outside the home and women's employment inside. She herself had paid a terrible price for this way of life and knew that it was a price most women, as wives and mothers, were forced to pay.*

The selection included here, "Women and Economics: Cupid-in-the-Kitchen," establishes some basic points that help us understand the character of life in 1898 for the average Victorian woman and that give us an insight into the norms of that society. Gilman saw the economic condition of women as inextricably linked to society's expectations of how gender determined occupation. She argued that the assumptions about who does what jobs affected the individuality of women in a way that robbed them of much of their freedom, independence, and creativity. What Gilman portrayed is a "Cupid-in-the-kitchen," who depends on her wage-earning husband, who spends all her time giving him what he likes—not what he needs—and who nourishes a family in a way that is not at all healthful. Gilman's exposition is detailed, wide-ranging, and carefully thought-out.

Gilman was not a professional economist like Veblen, Keynes, or Galbraith. Indeed, her gender precluded that possibility. She was dealing with economic issues that simply did not interest male econ-

omists. *These economists were, after all, the beneficiaries of a soci*
ety that was structured, as she tells us, on the premise that the
woman do all the dirty jobs in the house. Gilman reminds us that
women in their own homes are domestic servants who are not paid a
wage. They depend on the generosity of their husbands to survive and
so must do their best to please them and to merit support. Among the
wealthy, according to Gilman, the situation is possibly at its worst:
"It is here that the economic dependence of women is carried to its
extreme. The daughters and wives of the rich fail to perform even the
domestic service expected of the women of poorer families. They are
from birth to death absolutely non-productive in goods or labor of
economic value, and consumers of such goods and labor to an extent
limited only by the purchasing power of their male relatives." She
was quick to point out that it is not the fact of maternity that puts
women in this situation, but the assumption that people make about
what a woman ought to do with her life.

GILMAN'S RHETORIC

Gilman is careful to proceed in a detailed fashion, using the most
direct language and avoiding decoration or complexity. She is or-
dered, rational, and detailed. Her method consists of proposing what
she feels is an agreed-upon truth and then analyzing its elements so
as to produce consent on the part of her reader. She does not assume
a reader who agrees with her, and for that reason she proceeds very
cautiously, making sure not to claim too much and not to press her
reasoning to unlikely limits.

She begins her discussion of the way food is prepared by making
a brief, axiomatic statement: "Human nutrition is a long process."
From this observation arise many more that might challenge her au-
dience's basic opinions. For example, she complains that in a nation
in which half the people are amateur cooks feeding the other half, we
cannot expect the standard of nutrition to be high. The kind of food
women are likely to prepare will not be healthful, because women
are anxious to please their husbands—on whom they depend—and
their job, as society defines it, is to give their husbands the kind of
food that they want, not to decide independently what is best for
their husbands.

Gilman then extends her observations to the question of house-
cleaning. Professional cleaning, she claims, would be an improve-
ment over relying on amateurs—housewives. Eventually, she follows

the implications of her statements and proposes a new way of living. She suggests that people might live in houses or apartments without kitchens; they might live instead in congregate fashion, eating in common dining-rooms run by professionals. Her utopian views have rarely been implemented, even in this century, and she remains far ahead of her time in her vision of ways to live.

Gilman also appeals to scientific authority for an evaluation of the way men and women shape their domestic lives. She compares the way apes and other animals live together, concluding that in the natural world there is a greater sharing of jobs than in the world we human beings have made. The analogy she examines (para. 15) effectively advances her argument.

Gilman's tone is cool, exact, controlled. What she says is generally direct, clear, and meticulously expressed. She avoids giving vent to rage and never relies on personal observation or example to drive her point home. She is occasionally pedestrian in style and risks dullness at times, but she does so in order that the most thoughtful of her readers pay close attention to her argument.

She attracted many followers with this book, especially among women interested in women's rights. More importantly, this essay tells us a great deal about the condition of American women in Gilman's time. Gilman gives us insight into a problem that, for many, seems to have arisen only within years of today, when in fact it remains one of the oldest problems that we still face in the modern world.

Women and Economics: Cupid-in-the-Kitchen

As a natural consequence of our division of labor on sex-lines, giving to woman the home and to man the world in which to work, we have come to have a dense prejudice in favor of the essential womanliness of the home duties, as opposed to the essential manliness of every other kind of work. We have assumed that the preparation and serving of food and the removal of dirt, the nutritive and excretive processes of the family, are feminine functions; and we have also assumed that these processes must go on in what we call the home, which is the external expression of the family. In the home the human individual is fed, cleaned, warmed, and generally cared for, while not engaged in working in the world.

Human nutrition is a long process. There's many a ship 'twixt the cup and the lip, to paraphrase an old proverb. Food is produced by the human race collectively—not by individuals for their own consumption, but by interrelated groups of individuals, all over the world, for the world's consumption. This collectively produced food circulates over the earth's surface through elaborate processes of transportation, exchange, and preparation, before it reaches the mouths of the consumers; and the final processes of selection and preparation are in the hands of woman. She is the final purchaser: she is the final handler in that process of human nutrition known as cooking, which is a sort of extraorganic digestion proven advantageous to our species. This department of human digestion has become a sex-function, supposed to pertain to women by nature.

If it is to the advantage of the human race that its food supply should be thus handled by a special sex, this advantage should be shown in superior health and purity of habit. But no such advantage is visible. In spite of all our power and skill in the production and preparation of food we remain "the sickest beast alive" in the matter of eating. Our impotent outcries against adulteration prove that part of the trouble is in the food products as offered for purchase, the pathetic reiteration of our numerous cook-books proves that part of the trouble is in the preparation of those products, and the futile exhortations of physicians and mothers prove that part of the trouble is in our morbid tastes and appetites. It would really seem as if the human race after all its long centuries had not learned how to prepare good food, nor how to cook it, nor how to eat it—which is painfully true.

This great function of human nutrition is confounded with the sex-relation, and is considered a sex-function: it is in the helpless hands of that amiable but abortive agent, the economically dependent women; and the essential incapacity of such an agent is not hard to show. In her position as private house-steward she is the last purchaser of the food of the world, and here we reach the governing factor in our incredible adulteration of food products.

All kinds of deceit and imposition in human service are due to that desire to get without giving, which, as has been shown in previous chapters, is largely due to the training of women as non-productive consumers. But the particular form of deceit and imposition practised by a given dealer is governed by the intelligence and power of the buyer. The dilution and adulteration of food products is a particularly easy path to profit, because the ultimate purchaser has almost no power and very little intelligence. The individual housewife must buy at short intervals and in small quantities. This operates to her pecuniary disadvantage, as is well known; but its effect on the quality of her purchases is not so commonly observed. Not unless she becomes the head of a wealthy household, and so purchases in quantity for family, servants, and guests, is her trade of sufficient value to have force in the market. The dealer who sells to a hundred poor women can and does sell a much lower quality of food than he who sells an equal amount to one purchaser. Therefore, the home, as a food agency, holds an essentially and permanently unfavorable position as a purchaser; and it is thereby the principal factor in maintaining the low standard of food products against which we struggle with the cumbrous machinery of legislation.

Most housekeepers will innocently prove their ignorance of these matters by denying that the standard of food products is so low. Let such offended ladies but examine the statutes and ordinances of their own cities—of any civilized city—and see how the bread, the milk, the meat, the fruit, are under a steady legislative inspection which endeavors to protect the ignorance and helplessness of the individual purchaser. If the private housekeeper had the technical intelligence as purchaser which is needed to discriminate in the selection of foods, if she were prepared to test her milk, to detect the foreign substance in her coffee and spices, rightly to estimate the quality of her meat and the age of her fruit and vegetables, she would then be able at least to protest against her supply, and to seek, as far as time, distance, and funds allowed, a better market. This technical intelligence, however, is only to be obtained by special study and experience; and its attainment only involves added misery and difficulty to the private purchaser, unless accompanied by the power to enforce what the intelligence demands. 6

As it is, woman brings to her selection from the world's food only the empirical experience gained by practising upon her helpless family, and this during the very time when her growing children need the wise care which she is only able to give them in later years. This experience, with its pitiful limitation and its practical check by the personal taste and pecuniary standing of the family, is lost where it was found. Each mother slowly acquires some knowledge of her business by practising it upon the lives and health of her family and by observing its effect on the survivors; and each daughter begins again as ignorant as her mother was before her. This "rule of thumb" is not transmissible. 7

It is not a genuine education such as all important work demands, but a slow animal process of soaking up experience—hopelessly ineffectual in protecting the health of society. As the ultimate selecting agent in feeding humanity, the private housewife fails, and this not by reason of any lack of effort on her part, but by the essential defect of her position as individual purchaser. Only organization can oppose such evils as the wholesale adulteration of food; and woman, the house-servant, belongs to the lowest grade of unorganized labor.

Leaving the selection of food, and examining its preparation, one 8 would naturally suppose that the segregation of an entire sex to the fulfilment of this function would insure most remarkable results. It has, but they are not so favorable as might be expected. The art and science of cooking involve a large and thorough knowledge of nutritive value and of the laws of physiology and hygiene. As a science, it verges on preventive medicine. As an art, it is capable of noble expression within its natural bounds. As it stands among us today, it is so far from being a science and akin to preventive medicine, that it is the lowest of amateur handicrafts and a prolific source of disease; and, as an art, it has developed under the peculiar stimulus of its position as a sex-function into a voluptuous profusion as false as it is evil. Our innocent proverb, "The way to a man's heart is through his stomach," is a painfully plain comment on the way in which we have come to deprave our bodies and degrade our souls at the table.

On the side of knowledge it is permanently impossible that half 9 the world, acting as amateur cooks for the other half, can attain any high degree of scientific accuracy or technical skill. The development of any human labor requires specialization, and specialization is for-bidden to our cook-by-nature system. What progress we have made in the science of cooking has been made through the study and experi-ence of professional men cooks and chemists, not through the Sisyphean[1] labors of our endless generations of isolated women, each beginning again where her mother began before her.

Here, of course, will arise a pained outcry along the "mother's 10 doughnuts" line, in answer to which we refer to our second premise in the last chapter. The fact that we like a thing does not prove it to be right. A Missouri child may regard his mother's saleratus[2] biscuit with fond desire, but that does not alter their effect upon his spirits or

---

[1]**Sisyphean** Arduously repetitive, as in the labors of Sisyphus, a Greek mythical figure who was condemned eternally to roll a great stone to the top of a hill, only to have it roll back down when he neared his goal. See Homer's *Iliad* (Vi.153).

[2]**saleratus** Salt biscuit.

his complexion. Cooking is a matter of law, not the harmless play of fancy. Architecture might be more sportive and varied if every man built his own house, but it would not be the art and science that we have made it; and, while every woman prepares food for her own family, cooking can never rise beyond the level of the amateur's work.

But, low as is the status of cooking as a science, as an art it is 11 lower. Since the wife-cook's main industry is to please—that being her chief means of getting what she wants or of expressing affection—she early learned to cater to the palate instead of faithfully studying and meeting the needs of the stomach. For uncounted generations the grown man and the growing child have been subject to the constant efforts of her who cooked from affection, not from knowledge—who cooked to please. This is one of the widest pathways of evil that has ever been opened. In every field of life it is an evil to put the incident before the object, the means before the end; and here it has produced that familiar result whereby we live to eat instead of eating to live.

This attitude of the woman has developed the rambling excess 12 called "fancy cookery"—a thing as far removed from true artistic development as a swinging ice-pitcher from a Greek vase. Through this has come the limitless unhealthy folly of high living, in which human labor and time and skill are wasted in producing what is neither pure food nor pure pleasure, but an artificial performance, to be appreciated only by the virtuoso. Lower living could hardly be imagined than that which results from this unnatural race between artifice and appetite, in which body and soul are both corrupted.

In the man, the subject of all this dining-room devotion, has been 13 developed and maintained that cultivated interest in his personal tastes and their gratification—that demand for things which he likes rather than for things which he knows to be good, wherein lies one of the most dangerous elements in character known to the psychologist. The sequences of this affectionate catering to physical appetites may be traced far afield to its last result in the unchecked indulgence in personal tastes and desires, in drug habits and all intemperance. The temperament which is unable to resist these temptations is constantly being bred at home.

As the concentration of woman's physical energies on the sex-func- 14 tions, enforced by her economic dependence, has tended to produce and maintain man's excess in sex-indulgence, to the injury of the race; so the concentration of woman's industrial energies on the close and constant service of personal tastes and appetites has tended to produce and maintain an excess in table indulgence, both in eating and drinking, which is also injurious to the race. It is not here alleged that this is the only cause of our habits of this nature; but it is one of primal importance, and of ceaseless action.

We can perhaps see its working better by a light-minded analogy 15 than by a bold statement. Suppose two large, healthy, nimble apes. Suppose that the male ape did not allow the female ape to skip about and pluck her own cocoanuts, but brought to her what she was to have. Suppose that she was then required to break the shell, pick out the meat, prepare for the male what he wished to consume; and suppose, further, that her share in the dinner, to say nothing of her chance of a little pleasure excursion in the treetops afterward, was dependent on his satisfaction with the food she prepared for him. She, as an ape of intelligence, would seek, by all devices known to her, to add stimulus and variety to the meals she arranged, to select the bits he specially preferred to please his taste and to meet his appetite; and he, developing under this agreeable pressure, would gradually acquire a fine discrimination in foods, and would look forward to his elaborate feasts with increasing complacency. He would have a new force to make him eat—not only his need of food, with its natural and healthy demands, but her need of—everything, acting through his need of food.

This sounds somewhat absurd in a family of apes, but it is precisely 16 what has occurred in the human family. To gratify her husband has been the woman's way of obtaining her own ends, and she has of necessity learned how to do it; and, as she has been in general an uneducated and unskilled worker, she could only seek to please him through what powers she had—mainly those of house service. She has been set to serve two appetites, and to profit accordingly. She has served them well, but the profit to either party is questionable.

On lines of social development we are progressing from the gross 17 gorging of the savage on whatever food he could seize, toward the discriminating selection of proper foods, and an increasing delicacy and accuracy in their use. Against this social tendency runs the cross-current of our sexuo-economic relation, making the preparation of food a sex-function, and confusing all its processes with the ardor of personal affection and the dragging weight of self-interest. This method is applied, not only to the husband, but, in a certain degree, to the children; for, where maternal love and maternal energy are forced to express themselves mainly in the preparation of food, the desire properly to feed the child becomes confounded with an unwise desire to please, and the mother degrades her high estate by catering steadily to the lower tastes of humanity instead of to the higher.

Our general notion is that we have lifted and ennobled our eating 18 and drinking by combining them with love. On the contrary, we have lowered and degraded our love by combining it with eating and drinking; and, what is more, we have lowered these habits also. Some progress has been made, socially; but this unhappy mingling of sex-interest and self-interest with normal appetites, this Cupid-in-the-kitchen arrangement, has gravely impeded that progress. Professional cooking has taught us much. Commerce and manufacture have added to our range of supplies. Science has shown us what we need, and how and when we need it. But the affectionate labor of wife and mother is little touched by these advances. If she goes to the cooking school, it is to learn how to make the rich delicacies that will please rather than to study the nutritive value of food in order to guard the health of the household. From the constantly enlarging stores opened to her through man's activities she chooses widely, to make "a variety" that shall kindle appetite, knowing nothing of the combination best for physical needs. As to science, chemistry, hygiene they are but names to her. "John likes it so." "Willie won't eat it so." "Your father never could bear cabbage." She must consider what he likes, not only because she loves to please him or because she profits by pleasing him, but because he pays for the dinner, and she is a private servant.

Is it not time that the way to a man's heart through his stomach 19 should be relinquished for some higher avenue? The stomach should be left to its natural uses, not made a thoroughfare for stranger passions and purposes; and the heart should be approached through higher channels. We need a new picture of our overworked blind god—fat, greasy, pampered with sweetmeats by the poor worshippers long forced to pay their devotion through such degraded means.

No, the human race is not well nourished by making the process 20 of feeding it a sex-function. The selection and preparation of food should be in the hands of trained experts. And woman should stand beside man as the comrade of his soul, not the servant of his body.

This will require large changes in our method of living. To feed the 21 world by expert service, bringing to that great function the skill and experience of the trained specialist, the power of science, and the beauty of art, is impossible in the sexuo-economic relation. While we treat cooking as a sex-function common to all women and eating as a family function not otherwise rightly accomplished, we can develop no farther. We are spending much earnest study and hard labor today on the problem of teaching and training women in the art of cooking, both the wife and the servant; for, with our usual habit of considering voluntary individual conduct as the cause of conditions, we seek to modify conditions by changing individual conduct.

What we must recognize is that, while the conditions remain, the 22
conduct cannot be altered. Any trade or profession, the development
of which depended upon the labor of isolated individuals, assisted only
by hired servants more ignorant than themselves, would remain at a
similarly low level.

So far as health can be promoted by public means, we are steadily 23
improving by sanitary regulations and medical inspection, by profes-
sionally prepared "health foods" and by the literature of hygiene, by
special legislation as to contagious diseases and dangerous trades; but
the health that lies in the hands of the housewife is not reached by
these measures. The nine-tenths of our women who do their own work
cannot be turned into proficient purchasers and cooks any more than
nine-tenths of our men could be turned into proficient tailors with no
better training or opportunity than would be furnished by clothing
their own families. The alternative remaining to the women who comprise the other tenth is that peculiar survival of earlier labor methods
known as "domestic service."

As a method of feeding humanity, hired domestic service is inferior 24
even to the service of the wife and mother, and brings to the art of
cooking an even lower degree of training and a narrower experience.
The majority of domestic servants are young girls who leave this form
of service for marriage as soon as they are able; and we thus intrust
the physical health of human beings, so far as cooking affects it, to the
hands of untrained, immature women, of the lowest social grade, who
are actuated by no higher impulse than that of pecuniary necessity.
The love of the wife and mother stimulates at least her desire to feed
her family well. The servant has no such motive. The only cases in
which domestic cooking reaches anything like proficiency are those in
which the wife and mother is "a natural-born cook," and regales her
family with the products of genius, or those in which the households
of the rich are able to command the service of professionals.

There was a time when kings and lords retained their private poets 25
to praise and entertain them; but the poet is not truly great until he
sings for the world. So the art of cooking can never be lifted to its true
place as a human need and a social function by private service. Such
an arrangement of our lives and of our houses as will allow cooking to
become a profession is the only way in which to free this great art
from its present limitations. It should be a reputable, well-paid profession, wherein those women or those men who were adapted to this
form of labor could become cooks, as they would become composers
or carpenters. Natural distinctions would be developed between the

mere craftsman and the artist; and we should have large, new avenues of lucrative and honorable industry, and a new basis for human health and happiness.

This does not involve what is known as "co-operation." Co-operation, in the usual sense, is the union of families for the better performance of their supposed functions. The process fails because the principle is wrong. Cooking and cleaning are not family functions. We do not have a family mouth, a family stomach, a family face to be washed. Individuals require to be fed and cleaned from birth to death, quite irrespective of their family relations. The orphan, the bachelor, the childless widower, have as much need of these nutritive and excretive processes as any patriarchal parent. Eating is an individual function. Cooking is a social function. Neither is in the faintest degree a family function. That we have found it convenient in early stages of civilization to do our cooking at home proves no more than the allied fact that we have also found it convenient in such stages to do our weaving and spinning at home, our soap and candle making, our butchering and pickling, our baking and washing. 26

As society develops, its functions specialize; and the reason why this great race-function of cooking has been so retarded in its natural growth is that the economic dependence of women has kept them back from their share in human progress. When women stand free as economic agents, they will lift and free their arrested functions, to the much better fulfilment of their duties as wives and mothers and to the vast improvement in health and happiness of the human race. 27

Co-operation is not what is required for this, but trained professional service and such arrangement of our methods of living as shall allow us to benefit by such service. When numbers of people patronize the same tailor or baker or confectioner, they do not co-operate. Neither would they co-operate in patronizing the same cook. The change must come from the side of the cook, not from the side of the family. It must come through natural functional development in society, and it is so coming. Woman, recognizing that her duty as feeder and cleaner is a social duty, not a sexual one, must face the requirements of the situation, and prepare herself to meet them. A hundred years ago this could not have been done. Now it is being done, because the time is ripe for it. 28

If there should be built and opened in any of our large cities today a commodious and well-served apartment house for professional women with families, it would be filled at once. The apartments would be without kitchens; but there would be a kitchen belonging to the house from which meals could be served to the families in their 29 rooms or in a common dining-room, as preferred. It would be a home where the cleaning was done by efficient workers, not hired separately by the families, but engaged by the manager of the establishment; and a roof-garden, day nursery, and kindergarten, under well-trained professional nurses and teachers, would insure proper care of the children. The demand for such provision is increasing daily, and must soon be met, not by a boarding-house or a lodging-house, a hotel, a restaurant, or any makeshift patching together of these; but by a permanent provision for the needs of women and children, of family privacy with collective advantage. This must be offered on a business basis to prove a substantial business success; and it will so prove, for it is a growing social need.

There are hundreds of thousands of women in New York City 30
alone who are wage-earners, and who also have families; and the number increases. This is true not only among the poor and unskilled, but more and more among business women, professional women, scientific, artistic, literary women. Our school-teachers, who form a numerous class, are not entirely without relatives. To board does not satisfy the needs of a human soul. These women want homes, but they do not want the clumsy tangle of rudimentary industries that are supposed to accompany the home. The strain under which such women labor is no longer necessary. The privacy of the home could be as well maintained in such a building as described as in any house in a block, any room, flat, or apartment, under present methods. The food would be better, and would cost less; and this would be true of the service and of all common necessities.

In suburban homes this purpose could be accomplished much bet- 31
ter by a grouping of adjacent houses, each distinct and having its own yard, but all kitchenless, and connected by covered ways with the eating-house. No detailed prophecy can be made of the precise forms which would ultimately prove most useful and pleasant; but the growing social need is for the specializing of the industries practised in the home and for the proper mechanical provision for them.

The cleaning required in each house would be much reduced by 32
the removal of the two chief elements of household dirt—grease and ashes.

Meals could of course be served in the house as long as desired; 33
but, when people become accustomed to pure, clean homes, where no steaming industry is carried on, they will gradually prefer to go to their food instead of having it brought to them. It is a perfectly natural process, and a healthful one, to go to one's food. And, after all, the changes between living in one room, and so having the cooking most

absolutely convenient; going as far as the limits of a large house permit, to one's own dining-room; and going a little further to a dining-room not in one's own house, but near by—these differ but in degree. Families could go to eat together, just as they can go to bathe together or to listen to music together; but, if it fell out that different individuals presumed to develop an appetite at different hours, they could meet it without interfering with other people's comfort or sacrificing their own. Any housewife knows the difficulty of always getting a family together at meals. Why try? Then arises sentiment, and asserts that family affection, family unity, the very existence of the family, depend on their being together at meals. A family unity which is only bound together with table-cloth is of questionable value.

There are several professions involved in our clumsy method of housekeeping. A good cook is not necessarily a good manager, nor a good manager an accurate and thorough cleaner, nor a good cleaner a wise purchaser. Under the free development of these branches a woman could choose her position, train for it, and become a most valuable functionary in her special branch, all the while living in her own home; that is, she would live in it as a man lives in his home, spending certain hours of the day at work and others at home. 34

This division of the labor of housekeeping would require the service of fewer women for fewer hours a day. Where now twenty women in twenty homes work all the time, and insufficiently accomplish their varied duties, the same work in the hands of specialists could be done in less time by fewer people; and the others would be left free to do other work for which they were better fitted, thus increasing the productive power of the world. Attempts at co-operation so far have endeavored to lessen the existing labors of women without recognizing their need for other occupation, and this is one reason for their repeated failure. 35

It seems almost unnecessary to suggest that women as economic producers will naturally choose those professions which are compatible with motherhood, and there are many professions much more in harmony with that function than the household service. Motherhood is not a remote contingency, but the common duty and the common glory of womanhood. If women did choose professions unsuitable to maternity, Nature would quietly extinguish them by her unvarying process. Those mothers who persisted in being acrobats, horse-breakers, or sailors before the mast, would probably not produce vigorous and numerous children. If they did, it would simply prove that such work did not hurt them. There is no fear to be wasted on the danger of women's choosing wrong professions, when they are free to choose. 36

Many women would continue to prefer the very kinds of work which they are doing now, in the new and higher methods of execution. Even cleaning, rightly understood and practised, is a useful, and therefore honorable, profession. It has been amusing heretofore to see how this least desirable of labors has been so innocently held to be woman's natural duty. It is woman, the dainty, the beautiful, the beloved wife and revered mother, who has by common consent been expected to do the chamber-work and scullery work of the world. All that is basest and foulest she in the last instance must handle and remove. Grease, ashes, dust, foul linen, and sooty ironware—among these her days must pass. As we socialize our functions, this passes from her hands into those of man. The city's cleaning is his work. And even in our houses the professional cleaner is more and more frequently a man.

The organization of household industries will simplify and central- 37 ize its cleaning processes, allowing of many mechanical conveniences and the application of scientific skill and thoroughness. We shall be cleaner than we ever were before. There will be less work to do, and far better means of doing it. The daily needs of a well-plumbed house could be met easily by each individual in his or her own room or by one who liked to do such work; and the labor less frequently required would be furnished by an expert, who would clean one home after another with the swift skill of training and experience. The home would cease to be to us a workshop or a museum, and would become far more the personal expression of its occupants—the place of peace and rest, of love and privacy—than it can be in its present condition of arrested industrial development. And women will fill her place in those industries with far better results than are now provided by her ceaseless struggles, her conscientious devotion, her pathetic ignorance and inefficiency.

QUESTIONS

1. Do you think that Gilman is overstating when she says that Victorian housewives were amateur cooks? Given that they were amateur cooks, do you consider this a legitimate concern?
2. Do you think it is still true that women feel the best way to a man's heart is through his stomach? If so, why do you believe this to be true?
3. Why would Victorian housewives generally cook the kind of food that their husbands wanted rather than the kind of food that was best for them? Is this an issue today?
4. Why did Gilman worry over the quality of food that the average family bought?

5. What does it mean to "live to eat instead of eating to live"? Would Gilman approve of this idea? Do you approve?
6. Is it possible that we have "ennobled our eating and drinking by combining them with love"? If so, how would this affect Gilman's argument?
7. How serious an economic issue has Gilman raised in this essay? Are there ramifications that she has not considered that are important to you, regarding gender distinctions operative in your society?
8. To what extent is our socioeconomic structure based on gender distinctions of the kind Gilman describes?

WRITING ASSIGNMENTS

1. What is the economic situation of a woman in our society? Has she become an equal partner with her husband, as Gilman hoped she would? If you feel she has not, how different is her situation in the last decade of the twentieth century compared with 1898?
2. To what extent is it true that the preparation of food and the care of children is a sex-related function in our society? What functions do you see as sex-related? What effect do they have on the nature of your economy?
3. The concept of "Cupid-in-the-Kitchen" implies that the housewife is trying to please her husband sexually through performing well in the kitchen. Is this description accurate today? What would be the natural results of such a concept? To what extent are these results negative from an economic standpoint? To what extent would a woman who subscribed to this view contribute to her own economic deprivation?
4. To what degree do you concur with Gilman (para. 26) when she says that "Cooking and cleaning are not family functions"? Is this generally true, or is it true only in a limited number of cases? If cooking and cleaning are not family functions, then what are they? Why would society so completely perceive them as family functions if they are not so?
5. How well do you feel Gilman's proposal for dormitory-like structures to house families would work? What would be the advantages of living in such a situation? What would be the arguments against such a living situation? Would it be successful today?
6. In what ways does the thinking of Charlotte Perkins Gilman agree with the thinking of Mary Wollstonecraft? Examine the political implications of Gilman's argument as Wollstonecraft might understand them. Then apply the economic implications of Gilman's views to those of Wollstonecraft. Describe how each interprets the economic situation of women in their respective eras. In your discussion, explain what you understand to be the condition of women in both Wollstonecraft's and Gilman's lifetimes.

THORSTEIN VEBLEN

Pecuniary Emulation

THORSTEIN VEBLEN (1857–1929) *is one of America's most power-fully original thinkers in the areas of economics, business, and soci-ology. A product of the Scandinavian settlements of the Midwest, he was educated at Carleton College in Northfield, Minnesota, and was awarded the Ph.D. in philosophy at Yale University. One of the inter-esting ironies of his career is that, brilliant though he was, he did not immediately proceed to an academic appointment. He languished for seven years on his father's farm in Minnesota, reading—a fate similar to that of the great seventeenth-century English poet John Mil-ton, who spent a period of time on his father's estate before moving into a worldly career.*

The reasons that Veblen had been ignored by the academic world seem to have centered on his difficult personality and on his ex-tremely unpopular views of the direction of the American economy and of the nation's overall social structure. He was profoundly critical of the dominance of business interests over the interests of social bet-terment. He castigated the nation for its slavish worship of the canons of consumption. The passage included here is from his most famous

From *The Theory of the Leisure Class.* The Portable Veblen.

book, The Theory of the Leisure Class (1899), in which he develops a fascinating view of America as a culture that delights in abundance, waste, and conspicuous consumption. Conspicuous consumption is economic showing off. As a modern slogan puts it approvingly, "If you've got it, flaunt it."

Veblen felt that "flaunting it" was central to the American way of life, especially the way of life the leisure class that the American economics of abundance had produced. He condemned conspicuous consumption as fundamentally wasteful and as risking an ultimate financial collapse and a terrible fate for those who were poor. Interestingly, Veblen died in the year in which the spiraling economy, inflated by waves of selfish enthusiasm and reckless speculation, crashed so resoundingly that much of the nation was plunged into a decade of poverty.

It is no wonder that such a telling critic should at first have been kept from the rewards of academic life: he was too savage a gadfly to be tolerated. Yet he eventually succeeded. He taught at the University of Chicago after graduate studies in economics at Cornell. He taught at the New School for Social Research in New York City, at Stanford University in California for a short time, and at the University of Missouri. But the sad fact is that he was never a popular teacher: he begrudged his students their grades, usually marking them all C. He was a classroom mumbler, a monotone dryasdust. Yet, he had one of the most sparkling minds of his generation. Those students who persisted and got through the dull classroom periods were rewarded with an experience so intense that later many of them wrote remarkable memoirs.

Among his many publications, virtually all are of more interest now than they were while he was alive. His greatest fame was posthumous. It was after his death that his views began to be appreciated as those of a farseeing economics savant. One of his books, The Higher Learning in America (1918), is a biting attack on the willingness of America's universities to be dominated by capitalist businesses. The subservience of the universities to the demands of profits resulted in the universities' goals of producing passive, malleable, and acceptable workers for the needs of business and industry. Veblen would much rather have had the universities forsake the world of business and concentrate on the goals of thorough education, even if such a change in focus would have produced graduates likely to be uncomfortable in the then repressive structure of American business. His book is obviously as relevant today as ever, and his views are certainly as unwelcome as they were in his own time.

His "Pecuniary Emulation" discusses the question of the develop-ment of the urge to accumulate wealth. In Veblen's America, huge fortunes had been amassed by innumerable American tycoons, among them the group often known as robber barons, those who de-fied most common ethical principles of decency and fairness in order to make themselves almost unbelievably wealthy. Veblen saw these men as predatory and was led to compare their behavior with the predatory beasts of the wilderness. This, in turn, led him to the anal-ogy with Darwinian evolution and the "survival of the fittest."

Veblen's study includes ideas of evolutionary progress in econom-ics. Interestingly, Marx too had such views. Yet Veblen did not have Marx's purposes of recommending communism as the final stage of evolution of the modern state. Rather, he wanted to show that the question of ownership is susceptible to analysis in evolutionary terms. That is, if one examined its beginnings, he or she would be able to understand in depth the drive (clearly evident in his own time) of people to accumulate far more wealth and goods than they could ever use.

Like many of his expressions, the term "pecuniary emulation" be-comes clear as we progress through the selection. People live in a so-cial milieu; their behavior is understood and measured in terms of their neighbors. They emulate each other in their own social sphere; and when they indulge in pecuniary emulation, they are indulging in amassing money in order to be like their neighbors. As he says, "The currently accepted legitimate end of effort becomes the achievement of a favorable comparison with other men; and therefore the repug-nance to futility to a good extent coalesces with the incentive of em-ulation" (para. 19). In other words, the desire for achievement and the fear of failure (repugnance to futility) derive largely from the em-ulation of others who have been successful and the need to compare oneself with them. As he says in the same paragraph: "Among the motives which lead men to accumulate wealth, the primacy, both in scope and intensity, therefore, continues to belong to this motive of pecuniary emulation."

The section analyzes the sociological implications of a drive to-ward wealth, resting primarily on a comparison of contemporary practices with those of the earliest forms of society. Veblen traces the development of the concept of individual property, distinguishes ownership from simple appropriation (something like owning a river rather than simply using it), and attempts an analysis of the need to accumulate more than can be consumed. Such accumulation is, after all, what wealth is. For Veblen it therefore represents an unusual and

curious fact. His analysis is as pertinent for us as it was for his con-
temporaries at the end of the century.

VEBLEN'S RHETORIC

In something of the manner of Gilman, Veblen argues a position
based upon an entirely hypothetical construct: the primitive societies
from which we developed. He hypothesizes an evolutionary develop-
ment from a barbarian culture, as he puts it, to the current industrial
model. His analysis is detailed and his argument follows conclusively
from his postulation.

Another uncommon quality is the use of unusual terminology that
does not become clear until one is relatively deep into the essay.
Thus, "pecuniary emulation" is an opaque expression until one be-
gins to sort out the terminology near the end of the essay. The same
is true of the term "invidious comparison," which usually implies
simply a comparison that casts the thing compared in a dark light.
"Invidious" means "obnoxious or repugnant." But Veblen is using the
term simply to suggest a profound difference. A man of wealth be-
comes wealthy in order to create an "invidious comparison" with
neighbors: the wealthy man makes himself very different from his
neighbor.

Finally, Veblen reveals a bit of crustiness—and probably some of
the qualities that made him an unpopular teacher—in his delight in
complex words. His use of language is not so brilliant as to cast him
into the company of the English men of letters Matthew Arnold
(1822–1888) and William Hazlitt (1778–1830), to name two who in-
fluenced him; but he is certainly compelling and demanding. His
views are of great moment; he demands that we rise to his level, and
he refuses to lower himself to ours. The result of this rhetorical ap-
proach to style is to set him apart, to make him appear more difficult
than he is, and ultimately to reward us with a view of an interesting
mind commanding an unusual vocabulary for the purposes of making
us sit up and take notice. Veblen rewards our efforts with the product
of insights that actually change our way of thinking about social is-
sues and about the drive toward accumulation that we call the need
for creating wealth.

Pecuniary Emulation

In the sequence of cultural evolution the emergence of a leisure 1
class coincides with the beginning of ownership. This is necessarily
the case, for these two institutions result from the same set of economic forces. In the inchoate phase[1] of their development they are but
different aspects of the same general facts of social structure.

It is as elements of social structure—conventional facts—that lei- 2
sure and ownership are matters of interest for the purpose in hand. An
habitual neglect of work does not constitute a leisure class; neither
does the mechanical fact of use and consumption constitute ownership. The present inquiry, therefore, is not concerned with the beginning of indolence, nor with the beginning of the appropriation of useful articles to individual consumption. The point in question is the
origin and nature of a conventional leisure class on the one hand and
the beginnings of individual ownership as a conventional right or equitable claim on the other hand.

The early differentiation out of which the distinction between a 3
leisure and a working class arises is a division maintained between
men's and women's work in the lower stages of barbarism. Likewise
the earliest form of ownership is an ownership of the women by the
able-bodied men of the community. The facts may be expressed in
more general terms, and truer to the import of the barbarian theory of
life, by saying that it is an ownership of the woman by the man.

There was undoubtedly some appropriation of useful articles before 4
the custom of appropriating women arose. The usages of existing archaic communities in which there is no ownership of women is warrant for such a view. In all communities the members, both male and
female, habitually appropriate to their individual use a variety of useful things; but these useful things are not thought of as owned by the
person who appropriates and consumes them. The habitual appropriation and consumption of certain slight personal effects goes on without raising the question of ownership; that is to say, the question of a
conventional, equitable claim to extraneous things.

The ownership of women begins in the lower barbarian stages of 5

---

[1]**inchoate phase** The early, languageless phase, before things are codified, set up,
and explained.

culture, apparently with the seizure of female captives. The original reason for the seizure and appropriation of women seems to have been their usefulness as trophies. The practice of seizing women from the enemy as trophies gave rise to a form of ownership-marriage, resulting in a household with a male head. This was followed by an extension of slavery to other captives and inferiors, besides women, and by an extension of ownership-marriage to other women than those seized from the enemy. The outcome of emulation under the circumstances of a predatory life, therefore, has been on the one hand a form of marriage resting on coercion, and on the other hand the custom of ownership. The two institutions are not distinguishable in the initial phase of their development; both arise from the desire of the successful men to put their prowess in evidence by exhibiting some durable result of their exploits. Both also minister to that propensity for mastery which pervades all predatory communities. From the ownership of women the concept of ownership extends itself to include the products of their industry, and so there arises the ownership of things as well as of persons.

In this way a consistent system of property in goods is gradually 6 installed. And although in the latest stages of the development, the serviceability of goods for consumption has come to be the most obtrusive element of their value, still, wealth has by no means yet lost its utility as an honorific evidence of the owner's prepotence.[2]

Wherever the institution of private property is found, even in a 7 slightly developed form, the economic process bears the character of a struggle between men for the possession of goods. It has been customary in economic theory, and especially among those economists who adhere with least faltering to the body of modernized classical doctrines, to construe this struggle for wealth as being substantially a struggle for subsistence. Such is, no doubt, its character in large part during the earlier and less efficient phases of industry. Such is also its character in all cases where the "niggardliness of nature" is so strict as to afford but a scanty livelihood to the community in return for strenuous and unremitting application to the business of getting the means of subsistence. But in all progressing communities an advance is presently made beyond this early stage of technological development. Industrial efficiency is presently carried to such a pitch as to afford something appreciably more than a bare livelihood to those engaged in the industrial process. It has not been unusual for economic theory to

---

[2] **prepotence** Superior power.

speak of the further struggle for wealth on this new industrial basis as a competition for an increase of the comforts of life—primarily for an increase of the physical comforts which the consumption of goods affords.

The end of acquisition and accumulation is conventionally held to be the consumption of the goods accumulated—whether it is consumption directly by the owner of the goods or by the household attached to him and for this purpose identified with him in theory. This is at least felt to be the economically legitimate end of acquisition, which alone it is incumbent on the theory to take account of. Such consumption may of course be conceived to serve the consumer's physical wants—his physical comfort—or his so-called higher wants—spiritual, aesthetic, intellectual, or what not; the latter class of wants being served indirectly by an expenditure of goods, after the fashion familiar to all economic readers. 8

But it is only when taken in a sense far removed from its naïve meaning that consumption of goods can be said to afford the incentive from which accumulation invariably proceeds. The motive that lies at the root of ownership is emulation; and the same motive of emulation continues active in the further development of the institution to which it has given rise and in the development of all those features of the social structure which this institution of ownership touches. The possession of wealth confers honor; it is an invidious distinction. Nothing equally cogent can be said for the consumption of goods, nor for any other conceivable incentive to acquisition, and especially not for any incentive to the accumulation of wealth. 9

It is of course not to be overlooked that in a community where nearly all goods are private property the necessity of earning a livelihood is a powerful and ever-present incentive for the poorer members of the community. The need of subsistence and of an increase of physical comfort may for a time be the dominant motive of acquisition for those classes who are habitually employed at manual labor, whose subsistence is on a precarious footing, who possess little and ordinarily accumulate little; but it will appear in the course of the discussion that even in the case of these impecunious classes the predominance of the motive of physical want is not so decided as has sometimes been assumed. On the other hand, so far as regards those members and classes of the community who are chiefly concerned in the accumulation of wealth, the incentive of subsistence or of physical comfort never plays a considerable part. Ownership began and grew into a human institution on grounds unrelated to the subsistence minimum. The dominant incentive was from the outset the invidious distinction 10 attaching to wealth, and, save temporarily and by exception, no other motive has usurped the primacy at any later stage of the development.

Property set out with being booty held as trophies of the successful 11 raid. So long as the group had departed but little from the primitive communal organization, and so long as it still stood in close contact with other hostile groups, the utility of things or persons owned lay chiefly in an invidious comparison between their possessor and the enemy from whom they were taken. The habit of distinguishing between the interests of the individual and those of the group to which he belongs is apparently a later growth. Invidious comparison between the possessor of the honorific booty and his less successful neighbors within the group was no doubt present early as an element of the utility of the things possessed, though this was not at the outset the chief element of their value. The man's prowess was still primarily the group's prowess, and the possessor of the booty felt himself to be primarily the keeper of the honor of his group. This appreciation of exploit from the communal point of view is met with also at later stages of social growth, especially as regards the laurels of war.[3]

But so soon as the custom of individual ownership begins to gain 12 consistency, the point of view taken in making the invidious comparison on which private property rests will begin to change. Indeed, the one change is but the reflex of the other. The initial phase of ownership, the phase of acquisition by naïve seizure and conversion, begins to pass into the subsequent stage of an incipient organization of industry on the basis of private property (in slaves); the horde develops into a more or less self-sufficing industrial community; possessions then come to be valued not so much as evidence of successful foray, but rather as evidence of the prepotence of the possessor of these goods over other individuals within the community. The invidious comparison now becomes primarily a comparison of the owner with the other members of the group. Property is still of the nature of trophy, but, with the cultural advance, it becomes more and more a trophy of successes scored in the game of ownership carried on between the members of the group under the quasi-peaceable methods of nomadic life.

Gradually, as industrial activity further displaces predatory activity 13 in the community's everyday life and in men's habits of thought, accumulated property more and more replaces trophies of predatory exploit as the conventional exponent of prepotence and success. With

---

[3]*laurels of war*   The term is mildly ironic and refers to the honors or prizes of war. Veblen means a man's military exploits are especially significant in society.

the growth of settled industry, therefore, the possession of wealth gains in relative importance and effectiveness as a customary basis of repute and esteem. Not that esteem ceases to be awarded on the basis of other, more direct evidence of prowess; not that successful predatory aggression or warlike exploit ceases to call out the approval and admiration of the crowd, or to stir the envy of the less successful competitors; but the opportunities for gaining distinction by means of this direct manifestation of superior force grow less available both in scope and frequency. At the same time opportunities for industrial aggression, and for the accumulation of property by the quasi-peaceable methods of nomadic industry, increase in scope and availability. And it is even more to the point that property now becomes the most easily recognized evidence of a reputable degree of success as distinguished from heroic or signal achievement. It therefore becomes the conventional basis of esteem. Its possession in some amount becomes necessary in order to attain any reputable standing in the community. It becomes indispensable to accumulate, to acquire property, in order to retain one's good name. When accumulated goods have in this way once become the accepted badge of efficiency, the possession of wealth presently assumes the character of an independent and definitive basis of esteem. The possession of goods, whether acquired aggressively by one's own exertion or passively by transmission through inheritance from others, becomes a conventional basis of reputability. The possession of wealth, which was at the outset valued simply as an evidence of efficiency, becomes, in popular apprehension, itself a meritorious act. Wealth is now itself intrinsically honorable and confers honor on its possessor. By a further refinement, wealth acquired passively by transmission from ancestors or other antecedents presently becomes even more honorific than wealth acquired by the possessor's own effort; but this distinction belongs at a later stage in the evolution of the pecuniary culture and will be spoken of in its place.

Prowess and exploit may still remain the basis of award of the highest popular esteem, although the possession of wealth has become the basis of commonplace reputability and of a blameless social standing. The predatory instinct and the consequent approbation of predatory efficiency are deeply ingrained in the habits of thought of those peoples who have passed under the discipline of a protracted predatory culture. According to popular award, the highest honors within human reach may, even yet, be those gained by an unfolding of extraordinary predatory efficiency in war, or by a quasi-predatory efficiency in statecraft; but for the purposes of a commonplace decent standing in the community these means of repute have been replaced by the acquisi-

14

tion and accumulation of goods. In order to stand well in the eyes of the community, it is necessary to come up to a certain, somewhat indefinite, conventional standard of wealth; just as in the earlier predatory stage it is necessary for the barbarian man to come up to the tribe's standard of physical endurance, cunning, and skill at arms. A certain standard of wealth in the one case, and of prowess in the other, is a necessary condition of reputability, and anything in excess of this normal amount is meritorious.

Those members of the community who fall short of this, somewhat indefinite, normal degree of prowess or of property suffer in the esteem of their fellow-men; and consequently they suffer also in their own esteem, since the usual basis of self-respect is the respect accorded by one's neighbors. Only individuals with an aberrant temperament can in the long run retain their self-esteem in the face of the disesteem of their fellows. Apparent exceptions to the rule are met with, especially among people with strong religious convictions. But these apparent exceptions are scarcely real exceptions, since such persons commonly fall back on the putative approbation[4] of some supernatural witness of their deeds.

So soon as the possession of property becomes the basis of popular esteem, therefore, it becomes also a requisite to that complacency which we call self-respect. In any community where goods are held in severalty[5] it is necessary, in order to his own peace of mind, that an individual should possess as large a portion of goods as others with whom he is accustomed to class himself; and it is extremely gratifying to possess something more than others. But as fast as a person makes new acquisitions, and becomes accustomed to the resulting new standard of wealth, the new standard forthwith ceases to afford appreciably greater satisfaction than the earlier standard did. The tendency in any case is constantly to make the present pecuniary standard the point of departure for a fresh increase of wealth; and this in turn gives rise to a new standard of sufficiency and a new pecuniary classification of one's self as compared with one's neighbors. So far as concerns the present question, the end sought by accumulation is to rank high in comparison with the rest of the community in point of pecuniary strength. So long as the comparison is distinctly unfavorable to himself, the normal, average individual will live in chronic dissatisfaction with his present lot; and when he has reached what may be called the

15

16

---

[4]*putative approbation* Supposed approval.
[5]*held in severalty* Goods that are owned by individuals, not shared with others.

normal pecuniary standard of the community, or of his class in the community, this chronic dissatisfaction will give place to a restless straining to place a wider and ever-widening pecuniary interval between himself and this average standard. The invidious comparison can never become so favorable to the individual making it that he would not gladly rate himself still higher relatively to his competitors in the struggle for pecuniary reputability.

In the nature of the case, the desire for wealth can scarcely be satiated in any individual instance, and evidently a satiation of the average or general desire for wealth is out of the question. However widely, or equally, or "fairly," it may be distributed, no general increase of the community's wealth can make any approach to satiating this need, the ground of which is the desire of everyone to excel everyone else in the accumulation of goods. If, as is sometimes assumed, the incentive to accumulation were the want of subsistence or of physical comfort, then the aggregate economic wants of a community might conceivably be satisfied at some point in the advance of industrial efficiency; but since the struggle is substantially a race for reputability on the basis of an invidious comparison, no approach to a definitive attainment is possible. 17

What has just been said must not be taken to mean that there are no other incentives to acquisition and accumulation than this desire to excel in pecuniary standing and so gain the esteem and envy of one's fellow-men. The desire for added comfort and security from want is present as a motive at every stage of the process of accumulation in a modern industrial community; although the standard of sufficiency in these respects is in turn greatly affected by the habit of pecuniary emulation. To a great extent this emulation shapes the methods and selects the objects of expenditure for personal comfort and decent livelihood. 18

Besides this, the power conferred by wealth also affords a motive to accumulation. That propensity for purposeful activity and that repugnance to all futility of effort which belong to man by virtue of his character as an agent do not desert him when he emerges from the naïve communal culture where the dominant note of life is the unanalyzed and undifferentiated solidarity of the individual with the group with which his life is bound up. When he enters upon the predatory stage, where self-seeking in the narrower sense becomes the dominant note, this propensity goes with him still, as the pervasive trait that shapes his scheme of life. The propensity for achievement and the repugnance to futility remain the underlying economic motive. The propensity changes only in the form of its expression and in the proxi- 19 mate objects to which it directs the man's activity. Under the régime of individual ownership the most available means of visibly achieving a purpose is that afforded by the acquisition and accumulation of goods; and as the self-regarding antithesis between man and man[6] reaches fuller consciousness, the propensity for achievement—the instinct of workmanship—tends more and more to shape itself into a straining to excel others in pecuniary achievement. Relative success, tested by an invidious pecuniary comparison with other men, becomes the conventional end of action. The currently accepted legitimate end of effort becomes the achievement of a favorable comparison with other men; and therefore the repugnance to futility to a good extent coalesces with the incentive of emulation. It acts to accentuate the struggle for pecuniary reputability by visiting with a sharper disapproval all shortcoming and all evidence of shortcoming in point of pecuniary success. Purposeful effort comes to mean, primarily, effort directed to or resulting in a more creditable showing of accumulated wealth. Among the motives which lead men to accumulate wealth, the primacy, both in scope and intensity, therefore, continues to belong to this motive of pecuniary emulation.

In making use of the term "invidious," it may perhaps be unnec- 20
essary to remark, there is no intention to extol or depreciate, or to commend or deplore any of the phenomena which the word is used to characterize. The term is used in a technical sense as describing a comparison of persons with a view to rating and grading them in respect of relative worth or value—in an aesthetic or moral sense—and so awarding and defining the relative degrees of complacency with which they may legitimately be contemplated by themselves and by others. An invidious comparison is a process of valuation of persons in respect of worth.

---

[6]*antithesis between man and man*   Vying or competition between men.

QUESTIONS

1. What is your interpretation of the term "pecuniary emulation"? What makes the term difficult to understand at first? Does Veblen achieve any advantage because of its complexity?
2. Veblen assumes that humanity has experienced a cultural evolution. Explain what he means by this and try to decide if he is right.

3. Veblen often refers to the leisure class. What do you think he means by this term? Do you think there were many people who fit into this class? Do you think they were aware they were members of it?
4. At the end of this selection, Veblen says he is not judging but simply describing the facts. Does the essay bear this out?
5. What are Veblen's most valid criticisms of modern industrial economies? Are they any less valid for today's economy than they seem to have been for his?
6. To what extent is Veblen interested in the possibility of government interference with the economic activities of individuals?
7. Which passages suggest that Veblen was aware of Karl Marx and *The Communist Manifesto?* Does Veblen seem to agree with Marx on any key issues?

WRITING ASSIGNMENTS

1. In paragraph 6, Veblen says, "wealth has by no means yet lost its utility as an honorific evidence of the owner's prepotence." This was said of the culture of America in 1899. Is it any less true today? What signs do you see of the fact that wealth seems to impart a sense of potency or power to the wealthy? In what ways do the wealthy most use their power or potency?
2. In the early part of the essay, Veblen speculates about a barbarian way of life in which people appropriated objects, such as tools, but did not conceive of ownership until male warriors carried off women prisoners as booty. They then owned the women and regarded them as trophies. Examine Veblen's reasoning on this point by explaining what his theories are and then by considering the evidence or reasons on which he bases his views. Is his theory convincing? Once you have determined what his theory is, offer your own views on the subject. How do you think mankind first began to develop the concept of ownership?
3. What would society be like today if the concept of individual ownership had never developed? What might have developed instead? Write an essay that describes a hypothetical society in which nothing could be owned by an individual and in which no individual would ever wish to own anything. Would such a society be possible? Would it be better or worse than the kind of society we have today? Would you want to live in it? Do you know of any such society in either the past or the present?
4. One of Veblen's basic assumptions is that our economic system evolved from early stages to the stage it has now reached. Examine this view by establishing what you think these stages are and then hypothesize about what the next stage of economic and social evolution is likely to be for

our "postindustrial" phase of development. What will our economic and social system be like in the next stage? How long do you think it will take to reach it?

5. In paragraph 13, Veblen says that, in the latest stages of industrial society, "the possession of wealth . . . becomes . . . itself a meritorious act. Wealth is now itself intrinsically honorable and confers honor on its possessor. By a further refinement, wealth acquired passively by transmission from ancestors or other antecedents presently becomes even more honorific than wealth acquired by the possessor's own effort." To what extent is Veblen correct in his evaluation? Is it true that inherited wealth imparts greater honor than wealth that is acquired through labor? Remember that we sometimes call people who have made their own fortune the nouveau riche and that the term is never meant as a compliment. Why do people use such a term for those who have acquired wealth? Why is inherited wealth thought to be so much more honorific than acquired wealth? Do you think that wealth should be honorific at all?

6. Veblen says, "A certain standard of wealth in the one case, and of prowess in the other, is a necessary condition of reputability, and anything in excess of this normal amount is meritorious" (para. 14). What is this standard in our society? He admits that it is "somewhat indefinite" (para. 15), but is it possible to discuss it well enough so that others can understand that it does indeed exist? What signs give evidence of it? In paragraph 15 he also says that when men fall in the esteem of others by not reaching the indefinite level, they also fall in self-esteem. Moreover, "the usual basis of self-respect is the respect accorded by one's neighbors." Examine these points and show, by example and description, the extent to which Veblen is correct in describing the society you know.

7. Given that Veblen does not wholly approve of the behavior of many people who possess great wealth, what kinds of recommendations would he make to a government in order to bring reform into play? Does Veblen have faith in government's capacity to institute economic change, or does he believe that an economic system is beyond the power of a government's capacity for management?

JOHN MAYNARD KEYNES

The End of Laissez-Faire

JOHN MAYNARD KEYNES (1883–1946) became one of the most influential economists in modern times after his extraordinary analyses of economic decisions following World War I. He advised his own government, Great Britain, between the two world wars and during and after World War II. His advice to the United States government was responsible for policies that helped to restore economic prosperity in Europe.

His first famous book, The Economic Consequences of the Peace (1919), was written after he left his official position with the government in Britain during negotiations leading to the Treaty of Versailles. That document clarified the political and economic terms of the surrender of Germany and its allies at the end of World War I. He was outraged at the plans for demanding reparations from Germany for damages during the war, and he was especially appalled at the behavior of President Woodrow Wilson, whom he thought was both ignorant and hypocritical. The publication of The Economic Consequences of the Peace immediately established him not only as the most original economic mind of his generation but also as a kind of

From *Essays in Persuasion.*

prophet. He pointed out that the economic strictures imposed on Germany would produce economic collapse and social disorder. He, like many others, was fearful that Germany might become Communist— as Karl Marx predicted it would—as did Russia during a period of war and social upheaval.

His views were prophetic, but his analysis of the situation in Germany was not completely accurate. He felt that the Treaty of Versailles had been motivated by political and military considerations and that it had ignored the impact of economic issues. This he feared would lead to collapse, and to an extent it did. But the fact is that Britain and France had modified their demands for reparations, and the economic conditions of most Germans before the Great Depression of 1929 were not as bad as he predicted they would be.

"The End of Laissez-Faire" was written before the Great Depression and in anticipation of important changes in the nature of modern democratic capitalism. With Great Britain and other European nations bearing immense debts after the First World War, certain radical "socialist" moves, such as the nationalization of the railroads, were being taken in England.

Laissez-faire is a policy on the part of government to leave business alone to do what it will, including committing various abuses of the kind that Marx complained of. If a government will not regulate business, then government must let it go; Keynes realized that the period of unregulated business was over. Socialism implies complete control of an economic system and of business; although this occurred to a large degree in England after the Second World War, at the time Keynes wrote, the country was not yet ready for such socialization. But the essay, as he said later, was prophetic.

One of his chief points was that the corporation stood as a structure intermediate in size between the state and the individual, and that corporate groups might best represent the interests of both. Certainly, as Keynes explained, the problems of the economy are beyond the power of the individual to control. Corporations are, he noted , "a mode of government" and a more manageable mode than the state itself. However, he also pointed out that management of corporations is rarely responsible to the owners of its capital, the shareholders, in a direct way. Indeed, corporations sometimes downplay the individual interest so that they appear to be socializing themselves.

Keynes, like Marx, Gilman, and Veblen, saw an evolutionary pattern to economics. He expressed this by in part looking backward to the corporate structures of guilds and abbeys in the medieval pe-

riod and looking forward to what he called a "natural line of evolution." Socialism is winning out "against unlimited private profit." Keynes interpreted the kind of changes that were occurring as an end to laissez-faire but also as a continuance of some qualities of laissez-faire—those qualities that stimulated the growth of wealth, such as individual initiative.

KEYNES'S RHETORIC

Keynes's technique is based on a principle of separating issues into two parts. He begins the essay with a quick analysis of whether or not the policies of laissez-faire—doing economically as you will with regard only to personal profit—is a God-given right. Then he moves to the question of what the state ought to be doing in regard to managing an economic system. He refers to Jeremy Bentham's terms: Agenda *and* Non-Agenda. *These translate into what government should do versus what it should not do. Then he moves to the proposition that we should begin to rely on "forms of Government within a Democracy" that can actually accomplish what is on the agenda. These forms center on the corporation. At that point (para. 3) the discussion focuses on two examples: first, the nature of the corporation and second (para. 9), on the distinctions between the social and the individual aspects of the agenda.*

Within each of these two relatively brief discussions, Keynes offers analyses of the economic situations that he knows best. He examines socialism in some detail, then examines the state in relation to the individual. He sees that the powerful individual can serve the society badly and that some kind of regulation may be essential. To Keynes, such regulation falls short of socialism. He is very intent on assuring us that whatever government does, it should be something that the individual is not doing. In this way, the government will have a chance of being effective without displacing individual initiative.

Keynes's primary rhetorical stance is analytic. He examines an element, weighs it, compares it with other elements, then makes a pronouncement on its value and potential effectiveness. His is one of the most comprehensive and farseeing minds of our time.

The End of Laissez-Faire

Let us clear from the ground the metaphysical or general principles   1
upon which, from time to time, *laissez-faire*[1] has been founded. It is
not true that individuals possess a prescriptive "natural liberty" in
their economic activities. There is *no* "compact" conferring perpetual
rights on those who Have or on those who Acquire. The world is *not*
so governed from above that private and social interest always coincide. It is *not* so managed here below that in practice they coincide. It
is *not* a correct deduction from the Principles of Economics that enlightened self-interest always operates in the public interest. Nor is it
true that self-interest generally *is* enlightened; more often individuals
acting separately to promote their own ends are too ignorant or too
weak to attain even these. Experience does *not* show that individuals,
when they make up a social unit, are always less clear-sighted than
when they act separately.

We cannot, therefore, settle on abstract grounds, but must handle   2
on its merits in detail, what Burke[2] termed "one of the finest problems
in legislation, namely, to determine what the State ought to take upon
itself to direct by the public wisdom, and what it ought to leave, with
as little interference as possible, to individual exertion." We have to
discriminate between what Bentham,[3] in his forgotten but useful no-
menclature, used to term *Agenda* and *Non-Agenda*, and to do this
without Bentham's prior presumption that interference is, at the same
time, "generally needless" and "generally pernicious."[4] Perhaps the
chief task of Economists at this hour is to distinguish afresh the

---

[1]*laissez-faire* An economic environment in which government leaves businesses
unregulated and unrestrained.

[2]*Edmund Burke* (**1729–1797**) Anglo-Irish statesman who wrote *Reflections on the
French Revolution* (1790). His views were largely responsible for England's failure to support the Revolution.

[3]*Jeremy Bentham* (**1748–1832**) English philosopher, whose *An Introduction to the
Principles and Morals of Legislation* (1789) with its notion of "the greatest happiness for
the greatest number" was a major influence on English law in the mid-nineteenth century.

[4]Bentham's *Manual of Political Economy*, published posthumously, in Bowring's
edition (1843). [Keynes's note]

Agenda of Government from the *Non-Agenda;* and the companion
task of Politics is to devise forms of Government within a Democracy
which shall be capable of accomplishing the *Agenda.* I will illustrate
what I have in mind by two examples.

[1] I believe that in many cases the ideal size for the unit of control   3
and organization lies somewhere between the individual and the modern State. I suggest, therefore, that progress lies in the growth and the
recognition of semiautonomous bodies within the State—bodies
whose criterion of action within their own field is solely the public
good as they understand it, and from whose deliberations motives of
private advantage are excluded, though some place it may still be necessary to leave, until the ambit of men's altruism grows wider, to the
separate advantage of particular groups, classes, or faculties—bodies
which in the ordinary course of affairs are mainly autonomous within
their prescribed limitations, but are subject in the last resort to the
sovereignty of the democracy expressed through Parliament.

I propose a return, it may be said, towards mediaeval conceptions   4
of separate autonomies. But, in England at any rate, corporations are a
mode of government which has never ceased to be important and is
sympathetic to our institutions. It is easy to give examples, from what
already exists, of separate autonomies which have attained or are approaching the mode I designate—the Universities, the Bank of England, the Port of London Authority, even perhaps the Railway Com-
panies.

But more interesting than these is the trend of Joint Stock Institu-   5
tions, when they have reached a certain age and size, to approximate
to the status of public corporations rather than that of individualistic
private enterprise. One of the most interesting and unnoticed developments of recent decades has been the tendency of big enterprise to
socialize itself. A point arrives in the growth of a big institution—
particularly a big railway or big public utility enterprise, but also a big
bank or a big insurance company—at which the owners of the capital,
i.e., the shareholders, are almost entirely dissociated from the management, with the result that the direct personal interest of the latter in
the making of great profit becomes quite secondary. When this stage
is reached, the general stability and reputation of the institution are
more considered by the management than the maximum of profit for
the shareholders. The shareholders must be satisfied by conventionally
adequate dividends; but once this is secured, the direct interest of the
management often consists in avoiding criticism from the public and
from the customers of the concern. This is particularly the case if their
great size or semimonopolistic position renders them conspicuous in

the public eye and vulnerable to public attack. The extreme instance, perhaps, of this tendency in the case of an institution, theoretically the unrestricted property of private persons, is the Bank of England. It is almost true to say that there is no class of persons in the Kingdom of whom the Governor of the Bank of England thinks less when he decides on his policy than of his shareholders. Their rights, in excess of their conventional dividend, have already sunk to the neighborhood of zero. But the same thing is partly true of many other big institutions. They are, as time goes on, socializing themselves.

Not that this is unmixed gain. The same causes promote conser- 6
vatism and a waning of enterprise. In fact, we already have in these cases many of the faults as well as the advantages of State Socialism. Nevertheless we see here, I think, a natural line of evolution. The battle of Socialism against unlimited private profit is being won in detail hour by hour. In these particular fields—it remains acute elsewhere— this is no longer the pressing problem. There is, for instance, no so-called important political question so really unimportant, so irrelevant to the reorganization of the economic life of Great Britain, as the Nationalization of the Railways.

It is true that many big undertakings, particularly Public Utility 7
enterprises and other business requiring a large fixed capital, still need to be semisocialized. But we must keep our minds flexible regarding the forms of this semisocialism. We must take full advantage of the natural tendencies of the day, and we must probably prefer semiautonomous corporations to organs of the Central Government for which Ministers of State are directly responsible.

I criticize doctrinaire State Socialism, not because it seeks to en- 8
gage men's altruistic impulses in the service of Society, or because it departs from *laissez-faire,* or because it takes away from man's natural liberty to make a million, or because it has courage for bold experiments. All these things I applaud. I criticize it because it misses the significance of what is actually happening; because it is, in fact, little better than a dusty survival of a plan to meet the problems of fifty years ago, based on a misunderstanding of what some one said a hundred years ago. Nineteenth-century State Socialism sprang from Bentham, free competition, etc., and is in some respects a clearer, in some respects a more muddled, version of just the same philosphy as underlies nineteenth-century individualism. Both equally laid all their stress on freedom, the one negatively to avoid limitations on existing freedom, the other positively to destroy natural or acquired monopolies. They are different reactions to the same intellectual atmosphere.

(2) I come next to a criterion of *Agenda* which is particularly rele- 9
vant to what it is urgent and desirable to do in the near future. We
must aim at separating those services which are *technically social*
from those which are *technically individual*. The most important
Agenda of the State relate not to those activities which private individuals are already fulfilling, but to those functions which fall outside
the sphere of the individual, to those decisions which are made by *no
one* if the State does not make them. The important thing for Government is not to do things which individuals are doing already, and to
do them a little better or a little worse; but to do those things which
at present are not done at all.

It is not within the scope of my purpose on this occasion to develop 10
practical policies. I limit myself, therefore, to naming some instances
of what I mean from among those problems about which I happen to
have thought most.

Many of the greatest economic evils of our time are fruits of risk, 11
uncertainty, and ignorance. It is because particular individuals, fortunate in situation or in abilities, are able to take advantage of uncertainty
and ignorance, and also because for the same reason big business is
often a lottery, that great inequalities of wealth come about; and these
same factors are also the cause of the Unemployment of Labor, or the
disappointment of reasonable business expectations, and of the impair-
ment of efficiency and production. Yet the cure lies outside the oper-
ations of individuals; it may even be to the interest of individuals to
aggravate the disease. I believe that the cure for these things is partly
to be sought in the deliberate control of the currency and of credit by
a central institution, and partly in the collection and dissemination on
a great scale of data relating to the business situation, including the
full publicity, by law if necessary, of all business facts which it is useful to know. These measures would involve Society in exercizing di-
rective intelligence through some appropriate organ of action over
many of the inner intricacies of private business, yet it would leave
private initiative and enterprise unhindered. Even if these measures
prove insufficient, nevertheless they will furnish us with better
knowledge than we have now for taking the next step.

My second example relates to Savings and Investment. I believe 12
that some co-ordinated act of intelligent judgment is required as to the
scale on which it is desirable that the community as a whole should
save, the scale on which these savings should go abroad in the form of
foreign investments, and whether the present organization of the investment market distributes savings along the most nationally produc-

tive channels. I do not think that these matters should be left entirely to the chances of private judgment and private profits, as they are at present.

My third example concerns Population. The time has already come 13 when each country needs a considered national policy about what size of Population, whether larger or smaller than at present or the same, is most expedient. And having settled this policy, we must take steps to carry it into operation. The time may arrive a little later when the community as a whole must pay attention to the innate quality as well as to the mere numbers of its future members.

These reflections have been directed towards possible improve- 14 ments in the technique of modern Capitalism by the agency of collective action. There is nothing in them which is seriously incompatible with what seems to me to be the essential characteristic of Capitalism, namely the dependence upon an intense appeal to the money-making and money-loving instincts of individuals as the main motive force of the economic machine. Nor must I, so near to my end, stray towards other fields. Nevertheless, I may do well to remind you, in conclusion, that the fiercest contests and the most deeply felt divisions of opinion are likely to be waged in the coming years not round technical questions, where the arguments on either side are mainly economic, but round those which, for want of better words, may be called psychological or, perhaps, moral.

In Europe, or at least in some parts of Europe—but not, I think, in 15 the United States of America—there is a latent reaction, somewhat widespread, against basing Society to the extent that we do upon fostering, encouraging, and protecting the money-motives of individuals. A preference for arranging our affairs in such a way as to appeal to the money-motive as little as possible, rather than as much as possible, need not be entirely *a priori*, but may be based on the comparison of experiences. Different persons, according to their choice of profession, find the money-motive playing a large or a small part in their daily lives, and historians can tell us about other phases of social organization in which this motive has played a much smaller part than it does now. Most religions and most philosophies deprecate, to say the least of it, a way of life mainly influenced by considerations of personal money profit. On the other hand, most men today reject ascetic notions and do not doubt the real advantages of wealth. Moreover it seems obvious to them that one cannot do without the money-motive, and that, apart from certain admitted abuses, it does its job well. In the result the average man averts his attention from the problem, and has no clear idea what he really thinks and feels about the whole confounded matter.

Confusion of thought and feeling leads to confusion of speech. 16 Many people, who are really objecting to Capitalism as a way of life, argue as though they were objecting to it on the ground of its inefficiency in attaining its own objects. Contrariwise, devotees of Capitalism are often unduly conservative, and reject reforms in its technique, which might really strengthen and preserve it, for fear that they may prove to be first steps away from Capitalism itself. Nevertheless a time may be coming when we shall get clearer than at present as to when we are talking about Capitalism as an efficient or inefficient technique, and when we are talking about it as desirable or objectionable in itself. For my part, I think that Capitalism, wisely managed, can probably be made more efficient for attaining economic ends than any alternative system yet in sight, but that in itself it is in many ways extremely objectionable. Our problem is to work out a social organization which shall be as efficient as possible without offending our notions of a satisfactory way of life.

The next step forward must come, not from political agitation or 17 premature experiments, but from thought. We need by an effort of the mind to elucidate our own feelings. At present our sympathy and our judgment are liable to be on different sides, which is a painful and paralysing state of mind. In the field of action reformers will not be successful until they can steadily pursue a clear and definite object with their intellects and their feelings in tune. There is no party in the world at present which appears to me to be pursuing right aims by right methods. Material Poverty provides the incentive to change precisely in situations where there is very little margin for experiments. Material Prosperity removes the incentive just when it might be safe to take a chance. Europe lacks the means, America the will, to make a move. We need a new set of convictions which spring naturally from a candid examination of our own inner feelings in relation to the outside facts.

QUESTIONS

1. Does the economic future seem to have been especially uncertain in 1926, when Keynes wrote this essay?
2. How would you explain the meaning of "laissez-faire" to someone unfamiliar with the term?

3. Why does Keynes feel it is beyond his scope to "develop practical policies"? What is one practical policy he might have developed?
4. Is a corporation a form of government? Should it be?
5. What economic rights does an individual have in terms of making a great deal of money—as Keynes sees it?
6. Which points do you find yourself in disagreement over with Keynes? Which points do you agree with him on?
7. What does Keynes mean by the terms *Agenda* and *Non-Agenda?*
8. Under what conditions is it necessary for a nation to control the quantity and quality of its population (para. 13)?

WRITING ASSIGNMENTS

1. Keynes is very concerned with distinguishing between what the government should do to affect the economy and what the individual should do. When he says that he does not want the government to perform those functions that individuals are already performing, he implies that individuals are leaving undone much that would improve the economy. What would you recommend that the government do today that individuals are currently not doing? And how would the government's actions benefit the economy?
2. In paragraph 8 Keynes refers to man's "natural liberty to make a million." Do you believe that such a liberty exists and that it is natural? What are the results of such a liberty, and how could any government guarantee it?
3. Which services are technically social and technically individual in economics? That is, what can you do as an individual that government either cannot or will not do? In what senses can these two services conflict, and how can such conflict create an unhealthy economic situation? Have you had any experience in such a conflict?
4. How comfortable are you concerning the nature of the corporation as a government of sorts? Is it as good a development as Keynes seems to feel it is? Is this development in any way a substitute for government? In reading the business section of your newspaper, do you see evidence of corporate activity that can be in any way interpreted as governmental? Is the result desirable? Is it the result Keynes seems to have hoped for?
5. In paragraph 12, Keynes reminds us that the extent to which individuals save money affects the general health of the economy. He says he believes that "a co-ordinated act of intelligent judgement" is required to establish a national policy of savings. The United States has long been behind nations such as Japan in terms of the individual's goal to save. Do you feel that the government should intervene in the lives of individuals and determine how much they should save? How could any government achieve that end?

JOHN KENNETH GALBRAITH

The Position of Poverty

JOHN KENNETH GALBRAITH (b. 1908) was born in Canada but has been an American citizen since 1937. His Canadian background was rural, and his early experiences were connected with farming in Ontario, which helps to explain his having taken his first university degree in agricultural science. It may also help to explain why, in his many books on subjects such as economics, the State Department, Indian art, and government, he has always been praised for helping a layperson understand complex concepts. Sometimes, of course, he has been criticized for oversimplifying some issues, but on the whole, he has made a brilliant success of writing with wit and up-tempo humor about issues that are basically perplexing and sometimes troubling.

Galbraith was professor of economics at Harvard University for many years. During the presidential campaigns of Adlai Stevenson in 1952 and 1956, he assisted the Democrats as a speech writer and economics adviser. He performed the same tasks for John F. Kennedy in 1960, including drafting Kennedy's inaugural address. Kennedy appointed Galbraith ambassador to India, a post that he maintained for a little over two years, including the period during which India

---

From *The Affluent Society.*

and China fought a border war. His experiences in India resulted in Ambassador's Journal: A Personal Account of the Kennedy Years (1969). Kennedy called Galbraith his finest ambassadorial appointment, and since Kennedy's own father had been an ambassador, that constitutes significant praise.

Galbraith's involvement with politics was somewhat unusual for an academic economist at that time. It seems to have stemmed from strongly held personal views on the social issues of his time. One of the most important contributions of his best-known and probably most significant book, The Affluent Society (1958; rev. eds. 1969, 1976, 1984), presented his analysis of America's economic ambitions. He pointed out that at that time the welfare of the economy was entirely tied up in the measurement and growth of the gross national product. Economists and government officials concentrated on boosting output. He tried to help people see that, by itself, this goal was misdirected. The result, he said, would be a profusion of products that people really did not need and would not benefit from. It would result in creating artificial needs for things that had no ultimate value. Concentrating on bigger, more luxurious automobiles and building in a "planned obsolescence" that essentially put consumers in an economic squirrel cage seemed to him to be wasteful and ultimately destructive.

Galbraith suggested that America concentrate on genuine needs and satisfy them immediately. He was deeply concerned about the environment and suggested that clean air was a priority that took precedence over all consumer goods. He supported development of the arts and stressed that the improvement of housing across the nation was of first importance. His effort was directed at trying to help Americans change certain basic values. He wished to help them give up the pursuit of useless consumer novelties and to substitute a program of genuine development of the society. The commitment to consumer products as the basis of the economy naturally argued against a redirection of effort toward the solution of social problems.

"The Position of Poverty" is interesting because it is among the few statements made in economics on the question of what the country can or should do about the poor. As Galbraith points out at the beginning of the selection, economists generally comment on the entire economy and, when they do, give only lip service to the problem of poverty. The result is that we do not understand poverty very well, and we are not likely to make much progress in ridding it from society.

Galbraith is exceptionally clear in his essay so that little commen-

tary is needed to establish its importance. He is insightful in clarifying two kinds of poverty: case poverty and insular poverty. Case poverty is restricted to an individual and his or her family. Alcoholism, ignorance, mental deficiency, discrimination, or specific handicaps seem to be the cause of such poverty. It is an individual, not a group disorder. Insular poverty affects a group in a given area—an "island" within the larger society. He points to poverty in Appalachia and in the slums of major cities, where most of the people in those "islands" are at or below the poverty level. Insular poverty is linked to the environment, and its causes are somehow derived from that environment.

His analysis is perceptive and influential, and while little or no progress has been made in solving the problem of poverty since 1959, he assures us that there are things that can be done to help eradicate it. He also warns that it demands the nation's will, however, and that the nation may lack the will. As he wisely pointed out, the cause of the impoverished was not likely to be a popular political issue in 1958. Because the poverty-stricken are a minority, few politicians, he reasoned, would make them a campaign issue. Actually, he was wrong. Kennedy in 1960, Lyndon Johnson in 1964, and Jimmy Carter in 1972 made programs for the poor central among their governmental concerns. Because of the war in Vietnam and other governmental policies, however, the 1960s and early 1970s were a time of staggering inflation that wiped out any of the advances the poverty-stricken had made. The extent to which this is true is observable instantly on reading the work; the income figures for 1959 seem so unbelievably low as to make us think we are reading about the last century rather than the mid-twentieth century.

GALBRAITH'S RHETORIC

The most important rhetorical achievement of the piece is its style. This is an example of the elevated plain style: a clear, direct, and basically simple approach to language that only occasionally admits a somewhat learned vocabulary—as in the use of a very few words such as "opulent," "unremunerative," and "ineluctable." The vast majority of words he uses are ordinary ones.

He breaks the essay into six carefully numbered sections. This is a way of highlighting its basic structure and subtly reminding us that he has clearly separated its elements into related groups so that he can speak directly to aspects of his subject rather than to the entire subject. *Rhetoricians sometimes call this technique division, and its effect is to impart clarity and to confer a sense of authority on the writer.*

Galbraith relies on statistical information that the reader can examine if necessary. This information is treated in the early stages of the piece as a prologue. Once such information has been given, Galbraith draws some conclusions from it, proceeding in the manner of a logician establishing premises and deriving the necessary conclusions. The subject is sober and sobering, and so is the style. The issues are complex, uncertain, and difficult, but the style is direct, confident, and essentially simple. This is the secret of the success of the book from which this selection comes. The Affluent Society has been translated into well over a dozen languages and has been a bestseller around the globe. And despite the fact that the statistical information is outdated, it remains an influential book. Its fundamental insights are such that it is likely to be relevant to our economic circumstances for generations to come.

The Position of Poverty

"The study of the causes of poverty," Alfred Marshall[1] observed at the turn of the century, "is the study of the causes of the degradation of a large part of mankind." He spoke of contemporary England as well as of the world beyond. A vast number of people both in town and country, he noted, had insufficient food, clothing and house-room; they were: "Overworked and undertaught, weary and careworn, without quiet and without leisure." The chance of their succor, he concluded, gave to economic studies, "their chief and their highest interest."

No contemporary economist would be likely to make such an observation about the United States. Conventional economic discourse makes obeisance to the continued existence of some poverty. "We must remember that we still have a great many poor people." In the nineteen-sixties, poverty promised, for a time, to become a subject of

1

2

---

[1] **Alfred Marshall (1842–1924)** An English economist whose *Principles of Economics* (1890) was long a standard text and is still relied on by some economists for its theories of costs, value, and distribution.

serious political concern. Then war came and the concern evaporated or was displaced. For economists of conventional mood, the reminders that the poor still exist are a useful way of allaying uneasiness about the relevance of conventional economic goals. For some people, wants must be synthesized. Hence, the importance of the goods to them is not *per se* very high. So much may be conceded. But others are far closer to physical need. And hence we must not be cavalier about the urgency of providing them with the most for the least. The sales tax may have merit for the opulent, but it still bears heavily on the poor. The poor get jobs more easily when the economy is expanding. Thus, poverty survives in economic discourse partly as a buttress to the conventional economic wisdom.

The privation of which Marshall spoke was, a half century ago, the 3 common lot at least of all who worked without special skill. As a general affliction, it was ended by increased output which, however imperfectly it may have been distributed, nevertheless accrued in substantial amount to those who worked for a living. The result was to reduce poverty from the problem of a majority to that of a minority. It ceased to be a general case and became a special case. It is this which has put the problem of poverty into its peculiar modern form.

For poverty does survive. In part, it is a physical matter; those af- 4 flicted have such limited and insufficient food, such poor clothing, such crowded, cold and dirty shelter that life is painful as well as comparatively brief. But just as it is far too tempting to say that, in matters of living standards, everything is relative, so it is wrong to rest everything on absolutes. People are poverty-stricken when their income, even if adequate for survival, falls radically behind that of the community. Then they cannot have what the larger community regards as the minimum necessary for decency; and they cannot wholly escape, therefore, the judgment of the larger community that they are indecent. They are degraded for, in the literal sense, they live outside the grades or categories which the community regards as acceptable.

Since the first edition of this book appeared, and one hopes how- 5 ever slightly as a consequence, the character and dimension of this degradation have become better understood. There have also been fulsome promises that poverty would be eliminated. The performance on these promises has been less eloquent.

The degree of privation depends on the size of the family, the place 6 of residence—it will be less with given income in rural areas than in the cities—and will, of course, be affected by changes in living costs. The Department of Health, Education and Welfare has established rough standards, appropriately graded to family size, location and changing prices, to separate the poor from the less poor and the affluent. In 1972, a non-farm family of four was deemed poor if it had an income of $4275; a couple living otherwise than on a farm was called poor if it had less than $2724 and an unattached individual if receiving less than $2109. A farm family of four was poor with less than $3639; of two with less than $2315.[2]

By these modest standards, 24.5 million households, including individuals and families, were poor in 1972 as compared with 13.4 million in 1959. Because of the increase in population, and therewith in the number of households, in these years the reduction in the number of poor households, as a proportion of all households, was rather greater—from 24 percent in 1959 to 12 percent in 1972.[3]   7

One can usually think of the foregoing deprivation as falling into two broad categories. First, there is what may be called *case* poverty. This one encounters in every community, rural or urban, however prosperous that community or the times. Case poverty is the poor farm family with the junk-filled yard and the dirty children playing in the bare dirt. Or it is the gray-black hovel beside the railroad tracks. Or it is the basement dwelling in the alley.   8

Case poverty is commonly and properly related to some characteristic of the individuals so afflicted. Nearly everyone else has mastered his environment; this proves that it is not intractable. But some quality peculiar to the individual or family involved—mental deficiency, bad health, inability to adapt to the discipline of industrial life, uncontrollable procreation, alcohol, discrimination involving a very limited minority, some educational handicap unrelated to community shortcoming, or perhaps a combination of several of these handicaps—has kept these individuals from participating in the general well-being.   9

Second, there is what may be called *insular* poverty—that which manifests itself as an "island" of poverty. In the island, everyone or nearly everyone is poor. Here, evidently, it is not easy to explain matters by individual inadequacy. We may mark individuals down as intrinsically deficient in social performance; it is not proper or even wise so to characterize an entire community. The people of the island have been frustrated by some factor common to their environment.   10

Case poverty exists. It has also been useful to those who have needed a formula for keeping the suffering of others from causing suffering to themselves. Since this poverty is the result of the deficien-   11

---

[2]*Statistical Abstract of the United States*, 1974, p. 389. [Galbraith's note]
[3]*Statistical Abstract*, p. 389. [Galbraith's note]

cies, including the moral shortcomings, of the persons concerned, it is possible to shift the responsibility to those involved. They are worthless and, as a simple manifestation of social justice, they suffer for it. Or, at a somewhat higher level of social perception and compassion, it means that the problem of poverty is sufficiently solved by private and public charity. This rescues those afflicted from the worst consequences of their inadequacy or misfortune; no larger social change or reorganization is suggested. Except as it may be insufficient in its generosity, the society is not at fault.

Insular poverty yields to no such formulas. In earlier times, when agriculture and extractive industries were the dominant sources of livelihood, something could be accomplished by shifting the responsibility for low income to a poor natural endowment and thus, in effect, to God. The soil was thin and stony, other natural resources absent and hence the people were poor. And, since it is the undoubted preference of many to remain in the vicinity of the place of their birth, a homing instinct that operates for people as well as pigeons, the people remained in the poverty which heaven had decreed for them. It is an explanation that is nearly devoid of empirical application. Connecticut is very barren and stony and incomes are very high. Similarly Wyoming. West Virginia is well watered with rich mines and forests and the people are very poor. The South is much favored in soil and climate and similarly poor and the very richest parts of the South, such as the Mississippi-Yazoo Delta, have long had a well-earned reputation for the greatest deprivation. Yet so strong is the tendency to associate poverty with natural causes that even individuals of some modest intelligence will still be heard, in explanation of insular poverty, to say, "It's basically a poor country." "It's a pretty barren region."

Most modern poverty is insular in character and the islands are the rural and urban slums. From the former, mainly in the South, the southern Appalachians and Puerto Rico, there has been until recent times a steady flow of migrants, some white but more black, to the latter. Grim as life is in the urban ghetto, it still offers more hope, income and interest than in the rural slum. Largely in consequence of this migration, the number of poor farm families—poor by the standards just mentioned—declined between 1959 and 1973 from 1.8 million to 295,000. The decline in the far larger number of poor non-farm households in these years was only from 6.5 million to 4.5 million.[4]

12

13

---

[4]U.S. Department of Commerce, *Current Population Reports*, "Consumer Income," Series P-60, No. 98 (Washington, D.C.: U.S. Government Printing Office, 1975). [Galbraith's note]

This is not the place to provide a detailed profile of this poverty. 14
More than half of the poor households are headed by a woman, although in total women head only 9 percent of families. Over 30 percent are black, another 10 percent are of Spanish origin. A very large
proportion of all black households (31 percent in 1973 as compared
with 8 percent of whites) fall below the poverty line. Especially on the
farms, where the young have departed for the cities, a disproportionate
number of the poor are old. More often than not, the head of the
household is not in the labor force at all.

But the more important characteristic of insular poverty is forces, 15
common to all members of the community, which restrain or prevent
participation in economic life at going rates of return. These restraints
are several. Race, which acts to locate people by their color rather than
by the proximity to employment, is obviously one. So are poor educational facilities. (And this effect is further exaggerated when the poorly
educated, endemically a drug on the labor market, are brought together
in dense clusters by the common inadequacy of the schools available
to blacks and the poor.) So is the disintegration of family life in the
slum which leaves households in the hands of women. Family life itself is in some measure a manifestation of affluence. And so, without
doubt, is the shared sense of helplessness and rejection and the resulting demoralization which is the product of the common misfortune.

The most certain thing about this poverty is that it is not remedied 16
by a general advance in income. Case poverty is not remedied because
the specific individual inadequacy precludes employment and participation in the general advance. Insular poverty is not directly alleviated
because the advance does not remove the specific frustrations of environment to which the people of these islands are subject. This is not
to say that it is without effect. If there are jobs outside the ghetto or
away from the rural slum, those who are qualified, and not otherwise
constrained, can take them and escape. If there are no such jobs, none
can escape. But it remains that advance cannot improve the position
of those who, by virtue of self or environment, cannot participate.

With the transition of the very poor from a majority to a compara- 17
tive minority position, there has been a change in their political position. Any tendency of a politician to identify himself with those of the
lowest estate usually brought the reproaches of the well-to-do. Political pandering and demagoguery were naturally suspected. But, for the
man so reproached, there was the compensating advantage of align-
ment with a large majority. Now any politician who speaks for the
very poor is speaking for a small and generally inarticulate minority.

As a result, the modern liberal politician regularly aligns himself not with the poverty-ridden members of the community but with the far more numerous people who enjoy the far more affluent income of (say) the modern trade union member or the intellectual. Ambrose Bierce, in *The Devil's Dictionary*, called poverty "a file provided for the teeth of the rats of reform."[5] It is so no longer. Reform now concerns itself with the needs of people who are relatively well-to-do—whether the comparison be with their own past or with those who are really at the bottom of the income ladder.

In consequence, a notable feature of efforts to help the very poor is their absence of any very great political appeal.[6] Politicians have found it possible to be indifferent where they could not be derisory. And very few have been under a strong compulsion to support these efforts. 18

The concern for inequality and deprivation had vitality only so long as the many suffered while a few had much. It did not survive as a decisive political issue in a time when the many had much even though others had much more. It is our misfortune that when inequality declined as an issue, the slate was not left clean. A residual and in some ways rather more hopeless problem remained. 19

An affluent society, that is also both compassionate and rational would, no doubt, secure to all who needed it the minimum income essential for decency and comfort. The corrupting effect on the human spirit of unearned revenue has unquestionably been exaggerated as, indeed, have the character-building values of hunger and privation. To secure to each family a minimum income, as a normal function of the society, would help ensure that the misfortunes of parents, deserved or otherwise, were not visited on their children. It would help ensure that poverty was not self-perpetuating. Most of the reaction, which no doubt would be adverse, is based on obsolete attitudes. When poverty was a majority phenomenon, such action could not be afforded. A poor society, as this essay has previously shown, had to enforce the rule that the person who did not work could not eat. And possibly it was justified in the added cruelty of applying the rule to those who could not work or whose efficiency was far below par. An affluent society has no similar excuse for such rigor. It can use the forthright remedy of providing income for those without. Nothing requires such a society 20

---

[5]**Ambrose Bierce (1842–1914?)** A southern American writer noted for satirical writings such as the one quoted.

[6]This was true of the Office of Economic Opportunity—the so-called poverty program—and was ultimately the reason for its effective demise. [Galbraith's note]

to be compassionate. But it no longer has a high philosophical justification for callousness.

The notion that income is a remedy for indigency has a certain 21
forthright appeal.[7] As elsewhere argued, it would also ease the problems of economic management by reducing the reliance on production as a source of income. The provision of such a basic source of income must henceforth be the first and the strategic step in the attack on poverty.

But it is only one step. In the past, we have suffered from the sup- 22
position that the only remedy for poverty lies in remedies that allow people to look after themselves—to participate in the economy. Nothing has better served the conscience of people who wished to avoid inconvenient or expensive action than an appeal, on this issue, to Calvinist precept—"The only sound way to solve the problem of poverty is to help people help themselves." But this does not mean that steps to allow participation and to keep poverty from being self-perpetuating are unimportant. On the contrary. It requires that the investment in children from families presently afflicted be as little below normal as possible. If the children of poor families have first-rate schools and school attendance is properly enforced; if the children, though badly fed at home, are well nourished at school; if the community has sound health services, and the physical well-being of the children is vigilantly watched; if there is opportunity for advanced education for those who qualify regardless of means; and if, especially in the case of urban communities, housing is ample and housing standards are enforced, the streets are clean, the laws are kept, and recreation is adequate—then there is a chance that the children of the very poor will come to maturity without inhibiting disadvantage. In the case of insular poverty, this remedy requires that the services of the community be assisted from outside. Poverty is self-perpetuating partly because the poorest communities are poorest in the services which would eliminate it. To eliminate poverty efficiently, we must, indeed, invest more than proportionately in the children of the poor community. It is there that high quality schools, strong health services, special provision for nutrition and recreation are most needed to compensate for the very low investment which families are able to make in their own offspring.

The effect of education and related investment in individuals is to 23
help them overcome the restraints that are imposed by their environ-

---

[7]As earlier noted, in the first edition, the provision of a guaranteed income was discussed but dismissed as "beyond reasonable hope." [Galbraith's note]

ment. These need also to be attacked even more directly—by giving the mobility that is associated with plentiful, good and readily available housing, by provision of comfortable, efficient and economical mass transport, by making the environment pleasant and safe, and by eliminating the special health handicaps that afflict the poor.

Nor is case poverty entirely resistant to such remedies. Much can 24 be done to treat those characteristics which cause people to reject or be rejected by the modern industrial society. Educational deficiencies can be overcome. Mental deficiencies can be treated. Physical handicaps can be remedied. The limiting factor is not a lack of knowledge of what can be done. Overwhelmingly, it is a shortage of money.

It will be clear that, to a remarkable extent, the remedy for poverty 25 leads to the same requirements as those for social balance. The restraints that confine people to the ghetto are those that result from insufficient investment in the public sector. And the means to escape from these constraints and to break their hold on subsequent generations just mentioned—better nutrition and health, better education, more and better housing, better mass transport, an environment more conducive to effective social participation—all, with rare exceptions, call for massively greater investment in the public sector. In recent years, the problems of the urban ghetto have been greatly discussed but with little resultant effect. To a certain extent, the search for deeper social explanations of its troubles has been motivated by the hope that these (together with more police) might lead to solutions that would somehow elide the problem of cost. It is an idle hope. The modern urban household is an extremely expensive thing. We have not yet taken the measure of the resources that must be allocated to its public tasks if it is to be agreeable or even tolerable. And first among the symptoms of an insufficient allocation is the teeming discontent of the modern ghetto.

A further feature of these remedies is to be observed. Their conse- 26 quence is to allow participation in the economic life of the larger community—to make people and the children of people who are now idle productive. This means that they will add to the total output of goods and services. We see once again that even by its own terms the present preoccupation with the private sector of the economy as compared with the whole spectrum of human needs is inefficient. The parallel with investment in the supply of trained and educated manpower discussed above will be apparent.

But increased output of goods is not the main point. Even to the 27 most intellectually reluctant reader, it will now be evident that enhanced productive efficiency is not the motif of this volume. The very fact that increased output offers itself as a by-product of the effort to eliminate poverty is one of the reasons. No one would be called up to write at such length on a problem so easily solved as that of increasing production. The main point lies elsewhere. Poverty—grim, degrading and ineluctable—is not remarkable in India. For few, the fate is otherwise. But in the United States, the survival of poverty is remarkable. We ignore it because we share with all societies at all times the capacity for not seeing what we do not wish to see. Anciently this has enabled the nobleman to enjoy his dinner while remaining oblivious to the beggars around his door. In our own day, it enables us to travel in comfort by Harlem and into the lush precincts of midtown Manhattan. But while our failure to notice can be explained, it cannot be excused. "Poverty," Pitt[8] exclaimed, "is no disgrace but it is damned annoying." In the contemporary United States, it is not annoying but it is a disgrace.

---

[8]*William Pitt (1759–1806)* British prime minister from 1783 to 1801 and, briefly, again in 1804 and 1805.

QUESTIONS

1. What is the fundamental difference between the attitude Alfred Marshall held toward the poor (para. 1) and the attitude contemporary economists hold?
2. Galbraith avoids a specific definition of poverty because he says it changes from society to society. How would you define poverty as it exists in our society? What are its major indicators?
3. According to Galbraith, what is the relationship of politics to poverty?
4. What, according to this essay, seem to be the causes of poverty?
5. Clarify the distinctions Galbraith makes between case poverty and insular poverty. Are they reasonable distinctions?
6. Does Galbraith oversimplify the issues of poverty in America?
7. Galbraith first published this piece in 1958. How much has changed in our attitudes toward poverty since then? What kinds of progress seem to have been made on the question of poverty?

WRITING ASSIGNMENTS

1. In paragraph 4, Galbraith says, "People are poverty-stricken when their income, even if adequate for survival, falls radically behind that of the com-

munity. Then they cannot have what the larger community regards as the minimum necessary for decency; and they cannot wholly escape, therefore, the judgment of the larger community that they are indecent. They are degraded for, in the literal sense, they live outside the grades or categories which the community regards as acceptable." Examine what he says here and explain what he means. Is this an accurate description of poverty? Would you amend it? If so, in what ways? If you accept his description of poverty, what public policy would you recommend to deal with it? What would be the consequences of accepting Galbraith's description?

2. Galbraith points out some anomalies of poverty and place. For example, he notes that West Virginia is rich in resources but that its people have been notable for their poverty. Connecticut, on the other hand, is poor in resources, with stony, untillable land, and its people have been notable for their wealth. Some economists have also pointed out that, when the Americas were settled, South America had the gold, the lush tropics that yielded food and fruit for the asking, and that it held the promise of immense wealth. North America had a harsh climate, stubborn soil conditions, and dense forests that needed clearing. Yet North America has less poverty than does South America. Write a brief essay in which you consider whether what is said above is too simplified to be useful. If it is not, what do you think is the reason for the economic distinctions that Galbraith and others point out?

3. What personal experiences have you had with poverty? Are you familiar with examples of case poverty? If so, describe them in such a way as to help others understand them. Do you have any insight into the causes that produced the poverty? How could poor people in this category be rescued from poverty? What is their social situation in the community?

4. Examine the newspapers for the last several days and look through back issues of magazines such as *Time, Newsweek,* the *New Republic, The New Leader,* or *U.S. News and World Report.* How much attention do they pay to the question of poverty? Present a survey of the views you find and compare them with Galbraith's. How much agreement or disagreement is there? Would the level of the nation's concern with poverty please Galbraith?

5. Write a brief essay in which you delineate what you think is the current political attitude toward poverty. If possible, gather some recent statements made by politicians. Analyze them to see how closely they tally with Galbraith's concerns and views. Do any specific politicians act as spokespeople for the poor?

6. Galbraith says that the position of poverty has resulted from a dramatic change in our society, from a circumstance in which most people were poor and only a few were affluent to one in which most people are affluent and only a few are poor. Is Galbraith correct in this assessment? Interview your parents and grandparents and their friends. By this means, establish the validity of Galbraith's claim, then explain what you feel are the prob-

lems the poor face as a result of their minority status. If possible, during your interviews ask what feelings your parents and their friends have about the poverty-stricken. What feelings do you have? Are they shared by your friends?

PART THREE

IDEAS IN THE WORLD OF PSYCHOLOGY

WHAT DETERMINES OUR PSYCHOLOGICAL IDENTITY? HOW ARE OUR PSYCHOLOGY AND OUR SEXUALITY CONNECTED?

Sigmund Freud
Carl Jung
Karen Horney
B. F. Skinner
Simone de Beauvoir

INTRODUCTION

PSYCHOLOGY has often been described as a science in its infancy; however, it has done an immense amount of growing in the twentieth century. All the psychologists in this part are modern primarily because most of the exciting discoveries in psychology were made during their professional careers. The most important discovery is probably that of the unconscious mind, which was first discussed in the works of the American psychologist William James (1842–1910). But it was the work of Sigmund Freud around the turn of the century that most startled the world of psychology, since he began to suggest the functions of the unconscious mind as a repository of painful emotions and repressed thoughts. He also suggested means by which the unconscious mind could be apprehended—through the complex symbolic language of dreams and through free-associating during conversation with an analyst. Thus, his psychoanalytic methods are based upon the analysis of a patient's dreams and of the patient's free association while lying on a couch and talking with a doctor.

One of Freud's most controversial theories is that nervous disorders are sexual in origin. He probably most alarmed the psychological community by his theories of infantile sexuality, in which he demonstrated that even infants have sexual urges and needs. He also postulated certain theories concerning instincts that are natural to human beings. For a time, it was exceedingly controversial to suggest that humans, like other animals, had instincts. Freud, however, dared to assert that our sexual needs, as well as our need for sustenance, was instinctive and that because we all live in a regulated community, we are bound to have conflicts between our instinctual and our social needs.

What Sigmund Freud has to say in his essay on infantile sexuality seems fairly tame and perhaps even a bit obvious to us today. But it was a bombshell in its own day. People had always thought that children had no psychosexual awareness or drives until after puberty. Freud demonstrated that the sexual drive, which he had predicated as the strongest of psychic drives, was present even in the infant. His study was a pioneering effort that changed the nature of psychology entirely.

Freud's most distinguished follower was Carl Jung, who eventually broke away from Freud's influence and developed his own distinctive approach to psychology. Whereas Freud concentrated on the unique qualities of the individual's unconscious, Jung began to conceive of the unconscious as a repository of racial awareness, akin to the memory of the human species. In the process, he became aware of the feminine aspects of the personality of his male patients and the masculine aspects of his female patients. His views in "Anima and Animus" are unsettling to many people, because they imply that all people have the psychological qualities of both sexes in their subconscious. One of the unnerving aspects of the split that Jung observed was the potential for each part of the psyche to be at war with the other. Jung's insights now guide a growing school of psychology that has been very productive in the fields of art criticism, literature, and psychiatry. Jung deepened our sense of the nature of the unconscious by pointing us in totally unexpected directions.

Karen Horney, a contemporary of both Freud and Jung, responded in her work to some of Freud's theories concerning the sexual development of women. One of his theories was that girls naturally developed penis envy when they realized that they lacked the anatomical feature that boys possessed. Horney, after reflecting on the behavior of primitive tribespeople, theorized in turn that the envy was more on the part of men than of women. She asserted that men are envious of the power of women to create a human life out of their bodies and that as a result, throughout history, men have ascribed extraordinary powers to female deities.

However, Horney did not necessarily disagree entirely with Freud. As her daughter, Marianne Horney Eckardt, put it: "Her early writing did focus on such topics as penis envy among other issues. Her observations concluded that penis envy and other feminine symptomatology did exist, but were determined by cultural factors rather than libidinal conflicts." In Dr. Eckardt's words, then, Horney's interest in feminine psychology as such centered more on the cultural than on the purely psychiatric.

B. F. Skinner, a quite different psychologist, assumed that human beings are like all animals: a product of the interaction between psychology and environment. He believed that in our society, the price we pay for the freedom to do as we want as individuals may be too great and that we may have to surrender much of this freedom in order to achieve greater stability and happiness.

His theories are called behaviorist because they state that the individual adapts behavior to the environment according to a pattern of rewards and punishments. If this is so (and Skinner's views have achieved widespread acceptance), the issues of sexuality and the psyche are deeply connected to the structure of society and the environmental rewards and punishments associated with the behavior of males and females. Any balanced view of psychology must take these opinions into account.

Skinner was not concerned in this essay with sexuality. Here, the issues of psychology are based on environment, not on genetic or psychogenetic displacement, and so he tended to sidestep Freud, Jung, and Horney. Skinner's efforts were directed at producing what he felt was a higher level of scientific discourse, a discourse illustrated by considerable laboratory experiment and detailed observation.

In her critique of modern psychology, Simone de Beauvoir reviewed the positions taken by several major psychologists and made an attempt to find a view that properly accounted for women. She examined biological and psychological concerns, asserting that Freud's model for feminine psychology was based on his model for masculine psychology and was therefore in need of revision. She also suggested that the general models of feminine psychological behavior are unrealistic, because they are usually masculine in origin.

Beauvoir drew some important conclusions regarding the effects of modern psychology on women by analyzing the current theories and their limitations. But she also recommended ways that women could transcend the limitations of psychology and realize themselves. She knew that psychology could help to illuminate the future perhaps even more than explain the past, and so her concerns dealt as much with the future as with the past.

The quality of writing in these pieces varies not only because many are translations but also because not all of these writers were preoccupied with the surfaces of their styles. Yet, the writers are worthy of note for their efforts toward clarifying complex and sometimes unyielding problems. In other words, these writers are all exceptionally skillful, but not necessarily great stylists. They write an expository prose that strives to be as clear as possible while also convincing us of the truth of their position. None of these writers makes an emotional appeal to us; each relies on evidence, reasoning, and cautious conclusion.

SIGMUND FREUD

Infantile Sexuality

SIGMUND FREUD (1856–1939) is, in the minds of many, the founder of modern psychiatry. He developed the psychoanalytic method, the examination of the mind using methods of dream analysis, the analysis of the unconscious through free association, and the correlation of findings with attitudes toward sexuality and sexual development. His theories changed the way people treated neurosis and most other mental disorders. Today his theories are spread all over the world.

Freud was born in Freiberg, Moravia (now in Czechoslovakia), and moved to Vienna, Austria, when he was four. He lived and worked in Vienna until he was put under house arrest by the Nazis. He was released in 1938 and moved to London. The psychoanalytic movement of the twentieth century has often been described as a Viennese movement, or at least as a movement closely tied to the prosperity of the Viennese middle-class intellectuals of the time.

As a movement, psychoanalysis shocked most of the world by postulating a superego, which establishes high standards of behavior;

From *Three Essays on the Theory of Sexuality*. Translated by A. A. Brill.

an ego, which corresponds to the apparent personality; an id, which includes the deepest primitive forces of life; and an unconscious into which thoughts and memories we cannot face are "repressed" or "sublimated." The origin of much mental illness, the theory presumes, is in the inability of the mind to find a way to sublimate—express in harmless and often creative ways—the painful thoughts which have been repressed. Dreams and unconscious actions sometimes act as "releases" or harmless expressions of these thoughts and memories.

Difficult as some of these ideas were to accept, they did not cause quite the furor of the present excerpt, from a book that was hotly debated and sometimes violently rejected: Three Essays on the Theory of Sexuality, (1905 tr. 1953). At that time, Freud had become convinced by his work with neurotic patients that much of what disturbed them was connected with their sexuality. That led him to review the research on infantile sexuality and add to it with his own findings. It was also natural to his way of thinking to produce a theory of behavior built upon his researches.

What infuriated people so much was the suggestion that tiny children, even infants, had a sexual life. That it should also figure in the psychological health of the adult was almost as serious. Most people rejected the idea out of hand because it did not square with what they already believed or with what they felt they observed. The typical Freudian habit of seeing psychoanalytic "meaning" in otherwise innocent gestures, such as thumbsucking and bed-wetting, was brought into play in his observations on the sexuality of infants. Freud had a gift for interpretation—analysis—of apparently meaningless events. His capacity to find meaning in such events is still resented by many readers, but that is in part because they do not accept Freud's view that the psychological being—the person— makes every word, gesture, and act "meaningful" to his whole being. For Freud there are no accidents; there are unconscious intentions. When we understand those intentions, we begin to understand ourselves.

Freud believed that sexuality was perhaps the most powerful force in the psyche. He knew that middle-class propriety would be revolted by having to contemplate the concepts he presents in this piece. It is doubtful that he expected the middle class to accept his views. Yet he was rightly convinced that his views were too important to be swept aside in fear that society might be offended.

FREUD'S RHETORIC

Because this treatise is not aimed at a general public, Freud is free to address a general scientific community. He spares them no details regarding bodily functions; he adds little color to an already graceful style. His rhetorical technique is quite simple: he establishes a theory, reviews the evidence which he and others have gathered, then derives certain conclusions from his process.

One would not think of this piece as having a beginning, a middle, and a conclusion. It has rather independent sections that treat specific problems and observations. All of the sections come under the general heading of infantile sexuality, and all relate to the general theory that Freud develops: that there is a connection between infantile sexuality and mature sexuality and that it is revealed in the common amnesia—the forgetting or repressing from conscious memory—of experiences related to sexual awareness in both the infant and the hysteric patient.

If one had to give a name to his rhetorical approach, it might best be called the process of evidence and inference. In this sense, it is similar to the accepted methods of science in most fields. Evidence points to an inference, which then must be tested by analysis. We observe the process as we read Freud's work.

This method sounds very straightforward and artless. Freud's writing is generally marked by those qualities. But there is one rhetorical technique which he is the master of: the memorable phrase. For example, the term "psychoanalysis," which we take so much for granted, was invented by Freud when he was thirty-nine; it is now universally used. The term "Oedipus complex," describing the condition of wishing your same-sex parent dead so that you will be left to "marry" your opposite-sex parent, is also universal now. "Penis envy," used in this selection, is known worldwide, as is the "castration complex." Freud changed both our language and our world.

Infantile Sexuality

The Neglect of the Infantile. It is a part of popular belief about the   1
sexual instinct that it is absent in childhood and that it first appears
in the period of life known as puberty. This, though a common error,
is serious in its consequences and is chiefly due to our ignorance of
the fundamental principles of the sexual life. A comprehensive study
of the sexual manifestations of childhood would probably reveal to us
the essential features of the sexual instinct and would show us its
development and its composition from various sources.

It is quite remarkable that those writers who endeavor to explain   2
the qualities and reactions of the adult individual have given so much
more attention to the ancestral period than to the period of the individual's own existence—that is, they have attributed more influence
to heredity than to childhood. As a matter of fact, it might well be
supposed that the influence of the latter period would be easier to understand, and that it would be entitled to more consideration than heredity. To be sure, one occasionally finds in medical literature notes
on the premature sexual activities of small children, about erections
and masturbation and even reactions resembling coitus, but these are
referred to merely as exceptional occurrences, as curiosities, or as
deterring[1] examples of premature perversity. No author has, to my
knowledge, recognized the normality of the sexual instinct in childhood, and in the numerous writings on the development of the child
the chapter on "Sexual Development" is usually passed over.

Infantile Amnesia. The reason for this remarkable negligence I seek   3
partly in conventional considerations, which influence writers because
of their own bringing up, and partly to a psychic phenomenon which
thus far has remained unexplained. I refer to the peculiar amnesia
which veils from most people (not from all) the first years of their
childhood, usually the first six or eight years. So far, it has not occurred to us that this amnesia should surprise us, though we have good
reasons for it. For we are informed that during those years which have
left nothing except a few incomprehensible memory fragments, we

---

[1]*deterring* Frightening.

have vividly reacted to impressions, that we have manifested human pain and pleasure and that we have expressed love, jealousy and other passions as they then affected us. Indeed, we are told that we have uttered remarks which proved to grown-ups that we possessed understanding and a budding power of judgment. Still we know nothing of all this when we become older. Why does our memory lag behind all our other psychic activities? We really have reason to believe that at no time of life are we more capable of impressions and reproductions[2] than during the years of childhood.

On the other hand we must assume, or we may convince ourselves   4
through psychological observations on others, that the very impressions which we have forgotten have nevertheless left the deepest traces in our psychic life, and acted as determinants for our whole future development. We conclude therefore that we do not deal with a real forgetting of infantile impressions but rather with an amnesia similar to that observed in neurotics for later experiences, the nature of which consists in their being kept away from consciousness (repression). But what forces bring about this repression of the infantile impressions? He who can solve this riddle will also explain hysterical amnesia.[3]

We shall not, however, hesitate to assert that the existence of the   5
infantile amnesia gives us a new point of comparison between the psychic states of the child and those of the psychoneurotic. We have already encountered another point of comparison when confronted by the fact that the sexuality of the psychoneurotic preserves the infantile character or has returned to it. May there not be an ultimate connection between the infantile and the hysterical amnesias?

The connection between infantile and hysterical amnesias is really   6
more than a mere play of wit. Hysterical amnesia which serves the repression can only be explained by the fact that the individual already possesses a sum of memories which were withdrawn from conscious disposal and which by associative connection now seize that which is acted upon by the repelling forces of the repression emanating from consciousness. We may say that without infantile amnesia there would be no hysterical amnesia.

I therefore believe that the infantile amnesia which causes the in-   7
dividual to look upon his childhood as if it were a *prehistoric* time and

---

[2]***reproductions*** Imitations, such as mimicry.
[3]***hysterical amnesia*** The forgetfulness induced by psychological shock; Freud sees a connection between it and the fact that we forget most of our earliest experience, even though it is of crucial importance to our growth.

conceals from him the beginning of his own sexual life—that this amnesia, is responsible for the fact that one does not usually attribute any value to the infantile period in the development of the sexual life. One single observer cannot fill the gap which has been thus produced in our knowledge. As early as 1896, I had already emphasized the significance of childhood for the origin of certain important phenomena connected with the sexual life, and since then I have not ceased to put into the foreground the importance of the infantile factor for sexuality.

The Sexual Latency Period of Childhood and Its Interruptions

The extraordinary frequent discoveries of apparently abnormal and exceptional sexual manifestations in childhood, as well as the discovery of infantile reminiscences in neurotics, which were hitherto unconscious, allow us to sketch the following picture of the sexual behavior of childhood. It seems certain that the newborn child brings with it the germs of sexual feelings which continue to develop for some time and then succumb to a progressive suppression, which may in turn be broken through by the regular advances of the sexual development or may be checked by individual idiosyncrasies. Nothing is known concerning the laws and periodicity of this oscillating course of development. It seems, however, that the sexual life of the child mostly manifests itself in the third or fourth year in some form accessible to observation. 8

Sexual Inhibition. It is during this period of total or at least partial latency[4] that the psychic forces develop which later act as inhibitions on the sexual life, and narrow its direction like dams. These psychic forces are loathing, shame, and moral and esthetic ideal demands. We may gain the impression that the erection of these dams in the civilized child is the work of education; and surely education contributes much to it. In reality, however, this development is organically determined and can occasionally be produced without the help of education. Indeed education remains properly within its assigned domain if 9

[4]*latency* Period when sexual interests are not evident, as before puberty.

it strictly follows the path laid out by the organic,[5] and only imprints it somewhat cleaner and deeper.

Reaction Formation and Sublimation. What are the means that ac- 10 complish these very important constructions so important for the later personal culture and normality? They are probably brought about at the cost of the infantile sexuality itself. The influx of this sexuality does not stop even in this latency period, but its energy is deflected either wholly or partially from sexual utilization and conducted to other aims. The historians of civilization seem to be unanimous in the opinion that such deflection of sexual motive powers from sexual aims to new aims, a process which merits the name of *sublimation*,[6] has furnished powerful components for all cultural accomplishments. We will, therefore, add that the same process acts in the development of every individual, and that it begins to act in the sexual latency period.

We can also venture an opinion about the mechanisms of such sub- 11 limation. The sexual feelings of these infantile years would on the one hand be unusable, since the procreating functions are postponed—this is the chief character of the latency period; on the other hand, they would as such be perverse, as they would emanate from erogenous zones and from impulses which in the individual's course of development could only evoke a feeling of displeasure. They, therefore, awaken psychic counterforces (feelings of reaction), which build up the already mentioned psychical dams of disgust, shame and morality.

The Interruptions of the Latency Period. Without deluding ourselves 12 as to the hypothetical nature and deficient clearness of our understanding regarding the infantile period of latency and delay, we will return to reality and state that such a utilization of the infantile sexuality represents an ideal bringing up from which the development of the individual usually deviates in some measure, often very considerably. A part of the sexual manifestation which has withdrawn from sublimation occasionally breaks through, or a sexual activity remains throughout the whole duration of the latency period until the rein-

---

[5]*the organic* Freud means that the organism—the person—comes to certain understandings as a factor of growth and development. Education must respect organic growth and try not to get "out of order" with it.

[6]**sublimation** A psychological process whereby drives, such as the sexual drive, are transformed into different expressions, such as transforming a powerful sexual drive into a drive to make money or to excel in a given field.

forced breaking through of the sexual instinct in puberty. In so far as they have paid any attention to infantile sexuality, the educators behave as if they shared our views concerning the formation of the moral defense forces at the cost of sexuality. They seem to know that sexual activity makes the child uneducable, for they consider all sexual manifestations of the child as an "evil" in the face of which little can be accomplished. We have, however, every reason for directing our attention to those phenomena so much feared by the educators, for we expect to find in them the solution of the primary structure of the sexual instinct.

The Manifestations of
Infantile Sexuality

Thumbsucking. For reasons which we shall discuss later, we will take   13
as a model of the infantile sexual manifestations thumbsucking, to which the Hungarian pediatrist, Lindner, has devoted an excellent essay.

Thumbsucking, which manifests itself in the nursing baby and   14
which may be continued till maturity or throughout life, consists in a rhythmic repetition of sucking contact with the mouth (the lips), wherein the purpose of taking nourishment is excluded. A part of the lip itself, the tongue, which is another preferable skin region within reach, and even the big toe—may be taken as objects for sucking. Simultaneously, there is also a desire to grasp things, which manifests itself in a rhythmical pulling of the ear lobe and which may cause the child to grasp a part of another person (generally the ear) for the same purpose. The pleasure-sucking is connected with a full absorption of attention and leads to sleep or even to a motor reaction in the form of an orgasm. Pleasure-sucking is often combined with a rubbing contact with certain sensitive parts of the body, such as the breast and external genitals. It is by this path that many children go from thumbsucking to masturbation.

Lindner himself clearly recognized the sexual nature of this activ-   15
ity and openly emphasized it. In the nursery, thumbsucking is often treated in the same way as any other sexual "naughtiness" of the child. A very strong objection was raised against this view by many pediatrists and neurologists, which in part is certainly due to the confusion between the terms "sexual" and "genital." This contradiction raises the difficult question, which cannot be avoided, namely, in what general traits do we wish to recognize the sexual expression of the child.

I believe that the association of the manifestations into which we have gained an insight through psychoanalytic investigation justifies us in claiming thumbsucking as a sexual activity. Through thumbsucking we can study directly the essential features of infantile sexual activities.

Autoerotism. It is our duty here to devote more time to this manifestation. Let us emphasize the most striking character of this sexual activity which is, that the impulse is not directed to other persons but that the child gratifies himself on his own body; to use the happy term invented by Havelock Ellis, we will say that he is *autoerotic.*[7]   16

It is, moreover, clear that the action of the thumbsucking child is determined by the fact that he seeks a pleasure which he has already experienced and now remembers. Through the rhythmic sucking on a portion of the skin or mucous membrane, he finds gratification in the simplest way. It is also easy to conjecture on what occasions the child first experienced this pleasure which he now strives to renew. The first and most important activity in the child's life, the sucking from the mother's breast (or its substitute), must have acquainted him with this pleasure. We would say that the child's lips behaved like an *erogenous zone,* and that the stimulus from the warm stream of milk was really the cause of the pleasurable sensation. To be sure, the gratification of the erogenous zone was at first united with the gratification of the need for nourishment. The sexual activity leans first on one of the self-preservative functions and only later makes itself independent of it. He who sees a satiated child sink back from the mother's breast and fall asleep with reddened cheeks and blissful smile, will have to admit that this picture remains as typical of the expression of sexual gratification in later life. But the desire for repetition of sexual gratification is then separated from the desire for taking nourishment; a separation which becomes unavoidable with the appearance of teeth when the nourishment is no longer sucked but chewed. The child does not make use of a strange object for sucking but prefers his own skin, because it is more convenient, because it thus makes himself independent of the outer world which he cannot control, and because in this way he creates for himself, as it were, a second, even if an inferior, erogenous zone. This inferiority of this second region urges him later to seek the same parts, the lips of another person. ("It is a pity that I cannot kiss myself," might be attributed to him.)   17

---

[7]**autoerotic**   English psychologist Havelock Ellis (1859–1939) used the term to refer to masturbatory behavior.

Not all children suck their thumbs. It may be assumed that it is 18
found only in children in whom the erogenous significance of the lip-
zone is constitutionally reinforced. If the latter is retained in some
children, they develop into kissing epicures with a tendency to perverse kissing, or as men, they show a strong desire for drinking and
smoking. But should repression come into play, they then show disgust for eating and evince hysterical vomiting. By virtue of the community of the lip-zone, the repression encroaches upon the instinct of
nourishment. Many of my female patients showing disturbances in
eating, such as *hysterical globus*,[8] choking sensations and vomiting
have been energetic thumbsuckers in infancy.

In thumbsucking or pleasure-sucking, we are already able to ob- 19
serve the three essential characters of an infantile sexual manifestation. It has its origin in an *anaclitic*[9] relation to a physical function
which is very important for life; it does not yet know any sexual object, that is, it is *autoerotic*, and its sexual aim is under the control of
an *erogenous zone*. Let us assume for the present that these characteristics also hold true for most of the other activities of the infantile
sexual instinct.

The Sexual Aim of
the Infantile Sexuality

Characteristic Erogenous Zones. From the example of thumbsucking, 20
we may gather a great many points useful for distinguishing an erogenous zone. It is a portion of skin or mucous membrane in which stimuli produce a feeling of pleasure of definite quality. There is no doubt
that the pleasure-producing stimuli are governed by special conditions;
as yet we do not know them. The rhythmic characters must play some
part and this strongly suggests an analogy to tickling. It does not, however, appear so certain whether the character of the pleasurable feeling
evoked by the stimulus can be designated as "peculiar," and in what
part of this peculiarity the sexual factor consists. Psychology is still
groping in the dark when it concerns matters of pleasure and pain, and
the most cautious assumption is therefore the most advisable. We may
perhaps later come upon reasons which seem to support the peculiar
quality of the sensation of pleasure.

---

[8]**hysterical globus**   Abnormal reaction to putting things in the mouth.
[9]**anaclitic**   Characterized by a strong emotional—but not sexual—dependence.

The erogenous quality may adhere most notably to definite regions 21
of the body. As is shown by the example of thumbsucking, there are
predestined erogenous zones. But the same example also shows that
any other region of skin or mucous membrane may assume the function of an erogenous zone, hence it must bring along a certain adapt-
ability for it. The production of the sensation of pleasure therefore depends more on the quality of the stimulus than on the nature of the
bodily region. The thumbsucking child looks around on his body and
selects any portion of it for pleasure-sucking, and becoming accustomed to this particular part, he then prefers it. If he accidentally
strikes upon a predestined region, such as breast, nipple or genitals, it
naturally gets the preference. A very analogous tendency to displacement is again found in the symptomatology of hysteria. In this neurosis, the repression mostly affects the genital zones proper, and they
in turn transmit their excitability to the other zones which are usually
dormant in adult life, but then behave exactly like genitals. But besides this, just as in thumbsucking, any other region of the body may
become endowed with the excitation of the genitals and raised to an
erogenous zone. Erogenous and hysterogenous zones show the same
characters.[10]

The Infantile Sexual Aim. The sexual aim of the infantile impulse 22
consists in the production of gratification through the proper excitation of this or that selected erogenous zone. To have a desire for its
repetition, this gratification must have been previously experienced,
and we may be sure that nature has devised definite means so as not
to leave this experience of gratification to mere chance. The arrangement which has fulfilled this purpose for the lip-zone, we have already
discussed; it is the simultaneous connection of this part of the body
with the taking of nourishment. We shall also meet other similar
mechanisms as sources of sexuality. The state of desire for repetition
of gratification can be recognized through a peculiar feeling of tension
which in itself is rather of a painful character, and through a *centrally-
conditioned* feeling of itching or sensitiveness which is projected into
the peripheral erogenous zone. The sexual aim may therefore be formulated by stating that the main object is to substitute for the projected feeling of sensitiveness in the erogenous zone that outer stimulus which removes the feeling of sensitiveness by evoking the feeling

---

[10]Further reflection and evaluation of other observations lead me to attribute the
quality of erotism to all parts of the body and inner organs. [Freud's note]

of gratification. This external stimulus consists usually in a manipulation which is analogous to sucking.

It is in full accord with our physiological knowledge, if the need 23
happens to be awakened also peripherally, through an actual change in the erogenous zone. The action is puzzling only to some extent, as one stimulus seems to want another applied to the same place for its own abrogation.

The Masturbatic Sexual Manifestations

It is a matter of great satisfaction to know that there is nothing 24
further of great importance to learn about the sexual activity of the child, after the impulse of one erogenous zone has become comprehensible to us. The most pronounced differences are found in the action necessary for the gratification, which consists in sucking for the lip-zone, and which must be replaced by other muscular actions in the other zones, depending on their situation and nature.

The Activity of the Anal Zone. Like the lip-zone, the anal zone is, 25
through its position, adapted to produce an anaclisis of sexuality to other functions of the body. It should be assumed that the erogenous significance of this region of the body was originally very strong. Through psychoanalysis, one finds, not without surprise, the many transformations that normally take place in the sexual excitations emanating from here, and that this zone often retains for life a considerable fragment of genital irritability. The intestinal catarrhs[11] which occur quite frequently during infancy, produce sensitive irritations in this zone, and we often hear it said that intestinal catarrh at this delicate age causes "nervousness." In later neurotic diseases, they exert a definite influence on the symptomatic expression of the neurosis, placing at its disposal the whole sum of intestinal disturbances. Considering the erogenous significance of the anal zone which has been retained at least in transformation, one should not laugh at the hemorrhoidal influences to which the old medical literature attached so much weight in the explanation of neurotic states.

Children utilizing the erogenous sensitiveness of the anal zone, can 26
be recognized by their holding back of fecal masses until through ac-

---

[11]*catarrhs* Inflammation of the membrane.

cumulation there result violent muscular contractions; the passage of these masses through the anus is apt to produce a marked irritation of the mucous membrane. Besides the pain, this must also produce a sensation of pleasure. One of the surest premonitions of later eccentricity or nervousness is when an infant obstinately refuses to empty his bowel when placed on the chamber by the nurse, and controls this function at his own pleasure. It naturally does not concern him that he will soil his bed; all he cares for is not to lose the subsidiary pleasure in defecating. Educators have again shown the right inkling when they designate children who withhold these functions as naughty.

The content of the bowel which acts as a stimulus to the sexually 27 sensitive surface of mucous membrane, behaves like the precursor of another organ which does not become active until after the phase of childhood. In addition, it has other important meanings to the nursling. It is evidently treated as an additional part of the body; it represents the first "donation," the disposal of which expresses the pliability while the retention of it can express the spite of the little being towards his environment. From the idea of "donation," he later derives the meaning of the "babe," which according to one of the infantile sexual theories, is supposed to be acquired through eating, and born through the bowel.

The retention of fecal masses, which is at first intentional in order 28 to utilize them, as it were, for masturbatic excitation of the anal zone, is at least one of the roots of constipation so frequent in neurotics. The whole significance of the anal zone is mirrored in the fact that there are but few neurotics who have not their special scatologic[12] customs, ceremonies, etc., which they retain with cautious secrecy.

Real masturbatic irritation of the anal zone by means of the fingers, 29 evoked through either centrally or peripherally supported itching, is not at all rare in older children.

The Activity of the Genital Zone. Among the erogenous zones of the 30 child's body, there is one which certainly does not play the first role, and which cannot be the carrier of the earliest sexual feeling, which, however, is destined for great things in later life. In both male and female, it is connected with the voiding of urine (penis, clitoris), and in the former, it is enclosed in a sack of mucous membrane, probably in order not to miss the irritations caused by the secretions which may arouse sexual excitement at an early age. The sexual activities of this

---

[12]*scatologic* Pertaining to excrement, waste, or feces.

erogenous zone, which belongs to the real genitals, are the beginning of the later "normal" sexual life.

Owing to the anatomical position, the overflowing of secretions, 31 the washing and rubbing of the body, and to certain accidental excitements (the wandering of intestinal worms in the girl), it happens that the pleasurable feeling which these parts of the body are capable of producing makes itself noticeable to the child, even during the sucking age, and thus awakens a desire for repetition. When we consider the sum of all these arrangements and bear in mind that the measures for cleanliness hardly produce a different result than uncleanliness, we can scarcely ignore the fact that the infantile masturbation from which hardly anyone escapes, forms the foundation for the future primacy of this erogenous zone for sexual activity. The action of removing the stimulus and setting free the gratification consists in a rubbing contiguity with the hand or in a certain previously-formed pressure reflex, effected by the closure of the thighs. The latter procedure seems to be the more common in girls. The preference for the hand in boys already indicates what an important part of the male sexual activity will be accomplished in the future by the mastery impulse.

I can only make it clearer if I state that the infantile masturbation 32 should be divided into three phases. The first phase belongs to the nursing period, the second to the short flourishing period of sexual activity at about the fourth year, and only the third corresponds to the one which is often considered exclusively as masturbation of puberty.

Second Phase of Childhood Masturbation. Infantile masturbation 33 seems to disappear after a brief time, but it may continue uninterruptedly till puberty and thus represent the first marked deviation from that development which is desirable for civilized man. At some time during childhood after the nursing period, the sexual instinct of the genitals re-awakens and continues active for some time until it is again suppressed, or it may continue without interruption. The possible relations are very diverse and can only be elucidated through a more precise analysis of individual cases. The details, however, of this *second* infantile sexual activity leave behind the profoundest (unconscious) impressions in the person's memory; if the individual remains healthy they determine his character and if he becomes sick after puberty, they determine the symptomatology of his neurosis. In the latter case, it is found that this sexual period is forgotten and the conscious reminiscences pointing to it are displaced; I have already mentioned that I would like to connect the normal infantile amnesia with this infantile sexual activity. By psychoanalytic investigation, it is possible to bring to consciousness the forgotten material and thereby to remove a compulsion which emanates from the unconscious psychic material.

The Return of Infantile Masturbation. The sexual excitation of the nursing period returns during the designated years of childhood as a centrally determined tickling sensation demanding masturbatic gratification, or as a pollution-like process which, analogous to the pollution of maturity, may attain gratification without the aid of any action. The latter case is more frequent in girls and in the second half of childhood; its determinants are not well understood, but it often, though not regularly, seems to have as a basis a period of early active masturbation. The symptomatology of this sexual manifestation is poor; the genital apparatus is still undeveloped and all signs are therefore displayed by the urinary apparatus which is, so to say, the guardian of the genital apparatus. Most of the so-called bladder disturbances of this period are of a sexual nature; whenever the *enuresis nocturna*[13] does not represent an epileptic attack, it corresponds to a pollution. 34

The return of the sexual activity is determined by inner and outer causes, which can be conjectured from the formation of the neurotic symptoms and can be definitely revealed by psychoanalytic investigations. The internal causes will be discussed later; the accidental outer causes attain at this time a great and permanent importance. As the first outer cause, there is the influence of seduction which prematurely treats the child as a sexual object; under conditions favoring impressions, this teaches the child the gratification of the genital zones and thus, usually forces it to repeat this gratification in masturbation. Such influences can come from adults or other children. I cannot admit that I overestimated its frequency or its significance in my contributions to the etiology[14] of hysteria, though I did not know then that normal individuals may have the same experiences in their childhood, and hence placed a higher value on seductions than on the factors found in the sexual constitution and development. It is quite obvious that no seduction is necessary to awaken the sexual life of the child, that such an awakening may come on spontaneously from inner sources. 35

Polymorphous-Perverse Disposition. It is instructive to know that under the influence of seduction, the child may become polymorphous- 36

---

[13]**enuresis nocturna**   Nighttime bed-wetting.
[14]*etiology*   The source or cause of something, especially of a disease.

perverse[15] and may be misled into all sorts of transgressions. This goes to show that the child carries along the adaptation for them in his disposition. The formation of such perversions meets but slight resistance because the psychic dams against sexual transgressions, such as shame, loathing and morality—which depend on the age of the child—are not yet erected or are only in the process of formation. In this respect, the child perhaps does not behave differently from the average uncultured woman in whom the same polymorphous-perverse disposition exists. Such a woman may remain sexually normal under usual conditions, but under the guidance of a clever seducer, she will find pleasure in every perversion and will retain it as her sexual activity. The same polymorphous or infantile disposition fits the prostitute for her professional activity, still it is absolutely impossible not to recognize in the uniform disposition to all perversions, as shown by an enormous number of prostitutes and by many women who do not necessarily follow this calling, a universal and primitive human tendency.

Partial Impulses. For the rest, the influence of seduction does not aid 37 us in unravelling the original relations of the sexual instinct, but rather confuses our understanding of the same, inasmuch as it prematurely supplies the child with a sexual object at a time when the infantile sexual instinct does not yet evince any desire for it. We must admit, however, that the infantile sexual life, though mainly under the control of erogenous zones, also shows components which from the very beginning point to other persons as sexual objects. Among these, we may mention the impulses for looking, showing off, and for cruelty, which manifest themselves somewhat independently of the erogenous zones and only later enter into intimate relationship with the sexual life; but along with the erogenous sexual activity they are noticeable even in the infantile years, as separate and independent strivings. The little child is, above all, shameless, and during his early years, he evinces definite pleasure in displaying his body and especially his sex organs. A counterpart to this perverse desire, the curiosity to see other persons' genitals, probably appears first in the later years of childhood when the hindrance of the feeling of shame has already reached a certain development. Under the influence of seduction, the looking perversion may attain great importance for the sexual life of the child. Still, from my investigations of the childhood years

---

[15]*polymorphous-perverse* Freud's term for a person whose sexual expression is oral, anal, and genital rather than the usual adult expression, essentially genital.

of normal and neurotic patients, I must conclude that the impulse for looking can appear in the child as a spontaneous sexual manifestation. Small children, whose attention has once been directed to their own genitals—usually by masturbation—are wont to progress in this direction without outside interference and to develop a vivid interest in the genitals of their playmates. As the occasion for the gratification of such curiosity is generally afforded during the gratification of both excrementitious needs, such children become *voyeurs*[16] and are zealous spectators at the voiding of urine and feces of others. After this tendency has been repressed, the curiosity to see the genitals of others (one's own or those of the other sex) remains as a tormenting desire which in some neurotic cases, furnishes the strongest motive-power for the formation of symptoms.

The cruelty component of the sexual instinct develops in the child 38 with still greater independence of those sexual activities which are connected with erogenous zones. Cruelty is intimately related to the childish character, since the inhibition which restrains the mastery impulse before it causes pain to others—that is, the capacity for sympathy—develops comparatively late. As we know that a thorough psychological analysis of this impulse has not as yet been successfully done, we may assume that the feelings of cruelty emanate from the mastery impulse and appear at a period in the sexual life before the genitals have taken on their later role. This feeling then dominates a phase of the sexual life which we shall later describe as the pregenital organization. Children who are distinguished for evincing especial cruelty to animals and playmates may be justly suspected of an intensive and a premature sexual activity which emanates from the erogenous zones. But in a simultaneous prematurity of all sexual impulses, the erogenous sexual activity surely seems to be primary. The absence of the barrier of sympathy carries with it the danger that a connection formed in childhood between cruelty and the erogenous impulses will not be broken in later life.

An erogenous source of the passive impulse for cruelty (masoch- 39 ism) is found in the painful irritation of the gluteal region,[17] which is familiar to all educators since the confessions of J. J. Rousseau. This has justly caused them to demand that physical punishment, which is usually directed to this part of the body, should be withheld from all

---

[16]**voyeurs**   Those who get special pleasure from looking on, especially at something secret or private.

[17]**gluteal region**   The buttocks, where children are spanked. Rousseau in his *Confessions* (1781, 1788) admits a certain pleasure in corporal punishment.

children in whom the libido might be forced into collateral roads by the later demands of cultural education.

Study of Infantile
Sexual Investigation

Inquisitiveness. About the same time as the sexual life of the child 40 reaches its first rich development, from the age of three to the age of five, there appear the beginnings of that activity which are ascribed to the impulse for knowledge and investigation. The desire for knowledge can neither be reckoned among the elementary instinctive components, nor can it be altogether subsumed under sexuality. Its activity corresponds, on the one hand, to a sublimated form of acquisition, and on the other hand, the energy with which it works comes from the looking impulse. Its relation to the sexual life, however, is of particular importance, for we have learned from psychoanalysis that the inquisitiveness of children is directed to sexual problems unusually early and in an unexpectedly intensive manner; indeed, curiosity may perhaps first be awakened by sexual problems.

The Riddle of the Sphinx. It is not theoretical but practical interests, 41 which start the work of the child's investigation activity. The menace to the conditions of his existence through the actual or expected arrival of a new child, the fear of losing the care and love which is connected with this event, cause the child to become thoughtful and sagacious.[18] Corresponding with the history of this awakening, the first problem with which he occupies himself is not the question as to the difference between the sexes, but the riddle: Where do children come from? In a distorted form which can easily be unravelled, this is the same riddle which was proposed by the Theban Sphinx.[19] The fact of the two sexes is usually first accepted by the child without struggle and hesitation. It is quite natural for the male child to presuppose in all persons he knows a genital like his own, and to find it impossible to harmonize the lack of it with his conception of others.

The Castration Complex and Penis Envy. This conviction is energet- 42 ically adhered to by the boy and stubbornly defended against the con-

---

[18]*sagacious* Shrewd, cunning.

[19]**Theban Sphinx** The sphinx, with the face of a woman, body of a lion, and wings of a bird, waited outside Thebes for years, killing all who passed by and could not solve its riddle. Oedipus answered the riddle: "What walks on four legs in the morning, two legs in the day, and three legs in the evening?" The answer: man, who crawls in infancy, walks upright in his prime, and uses a cane in old age.

tradictions which soon result, and is only given up after severe internal struggles (castration complex). The substitute formations of this lost penis on the part of the woman play a great role in the formation of many perversions.[20]

The assumption of the same (male) genital in all persons is the first 43 of the remarkable and consequential infantile sexual theories. It is of little help to the child when biological science agrees with his preconceptions and recognizes the feminine clitoris as the real substitute for the penis. The little girl does not react with similar rejections when she sees the differently formed genital of the boy. She is immediately prepared to recognize it and soon becomes envious of the penis; this envy reaches its highest point in the consequentially important wish that she also should be a boy.

Birth Theories. Many people can remember distinctly how intensely 44 they interested themselves, in the prepubescent period, in the question of where children came from. The anatomical solutions at that time read very differently; the children come out of the breast or are cut out of the body, or the navel opens itself to let them out. Outside of analysis, one only seldom remembers this investigation from early childhood years, for it had long since merged into repression; its results, however, are thoroughly uniform. One gets children by eating something special (as in the fairy tale) or they are born through the bowel, like a passage. These infantile theories recall the structures in the animal kingdom, especially the *cloaca*[21] of those animals which are on a lower scale than mammals.

Sadistic Conception of the Sexual Act. If children at so tender an age 45 witness the sexual act between adults, for which an occasion is furnished by the conviction of the adults that little children cannot understand anything sexual, they cannot help conceiving the sexual act as a kind of maltreating or overpowering; that is, it impresses them in a sadistic sense. Psychoanalysis teaches us also that such an early childhood impression contributes much to the disposition for a later sadistic displacement of the sexual aim. Besides this, children also oc-

---

[20]One has the right to speak also of a castration complex in women. Male and female children form the theory that originally the woman, too, had a penis, which has been lost through castration. The conviction finally won (that the woman has no penis) often produces in the male a lasting depreciation of the other sex. [Freud's note]

[21]**cloaca**   All-purpose anal opening (as in a frog). The Latin word literally means a sewer.

cupy themselves with the problem of what the sexual act consists, or, as they grasp it, of what marriage consists, and seek the solution to the mystery usually in an intimacy carried on through the functions of urination and defecation.

The Typical Failure of the Infantile Sexual Investigation. It can be 46 stated in general about infantile sexual theories that they are models of the child's own sexual constitution, and that despite their grotesque mistakes, they show more understanding of the sexual processes than is credited to their creators. Children also notice the pregnancy of their mother and know how to interpret it correctly. The stork fable is very often related before auditors who respond with a deep, but mostly mute suspicion. Inasmuch as two elements remain unknown to infantile sexual investigation, namely, the role of the fructifying semen and the existence of the female genital opening—precisely the same points in which the infantile organization is still backward—the effort of the infantile mind regularly remains fruitless and ends in a rejection, which not infrequently leaves a lasting injury to the desire for knowledge. The sexual investigation of these early childhood years is always conducted alone; it signifies the first step towards an independent orientation of the world, and causes a marked estrangement between the child and the persons of his environment who formerly enjoyed his full confidence.

QUESTIONS

1. Freud begins with the question of the neglect of the infantile, the fact that most people paid little attention to the individual child's development (paras. 1–7). Explain what he means in these first seven paragraphs.
2. Children are said to go through a period of sexual latency. Clarify Freud's views on this question.
3. What kinds of sexual instincts are described in this selection? Are they recognizably sexual? Instinctual?
4. What are erogenous zones? Consult paragraph 20 and following.
5. Referring to paragraphs 42–43, clarify what Freud means by "castration complex" and "penis envy." What is their bearing on infantile sexuality?
6. What kind of audience would have found this work interesting and provocative? What kind would have found it repulsive? What kind would have found it unbelievable? Does Freud feel he must convince an unfriendly audience?

WRITING ASSIGNMENTS

1. Freud's complaint concerning the neglect of research and investigation into infantile behavior was written in 1905. Have things changed since then? What makes you feel that there is as much, less, or more neglect now than at that time? Do you feel that most people accept Freud's views on infantile sexuality now? Do you yourself accept his views?

2. Even the general educated public of 1905 found the theories expressed in this work utterly unacceptable. They were revolted both by Freud's views and by his methods of research. What would be distressing, alarming, or revolting about this piece? What could possibly cause people to react violently to Freud's views? Are there still people who would have such a reaction?

3. Take an aspect of Freud's theories with which you disagree and present your own argument. You may resort to your own childhood memories or those of friends. Refer directly to the aspects of Freud's thinking that seem least convincing to you and explore your reasons for rejecting them.

4. In paragraph 18, Freud refers to "kissing epicures." Establish just what is meant by that term, then clarify such persons' behavior. Do such epicures exist today? What is their current behavior? Have you known any? You may wish to supplement your personal knowledge by conducting two or three interviews with people who do know them. Be sure to try to connect your information with Freud's thoughts.

5. You may wish to offer your own theories concerning infantile sexuality. If so, you may use Freud's subject headings (where relevant to your theories) and rewrite the sections using your own thinking, your own evidence, and your own theories. Choose those subject headings that you feel are most important to your ideas. Headings such as "The Sexual Latency Period of Childhood and Its Interruptions," "Sexual Inhibition," and "The Sexual Aim of the Infantile Sexuality" may be of use to you. Naturally, you may make up your own headings if you wish.

6. The concepts of the castration complex and penis envy are both quite controversial. After establishing what Freud means by the terms, examine them to find out whether they are reasonable theories of behavior or whether they are not fully tenable. Moreover, consider the effect of holding such theories on matters related to social behavior—controversies related to feminism, for instance. Gather reactions from your friends. Do their views support Freud's theories or not? Do their views matter to you?

CARL JUNG

─────◦≈◦─────

Anima and Animus

CARL GUSTAV JUNG (1875–1961), *probably the most famous disciple of Freud, was a Swiss physician who collaborated with Freud between 1907 and 1912. He broke with Freud over important disagreements concerning the makeup of the unconscious. Jung was convinced that the unconscious was composed of more than ego, superego, and id. He defined the unconscious as a collection of archetypal images that could be inherited by members of the same group. Experience clarified these images, but the images, in turn, directed experience.*

In his famous essay on the collective unconscious, for example, he asserted that the great myths are expressions of the archetypes of actions and heroes that are stored in the unconscious. The myths give expression to the archetypes and help elucidate them for the individual and the society. Jung's view was that the archetypes that revealed themselves in the myths had to be adapted to by the individual if that individual were to be psychically healthy.

The archetypes that Jung describes in this selection are subtle and controversial. The anima is the female archetype that a man carries

From *Aspects of the Feminine.*

always within his subconscious. Jung refers to it as an imago, *a term that has been interpreted in psychoanalysis as "primordial image" and "archetype of the parent." An archetype is the basic pattern against which all other similar experiences are measured; so, the anima constitutes an archetype against which the idea of woman is measured. But it is also much more.*

According to Jung, one's personality is not characterized by an absolute unity. In fact, one has several personalities, including a mask that one adopts and presents to the world. This mask hides some of the important truths about oneself, truths that might be embarrassing. The female part of a man (the anima) has its own demands and is shaped by the parental model (or a substitute in youth) of the mother. It must be accounted for in the construction of the persona—the essential personality that one feels is one's own.

The same is true of the animus in the case of women. The parental model provides the immediate archetype, although in many cases there may be other sources for the archetype. It makes significant demands on a woman and must be reckoned with and adapted to if the woman is to be healthy. Jung cites the characteristics of the animus in some detail in this selection and goes on to examine some of the problems that can arise when the animus is not properly balanced in relationship to the persona.

Jung regarded the personality as a very complex structure, balancing the ego, the persona, the animus and anima, and possibly other archetypal images that may exist in the individual. Balancing these various segments of the personality is the job of the healthy person. When one segment becomes overpowering—as in the case of the animus in the personality of a woman—a pattern of psychic difficulties will be revealed. In other words, the animus can become dominant and overwhelm the personality of the woman. Much the same can happen in the case of a dominant anima in a man.

All of this leads to the curious question of what a person's "true personality" is. Jung attempted to answer this question, but his answer is not necessarily reassuring. He suggested that our personalities are multiform, consisting of numerous "autonomous complexes." An autonomous complex is a self-directed component of the psyche. The ego, for example, is an autonomous complex, as is the anima. Jung reserves the term "self" for the collection of autonomous complexes that make up the conscious and the unconscious mind of any individual.

Like Freud, Jung agreed that the human psyche is composed of a conscious element, characterized best by the ego, and an unconscious element that is filled with archetypal images and autonomous complexes. Jung asserted that "the unconscious is a psychological boundary-concept which covers all those psychic contents or processes which are not conscious, i.e., not related to the ego in a perceptible way." Jung described his proof of the evidence of the unconscious through his examination of patients, his use of hyponosis, and his experience with amnesiac hysterics. His lifetime of clinical work gave him the insights that he offers us in this discussion.

The portrait that Jung painted of the archetype of men and women may not please all readers. In many ways he is profoundly traditional in his description of gender types, and for that reason some feminists have difficulty with this work. His description of the anima and the animus—as well as his clinical observations about what seemed true to him about the two sexes—tended to be conservative by our modern standards. He made flat assertions concerning the basic nature of women and men and seemed to have shared his society's views about the way men and women should behave.

JUNG'S RHETORIC

This subject is difficult, even for Jung, and he labors to avoid abstractions that would make his text more difficult to understand. His discussion reprinted here is drawn from a longer chapter in which Jung tries to clarify some of the more elusive ideas as he proceeds. For that reason, Jung is very patient to make his points, explain them, and then illustrate them. Yet, despite his care, these knotty issues and fascinating ideas still require that we be patient and attentive in our reading.

One of his primary techniques consists of defining his terms as he writes. For example, he opens by identifying what he means by personality, a definition that may turn out to be surprising or alarming to his readers. For instance, in this case he postulates two or even more personalities—indeed, he imagines a situation in which the ego may be confused over which is the "true" personality.

Jung then goes on to discuss the anima, relating it to the mother and reminding us that it is an autonomous complex, with many of the characteristics of a personality in its own right. Jung frequently illustrates his points by reference to tribal behavior and tribal rites, because he sees in them a public recognition of the presence of the *unconscious complexes. In tribal people, these complexes are accorded the status of spirits, but for Jung, they are projections of the complexes that lie within each of us.*

Jung also uses situations that are familiar to all of us. He discusses the patterns of marriage that we know, but cites instances in which the imago of the mother is transferred to a man's wife. The pattern of behavior is described in enough detail so as to be verifiable (or not) in the mind of the reader. Therefore, although Jung works with a highly complex system of ideas, his efforts to be clear and lucid generally result in the reader's greater understanding.

———⚬———

Anima and Animus

It is probably no accident that our modern notions of "personal" and "personality" derive from the word *persona*. I can assert that my ego is personal or a personality, and in exactly the same sense I can say that my persona is a personality with which I identify myself more or less. The fact that I then possess two personalities is not so remarkable, since every autonomous or even relatively autonomous complex has the peculiarity of appearing as a personality, i.e., of being personified. This can be observed most readily in the so-called spiritualistic manifestations of automatic writing and the like. The sentences produced are always personal statements and are propounded in the first person singular, as though behind every utterance there stood an actual personality. A naïve intelligence at once thinks of spirits. The same sort of thing is also observable in the hallucinations of the insane, although these, more clearly than the first, can often be recognized as mere thoughts or fragments of thoughts whose connection with the conscious personality is immediately apparent to everyone. 1

The tendency of the relatively autonomous complex to direct personification also explains why the persona exercises such a "personal" effect that the ego is all too easily deceived as to which is the "true" personality. 2

Now, everything that is true of the persona and of all autonomous complexes in general also holds true of the anima. She likewise is a personality, and this is why she is so easily projected upon a woman. 3

So long as the anima is unconscious she is always projected, for every-thing unconscious is projected. The first bearer of the soul-image is always the mother; later it is borne by those women who arouse the man's feelings, whether in a positive or a negative sense. Because the mother is the first bearer of the soul-image, separation from her is a delicate and important matter of the greatest educational significance. Accordingly among primitives we find a large number of rites designed to organize this separation. The mere fact of becoming adult, and of outward separation, is not enough; impressive initiations into the "men's house" and ceremonies of rebirth are still needed in order to make the separation from the mother (and hence from childhood) en-tirely effective.

Just as the father acts as a protection against the dangers of the external world and thus serves his son as a model persona, so the mother protects him against the dangers that threaten from the dark-ness of his psyche. In the puberty rites, therefore, the initiate receives instruction about these things of "the other side," so that he is put in a position to dispense with his mother's protection 4

The modern civilized man has to forgo this primitive but nonethe-less admirable system of education. The consequence is that the an-ima, in the form of the mother-imago, is transferred to the wife; and the man, as soon as he marries, becomes childish, sentimental, depen-dent, and subservient, or else truculent, tyrannical, hypersensitive, al-ways thinking about the prestige of his superior masculinity. The last is of course merely the reverse of the first. The safeguard against the unconscious, which is what his mother meant to him, is not replaced by anything in the modern man's education; unconsciously, therefore, his ideal of marriage is so arranged that his wife has to take over the magical role of the mother. Under the cloak of the ideally exclusive marriage he is really seeking his mother's protection, and thus he plays into the hands of his wife's possessive instincts. His fear of the dark incalculable power of the unconscious gives his wife an illegitimate authority over him, and forges such a dangerously close union that the marriage is permanently on the brink of explosion from internal ten-sion—or else, out of protest, he flies to the other extreme, with the same results. 5

I am of the opinion that it is absolutely essential for a certain type of modern man to recognize his distinction not only from the persona, but from the anima as well. For the most part our consciousness, in true Western style, looks outwards, and the inner world remains in darkness. But this difficulty can be overcome easily enough, if only we will make the effort to apply the same concentration and criticism to 6 the psychic material which manifests itself, not outside, but in our private lives. So accustomed are we to keep a shamefaced silence about this other side—we even tremble before our wives, lest they betray us!—and, if found out, to make rueful confessions of "weakness," that there would seem to be only one method of education, namely, to crush or repress the weaknesses as much as possible or at least hide them from the public. But that gets us nowhere.

Perhaps I can best explain what has to be done if I use the persona   7
as an example. Here everything is plain and straightforward, whereas with the anima all is dark, to Western eyes anyway. When the anima continually thwarts the good intentions of the conscious mind, by contriving a private life that stands in sorry contrast to the dazzling persona, it is exactly the same as when a naïve individual, who has not the ghost of a persona, encounters the most painful difficulties in his passage through the world. There are indeed people who lack a developed persona—"Canadians who know not Europe's sham polite-ness"—blundering from one social solecism to the next, perfectly harmless and innocent, soulful bores or appealing children, or, if they are women, spectral Cassandras[1] dreaded for their tactlessness, eter-nally misunderstood, never knowing what they are about, always tak-ing forgiveness for granted, blind to the world, hopeless dreamers. From them we can see how a neglected persona works, and what one must do to remedy the evil. Such people can avoid disappointments and an infinity of sufferings, scenes, and social catastrophes only by learning to see how men behave in the world. They must learn to understand what society expects of them; they must realize that there are factors and persons in the world far above them; they must know that what they do has a meaning for others, and so forth. Naturally all this is child's play for one who has a properly developed persona. But if we reverse the picture and confront the man who possesses a bril-liant persona with the anima, and, for the sake of comparison, set him beside the man with no persona, then we shall see that the latter is just as well informed about the anima and her affairs as the former is about the world. The use which either makes of his knowledge can just as easily be abused, in fact it is more than likely that it will be.

The man with the persona is blind to the existence of inner reali-   8
ties, just as the other is blind to the reality of the world, which for him has merely the value of an amusing or fantastic playground. But the fact of inner realities and their unqualified recognition is obviously

---

[1]**Cassandra** A prophetess of doom in Homer's *Iliad* and Aeschylus's *Agamemnon*.

the *sine qua non*[2] for a serious consideration of the anima problem. If the external world is, for me, simply a phantasm, how should I take the trouble to establish a complicated system of relationship and adaptation to it? Equally, the "nothing but fantasy" attitude will never persuade me to regard my anima manifestations as anything more than fatuous weakness. If, however, I take the line that the world is outside *and* inside, that reality falls to the share of both, I must logically accept the upsets and annoyances that come to me from inside as symptoms of faulty adaptation to the conditions of that inner world. No more than the blows rained on the innocent abroad can be healed by moral repression will it help him resignedly to catalogue his "weaknesses." Here are reasons, intentions, consequences, which can be tackled by will and understanding. Take, for example, the "spotless" man of honor and public benefactor, whose tantrums and explosive moodiness terrify his wife and children. What is the anima doing here?

We can see it at once if we just allow things to take their natural course. Wife and children will become estranged; a vacuum will form about him. At first he will bewail the hard-heartedness of his family, and will behave if possible even more vilely than before. That will make the estrangement absolute. If the good spirits have not utterly forsaken him, he will after a time notice his isolation, and in his loneliness he will begin to understand how he caused the estrangement. Perhaps, aghast at himself, he will ask, "What sort of devil has got into me?"—without of course seeing the meaning of this metaphor. Then follow remorse, reconciliation, oblivion, repression, and, in next to no time, a new explosion. Clearly, the anima is trying to enforce a separation. This tendency is in nobody's interest. The anima comes between them like a jealous mistress who tries to alienate the man from his family. An official post or any other advantageous social position can do the same thing, but there we can understand the force of the attraction. Whence does the anima obtain the power to wield such enchantment? On the analogy with the persona there must be values or some other important and influential factors lying in the background like seductive promises. In such matters we must guard against rationalizations. Our first thought is that the man of honor is on the lookout for another woman. That might be—it might even be arranged by the anima as the most effective means to the desired end. Such an arrangement should not be misconstrued as an end in itself, for the blameless gentleman who is correctly married according to the law can

9

---

[2]**sine qua non**   Something absolutely essential and necessary.

be just as correctly divorced according to the law, which does not alter his fundamental attitude one iota. The old picture has merely received a new frame.

As a matter of fact, this arrangement is a very common method of implementing a separation—and of hampering a final solution. Therefore it is more reasonable not to assume that such an obvious possibility is the end-purpose of the separation. We would be better advised to investigate what is behind the tendencies of the anima. The first step is what I would call the objectivation of the anima, that is, the strict refusal to regard the trend towards separation as a weakness of one's own. Only when this has been done can one face the anima with the question, "Why do you want this separation?" To put the question in this personal way has the great advantage of recognizing the anima as a personality, and of making a relationship possible. The more personally she is taken the better. 10

To anyone accustomed to proceed purely intellectually and rationally, this may seem altogether too ridiculous. It would indeed be the height of absurdity if a man tried to have a conversation with his persona, which he recognized merely as a psychological means of relationship. But it is absurd only for the man who *has* a persona. If he has none, he is in this point no different from the primitive who, as we know, has only one foot in what we commonly call reality. With the other foot he stands in a world of spirits, which is quite real to him. Our model case behaves, in the world, like a modern European; but in the world of spirits he is the child of a troglodyte.[3] He must therefore submit to living in a kind of prehistoric kindergarten until he has got the right idea of the powers and factors which rule that other world. Hence he is quite right to treat the anima as an autonomous personality and to address personal questions to her. 11

I mean this as an actual technique. We know that practically every one has not only the peculiarity, but also the faculty, of holding a conversation with himself. Whenever we are in a predicament we ask ourselves (or whom else?), "What shall I do?" either aloud or beneath our breath, and we (or who else?) supply the answer. Since it is our intention to learn what we can about the foundations of our being, this little matter of living in a metaphor should not bother us. We have to accept it as a symbol of our primitive backwardness (or of such naturalness as is still, mercifully, left to us) that we can, like the Negro, discourse personally with our "snake." The psyche not being a unity 12

---

[3]***troglodyte*** A prehistoric cave dweller.

but a contradictory multiplicity of complexes, the dissociation required for our dialectics with the anima is not so terribly difficult. The art of it consists only in allowing our invisible partner to make herself heard, in putting the mechanism of expression momentarily at her disposal, without being overcome by the distaste one naturally feels at playing such an apparently ludicrous game with oneself, or by doubts as to the genuineness of the voice of one's interlocutor. This latter point is technically very important: we are so in the habit of identifying ourselves with the thoughts that come to us that we invariably assume we have made them. Curiously enough, it is precisely the most impossible thoughts for which we feel the greatest subjective responsibility. If we were more conscious of the inflexible universal laws that govern even the wildest and most wanton fantasy, we might perhaps be in a better position to see these thoughts above all others as objective occurrences, just as we see dreams, which nobody supposes to be deliberate or arbitrary inventions. It certainly requires the greatest objectivity and absence of prejudice to give the "other side" the opportunity for perceptible psychic activity. As a result of the repressive attitude of the conscious mind, the other side is driven into indirect and purely symptomatic manifestations, mostly of an emotional kind, and only in moments of overwhelming affectivity can fragments of the unconscious come to the surface in the form of thoughts or images. The inevitable accompanying symptom is that the ego momentarily identifies with these utterances, only to revoke them in the same breath. And, indeed, the things one says when in the grip of an affect sometimes seem very strange and daring. But they are easily forgotten, or wholly denied. This mechanism of deprecation and denial naturally has to be reckoned with if one wants to adopt an objective attitude. The habit of rushing in to correct and criticize is already strong enough in our tradition, and it is as a rule further reinforced by fear—a fear that can be confessed neither to oneself nor to others, a fear of insidious truths, of dangerous knowledge, of disagreeable verifications, in a word, fear of all those things that cause so many of us to flee from being alone with ourselves as from the plague. We say that it is egoistic or "morbid" to be preoccupied with oneself; one's own company is the worst, "it makes you melancholy"—such are the glowing testimonials accorded to our human makeup. They are evidently deeply ingrained in our Western minds. Whoever thinks in this way has obviously never asked himself what possible pleasure other people could find in the company of such a miserable coward. Starting from the fact that in a state of affect one often surrenders involuntarily to the truths of the other side, would it not be far better to make use of an affect so as to give the other side an opportunity to speak? It could therefore be said just as truly that one should cultivate the art of conversing with oneself in the setting provided by an affect, as though the affect itself were speaking without regard to our rational criticism. So long as the affect is speaking, criticism must be withheld. But once it has presented its case, we should begin criticizing as conscientiously as though a real person closely connected with us were our interlocutor. Nor should the matter rest there, but statement and answer must follow one another until a satisfactory end to the discussion is reached. Whether the result is satisfactory or not, only subjective feeling can decide. Any humbug is of course quite useless. Scrupulous honesty with oneself and no rash anticipation of what the other side might conceivably say are the indispensable conditions of this technique for educating the anima.

There is, however, something to be said for this characteristically 13 Western fear of the other side. It is not entirely without justification, quite apart from the fact that it is real. We can understand at once the fear that the child and the primitive have of the great unknown. We have the same childish fear of our inner side, where we likewise touch upon a great unknown world. All we have is the affect, the fear, without knowing that this is a world-fear—for the world of affects is invisible. We have either purely theoretical prejudices against it, or superstitious ideas. One cannot even talk about the unconscious before many educated people without being accused of mysticism. The fear is legitimate in so far as our rational *Weltanschauung*[4] with its scientific and moral certitudes—so hotly believed in because so deeply questionable—is shattered by the facts of the other side. If only one could avoid them, then the emphatic advice of the Philistine to "let sleeping dogs lie" would be the only truth worth advocating. And here I would expressly point out that I am not recommending the above technique as either necessary or even useful to any person not driven to it by necessity. The stages, as I said, are many, and there are greybeards who die as innocent as babes in arms, and in this year of grace troglodytes are still being born. There are truths which belong to the future, truths which belong to the past, and truths which belong to no time.

I can imagine someone using this technique out of a kind of holy 14 inquisitiveness, some youth, perhaps, who would like to set wings to

---

[4]**Weltanschauung** A German term for a comprehensive understanding of the world, especially from a specific point of view.

his feet, not because of lameness, but because he yearns for the sun. But a grown man, with too many illusions dissipated, will submit to this inner humiliation and surrender only if forced, for why should he let the terrors of childhood again have their way with him? It is no light matter to stand between a day-world of exploded ideas and discredited values, and a night-world of apparently senseless fantasy. The weirdness of this standpoint is in fact so great that there is probably nobody who does not reach out for security, even though it be a reaching back to the mother who shielded his childhood from the terrors of night. Whoever is afraid must needs be dependent; a weak thing needs support. That is why the primitive mind, from deep psychological necessity, begot religious instruction and embodied it in magician and priest. *Extra ecclesiam nulla salus,*[5] is still a valid truth today—for those who can go back to it. For the few who cannot, there is only dependence upon a human being, a humbler and a prouder dependence, a weaker and a stronger support, so it seems to me, than any other. What can one say of the Protestant? He has neither church nor priest, but only God—and even God becomes doubtful.

The reader may ask in some consternation, "But what on earth   15 does the anima do, that such double insurances are needed before one can come to terms with her?" I would recommend my reader to study the comparative history of religion so intently as to fill these dead chronicles with the emotional life of those who lived these religions. Then he will get some idea of what lives on the other side. The old religions with their sublime and ridiculous, their friendly and fiendish symbols did not drop from the blue, but were born of this human soul that dwells within us at this moment. All those things, their primal forms, live on in us and may at any time burst in upon us with annihilating force, in the guise of mass-suggestions against which the individual is defenseless. Our fearsome gods have only changed their names: they now rhyme with *ism*. Or has anyone the nerve to claim that the World War or Bolshevism was an ingenious invention? Just as outwardly we live in a world where a whole continent may be submerged at any moment, or a pole be shifted, or a new pestilence break out, so inwardly we live in a world where at any moment something similar may occur, albeit in the form of an idea, but no less dangerous and untrustworthy for that. Failure to adapt to this inner world is a negligence entailing just as serious consequences as ignorance and ineptitude in the outer world. It is after all only a tiny fraction of hu-

---

[5]**Extra ecclesiam nulla salus**   "There is no health outside the church."

manity, living mainly on that thickly populated peninsula of Asia which juts out into the Atlantic Ocean,[6] and calling themselves "cultured," who, because they lack all contact with nature, have hit upon the idea that religion is a peculiar kind of mental disturbance of undiscoverable purport. Viewed from a safe distance, say from central Africa or Tibet, it would certainly look as if this fraction had projected its own unconscious mental derangements upon nations still possessed of healthy instincts.

Because the things of the inner world influence us all the more 16 powerfully for being unconscious, it is essential for anyone who intends to make progress in self-culture (and does not all culture begin with the individual?) to objectivate the effects of the anima and then try to understand what contents underlie those effects. In this way he adapts to, and is protected against, the invisible. No adaptation can result without concessions to both worlds. From a consideration of the claims of the inner and outer worlds, or rather, from the conflict between them, the possible and the necessary follows. Unfortunately our Western mind, lacking all culture in this respect, has never yet devised a concept, nor even a name, for the *union of opposites through the middle path*, that most fundamental item of inward experience, which could respectably be set against the Chinese concept of Tao. It is at once the most individual fact and the most universal, the most legitimate fulfilment of the meaning of the individual's life.

In the course of my exposition so far, I have kept exclusively to 17 *masculine* psychology. The anima, being of feminine gender, is exclusively a figure that compensates the masculine consciousness. In woman the compensating figure is of a masculine character, and can therefore appropriately be termed the *animus*. If it was no easy task to describe what is meant by the anima, the difficulties become almost insuperable when we set out to describe the psychology of the animus.

The fact that a man naïvely ascribes his anima reactions to him- 18 self, without seeing that he really cannot identify himself with an autonomous complex, is repeated in feminine psychology, though if possible in even more marked form. This identification with an autonomous complex is the essential reason why it is so difficult to understand and describe the problem, quite apart from its inherent obscurity and strangeness. We always start with the naïve assumption that we are masters in our own house. Hence we must first accustom ourselves to the thought that, in our most intimate psychic life as

---

[6]*peninsula . . . Atlantic Ocean* Europe.

well, we live in a kind of house which has doors and windows to the world, but that, although the objects or contents of this world act upon us, they do not belong to us. For many people this hypothesis is by no means easy to conceive, just as they do not find it at all easy to understand and to accept the fact that their neighbour's psychology is not necessarily identical with their own. My reader may think that the last remark is something of an exaggeration, since in general one is aware of individual differences. But it must be remembered that our individual conscious psychology develops out of an original state of unconsciousness and therefore of nondifferentiation (termed by Lévy-Bruhl[7] *participation mystique*). Consequently, consciousness of differentiation is a relatively late achievement of mankind, and presumably but a relatively small sector of the indefinitely large field of original identity. Differentiation is the essence, the *sine qua non* of consciousness. Everything unconscious is undifferentiated, and everything that happens unconsciously proceeds on the basis of nondifferentiation—that is to say, there is no determining whether it belongs or does not belong to oneself. It cannot be established *a priori*[8] whether it concerns me, or another, or both. Nor does feeling give us any sure clues in this respect.

An inferior consciousness cannot *eo ipso*[9] be ascribed to women; it is merely different from masculine consciousness. But, just as a woman is often clearly conscious of things which a man is still groping for in the dark, so there are naturally fields of experience in a man which, for woman, are still wrapped in the shadows of nondifferentiation, chiefly things in which she has little interest. Personal relations are as a rule more important and interesting to her than objective facts and their interconnections. The wide fields of commerce, politics, technology, and science, the whole realm of the applied masculine mind, she relegates to the penumbra of consciousness; while, on the other hand, she develops a minute consciousness of personal relationships, the infinite nuances of which usually escape the man entirely. 19

We must therefore expect the unconscious of woman to show aspects essentially different from those found in man. If I were to attempt to put in a nutshell the difference between man and woman in this respect, i.e., what it is that characterizes the animus as opposed 20

---

[7] *Lucien Lévy-Bruhl (1857–1939)* French philosopher, psychologist, and ethnologist. He is especially well known for his studies of the psychology of preliterate peoples.

[8] **a priori** Beforehand.

[9] **eo ipso** In and of itself.

to the anima, I could only say this: as the anima produces *moods,* so the animus produces *opinions;* and as the moods of a man issue from a shadowy background, so the opinions of a woman rest on equally unconscious prior assumptions. Animus opinions very often have the character of solid convictions that are not lightly shaken, or of principles whose validity is seemingly unassailable. If we analyze these opinions, we immediately come upon unconscious assumptions whose existence must first be inferred; that is to say, the opinions are apparently conceived *as though* such assumptions existed. But in reality the opinions are not thought out at all; they exist ready made, and they are held so positively and with so much conviction that the woman never has the shadow of a doubt about them.

One would be inclined to suppose that the animus, like the anima, 21 personifies itself in a single figure. But this, as experience shows, is true only up to a point, because another factor unexpectedly makes its appearance, which brings about an essentially different situation from that existing in a man. The animus does not appear as one person, but as a plurality of persons. In H. G. Wells' novel *Christina Alberta's Father,* the heroine, in all that she does or does not do, is constantly under the surveillance of a supreme moral authority, which tells her with remorseless precision and dry matter-of-factness what she is doing and for what motives. Wells calls this authority a "Court of Conscience." This collection of condemnatory judges, a sort of College of Preceptors, corresponds to a personification of the animus. The animus is rather like an assembly of fathers or dignitaries of some kind who lay down incontestable, "rational," *ex cathedra*[10] judgments. On closer examination these exacting judgments turn out to be largely sayings and opinions scraped together more or less unconsciously from childhood on, and compressed into a canon of average truth, justice, and reasonableness, a compendium of preconceptions which, whenever a conscious and competent judgment is lacking (as not infrequently happens), instantly obliges with an opinion. Sometimes these opinions take the form of so-called sound common sense, sometimes they appear as principles which are like a travesty of education: "People have always done it like this," or "Everybody says it is like that."

It goes without saying that the animus is just as often projected as 22 the anima. The men who are particularly suited to these projections are either walking replicas of God himself, who know all about everything, or else they are misunderstood word-addicts with a vast and

---

[10]**ex cathedra**   From a seat of authority.

windy vocabulary at their command, who translate common or garden reality into the terminology of the sublime. It would be insufficient to characterize the animus merely as a conservative, collective conscience; he is also a neologist who, in flagrant contradiction to his correct opinions, has an extraordinary weakness for difficult and unfamiliar words which act as a pleasant substitute for the odious task of reflection.

Like the anima, the animus is a jealous lover. He is an adept at 23 putting, in place of the real man, an opinion about him, the exceedingly disputable grounds for which are never submitted to criticism. Animus opinions are invariably collective, and they override individuals and individual judgments in exactly the same way as the anima thrusts her emotional anticipations and projections between man and wife. If the woman happens to be pretty, these animus opinions have for the man something rather touching and childlike about them, which makes him adopt a benevolent, fatherly, professorial manner. But if the woman does not stir his sentimental side, and competence is expected of her rather than appealing helplessness and stupidity, then her animus opinions irritate the man to death, chiefly because they are based on nothing but opinion for opinion's sake, and "everybody has a right to his own opinions." Men can be pretty venomous here, for it is an inescapable fact that the animus always plays up the anima—and *vice versa*, of course—so that all further discussion becomes pointless.

In intellectual women the animus encourages a critical disputa- 24 tiousness and would-be highbrowism, which, however, consists essentially in harping on some irrelevant weak point and nonsensically making it the main one. Or a perfectly lucid discussion gets tangled up in the most maddening way through the introduction of a quite different and if possible perverse point of view. Without knowing it, such women are solely intent upon exasperating the man and are, in consequence, the more completely at the mercy of the animus. "Unfortunately I am always right," one of these creatures once confessed to me.

However, all these traits, as familiar as they are unsavory, are sim- 25 ply and solely due to the extraversion of the animus. The animus does not belong to the function of conscious relationship; his function is rather to facilitate relations with the unconscious. Instead of the woman merely associating opinions with external situations—situations which she ought to think about consciously—the animus, as an associative function, should be directed inwards, where it could associate the contents of the unconscious. The technique of coming to terms with the animus is the same in principle as in the case of the anima; only here the woman must learn to criticize and hold her opinions at a distance; not in order to repress them, but, by investigating their origins, to penetrate more deeply into the background, where she will then discover the primordial images, just as the man does in his dealings with the anima. The animus is the deposit, as it were, of all woman's ancestral experiences of man—and not only that, he is also a creative and procreative being, not in the sense of masculine creativity, but in the sense that he brings forth something we might call the λόγος σπερματικός, the spermatic word. Just as a man brings forth his work as a complete creation out of his inner feminine nature, so the inner masculine side of a woman brings forth creative seeds which have the power to fertilize the feminine side of the man. This would be the *femme inspiratrice*[11] who, if falsely cultivated, can turn into the worst kind of dogmatist and high-handed pedagogue—a regular "animus hound," as one of my women patients aptly expressed it.

A woman possessed by the animus is always in danger of losing 26 her femininity, her adapted feminine persona, just as a man in like circumstances runs the risk of effeminacy. These psychic changes of sex are due entirely to the fact that a function which belongs inside has been turned outside. The reason for this perversion is clearly the failure to give adequate recognition to an inner world which stands autonomously opposed to the outer world, and makes just as serious demands on our capacity for adaptation.

With regard to the plurality of the animus as distinguished from 27 what we might call the "uni-personality" of the anima, this remarkable fact seems to me to be a correlate of the conscious attitude. The conscious attitude of woman is in general far more exclusively personal than that of man. Her world is made up of fathers and mothers, brothers and sisters, husbands and children. The rest of the world consists likewise of families, who nod to each other but are, in the main, interested essentially in themselves. The man's world is the nation, the state, business concerns, etc. His family is simply a means to an end, one of the foundations of the state, and his wife is not necessarily *the* woman for him (at any rate not as the woman means it when she says "my man"). The general means more to him than the personal; his world consists of a multitude of co-ordinated factors, whereas her world, outside her husband, terminates in a sort of cosmic mist. A passionate exclusiveness therefore attaches to the man's anima, and

---

[11]**femme inspiratrice** Inspirational woman.

an indefinite variety to the woman's animus. Whereas the man has, floating before him, in clear outlines, the alluring form of a Circe or a Calypso, the animus is better expressed as a bevy of Flying Dutchmen[12] or unknown wanderers from over the sea, never quite clearly grasped, protean, given to persistent and violent motion. These personifications appear especially in dreams, though in concrete reality they can be famous tenors, boxing champions, or great men in faraway, unknown cities.

These two crepuscular figures from the dark hinterland of the psyche—truly the semigrotesque "guardians of the threshold," to use the pompous jargon of theosophy—can assume an almost inexhaustible number of shapes, enough to fill whole volumes. Their complicated transformations are as rich and strange as the world itself, as manifold as the limitless variety of their conscious correlate, the persona. They inhabit the twilight sphere, and we can just make out that the autonomous complex of anima and animus is essentially a psychological function that has usurped, or rather retained, a "personality" only because this function is itself autonomous and undeveloped. But already we can see how it is possible to break up the personifications, since by making them conscious we convert them into bridges to the unconscious. It is because we are not using them purposefully as functions that they remain personified complexes. So long as they are in this state they must be accepted as relatively independent personalities. They cannot be integrated into consciousness while their contents remain unknown. The purpose of the dialectical process is to bring these contents into the light; and only when this task has been completed, and the conscious mind has become sufficiently familiar with the unconscious processes reflected in the anima, will the anima be felt simply as a function.

I do not expect every reader to grasp right away what is meant by animus and anima. But I hope he will at least have gained the impression that it is not a question of anything "metaphysical," but far rather of empirical facts which could equally well be expressed in rational and abstract language. I have purposely avoided too abstract a terminology because, in matters of this kind, which hitherto have been so inaccessible to our experience, it is useless to present the reader with an intellectual formulation. It is far more to the point to give him

---

[12]*Circe . . . Calypso . . . Flying Dutchmen* Circe and Calypso are temptresses in Homer's *Odyssey* who detained or trapped passing seamen. The Flying Dutchman is the captain of a legendary ghost ship; in his ship of the same name, he was condemned to sail the seas until Judgment Day.

some conception of what the actual possibilities of experience are. Nobody can really understand these things unless he has experienced them himself. I am therefore much more interested in pointing out the possible ways to such experience than in devising intellectual formulae which, for lack of experience, must necessarily remain an empty web of words. Unfortunately there are all too many who learn the words by heart and add the experiences in their heads, thereafter abandoning themselves, according to temperament, either to credulity or to criticism. We are concerned here with a new questioning, a new—and yet age-old—field of psychological experience. We shall be able to establish relatively valid theories about it only when the corresponding psychological facts are known to a sufficient number of people. The first things to be discovered are always facts, not theories. Theory-building is the outcome of discussion among many.

QUESTIONS

1. What is Jung's view of the makeup of the personality? Do you feel it is a plausible view?
2. How does Jung define the anima? How does he define the animus?
3. Are you in any way aware of possessing an anima or an animus? Can you detect its presence in others?
4. What is your sense of the unconscious? Have you ever become aware of possessing an unconscious? What can you tell about its nature?
5. Jung uses the term "the other side" in paragraph 13 and elsewhere. What does he seem to mean by it?
6. Is it reasonable to think that the behavior of primitive peoples will give us insights into our psyches? What is Jung's position?
7. Do you agree with Jung that the psyche is not a unity? What convinces you one way or the other?
8. How is the anima "a figure that compensates the masculine consciousness" (para. 17)? In what ways can the animus compensate the feminine consciousness?

WRITING ASSIGNMENTS

1. What is the archetype of the woman for you? Describe the most womanly female you can imagine, considering appearance, special qualities of behavior, effects on the environment and on other people, and kinds of functions that she might fulfill in society. Do you feel that your sense of the archetypal woman is shared by most of the people in your social group?

2. What is the archetype of the man for you? Follow the directions for writing assignment 1, but establish the ideal man rather than the ideal woman.

3. Judging from the films that you regard as classic—films being similar to the myths that ancient peoples believed in—what do you feel are your society's archetypes of male and female? Consider not only their appearance, but also how men and women act and relate to one another. Do you feel it is possible that our society projects its collective archetypes into the films that we all see? What insights into the psychic nature of the society can be gained by examining these projections?

4. One of the possible projections of the anima in Western culture is the witch, the female who possesses mysterious powers and communicates with spirits. Examine the typical pattern of the witch in order to connect it as well as you can to the model of the parent. How similar are the powers of witches to the powers of the mothers of small boys? Is it possible that the archetype of the witch is an expression of the anima?

5. Define the ways in which the anima and the animus seem to function in the psyches of men and women. What does Jung see the anima and the animus doing, and what kinds of problems can each cause? Particularly examine paragraph 20 and the following discussion of the way the animus expresses itself in women.

6. Jung asserts that the psyche is not a unity. His analysis of personality implies a multitude of personalities, as well as the presence of autonomous complexes, such as the animus and the anima. Examine your psyche as frankly as possible and determine whether or not there is evidence in your makeup of a multiplicity of personalities or expressions of personality. If you feel it is impossible to examine your psyche, examine that of someone you know well, preferably someone your age.

7. In what sense can it be said that Jung's views are based on distinctions between the sexes apparent to him? Do you feel these distinctions are as prominent as he makes them out to be? Do you think that they are prominent enough to warrant his identification of the anima and the animus as significant parts of the psyche of every human being?

KAREN HORNEY

---·⟨∞⟩·---

The Distrust
Between the Sexes

KAREN HORNEY (1885–1952) was a distinguished psychiatrist who developed her career somewhat independently of the influence of Sigmund Freud. In her native Germany, she taught in the Berlin Psychoanalytic Institute from the end of World War I until 1932, a year before Hitler officially came to power. She was naturally influenced by Freud's work—as was every other psychoanalyst. But she found that, brilliant as it was, it did not satisfy her on important issues regarding female sexuality.

In Germany, Horney's early research was centered on questions about female psychology. This selection, first published in German in 1931, is part of these early studies. Horney's conclusion was that penis envy, like many other feminine psychological issues, was determined by cultural factors, and that they were not purely psychological or libidinal in origin. She thought Freud oversimplified female sexuality and that the truth, demonstrated through her own analysis, was vastly different. She began a significant theoretical shift that saw neurosis as a product of both psychological and cultural conflicts rather than simply as a product of psychological stress.

She emigrated to America in 1932, and she began writing a distinguished series of publications on neurosis. Her career in Chicago was

From *Feminine Psychology* (1967).

remarkable. Not only did she found the American Institute for Psychoanalysis (1941) and the American Journal of Psychoanalysis, but she also produced such important books as The Neurotic Personality of Our Time (1937); New Ways in Psychoanalysis (1939); and Self-Analysis (1942). Her work was rooted in cultural studies, and among her principal points was the fact that neuroses, including sexual problems, are caused by cultural influences and pressures that the individual simply cannot deal with. Freud thought the reverse, placing the causal force of neuroses in sexuality.

Her studies constantly brought her back to the question of interpersonal relations, and she saw the pressures of failed relationships as resulting from, in many cases, neurotic patterns that developed in childhood. The selection focuses particularly on the relationship that individuals establish with their mother or their father. Her insistence that childhood patterns affect adult behavior is consonant with Freudianism; however, her interpretations are somewhat different. Unlike Freud, she looks toward anthropological studies of behavior to help interpret behavior of modern people in light of such studies.

Horney claims that the distrust between the sexes cannot be explained away as existing only in individuals; rather, it is a widespread fact that must arise because of psychological forces that exist in men and women. She discusses a number of cultural practices in primitive peoples in an effort to suggest that even without the modern cultural trappings that we feel ourselves burdened by, the two sexes suffer anxieties in their relationships. She also looks at the normal relationship of the individual in a family setting, showing that normal expectations of relations between child and parent can sometimes be frustrated and that the result can be seriously harmful.

In addition, she examines the nature of culture, reminding us that early societies were often matriarchal; that is, they were centered not on men and manly activities but on women. Her views about matriarchy are quite suggestive in psychological terms. The mystery of a woman is connected with her biologically creative nature. The envy, as she sees it, is on the part of men, who, in order to compensate for women's capacity to create life, spend their energies creating "state, religion, art, and science" (para. 14).

Horney speaks directly about sexual matters and about what she sees as male anxieties. She holds that there are distinct areas of conflict between men and women, and she contends that they are psychological in origin.

HORNEY'S RHETORIC

This is an expository essay, establishing the truth of hypothesis by pointing to a range of evidence from a variety of sources. Horney's view is that the distrust between the sexes is the result of cultural forces that the individual is only dimly aware of. In this sense, she aligns herself with the Freudians, who constantly point to influences on the individual that are subconscious in nature and, therefore, are not part of the individual's self-awareness.

In a sense, her essay is itself an analysis of the relationship between men and women, with a look back at the history of culture. Her technique—a review of older societies—establishes that the current nature of the relationship between men and women is colored by the fact that modern society is dominated by patriarchal institutions. In ancient times, however, society may well have been matriarchal.

This selection was originally delivered as a lecture to the German Women's Medical Association in November 1930, and most of the audience was female. Consequently, the nature of the imagery, the frankness of the discourse, and the cultural focus is given to issues that would have a distinct impact on women. When we read this essay, we realize that Karen Horney is speaking with particular directness that, were she speaking to a mixed audience, she might have modified.

Her method of writing is analytical, as she tells us several times. She is searching for causes within the culture as well as within the individual, and this is the procedure used in her analysis. Her range of causal analysis is wide, including the comparative study of cultures (ethnology) as well as personal psychology. Her capacity to call on earlier writers and cultures shows an enormous scope. It also helps convince us of the seriousness of her inquiry.

The Distrust
Between the Sexes

As I begin to talk to you today about some problems in the rela- 1
tionship between the sexes, I must ask you not to be disappointed. I

will not concern myself primarily with the aspect of the problem that is most important to the physician. Only at the end will I briefly deal with the question of therapy. I am far more concerned with pointing out to you several psychological reasons for the distrust between the sexes.

The relationship between men and women is quite similar to that 2 between children and parents, in that we prefer to focus on the positive aspects of these relationships. We prefer to assume that love is the fundamentally given factor and that hostility is an accidental and avoidable occurrence. Although we are familiar with slogans such as "the battle of the sexes" and "hostility between the sexes," we must admit that they do not mean a great deal. They make us overfocus on sexual relations between men and women, which can very easily lead us to a too one-sided view. Actually, from our recollection of numerous case histories, we may conclude that love relationships are quite easily destroyed by overt or covert hostility. On the other hand we are only too ready to blame such difficulties on individual misfortune, on incompatibility of the partners, and on social or economic causes.

The individual factors, which we find causing poor relations be- 3 tween men and women, may be the pertinent ones. However, because of the great frequency, or better, the regular occurrence of disturbances in love relations, we have to ask ourselves whether the disturbances in the individual cases might not arise from a common background; whether there are common denominators for this easily and frequently arising suspiciousness between the sexes?

It is almost impossible to attempt within the framework of a brief 4 lecture to give you a complete survey of so large a field. I therefore will not even mention such factors as the origin and effects of such social institutions as marriage. I merely intend to select at random some of the factors that are psychologically understandable and pertain to the causes and effects of the hostility and tension between the sexes.

I would like to start with something very commonplace—namely, 5 that a good deal of this atmosphere of suspiciousness is understandable and even justifiable. It apparently has nothing to do with the individual partner, but rather with the intensity of the affects[1] and with the difficulty of taming them.

We know or may dimly sense, that these affects can lead to ecstasy, 6 to being beside oneself, to surrendering oneself, which means a leap into the unlimited and the boundless. This is perhaps why real passion

---

[1] *affects* Feelings, emotions, or passions.

is so rare. For like a good businessman, we are loath to put all our eggs in one basket. We are inclined to be reserved and ever ready to retreat. Be that as it may, because of our instinct for self preservation, we all have a natural fear of losing ourselves in another person. That is why what happens to love, happens to education and psychoanalysis; everybody thinks he knows all about them, but few do. One is inclined to overlook how little one gives of oneself, but one feels all the more this same deficiency in the partner, the feeling of "You never really loved me." A wife who harbors suicidal thoughts because her husband does not give her all his love, time, and interest, will not notice how much of her own hostility, hidden vindictiveness, and aggression are expressed through her attitude. She will feel only despair because of her abundant "love," while at the same time she will feel most intensely and see most clearly the lack of love in her partner. Even Strindberg[2] [who was a misogynist] defensively managed to say on occasion that he was no woman hater, but that women hated and tortured him.

Here we are not dealing with pathological phenomena at all. In 7 pathological cases we merely see a distortion and exaggeration of a general and normal occurrence. Anybody, to a certain extent, will be inclined to overlook his own hostile impulses, but under pressure of his own guilty conscience, may project them onto the partner. This process must, of necessity, cause some overt or covert distrust of the partner's love, fidelity, sincerity, or kindness. This is the reason why I prefer to speak of distrust between the sexes and not of hatred; for in keeping with our own experience we are more familiar with the feeling of distrust.

A further, almost unavoidable, source of disappointment and dis- 8 trust in our normal love life derives from the fact that the very intensity of our feelings of love stirs up all of our secret expectations and longings for happiness, which slumber deep inside us. All our unconscious wishes, contradictory in their nature and expanding boundlessly on all sides, are waiting here for their fulfillment. The partner is supposed to be strong, and at the same time helpless, to dominate us and be dominated by us, to be ascetic and to be sensuous. He should rape us and be tender, have time for us exclusively and also be intensely involved in creative work. As long as we assume that he could actually fulfill all these expectations, we invest him with the glitter of sexual overestimation. We take the magnitude of such overvaluation for the

---

[2]*August Strindberg (1849–1912)* A Swedish playwright and novelist whose portraits of women were dark and influenced by his misogyny (hatred of women).

measure of our love, while in reality it merely expresses the magnitude of our expectations. The very nature of our claims makes their fulfillment impossible. Herein lies the origin of the disappointments with which we may cope in a more or less effective way. Under favorable circumstances we do not even have to become aware of the great number of our disappointments, just as we have not been aware of the extent of our secret expectations. Yet there remain traces of distrust in us, as in a child who discovers that his father cannot get him the stars from the sky after all.

Thus far, our reflections certainly have been neither new nor specifically analytical and have often been better formulated in the past. The analytical approach begins with the question: What special factors in human development lead to the discrepancy between expectations and fulfillment and what causes them to be of special significance in particular cases? Let us start with a general consideration. There is a basic difference between human and animal development—namely, the long period of the infant's helplessness and dependency. The paradise of childhood is most often an illusion with which adults like to deceive themselves. For the child, however, this paradise is inhabited by too many dangerous monsters. Unpleasant experiences with the opposite sex seem to be unavoidable. We need only recall the capacity that children possess, even in their very early years, for passionate and instinctive sexual desires similar to those of adults and yet different from them. Children are different in the aims of their drives, but above all, in the pristine integrity of their demands. They find it hard to express their desires directly, and where they do, they are not taken seriously. Their seriousness sometimes is looked upon as being cute, or it may be overlooked or rejected. In short, children will undergo painful and humiliating experiences of being rebuffed, being betrayed, and being told lies. They also may have to take second place to a parent or sibling, and they are threatened and intimidated when they seek, in playing with their own bodies, those pleasures that are denied them by adults. The child is relatively powerless in the face of all this. He is not able to ventilate his fury at all, or only to a minor degree, nor can he come to grips with the experience by means of intellectual comprehension. Thus, anger and aggression are pent up within him in the form of extravagant fantasies, which hardly reach the daylight of awareness, fantasies that are criminal when viewed from the standpoint of the adult, fantasies that range from taking by force and stealing, to those about killing, burning, cutting to pieces, and choking. Since the child is vaguely aware of these destructive forces within

him, he feels, according to the talion law,[3] equally threatened by the
adults. Here is the origin of those infantile anxieties of which no child
remains entirely free. This already enables us to understand better the
fear of love of which I have spoken before. Just here, in this most irrational of all areas, the old childhood fears of a threatening father or
mother are reawakened, putting us instinctively on the defensive. In
other words, the fear of love will always be mixed with the fear of
what we might do to the other person, or what the other person might
do to us. A lover in the Aru Islands,[4] for example, will never make a
gift of a lock of hair to his beloved, because should an argument arise,
the beloved might burn it, thus causing the partner to get sick.

I would like to sketch briefly how childhood conflicts may affect   10
the relationship to the opposite sex in later life. Let us take as an example a typical situation: The little girl who was badly hurt through
some great disappointment by her father, will transform her innate
instinctual wish to receive from the man, into a vindictive one of taking from him by force. Thus the foundation is laid for a direct line of
development to a later attitude, according to which she will not only
deny her maternal instincts, but will have only one drive, i.e., to harm
the male, to exploit him, and to suck him dry. She has become a vam-
pire. Let us assume that there is a similar transformation from the
wish to receive to the wish to take away. Let us further assume that
the latter wish was repressed due to anxiety from a guilty conscience;
then we have here the fundamental constellation for the formation of
a certain type of woman who is unable to relate to the male because
she fears that every male will suspect her of wanting something from
him. This really means that she is afraid that he might guess her repressed desires. Or by completely projecting onto him her repressed
wishes, she will imagine that every male merely intends to exploit her,
that he wants from her only sexual satisfaction, after which he will
discard her. Or let us assume that a reaction formation of excessive
modesty will mask the repressed drive for power. We then have the
type of woman who shies away from demanding or accepting anything
from her husband. Such a woman, however, due to the return of the
repressed, will react with depression to the nonfulfillment of her unex-

---

[3]***talion law*** Law which demands that the criminal be given the same punishment
as was suffered by the victim—an eye for an eye.
[4]***Aru Islands*** Islands in Indonesia that were especially interesting for modern anthro-
pologists.

pressed, and often unformulated, wishes. She thus unwittingly jumps from the frying pan into the fire, as does her partner, because a depression will hit him much harder than direct aggression. Quite often the repression of aggression against the male drains all her vital energy. The woman then feels helpless to meet life. She will shift the entire responsibility for her helplessness onto the man, robbing him of the very breath of life. Here you have the type of woman who, under the guise of being helpless and childlike, dominates her man.

These are examples that demonstrate how the fundamental atti- 11
tude of women toward men can be disturbed by childhood conflicts. In an attempt to simplify matters, I have stressed only one point, which, however, seems crucial to me—the disturbance in the development of motherhood.

I shall now proceed to trace certain traits of male psychology. I do 12
not wish to follow individual lines of development, though it might be very instructive to observe analytically how, for instance, even men who consciously have a very positive relationship with women and hold them in high esteem as human beings, harbor deep within themselves a secret distrust of them; and how this distrust relates back to feelings toward their mothers, which they experienced in their formative years. I shall focus rather on certain typical attitudes of men toward women and how they have appeared during various eras of history and in different cultures, not only as regards sexual relationships with women, but also, and often more so, in nonsexual situations, such as in their general evaluation of women.

I shall select some random examples, starting with Adam and Eve. 13
Jewish culture, as recorded in the Old Testament, is outspokenly patriarchal. This fact reflects itself in their religion, which has no maternal goddesses; in their morals and customs, which allow the husband the right to dissolve the marital bond simply by dismissing his wife. Only by being aware of this background can we recognize the male bias in two incidents of Adam's and Eve's history. First of all, woman's capacity to give birth is partly denied and partly devaluated: Eve was made of Adam's rib and a curse was put on her to bear children in sorrow. In the second place, by interpreting her tempting Adam to eat of the tree of knowledge as a sexual temptation, woman appears as the sexual temptress, who plunges man into misery. I believe that these two elements, one born out of resentment, the other out of anxiety, have damaged the relationship between the sexes from the earliest times to the present. Let us follow this up briefly. Man's fear of woman is deeply rooted in sex, as is shown by the simple fact that it is only the sexually attractive woman of whom he is afraid and who,

although he strongly desires her, has to be kept in bondage. Old women, on the other hand, are held in high esteem, even by cultures in which the young woman is dreaded and therefore suppressed. In some primitive cultures the old woman may have the decisive voice in the affairs of the tribe; among Asian nations also she enjoys great power and prestige. On the other hand, in primitive tribes woman is surrounded by taboos during the entire period of her sexual maturity. Women of the Arunta tribe are able to magically influence the male genitals. If they sing to a blade of grass and then point it at a man or throw it at him, he becomes ill or loses his genitals altogether. Women lure him to his doom. In a certain East African tribe, husband and wife do not sleep together, because her breath might weaken him. If a woman of a South African tribe climbs over the leg of a sleeping man, he will be unable to run; hence the general rule of sexual abstinence two to five days prior to hunting, warfare, or fishing. Even greater is the fear of menstruation, pregnancy, and childbirth. Menstruating women are surrounded by extensive taboos—a man who touches a menstruating woman will die. There is one basic thought at the bottom of all this: Woman is a mysterious being who communicates with spirits and thus has magic powers that she can use to hurt the male. He must therefore protect himself against her powers by keeping her subjugated. Thus the Miri in Bengal do not permit their women to eat the flesh of the tiger, lest they become too strong. The Watawela of East Africa keep the art of making fire a secret from their women, lest women become their rulers. The Indians of California have ceremonies to keep their women in submission; a man is disguised as a devil to intimidate the women. The Arabs of Mecca exclude women from religious festivities to prevent familiarity between women and their overlords. We find similar customs during the Middle Ages—the Cult of the Virgin[5] side by side with the burning of witches; the adoration of "pure" motherliness, completely divested of sexuality, next to the cruel destruction of the sexually seductive woman. Here again is the implication of underlying anxiety, for the witch is in communication with the devil. Nowadays, with our more humane forms of aggression, we burn women only figuratively, sometimes with undisguised hatred,

---

[5]**Cult of the Virgin** During the Medieval period (c. 700–1300), the Roman Catholic Church promoted a strong emotional attachment to the Virgin Mary, which resulted in the production of innumerable paintings and sculptures. Horney points out the irony of venerating the mother of God while tormenting human women by burning them at the stake.

sometimes with apparent friendliness. In any case "The Jew must burn."[6] In friendly and secret autos-da-fé,[7] many nice things are said about women, but it is just unfortunate that in her God-given natural state, she is not the equal of the male. Moebius[8] pointed out that the female brain weighs less than the male one, but the point need not be made in so crude a way. On the contrary, it can be stressed that woman is not at all inferior, only different, but that unfortunately she has fewer or none of those human or cultural qualities that man holds in such high esteem. She is said to be deeply rooted in the personal and emotional spheres, which is wonderful; but unfortunately, this makes her incapable of exercising justice and objectivity, therefore disqualifying her for positions in law and government and in the spiritual community. She is said to be at home only in the realm of eros. Spiritual matters are alien to her innermost being, and she is at odds with cultural trends. She therefore is, as Asians frankly state, a second-rate being. Woman may be industrious and useful but is, alas, incapable of productive and independent work. She is, indeed, prevented from real accomplishment by the deplorable, bloody tragedies of menstruation and childbirth. And so every man silently thanks his God, just as the pious Jew does in his prayers, that he was not created a woman.

Man's attitude toward motherhood is a large and complicated chapter. One is generally inclined to see no problem in this area. Even the misogynist is obviously willing to respect woman as a mother and to venerate her motherliness under certain conditions, as mentioned above regarding the Cult of the Virgin. In order to obtain a clearer picture, we have to distinguish between two attitudes: men's attitudes toward motherliness, as represented in its purest form in the Cult of the Virgin, and their attitude toward motherhood as such, as we encounter it in the symbolism of the ancient mother goddesses. Males will always be in favor of motherliness, as expressed in certain spiritual qualities of women, i.e., the nurturing, selfless, self-sacrificing mother; for she is the ideal embodiment of the woman who could ful-

14

---

[6]**"The Jew must burn."**　This is a quote from *Nathan the Wise* by the eighteenth-century German author Gotthold Ephraim Lessing, a humanist and a spokesman for enlightenment and rationality. The expression became a colloquialism. It meant no matter how worthy and well-intentioned his acts, by virtue of being a Jew, a man was guilty. [Translator's note]

[7]*autos-da-fé*　Literally, acts of faith. It was a term used to refer to the hearing at which the Holy Inquisition gave its judgment on a case of heresy, and its most common use is to refer to the burning of heretics at the stake.

[8]*Paul Julius Möbius (1853–1907)*　German neurologist and student of the pathological traits of geniuses such as Rousseau, Goethe, Schopenhauer, and Nietzsche.

fill all his expectations and longings. In the ancient mother goddesses, man did not venerate motherliness in the spiritual sense, but rather motherhood in its most elemental meaning. Mother goddesses are earthy goddesses, fertile like the soil. They bring forth new life and they nurture it. It was this life-creating power of woman, an elemental force, that filled man with admiration. And this is exactly the point where problems arise. For it is contrary to human nature to sustain appreciation without resentment toward capabilities that one does not possess. Thus, a man's minute share in creating new life became, for him, an immense incitement to create something new on his part. He has created values of which he might well be proud. State, religion, art, and science are essentially his creations, and our entire culture bears the masculine imprint.

However, as happens elsewhere, so it does here; even the greatest   15
satisfactions or achievements, if born out of sublimation, cannot fully make up for something for which we are not endowed by nature. Thus there has remained an obvious residue of general resentment of men against women. This resentment expresses itself, also in our times, in men's distrustful defensive maneuvers against the threat of women's invasion of their domains; hence their tendency to devalue pregnancy and childbirth and to overemphasize male genitality. This attitude does not express itself in scientific theories alone, but is also of far-reaching consequence for the entire relationship between the sexes, and for sexual morality in general. Motherhood, especially illegitimate motherhood, is very insufficiently protected by law—with the one exception of a recent attempt at improvement in Russia. Conversely, there is ample opportunity for the fulfillment of the male's sexual needs. Emphasis on irresponsible sexual indulgence, and devaluation of women to an object of purely physical needs, are further consequences of this masculine attitude.

From Bachofen's[9] investigations we know that this state of the cul-   16
tural supremacy of the male has not existed since the beginning of time, but that women once occupied a central position. This was the era of the so-called matriarchy, when law and custom were centered around the mother. Matricide was then, as Sophocles[10] showed in the *Eumenides*, the unforgivable crime, while patricide, by comparison,

---

[9]*J. J. Bachofen (1815–1887)* One of the earliest German ethnologists who proposed, in 1861, that a pattern of matriarchy—in which the female was the dominant figure in society—had existed in the earliest societies.

[10]*Sophocles (496?–406 B.C.)* A great Greek tragedian. However, Horney is probably referring to Aeschylus (525–456 B.C.), who wrote the *Eumenides*, the play she mentions.

was a minor offense. Only in recorded historical times have men begun, with minor variations, to play the leading role in the political, economical, and judicial fields, as well as in the area of sexual morality. At present we seem to be going through a period of struggle in which women once more dare to fight for their equality. This is a phase, the duration of which we are not yet able to survey.

I do not want to be misunderstood as having implied that all disaster results from male supremacy and that relations between the sexes would improve if women were given the ascendency. However, we must ask ourselves why there should have to be any power struggle at all between the sexes. At any given time, the more powerful side will create an ideology suitable to help maintain its position and to make this position acceptable to the weaker one. In this ideology the differentness of the weaker one will be interpreted as inferiority, and it will be proven that these differences are unchangeable, basic, or God's will. It is the function of such an ideology to deny or conceal the existence of a struggle. Here is one of the answers to the question raised initially as to why we have so little awareness of the fact that there is a struggle between the sexes. It is in the interest of men to obscure this fact; and the emphasis they place on their ideologies has caused women, also, to adopt these theories. Our attempt at resolving these rationalizations and at examining these ideologies as to their fundamental driving forces, is merely a step on the road taken by Freud.[11]

I believe that my exposition shows more clearly the origin of resentment than the origin of dread, and I therefore want to discuss briefly the latter problem. We have seen that the male's dread of the female is directed against her as a sexual being. How is this to be understood? The clearest aspect of this dread is revealed by the Arunta tribe. They believe that the woman has the power to magically influence the male genital. This is what we mean by castration anxiety in analysis. It is an anxiety of psychogenic origin that goes back to feelings of guilt and old childhood fears. Its anatomical-psychological nucleus lies in the fact that during intercourse the male has to entrust his genitals to the female body, that he presents her with his semen and interprets this as a surrender of vital strength to the woman, similar to his experiencing the subsiding of erection after intercourse as evidence of having been weakened by the woman. Although the following idea has not been thoroughly worked through yet, it is highly probable, according to analytical and ethnological data, that the relationship to the mother is more strongly and directly associated with

17

18

---

[11]**Sigmund Freud (1856–1939)**   See the introduction to his selection in this part.

the fear of death than the relationship to the father. We have learned to understand the longing for death as the longing for reunion with the mother. In African fairy tales it is a woman who brings death into the world. The great mother goddesses also brought death and destruction. It is as though we were possessed by the idea that the one who gives life is also capable of taking it away. There is a third aspect of the male's dread of the female that is more difficult to understand and to prove, but that can be demonstrated by observing certain recurrent phenomena in the animal world. We can see that the male is quite frequently equipped with certain specific stimulants for attracting the female, or with specific devices for seizing her during sexual union. Such arrangements would be incomprehensible if the female animal possessed equally urgent or abundant sexual needs as does the male. As a matter of fact, we see that the female rejects the male unconditionally, after fertilization has occurred. Although examples taken from the animal world may be applied to human beings only with the greatest of caution, it is permissible, in this context, to raise the following question: Is it possible that the male is sexually dependent on the female to a higher degree than the woman is on him, because in women part of the sexual energy is linked to generative processes? Could it be that men, therefore, have a vital interest in keeping women dependent on them? So much for the factors that seem to be at the root of the great power struggle between men and women, insofar as they are of a psychogenic nature and related to the male.

That many-faceted thing called love succeeds in building bridges 19 from the loneliness on this shore to the loneliness on the other one. These bridges can be of great beauty, but they are rarely built for eternity and frequently they cannot tolerate too heavy a burden without collapsing. Here is the other answer to the question posed initially of why we see love between the sexes more distinctly than we see hate— because the union of the sexes offers us the greatest possibilities for happiness. We therefore are naturally inclined to overlook how powerful are the destructive forces that continually work to destroy our chances for happiness.

We might ask in conclusion, how can analytical insights contribute 20 to diminish the distrust between the sexes? There is no uniform answer to this problem. The fear of the power of the affects and the difficulty in controlling them in a love relationship, the resulting conflict between surrender and self-preservation, between the I and the Thou[12]

---

[12]*the I and the Thou*   A reference to Martin Buber's book *I and Thou*. Buber (1878–1965), a Jewish theologian and philosopher, is associated with modern existentialism.

is an entirely comprehensible, unmitigatable, and as it were, normal phenomenon. The same thing applies in essence to our readiness for distrust, which stems from unresolved childhood conflicts. These childhood conflicts, however, can vary greatly in intensity, and will leave behind traces of variable depth. Analysis not only can help in individual cases to improve the relationship with the opposite sex, but it can also attempt to improve the psychological conditions of childhood and forestall excessive conflicts. This, of course, is our hope for the future. In the momentous struggle for power, analysis can fulfill an important function by uncovering the real motives of this struggle. This uncovering will not eliminate the motives, but it may help to create a better chance for fighting the struggle on its own ground instead of relegating it to peripheral issues.

QUESTIONS

1. Is it true that there is hostility between the sexes?
2. What are some of the most important childhood experiences that can affect adult behavior toward the opposite sex?
3. This selection was a lecture delivered in Germany in 1930. To what extent do its concerns seem to be no longer relevant? To what extent are the concerns Horney cites still relevant?
4. Do you think this essay will promote better relations between men and women?
5. What kinds of expectations do women seem to have of men? What kinds do men have of women? Do their expectations tend to contribute to hostility in specific ways? Think about Horney's description of expectations in paragraph 8.
6. How do the examples of behavior in primitive cultures contribute to an understanding of the relationship between the sexes in our culture?
7. Is Horney pessimistic or optimistic about relationships between the sexes?

WRITING ASSIGNMENTS

1. In paragraph 9, Horney says that unpleasant experiences with the opposite sex are unavoidable. Is this true? What unpleasant experiences have you had with the opposite sex? What unpleasant experiences have you observed?
2. Horney mentions that the intensity of our feelings can stir up secret longings for, and expectations of, the opposite sex (para. 8). What kinds of secret expectations do you feel each sex might have about the other in a

relationship? Why would such expectations remain secret? Does the fact of secrecy contribute to problems? Does it contribute to hostility?

3. Deep in the essay, in paragraph 14, Horney talks about the possibility of envy contributing to the hostility between the sexes. She says, "For it is contrary to human nature to sustain appreciation without resentment toward capabilities that one does not possess." Do you think she is correct? And do you think she is correct in assuming that envy may have something to do with the hostility between the sexes? Examine your own experience to see whether you recall instances of envy on your part toward a member of the opposite sex (or vice versa).

4. At one point Horney says that "Man's fear of woman is deeply rooted in sex" (para. 13). Is this true? Is woman's fear of man deeply rooted in sex? Examine this question by comparing at least two, and preferably four, magazines for their revelations concerning the psychology of men and women. Choose two men's magazines and two women's magazines. Compare their visual material, particularly photographs of members of the opposite sex. Also compare the fiction and look for signs of a specifically male or female form of fantasy. Compare the advertising to see how distinct the interests of men and women are—and try to relate these to psychological concerns.

5. Horney is very direct in her discussion of male dominance in society, saying not only that it exists but asking "could it be that men, therefore, have a vital interest in keeping women dependent on them?" (para. 18). Do you feel this is true? Conduct an interview with one man and one woman. Find out whether they feel the same or whether they feel differently about this question. Ask them if they see an effort on the part of men to keep women dependent, and then ask them what form any such dependency takes. Do their opinions agree? Where do you stand on this issue?

6. At one point, Horney discusses the question of how different men are from women. Write an essay in which you show the extent to which women are different from men. If possible, sample others' opinions and see if they feel that there are important differences. To what extent would differences between men and women contribute toward hostility?

7. How would you characterize Horney's disagreements with Freud and Jung? What are the issues that she most clearly targets, and what success do you feel she has achieved in her debate? Do you find that Horney agrees more with Simone de Beauvoir, or is she in a camp all by herself? Isolate three or more specific issues from her discussion that might elucidate her position in relation to Freud, Jung, or Beauvoir.

B. F. SKINNER

What Is Man?

BURRHUS FREDERIC SKINNER (b. 1904) is an experimental psychologist known for his theories of behaviorism. Behavioral psychology focuses on the ways animals and people behave in response to the myriad complexities of their physical and psychological environment. Skinner's thought has moved in interesting directions, particularly in dealing with the questions of freedom. To some extent, he holds, freedom is not entirely desirable in modern society. It is something that we can outgrow.

Skinner's emphasis is on the reaction of the individual to the world in which he is placed, and to some extent Skinner sees the individual as a function of that world, as a person whose behavior is essentially created by reinforcement. Reinforcement may be aversive: punishment, such as a spanking, loss of a job, imprisonment. It may be positive: praise, a new job, greater privileges. The "contingencies of reinforcement," an expression he uses often in the present selection, can be aversive, positive, or both. Whatever form they take, they will create the personal behavior of most (if not all) individuals. In posing the question "What is man?" Skinner consciously raises

From *Beyond Freedom and Dignity* (1971).

questions that have been addressed throughout the ages, from ancient Greek philosophers to modern theologians. In answering the
question, he is trying to point the way to a new vision.

He calls his vision a scientific view of mankind. By calling it that
he includes in his thinking the results of a considerable body of research into the behavior of lower animals as well as of human beings.
He has studied the contingencies of reinforcement that have produced
learning, which has, in turn, produced behavior of various sorts. To
some extent, Skinner's scientific approach has postulated a view of
the individual as not being the autonomous agent one would ordinarily assume. The "autonomous agent"—another of Skinner's key terms
in this selection—feels able to do anything that free will dictates. The
autonomous agent seems to be free and independent. But Skinner
points out that such freedom and independence are to some extent
illusions. The culture, the family, the peer group, even the prejudices and ignorances of the individual—all combine as contingencies
of reinforcement not only to reduce but actually to erase the autonomy of the individual. "Autonomy," in this sense, refers to the individual, personally controlled behavior that each person (as well as
each squirrel, rat, and lower animal) feels he or she has.

Naturally, Skinner's views are not wholeheartedly endorsed by
most people who adhere to a more traditional view of humankind.
Skinner seems heartless and, perhaps, merely scientific. Yet, Skinner's claims suggest that he is most interested in pulling aside the veil
of illusion that makes us feel we are free and makes us accept the
unconsciously imposed limits on freedom that most of us do. As he
points out, cultures have long agreed to maintain certain fictions in
order to explain something about the forces that act on people. The
Greeks concerned themselves with the gods and with fate. The Christian view focuses on Jesus and God's providence. The eighteenth-century philosophers thought of the world in terms of a machine and
believed that there was an ascertainable range of causes and effects
that controls people's behavior. Skinner's view is different. He sees
people as learning to adapt to an environment without even realizing
that they do so. The invisible or unconscious aspects of this process
of adaptation are the things that Skinner hopes we will begin to understand.

SKINNER'S RHETORIC

The most obvious rhetorical device Skinner uses is the rhetorical
question: What is man? The rest of the essay is, quite logically, an

answer to that question. In the first sentences of the first paragraph, Skinner shifts the ground of the discussion by establishing that the question must be answered, not by looking mainly at the person, but by looking at the environment in which the person thrives. However, used to criticism of the simplified environmentalism that dominated nineteenth-century thought, he begins to clarify the entire nature of environment by examining the ways in which it begins to take over the function of direction, which had been thought to be the preserve only of the individual. He then goes on to examine traits of character, which are generally thought to reside only within the individual, and to show how they, too, are dependent upon the environment.

Even the extent to which the world can be known is brought into question by Skinner (paras. 8–18), and the issues concerning words and the way they work to affect our sense of knowledge are clarified. From there, Skinner addresses the question of thinking, which he calls "the last stronghold of autonomous man." Thinking is something people share with other beings, as Skinner shows, and certain kinds of misunderstanding, shown to be buried in the "metaphor of storage" (paras. 23–29) in which it is assumed that a person can "possess" knowledge, his or her past, culture, even his or her character. This thinking leads to a consideration of the self (paras. 32–38) and to a rejection of low-grade views of man as a machine (paras. 39–41). In four paragraphs, Skinner discusses the question of direction and purpose in life (paras. 42–45), and then he springs an interesting trap. The chapter to that point had been clearly predicting the doom of autonomous man, with whom the reader has been led to identify. But in the beginning of paragraph 46 he says, "It is only autonomous man who has reached a dead end. Man himself may be controlled by his environment, but it is an environment which is almost wholly of his own making."

The point Skinner wishes to make in answering the question he poses is that until we realize the truth of what it means for autonomous man to be given up as a worn-out fiction, we will misunderstand our own nature. When Socrates insisted that we must know ourselves in order to function in the world, he raised the same issues Skinner has raised. But Skinner's answers to the most basic question—What is man?—are somewhat different from any we have heard before.

What Is Man?

As a science of behavior adopts the strategy of physics and biology, 1
the autonomous agent[1] to which behavior has traditionally been attributed is replaced by the environment—the environment in which the
species evolved and in which the behavior of the individual is shaped
and maintained. The vicissitudes of "environmentalism" show how
difficult it has been to make this change. That a man's behavior owes
something to antecedent events and that the environment is a more
promising point of attack than man himself has long been recognized.
As Crane Brinton observed, "a program to change things not just to
convert people" was a significant part of the English, French, and Russian revolutions.[2] It was Robert Owen,[3] according to Trevelyan, who
first "clearly grasped and taught that environment makes character and
that environment is under human control" or, as Gilbert Seldes[4]
wrote, "that man is a creature of circumstance, that if you changed the
environments of thirty little Hottentots and thirty little aristocratic
English children, the aristocrats would become Hottentots, for all
practical purposes, and the Hottentots little conservatives."

The evidence for a crude environmentalism is clear enough. People 2
are extraordinarily different in different places, and possibly just because of the places. The nomad on horseback in Outer Mongolia and
the astronaut in outer space are different people, but, as far as we
know, if they had been exchanged at birth, they would have taken each
other's place. (The expression "change places" shows how closely we

---

[1]*autonomous agent* Skinner's term for the individual who feels he is a free agent
directed by his own will and basically undirected by outside forces.

[2]*revolutions* The English "Glorious Revolution" of 1688 introduced a constitutional
monarchy; the French Revolution, 1789, created a republic (for a time); the Russian Revolution, 1917, introduced a communist government.

[3]*Robert Owen (1771–1858)* A Welsh industrialist and reformer who brought better living conditions and education to workers at his cotton mills in New Lanark, England, agitated for improved working conditions throughout England, and supported the
new labor union movement. Owen's social thought can be seen in his *A New View of
Society* (1813). In 1825 he founded a utopian community in the United States, at New
Harmony, Indiana, but it failed, and he lost most of his fortune.

[4]*. . . Gilbert Seldes* Crane Brinton, G. M. Trevelyan, and Seldes are all writers
on history, behavior, and thought.

identify a person's behavior with the environment in which it occurs.) But we need to know a great deal more before that fact becomes useful. What is it about the environment that produces a Hottentot? And what would need to be changed to produce an English conservative instead?

Both the enthusiasm of the environmentalist and his usually ig- 3
nominious failure are illustrated by Owen's utopian experiment at New Harmony. A long history of environmental reform—in education, penology, industry, and family life, not to mention government and religion—has shown the same pattern. Environments are constructed on the model of environments in which good behavior has been observed, but the behavior fails to appear. Two hundred years of this kind of environmentalism has very little to show for itself, and for a simple reason. We must know how the environment works before we can change it to change behavior. A mere shift in emphasis from man to environment means very little.

Let us consider some examples in which the environment takes 4
over the function and role of autonomous man. The first, often said to involve human nature, is *aggression.* Men often act in such a way that they harm others, and they often seem to be reinforced by signs of damage to others. The ethologists[5] have emphasized contingencies of survival which would contribute these features to the genetic endowment of the species, but the contingencies of reinforcement in the lifetime of the individual are also significant, since anyone who acts aggressively to harm others is likely to be reinforced in other ways—for example, by taking possession of goods. The contingencies explain the behavior quite apart from any state or feeling of aggression or any initiating act by autonomous man.

Another example involving a so-called "trait of character" is *indus-* 5
try. Some people are industrious in the sense that they work energetically for long periods of time, while others are lazy and idle in the sense that they do not. "Industry" and "laziness" are among thousands of so-called "traits." The behavior they refer to can be explained in other ways. Some of it may be attributed to genetic idiosyncrasies (and subject to change only through genetic measures), and the rest to environmental contingencies, which are much more important than is usually realized. Regardless of any normal genetic endowment, an organism will range between vigorous activity and complete quiescence

---

[5]*ethologists* Those who study the formation and evolution of the human *ethos,* that is, the moral nature or guiding principles of a human group.

depending upon the schedules on which it has been reinforced. The explanation shifts from a trait of character to an environmental history of reinforcement.

A third example, a "cognitive" activity, is *attention*. A person responds only to a small part of the stimuli impinging upon him. The traditional view is that he himself determines which stimuli are to be effective by "paying attention" to them. Some kind of inner gatekeeper is said to allow some stimuli to enter and to keep all others out. A sudden or strong stimulus may break through and "attract" attention, but the person himself seems otherwise to be in control. An analysis of the environmental circumstances reverses the relation. The kinds of stimuli which break through by "attracting attention" do so because they have been associated in the evolutionary history of the species or the personal history of the individual with important—e.g., dangerous—things. Less forceful stimuli attract attention only to the extent that they have figured in contingencies of reinforcement. We can arrange contingencies which ensure that an organism—even such a "simple" organism as a pigeon—will attend to one object and not to another, or to one property of an object, such as its color, and not to another, such as its shape. The inner gatekeeper is replaced by the contingencies to which the organism has been exposed and which select the stimuli to which it reacts. 6

In the traditional view a person perceives the world around him and acts upon it to make it known to him. In a sense he reaches out and grasps it. He "takes it in" and possesses it. He "knows" it in the Biblical sense in which a man knows a woman. It has even been argued that the world would not exist if no one perceived it. The action is exactly reversed in an environmental analysis. There would, of course, be no perception if there were no world to be perceived, but an existing world would not be perceived if there were no appropriate contingencies. We say that a baby perceives his mother's face and knows it. Our evidence is that the baby responds in one way to his mother's face and in other ways to other faces or other things. He makes this distinction not through some mental act of perception but because of prior contingencies. Some of these may be contingencies of survival. Physical features of a species are particularly stable parts of the environment in which a species evolves. (That is why courtship and sex and relations between parent and offspring are given such a prominent place by ethologists.) The face and facial expressions of the human mother have been associated with security, warmth, food, and other important things, during both the evolution of the species and the life of the child. 7

We learn to perceive in the sense that we learn to respond to things   8
in particular ways because of the contingencies of which they are a
part. We may perceive the sun, for example, simply because it is an
extremely powerful stimulus, but it has been a permanent part of the
environment of the species throughout its evolution and more specific
behavior with respect to it could have been selected by contingencies
of survival (as it has been in many other species). The sun also figures
in many current contingencies of reinforcement: we move into or out
of sunlight depending on the temperature; we wait for the sun to rise
or set to take practical action; we talk about the sun and its effects;
and we eventually study the sun with the instruments and methods of
science. Our perception of the sun depends on what we do with respect
to it. Whatever we do, and hence however we perceive it, the fact remains that it is the environment which acts upon the perceiving person, not the perceiving person who acts upon the environment.

The perceiving and knowing which arise from verbal contingencies   9
are even more obviously products of the environment. We react to an
object in many practical ways because of its color; thus, we pick and
eat red apples of a particular variety but not green. It is clear that we
can "tell the difference" between red and green, but something more
is involved when we say that we *know* that one apple is red and the
other green. It is tempting to say that knowing is a cognitive process
altogether divorced from action, but the contingencies provide a more
useful distinction. When someone asks about the color of an object
which he cannot see, and we tell him that it is red, *we* do nothing
about the object in any other way. It is the person who has questioned
us and heard our answer who makes a practical response which depends on color. Only under verbal contingencies can a speaker respond
to an isolated property to which a nonverbal response cannot be made.
A response made to the property of an object without responding to
the object in any other way is called *abstract*. Abstract thinking is the
product of a particular kind of environment, not of a cognitive faculty.

As listeners we acquire a kind of knowledge from the verbal behav-   10
ior of others which may be extremely valuable in permitting us to
avoid direct exposure to contingencies. We learn from the experience
of others by responding to what they say about contingencies. When
we are warned against doing something or are advised to do something,
there may be no point in speaking of knowledge, but when we learn
more durable kinds of warnings and advice in the form of maxims or
rules, we may be said to have a special kind of knowledge about the
contingencies to which they apply. The laws of science are descriptions of contingencies of reinforcement, and one who knows a scien-

tific law may behave effectively without being exposed to the contingencies it describes. (He will, of course, have very different feelings about the contingencies, depending on whether he is following a rule or has been directly exposed to them. Scientific knowledge is "cold," but the behavior to which it gives rise is as effective as the "warm" knowledge which comes from personal experience.)

Isaiah Berlin has referred to a particular sense of knowing, said to   11
have been discovered by Giambattista Vico.[6] It is "the sense in which I know what it is to be poor, to fight for a cause, belong to a nation, to join or abandon a church or a party, to feel nostalgia, terror, the omnipresence of a god, to understand a gesture, a work of art, a joke, a man's character, that one is transformed or lying to oneself." These are the kinds of things one is likely to learn through direct contact with contingencies rather than from the verbal behavior of others, and special kinds of feelings are no doubt associated with them, but, even so, the knowledge is not somehow directly given. A person can know what it is to fight for a cause only after a long history during which he has learned to perceive and to know that state of affairs called fighting for a cause.

The role of the environment is particularly subtle when what is   12
known is the knower himself. If there is no external world to initiate knowing, must we not then say that the knower himself acts first? This is, of course, the field of consciousness, or awareness, a field which a scientific analysis of behavior is often accused of ignoring. The charge is a serious one and should be taken seriously. Man is said to differ from the other animals mainly because he is "aware of his own existence." He knows what he is doing; he knows that he has had a past and will have a future; he "reflects on his own nature"; he alone follows the classical injunction "Know thyself." Any analysis of human behavior which neglected these facts would be defective indeed. And some analyses do. What is called "methodological behaviorism" limits itself to what can be publicly observed; mental processes may exist, but they are ruled out of scientific consideration by their nature. The "behavioralists" in political science and many logical positivists[7] in philosophy have followed a similar line. But self-observation can be studied, and it must be included in any reasonably complete account

---

[6]*Giovanni Battista Vico (1668–1744)* Italian philosopher whose theories of history involve cycles of repetition of behavior. Sir Isaiah Berlin (b. 1909) is a British historian of ideas and philosopher.

[7]*logical positivists* Twentieth-century thinkers who felt human knowledge was limited to only those things that could be known from observation.

of human behavior. Rather than ignore consciousness, an experimental analysis of behavior has stressed certain crucial issues. The question is not whether a man can know himself but what he knows when he does so.

The problem arises in part from the indisputable fact of privacy: a 13 small part of the universe is enclosed within a human skin. It would be foolish to deny the existence of that private world, but it is also foolish to assert that because it is private it is of a different nature from the world outside. The difference is not in the stuff of which the private world is composed, but in its accessibility. There is an exclusive intimacy about a headache, or heartache, or a silent soliloquy. The intimacy is sometimes distressing (one cannot shut one's eyes to a headache), but it need not be, and it has seemed to support the doctrine that knowing is a kind of possession.

The difficulty is that although privacy may bring the knower closer 14 to what he knows, it interferes with the process through which he comes to know anything. As we saw in [an earlier chapter], the contingencies under which a child learns to describe his feelings are necessarily defective; the verbal community cannot use the procedures with which it teaches a child to describe objects. There are, of course, natural contingencies under which we learn to respond to private stimuli, and they generate behavior of great precision; we could not jump or walk or turn a handspring if we were not being stimulated by parts of our own body. But very little awareness is associated with this kind of behavior and, in fact, we behave in these ways most of the time without being aware of the stimuli to which we are responding. We do not attribute awareness to other species which obviously use similar private stimuli. To "know" private stimuli is more than to respond to them.

The verbal community specializes in self-descriptive contingen- 15 cies. It asks such questions as: What did you do yesterday? What are you doing now? What will you do tomorrow? Why did you do that? Do you really want to do that? How do you feel about that? The answers help people to adjust to each other effectively. And it is because such questions are asked that a person responds to himself and his behavior in the special way called knowing or being aware. Without the help of a verbal community all behavior would be unconscious. Consciousness is a social product. It is not only *not* the special field of autonomous man, it is *not* within range of a solitary man.

And it is not within the range of accuracy of anyone. The privacy 16 which seems to confer intimacy upon self-knowledge makes it impossible for the verbal community to maintain precise contingencies. Introspective vocabularies are by nature inaccurate, and that is one reason why they have varied so widely among schools of philosophy and psychology. Even a carefully trained observer runs into trouble when new private stimuli are studied. (Independent evidence of private stimulation—for example, through physiological measures—would make it possible to sharpen the contingencies which generate self-observation and would, incidentally, confirm the present interpretation. Such evidence would not, as we noted in [an earlier chapter], offer any support for a theory which attributed human behavior to an observable inner agent.)

Theories of psychotherapy which emphasize awareness assign a 17 role to autonomous man which is properly, and much more effectively, reserved for contingencies of reinforcement. Awareness may help if the problem is in part a lack of awareness, and "insight" into one's condition may help if one then takes remedial action, but awareness or insight alone is not always enough, and it may be too much. One need not be aware of one's behavior or the conditions controlling it in order to behave effectively—or ineffectively. On the contrary, as the toad's inquiry of the centipede demonstrates, constant self-observation may be a handicap. The accomplished pianist would perform badly if he were as clearly aware of his behavior as the student who is just learning to play.

Cultures are often judged by the extent to which they encourage 18 self-observation. Some cultures are said to breed unthinking men, and Socrates[8] has been admired for inducing men to inquire into their own nature, but self-observation is only a preliminary to action. The extent to which a man *should* be aware of himself depends upon the importance of self-observation for effective behavior. Self-knowledge is valuable only to the extent that it helps to meet the contingencies under which it has arisen.

Perhaps the last stronghold of autonomous man is that complex 19 "cognitive" activity called thinking. Because it is complex, it has yielded only slowly to explanation in terms of contingencies of reinforcement. When we say that a person *discriminates* between red and orange, we imply that discrimination is a kind of mental act. The

---

[8]*Socrates (469?–399 B.C.)* Greek philosopher. Socrates insisted upon rigorous self-examination no matter what the cost. He was put to death for "corrupting the youth" of Athens, which may indicate the problems inherent in promoting individualism in certain societies.

person himself does not seem to be doing anything; he responds in different ways to red and orange stimuli, but this is the result of discrimination rather than the act. Similarly, we say that a person *generalizes*—say, from his own limited experience to the world at large— but all we see is that he responds to the world at large as he has learned to respond to his own small world. We say that a person *forms a concept or an abstraction*, but all we see is that certain kinds of contingencies of reinforcement have brought a response under the control of a single property of a stimulus. We say that a person *recalls* or *remembers* what he has seen or heard, but all we see is that the present occasion evokes a response, possibly in weakened or altered form, acquired on another occasion. We say that a person *associates* one word with another, but all we observe is that one verbal stimulus evokes the response previously made to another. Rather than suppose that it is therefore autonomous man who discriminates, generalizes, forms concepts or abstractions, recalls or remembers, and associates, we can put matters in good order simply by noting that these terms do not refer to forms of behavior.

A person may take explicit action, however, when he solves a prob- 20 lem. In putting a jigsaw puzzle together he may move the pieces around to improve his chances of finding a fit. In solving an equation he may transpose, clear fractions, and extract roots to improve his chances of finding a form of the equation he has already learned how to solve. The creative artist may manipulate a medium until something of interest turns up. Much of this can be done covertly, and it is then likely to be assigned to a different dimensional system, but it can always be done overtly, perhaps more slowly but also often more effectively, and with rare exceptions it must have been learned in overt form. The culture promotes thinking by constructing special contingencies. It teaches a person to make fine discriminations by making differential reinforcement more precise. It teaches techniques to be used in solving problems. It provides rules which make it unnecessary to be exposed to the contingencies from which the rules are derived, and it provides rules for finding rules.

Self-control, or self-management, is a special kind of problem solv- 21 ing which, like self-knowledge, raises all the issues associated with privacy. We have discussed some techniques in connection with aversive control in [an earlier chapter]. It is always the environment which builds the behavior with which problems are solved, even when the problems are to be found in the private world inside the skin. None of this has been investigated in a very productive way, but the inadequacy of our analysis is no reason to fall back on a miracle-working mind. If our understanding of contingencies of reinforcement is not yet sufficient to explain all kinds of thinking, we must remember that the appeal to mind explains nothing at all.

In shifting control from autonomous man to the observable envi- 22 ronment we do not leave an empty organism. A great deal goes on inside the skin, and physiology will eventually tell us more about it. It will explain why behavior is indeed related to the antecedent events of which it can be shown to be a function. The assignment is not always correctly understood. Many physiologists regard themselves as looking for the "physiological correlates" of mental events. Physiological research is regarded as simply a more scientific version of introspection. But physiological techniques are not, of course, designed to detect or measure personalities, ideas, attitudes, feelings, impulses, thoughts, or purposes. (If they were, we should have to answer a third question in addition to those raised in [an earlier chapter]: How can a personality, idea, feeling, or purpose affect the instruments of the physiologist?) At the moment neither introspection nor physiology supplies very adequate information about what is going on inside a man as he behaves, and since they are both directed inward, they have the same effect of diverting attention from the external environment.

Much of the misunderstanding about an inner man comes from the 23 metaphor of storage. Evolutionary and environmental histories change an organism, but they are not stored within it. Thus, we observe that babies suck their mothers' breasts, and we can easily imagine that a strong tendency to do so has survival value, but much more is implied by a "sucking instinct" regarded as something a baby possesses which enables it to suck. The concept of "human nature" or "genetic endowment" is dangerous when taken in that sense. We are closer to human nature in a baby than in an adult, or in a primitive culture than in an advanced, in the sense that environmental contingencies are less likely to have obscured the genetic endowment, and it is tempting to dramatize that endowment by implying that earlier stages have survived in concealed form: man is a naked ape, and "the paleolithic bull which survives in man's inner self still paws the earth whenever a threatening gesture is made on the social scene." But anatomists and physiologists will not find an ape, or a bull, or for that matter instincts. They will find anatomical and physiological features which are the product of an evolutionary history.

The personal history of the individual is also often said to be stored 24 within him. For "instinct" read "habit." The cigarette habit is presumably something more than the behavior said to show that a person possesses it; but the only other information we have concerns the reinforcers and the schedules of reinforcement which make a person smoke a great deal. The contingencies are not stored; they have simply left a changed person.

The environment is often said to be stored in the form of memo- 25 ries: to recall something we search for a copy of it, which can then be seen as the original thing was seen. As far as we know, however, there are no copies of the environment in the individual *at any time*, even when a thing is present and being observed. The products of more complex contingencies are also said to be stored; the repertoire acquired as a person learns to speak French is called a "knowledge of French."

Traits of character, whether derived from contingencies of survival 26 or contingencies of reinforcement, are also said to be stored. A curious example occurs in Follett's *Modern American Usage:* "We say *He faced these adversities bravely,* aware without thought that the bravery is a property of the man, not of the facing; a brave act is poetic shorthand for the act of a person who shows bravery by performing it." But we call a man brave because of his acts, and he behaves bravely when environmental circumstances induce him to do so. The circumstances have changed his behavior; they have not implanted a trait or virtue.

Philosophies are also spoken of as things possessed. A man is said 27 to speak or act in certain ways because he has a particular philosophy—such as idealism, dialectical materialism, or Calvinism.[9] Terms of this kind summarize the effect of environmental conditions which it would now be hard to trace, but the conditions must have existed and should not be ignored. A person who possesses a "philosophy of freedom" is one who has been changed in certain ways by the literature of freedom.

The issue has had a curious place in theology. Does man sin be- 28 cause he is sinful, or is he sinful because he sins? Neither question points to anything very useful. To say that a man is sinful because he sins is to give an operational definition of sin. To say that he sins because he is sinful is to trace his behavior to a supposed inner trait. But whether or not a person engages in the kind of behavior called

---

[9]*idealism, dialectical materialism, or Calvinism Idealism* is the belief that reality is found in ideas rather than objects themselves; *dialectical materialism* is a Marxian belief in the conflict and resolution of powerful forces as well as a belief in material values and their reality; *Calvinism* is a strict Protestant religion which insists that people are totally depraved and only a few will be saved by the grace of God. All these philosophies have strong adherents today.

sinful depends upon circumstances which are not mentioned in either question. The sin assigned as an inner possession (the sin a person "knows") is to be found in a history of reinforcement. (The expression "God-fearing" suggests such a history, but piety, virtue, the immanence of God, a moral sense, or morality does not. As we have seen, man is not a moral animal in the sense of possessing a special trait or virtue; he has built a kind of social environment which induces him to behave in moral ways.)

These distinctions have practical implications. A recent survey of white Americans is said to have shown that "more than half blamed the inferior educational and economic status of blacks on 'something about Negroes themselves.'" The "something" was further identified as "lack of motivation," which was to be distinguished from *both* genetic and environmental factors. Significantly, motivation was said to be associated with "free will." To neglect the role of the environment in this way is to discourage any inquiry into the defective contingencies responsible for a "lack of motivation."   29

It is in the nature of an experimental analysis of human behavior that it should strip away the functions previously assigned to autonomous man and transfer them one by one to the controlling environment. The analysis leaves less and less for autonomous man to do. But what about man himself? Is there not something about a person which is more than a living body? Unless something called a self survives, how can we speak of self-knowledge or self-control? To whom is the injunction "Know thyself" addressed?   30

It is an important part of the contingencies to which a young child is exposed that his own body is the only part of his environment which remains the same *(idem)* from moment to moment and day to day. We say that he discovers his *identity* as he learns to distinguish between his body and the rest of the world. He does this long before the community teaches him to call things by name and to distinguish "me" from "it" or "you."   31

A self is a repertoire of behavior appropriate to a given set of contingencies. A substantial part of the conditions to which a person is exposed may play a dominant role, and under other conditions a person may report, "I'm not myself today," or, "I couldn't have done what you said I did, because that's not like me." The identity conferred upon a self arises from the contingencies responsible for the behavior. Two or more repertoires generated by different sets of contingencies compose two or more selves. A person possesses one repertoire appropriate to his life with his friends and another appropriate to his life   32 with his family, and a friend may find him a very different person if he sees him with his family or his family if they see him with his friends. The problem of identity arises when situations are intermingled, as when a person finds himself with both his family and his friends at the same time.

Self-knowledge and self-control imply two selves in this sense. The self-knower is almost always a product of social contingencies, but the self that is known may come from other sources. The controlling self (the conscience or superego) is of social origin, but the controlled self is more likely to be the product of genetic susceptibilities to reinforcement (the id, or the Old Adam). The controlling self generally represents the interests of others, the controlled self the interests of the individual.

The picture which emerges from a scientific analysis *is* not of a body with a person inside, but of a body which *is* a person in the sense that it displays a complex repertoire of behavior. The picture is, of course, unfamiliar. The man thus portrayed is a stranger, and from the traditional point of view he may not seem to be a man at all. "For at least one hundred years," said Joseph Wood Krutch,[10] "we have been prejudiced in every theory, including economic determinism, mechanistic behaviorism, and relativism, that reduces the stature of man until he ceases to be man at all in any sense that the humanists of an earlier generation would recognize." Matson has argued that "the empirical behavioral scientist . . . denies, if only by implication, that a unique being, called Man, exists." "What is now under attack," said Maslow, "is the 'being' of man." C. S. Lewis[11] put it quite bluntly: Man is being abolished.

There is clearly some difficulty in identifying the man to whom these expressions refer. Lewis cannot have meant the human species, for not only is it not being abolished, it is filling the earth. (As a result it may eventually abolish itself through disease, famine, pollution, or a nuclear holocaust, but that is not what Lewis meant.) Nor are individual men growing less effective or productive. We are told that what

33

34

35

---

[10]*Joseph Wood Krutch (1893–1970)* American critic and writer whose books and essays on nature were famed. His most famous book is *The Measure of Man* (1954). He also wrote *Henry David Thoreau* (1948), a highly regarded biography and appreciation.

[11]*Abraham Maslow (1908–1970) and C. S. Lewis (1898–1963)* Widely known as writers on human values. Maslow, an American psychologist, based his thinking on a hierarchy of human needs, from survival at the bottom to self-actualization at the top. Lewis, an English critic and novelist, was one of the foremost twentieth-century spokesmen for orthodox Christian belief.

is threatened is "man *qua*[12] man" or "man in his humanity," or "man as Thou not It," or "man as a person not a thing." These are not very helpful expressions, but they supply a clue. What is being abolished is autonomous man—the inner man, the homunculus,[13] the possessing demon, the man defended by the literatures of freedom and dignity.

His abolition has long been overdue. Autonomous man is a device used to explain what we cannot explain in any other way. He has been constructed from our ignorance, and as our understanding increases, the very stuff of which he is composed vanishes. Science does not de-humanize man, it de-homunculizes him, and it must do so if it is to prevent the abolition of the human species. To man *qua* man we read-ily say good riddance. Only by dispossessing him can we turn to the real causes of human behavior. Only then can we turn from the in-ferred to the observed, from the miraculous to the natural, from the inaccessible to the manipulable. 36

It is often said that in doing so we must treat the man who survives as a mere animal. "Animal" is a pejorative term, but only because "man" has been made spuriously honorific. Krutch has argued that whereas the traditional view supports Hamlet's exclamation, "How like a god!," Pavlov,[14] the behavioral scientist, emphasized "How like a dog!" But that was a step forward. A god is the archetypal pattern of an explanatory fiction, of a miracle-working mind, of the metaphysi-cal. Man is much more than a dog, but like a dog he is within range of a scientific analysis. 37

It is true that much of the experimental analysis of behavior has been concerned with lower organisms. Genetic differences are mini-mized by using special strains; environmental histories can be con-trolled, perhaps from birth; strict regimens can be maintained during long experiments; and very little of this is possible with human sub-jects. Moreover, in working with lower animals the scientist is less likely to put his own responses to the experimental conditions among his data, or to design contingencies with an eye to their effect on him rather than on the experimental organism he is studying. No one is disturbed when physiologists study respiration, reproduction, nutri-tion, or endocrine systems in animals; they do so to take advantage of very great similarities. Comparable similarities in behavior are being 38

---

[12]**qua**   As.

[13]***homunculus***   A tiny man; in Goethe's *Faust*, a kind of possessing spirit.

[14]***Ivan Pavlov (1849–1936)***   Russian physiologist who conditioned a dog to sali-vate upon the ringing of a bell. Much behaviorist psychology is based upon his experi-ments.

discovered. There is, of course, always the danger that methods designed for the study of lower animals will emphasize only those characteristics which they have in common with men, but we cannot discover what is "essentially" human until we have investigated nonhuman subjects. Traditional theories of autonomous man have exaggerated species differences. Some of the complex contingencies of reinforcement now under investigation generate behavior in lower organisms which, if the subjects were human, would traditionally be said to involve higher mental processes.

Man is not made into a machine by analyzing his behavior in mechanical terms. Early theories of behavior, as we have seen, represented man as a push-pull automaton, close to the nineteenth-century notion of a machine, but progress has been made. Man is a machine in the sense that he is a complex system behaving in lawful ways, but the complexity is extraordinary. His capacity to adjust to contingencies of reinforcement will perhaps be eventually simulated by machines, but this has not yet been done, and the living system thus simulated will remain unique in other ways. 39

Nor is man made into a machine by inducing him to use machines. Some machines call for behavior which is repetitious and monotonous, and we escape from them when we can, but others enormously extend our effectiveness in dealing with the world around us. A person may respond to very small things with the help of an electron microscope and to very large things with radiotelescopes, and in doing so he may seem quite inhuman to those who use only their unaided senses. A person may act upon the environment with the delicate precision of a micromanipulator or with the range and power of a space rocket, and his behavior may seen inhuman to those who rely only on muscular contractions. (It has been argued that the apparatus used in the operant laboratory misrepresents natural behavior because it introduces an external source of power, but men use external sources when they fly kites, sail boats, or shoot bows and arrows. They would have to abandon all but a small fraction of their achievements if they used only the power of their muscles.) People record their behavior in books and other media, and the use they make of the records may seem quite inhuman to those who can use only what they remember. People describe complex contingencies in the form of rules, and rules for manipulating rules, and they introduce them into electronic systems which "think" with a speed that seems quite inhuman to the unaided thinker. Human beings do all this with machines, and they would be less than human if they did not. What we now regard as machine-like behavior was, in fact, much commoner before the invention of these 40 devices. The slave in the cotton field, the bookkeeper on his high stool, the student being drilled by a teacher—these were the machine-like men.

Machines replace people when they do what people have done, and 41 the social consequences may be serious. As technology advances, machines will take over more and more of the functions of men, but only up to a point. We build machines which reduce some of the aversive features of our environment (grueling labor, for example) and which produce more positive reinforcers. We build them precisely because they do so. We have no reason to build machines to be reinforced by these consequences, and to do so would be to deprive ourselves of reinforcement. If the machines man makes eventually make him wholly expendable, it will be by accident, not design.

An important role of autonomous man has been to give human 42 behavior direction, and it is often said that in dispossessing an inner agent we leave man himself without a purpose. As one writer has put it, "Since a scientific psychology must regard human behavior objectively, as determined by necessary laws, it must represent human behavior as unintentional." But "necessary laws" would have this effect only if they referred exclusively to antecedent conditions. Intention and purpose refer to selective consequences, the effects of which can be formulated in "necessary laws." Has life, in all the forms in which it exists on the surface of the earth, a purpose, and is this evidence of intentional design? The primate hand evolved *in order that* things might be more successfully manipulated, but its purpose is to be found not in a prior design but rather in the process of selection. Similarly, in operant conditioning the purpose of a skilled movement of the hand is to be found in the consequences which follow it. A pianist neither acquires nor executes the behavior of playing a scale smoothly because of a prior intention of doing so. Smoothly played scales are reinforcing for many reasons, and they select skilled movements. In neither the evolution of the human hand nor in the acquired use of the hand is any prior intention or purpose at issue.

The argument for purpose seems to be strengthened by moving 43 back into the darker recesses of mutation. Jacques Barzun[15] has argued that Darwin and Marx both neglected not only human purpose but the creative purpose responsible for the variations upon which natural se-

---

[15]*Jacques Barzun (b. 1907)* A noted American scholar; Skinner is referring to his book, *Darwin, Marx, and Wagner.*

lection plays. It may prove to be the case, as some geneticists have argued, that mutations are not entirely random, but nonrandomness is not necessarily the proof of a creative mind. Mutations will not be random when geneticists explicitly design them in order that an organism will meet specific conditions of selection more successfully, and geneticists will then seem to be playing the role of the creative Mind in pre-evolutionary theory, but the purpose they display will have to be sought in their culture, in the social environment which has induced them to make genetic changes appropriate to contingencies of survival.

There is a difference between biological and individual purpose in that the latter can be felt. No one could have felt the purpose in the development of the human hand, whereas a person can in a sense feel the purpose with which he plays a smooth scale. But he does not play a smooth scale *because* he feels the purpose of doing so; what he feels is a by-product of his behavior in relation to its consequences. The relation of the human hand to the contingencies of survival under which it evolved is, of course, out of reach of personal observation; the relation of the behavior to contingencies of reinforcement which have generated it is not. **44**

A scientific analysis of behavior dispossesses autonomous man and turns the control he has been said to exert over to the environment. The individual may then seem particularly vulnerable. He is henceforth to be controlled by the world around him, and in large part by other men. Is he not then simply a victim? Certainly men have been victims, as they have been victimizers, but the word is too strong. It implies despoliation, which is by no means an essential consequence of interpersonal control. But even under benevolent control is the individual not at best a spectator who may watch what happens but is helpless to do anything about it? Is he not "at a dead end in his long struggle to control his own destiny"? **45**

It is only autonomous man who has reached a dead end. Man himself may be controlled by his environment, but it is an environment which is almost wholly of his own making. The physical environment of most people is largely man-made. The surfaces a person walks on, the walls which shelter him, the clothing he wears, many of the foods he eats, the tools he uses, the vehicles he moves about in, most of the things he listens to and looks at are human products. The social environment is obviously man-made—it generates the language a person speaks, the customs he follows, and the behavior he exhibits with respect to the ethical, religious, governmental, economic, educational, **46** and psychotherapeutic institutions which control him. The evolution of a culture is in fact a kind of gigantic exercise in self-control. As the individual controls himself by manipulating the world in which he lives, so the human species has constructed an environment in which its members behave in a highly effective way. Mistakes have been made, and we have no assurance that the environment man has constructed will continue to provide gains which outstrip the losses, but man as we know him, for better or for worse, is what man has made of man.

This will not satisfy those who cry "Victim!" C. S. Lewis protested: 47 ". . . the power of man to make himself what he pleases . . . means . . . the power of some men to make other men what they please." This is inevitable in the nature of cultural evolution. The controlling *self* must be distinguished from the controlled self, even when they are both inside the same skin, and when control is exercised through the design of an external environment, the selves are, with minor exceptions, distinct. The person who unintentionally or intentionally introduces a new cultural practice is only one among possibly billions who will be affected by it. If this does not seem like an act of self-control, it is only because we have misunderstood the nature of self-control in the individual.

When a person changes his physical or social environment "inten- 48 tionally"—that is, in order to change human behavior, possibly including his own—he plays two roles: one as a controller, as the designer of a controlling culture, and another as the controlled, as the product of a culture. There is nothing inconsistent about this; it follows from the nature of the evolution of a culture, with or without intentional design.

The human species has probably not undergone much genetic 49 change in recorded time. We have only to go back a thousand generations to reach the artists of the caves of Lascaux.[16] Features which bear directly on survival (such as resistance to disease) change substantially in a thousand generations, but the child of one of the Lascaux artists transplanted to the world of today might be almost indistinguishable from a modern child. It is possible that he would learn more slowly than his modern counterpart, that he could maintain only a smaller repertoire without confusion, or that he would forget more quickly;

---

[16]*caves of Lascaux*   Lascaux is in southwest France. The caves discovered there were painted with bison, elk, and other figures some 15,000 to 20,000 years ago. Other such caves have been found in Spain and elsewhere in France.

we cannot be sure. But we can be sure that a twentieth-century child transplanted to the civilization of Lascaux would not be very different from the children he met there, for we have seen what happens when a modern child is raised in an impoverished environment.

Man has greatly changed himself as a person in the same period of 50 time by changing the world in which he lives. Something of the order of a hundred generations will cover the development of modern religious practices, and something of the same order of magnitude modern government and law. Perhaps no more than twenty generations will account for modern industrial practices, and possibly no more than four or five for education and psychotherapy. The physical and biological technologies which have increased man's sensitivity to the world around him and his power to change that world have taken no more than four or five generations.

Man has "controlled his own destiny," if that expression means 51 anything at all. The man that man has made is the product of the culture man has devised. He has emerged from two quite different processes of evolution: the biological evolution responsible for the human species and the cultural evolution carried out by that species. Both of these processes of evolution may now accelerate because they are both subject to intentional design. Men have already changed their genetic endowment by breeding selectively and by changing contingencies of survival, and they may now begin to introduce mutations directly related to survival. For a long time men have introduced new practices which serve as cultural mutations, and they have changed the conditions under which practices are selected. They may now begin to do both with a clearer eye to the consequences.

Man will presumably continue to change, but we cannot say in 52 what direction. No one could have predicted the evolution of the human species at any point in its early history, and the direction of intentional genetic design will depend upon the evolution of a culture which is itself unpredictable for similar reasons. "The limits of perfection of the human species," said Étienne Cabet[17] in *Voyage en Icarie*, "are as yet unknown." But, of course, there are no limits. The human species will never reach a final state of perfection before it is exterminated—"some say in fire, some in ice," and some in radiation.

---

[17]*Étienne Cabet (1788–1856)* A French communist whose *Voyage en Icarie* (1840) offers a plan for a utopia which Cabet in 1848 tried to put into practice. He purchased land on the Red River in Texas, then sent 1,500 settlers there. The experiment failed. He later took his "Icarians" to Nauvoo, Illinois, a former Mormon settlement. He withdrew from the community in 1856 after dissension.

The individual occupies a place in a culture not unlike his place in 53
the species, and in early evolutionary theory that place was hotly debated. Was the species simply a type of individual, and if so, in what
sense could it evolve? Darwin himself declared species "to be purely
subjective inventions of the taxonomist." A species has no existence
except as a collection of individuals, nor has a family, tribe, race, nation, or class. A culture has no existence apart from the behavior of
the individuals who maintain its practices. It is always an individual
who behaves, who acts upon the environment and is changed by the
consequences of his action, and who maintains the social contingencies which *are* a culture. The individual is the carrier of both his
species and his culture. Cultural practices, like genetic traits, are
transmitted from individual to individual. A new practice, like a new
genetic trait, appears first in an individual and tends to be transmitted
if it contributes to his survival as an individual.

Yet, the individual is at best a locus in which many lines of devel- 54
opment come together in a unique set. His individuality is unques-
tioned. Every cell in his body is a unique genetic product, as unique as
that classic mark of individuality, the fingerprint. And even within the
most regimented culture every personal history is unique. No intentional culture can destroy that uniqueness, and, as we have seen, any
effort to do so would be bad design. But the individual nevertheless
remains merely a stage in a process which began long before he came
into existence and will long outlast him. He has no ultimate responsibility for a species trait or a cultural practice, even though it was he
who underwent the mutation or introduced the practice which became
part of the species or culture. Even if Lamarck[18] had been right in supposing that the individual could change his genetic structure through
personal effort, we should have to point to the environmental circumstances responsible for the effort, as we shall have to do when geneticists begin to change the human endowment. And when an individual
engages in the intentional design of a cultural practice, we must turn
to the culture which induces him to do so and supplies the art or science he uses.

One of the great problems of individualism, seldom recognized as 55
such, is death—the inescapable fate of the individual, the final assault
on freedom and dignity. Death is one of those remote events which
are brought to bear on behavior only with the aid of cultural practices.

---

[18]*Jean Baptiste Lamarck (1744–1829)* French scientist who thought that it was
possible to inherit acquired characteristics genetically.

What we see is the death of others, as in Pascal's[19] famous metaphor: "Imagine a number of men in chains, all under sentence of death, some of whom are each day butchered in the sight of the others; those remaining see their own condition in that of their fellows, and looking at each other with grief and despair await their turn. This is an image of the human condition." Some religions have made death more important by picturing a future existence in heaven or hell, but the individualist has a special reason to fear death, engineered not by a religion but by the literatures of freedom and dignity. It is the prospect of personal annihilation. The individualist can find no solace in reflecting upon any contribution which will survive him. He has refused to act for the good of others and is therefore not reinforced by the fact that others whom he has helped will outlive him. He has refused to be concerned for the survival of his culture and is not reinforced by the fact that the culture will long survive him. In the defense of his own freedom and dignity he has denied the contributions of the past and must therefore relinquish all claim upon the future.

Science has probably never demanded a more sweeping change in a 56 traditional way of thinking about a subject, nor has there ever been a more important subject. In the traditional picture a person perceives the world around him, selects features to be perceived, discriminates among them, judges them good or bad, changes them to make them better (or, if he is careless, worse), and may be held responsible for his action and justly rewarded or punished for its consequences. In the scientific picture a person is a member of a species shaped by evolutionary contingencies of survival, displaying behavioral processes which bring him under the control of the environment in which he lives, and largely under the control of a social environment which he and millions of others like him have constructed and maintained during the evolution of a culture. The direction of the controlling relation is reversed: a person does not act upon the world, the world acts upon him.

It is difficult to accept such a change simply on intellectual 57 grounds and nearly impossible to accept its implications. The reaction of the traditionalist is usually described in terms of feelings. One of these, to which the Freudians have appealed in explaining the resistance to psychoanalysis, is wounded vanity. Freud himself expounded,

---

[19]*Blaise Pascal (1623–1662)* French philosopher and scientist. He was generally enigmatic in his thought, particularly in his *Pensées* (1658), in which he begins to call all knowledge into doubt. Pascal was a devout Catholic, but the religious orthodoxy of his work is subject to debate.

as Ernest Jones[20] has said, "the three heavy blows which narcissism or self-love of mankind had suffered at the hands of science. The first was cosmological and was dealt by Copernicus;[21] the second was biological and was dealt by Darwin; the third was psychological and was dealt by Freud." (The blow was suffered by the belief that something at the center of man knows all that goes on within him and that an instrument called will power exercises command and control over the rest of one's personality.) But what are the signs or symptoms of wounded vanity, and how shall we explain them? What people *do* about such a scientific picture of man is call it wrong, demeaning, and dangerous, argue against it, and attack those who propose or defend it. They do so not out of wounded vanity but because the scientific formulation has destroyed accustomed reinforcers. If a person can no longer take credit or be admired for what he does, then he seems to suffer a loss of dignity or worth, and behavior previously reinforced by credit or admiration will undergo extinction. Extinction often leads to aggressive attack.

Another effect of the scientific picture has been described as a loss 58 of faith or "nerve," as a sense of doubt or powerlessness, or as discouragement, depression, or despondency. A person is said to feel that he can do nothing about his own destiny. But what he feels is a weakening of old responses which are no longer reinforced. People are indeed "powerless" when long-established verbal repertoires prove useless. For example, one historian has complained that if the deeds of men are "to be dismissed as simply the product of material and psychological conditioning," there is nothing to write about; "change must be at least partially the result of conscious mental activity."

Another effect is a kind of nostalgia. Old repertoires break through, 59 as similarities between present and past are seized upon and exaggerated. Old days are called the good old days, when the inherent dignity of man and the importance of spiritual values were recognized. Such fragments of outmoded behavior tend to be "wistful"—that is, they have the character of increasingly unsuccessful behavior.

These reactions to a scientific conception of man are certainly un- 60 fortunate. They immobilize men of good will, and anyone concerned with the future of his culture will do what he can to correct them. No

---

[20]**Ernest Jones (1879–1958)** A follower of Freud. His book *Hamlet and Oedipus* (1949) applies Freud's theory to a literary classic, Shakespeare's *Hamlet*.

[21]**Nicolaus Copernicus (1473–1543)** Polish astronomer who theorized that the earth revolved around the sun. His theory revolutionized astronomy and shook the foundations of Western thought.

theory changes what it is a theory about. Nothing is changed because we look at it, talk about it, or analyze it in a new way. Keats drank confusion to Newton[22] for analyzing the rainbow, but the rainbow remained as beautiful as ever and became for many even more beautiful. Man has not changed because we look at him, talk about him, and analyze him scientifically. His achievements in science, government, religion, art, and literature remain as they have always been, to be admired as one admires a storm at sea or autumn foliage or a mountain peak, quite apart from their origins and untouched by a scientific analysis. What does change is our chance of doing something about the subject of a theory. Newton's analysis of the light in a rainbow was a step in the direction of the laser.[23]

The traditional conception of man is flattering; it confers reinforc-   61
ing privileges. It is therefore easily defended and can be changed only with difficulty. It was designed to build up the individual as an instrument of countercontrol, and it did so effectively but in such a way as to limit progress. We have seen how the literatures of freedom and dignity, with their concern for autonomous man, have perpetuated the use of punishment and condoned the use of only weak nonpunitive techniques, and it is not difficult to demonstrate a connection between the unlimited right of the individual to pursue happiness and the catastrophes threatened by unchecked breeding, the unrestrained affluence which exhausts resources and pollutes the environment, and the imminence of nuclear war.

Physical and biological technologies have alleviated pestilence and   62
famine and many painful, dangerous, and exhausting features of daily life, and behavioral technology can begin to alleviate other kinds of ills. In the analysis of human behavior it is just possible that we are slightly beyond Newton's position in the analysis of light, for we are beginning to make technological applications. There are wonderful possibilities—and all the more wonderful because traditional approaches have been so ineffective. It is hard to imagine a world in which people live together without quarreling, maintain themselves

---

[22]*Sir Isaac Newton (1642–1727)* English scientist who invented differential and integral calculus and established the theory of gravity. His theories gave rise to a mechanical explanation of the universe in which all phenomena could be treated in terms of cause and effect. The English poet John Keats (1795–1821) reacted against Newton's analysis of the rainbow because he felt science was removing the romance and mystery from nature.

[23]*laser* A highly focused beam of electrons; a form of light. (The word is an acronym for *l*ight *a*mplification by *s*timulated *e*mission of *r*adiation.)

by producing the food, shelter, and clothing they need, enjoy themselves and contribute to the enjoyment of others in art, music, literature, and games, consume only a reasonable part of the resources of the world and add as little as possible to its pollution, bear no more children than can be raised decently, continue to explore the world around them and discover better ways of dealing with it, and come to know themselves accurately and, therefore, manage themselves effectively. Yet all this is possible, and even the slightest sign of progress should bring a kind of change which in traditional terms would be said to assuage wounded vanity, offset a sense of hopelessness or nostalgia, correct the impression that "we neither can nor need to do anything for ourselves," and promote a "sense of freedom and dignity" by building "a sense of confidence and worth." In other words, it should abundantly reinforce those who have been induced by their culture to work for its survival.

An experimental analysis shifts the determination of behavior from 63 autonomous man to the environment—an environment responsible both for the evolution of the species and for the repertoire acquired by each member. Early versions of environmentalism were inadequate because they could not explain how the environment worked, and much seemed to be left for autonomous man to do. But environmental contingencies now take over functions once attributed to autonomous man, and certain questions arise. Is man then "abolished"? Certainly not as a species or as an individual achiever. It is the autonomous inner man who is abolished, and that is a step forward. But does man not then become merely a victim or passive observer of what is happening to him? He is indeed controlled by his environment, but we must remember that it is an environment largely of his own making. The evolution of a culture is a gigantic exercise in self-control. It is often said that a scientific view of man leads to wounded vanity, a sense of hopelessness, and nostalgia. But no theory changes what it is a theory about; man remains what he has always been. And a new theory may change what can be done with its subject matter. A scientific view of man offers exciting possibilities. We have not yet seen what man can make of man.

QUESTIONS

1. Define the key terms of the chapter: "autonomous man," "contingencies of reinforcement," "environment," "the individual." Are there other key terms that need definition?

2. Skinner has not provided much of the scientific data on which his views are based because he wishes to address a general audience, one that can profit from the results, rather than the process, of scientific research. Should he have provided more scientific data? Is his audience a general audience? Would you like more data, more experimental information?
3. What are the most important ideas set forth in this piece? How do they relate to the area of psychology?
4. What kinds of different environments does Skinner take into account in the chapter? He mentions physical and social environments in paragraph 48. Are those the only ones there are?
5. Skinner believes that his view is scientific. Is he correct?

WRITING ASSIGNMENTS

1. One of the chief issues in the selection is concerned with the nature of the self. In an essay which uses Skinner's technique of the rhetorical question, answer the following question as carefully as he answers his: What is a self? Refer to paragraphs 32–34. Try to clarify what Skinner thinks the self is and offer, as you do so, your own views.
2. Examine the selection for reference to character traits. By referring to specific quotations, and by analyzing them carefully in relation to one another, explain what Skinner means by "character traits." Is his analysis of this term reasonable? Is he convincing in suggesting that character traits may not be "permanent" or "basic" as we had thought?
3. Look around you for examples of contingencies of reinforcement. What kind of person does your environment seem to encourage you to be? What kinds of reinforcement are available in your immediate environment? Be as specific as possible in answering these questions.
4. Answer the question: Am I an autonomous agent? Use Skinner's strategy of examining first the environment in which you live, giving special attention to the contingencies of reinforcement which you are aware of. Then proceed to examine your own inner nature—insofar as that is possible—to see what that will contribute to your autonomy. Consider, as you answer this question, the issues of identity that are raised in the selection in paragraph 32 and thereafter. Does the process of answering this question help you to a better insight into your own identity?
5. Answer the question: Are my friends autonomous agents? Using Skinner's theories of contingencies of reinforcement, examine the behavior of two or three of your friends (or one in depth). Do they feel that they are free to do as they wish? Do you believe that they are aware of the limits on their freedom or of the degree to which they react to the reinforcements in their environment? To what extent is their behavior predictable by an outside observer?

6. In this selection, Skinner is basically predicting the death knell of the concept of the individual as an autonomous agent. What does he see as the alternative to this concept? Analyze closely the section of the piece beginning with paragraph 45 and ending with paragraph 55. What exactly is Skinner saying in these paragraphs? What will replace the concept of man as an autonomous agent? Is Skinner's view acceptable to you? How would you describe his vision of the future? Establish what his thinking is on the nature of the individual in the future.

7. How would Freud or Jung regard Skinner's views? Skinner does not speak of "autonomous complexes," as Jung does nor of the sexual origins of psychological problems, as Freud does with his "Oedipus complex" and "penis envy." To what extent might Freud or Jung agree with Skinner; about which issues would Freud or Jung be likely to disagree with him? As you think about this question, also consider whether Karen Horney would agree or disagree with Skinner.

SIMONE DE BEAUVOIR

The Psychoanalytic
Point of View

SIMONE DE BEAUVOIR *(1908–1986) was one of the most important post–World War French intellectuals. Her work was basically philosophical, and she herself taught philosophy and lived with one of France's preeminent existentialist philosophers, Jean-Paul Sartre (1905–1980). Theirs was a highly charismatic romance: two attractive, independent, and dazzlingly brilliant leftist thinkers who represented the ideal couple to most intellectuals.*

Beauvoir met Sartre in 1929, while taking examinations for entrance to the school where she prepared as a teacher, the École Normale Superieure. Beauvoir taught in Marseilles, Rouen, and Paris, and all the while wrote novels, memoirs, and essays. Her best-known book remains Le Deuxième Sexe *(1949), published in English in 1953 as* The Second Sex, *which has been thought of as a beacon for the feminist movement. In it she discussed the implications of women being cast as the Other, the alienated of society. Beauvoir frequently discussed the implications of women being defined in relation to men—defined as what men are not, rather than as something in and of themselves.*

From *The Second Sex* (1953).

In the area of psychiatry, Beauvoir found some especially power-ful material to examine. She clarified Freud's position regarding women, demonstrating that his views also placed woman as the Other because his psychiatric theories are in the first place mascu-line, then modified and reexamined in feminine terms. In other words, as Karen Horney also implied, Freud did not create a separate feminine psychology based only on his observations of women; rather, he compared his observations with those that he made of masculine patients and then constructed a theory of feminine psy-chology. Beauvoir was quick to assert that this was an insufficient approach to psychology. Yet, she did not discard all of Freud's views but demonstrated what she felt was lacking in them.

Extremely frank, her discussion of sexuality was based on the view that men have a relatively simple erotic development, the center of erotic stimulation being located in the penis. According to Beauvoir, women possess two stages of erotic development. The first, and rela-tively simple stage, she called clitoral because in girlhood the center of erotic stimulation remains located in the clitoris. But later, and essen-tial to the full development of the woman if she is to avoid neurosis and become sexually more complete and more fully womanized, Beauvoir acknowledged the vagina as the center of erotic stimulation.

Beauvoir was careful to examine Freud's theories of penis envy and to suggest that they are not as clear and "simple" as Freud sug-gested. She, like Horney, recognized a cultural influence in the girl's envy of a boy's independence and activity. The penis, then, is sym-bolic for the freedom that society accords males, not a thing in it-self—certainly not something that females lack.

One of her most important statements was that a person is not born a woman, but that she makes herself a woman. This belief, worked out in the selection here, suggested that women are not nec-essarily dominated by the psychic contents of the unconscious and the inevitable Electra complex (the feminine version of the Oedipus complex) any more than they are dominated by the biological fact of their bodies and the absence of a penis. Women make choices and shape themselves as they wish: "Woman is a female to the extent that she feels herself as such" (para. 1).

In Beauvoir's words (para. 3), Freud was never concerned with the destiny of woman, but adapted his views on feminine psychology from his studies of "the destiny of man." Accordingly, the libido—the primordial sexual urge that exists in all people—is, in Freud's view, basically masculine and so he makes no clear differentiation of the feminine libido. This is a point that Beauvoir could not accept.

She refuted the idea that Freud might assume that woman is a "mutilated man" and she based her analysis (para. 7) on her sense of the limitation of psychiatry in relation to women.

Beauvoir was willing to admit (para. 12) that people are sexual beings, and that they may be dominated by sexual concerns. But she was unwilling to subscribe to Freud's interpretation of this situation. She understood shame, in other words, but did not acknowledge its source. She did not agree with the statement that "anatomy is destiny." In this essay at least, she expressed the view that one can control one's existence and that the individual existence precedes anatomy in importance.

BEAUVOIR'S RHETORIC

Beauvoir writes very directly. She analyzes her subject matter by relating it to the major theorists of the psychoanalytic position, then takes each in turn and examines the opinions that they present. Beauvoir is thorough, analytic, and careful, covering point after point to make herself understood.

She does not permit herself to be overly complicated in her beliefs or in her language. Instead, she tries to be direct and immediate. Beauvoir concentrates especially on establishing clearly the opinions of those with whom she disagrees. Freud's position is carefully detailed, then Adler's, then that of psychiatry in general. The entire argument would collapse if she did not accurately clarify these views, and clarify them from within the understanding and terminology of the original thinkers. For that reason, setting forth the positions against which she argues is one of Beauvoirs chief tasks in the essay.

Finally, in this essay Beauvoir presents a perspective that she believes has not been adequately established—that of women in general. At the time that she wrote this piece, Simone de Beauvoir was not known as a feminist. Indeed, in 1953 modern feminists were hardly known in the United States or in France. Later, in the 1970s, Beauvoir aligned herself with certain militant feminists, but already, in The Second Sex, she had provided a kind of rallying cry, a treatise that examined with great authority the representation of women in many different intellectual and cultural areas. For that reason, the book became memorable and a document of great political power. Its rhetoric is not especially patterned or self-conscious, but rather very simple and straightforward. The calm, reasonable, direct style contributes enormously to the selection's persuasiveness.

The Psychoanalytic
Point of View

The tremendous advance accomplished by psychoanalysis over psy- 1
chophysiology lies in the view that no factor becomes involved in the
psychic life without having taken on human significance; it is not the
body-object described by biologists that actually exists, but the body
as lived in by the subject. Woman is a female to the extent that she
feels herself as such. There are biologically essential features that
are not a part of her real, experienced situation: thus the structure
of the egg is not reflected in it, but on the contrary an organ of no
great biological importance, like the clitoris, plays in it a part of
the first rank. It is not nature that defines woman; it is she who
defines herself by dealing with nature on her own account in her emotional life.

An entire system has been built up in this perspective, which I do 2
not intend to criticize as a whole, merely examining its contribution
to the study of woman. It is not an easy matter to discuss psychoanalysis *per se.* Like all religions—Christiantity and Marxism, for example—it displays an embarrassing flexibility on a basis of rigid concepts.
Words are sometimes used in their most literal sense, the term *phallus,* for example, designating quite exactly that fleshy projection
which marks the male; again, they are indefinitely expanded and take
on symbolic meaning, the phallus now expressing the virile character
and situation *in toto.* If you attack the letter of his doctrine, the psychoanalyst protests that you misunderstand its spirit; if you applaud
its spirit, he at once wishes to confine you to the letter. The doctrine
is of no importance, says one, psychoanalysis is a method; but the
success of the method strengthens the doctrinaire in his faith. After
all, where is one to find the true lineaments of psychoanalysis if not
among the psychoanalysts? But there are heretics among these, just as
there are among Christians and Marxists; and more than one psychoanalyst has declared that "the worst enemies of psychoanalysis are
the psychoanalysts." In spite of a scholastic precision that often becomes pedantic, many obscurities remain to be dissipated. As Sartre

and Merleau-Ponty[1] have observed, the proposition "Sexuality is coextensive with existence" can be understood in two very different ways; it can mean that every experience of the existent has a sexual significance, or that every sexual phenomenon has an existential import. It is possible to reconcile these statements, but too often one merely slips from one to the other. Furthermore, as soon as the "sexual" is distinguished from the "genital," the idea of sexuality becomes none too clear. According to Dalbiez,[2] "the sexual with Freud is the intrinsic aptitude for releasing the genital." But nothing is more obscure than the idea of "aptitude"—that is, of possibility—for only realization gives indubitable proof of what is possible. Not being a philosopher, Freud has refused to justify his system philosophically; and his disciples maintain that on this account he is exempt from all metaphysical attack. There are metaphysical assumptions behind all his dicta, however, and to use his language is to adopt a philosophy. It is just such confusions that call for criticism, while making criticism difficult.

Freud never showed much concern with the destiny of woman; it is clear that he simply adapted his account from that of the destiny of man, with slight modifications. Earlier the sexologist Marañon[3] had stated that "As specific energy, we may say that the libido is a force of virile character. We will say as much of the orgasm." According to him, women who attain orgasm are "viriloid" women; the sexual impulse is "in one direction" and woman is only halfway along the road. Freud never goes to such an extreme; he admits that woman's sexuality is evolved as fully as man's; but he hardly studies it in particular. He writes: "The libido[4] is constantly and regularly male in essence, whether it appears in man or in woman." He declines to regard the feminine libido as having its own original nature, and therefore it will necessarily seem to him like a complex deviation from the human libido in general. This develops at first, he thinks, identically in the two sexes—each infant passes first through an oral phase that fixates it upon the maternal breast, and then through an anal phase; finally it reaches the genital phase, at which point the sexes become differentiated.

3

---

[1]*Jean-Paul Sarte (1905–1980); Maurice Merleau-Ponty (1908–1961)* Important French existentialist philosophers.

[2]*Roland Dalbiez* Twentieth-century French psychiatrist; interpreter of Freud.

[3]*Gregorio Marañon y Posadillo (1888–1960)* Spanish endocrinologist who studied the effects of sexual hormones on behavior.

[4]*libido* The sexual urge.

Freud further brought to light a fact the importance of which had   4
not been fully appreciated: namely, that masculine erotism is definitely located in the penis, whereas in woman there are two distinct
erotic systems: one the clitoral, which develops in childhood, the
other vaginal, which develops only after puberty. When the boy
reaches the genital phase, his evolution is completed, though he must
pass from the autoerotic inclination, in which pleasure is subjective,
to the heteroerotic inclination, in which pleasure is bound up with an
object, normally woman. This transition is made at the time of puberty through a narcissistic phase. But the penis will remain, as in
childhood, the specific organ of erotism. Woman's libido, also passing
through a narcissistic phase, will become objective, normally toward
man; but the process will be much more complex, because woman
must pass from clitoral pleasure to vaginal. There is only one genital
stage for man, but there are two for woman; she runs a much greater
risk of not reaching the end of her sexual evolution, of remaining at
the infantile stage and thus of developing neuroses.

While still in the autoerotic stage, the child becomes more or less   5
strongly attached to an object. The boy becomes fixed on his mother
and desires to identify himself with his father; this presumption terrifies him and he dreads mutilation at the hands of his father in punishment for it. Thus the castration complex springs from the Oedipus
complex. Then aggressiveness toward the father develops, but at the
same time the child interiorizes the father's authority; thus the superego is built up in the child and censures his incestuous tendencies.
These are repressed, the complex is liquidated, and the son is freed
from his fear of his father, whom he has now installed in his own
psyche under the guise of moral precepts. The superego is more powerful in proportion as the Oedipus complex has been more marked and
more rigorously resisted.

Freud at first described the little girl's history in a completely cor-   6
responding fashion, later calling the feminine form of the process the
Electra complex; but it is clear that he defined it less in itself than
upon the basis of his masculine pattern. He recognized a very important difference between the two, however: the little girl at first has a
mother fixation, but the boy is at no time sexually attracted to the
father. This fixation of the girl represents a survival of the oral phase.
Then the child identifies herself with the father; but toward the age of
five she discovers the anatomical difference between the sexes, and she
reacts to the absence of the penis by acquiring a castration complex—
she imagines that she has been mutilated and is pained at the thought.

Having then to renounce her virile pretensions, she identifies herself with her mother and seeks to seduce the father. The castration complex and the Electra complex thus reinforce each other. Her feeling of frustration is the keener since, loving her father, she wishes in vain to be like him; and, inversely, her regret strengthens her love, for she is able to compensate for her inferiority through the affection she inspires in her father. The little girl entertains a feeling of rivalry and hostility toward her mother. Then the superego is built up also in her, and the incestuous tendencies are repressed; but her superego is not so strong, for the Electra complex is less sharply defined than the Oedipus because the first fixation was upon the mother, and since the father is himself the object of the love that he condemns, his prohibitions are weaker than in the case of his son-rival. It can be seen that like her genital development the whole sexual drama is more complex for the girl than for her brothers. In consequence she may be led to react to the castration complex by denying her femininity, by continuing obstinately to covet a penis and to identify herself with her father. This attitude will cause her to remain in the clitoral phase, to become frigid, or to turn toward homosexuality.

The two essential objections that may be raised against this view 7 derive from the fact that Freud based it upon a masculine model. He assumes that woman feels that she is a mutilated man. But the idea of mutilation implies comparison and evaluation. Many psychoanalysts today admit that the young girl may regret not having a penis without believing, however, that it has been removed from her body; and even this regret is not general. It could not arise from a simple anatomical comparison; many little girls, in fact, are late in discovering the masculine construction, and if they do, it is only by sight. The little boy obtains from his penis a living experience that makes it an object of pride to him, but this pride does not necessarily imply a corresponding humiliation for his sisters, since they know the masculine organ in its outward aspect only—this outgrowth, this weak little rod of flesh can in itself inspire them only with indifference, or even disgust. The little girl's covetousness, when it exists, results from a previous evaluation of virility. Freud takes this for granted, when it should be accounted for. On the other hand, the concept of the Electra complex is very vague, because it is not supported by a basic description of the feminine libido. Even in boys the occurrence of a definitely genital Oedipus complex is by no means general; but, apart from very few exceptions, it cannot be admitted that the father is a source of genital excitation for his young daughter. One of the great problems of feminine eroticism is that clitoral pleasure is localized; and it is only toward puberty that a number of erogenous zones develop in various parts of the body, along with the growth of vaginal sensation. To say, then, that in a child of ten the kisses and caresses of her father have an "intrinsic aptitude" for arousing clitoral pleasure is to assert something that in most cases is nonsense. If it is admitted that the Electra complex has only a very diffuse emotional character, then the whole question of emotion is raised, and Freudianism does not help us in defining emotion as distinguished from sexuality. What deifies the father is by no means the feminine libido (nor is the mother deified by the desire she arouses in the son); on the contrary, the fact that the feminine desire (in the daughter) is directed toward a sovereign being gives it a special character. It does not determine the nature of its object; rather it is affected by the latter. The sovereignty of the father is a fact of social origin, which Freud fails to account for; in fact, he states that it is impossible to say what authority decided, at a certain moment in history, that the father should take precedence over the mother—a decision that, according to Freud, was progressive, but due to causes unknown. "It could not have been the patriarchal authority, since it is just this authority which progress conferred upon the father," as he puts it in his last work.

Adler[5] took issue with Freud because he saw the deficiency of a system that undertook to explain human life upon the basis of sexuality alone; he holds that sexuality should be integrated with the total personality. With Freud all human behavior seems to be the outcome of desire—that is, of the search for pleasure—but for Adler man appears to be aiming at certain goals; for the sexual urge he substitutes motives, purposes, projects. He gives so large a place to the intelligence that often the sexual has in his eyes only a symbolic value. According to his system, the human drama can be reduced to three elemental factors: in every individual there is a *will to power*, which, however, is accompanied by an *inferiority complex*; the resulting conflict leads the individual to employ a thousand ruses in a *flight from reality*—a reality with which he fears he may not be able to cope; the subject thus withdraws to some degree from the society of which he is apprehensive and hence becomes afflicted with the neuroses that involve disturbance of the social attitude. In woman the inferiority complex takes the form of a shamed rejection of her femininity. It is

8

---

[5]*Alfred Adler (1870–1937)* Austrian psychiatrist who was associated with Freud but who became increasingly critical of Freud's theories of sexuality.

not the lack of the penis that causes this complex, but rather woman's total situation; if the little girl feels penis envy it is only as the symbol of privileges enjoyed by boys. The place the father holds in the family, the universal predominance of males, her own education—everything confirms her in her belief in masculine superiority. Later on, when she takes part in sexual relations, she finds a new humiliation in the coital posture that places the woman underneath the man. She reacts through the "masculine protest": either she endeavors to masculinize herself, or she makes use of her feminine weapons to wage war upon the male. Through maternity she may be able to find an equivalent of the penis in her child. But this supposes that she begins by wholly accepting her role as woman and that she assumes her inferiority. She is divided against herself much more profoundly than is the male.

I shall not enlarge here upon the theoretical differences that sepa-   9
rate Adler and Freud nor upon the possibilities of a reconciliation; but this may be said: neither the explanation based upon the sexual urge nor that based upon motive is sufficient, for every urge poses a motive, but the motive is apprehended only through the urge—a synthesis of Adlerianism and Freudianism would therefore seem possible of realization. In fact, Adler retains the idea of psychic causation as an integral part of his system when he introduces the concepts of goal and of finality, and he is somewhat in accord with Freud in regard to the relation between drives and mechanism: the physicist always recognizes determinism when he is concerned with conflict or a force of attraction. The axiomatic proposition held in common by all psychoanalysts is this: the human story is to be explained by the interplay of determinate elements. And all the psychoanalysts allot the same destiny to woman. Her drama is epitomized in the conflict between her "viriloid" and her "feminine" tendencies, the first expressed through the clitoral system, the second in vaginal erotism. As a child she identifies herself with her father; then she becomes possessed with a feeling of inferiority with reference to the male and is faced with a dilemma: either to assert her independence and become virilized—which, with the underlying complex of inferiority, induces a state of tension that threatens neurosis—or to find happy fulfillment in amorous submission, a solution that is facilitated by her love for the sovereign father. He it is whom she really seeks in lover or husband, and thus her sexual love is mingled with the desire to be dominated. She will find her recompense in maternity, since that will afford her a new kind of independence. This drama would seem to be endowed with an energy, a dynamism, of its own; it steadily pursues its course through any and all distorting incidents, and every woman is passively swept along in it.

The psychoanalysts have had no trouble in finding empirical con- 10 firmation for their theories. As we know, it was possible for a long time to explain the position of the planets on the Ptolemaic system[6] by adding to it sufficiently subtle complications; and by superposing an inverse Oedipus complex upon the Oedipus complex, by disclosing desire in all anxiety, success has been achieved in integrating with the Freudian system the very facts that appear to contradict its validity. It is possible to make out a form only against a background, and the way in which the form is apprehended brings out the background behind it in positive detail; thus, if one is determined to describe a special case in a Freudian perspective, one will encounter the Freudian schema behind it. But when a doctrine demands the indefinite and arbitrary multiplication of secondary explanations, when observation brings to light as many exceptions as instances conformable to rule, it is better to give up the old rigid framework. Indeed, every psychoanalyst today is busily engaged after his fashion in making the Freudian concepts less rigid and in attempting compromises. For example, a contemporary psychoanalyst writes as follows: "Wherever there is a complex, there are by definition a number of components. . . . The complex consists in the association of these disparate elements and not in the representation of one among them by the others." But the concept of a simple association of elements is unacceptable, for the psychic life is not a mosaic, it is a single whole in every one of its aspects and we must respect that unity. This is possible only by our recovering through the disparate facts the original purposiveness of existence. If we do not go back to this source, man appears to be the battleground of compulsions and prohibitions that alike are devoid of meaning and incidental.

All psychoanalysts systematically reject the idea of *choice* and the 11 correlated concept of value, and therein lies the intrinsic weakness of the system. Having dissociated compulsions and prohibitions from the free choice of the existent, Freud fails to give us an explanation of their origin—he takes them for granted. He endeavored to replace the idea of value with that of authority; but he admits in *Moses and Monotheism* that he has no way of accounting for this authority. Incest, for example, is forbidden because the father has forbidden it—buy why did he forbid it? It is a mystery. The superego interiorizes, introjects commands and prohibitions emanating from an arbitrary tyranny, and the instinctive drives are there, we know not why: these two realities are

---

[6]***Ptolemaic system*** A system based on the speculations of the second-century Greek astronomer Ptolemy, who assumed the earth to be the center of the solar system.

unrelated because morality is envisaged as foreign to sexuality. The human unity appears to be disrupted, there is no thoroughfare from the individual to society; to reunite them Freud was forced to invent strange fictions, as in *Totem and Taboo*. Adler saw clearly that the castration complex could be explained only in a social context; he grappled with the problem of valuation, but he did not reach the source in the individual of the values recognized by society, and he did not grasp the fact that values are involved in sexuality itself, which led him to misjudge its importance.

Sexuality most certainly plays a considerable role in human life; it 12 can be said to pervade life throughout. We have already learned from physiology that the living activity of the testes and the ovaries is integrated with that of the body in general. The existent is a sexual, a sexuate body, and in his relations with other existents who are also sexuate bodies, sexuality is in consequence always involved. But if body and sexuality are concrete expressions of existence, it is with reference to this that their significance can be discovered. Lacking this perspective, psychoanalysis takes for granted unexplained facts. For instance, we are told that the little girl is *ashamed* of urinating in a squatting position with her bottom uncovered—but whence comes this shame? And likewise, before asking whether the male is proud of having a penis or whether his pride is expressed in his penis, it is necessary to know what pride is and how the aspirations of the subject can be incarnated in an object. There is no need of taking sexuality as an irreducible datum, for there is in the existent a more original "quest of being," of which sexuality is only one of the aspects. Sartre demonstrates this truth in *L'Être et le néant*,[7] as does Bachelard in his works on Earth, Air, and Water. The psychoanalysts hold that the primary truth regarding man is his relation with his own body and with the bodies of his fellows in the group; but man has a primordial interest in the substance of the natural world which surrounds him and which he tries to discover in work, in play, and in all the experiences of the "dynamic imagination." Man aspires to be at one concretely with the whole world, apprehended in all possible ways. To work the earth, to dig a hole, are activities as original as the embrace, as coition, and they deceive themselves who see here no more than sexual symbols. The hole, the ooze, the gash, hardness, integrity are primary real-

---

[7]**L'Être et le néant** Sartre's major philosophical work (1943), translated as *Being and Nothingness* (1956) . . . ***Gaston Bachelard (1884–1962)*** French philosopher of science who wrote works on the philosophical significance of the four classical elements: Earth, Air, Fire, and Water.

ities; and the interest they have for man is not dictated by the libido, but rather the libido will be colored by the manner in which he becomes aware of them. It is not because it symbolizes feminine virginity that integrity fascinates man; but it is his admiration for integrity that renders virginity precious. Work, war, play, art signify ways of being concerned with the world which cannot be reduced to any others; they disclose qualities that interfere with those which sexuality reveals. It is at once in their light and in the light of these erotic experiences that the individual exercises his power of choice. But only an ontological point of view, a comprehension of being in general, permits us to restore the unity of this choice.

It is this concept of choice, indeed, that psychoanalysis most vehemently rejects in the name of determinism and the "collective unconscious"; and it is this unconscious that is supposed to supply man with prefabricated imagery and a universal symbolism. Thus it would explain the observed analogies of dreams, of purposeless actions, of visions of delirium, of allegories, and of human destinies. To speak of liberty would be to deny oneself the possibility of explaining these disturbing conformities. But the idea of liberty is not incompatible with the existence of certain constants. If the psychoanalytic method is frequently rewarding in spite of the errors in its theory, that is because there are in every individual case certain factors of undeniable generality: situations and behavior patterns constantly recur, and the moment of decision flashes from a cloud of generality and repetition. "Anatomy is destiny," said Freud; and this phrase is echoed by that of Merleau-Ponty: "The body is generality." Existence is all one, bridging the gaps between individual existents; it makes itself manifest in analogous organisms, and therefore constant factors will be found in the bonds between the ontological and the sexual. At a given epoch of history the techniques, the economic and social structure of a society, will reveal to all its members an identical world, and there a constant relation of sexuality to social patterns will exist; analogous individuals, placed in analogous conditions, will see analogous points of significance in the given circumstances. This analogy does not establish a rigorous universality, but it accounts for the fact that general types may be recognized in individual case histories.

The symbol does not seem to me to be an allegory elaborated by a mysterious unconscious; it is rather the perception of a certain significance through the analogue of the significant object. Symbolic significance is manifested in the same way to numerous individuals, because of the identical existential situation connecting all the individual existents and the identical set of artificial conditions that all must confront. Symbolism did not come down from heaven nor rise up from subterranean depths—it has been elaborated, like language, by that human reality which is at once *Mitsein*[8] and separation; and this explains why individual invention also has its place, as in practice psychoanalysis has to admit, regardless of doctrine. Our perspective allows us, for example, to understand the value widely accorded to the penis. It is impossible to account for it without taking our departure from an existential fact: the tendency of the subject toward *alienation.* The anxiety that his liberty induces in the subject leads him to search for himself in things, which is a kind of flight from himself. This tendency is so fundamental that immediately after weaning, when he is separated from the Whole, the infant is compelled to lay hold upon his alienated existence in mirrors and in the gaze of his parents. Primitive people are alienated in mana, in the totem[9]; civilized people in their individual souls, in their egos, their names, their property, their work. Here is to be found the primary temptation to inauthenticity, to failure to be genuinely oneself. The penis is singularly adapted for playing this role of "double" for the little boy—it is for him at once a foreign object and himself; it is a plaything, a doll, and yet his own flesh; relatives and nurse-girls behave toward it as if it were a little person. It is easy to see, then, how it becomes for the child "an *alter ego* ordinarily more artful, more intelligent, and more clever than the individual." The penis is regarded by the subject as at once himself and other than himself, because the functions of urination and later of erection are processes midway between the voluntary and the involuntary, and because it is a capricious and as it were a foreign source of pleasure that is felt subjectively. The individual's specific transcendence takes concrete form in the penis and it is a source of pride. Because the phallus is thus set apart, man can bring into integration with his subjective individuality the life that overflows from it. It is easy to see, then, that the length of the penis, the force of the urinary jet, the strength of erection and ejaculation become for him the measure of his own worth.

Thus the incarnation of transcendence in the phallus is a constant; 15 and since it is also a constant for the child to feel himself transcended—that is to say, frustrated in his own transcendence by the father—we therefore continually come upon the Freudian idea of the

---

[8]***Mitsein*** Being with.

[9]***mana; in the totem*** By "mana," Beauvoir means in the tribal collective; by "in the totem," in the symbols of the tribe rather than being alienated as individuals distinct from the tribe.

"castration complex." Not having that *alter ego*, the little girl is not alienated in a material thing and cannot retrieve her integrity. On this account she is led to make an object of her whole self, to set up herself as the Other. Whether she knows that she is or is not comparable with boys is secondary; the important point is that, even if she is unaware of it, the absence of the penis prevents her from being conscious of herself as a sexual being. From this flow many consequences. But the constants I have referred to do not for all that establish a fixed destiny—the phallus assumes such worth as it does because it symbolizes a dominance that is exercised in other domains. If woman should succeed in establishing herself as subject, she would invent equivalents of the phallus; in fact, the doll, incarnating the promise of the baby that is to come in the future, can become a possession more precious than the penis. There are matrilineal societies in which the women keep in their possession the *masks* in which the group finds alienation; in such societies the penis loses much of its glory. The fact is that a true human privilege is based upon the anatomical privilege only in virtue of the total situation. Psychoanalysis can establish its truths only in the historical context.

Woman can be defined by her consciousness of her own femininity 16 no more satisfactorily than by saying that she is a female, for she acquires this consciousness under circumstances dependent upon the society of which she is a member. Interiorizing the unconscious and the whole psychic life, the very language of psychoanalysis suggests that the drama of the individual unfolds within him—such words as *complex, tendency,* and so on make that implication. But a life is a relation to the world, and the individual defines himself by making his own choices through the world about him. We must therefore turn toward the world to find answers for the questions we are concerned with. In particular psychoanalysis fails to explain why woman is the *Other.* For Freud himself admits that the prestige of the penis is explained by the sovereignty of the father, and, as we have seen, he confesses that he is ignorant regarding the origin of male supremacy.

We therefore decline to accept the method of psychoanalysis, with- 17 out rejecting *en bloc* the contributions of the science or denying the fertility of some of its insights. In the first place, we do not limit ourselves to regarding sexuality as something given. The insufficiency of this view is shown by the poverty of the resulting descriptions of the feminine libido; as I have already said, the psychoanalysts have never studied it directly, but only in taking the male libido as their point of departure. They seem to ignore the fundamental ambivalence of the attraction exerted on the female by the male. Freudians and Adlerians explain the anxiety felt by the female confronted by the masculine sex as being the inversion of a frustrated desire. Stekel[10] saw more clearly that an original reaction was concerned, but he accounts for it in a superficial manner. Woman, he says, would fear defloration, penetration, pregnancy, and pain, and such fear would restrain her desire—but this explanation is too rational. Instead of holding that her desire is disguised in anxiety or is contested by fear, we should regard as an original fact this blending of urgency and apprehension which is female desire: it is the indissoluble synthesis of attraction and repulsion that characterizes it. We may note that many female animals avoid copulation even as they are soliciting it, and we are tempted to accuse them of coquetry or hypocrisy; but it is absurd to pretend to explain primitive behavior patterns by asserting their similarity to complex modes of conduct. On the contrary, the former are in truth at the source of the attitudes that in woman are called coquetry and hypocrisy. The notion of a "passive libido" is baffling, since the libido has been defined, on the basis of the male, as a drive, an energy; but one would do no better to hold the opinion that a light could be at once yellow and blue—what is needed is the intuition of green. We would more fully encompass reality if instead of defining the libido in vague terms of "energy" we brought the significance of sexuality into relation with that of other human attitudes—taking, capturing, eating, making, submitting, and so forth; for it is one of the various modes of apprehending an object. We should study also the qualities of the erotic object as it presents itself not only in the sexual act but also to observation in general. Such an investigation extends beyond the frame of psychoanalysis, which assumes eroticism as irreducible.

Furthermore, I shall pose the problem of feminine destiny quite   18
otherwise: I shall place woman in a world of values and give her behavior a dimension of liberty. I believe that she has the power to choose between the assertion of her transcendence and her alienation as object; she is not the plaything of contradictory drives; she devises solutions of diverse ranking in the ethical scale. Replacing value with authority, choice with drive, psychoanalysis offers an *Ersatz*, a substitute, for morality—the concept of normality. This concept is certainly most useful in therapeutics, but it has spread through psychoanalysis in general to a disquieting extent. The descriptive schema is proposed as a law; and most assuredly a mechanistic psychology cannot accept

---

[10]***Wilhelm Stekel (1868–1940)*** A German psychiatrist who edited *Psyche and Eros*, a psychiatric journal.

the notion of moral invention; it can in strictness render an account of the *less* and never of the more; in strictness it can admit of checks, never of creations. If a subject does not show in his totality the development considered as normal, it will be said that his development has been arrested, and this arrest will be interpreted as a lack, a negation, but never as a positive decision. This it is, among other things, that makes the psychoanalysis of great men so shocking: we are told that such and such a transference, this or that sublimation, has not taken place in them; it is not suggested that perhaps they have refused to undergo the process, perhaps for good reasons of their own; it is not thought desirable to regard their behavior as possibly motivated by purposes freely envisaged; the individual is always explained through ties with his past and not in respect to a future toward which he projects his aims. Thus the psychoanalysts never give us more than an inauthentic picture, and for the inauthentic there can hardly be found any other criterion than normality. Their statement of the feminine destiny is absolutely to the point in this connection. In the sense in which the psychoanalysts understand the term, "to identify oneself" with the mother or with the father is to *alienate oneself* in a model, it is to prefer a foreign image to the spontaneous manifestation of one's own existence, it is to play at being. Woman is shown to us as enticed by two modes of alienation. Evidently to play at being a man will be for her a source of frustration; but to play at being a woman is also a delusion: to be a woman would mean to be the object, the *Other*—and the Other nevertheless remains subject in the midst of her resignation.

The true problem for woman is to reject these flights from reality 19 and seek self-fulfillment in transcendence. The thing to do, then, is to see what possibilities are opened up for her through what are called the virile and the feminine attitudes. When a child takes the road indicated by one or the other of its parents, it may be because the child freely takes up their projects; its behavior may be the result of a choice motivated by ends and aims. Even with Adler the will to power is only an absurd kind of energy; he denominates as "masculine protest" every project involving transcendence. When a little girl climbs trees it is, according to Adler, just to show her equality with boys; it does not occur to him that she likes to climb trees. For the mother her child is something quite other than an "equivalent of the penis." To paint, to write, to engage in politics—these are not merely "sublimations"; here we have aims that are willed for their own sakes. To deny it is to falsify all human history.

The reader will note a certain parallelism between this account and 20 that of the psychoanalysts. The fact is that from the male point of view—which is adopted by both male and female psychoanalysts—behavior involving alienation is regarded as feminine, that in which the subject asserts his transcendence as virile. Donaldson,[11] a historian of woman, remarked that the definitions: "man is a male human being, woman is a female human being," have been asymmetrically distorted; and it is among the psychoanalysts in particular that man is defined as a human being and woman as a female—whenever she behaves as a human being she is said to imitate the male. The psychoanalyst describes the female child, the young girl, as incited to identification with the mother and the father, torn between "viriloid" and "feminine" tendencies; whereas I conceive her as hesitating between the role of *object, Other* which is offered her, and the assertion of her liberty. Thus it is that we shall agree on a certain number of facts, especially when we take up the avenues of inauthentic flight open to women. But we accord them by no means the same significance as does the Freudian or the Adlerian. For us woman is defined as a human being in quest of values in a world of values, a world of which it is indispensable to know the economic and social structure.

---

[11]**Donaldson** Possibly a reference to Henry Herbert Donaldson (1857–1938), whose study of Laura Bridgman is a classic of neurology.

QUESTIONS

1. Do you agree that a person is not born a woman, but becomes a woman?
2. Is a woman a female to the extent that she feels herself as such?
3. What does it mean to regard the female in society as the Other?
4. How true is it that Freud's view of feminine psychology is built on his views of masculine psychology?
5. Beauvoir suggests that psychiatry is something like a religion (para. 2). Do you think she is right?
6. What does it mean to say that woman is a mutilated man? Would this tend to distort society's view of woman?
7. Is Beauvoir's view of the relation of little girls to their parents accurate as far as you can tell (see para. 6)?

WRITING ASSIGNMENTS

1. In paragraph 6 Beauvoir says that "the little girl entertains a feeling of rivalry and hostility toward her mother." Is this in any way supportable from your experience growing up? What is the nature of the girl's rivalry

with the mother? What denotes it, and what seems to be at its root? Is there a similar rivalry for a little boy with his father?

2. What is your view on the question of the little girl's supposed penis envy? Do little girls tend to envy the little boys in their lives? To what extent is that envy cultural, and to what extent is it biological. Is Beauvoir accurate in her assessment of the significance of this envy?

3. Define the Electra complex and how it seems to work, according to Beauvoir. You might look in the essay for a discussion of the complex, but paragraph 7 will get you started. How powerful is this complex? Were you in any way aware of it in yourself or your siblings as you grew up? Are you aware of it now?

4. What seems to be the evidence that supports the psychoanalytic views of Freud, Jung, and Beauvoir? Are you convinced that psychoanalysis is a science, or do you think it is something else? If it is something else, what might it be? Be sure to consider Beauvoir's discussion of the empirical evidence of psychoanalysis (para. 10).

5. One of the constant themes that Beauvoir returns to is the theme of choice (paras. 11 and 13). She believes that psychiatrists deny the validity of choice, but she herself feels that choice is one of the most powerful forces in a person's life. Taking the entire essay into account, how important do you feel choice is for determining your psychic fate?

6. One basic question that Beauvoir leaves us with is whether or not "Anatomy is destiny." Where do you stand? Do you feel that in your generation a person is directed by his or her anatomy? Will those born female find female roles in life? Will those born male find masculine roles? How significant is anatomy for directing your educational goals? How many decisions have you made—or have had made for you—that seem rooted in someone else's perception of your anatomy?

PART FOUR

IDEAS IN THE WORLD OF SCIENCE

HOW CAN WE KNOW THE
SECRETS OF NATURE? HOW
CAN WE *KNOW* THAT WE KNOW?

———⸲∞⸲———

Lucretius
Francis Bacon
Charles Darwin
Thomas Kuhn
Loren Eiseley
Stephen Jay Gould

INTRODUCTION

THE WORD "SCIENCE" is etymologically related to *scire*, "to know." The scientist wants to know about the world of experience, both that which is within the grasp and perception of the individual and that which is beyond the individual's grasp. For that reason, at its root science has always been concerned with developing a true knowledge of the nature of things. All the writers in Part Four are preoccupied with how the world works, what the nature of nature is, and how we can take advantage of that knowledge. Some of the writers, such as Francis Bacon and Thomas Kuhn, are interested in basic theories of how we know and how we make discoveries. Others, such as Charles Darwin and Stephen Jay Gould are interested in establishing what they feel is the truth about things. All are concerned with what we can know and whether we can trust our knowledge.

The Roman thinker Lucretius wrote *On the Nature of Things* to answer questions about the most basic things perceivable about the universe. His way of thinking is by our standards very limited since he had neither telescope nor microscope, but it is startling because of his accurate apprehension of such mysteries as vacuums and atoms. He had a tenacious mind that observed things carefully and drew responsible and remarkable conclusions. His book has been taken seriously for two thousand years; Lucretius continues to surprise readers with his knowledge.

The problem with knowing anything in the sciences, as Francis Bacon reminded his readers in "The Four Idols," is that human beings already have heads filled with presumptions and with methods of inquiry that are not necessarily the best tools for scientific examination. This is an important essay because in it Bacon confronts some of the basic issues in the sciences: what casts of mind are essential to gain knowledge? What in our makeup prevents us from seeing clearly? In an age before the advent of sophisticated instruments that permitted scientists to see directly into the way nature works, it was essential to probe first into the way in which we conceived problems and then set about to solve these problems. At the time Bacon wrote, the most sophisticated scientific instruments were the five senses.

Charles Darwin, in "Natural Selection," proposed a theory that is still controversial. While on a voyage around South America in the *Beagle*, Darwin had the opportunity to observe impressive similarities in the structures of various animals. He had the advantages of a good education, a deep knowledge of the Bible and theology (he was trained as a minister), and a systematic and inquiring mind. He kept scientific samples of insects and flowers and other forms of life and studied them closely in order to detect their resemblances. To explain the significance of his findings, he developed his theories of evolution. Explaining the nature of nature—or one aspect of nature, at least—as it functioned in human experience formed an essential element of Darwin's work.

Thomas Kuhn's "The Essential Tension" is a modern-day version of Francis Bacon's essay—at least in some ways. Kuhn was concerned with the kinds of mental functions that produced new knowledge. He speculated about whether there are presumptions that would actually impede discovery. What is the importance of old, accepted theories to the act of discovery? Kuhn makes us revise some of our preconceptions—even preconceptions that are informed by the essays in Part Four that precede this one. In his essay, Kuhn inquired into the science of science and for that reason, his ideas are important to how we look at science and those authors who write about it.

In "The Last Neanderthal," Loren Eiseley takes us on a meandering journey through observations that are exceptionally personal—in fact, autobiographical. It is a privilege to see a scientific mind at work, observing details and searching for meanings. The evolutionary issues that intrigued Darwin are here, just as are the issues of investigation that concerned Kuhn. This essay is relaxed and easy in appearance, but it contains most of the primary issues that bother all scientists: how can we know about the nature of things? How do our minds work in relation to the details of experience?

Stephen Jay Gould, in "Nonmoral Nature," examines the results of the kind of thinking that Bacon had deplored in the seventeenth century but that also flourished in the nineteenth century. If you interpreted the world of nature as if it were fashioned by someone with the same predilections as the Victorian scientist—who was usually, by the way, a minister as well as a scientist—then you would naturally see good and evil in animal and insect behavior. Even today most of us see the world in such terms, but Gould wants us to give that up in favor of a more rational approach. The world is the world; moral issues relate to us, not to dolphins or sharks. To learn that lesson is certainly difficult, but a scientific orientation should help us achieve the necessary detachment. The way we approach the evidence in front of our eyes, in other words, affects what we see just as much as what is there to be observed.

LUCRETIUS

Matter and Space

*T*ITUS LUCRETIUS CARUS *(c.100* B.C.–c.55 B.C.*) was a Roman poet who devoted his life to the teachings of the Greek philosopher Epicurus (c.341–270* B.C.*). In his celebrated work* On the Nature of Things, *Lucretius spelled out the consequences of belief in the Epicurean system. Unlike the philosopher Plato (see "The Allegory of the Cave," p. 517), the Epicureans assumed that the world was what it seemed to be, that the senses provided adequate knowledge of the world, and that the pleasurable things they did were in large measure the best rewards of life. Epicureans rarely spent their lives in public service or in roles that demanded self-sacrifice. Instead, they often lived in rural splendor, enjoying the good things of life.*

However, they were as interested in the nature of experience as anyone else, and by closely following the teachings of Epicurus, Lucretius was able to formulate a coherent scientific theory that is remarkable for its resemblance to much of modern thought. Lucretius did not have the advantage of scientific instruments, such as the microscope and the telescope, both of which were of primary impor-

---

From *On the Nature of Things*. Translated by R. E. Latham.

tance to the development of modern science. His only "instruments" were his five senses and his reasoning.

To us, his methods of reasoning are fascinating. He established a principle based on his observations and then demonstrated the likelihood of the truth of this principle by examining the available evidence and drawing the best conclusions possible. The procedure is quite scientific within its limitations, and if we were to imagine a modern scientist armed with experimental evidence attempting to draw a conclusion, we could imagine that the intellectual process would resemble that of Lucretius.

The most important point to observe about Lucretius may simply be the nature of his curiosity. What interested him were those things that we now think of as scientific: the nature of matter, the nature of space, the way natural phenomena exist and function. Few in his age were interested in such issues, and his voice is therefore singularly powerful.

The entire book is addressed to Memmius, believed to be a young man of aristocratic blood and great accomplishments. Of course, Lucretius expected his work to be read by others as well, and the principles he set down are as universal as he could make them. We must remember that there was no genuine marketplace for scientific ideas in Lucretius's time, and that, as he said, the earth lay "under the dead weight of superstition." For a treatise displaying the enlightenment of On the Nature of Things to evolve from this period is astonishing. All the more astonishing was it for Lucretius to virtually ignore the gods of Rome in his analysis of wordly experience. His strategy was to suggest that the gods existed but that they did not take notice of human life. Further, Lucretius thought that the classical concepts of soul and afterlife were fictions; his views, in many ways significantly materialistic, were also optimistic and encouraging for their emphasis on the value of human life and the excitement of human experience.

Perhaps one of the most striking and strikingly modern points he made was that matter is composed of invisible atoms. Such a statement seems to disregard common sense. Yet we know without question today that the atomic theory is true. Lucretius took the theory from another prominent Greek philosopher, Democritus (460?–?370 B.C.), and testing it by his careful analytic, he agreed that it was the only reasonable opinion that a person could maintain. It is staggering to think that in the century before Christ, Lucretius could have conceived these kinds of scientific positions in the face of what must have been the most profound skepticism and disbelief.

L U C R E T I U S ' S   R H E T O R I C

One of the most interesting rhetorical devices that Lucretius uses is the relaxed tone of personal communication. It is not appropriate to read this piece as if it were a letter, but it is similar to a letter. Memmius is an audience of one, and we may imagine that we are overhearing a piece intended for a personal audience, as when we read Martin Luther King, Jr.'s "Letter from Birmingham Jail." The result is that the tone is informal and the discussion relaxed. We are reading about science, but because there is no sense of being lectured to, we can relax and so pay attention more easily.

On the Nature of Things was originally written in poetic form. Such a form not only emphasizes the importance of the subject matter but also contributes to the work's gracefulness of expression. This translation makes it difficult for us to comprehend what On the Nature of Things *must have sounded like as poetry because there is little that is imagistic or patterned in the style of most poetry from that period. However, a structural pattern does hold throughout the piece.*

Lucretius uses an analytic approach. He selects six basic principles, or axioms, into which he divides his scientific doctrine. Then, within each of those principles, he structures a definition, a pattern of reasoning, and a list of examples. The rhetorical skill that is most evident in this piece is argumentation. Lucretius poses a position; he examines the evidence that points us to the position; and he dismisses counter positions and reviews the reasons why we should accept his argument. In this way, each of the six axioms is so well developed and elucidated that it is difficult for Memmius to perceive any viewpoint except *that of Lucretius.*

The six great principles Lucretius states are as follows:

1. *Nothing can ever be created by divine power out of nothing.*
2. *Nature resolves everything into its component atoms and never reduces anything to nothing.*
3. *There is vacuity in things.*
4. *Nothing exists that is distinct from body and from vacuity.*
5. *Material objects are of two kinds, atoms and compounds of atoms.*
6. *The atoms themselves cannot be swamped by any force, for they are preserved indefinitely by their absolute solidity.*

These principles, like Francis Bacon's Four Idols, guide the structure of the entire piece and achieve, in their presentation, a precision that is essential for good communication. Most of the writers on sci-

ence in Part Four of this book maintain clarity as their primary rhetorical aim; Lucretius, however, is one of the most lucid writers in
the entire book.

---◦∞◦---

Matter and Space

For what is to follow, my Memmius, lay aside your cares and lend 1
undistracted ears and an attentive mind to true reason. Do not scorn-
fully reject, before you have understood them, the gifts I have mar-
shalled for you with zealous devotion. I will set out to discourse to
you on the ultimate realities of heaven and the gods. I will reveal those
atoms from which nature creates all things and increases and feeds
them and into which, when they perish, nature again resolves them.
To these in my discourse I commonly give such names as the "raw
material," or "generative bodies" or "seeds" of things. Or I may call
them "primary particles," because they come first and everything else
is composed of them.

When human life lay grovelling in all men's sight, crushed to the 2
earth under the dead weight of superstition whose grim features loured
menacingly upon mortals from the four quarters of the sky, a man of
Greece[1] was first to raise mortal eyes in defiance, first to stand erect
and brave the challenge. Fables of the gods did not crush him, nor the
lightning flash and the growling menace of the sky. Rather, they
quickened his manhood, so that he, first of all men, longed to smash
the constraining locks of nature's doors. The vital vigor of his mind
prevailed. He ventured far out beyond the flaming ramparts of the
world and voyaged in mind throughout infinity. Returning victorious,
he proclaimed to us what can be and what cannot: how a limit is fixed
to the power of everything and an immovable frontier post. Therefore
superstition in its turn lies crushed beneath his feet, and we by his
triumph are lifted level with the skies.

---

[1]*a man of Greece* Epicurus.

One thing that worries me is the fear that you may fancy yourself 3
embarking on an impious course, setting your feet on the path of sin.
Far from it. More often it is this very superstition that is the mother
of sinful and impious deeds. Remember how at Aulis the altar of the
Virgin Goddess was foully stained with the blood of Iphigenia[2] by the
leaders of the Greeks, the patterns of chivalry. The headband was
bound about her virgin tresses and hung down evenly over both her
cheeks. Suddenly she caught sight of her father standing sadly in front
of the altar, the attendants beside him hiding the knife and her people
bursting into tears when they saw her. Struck dumb with terror, she
sank on her knees to the ground. Poor girl, at such a moment it did
not help her that she had been first to give the name of father to a
king. Raised by the hands of men, she was led trembling to the altar.
Not for her the sacrament of marriage and the loud chant of Hymen.[3]
It was her fate in the very hour of marriage to fall a sinless victim to
a sinful rite, slaughtered to her greater grief by a father's hand, so that
a fleet might sail under happy auspices. Such are the heights of
wickedness to which men are driven by superstition.

You yourself, if you surrender your judgment at any time to the 4
blood-curdling declamations of the prophets, will want to desert our
ranks. Only think what phantoms they can conjure up to overturn the
tenor of your life and wreck your happiness with fear. And not without
cause. For, if men saw that a term was set to their troubles, they would
find strength in some way to withstand the hocus-pocus and intimi-
dations of the prophets. As it is, they have no power of resistance,
because they are haunted by the fear of eternal punishment after death.
They know nothing of the nature of the spirit. Is it born, or is it implanted in us at birth? Does it perish with us, dissolved by death, or
does it visit the murky depths and dreary sloughs of Hades?[4] Or is it
transplanted by divine power into other creatures, as described in the
poems of our own Ennius, who first gathered on the delectable slopes
of Helicon[5] an evergreen garland destined to win renown among the
nations of Italy? Ennius indeed in his immortal verses proclaims that
there is also a Hell, which is peopled not by our actual spirits or bodies

---

[2] *Iphigenia* Maiden who was sacrificed by her father, Agamemnon, before he set
sail for the Trojan War.

[3] *Hymen* The god of marriage.

[4] *Hades* Underworld inhabited by the dead.

[5] *Ennius (239–169 B.C.)* Quintus Ennius, a Roman poet . . . *Helicon* The
mountain in Greece where the Muses, who presided over the arts, were said to dwell.

but only by shadowy images, ghastly pale. It is from this realm that he pictures the ghost of Homer,[6] of unfading memory, as appearing to him, shedding salt tears and revealing the nature of the universe.

I must therefore give an account of celestial phenomena, explaining   5 the movements of sun and moon and also the forces that determine events on earth. Next, and no less important, we must look with keen insight into the make-up of spirit and mind: we must consider those alarming phantasms that strike upon our minds when they are awake but disordered by sickness, or when they are buried in slumber, so that we seem to see and hear before us men whose dead bones lie in the embraces of earth.

I am well aware that it is not easy to elucidate in Latin verse the   6 obscure discoveries of the Greeks. The poverty of our language and the novelty of the theme compel me often to coin new words for the purpose. But your merit and the joy I hope to derive from our delightful friendship encourage me to face any task however hard. This it is that leads me to stay awake through the quiet of the night, studying how by choice of words and the poet's art I can display before your mind a clear light by which you can gaze into the heart of hidden things.

This dread and darkness of the mind cannot be dispelled by the   7 sunbeams, the shining shafts of day, but only by an understanding of the outward form and inner workings of nature. In tackling this theme, our starting-point will be this principle: *nothing can ever be created by divine power out of nothing*. The reason why all mortals are so gripped by fear is that they see all sorts of things happening on the earth and in the sky with no discernible cause, and these they attribute to the will of a god. Accordingly, when we have seen that nothing can be created out of nothing, we shall then have a clearer picture of the path ahead, the problem of how things are created and occasioned without the aid of the gods.

First then, if things were made out of nothing, any species could   8 spring from any source and nothing would require seed. Men could arise from the sea and scaly fish from the earth, and birds could be hatched out of the sky. Cattle and other domestic animals and every kind of wild beast, multiplying indiscriminately, would occupy cultivated and waste lands alike. The same fruits would not grow constantly on the same trees, but they would keep changing: any tree

---

[6] ***Homer (ninth century B.C.)*** Author of the epic poems *Iliad* and *Odyssey*, which recount the colorful exploits of gods and heroes.

might bear any fruit. If each species were not composed of its own generative bodies, why should each be born always of the same kind of mother? Actually, since each is formed out of specific seeds, it is born and emerges into the sunlit world only from a place where there exists the right material, the right kind of atoms. This is why everything cannot be born of everything, but a specific power of generation inheres in specific objects.

Again, why do we see roses appear in spring, grain in summer's 9 heat, grapes under the spell of autumn? Surely, because it is only after specific seeds have drifted together at their own proper time that every created thing stands revealed, when the season is favorable and the life-giving earth can safely deliver delicate growths into the sunlit world. If they were made out of nothing, they would spring up suddenly after varying lapses of time and at abnormal seasons, since there would of course be no primary bodies which could be prevented by the harshness of the season from entering into generative unions. Similarly, in order that things might grow, there would be no need of any lapse of time for the accumulation of seed. Tiny tots would turn suddenly into grown men, and trees would shoot up spontaneously out of the earth. But it is obvious that none of these things happens, since everything grows gradually, as is natural, from a specific seed and retains its specific character. It is a fair inference that each is increased and nourished by its own raw material.

Here is a further point. Without seasonable showers the earth can- 10 not send up gladdening growths. Lacking food, animals cannot reproduce their kind or sustain life. This points to the conclusion that many elements are common to many things, as letters are to words, rather than to the theory that anything can come into existence without atoms.

Or again, why has not nature been able to produce men on such a 11 scale that they could ford the ocean on foot or demolish high mountains with their hands or prolong their lives over many generations? Surely, because each thing requires for its birth a particular material which determines what can be produced. It must therefore be admitted that nothing can be made out of nothing, because everything must be generated from a seed before it can emerge into the unresisting air.

Lastly, we see that tilled plots are superior to untilled, and their 12 fruits are improved by cultivation. This is because the earth contains certain atoms which we rouse to productivity by turning the fruitful clods with the plowshare and stirring up the soil. But for these, you would see great improvements arising spontaneously without any aid from our labors.

The second great principle is this: *nature resolves everything into* 13
its component atoms and never reduces anything to nothing. If anything were perishable in all its parts, anything might perish all of a sudden and vanish from sight. There would be no need of any force to separate its parts and loosen their links. In actual fact, since everything is composed of indestructible seeds, nature obviously does not allow anything to perish till it has encountered a force that shatters it with a blow or creeps into chinks and unknits it.

If the things that are banished from the scene by age are annihi- 14
lated through the exhaustion of their material, from what source does Venus bring back the several races of animals into the light of life? And, when they are brought back, where does the inventive earth find each the special food required for its sustenance and growth? From what fount is the sea replenished by its native springs and the streams that flow into it from afar? Whence does the ether draw nutriment for the stars? For everything consisting of a mortal body must have been exhausted by the long day of time, the illimitable past. If throughout this bygone eternity there have persisted bodies from which the universe has been perpetually renewed, they must certainly be possessed of immortality. Therefore things cannot be reduced to nothing.

Again, all objects would regularly be destroyed by the same force 15
and the same cause, were it not that they are sustained by imperishable matter more or less tightly fastened together. Why, a mere touch would be enough to bring about destruction supposing there were no imperishable bodies whose union could be dissolved only by the appropriate force. Actually, because the fastenings of the atoms are of various kinds while their matter is imperishable, compound objects remain intact until one of them encounters a force that proves strong enough to break up its particular constitution. Therefore nothing returns to nothing, but everything is resolved into its constituent bodies.

Lastly, showers perish when father ether has flung them down into 16
the lap of mother earth. But the crops spring up fresh and gay; the branches on the trees burst into leaf; the trees themselves grow and are weighed down with fruit. Hence in turn man and brute draw nourishment. Hence we see flourishing cities blest with children and every leafy thicket loud with new broods of songsters. Hence in lush pastures cattle wearied by their bulk fling down their bodies, and the white milky juice oozes from their swollen udders. Hence a new generation frolic friskily on wobbly legs through the fresh grass, their young minds tipsy with undiluted milk. Visible objects therefore do not perish utterly, since nature repairs one thing from another and allows nothing to be born without the aid of another's death.

Well, Memmius, I have taught you that things cannot be created 17
out of nothing nor, once born, be summoned back to nothing. Perhaps,
however, you are becoming mistrustful of my words, because these
atoms of mine are not visible to the eye. Consider, therefore, this further evidence of *bodies whose existence you must acknowledge
though they cannot be seen.* First, wind, when its force is roused,
whips up waves, founders tall ships and scatters cloud-rack. Sometimes scouring plains with hurricane force it strews them with huge
trees and batters mountain peaks with blasts that hew down forests.
Such is wind in its fury, when it whoops aloud with a mad menace in
its shouting. Without question, therefore, there must be invisible particles of wind which sweep sea and land and the clouds in the sky,
swooping upon them and whirling them along in a headlong hurricane.
In the way they flow and the havoc they spread they are no different
from a torrential flood of water when it rushes down in a sudden spate
from the mountain heights, swollen by heavy rains, and heaps together
wreckage from the forest and entire trees. Soft though it is by nature,
the sudden shock of oncoming water is more than even stout bridges
can withstand, so furious is the force with which the turbid, storm-
flushed torrent surges against their piers. With a mighty roar it lays
them low, rolling huge rocks under its waves and brushing aside every
obstacle from its course. Such, therefore, must be the movement of
blasts of wind also. When they have come surging along some course
like a rushing river, they push obstacles before them and buffet them
with repeated blows; and sometimes, eddying round and round, they
snatch them up and carry them along in a swiftly circling vortex. Here
then is proof upon proof that winds have invisible bodies, since in
their actions and behavior they are found to rival great rivers, whose
bodies are plain to see.

Then again, we smell the various scents of things though we never 18
see them approaching our nostrils. Similarly, heat and cold cannot be
detected by our eyes, and we do not see sounds. Yet all these must be
composed of bodies, since they are able to impinge upon our senses.
For nothing can touch or be touched except body.

Again, clothes hung out on a surf-beaten shore grow moist. Spread 19
in the sun they grow dry. But we do not see how the moisture has
soaked into them, nor again how it has been dispelled by the heat. It
follows that the moisture is split up into minute parts which the eye
cannot possibly see.

Again, in the course of many annual revolutions of the sun a ring 20
is worn thin next to the finger with continual rubbing. Dripping water
hollows a stone. A curved plowshare, iron though it is, dwindles im-

perceptibly in the furrow. We see the cobble-stones of the highway
worn by the feet of many wayfarers. The bronze statues by the city
gates show their right hands worn thin by the touch of travellers who
have greeted them in passing. We see that all these are being diminished, since they are worn away. But to perceive what particles drop
off at any particular time is a power grudged to us by our ungenerous
sense of sight.

To sum up, whatever is added to things gradually by nature and the 21
passage of days, causing a cumulative increase, eludes the most attentive scrutiny of our eyes. Conversely, you cannot see what objects lose
by the wastage of age—sheer sea-cliffs, for instance, exposed to prolonged erosion by the mordant brine—or at what time the loss occurs.
It follows that nature works through the agency of invisible bodies.

On the other hand, things are not hemmed in by the pressure of 22
solid bodies in a tight mass. This is because *there is vacuity in things.*
A grasp of this fact will be helpful to you in many respects and will
save you from much bewildered doubting and questioning about the
universe and from mistrust of my teaching. Well then, by vacuity I
mean intangible and empty space. If it did not exist, things could not
move at all. For the distinctive action of matter, which is counterac-
tion and obstruction, would be in force always and everywhere. Nothing could proceed, because nothing would give it a starting-point by
receding. As it is, we see with our own eyes at sea and on land and
high up in the sky that all sorts of things in all sorts of ways are on
the move. If there were no empty space, these things would be denied
the power of restless movement—or rather, they could not possibly
have come into existence, embedded as they would have been in mo-
tionless matter.

Besides, there are clear indications that things that pass for solid 23
are in fact porous. Even in rocks a trickle of water seeps through into
caves, and copious drops ooze from every surface. Food percolates to
every part of an animal's body. Trees grow and bring forth their fruit
in season, because their food is distributed throughout their length
from the tips of the roots through the trunk and along every branch.
Noises pass through walls and fly into closed buildings. Freezing cold
penetrates to the bones. If there were no vacancies through which the
various bodies could make their way, none of these phenomena would
be possible.

Again, why do we find some things outweigh others of equal vol- 24
ume? If there is as much matter in a ball of wool as in one of lead, it
is natural that it should weigh as heavily, since it is the function of

matter to press everything downwards, while it is the function of space on the other hand to remain weightless. Accordingly, when one thing is not less bulky than another but obviously lighter, it plainly declares that there is more vacuum in it, while the heavier object proclaims that there is more matter in it and much less empty space. We have therefore reached the goal of our diligent inquiry: there is in things an admixture of what we call vacuity.

In case you should be misled on this question by the idle imagining 25 of certain theorists, I must anticipate their argument. They maintain that water yields and opens a penetrable path to the scaly bodies of fish that push against it, because they leave spaces behind them into which the yielding water can flow together. In the same way, they suppose, other things can move by mutually changing places, although every place remains filled. This theory has been adopted utterly without warrant. For how can the fish advance till the water has given way? And how can the water retire when the fish cannot move? There are thus only two alternatives: either all bodies are devoid of movement, or you must admit that things contain an admixture of vacuity whereby each is enabled to make the first move.

Lastly, if two bodies suddenly spring apart from contact on a broad 26 surface, all the intervening space must be void until it is occupied by air. However quickly the air rushes in all round, the entire space cannot be filled instantaneously. The air must occupy one spot after another until it has taken possession of the whole space. If anyone supposes that this consequence of such springing apart is made possible by the condensation of air, he is mistaken. For condensation implies that something that was full becomes empty, or *vice versa*. And I contend that air could not condense so as to produce this effect; or at any rate, if there were no vacuum, it could not thus shrink into itself and draw its parts together.

However many pleas you may advance to prolong the argument, 27 you must end by admitting that there is vacuity in things. There are many other proofs I could add to the pile in order to strengthen conviction; but for an acute intelligence these small clues should suffice to enable you to discover the rest for yourself. As hounds that range the hills often smell out the lairs of wild beasts screened in thickets, when once they have got on to the right trail, so in such questions one thing will lead on to another, till you can succeed by yourself in tracking down the truth to its lurking-places and dragging it forth. If you grow weary and relax from the chase, there is one thing, Memmius, that I can safely promise you: my honeyed tongue will pour from the treasury of my breast such generous drafts, drawn from inexhaustible

springs, that I am afraid slow-plodding age may creep through my
limbs and unbolt the bars of my life before the full flood of my arguments on any single point has flowed in verse through your ears.

To pick up the thread of my discourse, all nature as it is in itself 28
consists of two things—bodies and the vacant space in which the bodies are situated and through which they move in different directions.
The existence of bodies is vouched for by the agreement of the senses.
If a belief resting directly on this foundation is not valid, there will be
no standard to which we can refer any doubt on obscure questions for
rational confirmation. If there were no place and space, which we call
vacuity, these bodies could not be situated anywhere or move in any
direction whatever. This I have just demonstrated. It remains to show
that *nothing exists that is distinct both from body and from vacuity*
and could be ranked with the others as a third substance. For whatever
is must also be something. If it offers resistance to touch, however
light and slight, it will increase the mass of body by such amount,
great or small, as it may amount to, and will rank with it. If, on the
other hand, it is intangible, so that it offers no resistance whatever to
anything passing through it, then it will be that empty space which
we call vacuity. Besides, whatever it may be in itself, either it will act
in some way, or react to other things acting upon it, or else it will be
such that things can be and happen in it. But without body nothing
can act or react; and nothing can afford a place except emptiness and
vacancy. Therefore, besides matter and vacuity, we cannot include in
the number of things any third substance that can either affect our
senses at any time or be grasped by the reasoning of our minds.

You will find that anything that can be named is either a property 29
or an accident of these two. A *property* is something that cannot be
detached or separated from a thing without destroying it, as weight is
a property of rocks, heat of fire, fluidity of water, tangibility of all
bodies, intangibility of vacuum. On the other hand, servitude and liberty, poverty and riches, war and peace, and all other things whose
advent or departure leaves the essence of a thing intact, all these it is
our practice to call by their appropriate name, *accidents*.

Similarly, time by itself does not exist; but from things themselves 30
there results a sense of what has already taken place, what is now
going on and what is to ensue. It must not be claimed that anyone can
sense time by itself apart from the movement of things or their restful
immobility.

Again, when men say it *is* a fact that Helen was ravished or the 31
Trojans were conquered, do not let anyone drive you to the admission

that any such event *is* independently of any object, on the ground that the generations of men of whom these events were accidents have been swept away by the irrevocable lapse of time. For we could put it that whatever has taken place is an accident of a particular tract of earth or of the space it occupied. If there had been no matter and no space or place in which things could happen, no spark of love kindled by the beauty of Tyndareus' daughter would ever have stolen into the breast of Phrygian Paris to light that dazzling blaze of pitiless war; no Wooden Horse, unmarked by the sons of Troy, would have set the towers of Ilium aflame through the midnight issue of Greeks from its womb. So you may see that events cannot be said to *be* by themselves like matter or in the same sense as space. Rather, you should describe them as accidents of matter, or of the place in which things happen.

Material objects are of two kinds, atoms and compounds of at- 32 *oms. The atoms themselves cannot be swamped by any force, for they are preserved indefinitely by their absolute solidity.* Admittedly, it is hard to believe that anything can exist that is absolutely solid. The lightning stroke from the sky penetrates closed buildings, as do shouts and other noises. Iron glows molten in the fire, and hot rocks are cracked by untempered scorching. Hard gold is softened and melted by heat; and bronze, ice-like, is liquefied by flame. Both heat and piercing cold seep through silver, since we feel both alike when a cooling shower of water is poured into a goblet that we hold ceremonially in our hands. All these facts point to the conclusion that nothing is really solid. But sound reasoning and nature itself drive us to the opposite conclusion. Pay attention, therefore, while I demonstrate in a few lines that there exist certain bodies that are absolutely solid and indestructible, namely those atoms which according to our teaching are the seeds or prime units of things from which the whole universe is built up.

In the first place, we have found that nature is twofold, consisting 33 of two totally different things, matter and the space in which things happen. Hence each of these must exist by itself without admixture of the other. For, where there is empty space (what we call vacuity), there matter is not; where matter exists, there cannot be a vacuum. Therefore the prime units of matter are solid and free from vacuity.

Again, since composite things contain some vacuum, the surround- 34 ing matter must be solid. For you cannot reasonably maintain that anything can hide vacuity and hold it within its body unless you allow that the container itself is solid. And what contains the vacuum in things can only be an accumulation of matter. Hence matter, which possesses absolute solidity, can be everlasting when other things are decomposed.

Again, if there were no empty space, everything would be one solid 35
mass; if there were no material objects with the property of filling the space they occupy, all existing space would be utterly void. It is clear, then, that there is an alternation of matter and vacuity, mutually distinct, since the whole is neither completely full nor completely empty. There are therefore solid bodies, causing the distinction between empty space and full. And these, as I have just shown, can be neither decomposed by blows from without nor invaded and unknit from within nor destroyed by any other form of assault. For it seems that a thing without vacuum can be neither knocked to bits nor snapped nor chopped in two by cutting; nor can it let in moisture or seeping cold or piercing fire, the universal agents of destruction. The more vacuum a thing contains within it, the more readily it yields to these assailants. Hence, if the units of matter are solid and without vacuity, as I have shown, they must be everlasting.

Yet again, if the matter in things had not been everlasting, every- 36
thing by now would have gone back to nothing, and the things we see would be the product of rebirth out of nothing. But, since I have already shown that nothing can be created out of nothing nor any existing thing be summoned back to nothing, the atoms must be made of imperishable stuff into which everything can be resolved in the end, so that there may be a stock of matter for building the world anew. The atoms, therefore, are absolutely solid and unalloyed. In no other way could they have survived throughout infinite time to keep the world in being.

Furthermore, if nature had set no limit to the breaking of things, 37
the particles of matter in the course of ages would have been ground so small that nothing could be generated from them so as to attain in the fullness of time to the summit of its growth. For we see that anything can be more speedily disintegrated than put together again. Hence, what the long day of time, the bygone eternity, has already shaken and loosened to fragments could never in the residue of time be reconstructed. As it is, there is evidently a limit set to breaking, since we see that everything is renewed and each according to its kind has a fixed period in which to grow to its prime.

Here is a further argument. Granted that the particles of matter are 38
absolutely solid, we can still explain the composition and behavior of soft things—air, water, earth, fire—by their intermixture with empty space. On the other hand, supposing the atoms to be soft, we cannot account for the origin of hard flint and iron. For there would be no

foundation for nature to build on. Therefore there must be bodies strong in their unalloyed solidity by whose closer clustering things can be knit together and display unyielding toughness.

If we suppose that there is no limit set to the breaking of matter, 39 we must still admit that material objects consist of particles which throughout eternity have resisted the forces of destruction. To say that these are breakable does not square with the fact that they have survived throughout eternity under a perpetual bombardment of innumerable blows.

Again, there is laid down for each thing a specific limit to its 40 growth and its tenure of life, and the laws of nature ordain what each can do and what it cannot. No species is ever changed, but each remains so much itself that every kind of bird displays on its body its own specific markings. This is a further proof that their bodies are composed of changeless matter. For, if the atoms could yield in any way to change, there would be no certainty as to what could arise and what could not, at what point the power of everything was limited by an immovable frontier-post; nor could successive generations so regularly repeat the nature, behavior, habits and movements of their parents.

To proceed with our argument, there is an ultimate point in visible 41 objects which represents the smallest thing that can be seen. So also there must be an ultimate point in objects that lie below the limit of perception by our senses. This point is without parts and is the smallest thing that can exist. It never has been and never will be able to exist by itself, but only as one primary part of something else. It is with a mass of such parts, solidly jammed together in order, that matter is filled up. Since they cannot exist by themselves, they must needs stick together in a mass from which they cannot by any means be prized loose. The atoms therefore are absolutely solid and unalloyed, consisting of a mass of least parts tightly packed together. They are not compounds formed by the coalescence of their parts, but bodies of absolute and everlasting solidity. To these nature allows no loss or diminution, but guards them as seeds for things. If there are no such least parts, even the smallest bodies will consist of an infinite number of parts, since they can always be halved and their halves halved again without limit. On this showing, what difference will there be between the whole universe and the very least of things? None at all. For, however endlessly infinite the universe may be, yet the smallest things will equally consist of an infinite number of parts. Since true reason cries out against this and denies that the mind can believe it, you must needs give in and admit that there are least parts which themselves are partless. Granted that these parts exist, you must needs admit that the atoms they compose are also solid and everlasting. But, if all things were compelled by all-creating nature to be broken up into these least parts, nature would lack the power to rebuild anything out of them. For partless objects cannot have the essential properties of generative matter—those varieties of attachment, weight, impetus, impact and movement on which everything depends.

QUESTIONS

1. Lucretius tells Memmius that he is talking about "the ultimate realities of heaven and the gods" (para. 1). Is the truth of his statement evident from this passage?
2. Lucretius fears that Memmius may, in searching into the nature of things, feel that he is acting sinfully. Do people have that feeling about scientific inquiry even today?
3. What does Lucretius's view of religions seem to be? How religious does he seem himself?
4. What is Lucretius's definition of a vacuity (see paras. 33–35)? Does it seem to you a satisfactory definition?
5. Early in the selection, Lucretius is concerned with the seeds of things. Why does he spend so much time focusing on seeds? Does what he says make sense to you today?
6. How "scientific," in the modern sense, is Lucretius?

WRITING ASSIGNMENTS

1. Lucretius thought that atoms had to be absolutely solid rather than soft. He explains his reasoning in paragraph 38. Do you agree with his reasoning? Offer an alternative view that would explain why atoms could compose things as different as sponges and flint.
2. Examine Lucretius's comments (para. 32 onward) about vacuity and the motion of bodies. His opinion is that no bodies can move unless there is a vacuity that permits the objects near it to give way. This, he says, explains the motion of fish. Take an opposing view and explain why bodies can move without a vacuity.
3. Describe for someone who has not read the selection what Lucretius means by matter and space and why nature consists only of matter and space. Where is time in this view?
4. Choose one of the six "great principles": comment on the clarity of Lucretius's reasoning and then explain why you, from a modern perspective,

should be convinced by his argument. What do you feel is most up to date about his thinking?

5. How would Lucretius have explained the existence of electricity, television, and radio to Memmius? Use Lucretius's structure of proposing a statement and explaining it with observable examples. Which of Lucretius's six axioms would most closely explain these electrical phenomena?

6. If all of nature consists only of matter and space, then we have to admit that experience is wholly materialistic. What do you find in nature that is not matter or space? How important is this description and of what does nature consist if not matter and space? Would you be able to use Lucretius's description of nature to establish the existence of something that transcends matter?

FRANCIS BACON

The Four Idols

FRANCIS BACON, Lord Verulam (1561–1626), lived during some of the most exciting times in history. Among his contemporaries were the essayist Michel de Montaigne; the playwrights Christopher Marlowe and William Shakespeare; the adventurer Sir Francis Drake; and Queen Elizabeth I, in whose reign he held several high offices. He became lord high chancellor of England in 1618, but fell from power in 1621 through a complicated series of actions, among which was his complicity in a bribery scheme. Yet his so-called crimes were minor, despite the fact he paid dearly for them. His book of Essays (1597) was exceptionally popular during his lifetime, and when he found himself without a proper job, he devoted himself to what he declared to be his own true work, writing about philosophy and science.

His purposes in Novum Organum (The New Organon), published in 1620, were to replace the old organon, or instrument of thought, Aristotle's treatises on logic and thought. Despite the absolute stranglehold Aristotle held on sixteenth- and seventeenth-century minds through the fact that Aristotle's texts were used everywhere in schools

---

From *Novum Organum.*

and colleges, Bacon thought that his logic would produce error. In Novum Organum *he tried to set the stage for a new attitude toward logic and scientific inquiry. He proposed a system of reasoning usually referred to as induction. It is a quasi-scientific method involving the collecting and inventorying of a great mass of observations from nature. Once this mass of observations was gathered and organized, Bacon believed, the truth about what is observed would leap out at one.*

Bacon is often credited with having invented the scientific method, but this notion is not accurate. He was on the right track with respect to collecting and observing. What he was wrong about was the result of that gathering. After all, one could watch an infinite number of apples (and oranges, too) fall to the ground without having the slightest sense of why they do so. What Bacon failed to realize— and he died before he could get close enough to scientific observation to realize it—is the creative function of the scientist as expressed in the hypothesis. The hypothesis—a shrewd guess about why something happens—is then tested by the kinds of observations Bacon approved.

Nonetheless, "The Four Idols" is a brilliant work. It does establish the requirements for the kind of observation that produces true scientific knowledge. Bacon despaired of any science in his own day, in part because no one paid any attention to the ways in which the idols strangled thought, observation, and imagination. He realized that the would-be scientist was foiled even before he began. Bacon was a farsighted man. He was correct about the failures of science in his time; and he was correct, moreover, about the fact that scientific advance would depend on sensory perception and on aids to perception, such as microscopes and telescopes. The really brilliant aspect of "The Four Idols" is the fact that Bacon focuses, not on what is observed, but on the instrument of observation, the human mind. Only when the instrument is freed of error can its observations be relied upon.

BACON'S RHETORIC

Bacon was trained during the great age of English rhetoric, and his prose (even though it is translated from Latin) shows the clarity, balance, and organization that naturally characterize the prose writing of seventeenth-century England. The most basic device Bacon uses is enumeration: stating clearly that there are four idols and implying that he will treat each one in turn.

Enumeration is one of the most common and most reliable rhetorical devices. The listener hears a speaker say, "I have only three things I want to say today. . . ." And the listener is alerted to listen for all three, while being secretly grateful that there are only three. The reader, when encountering complex material, is always happy to have such "road signs" as, "The second aspect of this question is . . . ."

"The Four Idols" begins, after a three-paragraph introduction, with a single paragraph devoted to each idol, so that we have an early definition of each idol and a sense of what to look for. Paragraphs 8–16 cover only the issues related to the Idols of the Tribe: the problems all people have simply because they are people. Paragraphs 17–22 consider the Idols of the Cave, those particular fixations individuals have because of their special backgrounds or limitations. Paragraphs 23–26 treat of the questions related to Idols of the Marketplace, particularly those that deal with the way people misuse words and abuse definitions. The remainder of the selection treats of the Idols of the Theater, which relate entirely to philosophic systems and preconceptions—all of which tend to narrow the scope of research and understanding.

Enumeration works within each of these groups of paragraphs as well. Bacon often begins a paragraph with such statements as, "There is one principal . . . distinction between different minds" (para. 19). Or he says, "The idols imposed by words on the understanding are of two kinds" (para. 24). The effect is to ensure clarity where confusion could easily reign.

As an added means of achieving clarity, Bacon sets aside a single paragraph—the last—as a summary of the main points that have been made, and in the order in which they were made.

Within any section of this selection, Bacon depends upon observation, example, and reason to make his points. When he speaks of a given idol, he defines it, gives several examples to make it clearer, discusses its effects on thought, then dismisses it as dangerous. He then goes on to the next idol. In some cases, and where appropriate, he names those who are victims of a specific idol. In each case he tries to be thorough, explanatory, and convincing.

Not only is this work a landmark in thought; it is also, because of its absolute clarity, a beacon. We can still profit from its light.

The Four Idols

The idols[1] and false notions which are now in possession of the ⟶ 1
human understanding, and have taken deep root therein, not only so
beset men's minds that truth can hardly find entrance, but even after
entrance obtained, they will again in the very instauration[2] of the sciences meet and trouble us, unless men being forewarned of the danger
fortify themselves as far as may be against their assaults.

There are four classes of idols which beset men's minds. To these ⟶ 2
for distinction's sake I have assigned names—calling the first class
Idols of the Tribe; the second, *Idols of the Cave;* the third, *Idols of the
Marketplace;* the fourth, *Idols of the Theater.*

The formation of ideas and axioms by true induction[3] is no doubt ⟶ 3
the proper remedy to be applied for the keeping off and clearing away
of idols. To point them out, however, is of great use; for the doctrine
of idols is to the interpretation of nature what the doctrine of the re-
futation of sophisms[4] is to common logic.

The *Idols of the Tribe* have their foundation in human nature it- ⟶ 4
self, and in the tribe or race of men. For it is a false assertion that the
sense of man is the measure of things. On the contrary, all perceptions
as well of the sense as of the mind are according to the measure of the
individual and not according to the measure of the universe. And the
human understanding is like a false mirror, which, receiving rays irregularly, distorts and discolors the nature of things by mingling its
own nature with it.

The *Idols of the Cave* are the idols of the individual man. For ev- ⟶ 5

---

[1]*idols* By this term Bacon means phantoms or illusions (see note 21). The Greek
philosopher Democritus spoke of *eidola,* tiny representations of things that impressed
themselves on the mind.

[2]*instauration* Renewal; renovation.

[3]*induction* Bacon championed induction as the method by which new knowledge
is developed. As he saw it, induction involved a patient gathering, inventorying, and categorizing of facts in the hope that a large number of them would point to the truth. As a
process of gathering evidence from which inferences are drawn, induction is contrasted
with Aristotle's method, *deduction,* according to which a theory is established and the
truth deduced. Deduction places the stress on the authority of the expert; induction
places the stress on the facts themselves.

[4]*sophisms* Apparently intelligent statements that are wrong; false wisdom.

eryone (besides the errors common to human nature in general) has a cave or den of his own, which refracts[5] and discolors the light of nature; owing either to his own proper and peculiar nature; or to his education and conversation with others; or to the reading of books, and the authority of those whom he esteems and admires; or to the differences of impressions, accordingly as they take place in a mind preoccupied and predisposed or in a mind indifferent and settled; or the like. So that the spirit of man (according as it is meted out to different individuals) is in fact a thing variable and full of perturbation,[6] and governed as it were by chance. Whence it was well observed by Heraclitus[7] that men look for sciences in their own lesser worlds, and not in the greater or common world.

There are also idols formed by the intercourse and association of men with each other, which I call *Idols of the Marketplace,* on account of the commerce and consort of men there. For it is by discourse that men associate; and words are imposed according to the apprehension of the vulgar.[8] And therefore the ill and unfit choice of words wonderfully obstructs the understanding. Nor do the definitions or explanations wherewith in some things learned men are wont[9] to guard and defend themselves, by any means set the matter right. But words plainly force and overrule the understanding, and throw all into confusion and lead men away into numberless empty controversies and idle fancies. 6

Lastly, there are idols which have immigrated into men's minds from the various dogmas of philosophies, and also from wrong laws of demonstration.[10] These I call *Idols of the Theater;* because in my judgment all the received systems[11] are but so many stage-plays, representing worlds of their own creation after an unreal and scenic fashion. Nor is it only of the systems now in vogue, or only of the ancient sects and philosophies, that I speak; for many more plays of the same kind may yet be composed and in like artificial manner set forth; seeing 7

---

[5]*refracts* Deflects, bends back, alters.

[6]*perturbation* Uncertainty, disturbance. In astronomy, the motion caused by the gravity of nearby planets.

[7]*Heraclitus (535?–?475 B.C.)* Greek philosopher who believed that there was no reality except in change; all else was illusion. He also believed that fire was the basis of all the world and that everything we see is a transformation of it.

[8]*vulgar* Common people.

[9]*wont* Accustomed.

[10]*laws of demonstration* Bacon may be referring to Aristotle's logical system of syllogism and deduction.

[11]*received systems* Official or authorized views of scientific truth.

that errors the most widely different have nevertheless causes for the most part alike. Neither again do I mean this only of entire systems, but also of many principles and axioms in science, which by tradition, credulity, and negligence, have come to be received.

But of these several kinds of idols I must speak more largely and 8 exactly, that the understanding may be duly cautioned.

The human understanding is of its own nature prone to suppose 9 the existence of more order and regularity in the world than it finds. And though there be many things in nature which are singular and unmatched, yet it devises for them parallels and conjugates and relatives[12] which do not exist. Hence the fiction that all celestial bodies move in perfect circles; spirals and dragons being (except in name) utterly rejected. Hence too the element of fire with its orb is brought in, to make up the square with the other three which the sense perceives. Hence also the ratio of density[13] of the so-called elements is arbitrarily fixed at ten to one. And so on of other dreams. And these fancies affect not dogmas only, but simple notions also.

The human understanding when it has once adopted an opinion 10 (either as being the received opinion or as being agreeable to itself) draws all things else to support and agree with it. And though there be a greater number and weight of instances to be found on the other side, yet these it either neglects and despises, or else by some distinction sets aside and rejects; in order that by this great and pernicious predetermination the authority of its former conclusions may remain inviolate. And therefore it was a good answer that was made by one who when they showed him hanging in a temple a picture of those who had paid their vows as having escaped shipwreck, and would have him say whether he did not now acknowledge the power of the gods— "Ay," asked he again, "but where are they painted that were drowned after their vows?" And such is the way of all superstition, whether in astrology, dreams, omens, divine judgments, or the like; wherein men having a delight in such vanities, mark the events where they are fulfilled, but where they fail, though this happen much oftener, neglect and pass them by. But with far more subtlety does this mischief insinuate itself into philosophy and the sciences; in which the first conclu-

---

[12]*parallels and conjugates and relatives*   A reference to the habit of assuming that phenomena are regular and ordered, consisting of squares, triangles, circles, and other regular shapes.

[13]*ratio of density*   The false assumption that the relationship of mass or weight to volume was ten to one. This is another example of Bacon's complaint, establishing a convenient regular "relative" or relationship.

sion colors and brings into conformity with itself all that come after, though far sounder and better. Besides, independently of that delight and vanity which I have described, it is the peculiar and perpetual error of the human intellect to be more moved and excited by affirmatives than by negatives; whereas it ought properly to hold itself indifferently disposed towards both alike. Indeed, in the establishment of any true axiom, the negative instance is the more forcible of the two.

The human understanding is moved by those things most which 11 strike and enter the mind simultaneously and suddenly, and so fill the imagination; and then it feigns and supposes all other things to be somehow, though it cannot see how, similar to those few things by which it is surrounded. But for that going to and fro to remote and heterogeneous instances, by which axioms are tried as in the fire,[14] the intellect is altogether slow and unfit, unless it be forced thereto by severe laws and overruling authority.

The human understanding is unquiet; it cannot stop or rest, and 12 still presses onward, but in vain. Therefore it is that we cannot conceive of any end or limit to the world, but always as of necessity it occurs to us that there is something beyond. Neither again can it be conceived how eternity has flowed down to the present day; for that distinction which is commonly received of infinity in time past and in time to come can by no means hold; for it would thence follow that one infinity is greater than another, and that infinity is wasting away and tending to become finite. The like subtlety arises touching the infinite divisibility of lines,[15] from the same inability of thought to stop. But this inability interferes more mischievously in the discovery of causes:[16] for although the most general principles in nature ought

---

[14]***tried as in the fire*** Trial by fire is a figure of speech representing thorough, rigorous testing even to the point of risking what is tested. An axiom is a statement of apparent truth that has not yet been put to the test of examination and investigation.

[15]***infinite divisibility of lines*** This gave rise to the paradox of Zeno, the Greek philosopher of the fifth century B.C. who showed that it was impossible to get from one point to another because one had to pass the midpoint of the line determined by the two original points, and then the midpoint of the remaining distance, and then of that remaining distance, down to an infinite number of points. By using accepted truths to "prove" an absurdity about motion, Zeno actually hoped to prove that motion itself did not exist. This is the "subtlety" or confusion Bacon says is produced by the "inability of thought to stop."

[16]***discovery of causes*** Knowledge of the world was based on four causes: efficient (who made it?); material (what is it made of?); formal (what is its shape?); and final (what is its purpose?). The scholastics concentrated their thinking on the first and last, while the "middle causes," related to matter and shape, were the proper subject matter of science because they alone yielded to observation. (See paragraph 33.)

to be held merely positive, as they are discovered, and cannot with truth be referred to a cause; nevertheless, the human understanding being unable to rest still seeks something prior in the order of nature. And then it is that in struggling towards that which is further off, it falls back upon that which is more nigh at hand; namely, on final causes: which have relation clearly to the nature of man rather than to the nature of the universe, and from this source have strangely defiled philosophy. But he is no less an unskilled and shallow philosopher who seeks causes of that which is most general, than he who in things subordinate and subaltern[17] omits to do so.

The human understanding is no dry light, but receives an infusion 13 from the will and affections;[18] whence proceed sciences which may be called "sciences as one would." For what a man had rather were true he more readily believes. Therefore he rejects difficult things from impatience of research; sober things, because they narrow hope; the deeper things of nature, from superstition; the light of experience, from arrogance and pride, lest his mind should seem to be occupied with things mean and transitory; things not commonly believed, out of deference to the opinion of the vulgar. Numberless in short are the ways, and sometimes imperceptible, in which the affections color and infect the understanding.

But by far the greatest hindrance and aberration of the human un- 14 derstanding proceeds from the dullness, incompetency, and deceptions of the senses; in that things which strike the sense outweigh things which do not immediately strike it, though they be more important. Hence it is that speculation commonly ceases where sight ceases; insomuch that of things invisible there is little or no observation. Hence all the working of the spirits[19] enclosed in tangible bodies lies hid and unobserved of men. So also all the more subtle changes of form in the parts of coarser substances (which they commonly call alteration, though it is in truth local motion through exceedingly small spaces) is in like manner unobserved. And yet unless these two things just mentioned be searched out and brought to light, nothing great can be achieved in nature, as far as the production of works is concerned. So again the essential nature of our common air, and of all bodies less dense than air (which are very many) is almost unknown. For the sense by itself is a thing infirm and erring; neither can instruments for en-

---

[17]*subaltern* Lower in status.
[18]*will and affections* Human free will and emotional needs and responses.
[19]*spirits* The soul or animating force.

larging or sharpening the senses do much, but all the truer kind of interpretation of nature is effected by instances and experiments fit and apposite;[20] wherein the sense decides touching the experiment only, and the experiment touching the point in nature and the thing itself.

The human understanding is of its own nature prone to abstractions and gives a substance and reality to things which are fleeting. But to resolve nature into abstractions is less to our purpose than to dissect her into parts; as did the school of Democritus,[21] which went further into nature than the rest. Matter rather than forms should be the object of our attention, its configurations and changes of configuration, and simple action, and law of action or motion; for forms are figments of the human mind, unless you will call those laws of action forms.

Such then are the idols which I call *Idols of the Tribe;* and which take their rise either from the homogeneity of the substance of the human spirit,[22] or from its preoccupation, or from its narrowness, or from its restless motion, or from an infusion of the affections, or from the incompetency of the senses, or from the mode of impression.

The *Idols of the Cave* take their rise in the peculiar constitution, mental or bodily, of each individual; and also in education, habit, and accident. Of this kind there is a great number and variety; but I will instance those the pointing out of which contains the most important caution, and which have most effect in disturbing the clearness of the understanding.

Men become attached to certain particular sciences and speculations, either because they fancy themselves the authors and inventors thereof, or because they have bestowed the greatest pains upon them and become most habituated to them. But men of this kind, if they betake themselves to philosophy and contemplations of a general character, distort and color them in obedience to their former fancies; a thing especially to be noticed in Aristotle,[23] who made his natural

15

16

17

18

---

[20]***apposite*** Appropriate; well related.

[21]***Democritus (460?–?370 B.C.)*** Greek philosopher who thought the world was composed of atoms. Bacon felt such "dissection" to be useless because it was impractical. Yet Democritus's concept of the *eidola,* the mind's impressions of things, may have contributed to Bacon's idea of "the idol."

[22]***human spirit*** Human nature.

[23]***Aristotle (384–322 B.C.)*** Greek philosopher whose *Organon* (system of logic) dominated the thought of Bacon's time. Bacon sought to overthrow Aristotle's hold on science and thought.

philosophy[24] a mere bondservant to his logic, thereby rendering it contentious and well nigh useless. The race of chemists[25] again out of a few experiments of the furnace have built up a fantastic philosophy, framed with reference to a few things; and Gilbert[26] also, after he had employed himself most laboriously in the study and observation of the loadstone, proceeded at once to construct an entire system in accordance with his favorite subject.

There is one principal and, as it were, radical distinction between 19 different minds, in respect of philosophy and the sciences, which is this: that some minds are stronger and apter to mark the differences of things, others to mark their resemblances. The steady and acute mind can fix its contemplations and dwell and fasten on the subtlest distinctions: the lofty and discursive mind recognizes and puts together the finest and most general resemblances. Both kinds however easily err in excess, by catching the one at gradations, the other at shadows.

There are found some minds given to an extreme admiration of 20 antiquity, others to an extreme love and appetite for novelty; but few so duly tempered that they can hold the mean, neither carping at what has been well laid down by the ancients, nor despising what is well introduced by the moderns. This however turns to the great injury of the sciences and philosophy; since these affectations of antiquity and novelty are the humors[27] of partisans rather than judgments; and truth is to be sought for not in the felicity of any age, which is an unstable thing, but in the light of nature and experience, which is eternal. These factions therefore must be abjured,[28] and care must be taken that the intellect be not hurried by them into assent.

Contemplations of nature and of bodies in their simple form break 21 up and distract the understanding, while contemplations of nature and bodies in their composition and configuration overpower and dissolve the understanding: a distinction well seen in the school of Leucippus[29]

---

[24]*natural philosophy* The scientific study of nature in general—biology, zoology, geology, etc.

[25]*chemists* Alchemists had developed a "fantastic philosophy" from their experimental attempts to transmute lead into gold.

[26]*William Gilbert (1540–1603)* An English scientist who studied magnetism and codified many laws related to magnetic fields. He was particularly ridiculed by Bacon for being too narrow in his researches.

[27]*humors* Used in a medical sense to mean a distortion caused by imbalance.

[28]*abjured* Renounced, sworn off, repudiated.

[29]*Leucippus (fifth century B.C.)* Greek philosopher; teacher of Democritus and inventor of the atomistic theory. His works survive only in fragments.

and Democritus as compared with the other philosophies. For that school is so busied with the particles that it hardly attends to the structure; while the others are so lost in admiration of the structure that they do not penetrate to the simplicity of nature. These kinds of contemplation should therefore be alternated and taken by turns; that so the understanding may be rendered at once penetrating and comprehensive, and the inconveniences above mentioned, with the idols which proceed from them, may be avoided.

Let such then be our provision and contemplative prudence for 22 keeping off and dislodging the *Idols of the Cave,* which grow for the most part either out of the predominance of a favorite subject, or out of an excessive tendency to compare or to distinguish, or out of partiality for particular ages, or out of the largeness or minuteness of the objects contemplated. And generally let every student of nature take this as a rule—that whatever his mind seizes and dwells upon with peculiar satisfaction is to be held in suspicion, and that so much the more care is to be taken in dealing with such questions to keep the understanding even and clear.

But the *Idols of the Marketplace* are the most troublesome of all: 23 idols which have crept into the understanding through the alliances of words and names. For men believe that their reason governs words; but it is also true that words react on the understanding; and this it is that has rendered philosophy and the sciences sophistical and inactive. Now words, being commonly framed and applied according to the capacity of the vulgar, follow those lines of division which are most obvious to the vulgar understanding. And whenever an understanding of greater acuteness or a more diligent observation would alter those lines to suit the true divisions of nature, words stand in the way and resist the change. Whence it comes to pass that the high and formal discussions of learned men end oftentimes in disputes about words and names; with which (according to the use and wisdom of the mathematicians) it would be more prudent to begin, and so by means of definitions reduce them to order. Yet even definitions cannot cure this evil in dealing with natural and material things; since the definitions themselves consist of words, and those words beget others: so that it is necessary to recur to individual instances, and those in due series and order; as I shall say presently when I come to the method and scheme for the formation of notions and axioms.[30]

The idols imposed by words on the understanding are of two kinds. 24

---

[30]**notions and axioms** Conceptions and definitive statements of truth.

They are either names of things which do not exist (for as there are things left unnamed through lack of observation, so likewise are there names which result from fantastic suppositions and to which nothing in reality responds), or they are names of things which exist, but yet confused and ill-defined, and hastily and irregularly derived from realities. Of the former kind are Fortune, the Prime Mover, Planetary Orbits, Element of Fire, and like fictions which owe their origin to false and idle theories.[31] And this class of idols is more easily expelled, because to get rid of them it is only necessary that all theories should be steadily rejected and dismissed as obsolete.

But the other class, which springs out of a faulty and unskillful 25 abstraction, is intricate and deeply rooted. Let us take for example such a word as *humid;* and see how far the several things which the word is used to signify agree with each other; and we shall find the word *humid* to be nothing else than a mark loosely and confusedly applied to denote a variety of actions which will not bear to be reduced to any constant meaning. For it both signifies that which easily spreads itself round any other body; and that which in itself is indeterminate and cannot solidize; and that which readily yields in every direction; and that which easily divides and scatters itself; and that which easily unites and collects itself; and that which readily flows and is put in motion; and that which readily clings to another body and wets it; and that which is easily reduced to a liquid, or being solid easily melts. Accordingly when you come to apply the word—if you take it in one sense, flame is humid; if in another, air is not humid; if in another, fine dust is humid; if in another, glass is humid. So that it is easy to see that the notion is taken by abstraction only from water and common and ordinary liquids, without any due verification.

There are however in words certain degrees of distortion and error. 26 One of the least faulty kinds is that of names of substances, especially of lowest species and well-deduced (for the notion of *chalk* and of *mud* is good, of *earth* bad);[32] a more faulty kind is that of actions, as *to generate, to corrupt, to alter;* the most faulty is of qualities (except such as are the immediate objects of the sense), as *heavy, light, rare, dense,* and the like. Yet in all these cases some notions are of neces-

---

[31]*idle theories*   These are things that cannot be observed and thus do not exist. Fortune is fate; the Prime Mover is God or some "first" force; the notion that planets orbited the sun was considered as "fantastic" as these others, or as the idea that everything was made up of fire and its many permutations.

[32]**earth bad**   Chalk and mud were useful in manufacture; hence they were terms of approval. *Earth* is used here in the sense we use *dirt,* as in "digging in the dirt."

sity a little better than others, in proportion to the greater variety of subjects that fall within the range of the human sense.

But the *Idols of the Theater* are not innate, nor do they steal into the understanding secretly, but are plainly impressed and received into the mind from the play-books of philosophical systems and the perverted rules of demonstration.[33] To attempt refutations in this case would be merely inconsistent with what I have already said: for since we agree neither upon principles nor upon demonstrations, there is no place for argument. And this is so far well, inasmuch as it leaves the honor of the ancients untouched. For they are no wise disparaged—the question between them and me being only as to the way. For as the saying is, the lame man who keeps the right road outstrips the runner who takes a wrong one. Nay, it is obvious that when a man runs the wrong way, the more active and swift he is the further he will go astray.

27

But the course I propose for the discovery of sciences is such as leaves but little to the acuteness and strength of wits, but places all wits[34] and understandings nearly on a level. For as in the drawing of a straight line or perfect circle, much depends on the steadiness and practice of the hand, if it be done by aim of hand only, but if with the aid of rule or compass, little or nothing; so is it exactly with my plan. But though particular confutations[35] would be of no avail, yet touching the sects and general divisions of such systems I must say something; something also touching the external signs which show that they are unsound; and finally something touching the causes of such great infelicity and of such lasting and general agreement in error; that so the access to truth may be made less difficult, and the human understanding may the more willingly submit to its purgation and dismiss its idols.

28

Idols of the Theater, or of systems, are many, and there can be and perhaps will be yet many more. For were it not that now for many ages men's minds have been busied with religion and theology; and were it not that civil governments, especially monarchies, have been averse to such novelties, even in matters speculative; so that men labor therein to the peril and harming of their fortunes—not only unrewarded, but exposed also to contempt and envy; doubtless there would

29

---

[33]*perverted rules of demonstration*   Another complaint against Aristotle's logic as misapplied in Bacon's day.

[34]*wits*   Intelligence, reasoning powers.

[35]*confutations*   Specific counterarguments. Bacon means that he cannot offer particular arguments against each scientific sect; thus he offers a general warning.

have arisen many other philosophical sects like to those which in great variety flourished once among the Greeks. For as on the phenomena of the heavens many hypotheses may be constructed, so likewise (and more also) many various dogmas may be set up and established on the phenomena of philosophy. And in the plays of this philosophical theater you may observe the same thing which is found in the theater of the poets, that stories invented for the stage are more compact and elegant, and more as one would wish them to be, than true stories out of history.

In general, however, there is taken for the material of philosophy 30 either a great deal out of a few things, or a very little out of many things; so that on both sides philosophy is based on too narrow a foundation of experiment and natural history, and decides on the authority of too few cases. For the rational school of philosophers[36] snatches from experience a variety of common instances, neither duly ascertained nor diligently examined and weighed, and leaves all the rest to meditation and agitation of wit.

There is also another class of philosophers,[37] who having bestowed 31 much diligent and careful labor on a few experiments, have thence made bold to educe and construct systems; wresting all other facts in a strange fashion to conformity therewith.

And there is yet a third class,[38] consisting of those who out of faith 32 and veneration mix their philosophy with theology and traditions; among whom the vanity of some has gone so far aside as to seek the origin of sciences among spirits and genii.[39] So that this parent stock of errors—this false philosophy—is of three kinds; the sophistical, the empirical, and the superstitious. . . .

But the corruption of philosophy by superstition and an admixture 33 of theology is far more widely spread, and does the greatest harm,

---

[36]**rational school of philosophers** Platonists who felt that human reason alone could discover the truth and that experiment was unnecessary. Their observation of experience produced only a "variety of common instances" from which they reasoned.

[37]**another class of philosophers** William Gilbert (1540–1603) experimented tirelessly with magnetism, from which he derived numerous odd theories. Though Gilbert was a true scientist, Bacon thought of him as limited and on the wrong track.

[38]**a third class** Pythagoras (580?–?500 B.C.) was a Greek philosopher who experimented rigorously with mathematics and a tuned string. He is said to have developed the musical scale. His theory of reincarnation, or the transmigration of souls, was somehow based on his travels in India and his work with scales. The superstitious belief in the movement of souls is what Bacon complains of.

[39]**genii** Oriental demons or spirits; a slap at Pythagoras, who traveled in the Orient.

whether to entire systems or to their parts. For the human understanding is obnoxious to the influence of the imagination no less than to the influence of common notions. For the contentious and sophistical kind of philosophy ensnares the understanding; but this kind, being fanciful and tumid[40] and half poetical, misleads it more by flattery. For there is in man an ambition of the understanding, no less than of the will, especially in high and lofty spirits.

Of this kind we have among the Greeks a striking example in Pythagoras, though he united with it a coarser and more cumbrous superstition; another in Plato and his school,[41] more dangerous and subtle. It shows itself likewise in parts of other philosophies, in the introduction of abstract forms and final causes and first causes, with the omission in most cases of causes intermediate, and the like. Upon this point the greatest caution should be used. For nothing is so mischievous as the apotheosis of error; and it is a very plague of the understanding for vanity to become the object of veneration. Yet in this vanity some of the moderns have with extreme levity indulged so far as to attempt to found a system of natural philosophy on the first chapter of Genesis, on the book of Job, and other parts of the sacred writings; seeking for the dead among the living: which also makes the inhibition and repression of it the more important, because from this unwholesome mixture of things human and divine there arises not only a fantastic philosophy but also an heretical religion. Very meet it is therefore that we be sober-minded, and give to faith that only which is faith's. . . .

So much concerning the several classes of Idols, and their equipage: all of which must be renounced and put away with a fixed and solemn determination, and the understanding thoroughly freed and cleansed; the entrance into the kingdom of man, founded on the sciences, being not much other than the entrance into the kingdom of heaven, whereinto none may enter except as a little child.

34

35

---

[40]*tumid* Overblown, swollen.

[41]*Plato and his school* Plato's religious bent was further developed by Plotinus (205–270 A.D.) in his *Enneads*. Although Plotinus was not a Christian, his Neo-Platonism was welcomed as a philosophy compatible with Christianity.

QUESTIONS

1. Which of Bacon's idols is the most difficult to understand? Do your best to define it.
2. Which of these idols do we still need to worry about? Why? What dangers does it present?
3. What does Bacon mean by saying that our senses are weak (para. 14)? Is he correct in making that statement?
4. Occasionally Bacon says something in such a way that it seems a bit like an aphorism (see the introduction to Machiavelli). Find at least one such expression in this selection. Upon examination, does the expression have as much meaning as it seems to have?
5. What kind of readers did Bacon expect for this piece? What clues does his way of communicating provide regarding the nature of his anticipated readers?
6. Would Bacon agree with Lucretius's belief that all of nature consists only of matter and space?

WRITING ASSIGNMENTS

1. Compare Bacon's approach to reasoning with that of Lucretius. Is there a parallel to be made between Lucretius's "six great principles" and Bacon's Four Idols? To what extent would these great thinkers have agreed with each other, and to what extent would they have disagreed? Which of Lucretius's principles show evidence of his having avoided one or more of Bacon's Idols? Does Lucretius fall victim to any of the idols?
2. Which of Bacon's idols most seriously applies to you as a person? Using enumeration, put the idols in order of importance as you see them affecting your own judgment. If you prefer, you may write about which idol you believe is most important in impeding scientific investigation today.
3. Is it true, as Bacon says in paragraph 10, that people are in general more excited by affirmation than by negation? Do we really stress the positive and deemphasize the negative in the conduct of our general affairs? Find at least three instances in which people seem to gravitate toward the positive or the negative in a series of situations in daily life. Try to establish whether or not Bacon has, in fact, described what is a habit of mind.
4. In paragraph 13, Bacon states that the "will and affections" enter into matters of thought. By this he means that our understanding of what we observe is conditioned by what we want and what we feel. Thus, when he says, "For what a man had rather were true he more readily believes," he tells us that people tend to believe what they want to believe. Test this statement by means of observation. Find out, for example, how many older people are convinced that the world is deteriorating, how many younger people feel that there is a plot on the part of older people to hold them

back, how many women feel that men consciously oppress women, and how many men feel that feminists are not as feminine as they should be. What other beliefs can you discover that seem to have their origin in what people want to believe rather than in what is true?

5. Establish the extent to which the Idols of the Marketplace are relevant to issues in modern life. In particular, study the language used in the newspapers (and important magazines) to discuss nuclear warfare. To what extent are official words (those uttered by governments) designed to obscure issues? In what sense are they misleading? Consult the discussion in paragraph 23 and following paragraphs to answer this question. In what sense do "words stand in the way and resist . . . change" in regard to debate on nuclear war. If you wish to substitute another major issue (e.g., abortion, improving secondary schools, social welfare services, taxation, prayer in the schools), feel free to do so.

6. Bacon's views on religion have always been questionable. He grew up in a very religious time, but his writings rarely discuss religion positively. In this work he talks about giving "to faith only that which is faith's." He seems to feel that scientific investigation is something quite separate from religion. Examine this work carefully to establish what you think Bacon's view on this question is. Then take a stand on the issue of the relationship between religion and science. Should science be totally independent of religious concerns? Should religious issues control scientific experimentation? What does Bacon mean when he complains about the vanity of founding "a system of natural philosophy on the first chapter of Genesis, on the book of Job, and other parts of the sacred writings" (para. 34)? "Natural philosophy" means biology, chemistry, physics, and science in general. Are Bacon's complaints justified? Would his complaints be relevant today?

7. Bacon's purpose is to show how certain innate problems in our thinking can limit our ability to know the truth about the world of experience. He wants us to think scientifically. To what extent is Bacon's advice useful for thinking about experience that is other than scientific? Is he helpful in advising us how to think about religion, inner feelings, or spiritual awareness? How useful is the advice in "The Four Idols" for these areas of experience?

CHARLES DARWIN

Natural Selection

CHARLES DARWIN (1809–1882) was trained as a minister in the
Church of England, but he was also the grandson of one of England's
greatest horticulturists, Erasmus Darwin. Partly as a way of putting
off taking orders in the church, and partly because of his natural curiosity and scientific enterprise, Darwin managed to find himself performing the functions of a naturalist on the H.M.S. Beagle, which was
engaged in scientific explorations around South America during the
years 1831–1836. Darwin's fascinating book, Voyage of the Beagle
(1839), details the experiences he had and offers us some views of his
self-education as a naturalist.

His experiences on the Beagle led him to take note of variations in
species of animals he found in various separate locales, particularly
between remote islands and the mainland. Varieties—his term for
any visible (or invisible) differences in markings, coloration, size or

---

From On The Origin of Species by Means of Natural Selection. This text is from the
first edition, 1859. In the five subsequent editions, Darwin hedged more and more on his
theory, often introducing material in defense against objections. The first edition is vigorous and direct; this edition jolted the worlds of science and religion out of their com-
plaisance. In later editions, this chapter was titled "Natural Selection; or, Survival of the
Fittest."

shape of appendages, organs, or bodies—were of some peculiar use, he believed, for the animals in the environment in which he found them. He was not certain of what kind of use these varieties might be, and he did not know whether the changes that created the varieties resulted from the environment or from some chance operation of nature. Ultimately, he concluded that varieties in nature were caused by three forces: (1) natural selection, in which varieties occur spontaneously by chance but are then "selected" for because they are aids to survival; (2) direct action of the environment, in which nonadaptive varieties do not survive because of climate, food conditions, or the like; and (3) the effects of use or disuse of a variation (somewhat like the short beak of a bird in paragraph 9 in the extract). Sexual selection, which figures prominently in this work, was later thought to be less significant by Darwin.

The idea of evolution—the gradual change of species through some kind of modification of varieties—had been in the air for many years when Darwin began his work. The English scientists C.W. Wells in 1813 and Patrick Matthew in 1831 had both proposed theories of natural selection, although Darwin was unaware of their work. Alfred Russel Wallace (1823–1913), a younger English scientist, revealed in 1858 that he was about to propose the same theory of evolution as was Darwin. They joined and published their theories (in sketchy form) together, and the next year Darwin rushed his Origin of Species *to press.*

Darwin does not mention human beings as part of the evolutionary process in the selection. Because he was particularly concerned with the likelihood of adverse reactions on the part of theologians, he merely promised later discussion of that subject. It came in The Descent of Man *(1871), the companion to* On the Origin of Species.

When Darwin returned to England after completing his researches on the Beagle, *he supplemented his knowledge with information gathered from breeders of pigeons, livestock, dogs, and horses. This research, it must be noted, was rather limited, involving relatively few samples, and was conducted according to comparatively unscientific practices. Yet, it corresponded with his observations of nature. The fact was that man could cause changes in species; it was Darwin's task to show that nature—through the process of natural selection—could do the same thing.*

Naturally, The Descent of Man *stirred up a great deal of controversy between the church and Darwin's supporters. Note since the Roman Catholic Church denied the fact that the earth went around the sun, as Galileo had proved scientifically in 1632 (and was banished for his pains), had there been a more serious confrontation of science and religion. Darwin was ridiculed by ministers and doubted by older scientists; but he was stoutly defended by younger scientists, many of whom had arrived at conclusions similar to Darwin's. In the end, Darwin's views were accepted by the Church of England, and when he died in 1882 he was lionized and buried at Westminster Abbey in London. Only recently, controversy concerning his work has arisen again.*

DARWIN'S RHETORIC

Darwin's writing is fluent, smooth, and stylistically sophisticated. Yet, his material is burdensome, detailed, and in general not appealing. Despite these drawbacks, he manages to keep the reader engaged. His rhetorical method depends entirely upon the yoking of thesis and demonstration. He uses the topic of definition frequently, but he most frequently uses the topic of testimony, as he gathers information and instances, both real and imaginary, from many different sources.

Interestingly enough, Darwin said that he used Francis Bacon's method of induction in his researches. That means the gathering of evidence of many instances of a given phenomenon, from which the truth—or a natural law—will emerge. The fact is that Darwin did not quite follow this path. He did, as most modern scientists do, establish a hypothesis after a period of observation; then he looked for evidence that would confirm or disconfirm the hypothesis. He was careful to include examples that argued against his view, but like most scientists, he emphasized the importance of the positive samples.

Induction plays a part in the rhetoric of this selection in that the selection is dominated by examples. There are examples taken from the breeding of birds, from the condition of birds in nature, from domestic farm animals and their breeding; and there are many, many examples taken from botany, including the breeding of plants and the interdependence between certain insects and certain plants. Erasmus Darwin was famous for his work with plants, and it is natural that such observations would play an important part in his grandson's thinking.

The process of natural selection is carefully discussed, particularly in paragraph 8 and thereafter. Darwin emphasizes its positive nature and its differences from selection by human breeders. The topic of comparison, which appears frequently in the selection, is most conspicuous in these paragraphs. He postulates a nature in which the fittest survive because they are best adapted for survival, but he does not dwell on the fate of those who are unfit individuals. Later writers, often misapplying his theories, were to do that.

———•∽•———

Natural Selection

How will the struggle for existence . . . act in regard to varia- 1
tion? Can the principle of selection, which we have seen is so potent
in the hands of man, apply in nature? I think we shall see that it can
act most effectually. Let it be borne in mind in what an endless number of strange pecularities our domestic productions, and, in a lesser
degree, those under nature, vary; and how strong the hereditary tendency is. Under domestication, it may be truly said that the whole
organization becomes in some degree plastic.[1] Let it be borne in mind
how infinitely complex and close-fitting are the mutual relations of all
organic beings to each other and to their physical conditions of life.
Can it, then, be thought improbable, seeing that variations useful to
man have undoubtedly occurred, that other variations useful in some
way to each being in the great and complex battle of life, should sometimes occur in the course of thousands of generations? If such do occur, can we doubt (remembering that many more individuals are born
than can possibly survive) that individuals having any advantage, however slight, over others, would have the best chance of surviving and
or procreating their kind? On the other hand, we may feel sure that
any variation in the least degree injurious would be rigidly destroyed.
This preservation of favorable variations and the rejection of injurious
variations, I call Natural Selection. Variations neither useful nor injurious would not be affected by natural selection, and would be left a
fluctuating element, as perhaps we see in the species called polymorphic.[2]

---

[1]***plastic*** Capable of being shaped and changed.
[2]***species called polymorphic*** Species that have more than one form over the course
of their lives, such as butterflies.

We shall best understand the probable course of natural selection 2
by taking the case of a country undergoing some physical change, for
instance, of climate. The proportional numbers of its inhabitants
would almost immediately undergo a change, and some species might
become extinct. We may conclude, from what we have seen of the
intimate and complex manner in which the inhabitants of each country are bound together, that any change in the numerical proportions
of some of the inhabitants, independently of the change of climate
itself, would most seriously affect many of the others. If the country
were open on its borders, new forms would certainly immigrate, and
this also would seriously disturb the relations of some of the former
inhabitants. Let it be remembered how powerful the influence of a
single introduced tree or mammal has been shown to be. But in the
case of an island, or of a country partly surrounded by barriers, into
which new and better adapted forms could not freely enter, we should
then have places in the economy of nature which would assuredly be
better filled up, if some of the original inhabitants were in some manner modified; for, had the area been open to immigration, these same
places would have been seized on by intruders. In such case, every
slight modification, which in the course of ages chanced to arise, and
which in any way favored the individuals of any of the species, by
better adapting them to their altered conditions, would tend to be preserved; and natural selection would thus have free scope for the work
of improvement.

We have reason to believe . . . that a change in the conditions of 3
life, by specially acting on the reproductive system, causes or increases
variability; and in the foregoing case the conditions of life are supposed to have undergone a change, and this would manifestly be favorable to natural selection, by giving a better chance of profitable variations occurring; and unless profitable variations do occur, natural
selection can do nothing. Not that, as I believe, any extreme amount
of variability is necessary; as man can certainly produce great results
by adding up in any given direction mere individual differences, so
could Nature, but far more easily, from having incomparably longer
time at her disposal. Nor do I believe that any great physical change,
as of climate, or any unusual degree of isolation to check immigration,
is actually necessary to produce new and unoccupied places for natural
selection to fill up by modifying and improving some of the varying
inhabitants. For as all the inhabitants of each country are struggling
together with nicely balanced forces, extremely slight modifications in
the structure or habits of one inhabitant would often give it an advantage over others; and still further modifications of the same kind

would often still further increase the advantage. No country can be named in which all the native inhabitants are now so perfectly adapted to each other and to the physical conditions under which they live, that none of them could anyhow be improved; for in all countries, the natives have been so far conquered by naturalized productions, that they have allowed foreigners to take firm possession of the land. And as foreigners have thus everywhere beaten some of the natives, we may safely conclude that the natives might have been modified with advantage, so as to have better resisted such intruders.

As man can produce and certainly has produced a great result by his methodical and unconscious means of selection, what may not nature effect? Man can act only on external and visible characters; nature cares nothing for appearances, except in so far as they may be useful to any being. She can act on every internal organ, on every shade of constitutional difference, on the whole machinery of life. Man selects only for his own good; Nature only for that of the being which she tends. Every selected character is fully exercised by her; and the being is placed under well-suited conditions of life. Man keeps the natives of many climates in the same country; he seldom exercises each selected character in some peculiar and fitting manner; he feeds a long and a short beaked pigeon on the same food; he does not exercise a long-backed or long-legged quadruped in any peculiar manner; he exposes sheep with long and short wool to the same climate. He does not allow the most vigorous males to struggle for the females. He does not rigidly destroy all inferior animals, but protects during each varying season, as far as lies in his power, all his productions. He often begins his selection by some half-monstrous form; or at least by some modification prominent enough to catch his eye, or to be plainly useful to him. Under nature, the slightest difference of structure or constitution may well turn the nicely balanced scale in the struggle for life, and so be preserved. How fleeting are the wishes and efforts of man! how short his time! and consequently how poor will his products be, compared with those accumulated by nature during whole geological periods. Can we wonder, then, that nature's productions should be far "truer" in character than man's productions; that they should be infinitely better adapted to the most complex conditions of life, and should plainly bear the stamp of far higher workmanship? 4

It may be said that natural selection is daily and hourly scrutinizing, throughout the world, every variation, even the slightest; rejecting that which is bad, preserving and adding up all that is good; silently and insensibly working, whenever and wherever opportunity offers, at the improvement of each organic being in relation to its organic and 5 inorganic conditions of life. We see nothing of these slow changes in progress, until the hand of time has marked the long lapse of ages, and then so imperfect is our view into long past geological ages, that we only see that the forms of life are now different from what they formerly were.

Although natural selection can act only through and for the good 6 of each being, yet characters and structures, which we are apt to consider as of very trifling importance, may thus be acted on. When we see leaf-eating insects green, and bark-feeders mottled-grey; the alpine ptarmigan white in winter, the red-grouse the color of heather, and the black-grouse that of peaty earth, we must believe that these tints are of service to these birds and insects in preserving them from danger. Grouse, if not destroyed at some period of their lives, would increase in countless numbers; they are known to suffer largely from birds of prey; and hawks are guided by eyesight to their prey—so much so that on parts of the Continent[3] persons are warned not to keep white pigeons, as being the most liable to destruction. Hence I can see no reason to doubt that natural selection might be most effective in giving the proper color to each kind of grouse, and in keeping that color, when once acquired, true and constant. Nor ought we to think that the occasional destruction of an animal of any particular color would produce little effect; we should remember how essential it is in a flock of white sheep to destroy every lamb with the faintest trace of black. In plants, the down on the fruit and the color of the flesh are considered by botanists as characters of the most trifling importance; yet we hear from an excellent horticulturist, Downing,[4] that in the United States, smooth-skinned fruits suffer far more from a beetle, a curculio,[5] than those with down; that purple plums suffer far more from a certain disease than yellow plums; whereas another disease attacks yellow-fleshed peaches far more than those with other colored flesh. If, with all the aids of art, these slight differences make a great difference in cultivating the several varieties, assuredly, in a state of nature, where the trees would have to struggle with other trees and with a host of enemies, such differences would effectually settle which variety, whether a smooth or downy, a yellow or purple fleshed fruit, should succeed.

---

[3]**Continent** European continent; the contiguous land mass of Europe, excluding the British Isles.

[4]**Andrew Jackson Downing (1815–1852)** American horticulturist and specialist in fruit and fruit trees.

[5]**curculio** A weevil.

In looking at many small points of difference between species, 7
which, as far as our ignorance permits us to judge, seem to be quite
unimportant, we must not forget that climate, food, etc., probably produce some slight and direct effect. It is, however, far more necessary
to bear in mind that there are many unknown laws of correlation[6] of
growth, which, when one part of the organization is modified through
variation and the modifications are accumulated by natural selection
for the good of the being, will cause other modifications, often of the
most unexpected nature.

As we see that those variations which under domestication appear 8
at any particular period of life, tend to reappear in the offspring at the
same period—for instance, in the seeds of the many varieties of our
culinary and agricultural plants; in the caterpillar and cocoon stages of
the varieties of the silkworm; in the eggs of poultry, and in the color
of the down of their chickens; in the horns of our sheep and cattle
when nearly adult—so in a state of nature, natural selection will be
enabled to act on and modify organic beings at any age, by the accumulation of profitable variations at that age, and by their inheritance
at a corresponding age. If it profit a plant to have its seeds more and
more widely disseminated by the wind, I can see no greater difficulty
in this being effected through natural selection than in the cotton-
planter increasing and improving by selection the down in the pods on
his cotton-trees. Natural selection may modify and adapt the larva of
an insect to a score of contingencies, wholly different from those
which concern the mature insect. These modifications will no doubt
effect, through the laws of correlation, the structure of the adult; and
probably in the case of those insects which live only for a few hours,
and which never feed, a large part of their structure is merely the correlated result of successive changes in the structure of their larvae. So,
conversely, modifications in the adult will probably often affect the
structure of the larva; but in all cases natural selection will ensure that
modifications consequent on other modifications at a different period
of life, shall not be in the least degree injurious: for if they became so,
they would cause the extinction of the species.

Natural selection will modify the structure of the young in relation 9
to the parent, and of the parent in relation to the young. In social animals it will adapt the structure of each individual for the benefit of
the community; if each in consequence profits by the selected change.

---

[6]***laws of correlation*** In certain plants and animals, one condition relates to another, as in the case of blue-eyed white cats, which are always deaf; the reasons are not
clear.

What natural selection cannot do is to modify the structure of one species, without giving it any advantage, for the good of another species; and though statements to this effect may be found in works of natural history, I cannot find one case which will bear investigation. A structure used only once in an animal's whole life, if of high importance to it, might be modified to any extent by natural selection; for instance, the great jaws possessed by certain insects, and used exclusively for opening the cocoon—or the hard tip to the beak of nestling birds, used for breaking the egg. It has been asserted that of the best short-beaked tumbler-pigeons, more perish in the egg than are able to get out of it; so that fanciers[7] assist in the act of hatching. Now, if nature had to make the beak of a full-grown pigeon very short for the bird's own advantage, the process of modification would be very slow, and there would be simultaneously the most rigorous selection of the young birds within the egg, which had the most powerful and hardest beaks, for all with weak beaks would inevitably perish; or, more delicate and more easily broken shells might be selected, the thickness of the shell being known to vary like every other structure.

Sexual Selection

Inasmuch as peculiarities often appear under domestication in one 10 sex and become hereditarily attached to that sex, the same fact probably occurs under nature, and if so, natural selection will be able to modify one sex in its functional relations to the other sex, or in relation to wholly different habits of life in the two sexes, as is sometimes the case with insects. And this leads me to say a few words on what I call Sexual Selection. This depends, not on a struggle for existence, but on a struggle between the males for possession of the females; the result is not death to the unsuccessful competitor, but few or no offspring. Sexual selection is, therefore, less rigorous than natural selection. Generally, the most vigorous males, those which are best fitted for their places in nature, will leave most progeny. But in many cases, victory will depend not on general vigor, but on having special weapons, confined to the male sex. A hornless stag or spurless cock would have a poor chance of leaving offspring. Sexual selection by always allowing the victor to breed might surely give indomitable courage, length to the spur, and strength to the wing to strike in the spurred leg, as well as the brutal cock fighter,[8] who knows well that he can

---

[7]*fanciers* Amateurs who raise and race pigeons.

[8]*brutal cock fighter* Cockfights were a popular spectator sport in England, especially for gamblers; but many people considered them a form of horrible brutality.

improve his breed by careful selection of the best cocks. How low in the scale of nature this law of battle descends, I know not; male alligators have been described as fighting, bellowing, and whirling round, like Indians in a wardance, for the possession of the females; male salmons have been seen fighting all day long; male stag-beetles often bear wounds from the huge mandibles[9] of other males. The war is, perhaps, severest between the males of polygamous animals,[10] and these seem oftenest provided with special weapons. The males of carnivorous animals are already well armed; though to them and to others, special means of defense may be given through means of sexual selection, as the mane to the lion, the shoulder-pad to the boar, and the hooked jaw to the male salmon; for the shield may be as important for victory as the sword or spear.

Among birds, the contest is often of a more peaceful character. All 11 those who have attended to the subject believe that there is the severest rivalry between the males of many species to attract, by singing, the females. The rock-thrush of Guiana,[11] birds of paradise, and some others, congregate; and successive males display their gorgeous plumage and perform strange antics before the females, which standing by as spectators, at last choose the most attractive partner. Those who have closely attended to birds in confinement well know that they often take individual preferences and dislikes: thus Sir R. Heron[12] has described how one pied peacock was eminently attractive to all his hen birds. It may appear childish to attribute any effect to such apparently weak means: I cannot here enter on the details necessary to support this view; but if man can in a short time give elegant carriage and beauty to his bantams,[13] according to his standard of beauty, I can see no good reason to doubt that female birds, by selecting, during thousands of generations, the most melodious or beautiful males, according to their standard of beauty, might produce a marked effect. I strongly suspect that some well-known laws with respect to the plumage of male and female birds, in comparison with the plumage of the young, can be explained on the view of plumage having been chiefly modified by sexual selection, acting when the birds have come to the breeding

---

[9]*mandibles* Jaws.

[10]*polygamous animals* Animals that typically have more than one mate.

[11]*Guyana* Formerly British Guiana, on the northeast coast of South America.

[12]*Sir Robert Heron (1765–1854)* English politician who maintained a menagerie of animals.

[13]*bantams* Cocks bred for fighting.

age or during the breeding season; the modifications thus produced being inherited at corresponding ages or seasons, either by the males alone, or by the males and females; but I have not space here to enter on this subject.

Thus it is, as I believe, that when the males and females of any animal have the same general habits of life, but differ in structure, color, or ornament, such differences have been mainly caused by sexual selection; that is, individual males have had, in successive generations, some slight advantage over other males, in their weapons, means of defense, or charms; and have transmitted these advantages to their male offspring. Yet, I would not wish to attribute all such sexual differences to this agency: for we see peculiarities arising and becoming attached to the male sex in our domestic animals (as the wattle in male carriers, horn-like protuberances in the cocks of certain fowls, etc.), which we cannot believe to be either useful to the males in battle, or attractive to the females. We see analogous cases under nature, for instance, the tuft of hair on the breast of the turkey-cock, which can hardly be either useful or ornamental to this bird; indeed, had the tuft appeared under domestication, it would have been called a monstrosity.

Illustrations of the Action
of Natural Selection

In order to make it clear how, as I believe, natural selection acts, I must beg permission to give one or two imaginary illustrations. Let us take the case of a wolf, which preys on various animals, securing some by craft, some by strength, and some by fleetness; and let us suppose that the fleetest prey, a deer for instance, had from any change in the country increased in numbers, or that other prey had decreased in numbers, during that season of the year when the wolf is hardest pressed for food. I can under such circumstances see no reason to doubt that the swiftest and slimmest wolves would have the best chance of surviving, and so be preserved or selected, provided always that they retained strength to master their prey at this or at some other period of the year, when they might be compelled to prey on other animals. I can see no more reason to doubt this, than that man can improve the fleetness of his greyhounds by careful and methodical selection, or by that unconscious selection which results from each man trying to keep the best dogs without any thought of modifying the breed.

Even without any change in the proportional numbers of the ani- 14
mals on which our wolf preyed, a cub might be born with an innate
tendency to pursue certain kinds of prey. Nor can this be thought very
improbable; for we often observe great differences in the natural tendencies of our domestic animals; one cat, for instance, taking to catch
rats, another mice; one cat, according to Mr. St. John,[14] bringing home
winged game, another hares or rabbits, and another hunting on marshy
ground and almost nightly catching woodcocks or snipes. The tendency to catch rats rather than mice is known to be inherited. Now, if
any slight innate change of habit or of structure benefited an individual wolf, it would have the best chance of surviving and of leaving
offspring. Some of its young would probably inherit the same habits or
structure, and by the repetition of this process, a new variety might be
formed which would either supplant or coexist with the parent-form
of wolf. Or, again, the wolves inhabiting a mountainous district, and
those frequenting the lowlands, would naturally be forced to hunt different prey; and from the continued preservation of the individuals
best fitted for the two sites, two varieties might slowly be formed.
These varieties would cross and blend where they met; but to this
subject of intercrossing we shall soon have to return. I may add, that,
according to Mr. Pierce,[15] there are two varieties of the wolf inhabiting
the Catskill Mountains in the United States, one with a light grey-
hound-like form, which pursues deer, and the other more bulky, with
shorter legs, which more frequently attacks the shepherd's flocks.

Let us now take a more complex case. Certain plants excrete a 15
sweet juice, apparently for the sake of eliminating something injurious
from their sap; this is effected by glands at the base of the stipules[16]
in some Leguminosæ, and at the back of the leaf of the common laurel.
This juice, though small in quantity, is greedily sought by insects. Let
us now suppose a little sweet juice or nectar to be excreted by the
inner bases of the petals of a flower. In this case insects in seeking the
nectar would get dusted with pollen, and would certainly often transport the pollen from one flower to the stigma of another flower. The
flowers of two distinct individuals of the same species would thus get
crossed; and the act of crossing, we have good reason to believe (as
will hereafter be more fully alluded to), would produce very vigorous

---

[14]**Charles George William St. John (1809–1856)** An English naturalist whose
book, *Wild Sports and Natural History of the Highlands,* was published in 1846 and in
a second edition in 1848.

[15]**Pierce** Unidentified.

[16]**stipules** Spines at the base of a leaf.

seedlings, which consequently would have the best chance of flourishing and surviving. Some of these seedlings would probably inherit the nectar-excreting power. Those individual flowers which had the largest glands or nectaries, and which excreted most nectar, would be oftenest visited by insects, and would be oftenest crossed; and so in the long-run would gain the upper hand. Those flowers, also, which had their stamens and pistils[17] placed, in relation to the size and habits of the particular insects which visited them, so as to favor in any degree the transportal of their pollen from flower to flower, would likewise be favored or selected. We might have taken the case of insects visiting flowers for the sake of collecting pollen instead of nectar; and as pollen is formed for the sole object of fertilization, its destruction appears a simple loss to the plant; yet if a little pollen were carried, at first occasionally and then habitually, by the pollen-devouring insects from flower to flower, and a cross thus effected, although nine-tenths of the pollen were destroyed, it might still be a great gain to the plant; and those individuals which produced more and more pollen, and had larger and larger anthers,[18] would be selected.

When our plant, by this process of the continued preservation or natural selection of more and more attractive flowers, had been rendered highly attractive to insects, they would, unintentionally on their part, regularly carry pollen from flower to flower; and that they can most effectually do this, I could easily show by many striking instances. I will give only one—not as a very striking case, but as likewise illustrating one step in the separation of the sexes of plants, presently to be alluded to. Some holly-trees bear only male flowers, which have four stamens producing rather a small quantity of pollen, and a rudimentary pistil; other holly-trees bear only female flowers; these have a full-sized pistil, and four stamens with shrivelled anthers, in which not a grain of pollen can be detected. Having found a female tree exactly sixty yards from a male tree, I put the stigmas[19] of twenty flowers, taken from different branches, under the microscope, and on all, without exception, there were pollen-grains, and on some a profusion of pollen. As the wind had set for several days from the female to the male tree, the pollen could not thus have been carried. The weather had been cold and boisterous, and therefore not favorable to bees; nevertheless every female flower which I examined had been ef-

16

---

[17]***stamens and pistils*** Sexual organs of plants. The male and female organs appear together in the same flower.

[18]***anthers*** An anther is that part of the stamen that contains pollen.

[19]***stigmas*** Where the plant's pollen develops.

fectually fertilized by the bees, accidentally dusted with pollen, having flown from tree to tree in search of nectar. But to return to our imaginary case: as soon as the plant had been rendered so highly attractive to insects that pollen was regularly carried from flower to flower, another process might commence. No naturalist doubts the advantage of what has been called the "physiological division of labor"; hence we may believe that it would be advantageous to a plant to produce stamens alone in one flower or on one whole plant, and pistils alone in another flower or on another plant. In plants under culture and placed under new conditions of life, sometimes the male organs and sometimes the female organs become more or less impotent; now if we suppose this to occur in ever so slight a degree under nature, then as pollen is already carried regularly from flower to flower, and as a more complete separation of the sexes of our plant would be advantageous on the principle of the division of labor, individuals with this tendency more and more increased, would be continually favored or selected, until at last a complete separation of the sexes would be effected.

Let us now turn to the nectar-feeding insects in our imaginary case: 17 we may suppose the plant of which we have been slowly increasing the nectar by continued selection, to be a common plant; and that certain insects depended in main part on its nectar for food. I could give many facts, showing how anxious bees are to save time; for instance, their habit of cutting holes and sucking the nectar at the bases of certain flowers, which they can, with a very little more trouble, enter by the mouth. Bearing such facts in mind, I can see no reason to doubt that an accidental deviation in the size and form of the body, or in the curvature and length of the proboscis,[20] etc., far too slight to be appreciated by us, might profit a bee or other insect, so that an individual so characterized would be able to obtain its food more quickly, and so have a better chance of living and leaving descendants. Its descendants would probably inherit a tendency to a similar slight deviation of structure. The tubes of the corollas[21] of the common red and incarnate clovers (Trifolium pratense and incarnatum) do not on a hasty glance appear to differ in length; yet the hive-bee can easily suck the nectar out of the incarnate clover, but not out of the common red clover, which is visited by humble-bees[22] alone; so that whole fields of the red clover offer in vain an abundant supply of precious nectar to

---

[20]*proboscis* Snout.
[21]*corollas* Inner set of floral petals.
[22]*humble-bees* Bumblebees.

the hive-bee. Thus it might be a great advantage to the hive-bee to have a slightly longer or differently constructed proboscis. On the other hand, I have found by experiment that the fertility of clover greatly depends on bees visiting and moving parts of the corolla, so as to push the pollen on to the stigmatic surface. Hence, again, if humble-bees were to become rare in any country, it might be a great advantage to the red clover to have a shorter or more deeply divided tube to its corolla, so that the hive-bee could visit its flowers. Thus I can understand how a flower and a bee might slowly become, either simultaneously or one after the other, modified and adapted in the most perfect manner to each other, by the continued preservation of individuals presenting mutual and slightly favourable deviations of structure.

I am well aware that this doctrine of natural selection, exemplified 18
in the above imaginary instances, is open to the same objections which were at first urged against Sir Charles Lyell's noble views[23] on "the modern changes of the earth, as illustrative of geology"; but we now very seldom hear the action, for instance, of the coast-waves, called a trifling and insignificant cause, when applied to the excavation of gigantic valleys or to the formation of the longest lines of inland cliffs. Natural selection can act only by the preservation and accumulation of infinitesimally small inherited modifications, each profitable to the preserved being; and as modern geology has almost banished such views as the excavation of a great valley by a single diluvial[24] wave, so will natural selection, if it be a true principle, banish the belief of the continued creation of new organic beings, or of any great and sudden modification in their structure.

---

[23]*Sir Charles Lyell's noble views*   Lyell (1797–1875) was an English geologist whose landmark work, *Principles of Geology* (1830–1833), Darwin read while on the *Beagle*. The book inspired Darwin, and the two scientists became friends. Lyell was shown portions of *The Origin of Species* while Darwin was writing it.

[24]*diluvial*   Pertaining to a flood. Darwin means that geological changes, such as those which caused the Grand Canyon, were no longer thought of as being created instantly by flood (or other catastrophes), but were considered to have developed over a long period of time, as he imagines happened in the evolution of species.

QUESTIONS

1. Darwin's metaphor "battle of life" (para. 1) introduces issues that might be thought extraneous to a scientific inquiry. What is the danger of using such a metaphor? What is its advantage?

2. Many religious groups reject Darwin's concept of natural selection, but they heartily accept human selection. Why would there be such a difference between the two?

3. Do you feel that the theory of natural selection is a positive force? Could it be directed by divine power?

4. There is no reference to human beings in this work. Would you assume that the principles at work on animals would also be at work on people? Do you think that Darwin assumes so?

5. What distinguishes the way Darwin proposes and argues a view from Lucretius's method? Does either rely more heavily on sensory experience than the other?

6. When this chapter was published in a later edition, Darwin titled it "The Survival of the Fittest." What issues or emotions does that new title give rise to that "Natural Selection" does not?

WRITING ASSIGNMENTS

1. In paragraph 13, Darwin uses imaginary examples. Compare the value of his genuine examples and these imaginary ones. How effective is the use of imaginary examples in an argument? What requirements would an imaginary example have to have in order to be forceful in an argument? Do you find Darwin's imaginary examples to be strong or weak?

2. From paragraph 14 on, Darwin discusses the process of modification of a species through its beginning in the modification of an individual. Explain, insofar as you understand the concept, just how a species could be modified by a variation which would occur in just one individual. In your explanation, use Darwin's rhetorical technique of the imaginary example.

3. Write an essay which takes as its thesis statement the following sentence from paragraph 18: "Natural selection can act only by the preservation and accumulation of infinitesimally small inherited modifications, each profitable to the preserved being." Be sure to examine the work carefully to find other statements by Darwin that will give added strength, clarity, and meaning to this one. You may also employ the Darwinian device of presenting "imaginary instances" in your essay.

4. A controversy exists concerning the Darwinian theory of evolution. Explore the *Readers' Guide to Periodical Literature* for up-to-date information on the creationist-evolutionist conflict in schools. Look up either term or both to see what articles you can find. Establish the nature of the controversy and attempt to defend one side. Use your knowledge of natural selection gained from this piece. Remember, too, that Darwin was trained as a minister of the church and was very concerned about religious opinion.

5. When Darwin wrote this piece, he believed that sexual selection was of great importance in evolutionary changes in species. Assuming that this belief is true, establish the similarities between sexual selection in plants

and animals with sexual selection, as you have observed it, in people. Paragraphs 10–12 discuss this issue. Darwin does not discuss people, but it is clear that physical and stylistic distinctions between the sexes have some bearing on selection. Assuming that to be true, what qualities in people (physical and mental) are likely to survive? Why?

6. In the Middle Ages and earlier the official view of the church was that the world was flat. Columbus proved that the world was round, and the church agreed not to argue with him. The official view of the church was that the sun went around the earth. When Galileo proved otherwise, he was forced to deny his observations and then he was banished. Only later, in the face of overwhelming evidence, did the church back down. Regarding Darwin, the church held that all species were created on a specially appointed day; evolution was impossible. The Church of England and the Roman Catholic Church, after some struggle, seem to have accepted Darwin's views. Why is it still difficult for some religious organizations to accept Darwin's views? In order to deal with this question, you may have to interview some people connected with a church that holds that Darwin's views are inaccurate. You may also find some religious literature attacking Darwin. If so, establish what the concern of some churches and other religious organizations may be. Make as clear an argument for such organizations' point of view as you can.

7. What fundamental disagreements would Lucretius have had with the theory of evolution as Darwin describes it? One of Lucretius's basic principles is that divine intervention cannot produce life because everything grows from its own seed. Would Darwin's views be comforting to a critic of Lucretius who supported the theory of the creation of life by divine intervention? Darwin does not credit the seed with having the last word on what is created.

THOMAS S. KUHN

The Essential Tension: Tradition and Innovation in Scientific Research

THOMAS KUHN (b. 1922) began as a physicist but soon switched from research to the study of the history of science. His contributions in that field have been so striking as to represent a revolution in thought. His first book, The Structure of Scientific Revolutions *(1962; 1970; 3rd ed. 1982), was a landmark in the history of science. He followed that work with a book on the effects of the Copernican revolution on thought as well as a book of essays,* The Essential Tension *(1978), from which the selection presented here, a lecture first delivered in 1959, is taken.*

Kuhn, an educator and a scholar, has taught the history of science at Harvard University, the University of California at Berkeley, and Princeton University. He has been associated with the Institute for Advanced Study. Currently he teaches at the Massachusetts Institute of Technology (MIT). The talk which follows was delivered to a group of teachers and scholars at the University of Utah at a conference dedicated to discovering scientific talent in young people. As such, the conference was composed of people who were interested in creativity, imagination, and the intellectual problems involved with becoming a scientist.

Kuhn has an interesting concept buried deep within this talk, one that concerns the basic personality type that makes a good scientist.

This is not his focus, to be sure, nor does it directly enter into his thesis statement, but it underlies most of what he is saying. His conclusion is that the best scientist is that person who is most capable of working within the existing traditions of science. In fact, his conclusion is that in the long run such a person will be the most creative kind of scientist. Because this view is not quite what his audience expected to hear, it is buried rather than featured in his talk.

KUHN'S RHETORIC

Because Kuhn's presentation was given as a talk—and was only slightly altered for inclusion in his book—it has many of the typical rhetorical ingredients of a talk. One is the "signpost"—the statement of direction the speaker is taking. In paragraph 6 he points to time limitations which prevent him from giving a wide range of historical examples. He tells us in paragraph 7 that he will now "try briefly to epitomize the nature of education in the natural sciences." In paragraph 10 he tells us, "I shall shortly inquire about. . . ." In paragraph 18 he says, "and this is the point"; in paragraph 21, "What I have said so far. . ."; and in paragraph 26, "As first planned, my paper was to have ended at this point." All these signposts are set up to alert us to his direction, the moments of change of direction, the moments of summation, and the conclusion. Kuhn naturally refers to himself as "I," as most speakers do. Such a relaxed mode of address puts his listeners at ease and makes it simpler for him to explain what he is doing as he does it.

Kuhn also uses an age-old technique typical of a spoken address on a serious subject. He divides the talk into recognizable parts:

Introduction, in which he explains who he is and what he is going to talk about (paras. 1 and 2). His central thesis is stated at the end of paragraph 1.

Body, in which several subsections deal with separate issues:

1. A clarification of the tension between divergent and convergent thinking, with an emphasis on convergent thought (paras. 3–14). Paragraph 14 has a clear sense of a conclusion.

2. A discussion of the nature of education of scientists with an eye toward discovering what kind of personality the scientist should have (paras. 15–24), ending in another conclusion.

Conclusion, in which Kuhn adds a postscript, which is the final conclusion, summarizing his main argument (paras. 26–30).

Kuhn carefully considers theories that are contrary to his own, and while he does not use as many examples as, say, Darwin does, he offers a few key examples to help bolster his argument, as in his discussion of the wave–particle theories of light (para. 11), of science before Isaac Newton (para. 12), and his final discussion of Thomas Edison (1847–1931) in paragraph 29. All the while what he is doing is illustrating the essential tension between two kinds of thinking—the divergent thinking that his audience has already defined as necessary to creativity and the convergent thinking which he has deduced is essential to scientific progress. There must be a tension between these two kinds of thinking in the mind of the scientist who wishes to make creative discoveries. The topic of comparison is used implicitly throughout the essay.

Because his point is somewhat irregular—proposing that creativity comes directly out of the most complete commitment to tradition— Kuhn is careful to prepare his audience carefully for his conclusions. He realizes that what he is saying is a bit paradoxical, and he is cautious to make it clear that he is aware of the complexities of his position. What he wants most is to make his audience aware of the fact that looking only for examples of divergent thinking in prospective scientists is a mistake. Those whose thinking is essentially divergent in nature must accept the essential tension.

The Essential Tension:
Tradition and Innovation in
Scientific Research

I am grateful for the invitation to participate in this important con- 1
ference,[1] and I interpret it as evidence that students of creativity themselves possess the sensitivity to divergent approaches that they seek to
identify in others. But I am not altogether sanguine[2] about the outcome of your experiment with me. As most of you already know, I am
no psychologist, but rather an ex-physicist now working in the history
of science. Probably my concern is no less with creativity than your
own, but my goals, my techniques, and my sources of evidence are so
very different from yours that I am far from sure how much we do, or
even *should*, have to say to each other. These reservations imply no
apology: rather they hint at my central thesis. In the sciences, as I
shall suggest below, it is often better to do one's best with the tools at
hand than to pause for contemplation of divergent approaches.

If a person of my background and interests has anything relevant 2
to suggest to this conference, it will not be about your central concerns, the creative personality and its early identification. But implicit
in the numerous working papers distributed to participants in this
conference is an image of the scientific process and of the scientist;
that image almost certainly conditions many of the experiments you
try as well as the conclusions you draw; and about it the physicist-
historian may well have something to say. I shall restrict my attention
to one aspect of this image—an aspect epitomized as follows in one of
the working papers: The basic scientist "must lack prejudice to a degree where he can look at the most 'self-evident' facts or concepts
without necessarily accepting them, and, conversely, allow his imagination to play with the most unlikely possibilities.". . . In the more
technical language supplied by other working papers, . . . this aspect

---

[1] ***this important conference*** · It was a conference on the identification of scientific
talent held at the University of Utah in 1959.
[2] ***sanguine*** Hopeful or optimistic.

of the image recurs as an emphasis upon "divergent thinking, . . . the freedom to go off in different directions, . . . rejecting the old solution and striking out in some new direction."

I do not at all doubt that this description of "divergent thinking" 3 and the concomitant search for those able to do it are entirely proper. Some divergence characterizes all scientific work, and gigantic divergences lie at the core of the most significant episodes in scientific development. But both my own experience in scientific research and my reading of the history of sciences lead me to wonder whether flexibility and open-mindedness have not been too exclusively emphasized as the characteristics requisite for basic research. I shall therefore suggest below that something like "convergent thinking" is just as essential to scientific advance as is divergent. Since these two modes of thought are inevitably in conflict, it will follow that the ability to support a tension that can occasionally become almost unbearable is one of the prime requisites for the very best sort of scientific research.

I am elsewhere studying these points more historically, with em- 4 phasis on the importance to scientific development of "revolutions."[3] These are episodes—exemplified in their most extreme and readily recognized form by the advent of Copernicanism, Darwinism, or Einsteinianism—in which a scientific community abandons one time-honored way of regarding the world and of pursuing science in favor of some other, usually incompatible, approach to its discipline. I have argued in the draft that the historian constantly encounters many far smaller but structurally similar revolutionary episodes and that they are central to scientific advance. Contrary to a prevalent impression, most new discoveries and theories in the sciences are not merely additions to the existing stockpile of scientific knowledge. To assimilate them the scientist must usually rearrange the intellectual and manipulative equipment he has previously relied upon, discarding some elements of his prior belief and practice while finding new significances in and new relationships between many others. Because the old must be revalued and reordered when assimilating the new, discovery and invention in the sciences are usually intrinsically revolutionary. Therefore, they do demand just that flexibility and open-mindedness that characterize, or indeed define, the divergent thinker. Let us henceforth take for granted the need for these characteristics. Unless many scientists possessed them to a marked degree, there would be no scientific revolutions and very little scientific advance.

---

[3][Thomas Kuhn,] *The Structure of Scientific Revolutions* (Chicago, 1962). [Kuhn's note]

Yet flexibility is not enough, and what remains is not obviously 5
compatible with it. Drawing from various fragments of a project still
in progress, I must now emphasize that revolutions are but one of two
complementary aspects of scientific advance. Almost none of the research undertaken by even the greatest scientists is designed to be revolutionary, and very little of it has any such effect. On the contrary,
normal research, even the best of it, is a highly convergent activity
based firmly upon a settled consensus acquired from scientific education and reinforced by subsequent life in the profession. Typically, to
be sure, this convergent or consensus-bound research ultimately results in revolution. Then, traditional techniques and beliefs are abandoned and replaced by new ones. But revolutionary shifts of a scientific tradition are relatively rare, and extended periods of convergent
research are the necessary preliminary to them. As I shall indicate below, only investigations firmly rooted in the contemporary scientific
tradition are likely to break that tradition and give rise to a new one.
That is why I speak of an "essential tension" implicit in scientific
research. To do his job the scientist must undertake a complex set of
intellectual and manipulative commitments. Yet his claim to fame, if
he has the talent and good luck to gain one, may finally rest upon his
ability to abandon this net of commitments in favor of another of his
own invention. Very often the successful scientist must simultaneously display the characteristics of the traditionalist and of the
iconoclast.[4]

The multiple historical examples upon which any full documenta- 6
tion of these points must depend are prohibited by the time limitations of the conference. But another approach will introduce you to at
least part of what I have in mind—an examination of the nature of
education in the natural sciences. One of the working papers for this
conference . . . quotes Guilford's very apt description of scientific education as follows: "[It] has emphasized abilities in the areas of con-

---

[4]Strictly speaking, it is the professional group rather than the individual scientist that
must display both these characteristics simultaneously. In a fuller account of the ground
covered in this paper that distinction between individual and group characteristics would
be basic. Here I can only note that, though recognition of the distinction weakens the
conflict or tension referred to above, it does not eliminate it. Within the group some
individuals may be more traditionalistic, others more iconoclastic, and their contributions may differ accordingly. Yet education, institutional norms, and the nature of the
job to be done will inevitably combine to insure that all group members will, to a greater
or lesser extent, be pulled in both directions. [Kuhn's note] An *iconoclast* is not traditional, but likes to break with the past, often in very dramatic ways.

vergent thinking and evaluation, often at the expense of development in the area of divergent thinking. We have attempted to teach students how to arrive at 'correct' answers that our civilization has taught us are correct. . . . Outside the arts [and I should include most of the social sciences] we have generally discouraged the development of divergent-thinking abilities, unintentionally." That characterization seems to me eminently just, but I wonder whether it is equally just to deplore the product that results. Without defending plain bad teaching, and granting that in this country the trend to convergent thinking in all education may have proceeded entirely too far, we may nevertheless recognize that a rigorous training in convergent thought has been intrinsic to the sciences almost from their origin. I suggest that they could not have achieved their present state or status without it.

Let me try briefly to epitomize the nature of education in the natural sciences, ignoring the many significant yet minor differences between the various sciences and between the approaches of different educational institutions. The single most striking feature of this education is that, to an extent totally unknown in other creative fields, it is conducted entirely through textbooks. Typically, undergraduate *and* graduate students of chemistry, physics, astronomy, geology, or biology acquire the substance of their fields from books written especially for students. Until they are ready, or very nearly ready, to commence work on their own dissertations, they are neither asked to attempt trial research projects nor exposed to the immediate products of research done by others, that is, to the professional communications that scientists write for each other. There are no collections of "readings" in the natural sciences. Nor are science students encouraged to read the historical classics of their fields—works in which they might discover other ways of regarding the problems discussed in their textbooks, but in which they would also meet problems, concepts, and standards of solution that their future professions have long since discarded and replaced.

In contrast, the various textbooks that the student does encounter display different subject matters, rather than, as in many of the social sciences, exemplifying different approaches to a single problem field. Even books that compete for adoption in a single course differ mainly in level and in pedagogic detail, not in substance or conceptual structure. Last, but most important of all, is the characteristic technique of textbook presentation. Except in their occasional introductions, science textbooks do not describe the sorts of problems that the professional may be asked to solve and the variety of techniques available for their solution. Rather, these books exhibit concrete problem solutions that the profession has come to accept as paradigms,[5] and they then ask the student, either with a pencil and paper or in the laboratory, to solve for himself problems very closely related in both method and substance to those through which the textbook or the accompanying lecture has led him. Nothing could be better calculated to produce "mental sets" or *Einstellungen.*[6] Only in their most elementary courses do other academic fields offer as much as a partial parallel.

Even the most faintly liberal educational theory must view this   9
pedagogic technique as anathema. Students, we would all agree, must begin by learning a good deal of what is already known, but we also insist that education give them vastly more. They must, we say, learn to recognize and evaluate problems to which no unequivocal solution has yet been given; they must be supplied with an arsenal of techniques for approaching these future problems; and they must learn to judge the relevance of these techniques and to evaluate the possibly partial solutions which they can provide. In many respects these attitudes toward education seem to me entirely right, and yet we must recognize two things about them. First, education in the natural sciences seems to have been totally unaffected by their existence. It remains a dogmatic initiation in a pre-established tradition that the student is not equipped to evaluate. Second, at least in the period when it was followed by a term in an apprenticeship relation, this technique of exclusive exposure to a rigid tradition has been immensely productive of the most consequential sorts of innovations.

I shall shortly inquire about the pattern of scientific practice that   10
grows out of this educational initiation and will then attempt to say why that pattern proves quite so successful. But first, an historical excursion will reinforce what has just been said and prepare the way for what is to follow. I should like to suggest that the various fields of natural science have not always been characterized by rigid education in exclusive paradigms, but that each of them acquired something like that technique at precisely the point when the field began to make rapid and systematic progress. If one asks about the origin of our contemporary knowledge of chemical composition, of earthquakes, of biological reproduction, of motion through space, or of any other subject matter known to the natural sciences, one immediately encounters a

---

[5]***paradigms***   Patterns or models of thought; the established views of the way something works or is.
[6]***Einstellungen***   Outlook (German).

characteristic pattern that I shall here illustrate with a single example.

Today, physics textbooks tell us that light exhibits some properties 11
of a wave and some of a particle: both textbook problems and research
problems are designed accordingly. But both this view and these textbooks are products of an early twentieth-century revolution. (One
characteristic of scientific revolutions is that they call for the rewriting of science textbooks.) For more than half a century before 1900,
the books employed in scientific education had been equally unequivocal in stating that light was wave motion. Under those circumstances scientists worked on somewhat different problems and often
embraced rather different sorts of solutions to them. The nineteenth-
century textbook tradition does not, however, mark the beginning of
our subject matter. Throughout the eighteenth century and into the
early nineteenth, Newton's *Opticks*[7] and the other books from which
men learned science taught almost all students that light was particles, and research guided by this tradition was again different from that
which succeeded it. Ignoring a variety of subsidiary changes within
these three successive traditions, we may therefore say that our views
derive historically from Newton's views by way of two revolutions in
optical thought, each of which replaced one tradition of convergent
research with another. If we make appropriate allowances for changes
in the locus[8] and materials of scientific education, we may say that
each of these three traditions was embodied in the sort of education
by exposure to unequivocal paradigms that I briefly epitomized above.
Since Newton, education and research in physical optics have normally been highly convergent.

The history of theories of light does not, however, begin with New- 12
ton. If we ask about knowledge in the field before his time, we encounter a significantly different pattern—a pattern still familiar in the
arts and in some social sciences, but one which has largely disappeared
in the natural sciences. From remote antiquity until the end of the
seventeenth century there was no single set of paradigms for the study
of physical optics. Instead, many men advanced a large number of different views about the nature of light. Some of these views found few
adherents, but a number of them gave rise to continuing schools of

---

[7]***Opticks (1704)*** By Sir Isaac Newton (1642–1727); one of the most important
studies of light and color theory. The book began as a series of lectures in Trinity College,
Cambridge. Newton developed here his theory that light was composed of tiny individual
corpuscles, or particles.
[8]*locus* Place.

optical thought. Although the historian can note the emergence of new points of view as well as changes in the relative popularity of older ones, there was never anything resembling consensus. As a result, a new man entering the field was inevitably exposed to a variety of conflicting viewpoints; he was forced to examine the evidence for each, and there always was good evidence. The fact that he made a choice and conducted himself accordingly could not entirely prevent his awareness of other possibilities. This earlier mode of education was obviously more suited to produce a scientist without prejudice, alert to novel phenomena, and flexible in his approach to his field. On the other hand, one can scarcely escape the impression that, during the period characterized by this more liberal educational practice, physical optics made very little progress.[9]

13 The preconsensus (we might here call it the divergent) phase in the development of physical optics is, I believe, duplicated in the history of all other scientific specialties, excepting only those that were born by the subdivision and recombination of pre-existing disciplines. In some fields, like mathematics and astronomy, the first firm consensus is prehistoric. In others, like dynamics, geometric optics, and parts of physiology, the paradigms that produced a first consensus date from classical antiquity. Most other natural sciences, though their problems were often discussed in antiquity, did not achieve a first consensus until after the Renaissance. In physical optics, as we have seen, the first firm consensus dates only from the end of the seventeenth century; in electricity, chemistry, and the study of heat, it dates from the eighteenth; while in geology and the nontaxonomic[10] parts of biology no very real consensus developed until after the first third of the nineteenth century. This century appears to be characterized by the emergence of a first consensus in parts of a few of the social sciences.

14 In all the fields named above, important work was done before the achievement of the maturity produced by consensus. Neither the na-

---

[9]The history of physical optics before Newton has recently been well described by Vasco Ronchi in *Histoire de la lumière*, trans. J. Taton (Paris, 1956). His account does justice to the element I elaborate too little above. Many fundamental contributions to physical optics were made in the two millennia before Newton's work. Consensus is not prerequisite to a sort of progress in the natural sciences, any more than it is to progress in the social sciences or the arts. It is, however, prerequisite to the sort of progress that we now generally refer to when distinguishing the natural sciences from the arts and from most social sciences. [Kuhn's note]

[10]**nontaxonomic** Unrelated to the classification of plants and animals.

ture nor the timing of the first consensus in these fields can be understood without a careful examination of both the intellectual and the
manipulative techniques[11] developed before the existence of unique
paradigms. But the transition to maturity is not less significant because individuals practiced science before it occurred. On the contrary,
history strongly suggests that, though one can practice science—as one
does philosophy or art or political science—without a firm consensus,
this more flexible practice will not produce the pattern of rapid consequential scientific advance to which recent centuries have accustomed us. In that pattern, development occurs from one consensus to
another, and alternate approaches are not ordinarily in competition.
Except under quite special conditions, the practitioner of a mature science does not pause to examine divergent modes of explanation or experimentation.

I shall shortly ask how this can be so—how a firm orientation to- 15
ward an apparently unique tradition can be compatible with the practice of the disciplines most noted for the persistent production of
novel ideas and techniques. But it will help first to ask what the education that so successfully transmits such a tradition leaves to be
done. What can a scientist working within a deeply rooted tradition
and little trained in the perception of significant alternatives hope to
do in his professional career? Once again limits of time force me to
drastic simplification, but the following remarks will at least suggest
a position that I am sure can be documented in detail.

In pure or basic science[12]—that somewhat ephemeral category of 16
research undertaken by men whose most immediate goal is to increase
understanding rather than control of nature—the characteristic problems are almost always repetitions, with minor modifications, of problems that have been undertaken and partially resolved before. For example, much of the research undertaken within a scientific tradition
is an attempt to adjust existing theory or existing observation in order
to bring the two into closer and closer agreement. The constant examination of atomic and molecular spectra during the years since the
birth of wave mechanics, together with the design of theoretical ap-
proximations for the prediction of complex spectra, provides one important instance of this typical sort of work. Another was provided by

---

[11]***manipulative techniques*** Practical testing, as opposed to theorizing.
[12]***pure or basic science*** The distinction, pure and applied, is equivalent to the distinction between theoretical and practical science.

the remarks about the eighteenth-century development of Newtonian dynamics[13] in the paper on measurement supplied to you in advance of the conference.[14] The attempt to make existing theory and observation conform more closely is not, of course, the only standard sort of research problem in the basic sciences. The development of chemical thermodynamics[15] or the continuing attempts to unravel organic structure illustrate another type—the extension of existing theory to areas that it is expected to cover but in which it has never before been tried. In addition, to mention a third common sort of research problem, many scientists constantly collect the concrete data (e.g., atomic weights, nuclear moments[16]) required for the application and extension of existing theory.

These are normal research projects in the basic sciences, and they illustrate the sorts of work on which all scientists, even the greatest, spend most of their professional lives and on which many spend all. Clearly their pursuit is neither intended nor likely to produce fundamental discoveries or revolutionary changes in scientific theory. Only if the validity of the contemporary scientific tradition is assumed do these problems make much theoretical or any practical sense. The man who suspected the existence of a totally new type of phenomenon or who had basic doubts about the validity of existing theory would not think problems so closely modeled on textbook paradigms worth undertaking. It follows that the man who does undertake a problem of this sort—and that means all scientists at most times—aims to elucidate the scientific tradition in which he was raised rather than to change it. Furthermore, the fascination of his work lies in the difficulties of elucidation rather than in any surprises that the work is likely to produce. Under normal conditions the research scientist is not an innovator but a solver of puzzles, and the puzzles upon which he concentrates are just those which he believes can be both stated and solved within the existing scientific tradition.

Yet—and this is the point—the ultimate effect of this tradition-bound work has invariably been to change the tradition. Again and

---

[13]*Newtonian dynamics*   Newton's three laws of motion are: (1) An object stays at rest until an outside force moves it. (2) The change of motion is proportional to the force that moves it. (3) To every action there is an equal and opposite reaction.

[14]A revised version appeared in *Isis* 52 (1961): 161–93. [Kuhn's note]

[15]*chemical thermodynamics*   Laws determining motion, usually of gases, in relation to heat.

[16]*atomic weights, nuclear moments*   Atomic weight of an element is the average of its isotopes, the average number of atoms in its molecule. Nuclear moment is the axis of the molecule, its center.

again the continuing attempt to elucidate a currently received tradition has at last produced one of those shifts in fundamental theory, in
problem field,[17] and in scientific standards to which I previously referred as scientific revolutions. At least for the scientific community
as a whole, work within a well-defined and deeply ingrained tradition
seems more productive of tradition-shattering novelties than work in
which no similarly convergent standards are involved. How can this
be so? I think it is because no other sort of work is nearly so well
suited to isolate for continuing and concentrated attention those loci
of trouble or causes of crisis upon whose recognition the most fundamental advances in basic science depend.

As I have indicated in the first of my working papers, new theories 19
and, to an increasing extent, novel discoveries in the mature sciences
are not born *de novo*.[18] On the contrary, they emerge from old theories
and within a matrix[19] of old beliefs about the phenomena that the
world does *and does not* contain. Ordinarily such novelties are far too
esoteric and recondite[20] to be noted by the man without a great deal
of scientific training. And even the man with considerable training can
seldom afford simply to go out and look for them, let us say by explor-
ing those areas in which existing data and theory have failed to produce understanding. Even in a mature science there are always far too
many such areas, areas in which no existing paradigms seem obviously
to apply and for whose exploration few tools and standards are available. More likely than not the scientist who ventured into them, relying merely upon his receptivity to new phenomena and his flexibility to new patterns of organization, would get nowhere at all. He
would rather return his science to its preconsensus or natural history
phase.

Instead, the practitioner of a mature science, from the beginning of 20
his doctoral research, continues to work in the regions for which the
paradigms derived from his education and from the research of his contemporaries seem adequate. He tries, that is, to elucidate topographical
detail on a map whose main outlines are available in advance, and he
hopes—if he is wise enough to recognize the nature of his field—that
he will some day undertake a problem in which the anticipated does

---

[17]*problem field*   Theoretical questions.

[18]*de novo*   Over again; from the start.

[19]*matrix*   Interrelated group of, in this case, beliefs; when one changes, all are altered.

[20]*esoteric and recondite*   Designed for specially trained people and difficult to understand.

not occur, a problem that goes wrong in ways suggestive of a fundamental weakness in the paradigm itself. In the mature sciences the prelude to much discovery and to all novel theory is not ignorance, but the recognition that something has gone wrong with existing knowledge and beliefs.

What I have said so far may indicate that it is sufficient for the productive scientist to adopt existing theory as a lightly held tentative hypothesis, employ it *faute de mieux*[21] in order to get a start in his research, and then abandon it as soon as it leads him to a trouble spot, a point at which something has gone wrong. But though the ability to recognize trouble when confronted by it is surely a requisite for scientific advance, trouble must not be too easily recognized. The scientist requires a thoroughgoing commitment to the tradition with which, if he is fully successful, he will break. In part this commitment is demanded by the nature of the problems the scientist normally undertakes. These, as we have seen, are usually esoteric puzzles whose challenge lies less in the information disclosed by their solutions (all but its details are often known in advance) than in the difficulties of technique to be surmounted in providing any solution at all. Problems of this sort are undertaken only by men assured that there is a solution which ingenuity can disclose, and only current theory could possibly provide assurance of that sort. That theory alone gives meaning to most of the problems of normal research. To doubt it is often to doubt that the complex technical puzzles which constitute normal research have any solutions at all. Who, for example, would have developed the elaborate mathematical techniques required for the study of the effects of interplanetary attractions upon basic Keplerian orbits[22] if he had not assumed that Newtonian dynamics, applied to the planets then known, would explain the last details of astronomical observation? But without that assurance, how would Neptune have been discovered and the list of planets changed?

In addition, there are pressing practical reasons for commitment. Every research problem confronts the scientist with anomalies[23] whose sources he cannot quite identify. His theories and observations never quite agree; successive observations never yield quite the same

---

[21]**faute de mieux**   For want of something better.

[22]***Keplerian orbits***   Johannes Kepler (1571–1630) discovered that the planets move in elliptical, not circular orbits. He recognized the gravitational pull of the sun and planets and was noted for the care and exactitude of his measurements.

[23]***anomalies***   Unaccountable variations from what is expected.

results; his experiments have both theoretical and phenomenological[24] by-products which it would take another research project to unravel. Each of these anomalies or incompletely understood phenomena could conceivably be the clue to a fundamental innovation in scientific theory or technique, but the man who pauses to examine them one by one never completes his first project. Reports of effective research repeatedly imply that all but the most striking and central discrepancies could be taken care of by current theory if only there were time to take them on. The men who make these reports find most discrepancies trivial or uninteresting, an evaluation that they can ordinarily base only upon their faith in current theory. Without that faith their work would be wasteful of time and talent.

Besides, lack of commitment too often results in the scientist's undertaking problems that he has little chance of solving. Pursuit of an anomaly is fruitful only if the anomaly is more than nontrivial. Having discovered it, the scientist's first efforts and those of his profession are to do what nuclear physicists are now doing. They strive to generalize the anomaly, to discover other and more revealing manifestations of the same effect, to give it structure by examining its complex interrelationships with phenomena they still feel they understand. Very few anomalies are susceptible to this sort of treatment. To be so they must be in explicit and unequivocal conflict with some structurally central tenet of current scientific belief. Therefore, their recognition and evaluation once again depend upon a firm commitment to the contemporary scientific tradition.

This central role of an elaborate and often esoteric tradition is what I have principally had in mind when speaking of the essential tension in scientific research. I do not doubt that the scientist must be, at least potentially, an innovator, that he must possess mental flexibility, and that he must be prepared to recognize troubles where they exist. That much of the popular stereotype is surely correct, and it is important accordingly to search for indices of the corresponding personality characteristics. But what is no part of our stereotype and what appears to need careful integration with it is the other face of this same coin. We are, I think, more likely fully to exploit our potential scientific talent if we recognize the extent to which the basic scientist must also be a firm traditionalist, or, if I am using your vocabulary at all correctly, a convergent thinker. Most important of all, we must seek to understand

---

[24]***phenomenological*** Related to perceptible events.

how these two superficially discordant modes of problem solving can be reconciled both within the individual and within the group.

Everything said above needs both elaboration and documentation. 25 Very likely some of it will change in the process. This paper is a report on work in progress. But, though I insist that much of it is tentative and all of it incomplete, I still hope that the paper has indicated why an educational system best described as an initiation into an unequivocal tradition should be thoroughly compatible with successful scientific work. And I hope, in addition, to have made plausible the historical thesis that no part of science has progressed very far or very rapidly before this convergent education and correspondingly convergent normal practice became possible. Finally, though it is beyond my competence to derive personality correlates from this view of scientific development, I hope to have made meaningful the view that the productive scientist must be a traditionalist who enjoys playing intricate games by pre-established rules in order to be a successful innovator who discovers new rules and new pieces with which to play them.

As first planned, my paper was to have ended at this point. But 26 work on it, against the background supplied by the working papers distributed to conference participants, has suggested the need for a postscript. Let me therefore briefly try to eliminate a likely ground of misunderstanding and simultaneously suggest a problem that urgently needs a great deal of investigation.

Everything said above was intended to apply strictly only to basic 27 science, an enterprise whose practitioners have ordinarily been relatively free to choose their own problems. Characteristically, as I have indicated, these problems have been selected in areas where paradigms were clearly applicable but where exciting puzzles remained about how to apply them and how to make nature conform to the results of the application. Clearly the inventor and applied scientist are not generally free to choose puzzles of this sort. The problems among which they may choose are likely to be largely determined by social, economic, or military circumstances external to the sciences. Often the decision to seek a cure for a virulent disease, a new source of household illumination, or an alloy able to withstand the intense heat of rocket engines must be made with little reference to the state of the relevant science. It is, I think, by no means clear that the personality characteristics requisite for pre-eminence in this more immediately practical sort of work are altogether the same as those required for a great achievement in basic science. History indicates that only a few individuals, most of whom worked in readily demarcated areas, have achieved eminence in both.

I am by no means clear where this suggestion leads us. The troublesome distinctions between basic research,[25] applied research, and invention need far more investigation. Nevertheless, it seems likely, for example, that the applied scientist, to whose problems no scientific paradigm need be fully relevant, may profit by a far broader and less rigid education than that to which the pure scientist has characteristically been exposed. Certainly there are many episodes in the history of technology in which lack of more than the most rudimentary scientific education has proved to be an immense help. This group scarcely needs to be reminded that Edison's electric light[26] was produced in the face of unanimous scientific opinion that the arc light could not be "subdivided," and there are many other episodes of this sort.

This must not suggest, however, that mere differences in education will transform the applied scientist into a basic scientist or vice versa. One could at least argue that Edison's personality, ideal for the inventor and perhaps also for the "oddball" in applied science, barred him from fundamental achievements in the basic sciences. He himself expressed great scorn for scientists and thought of them as wooly-headed people to be hired when needed. But this did not prevent his occasionally arriving at the most sweeping and irresponsible scientific theories of his own. (The pattern recurs in the early history of electrical technology: both Tesla[27] and Gramme[28] advanced absurd cosmic schemes that they thought deserved to replace the current scientific knowledge of their day.) Episodes like this reinforce an impression that the per-

28

29

---

[25]***basic research*** Research designed to establish new theories. Other types of research attempt to put basic research to some practical use.

[26]***electric light*** Thomas Alva Edison (1847–1931) did not invent the electric light, but did the applied research that made it a practical commercial product, which it became in 1882.

[27]***Nikola Tesla (1856–1943)*** Electrical engineer of Croatian descent; inventor of carbon arc lighting, in which a huge electrical charge bridges a gap with a bright flash. He also invented alternating current. In later years he claimed to be able to communicate with distant planets and to be able to split the earth like an apple.

[28]***Zénobe-Théophile Gramme (1826–1901)*** A basically untrained Belgian scientist and inventor who worked with direct and alternating current. He held some wild and ignorant views of the power of magnetism.

sonality requisites of the pure scientist and of the inventor may be quite different, perhaps with those of the applied scientist lying somewhere between.[29]

Is there a further conclusion to be drawn from all this? One spec- 30 ulative thought forces itself upon me. If I read the working papers correctly, they suggest that most of you are really in search of the *inventive* personality, a sort of person who does emphasize divergent thinking but whom the United States has already produced in abundance. In the process you may be ignoring certain of the essential requisites of the basic scientist, a rather different sort of person, to whose ranks America's contributions have as yet been notoriously sparse. Since most of you are, in fact, Americans, this correlation may not be entirely coincidental.

---

[29]For the attitude of scientists toward the technical possibility of the incandescent light see Francis A. Jones, *Thomas Alva Edison* (New York, 1908), pp. 99–100, and Harold C. Passer, *The Electrical Manufacturers, 1875–1900* (Cambridge, Mass., 1953), pp. 82–83. For Edison's attitude toward scientists see Passer, ibid., pp. 180–81. For a sample of Edison's theorizing in realms otherwise subject to scientific treatments see Dagobert D. Runes, ed., *The Diary and Sundry Observations of Thomas Alva Edison* (New York, 1948), pp. 205–44, passim. [Kuhn's note]

QUESTIONS

1. What is divergent thinking? Give some examples from your own experience.
2. What is convergent thinking? Give some examples from your experience.
3. Assuming that Kuhn's audience was committed to the principles of divergent thinking before they heard his talk, do you feel that they would have changed their minds after hearing it? What are your reasons for thinking they would (or would not) have changed their minds?
4. Find all the signposts in the talk that explain where the argument is heading, what Kuhn is planning to do, and what he has done. How effective are these signposts for following his argument? Do you find them annoying or helpful? Are there any places where they are needed but not supplied?
5. Kuhn talks about reaching a consensus in science. What does he mean? See paragraphs 12–13.
6. Would Kuhn describe Darwin's research and conclusions as divergent or convergent thinking? Why?
7. Would Kuhn approve of Lucretius's ways of reasoning, or would he suggest some important changes in Lucretius's approach?

WRITING ASSIGNMENTS

1. Kuhn is interested in the kind of personality that would be best suited to doing creative work in science. After listening to his talk, if you were a member of the audience responsible for selecting a potential scientist from a group of young people, what personality characteristics would you look for? What, in Kuhn's view, are the intellectual and personal characteristics of scientists that are most likely to ensure scientific discovery in the future?

2. Much of what Kuhn has to say about thinking relates directly to the way in which education in the sciences is conducted. The student is asked to master the basic paradigms of a branch of science—theories, models, patterns, examples—that are at hand. What are your views on the nature of scientific education? Based on your own experience, what is praiseworthy about it? What is not praiseworthy about it? Is science education much as Kuhn describes it?

3. What is it about the very nature of science that suits it best to convergent thinking? Consider the discovery of facts, laws, and principles that really work and that do not admit of much variance. Why would science resist divergent thought? What would actually constitute divergent thought in science? Why is consensus such a deterrent to divergence? *Should* it be a deterrent to divergence? What are the alternatives, if any, to such consensus?

4. In paragraph 3, Kuhn asserts that "these two modes of thought" (divergence and convergence) "are inevitably in conflict." Is this statement necessarily true? Find examples in any area of inquiry—science, politics, religion, education, or any other area that interests you—which help you decide just what the nature of the conflict (if there is one) actually is. If you find that there is no conflict, explain why there is none. If you find that there is conflict, explain why there is. Use Kuhn's rhetorical techniques of beginning with an introduction, dividing your topic in the body of the essay, and ending with a summary conclusion. Structure your essay like a talk and offer some of the same kinds of signposts that Kuhn uses.

5. Look for examples of convergent and divergent thinking in your social life and write an essay based on your findings. Are most of your friends likely to be convergent or divergent in their thinking? Choose some specific persons and instances of their thinking. If possible, spend some time in observation of your friends (and yourself) to see which kind of thinking is more prevalent. How much tolerance do your friends have for divergent thinking? How much tolerance do older people seem to have for divergent thinking? What seem to be the most touchy issues with respect to divergent thinking? Make your essay into the shape of a talk like Kuhn's, using signposts, an introduction, a body, and a conclusion. Use the first person throughout.

6. What paradigms of thinking would Lucretius have been arguing against in his "Matter and Space"? Is it possible to know what he was afraid Memmius would believe instead of what Lucretius himself thought to be the truth? What kinds of thought patterns does Lucretius reject and accept in his writing? What would be Kuhn's critique of Lucretius?

LOREN EISELEY

The Last Neanderthal

LOREN EISELEY (1907–1977) is one of the most distinguished
American science writers. He was born in Nebraska, where he began
his schooling and planned to be a poet. That his abilities were considerable is evidenced by the fact that he published his first poetry at
age twenty in the respected literary magazine The Prairie Schooner.
He soon became a contributing editor of the journal, a position he
retained while pursuing his college education. He was drawn to anthropology while at the University of Nebraska and there participated
in a major archaeological dig, an experience he mentions in "The
Last Neanderthal." Next, he attended the University of Pennsylvania
to study for a graduate degree in anthropology. His friendship with
Frank Speck, the unconventional chairman of the department, probably confirmed his ambition to be a professional scientist. After receiving his Ph.D. at Pennsylvania, he taught at the University of
Kansas (1937–1944) and Oberlin College (1944–1947). Eventually, he
was asked to be chairman of the anthropology department at the University of Pennsylvania at a time when the department had lan-

---

From *The Star Thrower*.

guished, following the retirement of Frank Speck. Later, he was to serve for two years as provost of the university.

All this time he was writing. Among his distinguished books are The Immense Journey *(1957)*; Darwin's Century *(1958)*; The Firmament of Time *(1960)*; The Mind as Nature *(1962)*; The Unexpected Universe, The Brown Wasps *(both 1969)*; and The Star Thrower *(1978), from which this essay comes. This prodigious output represents only part of his work. His genius lies in meditating on the phenomena that surround humankind and finding in such phenomena a connection with nature. Eiseley always locates us in relation to our natural environment, reminding us that we are not here alone, and that we must seek to understand ourselves better, within our environment.*

Eiseley had a special respect for Francis Bacon and his vision of the relationship of humankind to nature. In 1961 Eiseley gave the Montgomery Series of Lectures at the University of Nebraska, focusing on the achievement of Bacon and paying special attention to Bacon's sense of time and his ability to find in the Greek myths wisdom that could illuminate contemporary thought. The lectures were published in 1963 under the title Francis Bacon and the Modern Dilemma by the University of Nebraska, but because of poor editing, the book was error-ridden and Eiseley demanded that it be withdrawn. Ten years later, it was corrected and republished under the title The Man Who Saw Through Time *(1973) which was also the title of his first essay on Bacon. Bacon, considered the inventor of scientific method because of his insistence on induction as a method of reasoning, forced people to look forward rather than simply backward in historical studies: he recognized that scientific discoveries would ultimately change the nature of the way we see the world.*

In "The Last Neanderthal," Eiseley approached a special kind of problem raised by his observations and by the conclusions that he felt he could draw from them. The Neanderthal was a human species that disappeared some thirty thousand years ago and whose skeletal remains date to ninety thousand years ago. Homo sapiens is a closely related species. He knew the dimensions of the Neanderthal skull because he had studied them—although he tells us that he had lost his notes and notebook. He had first seen a Neanderthal-like skull in a dissection room and noted its low forehead and heavy eye-sockets. On a dig searching for rhinoceros bones, he had observed a woman, who had visited their campsite, whose skull looked pronouncedly like that of a Neanderthal. His mind was taken with the possibility *that some of the Neanderthal genes might still be extant, showing up occasionally in a modern human such as this woman.*

Eiseley found the experience startling and began a long series of reflections on the differences between modern humans and the ancient Neanderthal. His musings implied that although the Neanderthal lost out in the evolutionary struggle of the fittest, there was much that was gentle and good about the Neanderthal and much that was lost to humanity when the Neanderthal became extinct.

What Eiseley gave us is a valuation of research observations. He derived his observations from several sources and from several historical epochs, then wove an elaborate and striking analysis that constituted a response to his own experience. He tried to establish what his musings might mean to us, what they might mean to science, and how they can help us better understand our situation as humans. In a way, he asks "What is the meaning of all this?"

EISELEY'S RHETORIC

Because Eiseley is a very poetic writer, his rhetoric is much different from what we find in most scientific writing. For one thing, he is able to recreate the sense of mood and location with an ease that is enviable, not to be found in other writers such as Lucretius or Bacon. Their writing is more factual, and their techniques more limited to enumeration: six great principles, for instance, and four idols. But Eiseley uses no such devices. Instead, he paints a picture using detail, description, and the touching moment: "The dog was little more than a skeleton but still articulated, one delicate bony paw laid gracefully—as though its owner merely slept, and would presently awaken—across a stone at the water's edge."

His images are evocative, concrete, and efficient. He sets a scene, brings us into it, and allows us to share with him some of his more intense memories. And since this is a record of memories, and in some ways a hymn to the human memory in general, his most interesting rhetorical device is the narrative. Telling us stories, we learn about the junkman of his youth, the drowned dog cast up on the coast, the locals who nosed around an archaeological dig. We get to see him as an actor in a drama: "As I turned upward into the hills beyond the beach I was faintly aware. . . ." (para. 6).

When he begins to tell us about the young woman he meets, we have the central narrative, the story that is designed to introduce us to the concept of the Neanderthal as it may still linger in the human race, in our genes. The view Eiseley gives us is both backward and forward. We look back through time to our origins but forward in time to our future. He ends his discussion with a vision of himself being consumed, as by a fire: the same metabolic power he marvels at in the opening paragraphs when he realizes that the thoughts of the human brain are produced as naturally by nature as the color of a flower. Eiseley's vision in this essay is unifying, powerful, and of the sort that forces us to think more deeply about our place in the universe.

———⚬———

The Last Neanderthal

For thou shalt be in league with the stones of the field: and the beasts of the field shall be at peace with thee.

JOB 5:23

It has long been the thought of science, particularly in evolutionary biology, that nature does not make extended leaps, that her creatures slip in slow disguise from one shape to another. A simple observation will reveal, however, that there are rocks in deserts that glow with heat for a time after sundown. Similar emanations may come from the writer or the scientist. The creative individual is someone upon whom mysterious rays have converged and are again reflected, not necessarily immediately, but in the course of years. That all of this wispy geometry of dreams and memories should be the product of a kind of slow-burning oxidation carried on in an equally diffuse and mediating web of nerve and sense cells is surprising enough, but that the emanations from the same particulate organ, the brain, should be so strikingly different as to disobey the old truism of an unleaping nature is quite surprising, once one comes to contemplate the reality.

The same incident may stand as a simple fact to some, an intangible hint of the nature of the universe to others, a useful myth to a savage, or any number of other things. The receptive mind makes all the difference, shadowing or lighting the original object. I was an observer, intent upon my own solitary hieroglyphics.[1]

It happened a long time ago at Curaçao, in the Netherlands Antilles, on a shore marked by the exposed ribs of a wrecked freighter. The place was one where only a student of desolation would find cause to linger. Pelicans perched awkwardly on what remained of a rusted prow. On the edge of the littered beach beyond the port I had come upon a dead dog wrapped in burlap, obviously buried at sea and drifted in by the waves. The dog was little more than a skeleton but still articulated, one delicate bony paw laid gracefully—as though its owner merely slept, and would presently awaken—across a stone at the water's edge. Around his throat was a waterlogged black strap that showed he had once belonged to someone. This dog was a mongrel whose life had been spent among the island fishermen. He had known only the small sea-beaten boats that come across the strait from Venezuela. He had romped briefly on shores like this to which he had been returned by the indifferent sea.

I stepped back a little hesitantly from the smell of death, but still I paused reluctantly. Why, in this cove littered with tin cans, bottles, and cast-off garments, did I find it difficult, if not a sacrilege, to turn away? Because, the thought finally came to me, this particular tattered garment had once lived. Scenes on the living sea that would never in all eternity recur again had streamed through the sockets of those vanished eyes. The dog was young, the teeth in its jaws still perfect. It was of that type of loving creature who had gamboled happily about the legs of men and striven to partake of their endeavors.

Someone had seen crudely to his sea burial, but not well enough to prevent his lying now where came everything abandoned. Nevertheless, vast natural forces had intervened to clothe him with a pathetic dignity. The tide had brought him quietly at night and placed what remained of him asleep upon the stones. Here at sunrise I had stood above him in a light he would never any longer see. Even if I had had a shovel the stones would have prevented his burial. He would wait for a second tide to spirit him away or lay him higher to bleach starkly upon coral and conch shells, mingling the little lime of his bones with all else that had once stood upright on these shores.

---

[1]**hieroglyphics** A system of writing, particularly that of ancient Egypt, which uses pictorial symbols to represent words and sounds; hence, writing that is difficult to decipher.

As I turned upward into the hills beyond the beach I was faintly   6
aware of a tracery of lizard tails amidst the sand and the semi-desert
shrubbery. The lizards were so numerous on the desert floor that their
swift movement in the bright sun left a dizzying impression, like spots
dancing before one's eyes. The creatures had a tangential way of darting off to the side like inconsequential thoughts that never paused long
enough to be fully apprehended. One's eyesight was oppressed by subtly moving points where all should have been quiet. Similar darting
specks seemed to be invading my mind. Offshore I could hear the sea
wheezing and suspiring in long gasps among the cavern of the coral.
The equatorial sun blazed on my unprotected head and hummingbirds
flashed like little green flames in the underbrush. I sought quick shelter under a manzanillo tree, whose poisoned apples had tempted the
sailors of Columbus.

I suppose the apples really made the connection. Or perhaps merely   7
the interior rustling of the lizards as I passed some cardboard boxes
beside a fence brought the thing to mind. Or again, it may have been
the tropic sun, lending its flames to life with a kind of dreadful indifference as to the result. At any rate, as I shielded my head under the
leaves of the poison tree, the darting lizard points began to run together into a pattern.

Before me passed a broken old horse plodding before a cart laden   8
with bags of cast-off clothing, discarded furniture, and abandoned
metal. The horse's harness was a makeshift combination of straps
mended with rope. The bearded man perched high in the driver's seat
looked as though he had been compounded from the assorted junk
heap in the wagon bed. What finally occupied the center of my attention, however, was a street sign and a year—a year that scurried into
shape with the flickering alacrity of the lizards. "R Street," they
spelled, and the year was 1923.

By now the man on the wagon is dead, his cargo dispersed, never   9
to be reassembled. The plodding beast has been overtaken by whatever
fate comes upon a junkman's horse. Their significance upon that particular day in 1923 had been resolved to this, just this: The wagon had
been passing the intersection between R and Fourteenth streets when
I had leaned from a high-school window a block away, absorbed as
only a sixteen-year-old may sometimes be with the sudden discovery
of time. It is all going, I thought with the bitter desperation of the
young confronting history. No one can hold us. Each and all, we are
riding into the dark. Even living, we cannot remember half the events
of our own days.

At that moment my eye had fallen upon the junk dealer passing 10
his fateful corner. Now, I had thought instantly, now, save him, im-
mortalize the unseizable moment. The junkman is the symbol of all
that is going or is gone. He is passing the intersection into nothingness. Say to the mind, "Hold him, do not forget."

The darting lizard points beyond the manzanillo tree converged and 11
tightened. The phantom horse and the heaped, chaotic wagon were
still jouncing across the intersection upon R Street. They had never
crossed it; they would not. Forty-five years had fled away. I was not
wrong about the powers latent in the brain. The scene was still in
process.

I estimated the lowering of the sun with one eye while at the back 12
of my mind the lizard rustling continued. The blistering apples of the
manzanillo reminded me of an inconsequential wild-plum fall far
away in Nebraska. They were not edible but they contained the same,
if a simpler, version of the mystery hidden in our heads. They were
hoarding and dispersing energy while the inanimate universe was running down around us.

"We must regard the organism as a configuration contrived to 13
evade the tendency of the universal laws of nature," John Joly the geologist had once remarked. Unlike the fire in a thicket, life burned
cunningly and hoarded its resources. Energy provisions in the seed provided against individual death. Of all the unexpected qualities of an
unexpected universe, the sheer organizing power of animal and plant
metabolism is one of the most remarkable, but, as in the case of most
everyday marvels, we take it for granted. Where it reaches its highest
development, in the human mind, we forget it completely. Yet out of
it history is made—the junkman on R Street is prevented from depart-
ing. Growing increasingly archaic, that phantom would be held at the
R Street intersection while all around him new houses arose and the
years passed unremembered. He would not be released until my own
mind began to crumble.

The power to free him is not mine. He is held enchanted because 14
long ago I willed a miniature of history, confined to a single brain.
That brain is devouring oxygen at a rate out of all proportion to the
rest of the body. It is involved in burning, evoking, and transposing
visions, whether of lizard tails, alphabets from the sea, or the realms
beyond the galaxy. So important does nature regard this unseen combustion, this smoke of the planet's autumn, that a starving man's brain
will be protected to the last while his body is steadily consumed. It is
a part of unexpected nature.

In the rational universe of the physical laboratory this sullen and 15
obstinate burning might not, save for our habit of taking the existent
for granted, have been expected. Nonetheless, it is here, and man is its
most tremendous manifestation. One might ask, Would it be possible
to understand humanity a little better if one could follow along just a
step of the evolutionary pathway in person? Suppose that there still
lived . . . but let me tell the tale, make of it what you will.

Years after the experience I am about to describe, I came upon a 16
recent but Neanderthaloid skull in the dissecting room—a rare-enough
occurrence, one that the far-out flitting of forgotten genes struggles
occasionally to produce, as if life sometimes hesitated and were inclined to turn back upon its pathway. For a time, remembering an
episode of my youth, I kept the indices of cranial measurement by me.

Today, thinking of that experience, I have searched vainly for my 17
old notebook. It is gone. The years have a way of caring for things that
do not seek the safety of print. The earlier event remains, however,
because it was not a matter of measurements or anthropological
indices but of a living person whom I once knew. Now, in my autumn,
the face of that girl and the strange season I spent in her neighborhood
return in a kind of hazy lesson that I was too young to understand.

It happened in the West, somewhere in that wide drought-ridden 18
land of empty coulees that carry in sudden spates of flood the boulders
of the Rockies toward the sea. I suppose that, with the outward flight
of population, the region is as wild now as it was then, some forty
years ago. It would be useless to search for the place upon a map,
though I have tried. Too many years and too many uncertain miles lie
behind all bone hunters. There was no town to fix upon a road map.
There was only a sod house tucked behind a butte, out of the prevailing wind. And there was a little spring-fed pond in a grassy meadow—
that I remember.

Bone hunting is not really a very romantic occupation. One walks 19
day after day along miles of frequently unrewarding outcrop. One
grows browner, leaner, and tougher, it is true, but one is far from the
bright lights, and the prospect, barring a big strike, like a mammoth,
is always to abandon camp and go on. It was really a gypsy profession,
then, for those who did the field collecting.

In this case, we did not go on. There was an eroding hill in the 20
vicinity, and on top of that hill, just below sod cover, were the foot
bones, hundreds of them, of some lost Tertiary species of American
rhinoceros. It is useless to ask why we found only foot bones or why
we gathered the mineralized things in such fantastic quantities that

they must still lie stacked in some museum storeroom. Maybe the creatures had been immured standing up in a waterhole and in the millions of succeeding years the rest of the carcasses had eroded away from the hilltop stratum. But there were the foot bones, and the orders had come down, so we dug carpals and metacarpals till we cursed like an army platoon that headquarters has forgotten.

There was just one diversion: the spring, and the pond in the 21 meadow. There, under the bank, we cooled our milk and butter purchased from the soddy inhabitants. There we swam and splashed after work. The country people were reserved and kept mostly to themselves. They were uninterested in the dull bones on the hilltop unenlivened by skulls or treasure. After all, there was reason for their reserve. We must have appeared, by their rural standards, harmless but undoubtedly touched in the head. The barrier of reserve was never broken. The surly farmer kept to his parched acres and estimated to his profit our damage to his uncultivated hilltop. The slatternly wife tended a few scrawny chickens. In that ever-blowing landscape their windmill largely ran itself.

Only a stocky barefoot girl of twenty sometimes came hesitantly 22 down the path to our camp to deliver eggs. Some sixty days had drifted by upon that hillside. I began to remember the remark of an old fossil hunter who in his time had known the Gold Coast and the African veldt. "When calico begins to look like silk," he had once warned over a fire in the Sierras, "it is time to go home."

But enough of that. We were not bad young people. The girl shyly 23 brought us the eggs, the butter, and the bacon and then withdrew. Only after some little time did her appearance begin to strike me as odd. Men are accustomed to men in their various color variations around the world. When the past intrudes into a modern setting, however, it is less apt to be visible, because to see it demands knowledge of the past, and the past is always camouflaged when it wears the clothes of the present.

The girl came slowly down the trail one evening, and it struck me 24 suddenly how alone she looked and how, well, *alien*, she also appeared. Our cook was stoking up the evening fire, and as the shadows leaped and flickered I, leaning invisibly against a rock, was suddenly transported one hundred thousand years into the past. The shadows and their dancing highlights were the cause of it. They had swept the present out of sight. That girl coming reluctantly down the pathway to the fire was removed from us in time, and subconsciously she knew it as I did. By modern standards she was not pretty, and the gingham dress she wore, if anything, defined the difference.

Short, thickset, and massive, her body was still not the body of a 25
typical peasant woman. Her head, thrust a little forward against the
light, was massive-boned. Along the eye orbits at the edge of the fron-
tal bone I could see outlined in the flames an armored protuberance
that, particularly in women, had vanished before the close of the
Würmian[2] ice. She swung her head almost like a great muzzle beneath
its curls, and I was struck by the low bun-shaped breadth at the back.
Along her exposed arms one could see a flash of golden hair.

No, we are out of time, I thought quickly. We are each and every 26
one displaced. She is the last Neanderthal, and she does not know
what to do. We are those who eliminated her long ago. It is like an old
scene endlessly re-enacted. Only the chipped stones and the dead game
are lacking.

I came out of the shadow then and spoke gently to her, taking the 27
packages. It was the most one could do across that waste of infinite
years. She spoke almost inaudibly, drawing an unconscious circle in
the dust with a splayed bare foot. I saw, through the thin dress, the
powerful thighs, the yearning fertility going unmated in this lonesome
spot. She looked up, and a trick of the fire accentuated the cavernous
eye sockets so that I saw only darkness within. I accompanied her a
short distance along the trail. "What is it you are digging for?" she
managed to ask.

"It has to do with time," I said slowly. "Something that happened 28
a long time ago."

She listened incuriously, as one at the morning of creation might 29
do.

"Do you like this?" she persisted. "Do you always just go from one 30
place to another digging these things? And who pays for it, and what
comes of it in the end? Do you have a home?" The soddy and her burly
father were looming in the dusk. I paused, but questions flung across
the centuries are hard to answer.

"I am a student," I said, but with no confidence. How could I say 31
that suddenly she herself and her ulnar-bowed[3] and golden-haired fore-
arms were a part of a long reach backward into time?

"Of what has been, and what will come of it we are trying to find 32
out. I am afraid it will not help one to find a home," I said, more to
myself than her. "Quite the reverse, in fact. You see—"

The dark sockets under the tumbled hair seemed somehow sadly 33

---

[2]***Würmian*** The fourth and final stage of glaciation in Europe during the Ice Age.

[3]***ulnar-bowed*** Neanderthal anatomy suggests that the ulnar—the inner bone stretching from elbow to wrist—is distinctively bow-shaped.

vacant. "Thank you for bringing the things," I said, knowing the customs of that land. "Your father is waiting. I will go back to camp now." With this I strode off toward our fire but went, on impulse, beyond it into the full-starred night.

This was the way of things along the Wild Cat escarpment. There 34 was sand blowing and the past mingling with the present in more ways than professional science chose to see. There were eroded farms no longer running cattle and a diminishing population waiting, as this girl was waiting, for something they would never possess. They were, without realizing it, huntsmen without game, women without warriors. Obsolescence was upon their way of life.

But about the girl lingered a curious gentleness that we know now 35 had long ago touched the vanished Neanderthals she so resembled. It would be her fate to marry eventually one of the illiterate hardeyed uplanders of my own kind. Whatever the subtle genes had resurrected in her body would be buried once more and hidden in the creature called *sapiens.* Perhaps in the end his last woman would stand unwanted before some fiercer, brighter version of himself. It would be no more than justice. I was farther out in the deep spaces than I knew, and the fire was embers when I returned.

The season was waning. There came, inevitably, a time when the 36 trees began to talk of winter in the crags above the camp. I have repeated all that can be said about so fragile an episode. I had exchanged in the course of weeks a few wistful, scarcely understood remarks. I had waved to her a time or so from the quarry hilltop. As the time of our departure neared I had once glimpsed her shyly surveying from a rise beyond the pond our youthful plungings and naked wallowings in the spring-fed water. Then suddenly the leaves were down or turning yellow. It was time to go. The fossil quarry and its interminable foot bones were at last exhausted.

But something never intended had arisen for me there by the dark- 37 ening water—some agonizing, lifelong nostalgia, both personal and, in another sense, transcending the personal. It was—how shall I say it?— the endurance in a single mind of two stages of man's climb up the energy ladder that may be both his triumph and his doom.

Our battered equipment was assembled in the Model T's, which, 38 in that time, were the only penetrators of deep-rutted upland roads. Morose good-byes were expressed; money was passed over the broken sod cover on the hilltop. Hundreds of once galloping rhinoceros foot bones were stowed safely away. And that was it. I stood by the running board and slowly, very slowly, let my eyes wander toward that massive, archaic, and yet tragically noble head—of a creature so far back in time it did not know it represented tragedy. I made, I think, some kind of little personal gesture of farewell. Her head raised in recognition and then dropped. The motors started. *Homo sapiens,* the energy devourer, was on his way once more.

What was it she had said, I thought desperately as I swung aboard. 39 Home, she had questioned, "Do you have a home?" Perhaps I once did, I was to think many times in the years that followed, but I, too, was a mental atavism.[4] I, like that lost creature, would never find the place called home. It lay somewhere in the past down that hundred-thousand-year road on which travel was impossible. Only ghosts with uncertain eyes and abashed gestures would meet there. Upon a surging tide of power first conceived in the hearth fires of dead caverns mankind was plunging into an uncontrolled future beyond anything the people of the Ice had known.

The cell that had somehow mastered the secret of controlled en- 40 ergy, of surreptitious burning to a purpose, had finally produced the mind, judiciously, in its turn, controlling the inconstant fire at the cave mouth. Beyond anything that lost girl could imagine, words in the mouth or immured in libraries would cause substance to vanish and the earth itself to tremble. The little increments of individual energy dissolving at death had been coded and passed through the centuries by human ingenuity. A climbing juggernaut of power was leaping from triumph to triumph. It threatened to be more than man and all his words could master. It was more and less than man.

I remembered those cavernous eye sockets whose depths were for- 41 ever hidden from me in the firelight. Did they contain a premonition of the end we had invited, or was it only that I was young and hungry for all that was untouchable? I have searched once more for the old notebooks but, again, in vain. They would tell me, at best, only how living phantoms can be anatomically compared with those of the past. They would tell nothing of that season of the falling leaves or how I learned under the night sky of the utter homelessness of man.

I have seen a tree root burst a rock face on a mountain or slowly 42 wrench aside the gateway of a forgotten city. This is a very cunning feat, which men take too readily for granted. Life, unlike the inanimate, will take the long way round to circumvent barrenness. A kind of desperate will resides even in a root. It will perform the evasive tactics of an army, slowly inching its way through crevices and hoard-

---

[4]*atavism* A throwback.

ing energy until someday it swells and a living tree upheaves the heaviest mausoleum. This covert struggle is part of the lifelong battle waged against the Second Law of Thermodynamics,[5] the heat death that has been frequently assumed to rule the universe. At the hands of man that hoarded energy takes strange forms, both in the methods of its accumulation and in the diverse ways of its expenditure.

For hundreds of thousands of years, a time longer than all we know 43 of recorded history, the kin of that phantom girl had lived without cities along the Italian Mediterranean or below the northern tentacles of the groping ice. The low archaic skull vault had been as capacious as ours. Neanderthal man had, we now know after long digging, his own small dreams and kindnesses. He had buried his dead with offerings—there were even evidences that they had been laid, in some instances, upon beds of wild flowers. Beyond the chipped flints and the fires in the cavern darkness his mind had not involved itself with what was to come upon him with our kind—the first bowmen, the great artists, the terrible creatures of his blood who were never still.

It was a time of autumn driftage that might have lasted and been 44 well forever. Whether it was his own heavy brow that changed in the chill nights or that somewhere his line had mingled with a changeling cuckoo brood who multiplied at his expense we do not know with certainty. We know only that he vanished, though sometimes, as in the case of my upland girl, a chance assemblage of archaic genes struggles to re-emerge from the loins of *sapiens*.

But the plucked flint had flown; the heavy sad girls had borne the 45 children of the conquerors. Rain and leaves washed over the cave shelters of the past. Bronze replaced flint, iron replaced bronze, while the killing never ceased. The Neanderthals were forgotten; their grottoes housed the oracles of later religions. Marble cities gleamed along the Mediterranean. The ice and the cave bear had vanished. White-robed philosophers discoursed in Athens. Armed galleys moved upon the waters. Agriculture had brought wealth and diversification of labor. It had also brought professional soldiery. The armored ones were growing and, with them, slavery, torture, and death upon all the seas of the world.

The energy that had once sufficed only to take man from one 46 camping place to another, the harsh but innocent world glimpsed by

---

[5]*Second Law of Thermodynamics* The reversible relationship of heat and mechanical energy in which mechanical energy converts into heat and heat back into mechanical energy.

Cook in the eighteenth century on the shores of Australia, century by century was driving toward a climax. The warriors with the tall foreheads given increasingly to fanatic religions and monumental art had finally grown to doubt the creations of their own minds.

The remnants of what had once been talked about in Athens and 47 been consumed in the flames of Alexandria hesitantly crept forth once more. Early in the seventeenth century Sir Francis Bacon asserted that "by the agency of man a new aspect of things, a new universe, comes into view." In those words he was laying the basis of what he came to call "the second world," that world which could be drawn out of the natural by the sheer power of the human mind. Man had, of course, unwittingly been doing something of the sort since he came to speak. Bacon, however, was dreaming of the new world of invention, of toleration, of escape from irrational custom. He was the herald of the scientific method itself. Yet that method demands history also—the history I as an eager student had long ago beheld symbolically upon a corner in the shape of a junkman's cart. Without knowledge of the past, the way into the thickets of the future is desperate and unclear.

Bacon's second world is now so much with us that it rocks our 48 conception of what the natural order was, or is, or in what sense it can be restored. A mathematical formula traveling weakly along the fibers of the neopallium[6] may serve to wreck the planet. It is a kind of metabolic energy never envisaged by the lichen attacking a rock face or dreamed of in the flickering shadows of a cave fire. Yet from these ancient sources man's hunger has been drawn. Its potential is to be found in the life of the world we call natural, just as its terrifying intricacy is the product of the second visionary world evoked in the brain of man.

The two exist on the planet in an increasingly uneven balance. Into 49 one or the other or into a terrifying nothing one of these two worlds must finally subside. Man, whose strange metabolism has passed beyond the search for food to the naked ingestion of power, is scarcely aware that the energy whose limited planetary store lies at the root of the struggle for existence has passed by way of his mind into another dimension. There the giant shadows of the past continue to contend. They do so because life is a furnace of concealed flame.

Some pages back I spoke of a wild-plum thicket. I did so because I 50

---

[6]***neopallium*** The part of the brain that developed in the process of mammalian evolution.

had a youthful memory of visiting it in autumn. All the hoarded juices of summer had fallen with that lush untasted fruit upon the grass. The tiny engines of the plant had painstakingly gathered throughout the summer rich stores of sugar and syrup from the ground. Seed had been produced; birds had flown away with fruit that would give rise to plum trees miles away. The energy dispersion was so beneficent on that autumn afternoon that earth itself seemed anxious to promote the process against the downward guttering of the stars. Even I, tasting the fruit, was in my animal way scooping up some of it into thoughts and dreams.

51 Long after the Antillean adventure I chanced on an autumn walk to revisit the plum thicket. I was older, much older, and I had come largely because I wondered if the thicket was still there and because this strange hoarding and burning at the heart of life still puzzled me. I have spoken figuratively of fire as an animal, as being perhaps the very *essence* of animal. Oxidation, I mean, as it enters into life and consciousness.

52 Fire, as we have learned to our cost, has an insatiable hunger to be fed. It is a nonliving force that can even locomote itself. What if now— and I half closed my eyes against the blue plums and the smoke drifting along the draw—what if now it is only concealed and grown slyly conscious of its own burning in this little house of sticks and clay that I inhabit? What if I am, in some way, only a sophisticated fire that has acquired an ability to regulate its rate of combustion and to hoard its fuel in order to see and walk?

53 The plums, like some gift given from no one to no one visible, continued to fall about me. I was old now, I thought suddenly, glancing at a vein on my hand. I would have to hoard what remained of the embers. I thought of the junkman's horse and tried to release him so that he might be gone.

54 Perhaps I had finally succeeded. I do not know. I remembered that star-filled night years ago on the escarpment and the heavy-headed dreaming girl drawing a circle in the dust. Perhaps it was time itself she drew, for my own head was growing heavy and the smoke from the autumn fields semed to be penetrating my mind. I wanted to drop them at last, these carefully hoarded memories. I wanted to strew them like the blue plums in some gesture of love toward the universe all outward on a mat of leaves. Rich, rich and not to be hoarded, only to be laid down for someone, anyone, no longer to be carried and remembered in pain like the delicate paw lying forever on the beach at Curaçao.

55 I leaned farther back, relaxing in the leaves. It was a feeling I had

never had before, and it was strangely soothing. Perhaps I was no longer *Homo sapiens,* and perhaps that girl, the last Neanderthal, had known as much from the first. Perhaps all I was, really, was a pile of autumn leaves seeing smoke wraiths through the haze of my own burning. Things get odder on this planet, no less so. I dropped my head finally and gazed straight up through the branches at the sun. It was all going, I felt, memories dropping away in that high indifferent blaze that tolerated no other light. I let it be so for a little, but then I felt in my pocket the flint blade that I had carried all those years from the gravels on the escarpment. It reminded me of a journey I would not complete and the circle in the dust around which I had magically traveled for so long.

I arose then and, biting a plum that tasted bitter, I limped off down the ravine. One hundred thousand years had made little difference—at least, to me. The secret was to travel always in the first world, not the second; or, at least, to know at each crossroad which world was which. I went on, clutching for stability the flint knife in my pocket. A blue smoke like some final conflagration swept out of the draw and preceded me. I could feel its heat. I coughed, and my eyes watered. I tried as best I could to keep pace with it as it swirled on. There was a crackling behind me as though I myself were burning, but the smoke was what I followed. I held the sharp flint like a dowser's twig, cold and steady in my hand. 56

QUESTIONS

1. What are the emanations of the brain with which Eiseley begins and ends the essay?
2. What is the point of the reminiscence concerning the dog that was cast onto the shore in the Netherlands Antilles (paras. 3–5)?
3. Why does Eiseley tell us about the junkman (para. 8)? How does he interpret the metaphor of junk in this essay (see para. 10)?
4. How would Eiseley know that a skull was or was not Neanderthaloid? See paragraph 16.
5. How much interest do the nearby people take in the dig that Eiseley describes? Is he surprised at their attitude?
6. Is there anything unscientific about Eiseley's interest in the girl whose skull seems to bear a resemblance to a Neanderthal?
7. Eiseley ends with a meditation on his being like a fire (para. 52) and autumn leaves consumed in flames (para. 55). What does he mean by this statement? How does it fit into his reflections on the metabolism of "slow-burning oxidation" in paragraph 1?

WRITING ASSIGNMENTS

1. Describe Eiseley's attitude toward the nature of his own memory. Consider the extent to which he connects his memory with the larger question of the earth's "memory" as it is recorded in archaeological evidence on a site such as that where he spent time digging up the bones of rhinoceros feet.

2. Using the evidence that Eiseley supplies, what can you assume about the Neanderthal in comparison with his nemesis, *Homo sapiens?* What are the facts that Eiseley tells us, and what are the expressions of his own feelings that seem associated with those facts? Explore his emotional response to the signs of the Neanderthal that he observed in the woman who spoke with him at the dig.

3. Compare the way in which Eiseley approaches scientific reasoning with the way Lucretius reasons. Is Eiseley's "scientific method" more or less scientific than Lucretius's? Examine Eiseley's thinking in relation to Francis Bacon's "The Four Idols." Is Eiseley guilty of depending on any of these idols?

4. What is the ultimate scientific purpose of Eiseley's inquiry in this essay? What is he hoping to understand more fully by means of his reflections? As an anthropologist, how can he contribute to our greater knowledge of the nature of humankind?

5. Examine Eiseley's essay for his awareness of Darwin's theories. Can you establish conclusively that Eiseley is Darwinian in his thinking? What difference would it make to his views if he opposed Darwin? Would Darwin find Eiseley's essay to his liking?

6. What is the implied comparison Eiseley makes between *Homo sapiens* and the Neanderthal? (The correct terminology is *Homo sapiens sapiens* and *Homo sapiens neanderthalensis*.) Throughout the essay, he reflects on the past—his personal past—then on the past of the natural world and next on that of the human species. What was the fate of the Neanderthal, and why? What bearing does the Neanderthal fate have on the world as we know it today?

STEPHEN JAY GOULD

·—————⚭·—————·

Nonmoral Nature

STEPHEN JAY GOULD *(b. 1941) is professor of geology at Harvard University, where his field of interest centers on the special evolutionary problems related to species of Bahamaian snails. He decided to become a paleontologist when he was five years old, after his father had taken him to the American Museum of Natural History in New York City, where he first saw reconstructed dinosaurs.*

Gould has become well known for his essays on science, essays that have had the clarity needed to explain complex concepts to a general audience but that have also been informed by a superb scientific understanding. His articles for Natural History *magazine have been widely quoted and also collected in book form. His books have been praised and have won prizes. With works such as* Ever Since Darwin *(1977),* The Panda's Thumb *(1980),* The Mismeasure of Man *(1981), and* The Flamingo's Smile *(1985), Gould has constantly pointed to the significance of the work of the scientist he most frequently praises, Charles Darwin. His books have been celebrated around the world, and in 1981 Gould won a MacArthur Fellowship— a stipend of more than $38,000 a year for five years that permitted him to do any work he wished.*

"Nonmoral Nature" concerns itself with a highly controversial issue: the religious "reading" of natural events. Gould has frequently given testimony at legislative hearings in which creationists have insisted that the Bible's version of creation be taught in science courses

as scientific fact. Gould opposes this position because he views the account of the creation in Genesis as a religious, not a scientific, one. He points out that Darwin (who was trained as a minister) did not think there was conflict between his theories and religious beliefs.

Gould's primary point in this selection is that the behavior of animals in nature—with ruthless and efficient predators inflicting pain on an essentially helpless prey—has presented theologians with very exacting problems. If God is good and if creation reveals his goodness, how does one account for the suffering of nature's victims?

Gould examines in great detail certain specific issues that plagued nineteenth-century theologians. The behavior of the ichneumon wasp, an efficient wasp that plants its egg in a host caterpillar or aphid, is his special concern, since the phenomenon epitomized by the ichneumon baffled theologians. There are so many species of ichneumons that it could not be regarded as an isolated phenomenon. Part of Gould's approach is to describe the behavior of the ichneumon in detail to make it plain that the total mechanism of the predatory, parasitic animal is complex, subtle, and brilliant.

It is almost impossible to read this selection without developing a sense of respect for the predator, something that was extremely difficult, if not impossible, for nineteenth-century theologians to do. Their problem, Gould asserts, was that they anthropomorphized the behavior of these insects. That is, they thought of them in human terms. The act of predation was seen in the same light as we see the acts of human thugs who toy with their victims, or as Gould puts it, the acts of official state-hired killers whose job was, in Renaissance England, to inflict as much pain as possible on traitors before killing them. This model is a kind of lens through which the behavior of predators was interpreted and understood. The ichneumons paralyze their host and then eat it from the inside out; they take great care not to permit a victim to die until the last morsel is consumed.

Instead of an anthropocentric—human-centered—view, Gould wants us to take a scientific view as well as to see the predators' behavior in the same sympathetic manner in which we observe the victims' behavior. If we do so, he asserts, we will come to think of the ichneumon as nonmoral—of nature as nonmoral—rather than to think of its act of predation in moral terms, as if predators were instruments of evil. The concept of evil, he says, is limited to human beings. The world of nature is unconcerned with it, and if we apply morality to nature, we end up merely seeing nature as a reflection of our own beliefs and values. Instead, he wishes us to conceive of nature as he thinks it is, something apart from strictly human values.

GOULD'S RHETORIC

Gould's writing is distinguished for its clarity and directness. In this essay, he relies on the testimony of renowned authorities, establishing at once a remarkable breadth of interest and revealing considerably detailed learning about his subject. He explores a number of theories with sympathy and care, demonstrating their limits before offering his own views.

Since his field of interest is advanced biology, he runs the risk of losing the general reader. He might have oversimplified his subject in order to avoid doing this, but he does not: he does not shrink from using Latin classifications to identify his subject matter, but he defines each specialized term when he first uses it. He clarifies each opposing argument and demonstrates, in his analysis, what its limitations and potentials are.

Interestingly, instead of employing a metaphor in order to help convince us of a significant fact or critical opinion, Gould "deconstructs" a metaphor that was once in wide use. In other words, he reveals the metaphor to us; he shows us how it has affected belief and then asks us to reject the metaphor so as to see the world as it actually is. The metaphor is simple: the animal world is comparable to the human world with respect to ethical (normal) behavior. Since the behavior of animals is metaphorically like that of people, the ethical issue must be deep in the grain of nature. This view is mistaken, Gould says. Maintaining the metaphor is inviting and can be irresistible. Yet we must resist it.

Gould also makes widespread use of the rhetorical device of metonymy in which a part of something stands for the whole. Thus, the details of nature, which is God's creation, are made to reflect the entirety, which is God. Therefore, the behavior of the ichneumon comes to stand for the nature of God; and because the ichneumon's behavior is adjudged evil by those who hold to the first metaphor, there is a terrible contradiction which cannot be rationalized by theological arguments.

Gould shows us just how difficult the problem of the theologian is. Then he shows us a way out. But it is a way out that depends on our capacity to think differently from the way we may be used to doing. It may demand a change on our part, and some may not be able to achieve it.

Nonmoral Nature

When the Right Honorable and Reverend Francis Henry, earl of Bridgewater,[1] died in February, 1829, he left £8,000 to support a series of books "on the power, wisdom and goodness of God, as manifested in the creation." William Buckland,[2] England's first official academic geologist and later dean of Westminster, was invited to compose one of the nine Bridgewater Treatises. In it he discussed the most pressing problem of natural theology: If God is benevolent and the Creation displays his "power, wisdom and goodness," then why are we surrounded with pain, suffering, and apparently senseless cruelty in the animal world?

Buckland considered the depredation of "carnivorous races" as the primary challenge to an idealized world in which the lion might dwell with the lamb. He resolved the issue to his satisfaction by arguing that carnivores actually increase "the aggregate of animal enjoyment" and "diminish that of pain." The death of victims, after all, is swift and relatively painless, victims are spared the ravages of decreptitude and senility, and populations do not outrun their food supply to the greater sorrow of all. God knew what he was doing when he made lions. Buckland concluded in hardly concealed rapture:

> The appointment of death by the agency of carnivora, as the ordinary termination of animal existence, appears therefore in its main results to be a dispensation of benevolence; it deducts much from the aggregate amount of the pain of universal death; it abridges, and almost annihilates, throughout the brute creation, the misery of disease, and accidental injuries, and lingering decay; and imposes such salutary restraint upon excessive increase of numbers, that the supply of food maintains perpetually a due ratio to the demand. The result is, that the surface of the land and depths of the waters are ever crowded with myriads of animated beings, the pleasures of whose life are co-extensive

---

[1] *Reverend Francis Henry, earl of Bridgewater (1756–1829)* He was the eighth and last earl of Bridgewater. He was also a naturalist and a Fellow at All Souls College, Oxford, before he became earl of Bridgewater in 1823. On his death, he left a fund to be used for the publication of the Bridgewater Treatises, essay discussions of the moral implications of scientific research and discoveries.

[2] *William Buckland (1784–1856)* An English clergyman and also a geologist. His essay, "Geology and Mineralogy," was a Bridgewater Treatise in 1836.

with its duration; and which throughout the little day of existence that is allotted to them, fulfill with joy the functions for which they were created.

We may find a certain amusing charm in Buckland's vision today, 3 but such arguments did begin to address "the problem of evil" for many of Buckland's contemporaries—how could a benevolent God create such a world of carnage and bloodshed? Yet these claims could not abolish the problem of evil entirely, for nature includes many phenomena far more horrible in our eyes than simple predation. I suspect that nothing evokes greater disgust in most of us than slow destruction of a host by an internal parasite—slow ingestion, bit by bit, from the inside. In no other way can I explain why *Alien*, an uninspired, grade-C, formula horror film, should have won such a following. That single scene of Mr. Alien, popping forth as a baby parasite from the body of a human host, was both sickening and stunning. Our nineteenth-century forebears maintained similar feelings. Their greatest challenge to the concept of a benevolent deity was not simple predation—for one can admire quick and efficient butcheries, especially since we strive to construct them ourselves—but slow death by parasitic ingestion. The classic case, treated at length by all the great naturalists, involved the so-called ichneumon fly. Buckland had sidestepped the major issue.

The ichneumon fly, which provoked such concern among natural 4 theologians, was a composite creature representing the habits of an enormous tribe. The Ichneumonoidea are a group of wasps, not flies, that include more species than all the vertebrates combined (wasps, with ants and bees, constitute the order Hymenoptera; flies, with their two wings—wasps have four—form the order Diptera). In addition, many related wasps of similar habits were often cited for the same grisly details. Thus, the famous story did not merely implicate a single aberrant species (perhaps a perverse leakage from Satan's realm), but perhaps hundreds of thousands of them—a large chunk of what could only be God's creation.

The ichneumons, like most wasps, generally live freely as adults 5 but pass their larval life as parasites feeding on the bodies of other animals, almost invariably members of their own phylum, Arthropoda. The most common victims are caterpillars (butterfly and moth larvae), but some ichneumons prefer aphids and others attack spiders. Most hosts are parasitized as larvae, but some adults are attacked, and many tiny ichneumons inject their brood directly into the egg of their host.

The free-flying females locate an appropriate host and then convert 6 it to a food factory for their own young. Parasitologists speak of ecto-parasitism when the uninvited guest lives on the surface of its host, and endoparasitism when the parasite dwells within. Among endoparasitic ichneumons, adult females pierce the host with their ovipositor and deposit eggs within it. (The ovipositor, a thin tube extending backward from the wasp's rear end, may be many times as long as the body itself.) Usually, the host is not otherwise inconvenienced for the moment, at least until the eggs hatch and the ichneumon larvae begin their grim work of interior excavation. Among ectoparasites, however, many females lay their eggs directly upon the host's body. Since an active host would easily dislodge the egg, the ichneumon mother often simultaneously injects a toxin that paralyzes the caterpillar or other victim. The paralysis may be permanent, and the caterpillar lies, alive but immobile, with the agent of its future destruction secure on its belly. The egg hatches, the helpless caterpillar twitches, the wasp larva pierces and begins its grisly feast.

Since a dead and decaying caterpillar will do the wasp larva no good, it eats in a pattern that cannot help but recall, in our inappropriate, anthropocentric interpretation, the ancient English penalty for treason—drawing and quartering, with its explicit object of extracting as much torment as possible by keeping the victim alive and sentient. As the king's executioner drew out and burned his client's entrails, so does the ichneumon larva eat fat bodies and digestive organs first, keeping the caterpillar alive by preserving intact the essential heart and central nervous system. Finally, the larva completes its work and kills its victim, leaving behind the caterpillar's empty shell. Is it any wonder that ichneumons, not snakes or lions, stood as the paramount challenge to God's benevolence during the heyday of natural theology?

As I read through the nineteenth- and twentieth-century literature on ichneumons, nothing amused me more than the tension between an intellectual knowledge that wasps should not be described in human terms and a literary or emotional inability to avoid the familiar categories of epic and narrative, pain and destruction, victim and vanquisher. We seem to be caught in the mythic structures of our own cultural sagas, quite unable, even in our basic descriptions, to use any other language than the metaphors of battle and conquest. We cannot render this corner of natural history as anything but story, combining the themes of grim horror and fascination and usually ending not so much with pity for the caterpillar as with admiration for the efficiency of the ichneumon.

I detect two basic themes in most epic descriptions: the struggles of prey and the ruthless efficiency of parasites. Although we acknowledge that we witness little more than automatic instinct or physiological reaction, still we describe the defenses of hosts as though they represented conscious struggles. Thus, aphids kick and caterpillars may wriggle violently as wasps attempt to insert their ovipositors. The pupa of the tortoise-shell butterfly (usually considered an inert creature silently awaiting its conversion from duckling to swan) may contort its abdominal region so sharply that attacking wasps are thrown into the air. The caterpillars of *Hapalia*, when attacked by the wasp *Apanteles machaeralis*, drop suddenly from their leaves and suspend themselves in air by a silken thread. But the wasp may run down the thread and insert its eggs nonetheless. Some hosts can encapsulate the injected egg with blood cells that aggregate and harden, thus suffocating the parasite.

J. H. Fabre,[3] the great nineteenth-century French entomologist,   10
who remains to this day the preeminently literate natural historian of insects, made a special study of parasitic wasps and wrote with an unabashed anthropocentrism about the struggles of paralyzed victims (see his books *Insect Life* and *The Wonders of Instinct*). He describes some imperfectly paralyzed caterpillars that struggle so violently every time a parasite approaches that the wasp larvae must feed with unusual caution. They attach themselves to a silken strand from the roof of their burrow and descend upon a safe and exposed part of the caterpillar:

> The grub is at dinner: head downwards, it is digging into the limp belly of one of the caterpillars. . . At the least sign of danger in the heap of caterpillars, the larva retreats . . . and climbs back to the ceiling, where the swarming rabble cannot reach it. When peace is restored, it slides down [its silken cord] and returns to table, with its head over the viands and its rear upturned and ready to withdraw in case of need.

In another chapter, he describes the fate of a paralyzed cricket: 11

> One may see the cricket, bitten to the quick, vainly move its antennae and abdominal styles, open and close its empty jaws, and even move a foot, but the larva is safe and searches its vitals with impunity. What an awful nightmare for the paralyzed cricket!

Fabre even learned to feed some paralyzed victims by placing a   12
syrup of sugar and water on their mouthparts—thus showing that they remained alive, sentient, and (by implication) grateful for any palliation of their inevitable fate. If Jesus, immobile and thirsting on the

---

[3]*Jean-Henri Fabre (1823–1915)* A French entomologist whose patient study of insects earned him the nickname, "the Virgil of Insects." His writings are voluminous and, at times, elegant.

cross, received only vinegar from his tormentors, Fabre at least could make an ending bittersweet.

The second theme, ruthless efficiency of the parasites, leads to the 13 opposite conclusion—grudging admiration for the victors. We learn of their skill in capturing dangerous hosts often many times larger than themselves. Caterpillars may be easy game, but the psammocharid wasps prefer spiders. They must insert their ovipositors in a safe and precise spot. Some leave a paralyzed spider in its own burrow. *Planiceps hirsutus*, for example, parasitizes a California trapdoor spider. It searches for spider tubes on sand dunes, then digs into nearby sand to disturb the spider's home and drive it out. When the spider emerges, the wasp attacks, paralyzes its victim, drags it back into its own tube, shuts and fastens the trapdoor, and deposits a single egg upon the spider's abdomen. Other psammocharids will drag a heavy spider back to a previously prepared cluster of clay or mud cells. Some amputate a spider's legs to make the passage easier. Others fly back over water, skimming a buoyant spider along the surface.

Some wasps must battle with other parasites over a host's body. 14 *Rhyssella curvipes* can detect the larvae of wood wasps deep within alder wood and drill down to its potential victims with its sharply ridged ovipositor. *Pseudorhyssa alpestris*, a related parasite, cannot drill directly into wood since its slender ovipositor bears only rudimentary cutting ridges. It locates the holes made by *Rhyssella*, inserts its ovipositor, and lays an egg on the host (already conveniently paralyzed by *Rhyssella*), right next to the egg deposited by its relative. The two eggs hatch at about the same time, but the larva of *Pseudorhyssa* has a bigger head bearing much larger mandibles. *Pseudorhyssa* seizes the smaller *Rhyssella* larva, destroys it, and proceeds to feast upon a banquet already well prepared.

Other praises for the efficiency of mothers invoke the themes of 15 early, quick, and often. Many ichneumons don't even wait for their hosts to develop into larvae, but parasitize the egg directly (larval wasps may then either drain the egg itself or enter the developing host larva). Others simply move fast. *Apanteles militaris* can deposit up to seventy-two eggs in a single second. Still others are doggedly persistent. *Aphidius gomezi* females produce up to 1,500 eggs and can parasitize as many as 600 aphids in a single working day. In a bizarre twist upon "often," some wasps indulge in polyembryony, a kind of iterated supertwinning. A single egg divides into cells that aggregate into as many as 500 individuals. Since some polyembryonic wasps parasitize caterpillars much larger than themselves and may lay up to six eggs in each, as many as 3,000 larvae may develop within, and feed upon, a single host. These wasps are endoparasites and do not paralyze their victims. The caterpillars writhe back and forth, not (one suspects) from pain, but merely in response to the commotion induced by thousands of wasp larvae feeding within.

The efficiency of mothers is matched by their larval offspring. I 16 have already mentioned the pattern of eating less essential parts first, thus keeping the host alive and fresh to its final and merciful dispatch. After the larva digests every edible morsel of its victim (if only to prevent later fouling of its abode by decaying tissue), it may still use the outer shell of its host. One aphid parasite cuts a hole in the belly of its victim's shell, glues the skeleton to a leaf by sticky secretions from its salivary gland, and then spins a cocoon to pupate within the aphid's shell.

In using inappropriate anthropocentric language in this romp 17 through the natural history of ichneumons, I have tried to emphasize just why these wasps became a preeminent challenge to natural theology—the antiquated doctrine that attempted to infer God's essence from the products of his creation. I have used twentieth-century examples for the most part, but all themes were known and stressed by the great nineteenth-century natural theologians. How then did they square the habits of these wasps with the goodness of God? How did they extract themselves from this dilemma of their own making?

The strategies were as varied as the practitioners; they shared only 18 the theme of special pleading for an a priori doctrine[4]—they knew that God's benevolence was lurking somewhere behind all these tales of apparent horror. Charles Lyell[5] for example, in the first edition of his epochal *Principles of Geology* (1830–1833), decided that caterpillars posed such a threat to vegetation that any natural checks upon them could only reflect well upon a creating deity, for caterpillars would destroy human agriculture "did not Providence put causes in operation to keep them in due bounds."

The Reverend William Kirby[6], rector of Barham and Britain's fore- 19

---

[4]**an a priori doctrine** *A priori* means beforehand, and Gould refers to those who approach a scientific situation with a preestablished view in mind. He is suggesting that such an approach prevents the kind of objectivity and fairness that scientific examination is supposed to produce.

[5]**Charles Lyell (1797–1875)** An English geologist who established the glacial layers of the Eocene (dawn of recent), Miocene (less recent), and Pliocene (more recent) epochs during his excavations of Tertiary period strata in Italy. He was influential in urging Darwin to publish his theories. His work is still respected.

[6]**The Reverend William Kirby (1759–1850)** An English specialist in insects. He was the author of a Bridgewater Treatise, *The History, Habits, and Instincts of Animals* (2 vols., 1835).

most entomologist, chose to ignore the plight of caterpillars and focused instead upon the virtue of mother love displayed by wasps in provisioning their young with such care.

> The great object of the female is to discover a proper nidus for her eggs. In search of this she is in constant motion. Is the caterpillar of a butterfly or moth the appropriate food for her young? You see her alight upon the plants where they are most usually to be met with, run quickly over them, carefully examining every leaf, and, having found the unfortunate object of her search, insert her sting into its flesh, and there deposit an egg. . . . The active Ichneumon braves every danger, and does not desist until her courage and address have insured subsistence for one of her future progeny.

Kirby found this solicitude all the more remarkable because the 20 female wasp will never see her child and enjoy the pleasures of parenthood. Yet her love compels her to danger nonetheless:

> A very large proportion of them are doomed to die before their young come into existence. But in these the passion is not extinguished. . . . When you witness the solicitude with which they provide for the security and sustenance of their future young, you can scarcely deny to them love for a progeny they are never destined to behold.

Kirby also put in a good word for the marauding larvae, praising 21 them for their forbearance in eating selectively to keep their caterpillar prey alive. Would we all husband our resources with such care!

> In this strange and apparently cruel operation one circumstance is truly remarkable. The larva of the Ichneumon, though every day, perhaps for months, it gnaws the inside of the caterpillar, and though at last it has devoured almost every part of it except the skin and intestines, carefully all this time it avoids injuring the vital organs, as if aware that its own existence depends on that of the insect upon which it preys! . . . What would be the impression which a similar instance amongst the race of quadrupeds would make upon us? If, for example, an animal . . . should be found to feed upon the inside of a dog, devouring only those parts not essential to life, while it cautiously left uninjured the heart, arteries, lungs, and intestines—should we not regard such an instance as a perfect prodigy, as an example of instinctive forbearance almost miraculous? [The last three quotes come from the 1856, and last pre-Darwinian, edition of Kirby and Spence's *Introduction to Entomology.*]

This tradition of attempting to read moral meaning from nature did 22 not cease with the triumph of evolutionary theory after Darwin published *On the Origin of Species* in 1859—for evolution could be read as God's chosen method of peopling our planet, and ethical messages might still populate nature. Thus, St. George Mivart,[7] one of Darwin's most effective evolutionary critics and a devout Catholic, argued that "many amiable and excellent people" had been misled by the apparent suffering of animals for two reasons. First, however much it might hurt, "physical suffering and moral evil are simply incommensurable." Since beasts are not moral agents, their feelings cannot bear any ethical message. But secondly, lest our visceral sensitivities still be aroused, Mivart assures us that animals must feel little, if any, pain. Using a favorite racist argument of the time—that "primitive" people suffer far less than advanced and cultured people—Mivart extrapolated further down the ladder of life into a realm of very limited pain indeed: Physical suffering, he argued,

> depends greatly upon the mental condition of the sufferer. Only during consciousness does it exist, and only in the most highly organized men does it reach its acme. The author has been assured that lower races of men appear less keenly sensitive to physical suffering than do more cultivated and refined human beings. Thus only in man can there really be any intense degree of suffering, because only in him is there that intellectual recollection of past moments and that anticipation of future ones, which constitute in great part the bitterness of suffering. The momentary pang, the present pain, which beasts endure, though real enough, is yet, doubtless, not to be compared as to its intensity with the suffering which is produced in man thorugh his high prerogative of self-consciousness [from *Genesis of Species*, 1871].

It took Darwin himself to derail this ancient tradition—in that gentle way so characteristic of his radical intellectual approach to nearly everything. The ichneumons also troubled Darwin greatly and he wrote of them to Asa Gray[8] in 1860:

> I own that I cannot see as plainly as others do, and as I should wish to do, evidence of design and beneficence on all sides of us. There seems

23

---

[7]***St. George Mivart (1827–1900)*** English anatomist and biologist who examined the comparative anatomies of insect-eating and meat-eating animals. A convert to Roman Catholicism in 1844, his inability to reconcile religious and evolutionary theories resulted in his excommunication from the church in 1900.

[8]***Asa Gray (1810–1888)*** America's most important botanist. His works, which are still considered important, are *Structural Botany* (1879) [originally published in 1842 as *Botanical Text-Book*], *The Elements of Botany* (1836), *How Plants Grow* (1858), and *How Plants Behave* (1872). Gray was a serious critic of Darwin and wrote a great number of letters to him; but he was also a firm believer in Darwinian evolution. Since he was also a well-known member of an evangelical Protestant faith, he was effective in countering religious attacks on Darwin by showing that there is no conflict between Darwinism and religion.

to me too much misery in the world. I cannot persuade myself that a beneficent and omnipotent God would have designedly created the Ichneumonidae with the express intention of their feeding within the living bodies of Caterpillars, or that a cat should play with mice.

Indeed, he had written with more passion to Joseph Hooker[9] in 1856: "What a book a devil's chaplain might write on the clumsy, wasteful, blundering, low, and horribly cruel works of nature!"

This honest admission—that nature is often (by our standards) cruel and that all previous attempts to find a lurking goodness behind everything represent just so much absurd special pleading—can lead in two directions. One might retain the principle that nature holds moral messages for humans, but reverse the usual perspective and claim that morality consists in understanding the ways of nature and doing the opposite. Thomas Henry Huxley[10] advanced this argument in his famous essay on *Evolution and Ethics* (1893):   24

> The practice of that which is ethically best—what we call goodness or virtue—involves a course of conduct which, in all respects, is opposed to that which leads to success in the cosmic struggle for existence. In place of ruthless self-assertion it demands self-restraint; in place of thrusting aside, or treading down, all competitors, it requires that the individual shall not merely respect, but shall help his fellows. . . . It repudiates the gladiatorial theory of existence. . . . Laws and moral precepts are directed to the end of curbing the cosmic process.

The other argument, more radical in Darwin's day but common now, holds that nature simply is as we find it. Our failure to discern the universal good we once expected does not record our lack of insight or ingenuity but merely demonstrates that nature contains no moral messages framed in human terms. Morality is a subject for philosophers, theologians, students of the humanities, indeed for all thinking people. The answers will not be read passively from nature; they do not, and cannot, arise from the data of science. The factual   25

---

[9]*Joseph Hooker (1817–1911)* English botanist who studied flowers in exotic locations such as Tasmania, the Antarctic, New Zealand, and India. He was, along with Charles Lyell, a friend of Darwin and one of those who urged him to publish *On the Origin of Species*. He was the director of London's Kew Gardens from 1865–1885.

[10]*Thomas Henry Huxley (1825–1895)* An English naturalist who, quite independent of organizations and formal support, became one of the most important scientists of his time. He searched for a theory of evolution that was based on a rigorous examination of the facts and found, in Darwin's work, the theory that he could finally respect. He was a strong champion of Darwin.

state of the world does not teach us how we, with our powers for good and evil, should alter or preserve it in the most ethical manner.

Darwin himself tended toward this view, although he could not, as   26
a man of his time, thoroughly abandon the idea that laws of nature might reflect some higher purpose. He clearly recognized that the specific manifestations of those laws—cats playing with mice, and ichneumon larvae eating caterpillars—could not embody ethical messages, but he somehow hoped that unknown higher laws might exist "with the details, whether good or bad, left to the working out of what we may call chance."

Since ichneumons are a detail, and since natural selection is a law   27
regulating details, the answer to the ancient dilemma of why such cruelty (in our terms) exists in nature can only be that there isn't any answer—and that the framing of the question "in our terms" is thoroughly inappropriate in a natural world neither made for us nor ruled by us. It just plain happens. It is a strategy that works for ichneumons and that natural selection has programmed into their behavioral repertoire. Caterpillars are not suffering to teach us something; they have simply been outmaneuvered, for now, in the evolutionary game. Perhaps they will evolve a set of adequate defenses sometime in the future, thus sealing the fate of ichneumons. And perhaps, indeed probably, they will not.

Another Huxley, Thomas's grandson Julian,[11] spoke for this posi-   28
tion, using as an example—yes, you guessed it—the ubiquitous ichneumons:

> Natural selection, in fact, though like the mills of God in grinding slowly and grinding small, has few other attributes that a civilized religion would call divine. . . . Its products are just as likely to be aesthetically, morally, or intellectually repulsive to us as they are to be attractive. We need only think of the ugliness of *Sacculina* or a bladderworm, the stupidity of a rhinoceros or a stegosaur, the horror of a female mantis devouring its mate or a brood of ichneumon flies slowly eating out a caterpillar.

It is amusing in this context, or rather ironic since it is too serious to be amusing, that modern creationists accuse evolutionists of preaching a specific ethical doctrine called secular humanism and thereby demand equal time for their unscientific and discredited views. If nature is nonmoral, then evolution cannot teach any ethical theory at all. The

---

[11]***Thomas's grandson, Julian*** Julian Huxley (1887–1975), an English biologist and a brother of the novelist Aldous Huxley.

assumption that it can has abetted a panoply of social evils that ideologues falsely read into nature from their beliefs—eugenics and (misnamed) social Darwinism prominently among them. Not only did Darwin eschew any attempt to discover an antireligious ethic in nature, he also expressly stated his personal bewilderment about such deep issues as the problem of evil. Just a few sentences after invoking the ichneumons, and in words that express both the modesty of this splendid man and the compatibility, through lack of contact, between science and true religion, Darwin wrote to Asa Gray,

> I feel most deeply that the whole subject is too profound for the human intellect. A dog might as well speculate on the mind of Newton. Let each man hope and believe what he can.

QUESTIONS

1. What does Gould reveal to us about the nature of insect life?
2. Scientifically speaking, what information does Gould provide us that is most valuable for telling us how nature works?
3. What does it mean to anthropomorphize nature? What are some concrete results of doing so?
4. Do you find yourself bothered, annoyed, or disconcerted by the knowledge of how the ichneumon wasp parasitizes its host?
5. Does the behavior of the ichneumon wasp put at stake any genuine religious questions of today?
6. Does the existence of predatory insects and animals at all threaten religious belief?
7. Is it difficult to accept Gould's view that nature is nonmoral?

WRITING ASSIGNMENTS

1. In a brief essay, try to answer the question Gould examines in paragraph 1: "Why are we surrounded with pain, suffering, and apparently senseless cruelty in the animal world?"
2. Is the fact of such pain, suffering, and apparently senseless cruelty a religious issue? If so, in what way is it? If not, demonstrate why.
3. In paragraph 17, Gould describes natural theology as "the antiquated doctrine that attempted to infer God's essence from the products of his creation." Is this a reasonable description of natural theology as you understand it? In the process of answering this question, clarify what a theology that based its claims in an observation of nature would be able to claim

about the essence of God. What kind of religion would be possible if all theology were based on the behavior of natural life, including ichneumons?

4. Thomas Henry Huxley, in paragraph 24, refers to a "gladiatorial theory of existence." What kind of theory of existence would develop from thinking of nature—both animal and human—in terms of the behavior of gladiators? Establish the gladiatorial theory of nature and then explain how it would alter human nature if we were to shape our lives by it.

5. Gould points out that even after having established his theory of evolution, Darwin could not "thoroughly abandon the idea that laws of nature might reflect some higher purpose" (para. 26). Assuming that you are in agreement with Darwin but that you also see the problems that Gould has presented us, clarify what the higher purpose of a nature such as Gould describes might be. Does Gould's description of the behavior of the ichneumon (or any other) predator in any way compromise the idea that nature has a higher purpose? Does Gould hold that it has a higher purpose?

6. Compare this essay with Francis Bacon's "The Four Idols." What intellectual issues does it share with Bacon's essay? Is there a common ground between them regarding science and their attitude toward religion? What is it? What might Francis Bacon have decided about the ultimate ethical issues raised by a consideration of the ichneumon? Do you think that Bacon would have held the same views about the ichneumon's predatory powers as did the nineteenth-century theologians? That is, would he have conceived of nature in ethical/moral terms?

7. Why would Gould's scientific subject matter involve issues of morality to a greater extent than, say, the subject matter of Lucretius, Charles Darwin, Loren Eiseley? Is it possible that the study of physics or anthropology is less fundamentally concerned with moral issues than the study of biology is? One result of Darwin's concerns is the possibility of apes and humans being related. Is this less worth considering from a moral viewpoint than the ichneumon wasp? What are the major moral issues in science that you observed from examining these writers?

IDEAS IN THE WORLD OF PHILOSOPHY

HOW CAN WE TELL THE GOOD
FROM THE BAD? IS THERE BUT ONE
TRUE PATH OF ETHICAL BEHAVIOR?

———— ❧ ————

Siddhārtha Gautama, the Buddha
Plato
Marcus Aurelius
St. Augustine
Friedrich Nietzsche
Simone Weil
Mary Daly

INTRODUCTION

THE SELECTIONS in Part Five center on issues of moral behavior and remind us that the pursuit of wisdom is a natural human activity that leads us toward happiness. Although some of these pieces were written by members of religious orders—the Buddha, St. Augustine, and Mary Daly, for example—the essays are not limited to religious issues. More importantly, these writers recognize the question of whether there exists a path to lead us to wisdom, or enlightenment. Such a question involves all of us, no matter what our gender, our age, or our station.

The wisdom of Siddhārtha Gautama, the Buddha directs our attention inward to the deepest resources of the individual. According to the Buddha, meditation is the path to enlightenment, revealing a moral life that follows an eight-fold path and eventually provides spiritual peace. Anticipating Plato, the Buddha recommended freeing oneself from the bondage of the senses and seeking moderation. He also looked forward to the teachings of St. Augustine and the Christian church in reminding his disciples of their final spiritual goals. For the Buddha, meditation remained the way to the essential goal of enlightenment, which in turn led to the accomplishment of an ethical life.

Plato instructed that the first requirement of finding the proper ethical path lay in knowing how to avoid being fooled by false appearances. For Plato, ethical issues could be distorted by a mistaken materialism that assumed the world of the senses is of primary importance. Materialism, he explained, is an illusion. The world of ideas is the only true world; it is the world of heavenly apprehension. Therefore, in order to achieve enlightenment, you must know how to choose properly. In other words, in order to choose the good, you have to know the good. Plato insisted that the choices that led to the good led away from the world of matter. So the first ethical choice involved choosing to know the truth. This message, by the way, is repeated in different ways by many of these philosophers.

The work of the second-century Roman emperor Marcus Aurelius, as seen in his "Stoicism and Self-Discipline," shows us that by imitating the order and calm of the universe, we can discover the ethical path that will guide us to proper conduct and a moral position. His philosophy, called Stoicism, had roots in ancient Greece and stressed duty as the ultimate goal of life. We now link most of the beliefs of Stoicism with religion rather than philosophy. In Marcus Aurelius's time, Roman religion was not based on concerns of ethical behavior but on mysteries and ceremonies designed to keep the state intact, strong, and favored in the eyes of the gods. Ethical and moral issues, however, were defined by philosophers such as Marcus Aurelius.

"Memory and the Happy Life," an excerpt from St. Augustine's *Confessions*, is more properly a meditation than are Marcus Aurelius's meditations. Marcus Aurelius tied together scattered thoughts and loosely related them to one another, but Augustine reflected deeply on a single idea and its ramifications. Augustine assured us that what is most important in finding the moral path is developing a true knowledge of ourselves, including our faults and our desires. Memory is indispensable to our gaining and retaining that knowledge. He demonstrated that memory, a faculty of the mind, is essential to acquiring the knowledge of goodness. A bishop of the Christian church in North Africa, Augustine was obviously concerned with specifically religious issues.

St. Augustine offered a powerful alternative to the discipline of meditation because he resisted the idea of emptying the mind. Instead, when he examined the concept of memory in his *Confessions*, Augustine promoted self-knowledge, which in his other works he clearly identified with the knowledge of God. For him, following God represented the only moral path.

In "Apollonianism and Dionysianism," Friedrich Nietzsche explored issues that were difficult for the Greeks to resolve. Greek philosophers usually recommended that on the path to enlightenment a person should avoid extremes and practice moderation. But Apollonianism, the rational life, and Dionysianism, the life of passion, are profound extremes that were regarded as forms of divine madness, the first associated with Apollo—god of music and poetry—and the second with Dionysus—god of wine. Nietzsche described, then, more than one appropriate path to pursue, and both were products of a special form of divinity.

These gods may be threatening to conventional thought, but Nietzsche argued that they are not immoral. He complicated the issue of morality by demanding consideration for the godliness of the individual and the virtues of inspiration. A divine madness is what he praised, something close to the ecstasy of the ancients, a path that he found more appealing than those of St. Augustine or the Buddha.

Simone Weil found her spiritual truth in Christianity, which apparently was thrust on her in a moment of intense revelation that recalls some of the revelatory moments recorded in the Bible. Yet her path was strewn with many personal considerations. Born a Jew but deeply attracted to the Christian church, Weil could not bring herself to accept the authoritarianism of Christianity. Her letter to her spiritual advisor, Father Perrin, is filled with questioning and an expression of spiritual concern. Weil was touched deeply by the suffering of others and increasingly participated in the fate of what Jesus called "the least of them." Her path to enlightenment led her to a life of self-sacrifice, a life that resembles a saint's.

In "The Qualitative Leap Beyond Patriarchal Religion," Mary Daly questions the basic patriarchal assumptions of most modern religions. Daly believes that most religions' adherence to imagery that praises the masculine ideal and condemns as evil the feminine does not inevitably produce the best ethical behavior. Toward this belief she cites religious wars and acts of oppression conducted under the disguise of patriarchal morality. Her ethics lead her to create a diarchy to replace the old-fashioned patriarchy so that the image of women can be renovated and the image of humanity celebrated universally.

Control is central in Mary Daly's essay, but she examines the implications of how the ethical behavior of an institution—the Church—affects individuals. According to Daly, the patriarchy of Christianity introduces a key ethical question on the nature of the religious institution that she served.

Because these essays concern themselves with ethical issues, they describe again and again the quest to perfect the self and to apply self-control as a means to achieve that perfection. Even when an essay explores varieties of divine madness and the value of loss of control, as in Friedrich Nietzsche's "Apollonianism and Dionysianism," the focus is still on questions of control, lack of control, and the benefits that can be derived from both.

These pieces are extraordinary for their differing attitudes toward the Good and the True. Ethical opinions can be complex and difficult to clarify—these writers show us some of the reasons why. They also remind us that to be human is to continually consider the ethical alternatives available to us and to remind us that we remain the only creatures for whom such alternatives have moral implications.

SIDDHĀRTHA GAUTAMA, THE BUDDHA

Meditation: Path to Enlightenment

SIDDHĀRTHA GAUTAMA (?563–?483 B.C.), *known as the Buddha (Sanskrit for "enlightened one"), was born in Kapilavastu, the chief town of Kapila in what is now Nepal. His family was petty royalty, and he himself a minor prince. One of his names is Sakyamuni, "sage of the Sakya clan." Early texts state that he was protected from knowledge of the outside world so that when he was twenty-nine, after finally witnessing the pain and difficulties of the poor, he renounced his aristocratic position and his wife and family. He left his home and wandered, living the ascetic religious life, until he reached Bodh Gaya, where he spent his time in meditation until he achieved enlightenment.*

His purpose in seeking enlightenment was to show the way to people so that they could relieve the misery of their own lives. In most versions of Buddhism, the Buddha is regarded as "Lord" Buddha. In other versions, he is regarded as a man who had reached a level of perfection that is possible for ordinary people to achieve. Some branches of Buddhism describe several Buddhas, or bodhisattvas—

Translated by Edward Conze.

those who enter different spiritual stages at different times and may be viewed as either great teachers or as heavenly saviors.

The religion that developed from the Buddha's teachings resembled the Stoic teachings of Marcus Aurelius, although it certainly had much different roots. In Buddhism, the purpose of life is to achieve the enlightenment that will enable the individual to end samsāra—the wandering of the soul from one becoming (incarnation) to another—and reach nirvana, a peace that lies beyond human understanding. In the selection that follows, nirvana is referred to as the end of being.

Because Buddhists hoped to achieve nirvana, they guided their lives by firm precepts. They believed that the existence they now enjoy was shaped and formed by the soul in a previous existence and that since their present way of life shaped existences to come, they needed to make their own karma. Karma is a Sanskrit word for "making," translated sometimes as "action." Therefore, Buddhists have established some careful rules of behavior for creating their karma. Called the noble Eightfold Path, it is marked by the following principles.

1. Right views—the avoidance of illusion
2. Right aims—purposive intentions to achieve nirvana
3. Right speech—preferring the truth
4. Right conduct—being honest, true, pure in behavior
5. Right living—avoiding hurting all beings and thus preferring a vegetarian diet
6. Self-control—preferring disciplined behavior
7. Right-mindedness—being aware and alert
8. Right meditation—deep contemplation of life

The ethical implications of Buddhism are evident in the eight admonitions of the noble Eightfold Path.

The Buddhist scriptures, from which this passage comes, were not written by the Buddha, but gathered from his teachings by disciples such as his personal follower, Ānanda. The scriptures date from the fifth century B.C. and were written down some time in the seventh century A.D. by monks who were fearful that the teachings, because of intense persecution of Buddhists, might be lost. Buddhism is rare in India today—located mainly in Sri Lanka—but it was transplanted to China and Japan, where it remains influential. Although Southeast Asia today is largely Buddhist, Buddhism coexists with many local religions, some of which contain quite opposing views.

The volume of Buddhist scriptures—hundreds of thousands of

pages—resulted from the contribution of many different schools of Buddhism, each with its own interpretation. In Japan, for example, several schools of Buddhism have been prominent. One is the Rinzai sect, a form of Buddhism that meditates on complex and baffling riddles, such as the question, What is the sound of one hand clapping? Such a riddle, called a koan, *is especially difficult for the Western mind to comprehend. Another is the Soto sect, which dates from the thirteenth century* A.D. *and emphasizes quiet sitting—zazen—as a means to enlightenment. Both of these sects are still vital in modern Buddhism.*

Buddhist meditation, which originated from the Zen school of Buddhism, depends on a willingness to remain quiet and suspend all logical thought, desire, and attachments. It is an extremely difficult discipline but is recognized by all Buddhists as the one true path to enlightenment, demanding the denial of the sensory world, of transitory events and values.

The following passage emphasizes the advantages of meditation as well as the advantages of introversion. The material world is seen as a distraction that incessantly robs people of their peace and their awareness of the truth about existence. Zen meditation is a radical technique for bringing the external world under the control of the spirit. However, it is closely related to Greek and Roman advice and therefore central to much that is basic to our views concerning spiritual values in modern times.

B U D D H I S T   R H E T O R I C

The material in this selection is not only translated from a language and a tradition quite foreign to English but also is derived from several sources. "The Advantages of Meditation" comes from a scripture called Milindapanha *and is rendered in prose. "The Practice of Introversion," however, originates from another text,* Shantideva, *and is rendered in poetry. The third section, "The Progressive Steps of Meditation," is from the* Ashvaghosha, *yet another important Buddhist text. That these texts differ in age and in approach makes the rhetorical situation unusual.*

However, certain qualities are present in all the texts. All are "how-to" texts, offering a step-by-step examination of the nature of meditation, its benefits, characteristics, and results. Typical of many Buddhist texts is the technique of enumeration: listing eight noble paths, twenty-eight advantages to meditation, and so on. Such a technique is especially useful for instruction because of its clear, progressive approach.

However, there is a further problem that the translator must resolve. As Edward Conze, the translator of these texts, explains, "For Buddhists the founder of their religion is the 'Lord Buddha,' a godlike being who has transcended the conditions of ordinary life, and his words are not those of a mere man, but a voice issuing from another world. It is therefore quite inconceivable that the Buddha should speak as ordinary people do." Therefore, the text as translated employs an elevated diction in a tone that is formal and distant. We might consider it priestlike. We usually expect and appreciate conversational, direct prose. But in confronting material that is so serious, dignified, and spiritual, it seems more appropriate that the level of diction be high and the tone formal.

However, the material here remains accessible. The scriptures aim at clarity and immediacy and invite us to take part in a fascinating spiritual journey.

———— ❦ ————

Meditation:
Path to Enlightenment

1. The Advantages of Meditation

Secluded meditation has many virtues. All the Tathagatas[1] have won their all-knowledge in a state of secluded meditation, and, even after their enlightenment, they have continued to cultivate meditation in the recollection of the benefits it brought to them in the past. It is just as a man who has received some boon from a king, and who would, in recollection of the benefits he has had, remain also in the future in attendance on that king.

There are, in fact, twenty-eight advantages to be gained from secluded meditation, and they are the reason why the Tathagatas have

1

2

---

[1] **Tathagata** One of Buddha's titles. It means "he who has thus come."

devoted themselves to it. They are as follows: secluded meditation guards him who meditates, lengthens his life, gives him strength, and shuts out faults; it removes illfame, and leads to good repute; it drives out discontent, and makes for contentment; it removes fear, and gives confidence; it removes sloth and generates vigor; it removes greed, hate, and delusion; it slays pride, breaks up preoccupations, makes thought one-pointed, softens the mind, generates gladness, makes one venerable, gives rise to much profit, makes one worthy of homage, brings exuberant joy, causes delight, shows the own-being of all conditioned things, abolishes rebirth in the world of becoming, and it bestows all the benefits of an ascetic life. These are the twenty-eight advantages of meditation which induce the Tathagatas to practice it.

And it is because the Tathagatas wish to experience the calm and   3
easeful delight of meditational attainments that they practice meditation with this end in view. Four are the reasons why the Tathagatas tend meditation: so that they may dwell at ease; on account of the manifoldness of its faultless virtues; because it is the road to all holy states without exception; and because it has been praised, lauded, exalted, and commended by all the Buddhas.

2. The Practice of Introversion

With his vigor grown strong, his mind should be placed in sama-   4
   dhi;[2]
For if thought be distracted we lie in the fangs of the passions.

No distractions can touch the man who's alone both in his body   5
   and mind.
Therefore renounce you the world, give up all thinking discursive!

Thirsting for gain, and loving the world, the people fail to renounce   6
   it.
But the wise can discard this love, reflecting as follows:

Through stillness joined to insight true,   7
His passions are annihilated.
Stillness must first of all be found.
That springs from disregarding worldly satisfactions.

---

[2]**Samadhi** Trancelike concentration.

Shortlived yourself, how can you think that others, quite as fleet-   8
    ing, are worthy of your love?
Thousands of births will pass without a sight of him you cherish
    so.

When unable to see your beloved, discontent disturbs your sama-   9
    dhi;
When you have seen, your longing, unsated as ever, returns as be-
    fore.

Then you forfeit the truth of the Real; your fallen condition shocks   10
    you no longer;
Burning with grief you yearn for reunion with him whom you cher-
    ish.

Worries like these consume a brief life—over and over again to no   11
    purpose;
You stray from the Dharma[3] eternal, for the sake of a transient
    friend.

To share in the life of the foolish will lead to the states of woe;   12
You share not, and they will hate you; what good comes from con-
    tact with fools?

Good friends at one time, of a sudden they dislike you,   13
You try to please them, quite in vain—the worldly are not easily
    contented!

Advice on their duties stirs anger; your own good deeds they   14
    impede;
When you ignore what they say they are angry, and head for a state
    of woe.

Of his betters he is envious, with his equals there is strife;   15
To inferiors he is haughty, mad for praise and wroth at blame;
Is there ever any goodness in these foolish common men?

Self-applause, belittling others, or encouragement to sin,   16
Some such evil's sure to happen where one fool another meets.

Two evils meet when fools consort together.   17
Alone I'll live, in peace and with unblemished mind.

---

[3]**Dharma**   Reality, divine law, virtue. This word has numerous meanings, depending
on its context.

Far should one flee from fools. When met, they should be won by 18
  kindness,
Not in the hope of intimacy, but so as to preserve an even, holy,
  mind.

Enough for Dharma's work I'll take from him, just as a bee takes 19
  honey from a flower.
Hidden and unknown, like the new moon, I will live my life.

The fools are no one's friends, so have the Buddhas taught us; 20
They cannot love unless their interest in themselves impels
  them.

Trees do not show disdain, and they demand no toilsome wooing; 21
Fain would I now consort with them as my companions.

Fain would I dwell in a deserted sanctuary, beneath a tree, or in a 22
  cave,
In noble disregard for all, and never looking back on what I left.

Fain would I dwell in spacious regions owned by no one, 23
And there, a homeless wanderer, follow my own mind,

A clay bowl as my only wealth, a robe that does not tempt the 24
  robbers,
Dwelling exempt from fear, and careless of my body.

Alone a man is born, and quite alone he also meets his death; 25
This private anguish no one shares; and friends can only bar true
  welfare.

Those who travel through Becoming should regard each incarna- 26
  tion
As no more than a passing station on their journey through Samsāra.[4]

So will I ever tend delightful and untroubled solitude, 27
Bestowing bliss, and stilling all distractions.

And from all other care released, the mind set on collecting my 28
  own spirit,
To unify and discipline my spirit I will strive.

---

[4]**Samsāra** The world of being and becoming.

3. The Progressive Steps
of Meditation

The restraint of the senses. By taking your stand on mindfulness you 29
must hold back from the sense-objects your senses, unsteady by nature. Fire, snakes, and lightning are less inimical to us than our own
senses, so much more dangerous. For they assail us all the time. Even
the most vicious enemies can attack only some people at some times,
and not at others, but everybody is always and everywhere weighed
down by his senses. And people do not go to hell because some enemy
has knocked them down and cast them into it; it is because they have
been knocked down by their unsteady senses that they are helplessly
dragged there. Those attacked by external enemies may, or may not,
suffer injury to their souls; but those who are weighed down by the
senses suffer in body and soul alike. For the five senses are rather like
arrows which have been smeared with the poison of fancies, have cares
for their feathers and happiness for their points, and fly about in the
space provided by the range of the sense-objects; shot off by Kama, the
God of Love, they hit men in their very hearts as a hunter hits a deer,
and if men do not know how to ward off these arrows they will be
their undoing; when they come near us we should stand firm in self-
control, be agile and steadfast, and ward them off with the great armor
of mindfulness. As a man who has subdued his enemies can everywhere live and sleep at ease and free from care, so can he who has
pacified his senses. For the senses constantly ask for more by way of
worldly objects, and normally behave like voracious dogs who can
never have enough. This disorderly mob of the senses can never reach
satiety, not by any amount of sense-objects; they are rather like the
sea, which one can go on indefinitely replenishing with water.

In this world the senses cannot be prevented from being active, 30
each in its own sphere. But they should not be allowed to grasp either
the general features of an object, or its particularities. When you have
beheld a sight-object with your eyes, you must merely determine the
basic element (which it represents, e.g., it is a "sight-object") and
should not under any circumstances fancy it as, say, a woman or a
man. But if now and then you have inadvertently grasped something
as a "woman" or a "man," you should not follow that up by determining the hairs, teeth, etc., as lovely. Nothing should be subtracted from
the datum, nothing added to it; it should be seen as it really is, as what
it is like in real truth.

If you thus try to look continually for the true reality in that which 31
the senses present to you, covetousness and aversion will soon be left

without a foothold. Coveting ruins those living beings who are bent
on sensuous enjoyment by means of pleasing forms, like an enemy
with a friendly face who speaks loving words, but plans dark deeds.
But what is called "aversion" is a kind of anger directed towards certain objects, and anyone who is deluded enough to pursue it is bound
to suffer for it either in this or a future life. Afflicted by their likes and
dislikes, as by excessive heat or cold, men will never find either happiness or the highest good as long as they put their trust in the unsteady senses.

How the senses cause bondage. A sense-organ, although it may have 32
begun to react to a sense-object, does not get caught up in it unless the
mind conceives imaginary ideas about the object. Both fuel and air
must be present for a fire to blaze up; so the fire of the passions is born
from a combination of a sense-object with imaginations. For people are
tied down by a sense-object when they cover it with unreal imaginations; likewise they are liberated from it when they see it as it really
is. The sight of one and the same object may attract one person, repel
another, and leave a third indifferent; a fourth may be moved to withdraw gently from it. Hence the sense-object itself is not the decisive
cause of either bondage or emancipation. It is the presence or absence
of imaginations which determines whether attachment takes place or
not. Supreme exertions should therefore be made to bring about a restraint of the senses; for unguarded senses lead to suffering and continued becomings. In all circumstances you should therefore watch out
for these enemies which cause so much evil, and you should always
control them, i.e., your seeing, hearing, smelling, tasting, and touching. Do not be negligent in this matter even for a moment. The onrush
of sense-experiences must be shut out with the sluice-gate of mindfulness.

Moderation in eating. Moreover you must learn to be moderate in eat- 33
ing, and eat only enough to remain healthy, and fit for trance. For excessive food obstructs the flow of the breath as it goes in and out,
induces lassitude and sleepiness, and kills all valor. And as too much
food has unfortunate consequences, so also starvation does not lead to
efficiency. For starvation drains away the body's volume, luster, firmness, performance, and strength. You should take food in accordance
with your individual capacity, neither too much, nor, from pride, too
little. As somebody with a running sore puts healing ointment on it,
so the man who seeks liberation should use food only to remove his
hunger. As the axle of a chariot must be lubricated so that it may work

properly, so the wise man employs food only to maintain his life. He takes care of his body, and carries it along with him, not because he has any affection for it, but simply because it enables him to cross the flood of suffering. The spiritual man offers food to his body merely to dispel hunger, and not from greed, or from any love for it.

The avoidance of sleep. After he has passed his day in keeping his 34
mind collected, the self-possessed man should shake off his sleepiness and spend also the night in the practice of Yoga.[5] When threatened with sleepiness you should constantly mobilize in your mind the factors of exertion and fortitude, of stamina and courage. You should repeat long passages from the Scriptures which you know by heart, expound them to others and reflect on them yourself. In order to keep awake all the time, wet your face with water, look round in all directions and fix your eyes on the stars. With your senses turned inwards, unmoved and well-controlled, with your mind undistracted, you should walk about or sit down at night. Fear, zest, and grief keep sleepiness away; therefore cultivate these three when you feel drowsy. Fear is best fostered by the thought of death coming upon you, zest by thinking of the blessings of the Dharma, grief by dwelling on the boundless ills which result from birth. These, and similar steps, my friend, you should take to keep awake. For what wise man would not regret sleeping away his life uselessly? In fact a wise man, who wants to be saved from the great danger, would not want to go to sleep while ignoring his faults, which are like vicious snakes that have crept into a house. Who would think of lying down to sleep undisturbed when the whole living world is like a house on fire, blazing with the flames of death, disease, and old age? Therefore you should recognize sleep as a darkening of your mind, and it would be unworthy of you to become absorbed in it while your faults are still with you and threaten you like enemies with their swords. The first three of the nine hours of the night you should spend in strenuous activity; then only should you rest your body, and lie down to sleep, but without relaxing your self-control. With a tranquil mind you should lie on your right side, you should look forward to the time when you will wake up and when the sun will shine again. In the third watch you should get up, and, either walking or sitting, with a pure mind and well-guarded senses, continue your practice of Yoga.

---

[5]**Yoga** Disciplined exercises designed to further self-control. A yogin is one who practices yoga.

Full awareness of the postures, etc. You are further asked to apply 35
mindfulness to your sitting, walking, standing, looking, speaking, and
so on, and to remain fully conscious in all your activities. The man
who has imposed strict mindfulness on all he does, and remains as
watchful as a gatekeeper at a city-gate, is safe from injury by the passions, just as a well-guarded town is safe from its foes. No defilement
can arise in him whose mindfulness is directed on all that concerns
his body. On all occasions he guards his thought, as a nurse guards a
child. Without the armor of mindfulness a man is an easy target for
the defilements, just as on a battlefield someone who has lost his armor is easily shot by his enemies. A mind which is not protected by
mindfulness is as helpless as a sightless man walking over uneven
ground without a guide. Loss of mindfulness is the reason why people
engage in useless pursuits, do not care for their own true interests, and
remain unalarmed in the presence of things which actually menace
their welfare. And, as a herdsman runs after his scattered cows, so
mindfulness runs after all the virtues, such as morality, etc., wherever
they can be found. The Deathless is beyond the reach of those who
disperse their attention, but it is within the grasp of those who direct
their mindfulness on all that concerns the body. Without mindfulness
no one can have the correct holy method; and in the absence of the
holy method he has lost the true Path. By losing the true Path he has
lost the road to the Deathless; the Deathless being outside his reach,
he cannot win freedom from suffering. Therefore you should superin-
tend your walking by thinking "I am walking," your standing by
thinking "I am standing," and so on; that is how you are asked to apply
mindfulness to all such activities.

The advantages of solitary meditation. Then, my friend, you should 36
find yourself a living-place which, to be suitable for Yoga, must be
without noise and without people. First the body must be placed in
seclusion; then detachment of the mind is easy to attain. But those
who do not like to live in solitude, because their hearts are not at
peace and because they are full of greed, they will hurt themselves
there, like someone who walks on very thorny ground because he cannot find the proper road. It is no easier to deny the urges of a man who
has not seen the real truth, and who finds himself standing in the
fairground of the sensory world, fascinated by its brightness, than it is
to deny those of a bull who is eating corn in the middle of a cornfield.
A brightly shining fire, when not stirred by the wind, is soon appeased;
so the unstimulated heart of those who live in seclusion wins peace
without much effort. One who delights in solitude is content with his

own company, eats wherever he may be, lodges anywhere, and wears just anything. To shun familiarity with others, as if they were a thorn in the flesh, shows a sound judgement, and helps to accomplish a useful purpose and to know the taste of a happy tranquillity. In a world which takes pleasure in worldly conditions and which is made unrestful by the sense-objects, he dwells in solitude indifferent to worldly conditions, as one who has attained his object, who is tranquil in his heart. The solitary man then drinks the nectar of the Deathless, he becomes content in his heart, and he grieves for the world made wretched by its attachment to sense-objects. If he is satisfied with living alone for a long time in an empty place, if he refrains from dallying with the agents of defilement, regarding them as bitter enemies, and if, content with his own company, he drinks the nectar of spiritual exultation, then he enjoys a happiness greater than that of paradise.

Concentration, and the forsaking of idle thoughts. Sitting cross-legged in some solitary spot, hold your body straight, and for a time keep your attention in front of you, either on the tip of the nose or the space on your forehead between the eyebrows. Then force your wandering mind to become wholly occupied with one object. If that mental fever, the preoccupation with sensuous desires, should dare to attack you, do not give your consent, but shake it off, as if it were dust on your clothes. Although, out of wise consideration, you may habitually eschew sense-desires, you can definitely rid yourself of them only through an antidote which acts on them like sunshine on darkness. There remains a latent tendency towards them, like a fire hidden under the ashes; this, like fire by water, must be put out by systematic meditation. As plants sprout forth from a seed, so sense-desires continue to come forth from that latent tendency; they will cease only when that seed is destroyed. When you consider what sufferings these sense-pleasures entail, by way of their acquisition, and so on, you will be prepared to cut them off at the root, for they are false friends. Sense-pleasures are impermanent, deceptive, trivial, ruinous, and largely in the power of others; avoid them as if they were poisonous vipers! The search for them involves suffering and they are enjoyed in constant disquiet; their loss leads to much grief, and their gain can never result in lasting satisfaction. A man is lost if he expects contentment from great possessions, the fulfilment of all his wishes from entry into heaven, or happiness from the sense-pleasures. These sense-pleasures are not worth paying any attention to, for they are unstable, unreal, hollow, and uncertain, and the happiness they can give is merely imaginary.

But if ill-will or the desire to hurt others should stir your mind,   38
purify it again with its opposite, which will act on it like a wishing
jewel on muddied water. Friendliness and compassionateness are, you
should know, their antidotes; for they are forever as opposed to hatred
as light is to darkness. A man who, although he has learned to abstain
from overt immoral acts, still persists in nursing ill-will, harms himself by throwing dirt over himself, like an elephant after his bath. For
a holy man forms a tender estimate of the true condition of mortal
beings, and how should he want to inflict further suffering on them
when they are already suffering enough from disease, death, old age,
and so on? With his malevolent mind a man may cause damage to
others, or he may not; in any case his own malevolent mind will be
forthwith burned up. Therefore you should strive to think of all that
lives with friendliness and compassion, and not with ill-will and a desire to hurt. For whatever a man thinks about continually, to that his
mind becomes inclined by the force of habit. Abandoning what is unwholesome, you therefore ought to ponder what is wholesome; for
that will bring you advantages in this world and help you to win the
highest goal. For unwholesome thoughts will grow when nursed in the
heart, and breed misfortunes for yourself and others alike. They not
only bring calamities to oneself by obstructing the way to supreme
beatitude, but they also ruin the affection of others, because one ceases
to be worthy of it.

You must also learn to avoid confusion in your mental actions, and   39
you should, my friend, never think even one single unwholesome
thought. All the ideas in your mind which are tainted by greed, hate,
and delusion deprive you of virtue and fashion your bondage. Delusion
injures others, brings hardship to oneself, soils the mind, and may well
lead to hell. It is better for you not to hurt yourself with such unwholesome thoughts! Just as an unintelligent person might burn precious aloe wood as if it were a piece of ordinary timber, so by not
observing the correct method which leads to emancipation you would
waste the rare opportunities offered by a human birth. To neglect the
most excellent Dharma, and instead to think demeritorious thoughts,
is like neglecting the jewels on a jewel-island and collecting lumps of
earth instead. A person who has won existence as a human being, and
who would pursue evil rather than good, is like a traveller to the Him-
alayas who would feed on deadly rather than on health-giving herbs.
Having understood this, try to drive out disturbing thoughts by means
of their appropriate antidotes, just as one pushes a wedge out of a cleft
in a log with the help of a slender counterwedge.

How to deal with thoughts concerning family and homeland. But if 40
you start worrying about the prosperity or difficulties of your relatives,
you should investigate the true nature of the world of the living, and
these ideas will disappear again. Among beings whom their Karma
drags along in the cycle of Samsara, who is a stranger, who a relation?
Delusion alone ties one person to another. For in the past the person
who is now one of your own people happened to be a stranger to you;
in the future the stranger of today will be one of your own people.
Over a number of lives a person is no more firmly associated with his
own people than birds who flock together at the close of day, some
here, some there. Relatives are no more closely united than travellers
who for a while meet at an inn, and then part again, losing sight of
each other. This world is by nature split up into disjointed parts; no
one really belongs to anyone else; it is held together by cause and effect, as loose sand by a clenched fist. And yet, a mother will cherish
her son because she expects that he will support her, and a son loves
his mother because she bore him in her womb. As long as relatives
agree with each other, they display affection; but disagreements turn
them into enemies. We see relatives behave unkindly, while nonrela-
tives may show us kindness. Men, indeed, make and break affections
according to their interests. As an artist becomes enamored of a
woman he has himself painted, so the affection, which a person has
for another with whom he feels at one, is entirely of his own making.
As for him who in another life was bound to you by ties of kinship,
and who was so dear to you then, what is he to you now or you to
him? Therefore it is unworthy of you to allow your mind to become
preoccupied with thoughts of your relatives. In the Samsaric world
there is no fixed division between your own people and other people.

And if you should hit on the idea that this or that country is safe, 41
prosperous, or fortunate, give it up, my friend, and do not entertain it
in any way; for you ought to know that the world everywhere is ablaze
with the fires of some faults or others. There is certain to be some
suffering, either from the cycle of the seasons, or from hunger, thirst,
or exhaustion, and a wholly fortunate country does not exist anywhere. Whether it be excessive cold or heat, sickness or danger, something always afflicts people everywhere; no safe refuge can thus be
found in the world. And in all countries of the world people are greatly
afraid of old age, disease, and death, and there is none where these
fears do not arise. Wherever this body may go, there suffering must
follow; there is no place in the world where it is not accompanied by
afflictions. However delightful, prosperous, and safe a country may appear to be, it should be recognized as a bad country if consumed by the

defilements. This world is smitten with countless ills, which affect
both body and mind, and we cannot go to any country which is safe
from them and where we can expect to live at ease.

Suffering is the lot of everyone, everywhere and all the time; there-　42
fore, my friend, do not hanker after the glittering objects of this world!
And, once this hankering is extinct in you, then you will clearly see
that this entire world of the living can be said to be on fire.

How to be mindful of death. But if you should make any plans that　43
do not reckon with the inevitability of death, you must make an effort
to lay them down again, as if they were an illness which attacks your
own self. Not even for a moment should you rely on life going on, for
Time, like a hidden tiger, lies in wait to slay the unsuspecting. There
is no point in your feeling too strong or too young to die, for death
strikes down people whatever their circumstances, and is no respecter
of youthful vitality. The body we drag along with us is a fertile soil for
all sorts of mishaps, and no sensible person would entertain any firm
expectation of well-being or of life. Who could ever be free from cares
as long as he has to bear with this body which, as a receptacle of the
four great elements, resembles a pot full of snakes at war with each
other? Consider how strange and wonderful it is that this man, on
drawing in his breath, can immediately afterwards breathe out again;
so little can life be trusted! And this is another strange and wonderful
thing that, having slept, he wakes up again, and that, having got up,
he goes to sleep again; for many are the adversities of those who have
a body. How can we ever feel secure from death, when from the womb
onwards it follows us like a murderer with his sword raised to kill us?
No man born into this world, however pious or strong he be, ever gets
the better of the King of Death, either now, or in the past or the future.
For when Death in all its ferocity has arrived on the scene, no bargain-
ing can ward him off, no gifts, no attempt at sowing dissension, no
force of arms and no restraint. Our hold on life is so uncertain that it
is not worth relying on. All the time Death constantly carries people
away, and does not wait for them to reach the age of seventy! Who,
unless he be quite mad, would make plans which do not reckon with
death, when he sees the world so unsubstantial and frail, like a water
bubble?

The four holy truths. Investigating the true nature of reality and di-　44
recting his mind towards the complete destruction of the Outflows,
the Yogin learns to understand correctly the four statements which
express the four Truths, i.e., suffering, and the rest. First there is the

ubiquitous fact of suffering, which can be defined as oppression; then the cause of suffering, which is the same as its origination; the extinction of suffering, which consists essentially in the definite escape from it; and finally the path which leads to tranquillity, and which has the essential function of saving. And those whose intellect has awakened to these four holy truths, and who have correctly penetrated to their meaning, their meditations shall overcome all the Outflows, they will gain the blessed calm, and no more will they be reborn. It is, on the other hand, through its failure to awaken to these four facts which summarize the essential nature of true reality, and through its inability to penetrate to their meaning, that the Samsaric world whirls round and round, that it goes from one becoming to another, and that it cannot win the blessed calm.

You should therefore, to explain it briefly, know with regard to the 45 fact of ill, that birth is the basis of all the other misfortunes, like old age, and so on; for as all plants grow on the earth, so all calamities grow on the soil of birth. For the birth of a body endowed with sense-organs leads of necessity to manifold ills, and the production of a person's physical existence automatically implies that of death and sickness. As food, whether good or bad, far from sustaining us becomes merely destructive when mixed with poison, so all birth into this world, whether among animals, or above or below them, tends to ill and not to ease. The numerous afflictions of living beings, such as old age and so on, are unavoidably produced wherever there is Worldly Activity; but even the most frightful gales could not possibly shake trees that have never been planted. Where there is a body, there must also be such sufferings as disease, old age, and so on, and likewise hunger, thirst, wetness, heat, cold, etc. And the mind which is dependent on the body involves us in such ills as grief, discontent, anger, fear, etc. Wherever there is a psycho-physical organism, suffering is bound to take place; but for him who is liberated from it there can be no suffering, either now, or in the past, or the future.

And that suffering which we find bound up with Worldly Activity 46 in this world is caused by the multitude of the defilements, such as craving, and the rest; but it is not due to a Creator, or Primordial Matter, or Time, or the Nature of things, or Fate, or Chance. And for that reason, i.e., because all Worldly Activity is a result of the defilements, we can be sure that the passionate and the dull will die, whereas those who are without passion and dullness will not be born again.

Therefore, once you have seen, my friend, that craving, etc., are the 47 causes of the manifold ills which follow on birth, remove those causes if you want to be free from suffering; for an effect ceases when its cause has been stopped, and so also suffering becomes extinct when its cause has been quite exhausted. You must therefore come face to face with the holy, calm, and fortunate Dharma, which through dispassion has turned away from craving, which is the supreme place of rest, wherein all Worldly Activity is stopped, a shelter which abides eternally and which nothing can ever take away; that secure place which is final and imperishable, and where there is no birth, old age, death, or disease, no conjunction with unpleasant things, no disappointment over one's wishes, nor separation from what is dear. When the flame of a lamp comes to an end, it does not go anywhere down in the earth or up in the sky, nor into any of the directions of space, but because its oil is exhausted it simply ceases to burn. So, when an accomplished saint comes to the end, he does not go anywhere down in the earth or up in the sky, nor into any of the directions of space, but because his defilements have become extinct he simply ceases to be disturbed.

The wise man who wishes to carry out the sacred precepts of tradition should, as a means for the attainment of this Dharma, develop the eightfold Path—three of its steps, i.e., right speech, right bodily action, and right livelihood concern morality; three, i.e., right views, right intentions, and right effort concern wisdom; two again, i.e., right mindfulness and right concentration promote tranquilizing concentration. As a result of morality the defilements no longer proliferate, as seeds no longer germinate after the right season for them has passed; for when a man's morality is pure, the vices attack his mind but half-heartedly, as if they had become ashamed. Concentration, in its turn, blocks the defilements, as a rock blocks the torrent of a mighty river; for the faults are unable to attack a man who is absorbed in trance, as if they were spell-bound snakes immobilized by mantras. Wisdom, finally, completely destroys the defilements, as a river, which in the rainy season overflows its banks, sweeps away the trees that grow on them; consumed by wisdom, the faults cease to thrive and grow, like a tree burnt up by the fire which flares up after it has been struck by a thunderbolt. By entering on this eightfold path, which has morality, concentration, and wisdom for its three divisions, and which is holy, incorruptible, and straight, one forsakes those faults which are the causes of suffering, and one attains the state of absolute peace. Ten qualities are required of those who proceed along it: steadfastness, sincerity, self-respect, vigilance, seclusion from the world, contentment with little, simplicity of tastes, nonattachment, aversion to Worldly Activity, and patience. For he who discovers the true nature of ill, its origin and its cessation, can advance on the holy path, in the company

48

of spiritual friends, towards Peace. It is like someone who correctly diagnoses a disease as a disease, and who correctly determines its cause and its cure; when treated by skilful friends he will soon be healthy again. You should therefore regard ill as a disease, the defilements as its cause, their cessation as the state of health, and the path as the remedy. What you must furthermore understand is that suffering is the same as Worldly Activity, and that it is kept going by the defilements; that their stopping is the same as inactivity, and that it is the path which leads to that. As though your turban or your clothes were on fire, so with a sense of urgency should you apply your intellect to the comprehension of the truths. It is because it fails to perceive the guidance given by these truths that the world of the living is being burnt alive. When therefore someone sees that his psycho-physical organism is something that ought to be extinguished, then he has the correct vision; in consequence of his correct insight he becomes disgusted with the things of the world; and as he is no longer drawn to them, his greed gradually exhausts itself. Solemnly I assure you that his mind is definitely liberated when passion and the hope of pleasure have become extinct; and that, once his mind is well freed of those two, there is nothing further that he has to do. For I proclaim it as a fact that the effective extinction of all the Outflows lies in seeing and discerning the own-being of the psychophysical personality, its cause and its disappearance.

QUESTIONS

1. What does it mean to restrain the senses?
2. Do you think restraining the senses will produce the results that the Buddha desires?
3. In paragraphs 29–31, the Buddha complains about the unsteadiness of the senses. What does he mean? Are you aware of the unsteadiness of the senses?
4. What seem to be the primary advantages of meditation? Are the advantages obviously religious, or are they secular as well?
5. What is the Buddhist attitude toward the body? How does it seem to differ from Western culture's current attitudes?
6. The Buddha recommends constant mindfulness. What does this entail?
7. Why should meditation be solitary? Are you convinced that solitariness is essential?
8. What does enlightenment seem to mean for the Buddha? Do you feel that it is possible for you to achieve it?

W R I T I N G   A S S I G N M E N T S

1. Follow the directions for meditation as closely as possible. Try to spend at least three days meditating for ten minutes a day or longer. Write a record of your experiences and establish what for you are the advantages of meditation. Reread paragraph 37 closely before beginning this experiment.

2. In paragraph 37, we find the statement: "Sense-pleasures are impermanent, deceptive, trivial, ruinous, and largely in the power of others; avoid them as if they were poisonous vipers!" Obviously, this is not the general attitude of modern-day Westerners. Clarify your position on the value or lack of value of the sense-pleasures. Are they as evil as the Buddha suggests, or do they possess value?

3. The Buddha suggests that ideas such as greed, hate, and delusion actually lead us into bondage. By referring to specific historical examples or examples from your own experience, explain how this observation is true. What is it about the ideas we hold that makes them potentially so damaging to us? Does the Buddha recommend ways that we can avoid holding such ideas? Fashion an essay that examines these questions.

4. In paragraph 44, the Buddha states that suffering is universal. He equates suffering with oppression. Examine his teachings on this question and relate the question of suffering to our modern society. Do you feel that oppression produces suffering today as it did in the Buddha's time? Is there a sense in which the Buddha's suggestions for the relief of suffering—implied in the techniques of meditation—would alleviate the sufferings of modern oppressed people?

5. The noble Eightfold Path is discussed in paragraph 48 as well as in the introduction to this selection. Determine its applicability to your life, and take a stand on whether you believe your life would improve if you were to follow this path. Be as specific as possible, referring to specific actions, either actual or potential, and specific relationships, either actual or potential, that would be altered in your life.

PLATO

The Allegory of the Cave

PLATO (428–347 B.C.) was born into an aristocratic Athenian family and educated according to the best precepts available. He eventually became a student of Socrates and later involved himself closely with Socrates' work and teaching. Plato was not only Socrates' finest student but was also the student who immortalized Socrates in his works. Most of Plato's works are philosophical essays, with Socrates as a character speaking in a dialogue with one or more students or listeners. Thus, Plato permits us the vision of Socrates written by one who knew him and listened carefully to what he said.

The times in which Plato lived were turbulent indeed. In 405 B.C. Athens was defeated by Sparta and was governed by tyrants. Political life in Athens was dangerous. Plato felt, however, that he could effect positive change in Athenian politics until, in 399 B.C., Socrates was tried unjustly for corrupting the youth of Athens and sentenced to death. After that, Plato withdrew from public life and devoted himself to writing and to the Academy which he founded in an olive grove in Athens. The Academy endured for almost a thousand years, which tells us how greatly Plato's thought was valued.

From *The Republic*. Translated by Benjamin Jowett.

Although it is not easy to condense Plato's views, he may be said to have held the world of sense perception as inferior to the world of ideal entities that exist only in a pure spiritual realm. These ideals, or forms, had been perceived directly by everyone before birth, and then dimly remembered here on earth. But the memory, even dim as it is, makes it possible for people to understand what is perceived by the senses despite the fact that the senses are so unreliable and perceptions are so imperfect.

This view of reality has long been important to philosophers because it gives a philosophical basis to antimaterialistic thought. It values the spirit first and frees people from the tyranny of sensory perception and sensory reward. In the case of love, Plato held that Eros leads us to a reverence for the body and its pleasures; but the thrust of his teaching is that the body is a metaphor for spiritual delights. Plato assures us that the body is only a starting point and that it can eventually lead both to spiritual fulfillment and to the appreciation of true beauty.

"The Allegory of the Cave" is, on the one hand, a discussion of politics—the Republic, from which it is taken, is a treatise on justice and the ideal government. On the other hand, it has long stood for a kind of demonstration of the fact that if our perceptions are what we must rely upon to know the truth about the world, then we actually know very little about it. We know what we perceive, but we have no way of knowing anything beyond that. Likewise, in order to live ethically, it is essential to know what is true and therefore what is important to us.

Plato's allegory has been persuasive for centuries and remains at the center of thought that attempts to counter the pleasures of the sensual life. Most religions aim for spiritual refinement and praise the qualities of the soul, which lies beyond perception. Thus, it comes as no surprise that Christianity and other religions have not only praised Plato but have developed systems of thought that bear a close resemblance to his. Later refinements of his thought, usually called Neo-Platonism, have been influential even into modern times.

PLATO'S RHETORIC

Two very important rhetorical techniques are at work in the following selection. The first and more obvious—at least on one level— is the reliance on the allegory, a story in which the characters and situations are meant to resemble people and situations in another context. It is a difficult technique to use well, although we have the example of Aesop's fables in which animals represent people and their foibles. The advantage of the technique is that a complex and sometimes unpopular argument can be fought and won before the audience realizes that an argument is being fought. The disadvantage of the technique is that the terms of the allegory may only approximate the situation which it reflects; thus, the argument may fail to be convincing.

Another rhetorical technique Plato uses is the dialogue. In fact, it is a hallmark of Plato's work, since most of his writings are called dialogues. The Symposium, Apology, Phaedo, Crito, Meno, and most of his famous works are written in dialogue form. Usually Socrates is speaking to a student or a friend about highly abstract issues. Socrates asks questions which require simple answers. Slowly, the questioning proceeds to elucidate the answers to the most complex of issues.

This use of the question-and-answer dialogue is basically the Socratic method. Socrates analyzes the answer to each question, examines the implications of those answers, then asserts the truth. The method is functional in part because Plato's theory is that people do not learn things; they remember them. That is, since people came originally from heaven, where they knew the truth, they already possess that knowledge and must recover it by means of the dialogue. Socrates' method is ideally suited to that purpose.

Beyond these techniques, however, we must look at Plato's style. It is true that he is working with very difficult ideas, but the style of the work is so clear, simple, and direct that few people would have trouble understanding what is said at any given moment. Considering the influence this work has had on world thought and the reputation Plato had earned by the time he came to write the Republic, it is remarkable that the style is so plain and so accessible. It is significant that such a great mind can express itself with such impressive clarity. Part of that capacity is due to Plato's respect for rhetoric and its proper uses.

The Allegory of the Cave

SOCRATES, GLAUCON. The den, the prisoners: the light at a distance;

And now, I said, let me show in a figure how far our 1
nature is enlightened or unenlightened:—Behold! human
beings living in an underground den, which has a mouth
open towards the light and reaching all along the den;
here they have been from their childhood, and have their
legs and necks chained so that they cannot move, and
can only see before them, being prevented by the chains
from turning round their heads. Above and behind them
a fire is blazing at a distance, and between the fire and
the prisoners there is a raised way; and you will see, if
you look, a low wall built along the way, like the screen
which marionette players have in front of them, over
which they show the puppets.

I see. 2

the low wall, and the moving figures of which the shadows are seen on the opposite wall of the den.

And do you see, I said, men passing along the wall 3
carrying all sorts of vessels, and statues and figures of
animals made of wood and stone and various materials,
which appear over the wall? Some of them are talking,
others silent.

You have shown me a strange image, and they are 4
strange prisoners.

Like ourselves, I replied; and they see only their own 5
shadows, or the shadows of one another, which the fire
throws on the opposite wall of the cave?

True, he said; how could they see anything but the 6
shadows if they were never allowed to move their heads?

And of the objects which are being carried in like 7
manner they would only see the shadows?

Yes, he said. 8

And if they were able to converse with one another, 9
would they not suppose that they were naming what was
actually before them?

Very true. 10

And suppose further that the prison had an echo 11
which came from the other side, would they not be sure

The prisoners would mistake the shadows for realities.

to fancy when one of the passers-by spoke that the voice which they heard came from the passing shadow?

No question, he replied. 12

To them, I said, the truth would be literally nothing 13 but the shadows of the images.

That is certain. 14

And now look again, and see what will naturally fol- 15 low if the prisoners are released and disabused of their error. At first, when any of them is liberated and compelled suddenly to stand up and turn his neck round and walk and look towards the light, he will suffer sharp pains; the glare will distress him, and he will be unable to see the realities of which in his former state he had seen the shadows; and then conceive some one saying to him, that what he saw before was an illusion, but that now, when he is approaching nearer to being and his eye is turned towards more real existence, he has a clearer

And when released, they would still persist in maintaining the superior truth of the shadows.

vision—what will be his reply? And you may further imagine that his instructor is pointing to the objects as they pass and requiring him to name them,—will he not be perplexed? Will he not fancy that the shadows which he formerly saw are truer than the objects which are now shown to him?

Far truer. 16

And if he is compelled to look straight at the light, 17 will he not have a pain in his eyes which will make him turn away to take refuge in the objects of vision which he can see, and which he will conceive to be in reality clearer than the things which are now being shown to him?

True, he said. 18

When dragged upwards, they would be dazzled by excess of light.

And suppose once more, that he is reluctantly 19 dragged up a steep and rugged ascent, and held fast until he is forced into the presence of the sun himself, is he not likely to be pained and irritated? When he approaches the light his eyes will be dazzled, and he will not be able to see anything at all of what are now called realities.

Not all in a moment, he said. 20

He will require to grow accustomed to the sight of 21 the upper world. And first he will see the shadows best, next the reflections of men and other objects in the water, and then the objects themselves; then he will gaze upon the light of the moon and the stars and the spangled heaven; and he will see the sky and the stars by night better than the sun or the light of the sun by day?

Certainly.   22

At length they will see the sun and understand his nature.

Last of all he will be able to see the sun, and not mere 23
reflections of him in the water, but he will see him in his own proper place, and not in another; and he will contemplate him as he is.

Certainly.   24

He will then proceed to argue that this is he who 25
gives the season and the years, and is the guardian of all that is in the visible world, and in a certain way the cause of all things which he and his fellows have been accustomed to behold?

Clearly, he said, he would first see the sun and then 26
reason about him.

They would then pity their old companions of the den.

And when he remembered his old habitation, and the 27
wisdom of the den and his fellow prisoners, do you not suppose that he would felicitate himself on the change, and pity them?

Certainly, he would.   28

And if they were in the habit of conferring honors 29
among themselves on those who were quickest to observe the passing shadows and to remark which of them went before, and which followed after, and which were together; and who were therefore best able to draw conclusions as to the future, do you think that he would care for such honors and glories, or envy the possessors of them? Would he not say with Homer,

Better to be the poor servant of a poor master,

and to endure anything, rather than think as they do and live after their manner?

Yes, he said, I think that he would rather suffer any- 30
thing than entertain these false notions and live in this miserable manner.

Imagine once more, I said, such an one coming sud- 31
denly out of the sun to be replaced in his old situation; would he not be certain to have his eyes full of darkness?

To be sure, he said.   32

But when they returned to the den they would see much worse than those who had never left it.

And if there were a contest, and he had to compete   33
in measuring the shadows with the prisoners who had
never moved out of the den, while his sight was still
weak, and before his eyes had become steady (and the
time which would be needed to acquire this new habit of
sight might be very considerable), would he not be ridiculous? Men would say of him that up he went and down
he came without his eyes; and that it was better not even
to think of ascending; and if any one tried to loose another and lead him up to the light, let them only catch
the offender, and they would put him to death.

No question, he said.   34

The prison is the world of sight, the light of the fire is the sun.

This entire allegory, I said, you may now append, dear   35
Glaucon, to the previous argument; the prison house is
the world of sight, the light of the fire is the sun, and
you will not misapprehend me if you interpret the journey upwards to be the ascent of the soul into the intellectual world according to my poor belief, which, at your
desire, I have expressed—whether rightly or wrongly God
knows. But, whether true or false, my opinion is that in
the world of knowledge the idea of good appears last of
all, and is seen only with an effort; and, when seen, is
also inferred to be the universal author of all things beautiful and right, parent of light and of the lord of light in
this visible world, and the immediate source of reason
and truth in the intellectual; and that this is the power
upon which he who would act rationally either in public
or private life must have his eye fixed.

I agree, he said, as far as I am able to understand you.   36

Moreover, I said, you must not wonder that those   37
who attain to this beatific vision are unwilling to descend to human affairs; for their souls are ever hastening
into the upper world where they desire to dwell; which
desire of theirs is very natural, if our allegory may be

Nothing extraordinary in the philosopher being unable to see in the dark.

trusted.

Yes, very natural.   38

And is there anything surprising in one who passes   39
from divine contemplations to the evil state of man, mis-
behaving himself in a ridiculous manner; if, while his
eyes are blinking and before he has become accustomed

to the surrounding darkness, he is compelled to fight in courts of law, or in other places, about the images or the shadows of images of justice, and is endeavoring to meet the conceptions of those who have never yet seen absolute justice?

Anything but surprising, he replied. 40

The eyes may be blinded in two ways, by excess or by defect of light.

Anyone who has common sense will remember that 41 the bewilderments of the eyes are of two kinds, and arise from two causes, either from coming out of the light or from going into the light, which is true of the mind's eye, quite as much as of the bodily eye; and he who remembers this when he sees anyone whose vision is perplexed and weak, will not be too ready to laugh; he will first ask whether that soul of man has come out of the brighter life, and is unable to see because unaccustomed to the dark, or having turned from darkness to the day is dazzled by excess of light. And he will count the one happy in his condition and state of being, and he will pity the other; or, if he have a mind to laugh at the soul which comes from below into the light, there will be more reason in this than in the laugh which greets him who returns from above out of the light into the den.

That, he said, is a very just distinction. 42

The conversion of the soul is the turning round the eye from darkness to light.

But then, if I am right, certain professors of education 43 must be wrong when they say that they can put a knowledge into the soul which was not there before, like sight into blind eyes.

They undoubtedly say this, he replied. 44

Whereas, our argument shows that the power and ca- 45 pacity of learning exists in the soul already; and that just as the eye was unable to turn from darkness to light without the whole body, so too the instrument of knowledge can only by the movement of the whole soul be turned from the world of becoming into that of being, and learn by degrees to endure the sight of being, and of the brightest and best of being, or in other words, of the good.

Very true. 46

And must there not be some art which will effect 47 conversion in the easiest and quickest manner; not implanting the faculty of sight, for that exists already, but has been turned in the wrong direction, and is looking away from the truth?

Yes, he said, such an art may be presumed.   48

The virtue of wisdom has a divine power which may be turned either towards good or towards evil.

And whereas the other so-called virtues of the soul   49 seem to be akin to bodily qualities, for even when they are not originally innate they can be implanted later by habit and exercise, the virtue of wisdom more than anything else contains a divine element which always remains, and by this conversion is rendered useful and profitable; or, on the other hand, hurtful and useless. Did you never observe the narrow intelligence flashing from the keen eye of a clever rogue—how eager he is, how clearly his paltry soul sees the way to his end; he is the reverse of blind, but his keen eyesight is forced into the service of evil, and he is mischievous in proportion to his cleverness?

Very true, he said.   50

But what if there had been a circumcision of such na-   51 tures in the days of their youth; and they had been severed from those sensual pleasures, such as eating and drinking, which, like leaden weights, were attached to them at their birth, and which drag them down and turn the vision of their souls upon the things that are below— if, I say, they had been released from these impediments and turned in the opposite direction, the very same faculty in them would have seen the truth as keenly as they see what their eyes are turned to now.

Very likely.   52

Neither the uneducated nor the overeducated will be good servants of the State.

Yes, I said; and there is another thing which is likely,   53 or rather a necessary inference from what has preceded, that neither the uneducated and uninformed of the truth, nor yet those who never make an end of their education, will be able ministers of State; not the former, because they have no single aim of duty which is the rule of all their actions, private as well as public; nor the latter, because they will not act at all except upon compulsion, fancying that they are already dwelling apart in the islands of the blessed.

Very true, he replied.   54

Then, I said, the business of us who are the founders   55 of the State will be to compel the best minds to attain that knowledge which we have already shown to be the greatest of all—they must continue to ascend until they arrive at the good; but when they have ascended and seen enough we must not allow them to do as they do now.

What do you mean? 56

Men should ascend to the upper world, but they should also return to the lower.

.I mean that they remain in the upper world: but this 57 must not be allowed; they must be made to descend again among the prisoners in the den, and partake of their labors and honors, whether they are worth having or not.

But is not this unjust? he said; ought we to give them 58 a worse life, when they might have a better?

You have again forgotten, my friend, I said, the inten- 59 tion of the legislator, who did not aim at making any one class in the State happy above the rest; the happiness was to be in the whole State, and he held the citizens together by persuasion and necessity, making them bene-factors of the State, and therefore benefactors of one an-other; to this end he created them, not to please them-selves, but to be his instruments in binding up the State.

True, he said, I had forgotten. 60

The duties of philosophers.

Observe, Glaucon, that there will be no injustice in 61 compelling our philosophers to have a care and provi-dence of others; we shall explain to them that in other States, men of their class are not obliged to share in the toils of politics: and this is reasonable, for they grow up at their own sweet will, and the government would rather not have them. Being self-taught, they cannot be expected to show any gratitude for a culture which they have never received. But we have brought you into the world to be rulers of the hive, kings of yourselves and of the other citizens, and have educated you far better and more perfectly than they have been educated, and you

Their obligations to their country will induce them to take part in her government.

are better able to share in the double duty. Wherefore each of you, when his turn comes, must go down to the general underground abode, and get the habit of seeing in the dark. When you have acquired the habit, you will see ten thousand times better than the inhabitants of the den, and you will know what the several images are, and what they represent, because you have seen the beautiful and just and good in their truth. And thus our State, which is also yours, will be a reality, and not a dream only, and will be administered in a spirit unlike that of other States, in which men fight with one another about shadows only and are distracted in the struggle for power, which in their eyes is a great good. Whereas the truth is that the State in which the rulers are most reluctant to govern is always the best and most quietly governed, and the State in which they are most eager, the worst.

Quite true, he replied. 62

And will our pupils, when they hear this, refuse to 63 take their turn at the toils of State, when they are allowed to spend the greater part of their time with one another in the heavenly light?

They will be willing but not anxious to rule.

Impossible, he answered; for they are just men, and 64 the commands which we impose upon them are just; there can be no doubt that every one of them will take office as a stern necessity, and not after the fashion of our present rulers of State.

The statesman must be provided with a better life than that of a ruler; and then he will not covet office.

Yes, my friend, I said; and there lies the point. You 65 must contrive for your future rulers another and a better life than that of a ruler, and then you may have a well-ordered State; for only in the State which offers this, will they rule who are truly rich, not in silver and gold, but in virtue and wisdom, which are the true blessings of life. Whereas if they go to the administration of public affairs, poor and hungering after their own private advantage, thinking that hence they are to snatch the chief good, order there can never be; for they will be fighting about office, and the civil and domestic broils which thus arise will be the ruin of the rulers themselves and of the whole State.

Most true, he replied. 66

And the only life which looks down upon the life of 67 political ambition is that of true philosophy. Do you know of any other?

Indeed, I do not, he said. 68

QUESTIONS

1. What is the relationship between Socrates and Glaucon? Are they equal in intellectual authority? Are they concerned with the same issues?
2. How does the allegory of the prisoners in the cave watching shadows on a wall relate to us today? What are the shadows that we see and how do they distort our sense of what is real?
3. Are we also prisoners in the sense that Plato's characters are prisoners?
4. From a scientific point of view—taking into account the thought of Lucretius, for example—what are the facts about our inabilities to perceive the reality of experience? Does the fact that the material world is composed of atoms imply that we are in a position similar to those in Plato's cave?
5. If Plato is right that the material world is an illusion, how would too great a reliance on materialism affect ethical decisions?
6. What ethical issues, if any, are raised by Plato's allegory?
7. In paragraph 49 Plato states that the virtue of wisdom "contains a divine element." What does this seem to mean? Do you agree with Plato? What is "a divine element"?
8. What distinctions does Plato make between the public and the private? Would you make the same distinctions (see paras. 53–55)?

WRITING ASSIGNMENTS

1. Analyze the allegory of the cave for its strengths and weaknesses. Consider what it is meant to imply for people living in a world of the senses and what Plato implies lies behind that world. Consider the extent to which people are like (or unlike) the figures in the cave. Consider the extent to which the world we know is like the cave. Consider, too, the "revelations" implied in the allegory and its contemplation.
2. Socrates ends the dialogue by saying that after rulers of the state have served their term they must be able to look forward to a better life than that of being rulers. He and Glaucon agree that there is only one life that "looks down upon the life of political ambition"—"that of true philosophy." What is the life of true philosophy? Is it superior to that of being a ruler (or anything else)? How would you define its superiority? What would its qualities be? What would its concerns be? Would you be happy leading such a life?
3. In what ways would a dependence on the material world for our highest moral values affect our ethical behavior? What is the connection between ethics and materialism? Write a brief essay that defends or attacks materialism as a basis for ethical action. How can we aspire to the good if we root our greatest pleasures in our sense? What alternatives do modern people have if we choose to base our actions on nonmaterialistic, or spiritual

values? What are those values? How can they guide our ethical behavior? Do you think they should?

4. In paragraph 61, Socrates outlines a program that would assure Athens of good rulers and good government. Clarify exactly what the program is, what its problems and benefits are, and how it would have to be put into action. Then decide whether or not the program would work. You may consider whether or not it would work for our time, for Socrates' time, or both. If possible, use examples (hypothetical or real) to bolster your argument.

5. Socrates states unequivocally that Athens should compel the best and the most intelligent young men to be rulers of the state. Review his reasons for saying so; consider what his concept of the state is; then take a stand on the issue. Is it right to want to compel the best and most intelligent young people to become rulers? If so, would it be proper to compel those well suited for the professions of law, medicine, teaching, or religion to follow those respective callings? Would we not have an ideal society if everyone were forced to practice the calling for which they had the best aptitude?

6. Plato has a great deal to say about goodness as it relates to government. Compare his views with those of Lao-Tzu, Machiavelli, and Rousseau. Which of those thinkers would Plato have agreed with most? Which do you feel he most emphatically influenced? In comparing these writers and their political views, consider what the nature of goodness in a ruler must be. Do you think that we hold similar attitudes today in our expectations for the goodness of our government?

MARCUS AURELIUS

Stoicism and Self-Discipline

MARCUS *AELIUS AURELIUS ANTONINUS (A.D. 121–180) was the kind of philosopher who molded his thinking in the arena of active, public service. Like Machiavelli, he was embroiled in politics and government, but unlike Machiavelli, he did not simply serve as an adjunct to the ruler. Marcus Aurelius was the ruler, the emperor of Rome from 161 until his death. While in the camps with his soldiers, defending the empire's distant borders against the incursions of the barbarians, he met his end from disease.*

The artistic representations of Marcus Aurelius that have survived usually depict him in warrior's harness, with armor breastplate and the short leather coverlet of the Roman legions. An active man who adhered to the Stoic belief of service to the state, he was never a robust athlete but managed to work at outdoor activities in order to build up his stamina and strength. He assumed command of the empire at the death of his adoptive father, Antoninus Pius, from whom over the years he had learned the business of government, finally emerging as a capable and clearheaded ruler.

His times, however, were dangerous. The tribes of people who

Translated by Maxwell Staniforth.

were spread throughout Europe and North Africa had grown stronger, while the Roman legions had grown weaker. In 160 Rome was breathing its last gasps of greatness. Only two hundred fifty years later, in 410, Rome itself was sacked by the Visigoths. During the reign of Marcus Aurelius, the dangers to Rome became serious enough to demand that he be on the frontiers with his troops, commanding them in battle.

In the midst of these turbulent campaigns, Marcus Aurelius began collecting the material he included in his Meditations, *a book that has inspired readers throughout the ages. The organization of the* Meditations *resembles more closely the accumulative approach that Lao-Tzu uses in his* Tao Te Ching *than the narrative style of Plato. Although he numbered the items for his convenience, the numbering also serves to remind us that these are separable paragraphs that loosely rather than tightly compose a whole. The subject consistently focuses on the question of how an individual should behave in daily life, but the details move in many different directions, depending on what Marcus Aurelius was reading or thinking. The text may be defined as meditations in the sense of jottings that reflect his response at a given moment to a specific thought or event.*

The title has been traditionally translated as "meditations" since its early English version in the seventeenth century, but the Greek may be better rendered as "conversations with himself." This point is important because it helps explain some of the sense we get that we are not reading a finished, rhetorically fashioned book with a beginning, a middle, and an end. Instead, we are reading the thoughts of a man whose primary work was not writing but ruling an empire.

Marcus Aurelius, a famous Stoic: states in the Meditations, *"nothing can be good for a man unless it helps to make him just, self-disciplined, courageous, and independent." In other words, whatever does not lead to these ends is therefore not good and should be avoided. Stoicism was a moral philosophy that insisted on self-control as the key to the fullest development of the individual. The pleasures of the senses, while not necessarily bad in and of themselves, led to behavior marked by excess, dilatoriness, and negligence.*

Originating in Greece, Stoicism became most fully developed in Rome during the early centuries of Christianity and indeed paralleled Christianity in many ways. Christians, in seeking to follow the teachings of Jesus, found that the Stoic moral values were positive and helpful in the pursuit of Christian goals. In fact, when Marcus Aurelius, a pagan, speaks of God, he often sounds Christian.

Stoicism appealed to Rome's leaders because it stressed individualism and public service. The competing philosophy, Epicureanism, emphasized personal pleasure over public service and self-discipline. Lucretius (95–55 B.C.) one of the most famous Epicureans, is proof that the Epicureans were capable of thinking deeply about the world of material experience. But generally, Epicureanism recommended retirement from Rome altogether and often promoted a life of self-indulgence. The great suburbs of Rome often had country villas populated with Epicureans who had retired from the public eye to enjoy a life devoted to pleasure.

Such a life was not for Marcus Aurelius, who examined his actions with a critical eye to ensure that his conduct would withstand public scrutiny. He emphasized nature and the natural because he believed that people were naturally good, naturally rational, naturally virtuous and should maintain self-control in order to avoid distracting themselves from such a state. When he asks (in paragraph 19) whether anyone could really think that we were created only for pleasure, he has the Epicurean view in mind, a view that he felt to be essentially destructive. More than one historian of Rome has agreed with him and has blamed the fall of Rome on the indulgences of Romans who disdained the virtues of Marcus Aurelius.

MARCUS AURELIUS'S RHETORIC

Marcus Aurelius wrote the Meditations *in Greek even though he was Roman because Greek was the learned language of the time. His use of it emphasized the seriousness and importance of what he wrote.*

One of the strengths of Marcus Aurelius's rhetoric is his ability to employ, as Francis Bacon did, an axiom or aphorism: "Make the best of today." "To each his own felicity." "Accept modestly; surrender gracefully." "A man's true delight is to do the things he was made for." He favors such statements because, striving as he did after truth and wisdom, such axioms compress and concentrate the truth most effectively. Wisdom for the ancient philosophers was often expressed in such "portable" observations.

In item 30, Marcus Aurelius tells us to "use language that is seemly but not rhetorical." His own work illustrates his advice. According to his translator, in the original Greek his language is sometimes a bit awkward, the awkwardness perhaps of one writing in for-

mal language that is not the language of conversation. However, in translation his language is straightforward, clear, precise, and unaffected. Much of his communication is interior, as he suggests to us in both his title and in the consistent pattern of address he maintains to a person who, we finally realize, is not another but himself.

Because Marcus Aurelius was a busy public figure, he did not have the leisure necessary to compose a formal, polished work like Plato or Machiavelli. Instead, he wrote in an abbreviated form: his paragraphs represent thoughts that occurred to him, ideas that appealed to him, or problems that he wanted to mull over. Such books came to be known as "commonplace books." Writers might find a quotation that appealed to them, write it down, and contemplate its meaning. Or perhaps they would reflect on a topic that stimulated their interest and jot down their thoughts on that topic. Today, some writers keep journals for the same purposes. In a sense, the rhetorical strategy consists of appearing to have no strategy. Rather, the emphasis of such writing is on creating a storehouse of ideas for future use.

The effect of this rhetorical emphasis is that we as readers can "drop in" anywhere in the book that we wish. With no continuous narrative, no story being told or position being argued, we can read with a kind of innocence. Our guard is down because we do not feel that we are being harangued, which makes us a desirable audience for a rhetorician who is arguing a case. And Marcus Aurelius is definitely arguing a case throughout his Meditations. He wants us to adopt a behavior that stresses our highest qualities as he interprets "highest": we must be virtuous, independent, and courageous. In the glory days of the Roman Empire, such qualities were much admired. Rome flourished when its leaders observed these qualities and suffered when its leaders became tyrants and abandoned them.

Of course, since he is largely speaking to himself, his need to develop an elaborate rhetorical argument is less serious. Clearly, he is preaching to the converted. The generations that have, for almost two thousand years, read his work have valued it because it appeals to the best in people. Even those who do not keep to the virtuous behavior that he recommends realize that it is positive and perhaps the best way to live. His works are admired almost as much by those who do not follow his advice as by those who do.

Stoicism
and Self-Discipline

It will tend to avert complacency if you remember that any claim   1
to have lived as a philosopher all your life, or even since reaching manhood, is now out of the question; indeed, it is as evident to many
others as it is to yourself that even today philosophy is still far beyond
you. Consequently your mind remains in a state of confusion, and it
grows no easier to earn the title of philosopher; also, your station in
life militates constantly against it. Once all this is seen in its true
light, you should banish any thoughts of how you may appear to others, and rest content if you can make the remainder of your life what
nature would have it to be. Learn to understand her will, and let nothing else distract you. Up to now, all your wanderings in search of the
good life have been unsuccessful; it was not be found in the casuistries
of logic,[1] nor in wealth, celebrity, worldly pleasures, or anything else.
Where, then, lies the secret? In doing what man's nature seeks. How
so? By adopting strict principles for the regulation of impulse and action. Such as? Principles regarding what is good or bad for us: thus, for
example, that nothing can be good for a man unless it helps to make
him just, self-disciplined, courageous, and independent; and nothing
bad unless it has the contrary effect.

Of any action, ask yourself, What will its consequences be to   2
me? Shall I repent of it? Before long I shall be dead and all will be forgotten; but in the meantime, if this undertaking is fit for a rational and social being, who is under the same law as God himself, why look for
more?

Alexander, Caesar, Pompey[2]—what were they beside Diogenes,   3

---

[1]*casuistries of logic* Specious or deceptive arguments about ethical issues. Casuis-
try is sometimes defined as a form of false argument.

[2]*Alexander . . . Pompey* All important generals and statesmen. Alexander the
Great (356–323 B.C.) was the first world conqueror; Julius Caesar (?100–44 B.C.), a great
Roman emperor; Pompey (106–48 B.C.), an ally and later an opponent of Julius Caesar
whom he defeated at Pharsalus in 48 B.C.

Heraclitus, Socrates?[3] These last looked at things and their causes and what they are made of; and their master-spirits were cast in one mold. But the others—what a host of cares, what an infinity of enslavements!

You may break your heart, but men will still go on as before.   4

The first rule is, to keep an untroubled spirit; for all things must   5
bow to Nature's law, and soon enough you must vanish into nothingness, like Hadrian and Augustus. The second is to look things in the face and know them for what they are, remembering that it is your duty to be a good man. Do without flinching what man's nature demands; say what seems to you most just—though with courtesy, modesty, and sincerity.

Universal Nature's task is to shuffle, transpose, interchange, re-   6
move from one state and transfer to another. Everywhere there is change; and yet we need fear nothing unexpected, for all things are ruled by age-long wont, and even the manner of apportioning them does not vary.

Every nature finds its satisfaction in the smooth pursuance of its   7
own road. To a nature endowed with reason, this means assenting to no impression that is misleading or obscure, giving rein to no impulse towards actions that are not social, limiting all desires or rejections to things that lie within its own power, and greeting every dispensation of Nature with an equal welcome. For these dispensations are as truly a part of her as a leaf's nature is part of the plant's; save that the leaf's is part of a nature which has no feelings or reason, and is capable of being frustrated, while man's nature is part of one which not only cannot be frustrated, but also is endowed with both intelligence and justice, since it assigns to all men equally their proper share of time, being, causation, activity, and experiences. (Do not look to find this equality, though, in any exact correspondence between one man and another in every particular, but rather in a general comparison of them both in their entirety.)

You cannot hope to be a scholar. But what you can do is to curb   8
arrogance; what you can do is to rise above pleasures and pains; you can be superior to the lure of popularity; you can keep your temper with the foolish and ungrateful, yes, and even care for them.

---

[3]***Diogenes . . . Socrates***   Diogenes (412–323 B.C.) was a Cynic philosopher; Heraclitus (c.540–c.480 B.C.) was a philosopher who thought fire was the basis of all things; Socrates (470?–399 B.C.) was a celebrated Athenian philosopher, the teacher of Plato and often the primary speaker in Plato's dialogues. All these philosophers were Greeks.

Let no one, not even yourself, ever hear you abusing court life 9
again.

Repentance is remorse for the loss of some helpful opportunity. 10
Now, what is good is always helpful, and must be the concern of every
good man; but an opportunity of pleasure is something no good man
would ever repent of having let pass. It follows, therefore, that pleasure
is neither good nor helpful.

Ask yourself, What is this thing in itself, by its own special consti- 11
tution? What is it in substance, and in form, and in matter? What is
its function in the world? For how long does it subsist?

When it is hard to shake off sleep, remind yourself that to be going 12
about the duties you owe society is to be obeying the laws of man's
nature and your own constitution, whereas sleep is something we
share with the unreasoning brute creation; and furthermore, that obedience to one's own nature is the more proper, the more suitable, and
indeed the more agreeable course.

If possible, make it a habit to discover the essential character of 13
every impression, its effects on the self, and its response to a logical
analysis.

No matter whom you meet, always begin by asking yourself, What 14
are his views on the goodness or badness of things? For then, if his
beliefs about pleasure and pain and their causes, or about repute and
disrepute, or life and death are of a certain type, I shall not be surprised
or scandalized to find his actions in keeping with them, I shall tell
myself that he has no choice.

Nobody is surprised when a fig-tree brings forth figs. Similarly, we 15
ought to be ashamed of our surprise when the world produces its normal crop of happenings. A physician or a shipmaster would blush to
be surprised if a patient proves feverish, or a wind contrary.

To change your mind and defer to correction is not to sacrifice your 16
independence; for such an act is your own, in pursuance of your own
impulse, your own judgement, and your own thinking.

If the choice is yours, why do the thing? If another's, where are you 17
to lay the blame for it? On gods? On atoms? Either would be insanity.
All thoughts of blame are out of place. If you can, correct the offender;
if not, correct the offence; if that too is impossible, what is the point
of recriminations? Nothing is worth doing pointlessly.

That which dies does not drop out of the world. Here it remains; 18
and here too, therefore, it changes and is resolved into its several particles; that is, into the elements which go to form the universe and
yourself. They themselves likewise undergo change, and yet from
them comes no complaint.

Everything—a horse, a vine—is created for some duty. This is noth- 19
ing to wonder at: even the sun-god himself will tell you, "There is a
work that I am here to do," and so will all the other sky-dwellers. For
what task, then, were you yourself created? For pleasure? Can such a
thought be tolerated?

Nature always has an end in view; and this aim includes a thing's 20
ending as much as its beginning or its duration. She is like the ball's
thrower. Is the ball itself bettered by its upward flight? Is it any worse
as it comes down, or as it lies after its fall? What does a bubble gain
by holding together, or lose by collapsing? The like is true of a candle,
too.

Turn this mortal body inside out, and now see the appearance it 21
presents. See what it comes to in old age, or sickness, or decay. How
fleeting are the lives of him alike who praises and him who is praised;
of the rememberer and the remembered; how small their little corner
of this terrestrial zone—and even there they are not all at peace with
one another. Nay, the whole earth is itself no more than the puniest
dot.

Give it the whole of your attention, whether it be a material object, 22
an action, a principle, or the meaning of what is being said.

This disappointment serves you right. You would rather hope for
goodness tomorrow than practice it today.

In what I do, I am to do it with reference to the service of mankind. 23
In what befalls me, I am to accept it with reference to the gods, and to
that universal source from which the whole close-linked chain of circumstance has its issue.

What do the baths bring to your mind? Oil, sweat, dirt, greasy wa- 24
ter, and everything that is disgusting. Such, then, is life in all its parts,
and such is every material thing in it.

Death robbed Lucilla of Verus,[4] and later claimed Lucilla too. 25
Death took Maximus from Secunda, then Secunda herself; Diotimus
from Epitynchanus, and Epitynchanus after him; Faustina from Antoninus, and Antoninus in his turn. So it is ever. Celer buries Hadrian,
and is buried himself. Those noble minds of old, those men of presci-

---

[4]Lucilla and Verus were Marcus's own parents. Maximus was the teacher to whom
he refers with gratitude in 1, 15, and Secunda that philosopher's wife. Epitynchanus and
Diotimus are unknown. The emperor Antoninus, who was married to Faustina, was the
adoptive father of Marcus. Celer was secretary to the emperor Hadrian. Of Charax we
know nothing. By Demetrius is perhaps meant Demetrius of Phaleron, the last of the
famous Athenian orators and statesmen, to whom Marcus alludes again in IX, 29. Eudaemon is said to have been an astrologer of repute. [Staniforth's note]

ence, those men of pride, where are they now? Keep wits like Charax, Demetrius the Platonist, Eudaemon, and others like them; all enduring but for a day, all now long since dead and gone; some forgotten as soon as dead, some passed into legend, some faded even out of legend itself. Bethink you then how either this complex body of your own must also one day be broken up in dispersion, or else the breath that animates it must be extinguished, or removed and translated elsewhere.

A man's true delight is to do the things he was made for. He was 26 made to show goodwill to his kind, to rise above the promptings of his senses, to distinguish appearances from realities, and to pursue the study of universal Nature and her works.

We have three relationships: one to this bodily shell which envel- 27 ops us, one to the divine Cause which is the source of everything in all things, and one to our fellow-mortals around us.

Pain must be an evil either to the body—in which case let the body 28 speak for itself—or if not, to the soul. But the soul can always refuse to consider it an evil, and so keep its skies unclouded and its calm unruffled. For there is no decision, no impulse, no movement of approach or recoil, but must proceed from within the self; and into this self no evil can force its way.

Erasing all fancies, keep on saying to yourself, "It lies in my own 29 hands to ensure that no viciousness, cupidity, or turmoil of any kind finds a home in this soul of mine; it lies with me to perceive all things in their true light, and to deal with each of them as it merits." Remember this authority, which is nature's gift to you.

Both in the senate and when addressing individuals, use language 30 that is seemly but not rhetorical. Be sane and wholesome in your speech.

Think of the court of Augustus: wife, daughter, children, grand- 31 sires, sister, Agrippa,[5] kindred, connections, friends, Areius, Maecenas, medical attendants, priests—an entire court, all vanished. Turn to other records of eclipse; extinctions not of individuals but of whole stocks—the Pompeys, for example—and the inscription we see on memorials, "The last of his house." Think of all the pains taken by their predecessors to leave an heir after them; and yet in the end someone must be the last, and one more whole race has perished.

Your every separate action should contribute towards an integrated 32

---

[5]Agrippa and Maecenas were the two chief ministers of Augustus, having between them the management of almost all public affairs. Areius the philosopher was his personal friend and counselor. [Staniforth's note]

life; and if each of them, so far as it can, does its part to this end, be satisfied; for that is something which nobody can prevent. "There will be interferences from without," you say? Even so, they will not affect the justice, prudence, and reasonableness of your intentions. "No, but some kind of practical action may be prevented." Perhaps; yet if you submit to the frustration with a good grace, and are sensible enough to accept what offers itself instead, you can substitute some alternative course which will be equally consistent with the integration we are speaking of.

Accept modestly; surrender gracefully. 33

You have perhaps seen a severed hand or foot, or a head lying by 34 itself apart from its body. That is the state to which a man is doing his best to reduce himself, when he refuses to accept what befalls him and breaks away from his fellows, or when he acts for selfish ends alone. Then you become an outcast from the unity of Nature; though born a part of it, you have cut yourself away with your own hand. Yet here is the beautiful thought: that it still lies in your own power to reunite yourself. No other part of creation has been so favored by God with permission to come together again, after once being sundered and divided. Behold, then, his goodness, with which he has dignified man: he has put it in his power, not only initially to keep himself inseparate from the whole, but afterwards, if separated, to return and be reunited and resume his membership as before.

When the Nature of all things rational equipped each rational being 35 with his powers, one of the faculties we received from her hand was this, that just as she herself transmutes every obstacle or opposition, fits it into its place in destiny's pattern, and assimilates it into herself, so a rational being has power to turn each hindrance into material for himself, and use it to set forward his own endeavors.

Never confuse yourself by visions of an entire lifetime at once. 36 That is, do not let your thoughts range over the whole multitude and variety of the misfortunes that may befall you, but rather, as you encounter each one, ask yourself, "What is there unendurable, so insupportable, in this?" You will find that you are ashamed to admit defeat. Again, remember that it is not the weight of the future or the past that is pressing upon you, but ever that of the present alone. Even this burden, too, can be lessened if you confine it strictly to its own limits, and are severe enough with your mind's inability to bear such a trifle.

Are Pantheia[6] or Pergamus still sitting to this day by the tomb of 37

---

[6]According to Lucian, Pantheia was the mistress, and Pergamus a freedman, of Verus, Marcus's imperial colleague. [Staniforth's note]

Verus? Chabrias or Diotimus by Hadrian's? Ridiculous! And supposing they were, would the dead be sensible of it? Or if sensible, pleased? Moreover, even if the dead themselves were pleased, could the mourners, for their part, be expected to go on living for ever? Were not they likewise doomed to become old men and old women, and to pass away in their turn?—and then what could the mourned do, when their mourners were no more? And all this for nothing more than a bagful of stench and corruption.

In the words of Crito the sage, "If thou has eyes to see, then see."   38

In the constitution of a rational being, I find no virtue implanted   39 for the combating of justice, but I do find self-control implanted for the combating of pleasure.

Subtract your own notions of what you imagine to be painful, and   40 then your self stands invulnerable. "My self—what is it?" Your reason. "But I am not all reason." So be it; in that case, at least let your reason forbear to give pain to itself, and if another part of you is in trouble, let its thoughts about itself be its own concern.

To the nature of the vital force animating our bodies, any frustra-   41 tion of the senses is an evil, and so is the frustration of any endeavor. The nature of a plant has likewise its own frustrations and its evils; and in the same way, any frustration of the mind is an evil to the nature of the mind. Apply all this to your own case. Does a pain affect you, or a pleasure? The senses will see to that. Have you been balked in an endeavor? It is true that if it was made without any allowance for possible failure, such frustration is indeed an evil to you as a rational being. However, once you accept that universal necessity, you can suffer no harm and no frustration. Within its own domain, there is nobody who can frustrate the mind. Fire, sword, oppression, calumny, and all else are powerless to touch it. "The globe, once orbed and true, remains a sphere."

I, who have never willfully pained another, have no business to   42 pain myself.

To each his own felicity. For me, soundness of my sovereign fac-   43 ulty, reason; no shrinking from mankind and its vicissitudes; the ability to survey and accept all things with a kindly eye, and to deal with them according to their deserts.

Make the best of today. Those who aim instead at tomorrow's plau-   44 dits fail to remember that future generations will be nowise different from the contemporaries who so try their patience now, and nowise less mortal. In any case, can it matter to you how the tongues of posterity may wag, or what views of yourself it may entertain?

Take me and cast me where you will; I shall still be possessor of   45 the divinity within me, serene and content so long as it can feel and act as becomes its constitution. Is the matter of such moment that my soul should be afflicted by it, and changed for the worse, to become a cowering craven thing, suppliant and spiritless? Could anything at all be of such consequence as that?

No event can happen to a man but what is properly incidental to 46 man's condition, nor to an ox, vine, or stone but what properly belongs to the nature of oxen, vines, and stones. Then if all things experience only what is customary and natural to them, why complain? The same Nature which is yours as well as theirs brings you nothing you cannot bear.

If you are distressed by anything external, the pain is not due to 47 the thing itself but to your own estimate of it; and this you have the power to revoke at any moment. If the cause of the trouble lies in your own character, set about reforming your principles; who is there to hinder you? If it is the failure to take some apparently sound course of action that is vexing you, then why not take it, instead of fretting? "Because there is an insuperable obstacle in the way." In that case, do not worry; the responsibility for inaction is not yours. "But life is not worth living with this thing undone." Why then, bid life a good-humored farewell; accepting the frustration gracefully, and dying like any other man whose actions have not been inhibited.

Remember that your higher Self becomes invincible when once it 48 withdraws into itself and calmly refuses to act against its will, even though such resistance may be wholly irrational. How much more, then, when its decision is based on reason and circumspection! Thus a mind that is free from passion is a very citadel; man has no stronger fortress in which to seek shelter and defy every assault. Failure to perceive this is ignorance; but to perceive it, and still not to seek its refuge, is misfortune indeed.

Never go beyond the sense of your original impressions. These tell 49 you that such-and-such a person is speaking ill of you; that was their message; they did not go on to say it has done you any harm. I see my child is ill; my eyes tell me that, but they do not suggest that his life is in danger. Always, then, keep to the original impressions; supply no additions of your own, and you are safe. Or at least, add only a recognition of the great world-order by which all things are brought to pass.

Is your cucumber bitter? Throw it away. Are there briars in your 50 path? Turn aside. That is enough. Do not go on to say, "Why were things of this sort ever brought into the world?" The student of nature will only laugh at you; just as a carpenter or a shoemaker would laugh, if you found fault with the shavings and scraps from their work which you saw in the shop. Yet they, at least, have somewhere to throw their litter; whereas Nature has no such out-place. That is the miracle of her workmanship: that in spite of this self-limitation, she nevertheless transmutes into herself everything that seems worn-out or old or useless, and re-fashions it into new creations, so as never to need either fresh supplies from without, or a place to discard her refuse. Her own space, her own materials and her own skill are sufficient for her.

Dilatory action, incoherent conversation, vague impressions; a soul 51 too inwardly cramped; a soul too outwardly effusive; a life without room for leisure—avoid such things. Martyrdom, mutilation, execration; how can they affect the mind's ability to remain pure, sane, temperate, just? A man may stand by a clear spring of sweet water and heap abusive words upon it, yet it still goes on welling up fresh and wholesome; he may even cast in mire and filth, but it will quickly dissolve them and wash them away, and show no stain. How be lord yourself of such a perennial fountain? By safeguarding the right to be your own master every hour of the day, in all charity, simplicity and modesty.

Without an understanding of the nature of the universe, a man can- 52 not know where he is; without an understanding of its purpose, he cannot know what he is, nor what the universe itself is. Let either of these discoveries be hid from him, and he will not be able so much as to give a reason for his own existence. So what are we to think of anyone who cares to seek or shun the applause of the shouting multitudes, when they know neither where they are nor what they are?

Would you wish for the praise of one who thrice an hour calls 53 down curses on his own head? Would you please one who cannot even please himself? And how can a man be pleased with himself, when he repents of well-nigh everything he does?

As your breathing partakes of the circumfluent air, so let your 54 thinking partake of the circumfluent Mind. For there is a mental Force which, for him who can draw it to himself, is no less ubiquitous and all-pervading than is the atmosphere for him who can breathe it.

The general wickedness of mankind cannot injure the universe; nor 55 can the particular wickedness of one man injure a fellow-man. It harms none but the culprit himself; and he can free himself from it as soon as he so chooses.

My neighbor's will is of no greater concern to my will than his 56 breath or his flesh. No matter how much we are made for one another, still each man's self has its own sovereign rights. Otherwise my neighbor's wickedness would become my evil; and God has not willed this, lest the ruin of my happiness should lie at another's disposal.

The sun is seen to pour down and expend itself in all directions, 57
yet is never exhausted. For this downpouring is but a self-extension;
sunbeams, in fact, derive their very name from a word signifying
"to be extended." To understand the property of a sunbeam, watch
the light as it streams into a darkened room through a narrow
chink. It prolongs itself forward in a straight line, until it is held
up by encountering some solid body which blocks its passage to
the air beyond; and then it remains at rest there, without slipping
off or falling away. The emission, and the diffusion, of thought should
be the counterpart of this: not exhausting, but simply extending itself;
not dashing violently or furiously against the obstacles it encounters,
nor yet falling away in despair; but holding its ground and lighting up
that upon which it rests. Failure to transmit it is mere self-deprivation
of light.

He who fears death either fears to lose all sensation or fears new 58
sensations. In reality, you will either feel nothing at all, and therefore
nothing evil, or else, if you can feel any new sensations, you will be a
new creature, and so will not have ceased to have life.

Men exist for each other. Then either improve them, or put up 59
with them.

An arrow travels in one fashion, but the mind in another. Even 60
when the mind is feeling its way cautiously and working round a problem from every angle, it is still moving directly onwards and making
for its goal.

Enter into the ruling principle of your neighbor's mind, and suffer 61
him to enter into yours.

QUESTIONS

1. What seem to be the chief Stoic virtues?
2. Is it clear that Marcus Aurelius is addressing himself, or do you think he
   is writing to another person?
3. Is there any evidence that Marcus Aurelius expected his book to be published and read by others?
4. What is Marcus Aurelius's attitude toward death?
5. Why does he constantly remind us of the shortness of life?
6. What does Marcus Aurelius mean by a "great world-order" in paragraph
   49?
7. Which advice seems to you the least valuable in this selection from the
   Meditations? Which seems of greatest value?
8. How important is ethical behavior to Marcus Aurelius? Of what value is
   ethical behavior to the individual?

WRITING ASSIGNMENTS

1. Marcus Aurelius tells us in paragraph 27 that "we have three relationships": one to our body; one to a divine power; and one to our "fellow-
mortals." Judging from what he tells us in this selection, which of these is
the most important relationship for him? Find evidence to support your
view, considering the general ranking of these three relationships as they
are emphasized in his work.

2. Establish the character of Marcus Aurelius's religious beliefs in this selection. Find all the passages that treat religion or that allude to religious
values. Is it clear, for example, that he believes in a single god, or does he
appear to believe in many gods? What is his concept of the divine? Do his
beliefs sound completely unlike those of a modern religious person? In a
brief essay, clarify his religious views.

3. Stoicism praises the rational qualities in people. To what extent does Marcus Aurelius value his rational faculties? In this selection do you find any
other human psychological qualities that he values significantly? Examine
the passage for observations on the rational faculties and clarify his views.
Is there evidence that he himself pays special attention to the rational in
his life?

4. How does the philosophy of Marcus Aurelius seem to differ from that of
Plato in "The Allegory of the Cave"? On which points would these philosophers agree and on which points would they disagree? How important is
ethical behavior and self-control for Plato? How important is sensory experience for Marcus Aurelius? Choose three or four important points made
by these philosophers and carefully compare their views.

5. In paragraph 40 Marcus Aurelius asks, "Myself—what is it?" How would
you answer this question? Why is it important for Marcus Aurelius to deal
with this issue in the first place? He suggests that reason may be an important component of the self. Is this view acceptable to you? How would
you define self? What has self to do with the material that Marcus Aurelius is developing in this selection?

6. Stoics are most stoical when facing death. Their philosophy permitted
them to accept sudden change and to accept the inevitable. However, they
did not believe in heaven, or any kind of afterlife. Examine this selection
for its discussions of death. In a brief essay, define Marcus Aurelius's position on death and explain how it directs his life. What ultimate effect
does his certain knowledge of his own death have on his everyday behavior?

7. In a brief essay, decide whether Marcus Aurelius is correct when he says
in paragraph 20 that "Nature always has an end in view; and this aim
includes a thing's ending as much as its beginning or its duration." What
evidence in nature do you perceive supports this position or qualifies it?
What effect would such a position have on human beings, if it were true?
What effect would it have if false? In what sense does it serve as a foundation for Marcus Aurelius's philosophy in the *Meditations*?

ST. AUGUSTINE

Memory and the Happy Life

ST. AUGUSTINE OF HIPPO (A.D. 354–430) was one of the most powerful intellects of the early Christian church. His parents sent him to study rhetoric in the city of Carthage, a large cosmopolitan center in North Africa. There he encountered the sins of the flesh, describing himself as degenerate. He lived with a woman who bore him a child in 372. It was not until he read the Stoic philosophy of the Roman writer Cicero (106–43 B.C.) that he began to take charge of his life. Eventually he joined the Manichaeans, a Roman cult. It was founded by Manes in Persia in A.D. 242 and spread rapidly, after considerable bouts with persecution. Augustine found it satisfying partly because it tended to relieve the sinner of the responsibility of sin. However, he soon found it lacking.

Manichaeism was a dualistic religion that insisted on a belief in an eternal struggle between the forces of darkness and the forces of light. The outcome of the struggle between good and evil was always in doubt, and Manichaeans devoted their lives to keeping on the side of good. All that sounds well enough, but the behavior of Manichaeans sometimes demanded extreme action in the name of the

---

Translated by J. G. Pilkington.

good—actions that by any standard verged on the criminal, like, for example, those of religious zealots who kill in the name of religion.

In 383, Augustine left Carthage, where he had been teaching rhetoric, and abandoned the cult. He traveled eventually to Milan, where he heard Ambrose, the bishop of Milan, preach—his first positive experience with Christianity. Also at Milan, Augustine was first exposed to Neoplatonism, a philosophical school that emphasized a spiritual reality beyond the Manichaean materialist struggle. His conversion to Christianity occurred in 386, and he and his son were baptized by Ambrose in 387. Eventually, he returned to Hippo in North Africa. The bishop there ordained him priest, and Augustine established a monastery and defended the Church against several important early heresies. Augustine had become one of the most eloquent and effective supporters of the Christian church. His early works included tracts attacking Manichaeism and other pagan cults.

The Confessions is one of the most original of his many books. It is not a handbook for behavior, such as Marcus Aurelius's Meditations. It does not collect the thoughts of others or try to establish a pattern of instruction, as the Buddhist texts. Neither does it explore strictly philosophical problems, as in Plato's works. Instead, Augustine examines his own personality, his own thinking, his own experience in order to understand the relationship between himself as an individual and his God. Such an autobiographical approach to thought was rare then, but today, in great part because of his pioneering work, it seems commonplace. We expect philosophers to contemplate their personal experience, examine their lives, and extrapolate from their reflections in order to understand the world around them. Augustine set about in the Confessions to examine his own life in an effort to understand who he was and to help other people learn about their own natures.

The Confessions relates the story of his life, including the details of his sins, his complaints about being unable to resist sexual longings, and his lack of discipline. It also describes how he first accepts, then rejects in disgust, the Manichaean cult and how he comes to embrace Christianity. Certainly, he created a first-rate drama out of his life.

The selection reprinted here, "Memory and the Happy Life," is from Book X, the first of four reflective books that are less autobiographical than analytic and imaginative. Throughout the Confessions, Augustine gave thanks to God for helping him to find the true faith, *and in his discussion of memory, he found himself struggling with intellectual issues that are akin to those of modern psychology.*

Augustine examined his memory for clues to his own nature. He treated forgetfulness as if it were an aspect of memory—for how could anyone know that something was forgotten unless memory supplied that information? Moreover, without memory, how could Augustine know himself at all? Augustine argued that one's own sense of self—identity and experience—depends on a keen memory and, by extension, one's knowledge of God. The entire fabric of the Confessions, *finally, depends on memory.*

ST. AUGUSTINE'S RHETORIC

Augustine was a competent teacher and practitioner of rhetoric, and his rhetorical performance in Book X is admirable. Even in translation, the Confessions *stands as a deeply moving and eloquent text. Augustine's model was Cicero, and to some extent his style emulates Cicero's. Augustine's approach to language includes the momentary digression from a subject. These digressions frequently address God directly, resembling miniature psalms: "What then am I, O my God? Of what nature am I?" His expostulations sound like those in the Book of Psalms.*

Along with his reliance on rhetorical questions, Augustine employs the patterned repetition that is one of the most important techniques of the trained writer: "I will pass beyond memory also, but where shall I find Thee, O Thou truly good and assured sweetness? But where shall I find Thee? If I find Thee without memory, then am I unmindful of Thee. And how now shall I find Thee, if I do not remember Thee?"

His comparisons of abstract ideas with concrete actions illustrate his points well. When he speculates how he can know God if he does not remember Him, he compares his search to that of a woman who has lost a drachma (para. 3) and recognizes the drachma when she finds it, because she remembers it. The comparison is concrete, homey, and recognizable. It is similar to the comparison of himself as soil in which a seed is planted (para. 1), with which the selection begins.

He especially excels in various combinations of balance and antithesis, as evidenced in sentences such as "For notwithstanding he rejoices to endure, he would rather there were naught for him to en-

dure." In the following sentence he uses the device of chiasmus, *in which the syntactic pattern* A *followed by* B *is repeated in the second part of the sentence in reverse, as* B *followed by* A: *"In adversity [A], I desire prosperity [B]; in prosperity [B], I fear adversity [A]."*

Even more complex patterning is achieved in a remarkable group of sentences such as "Thus, thus, truly thus doth the human mind, so blind and sick, so base and unseemly, desire to lie concealed, but wishes not that anything should be concealed from it. But the opposite is rendered unto it,—that itself is not concealed from the truth, but the truth is concealed from it." His manipulation of language leads us into an increasingly deep contemplation of many fascinating ideas, so that we feel that we have grown closer to the truth, or at least to Augustine's version of the truth.

Memory and the Happy Life

Truly, O Lord, I labor therein, and labor in myself. I am become a   1
troublesome soil that requires overmuch labor. For we are not now
searching out the tracts of heaven, or measuring the distances of the
stars, or inquiring about the weight of the earth. It is I myself—I, the
mind—who remember. It is not much to be wondered at, if what I
myself am not be far from me. But what is nearer to me than myself?
And, behold, I am not able to comprehend the force of my own memory, though I cannot name myself without it. For what shall I say
when it is plain to me that I remember forgetfulness? Shall I affirm
that that which I remember is not in my memory? Or shall I say that
forgetfulness is in my memory with the view of my not forgetting?
Both of these are most absurd. What third view is there? How can I
assert that the image of forgetfulness is retained by my memory, and
not forgetfulness itself, when I remember it? And how can I assert this,
seeing that when the image of anything is imprinted on the memory,
the thing itself must of necessity be present first by which that image
may be imprinted? For this do I remember Carthage; thus, all the
places to which I have been; thus, the faces of men whom I have seen,
and things reported by the other senses; thus, the health or sickness
of the body. For when these objects were present, my memory received

images from them, which, when they were present, I might gaze on and reconsider in my mind, as I remembered them when they were absent. If, therefore, forgetfulness is retained in the memory through its image, and not through itself, then itself was once present, that its image might be taken. But when it was present, how did it write its image on the memory, seeing that forgetfulness by its presence blots out even what it finds already noted? And yet, in whatever way, though it be incomprehensible and inexplicable, yet most certain I am that I remember also forgetfulness itself, whereby what we do remember is blotted out.

Great is the power of memory; very wonderful is it, O my God, a   2 profound and infinite manifoldness; and this thing is the mind, and this I myself am. What then am I, O my God? Of what nature am I? A life various and manifold, and exceeding vast. Behold, in the numberless fields, and caves, and caverns of my memory, full without number of numberless kinds of things, either through images, as all bodies are; or by the presence of the things themselves, as are the arts; or by some notion or observation, as the affections of the mind are, which, even though the mind doth not suffer, the memory retains, while whatsoever is in the memory is also in the mind: through all these do I run to and fro, and fly; I penetrate on this side and that, as far as I am able, and nowhere is there an end. So great is the power of memory, so great the power of life in man, whose life is mortal. What then shall I do, O Thou my true life, my God? I will pass even beyond this power of mine which is called memory—I will pass beyond it, that I may proceed to Thee, O Thou sweet Light. What sayest Thou to me? Behold, I am soaring by my mind towards Thee who remainest above me. I will also pass beyond this power of mine which is called memory, wishful to reach Thee whence Thou canst be reached, and to cleave unto Thee whence it is possible to cleave unto Thee. For even beasts and birds possess memory, else could they never find their lairs and nests again, nor many other things to which they are used; neither indeed could they become used to anything, but by their memory, I will pass, then, beyond memory also, that I may reach Him who has separated me from the four-footed beasts and the fowls of the air, making me wiser than they. I will pass beyond memory also, but where shall I find Thee, O Thou truly good and assured sweetness? But where shall I find Thee? If I find Thee without memory, then am I unmindful of Thee. And how now shall I find Thee, if I do not remember Thee?

For the woman who lost her drachma, and searched for it with a   3 lamp, unless she had remembered it, would never have found it. For when it was found, whence could she know whether it were the same, had she not remembered it? I remember to have lost and found many things; and this I know thereby, that when I was searching for any of them, and was asked, "Is this it?" "Is that it?" I answered "No," until such time as that which I sought were offered to me. Which had I not remembered,—whatever it were,—though it were offered me, yet would I not find it, because I could not recognize it. And thus it is always, when we search for and find anything that is lost. Notwithstanding, if anything be by accident lost from the sight, not from the memory,—as any visible body,—the image of it is retained within, and is searched for until it be restored to sight; and when it is found, it is recognized by the image which is within. Nor do we say that we have found what we had lost unless we recognize it; nor can we recognize it unless we remember it. But this, though lost to the sight, was retained in the memory.

But how is it when the memory itself loses anything, as it happens 4
when we forget anything and try to recall it? Where finally do we search, but in the memory itself? And there, if perchance one thing be offered for another, we refuse it, until we meet with what we seek; and when we do, we exclaim, "This is it!" which we should not do unless we knew it again, nor should we recognize it unless we remembered it. Assuredly, therefore, we had forgotten it. Or, had not the whole of it slipped our memory, but by the part by which we had hold was the other part sought for; since the memory perceived that it did not revolve together as much as it was accustomed to do, and halting, as if from the mutilation of its old habit, demanded the restoration of that which was wanting. For example, if we see or think of some man known to us, and, having forgotten his name, endeavor to recover it, whatsoever other thing presents itself is not connected with it; because it was not used to be thought of in connection with him, and is consequently rejected, until that is present whereon the knowledge reposes fittingly as its accustomed object. And whence, save from the memory itself, does that present itself? For even when we recognize it as put in mind of it by another, it is thence it comes. For we do not believe it as something new, but, as we recall it, admit what was said to be correct. But if it were entirely blotted out of the mind, we should not, even when put in mind of it, recollect it. For we have not as yet entirely forgotten what we remember that we have forgotten. A lost notion, then, which we have entirely forgotten, we cannot even search for.

How, then, do I seek Thee, O Lord? For when I seek Thee, my God, 5
I seek a happy life. I will seek Thee, that my soul may live. For my body liveth by my soul, and my soul liveth by Thee. How, then, do I

seek a happy life, seeing that it is not mine till I can say, "It is enough!" in that place where I ought to say it? How do I seek it? Is it by remembrance, as though I had forgotten it, knowing too that I had forgotten it? or, longing to learn it as a thing unknown, which either I had never known, or had so forgotten it as not even to remember that I had forgotten it? Is not a happy life the thing that all desire, and is there any one who altogether desires it not? But where did they acquire the knowledge of it, that they do desire it? Where have they seen it, that they so love it? Truly we have it, but how I know not. Yea, there is another way in which, when any one hath it, he is happy; and some there be that are happy in hope. These have it in an inferior kind to those that are happy in fact; and yet are they better off than they who are happy neither in fact nor in hope. And even these, had they it not in some way, would not so much desire to be happy, which that they do desire is most certain. How they come to know it, I cannot tell, but they have it by some kind of knowledge unknown to me, who am in much doubt as to whether it be in the memory; for if it be there, then have we been happy once; whether all individually, or as in that man who first sinned, in whom also we all died, and from whom we are all born with misery, I do not now ask; but I ask whether the happy life be in the memory? For did we not know it, we should not love it. We hear the name, and we all acknowledge that we desire the thing; for we are not delighted with the sound only. For when a Greek hears it spoken in Latin, he does not feel delighted, for he knows not what is spoken; but we are delighted, as he too would be if he heard it in Greek; because the thing itself is neither Greek nor Latin, which Greeks and Latins, men of all other tongues, long so earnestly to obtain. It is then known unto all, and could they with one voice be asked whether they wished to be happy, without doubt they would all answer that they would. And this could not be unless the thing itself, of which it is the name, were retained in their memory.

But is it so as one who has seen Carthage remembers it? No. For a happy life is not visible to the eye, because it is not a body. Is it, then, as we remember numbers? No. For he that hath these in his knowledge strives not to attain further; but a happy life we have in our knowledge, and, therefore, do we love it, while yet we wish further to attain it that we may be happy. Is it, then, as we remember eloquence? No. For although some, when they hear this name, call the thing to mind, who, indeed, are not yet eloquent, and many who wish to be so, whence it appears to be in their knowledge; yet have these by their bodily perceptions noticed that others are eloquent, and been delighted with it, and long to be so,—although they would not be delighted save

6

for some interior knowledge, nor desire to be so unless they were delighted,—but a happy life we can by no bodily perception make experience of in others. Is it, then, as we remember joy? It may be so; for my joy I remember, even when sad, like as I do a happy life when I am miserable. Nor did I ever with perception of the body either see, hear, smell, taste, or touch my joy; but I experienced it in my mind when I rejoiced; and the knowledge of it clung to my memory, so that I can call it to mind, sometimes with disdain and at others with desire, according to the difference of the things wherein I now remember that I rejoiced. For even from unclean things have I been bathed with a certain joy, which now calling to mind, I detest and execrate; at other times, from good and honest things, which, with longing, I call to mind, though perchance they be not nigh at hand, and then with sadness do I call to mind a former joy.

Where and when, then, did I experience my happy life, that I 7 should call it to mind, and love and long for it? Nor is it I alone or a few others who wish to be happy, but truly all; which, unless by certain knowledge we knew, we should not wish with so certain a will. But how is this, that if two men be asked whether they would wish to serve as soldiers, one, it may be, would reply that he would, the other that he would not; but if they were asked whether they would wish to be happy, both of them would unhesitatingly say that they would; and this one would wish to serve, and the other not, from no other motive but to be happy? Is it, perchance, that as one joys in this, and another in that, so do all men agree in their wish for happiness, as they would agree, were they asked, in wishing to have joy,—and this joy they call a happy life? Although, then, one pursues joy in this way, and another in that, all have one goal, which they strive to attain, namely, to have joy. This life, being a thing which no one can say he has not experienced, it is on that account found in the memory, and recognized whenever the name of a happy life is heard.

Let it be far, O Lord,—let it be far from the heart of Thy servant 8 who confesseth unto Thee; let it be far from me to think myself happy, be the joy what it may. For there is a joy which is not granted to the "wicked," but to those who worship Thee thankfully, whose joy Thou Thyself art. And the happy life is this,—to rejoice unto Thee, in Thee, and for Thee; this it is, and there is no other. But those who think there is another follow after another joy, and that not the true one. Their will, however, is not turned away from some shadow of joy.

It is not, then, certain that all men wish to be happy, since those 9 who wish not to rejoice in Thee, which is the only happy life, do not verily desire the happy life. Or do all desire this, but because "the flesh lusteth against the spirit, and the spirit against the flesh," so that they "cannot do the things that they would," they fall upon that which they are able to do, and with that are content; because that which they are not able to do, they do not so will as to make them able? For I ask of every man, whether he would rather rejoice in truth or in falsehood. They will no more hesitate to say, "in truth" than to say, "that they wish to be happy." For a happy life is joy in the truth. For this is joy in Thee, who art "the truth," O God, "my light," "the health of my countenance, and my God." All wish for this happy life; this life do all wish for, which is the only happy one; joy in the truth do all wish for. I have had experience of many who wished to deceive, but not one who wished to be deceived. Where, then, did they know this happy life, save where they knew also the truth? For they love it, too, since they would not be deceived. And when they love a happy life, which is naught else but joy in the truth, assuredly they love also the truth; which yet they would not love were there not some knowledge of it in the memory. Wherefore, then, do they not rejoice in it? Why are they not happy? Because they are more entirely occupied with other things which rather make them miserable, than that which would make them happy, which they remember so little of. For there is yet a little light in men; let them walk—let them "walk," that "the darkness" seize them not.

Why, then, doth truth beget hatred, and that man of thine, preach- 10 ing the truth, become an enemy unto them, whereas a happy life is loved, which is naught else but joy in the truth; unless that truth is loved in such a sort as that those who love aught else wish that to be the truth which they love, and, as they are willing to be deceived, are unwilling to be convinced that they are so? Therefore do they hate the truth for the sake of that thing which they love instead of the truth. They love truth when she shines on them, and hate her when she rebukes them. For, because they are not willing to be deceived, and wish to deceive, they love her when she reveals herself, and hate her when she reveals them. On that account shall she so requite them, that those who were unwilling to be discovered by her she both discovers against their will, and discovers not herself unto them. Thus, thus, truly thus doth the human mind, so blind and sick, so base and unseemly, desire to lie concealed, but wishes not that anything should be concealed from it. But the opposite is rendered unto it,—that itself is not concealed from the truth, but the truth is concealed from it. Yet, even while thus wretched, it prefers to rejoice in truth rather than in falsehood. Happy then will it be, when, no trouble intervening, it shall rejoice in that only truth by whom all things else are true.

Behold how I have enlarged in my memory seeking Thee, O Lord; 11 and out of it have I not found Thee. Nor have I found aught concerning Thee, but what I have retained in memory from the time I learned Thee. For from the time I learned Thee have I never forgotten Thee. For where I found truth, there found I my God, who is the Truth itself, which from the time I learned it have I not forgotten. And thus since the time I learned Thee, Thou abidest in my memory; and there do I find Thee whensoever I call Thee to remembrance, and delight in Thee. These are my holy delights, which Thou has bestowed upon me in mercy, having respect unto my poverty.

But where in my memory abidest Thou, O Lord, where dost Thou 12 there abide? What manner of chamber has Thou there formed for Thyself? What sort of sanctuary hast Thou erected for Thyself? Thou hast granted this honor to my memory, to take up Thy abode in it; but in what quarter of it Thou abidest, I am considering. For in calling Thee to mind, I soared beyond those parts of it which the beasts also possess, since I found Thee not there amongst the images of corporeal things; and I arrived at those parts where I had committed the affections of my mind, nor there did I find Thee. And I entered into the very seat of my mind, which it has in my memory, since the mind remembers itself also—nor wert Thou there. For as Thou art not a bodily image, nor the affection of a living creature, as when we rejoice, condole, desire, fear, remember, forget, or aught of the kind; so neither art Thou the mind itself, because Thou art the Lord God of the mind; and all these things are changed, but Thou remainest unchangeable over all, yet vouchsafest to swell in my memory, from the time I learned Thee. But why do I now seek in what part of it Thou dwellest, as if truly there were places in it? Thou dost dwell in it assuredly, since I have remembered Thee from the time I learned Thee, and I find Thee in it when I call Thee to mind.

Where, then, did I find Thee, so as to be able to learn Thee? For 13 Thou wert not in my memory before I learned Thee. Where, then, did I find Thee, so as to be able to learn Thee, but in Thee above me? Place there is none, we go both "backward" and "forward," and there is no place. Everywhere, O Truth, dost Thou direct all who consult Thee, and dost at once answer all, though they consult Thee on divers things. Clearly dost Thou answer, though all do not with clearness hear. All consult Thee upon whatever they wish, though they hear not always that which they wish. He is Thy best servant who does not so much look to hear that from Thee which he himself wisheth, as to wish that which he heareth from Thee.

Too late did I love Thee, O Fairness, so ancient, and yet so new! 14
Too late did I love Thee! For behold, Thou wert within, and I without,
and there did I seek Thee; I, unlovely, rushed heedlessly among the
things of beauty Thou madest. Thou wert with me, but I was not with
Thee. Those things kept me far from Thee, which, unless they were in
Thee, were not. Thou calledst, and criedst aloud, and forcedst upon
my deafness. Thou didst gleam and shine, and chase away my blindness. Thou didst exhale odors, and I drew in my breath and do pant
after Thee. I tasted, and do hunger and thirst. Thou didst touch me,
and I burned for Thy peace.

When I shall cleave unto Thee with all my being, then shall I in 15
nothing have pain and labor; and my life shall be a real life, being
wholly full of Thee. But now since he whom Thou fillest is the one
Thou liftest up, I am a burden to myself, as not being full of Thee. Joys
of sorrow contend with sorrows of joy; and on which side the victory
may be I know not. Woe is me! Lord, have pity on me. My evil sorrows
contend with my good joys; and on which side the victory may be I
know not. Woe is me! Lord, have pity on me. Woe is me! Lo, I hide
not my wounds; Thou art the Physician, I the sick; Thou merciful, I
miserable. Is not the life of man upon earth a temptation? Who is he
that wishes for vexations and difficulties? Thou commandest them to
be endured, not to be loved. For no man loves what he endures, though
he may love to endure. For notwithstanding he rejoices to endure, he
would rather there were naught for him to endure. In adversity, I desire
prosperity; in prosperity, I fear adversity. What middle place, then, is
there between these, where human life is not a temptation? Woe unto
the prosperity of this world, once and again, from fear of misfortune
and a corruption of joy! Woe unto the adversities of this world, once
and again, and for the third time, from the desire of prosperity; and
because adversity itself is a hard thing, and makes shipwreck of endurance! Is not the life of man upon earth a temptation, and that without
intermission?

And my whole hope is only in Thy exceeding great mercy. Give 16
what Thou commandest, and command what Thou wilt. Thou impos-
est continency upon us, "nevertheless, when I perceived," saith one,
"that I could not otherwise obtain her, except God gave her
me; . . . that was a point of wisdom also to know whose gift she
was." For by continency are we bound up and brought into one,
whence we were scattered abroad into many. For he loves Thee too
little who loves aught with Thee, which he loves not for Thee, O love,
who ever burnest, and art never quenched! O charity, my God, kindle

me! Thou commandest continency; give what Thou commandest, and command what Thou wilt.

Verily, Thou commandest that I should be continent from the "lust 17 of the flesh, and the lust of the eyes, and the pride of life." Thou hast commanded me to abstain from concubinage; and as to marriage itself, Thou hast advised something better than Thou hast allowed. And because Thou didst give it, it was done; and that before I became a dispenser of Thy sacrament. But there still exist in my memory—of which I have spoken much—the images of such things as my habits had fixed there; and these rush into my thoughts, though strengthless, when I am awake; but in sleep they do so not only so as to give pleasure, but even to obtain consent, and what very nearly resembles reality. Yea, to such an extent prevails the illusion of the image, both in my soul and in my flesh, that the false persuade me, when sleeping, unto that which the true are not able when waking. Am I not myself at that time, O Lord my God? And there is yet so much difference between myself and myself, in that instant wherein I pass back from waking to sleeping, or return from sleeping to waking! Where, then, is the reason which when waking resists such suggestions? And if the things themselves be forced on it, I remain unmoved. Is it shut up with the eyes? Or is it put to sleep with the bodily senses? But whence, then, comes it to pass, that even in slumber we often resist, and, bearing our purpose in mind, and continuing most chastely in it, yield no assent to such allurements? And there is yet so much difference that, when it happeneth otherwise, upon awaking we return to peace of conscience; and by this same diversity do we discover that it was not we that did it, while we still feel sorry that in some way it was done in us.

QUESTIONS

1. In what ways does St. Augustine's concept of memory agree with yours? Are there ways in which it does not?
2. Why is memory so important to the quest for self-knowledge?
3. What does memory contribute to a person's search for the truth?
4. Why does Augustine assert in paragraph 13 that God was not in his memory before he searched for Him?
5. Is this excerpt more about memory or about God?
6. Is St. Augustine's personality revealed in this selection?
7. St. Augustine writes, "Great is the power of memory." Does he convince you that he is right? What is memory's power?

WRITING ASSIGNMENTS

1. Examine your own memory and describe it to your peers. What do you notice about the way in which your memory works? What makes you remember something? Is it possible for you to forget things when you wish? What kinds of things do you forget even when you wish to remember them? Is your memory capricious, or is it dependable?

2. What is the relationship of that which you think of as your self to your memory? Is your memory distinct from your self, or is it a part of your self? When you say, "I remember . . . ," what in your psyche is that which you call "I"? Consider the speculations that Augustine raises in his first paragraph when he says, "It is I myself—I, the mind." Do you feel the same way? What is your reasoning on this point?

3. Augustine is unraveling a puzzle in paragraph 4 when he wonders where to search for that which is forgotten if not in the memory. How can it be forgotten if it is in the memory? Examine the process by which you search for information that you thought was in your memory, but that you have forgotten. Does the process bear a strong resemblance to the description that Augustine provides? Is forgetfulness a part of the memory or is it some kind of absence from the memory? Why is Augustine puzzled?

4. Beginning in paragraph 5, Augustine discusses the concept of a happy life extensively. What seems to be his view of the happy life, the life of joy? He connects it with the knowledge of God. What is the connection with memory and the knowledge of God, or of memory and the happy life? Do you feel that memory is a key component of the happy life? Why? In a brief essay, establish exactly what role the memory plays in defining what the happy life is for you.

5. Find the references to God in this selection. Then, in a brief essay, describe the concept of God that Augustine seems to hold. What kind of God does he imagine? Is his concept of God a modern concept, or do you feel it is markedly old-fashioned? Is it difficult for you to understand the relationship he has with God? What are its chief components? Why does he seem to have taken such joy in his knowledge of God?

FRIEDRICH NIETZSCHE

Apollonianism and Dionysianism

FRIEDRICH NIETZSCHE (1844–1900), *one of the most influential modern thinkers, was concerned that the rise of science in the modern world and the changes in attitudes toward religion and the nature of God would leave people with a loss of purpose. Like many historians and philosophers of the day, he feared that modern civilization itself was somehow hanging in the balance, and that unless people struggled to reclaim the leadership that brought progress and prosperity, the foundations of society would collapse.*

His solution for the malaise that he felt was settling on modern society involved a search for meaning through a form of introspection and self-understanding that might well have been intelligible to Buddha, Plato, or Marcus Aurelius. For Nietzsche, self-mastery was the key to transcending the confusion of modern thought. Realizing that self-domination was not an easy state to achieve, he named that man who succeeded in mastering himself "superman," a man who could create his own values instead of blindly following conventional or societal standards.

His own personal life was rather difficult. He was the son of a

---

From *The Birth of Tragedy from the Spirit of Music*. Translated by Francis Golffing.

minister, but his father died when he was four, and Nietzsche was raised by a gathering of family women. There is an antifemale tone to certain of the writings, and some critics have felt that it is a result of his upbringing. It may also be related to the fact that, when a young man, he may have contracted syphilis from a prostitute in Leipzig.

He was a brilliant student, particularly of the classics, and became a professor at the University of Basel at a very young age. His first book, The Birth of Tragedy from the Spirit of Music (1872), is the result of an effort to clarify certain aspects of the music of Richard Wagner, the contemporary composer of the Ring Cycle of operas based on Scandinavian mythology. Nietzsche eventually broke with Wagner on philosophical matters, but his regard for Wagner's music remained strong. The insight on which the work rests, presented in the selection, attempts to clarify the two basic psychological forces in humankind: Apollonian intellectuality and Dionysian passion. Both forces were present in ancient Greek society, which Nietzsche seems to take as a standard of high civilization, particularly in its Doric phase—a phase of clear, calm, beautiful works exemplified by the Parthenon in Athens. Although the Apollonian is opposed to the Dionysian, Nietzsche points out that the Greeks discovered that both forces need to be present together in a culture. The tragedy, he says, was the ground on which these forces were able to meet in ancient Greece. In Nietzsche's time—as he points out in a section not included here—they meet in the music of Richard Wagner.

The kind of behavior countenanced by these two gods is quite different, but each of them represents an aspect of divinity. The rational approximates the ideals of Plato and Marcus Aurelius, but the ecstatic qualities of Dionysianism come closer to the views of St. Augustine, who in his youth was an ecstatic sensualist, and only later in his life an equally ecstatic follower of God. Because these are psychological states of mind that can be experienced by the same person at different times, Nietzsche carefully describes the positive aspects of each kind of behavior.

Nietzsche relies on art to help him clarify the psychological types represented by each of these Greek gods. Apollo dominates intellectually. He demands clarity, order, reason, and calm. He is also the god of the individual. Dionysius, on the other hand, is the god of ecstasy and passion. Obscurity, disorder, irrational behavior, even hysteria are encouraged by Dionysius. He is the god of throngs and mobs. After reading this excerpt, we realize that most of us have both *capacities within us and that one of the challenges of life is learning how to balance them.*

NIETZSCHE'S RHETORIC

The most obvious rhetorical device Nietzsche uses is comparison and contrast. The Apollonian contrasts with the Dionysian; the Greek with the barbarian; the dream with the illusion; gods with people; the individual with the group; the one with the many; even life with death. In this sense, the subject at hand has governed the basic shape of the work.

Nietzsche's task was to explain the different polarities, how they express themselves, and what their effect is. Since these were terms which were quite new to most readers when he wrote this work, it took him some time to clarify the nature of the Apollonian and the Dionysian. In a sense, the first paragraphs are spent in the task of definition. Some of the paragraphs explore the topic of circumstance, a survey of past time, particularly in regard to Greek society. Once each polarity is defined, Nietzsche goes on to explain its sphere of influence, what we can expect of it, and what its implications are. Insofar as those qualities are present in the rhetoric, the essay is itself Apollonian.

There is a surprise in Nietzsche's use of rhetoric here, however. He also illustrates, through rhetorical techniques, some aspects of the Dionysian nature. There are passages in the selection, such as paragraph 5 when he is speaking of Dionysius, which can best be described as ecstatic, poetic—and, if not irrational, certainly obscure and difficult to grasp. The Dionysian aspects of the passage are based on feeling. We all know that there are poems we read which we cannot break down into other words—or even explain to others. What we get from such poems is not an understanding but a feeling or an impression. The same is true of the passages which we confront in this essay. They challenge us because we know that the general character of any essay must be Apollonian. When we are greeted by Dionysian verbal excursions, we are a bit thrown off. Yet, that is part of Nietzsche's point: verbal artifacts (such as Greek tragedy) can combine both forces.

In fact, it may be that Nietzsche's most important point is that both forces yearn to be joined in some kind of artifact. For the ancients it was in the work of the Greek tragedians. For the Elizabe-

thans it was in Shakespeare. For people of his own day it was in the Ring Cycle of Wagner. The ultimate effect of using the rhetorical device of comparison and contrast is to emphasize the fact that these two forces must be unified in the highest cultures. Diversity is everywhere in nature, as Nietzsche implies throughout, but that diversity has one deep longing: to be One with the One. As he says (para. 14), the eternal goal of the original Oneness is its redemption through illusion. Illusion is art, not just dream. The great psychologists who built twentieth-century theories understood both dream and illusion; they are projections of mental states and give access to the inner nature of humankind.

Apollonianism and Dionysianism

Much will have been gained for esthetics once we have succeeded 1
in apprehending directly—rather than merely *ascertaining*—that art owes its continuous evolution to the Apollonian-Dionysiac duality, even as the propagation of the species depends on the duality of the sexes, their constant conflicts and periodic acts of reconciliation. I have borrowed my adjectives from the Greeks, who developed their mystical doctrines of art through plausible *embodiments*, not through purely conceptual means. It is by those two art-sponsoring deities, Apollo and Dionysos,[1] that we are made to recognize the tremendous split, as regards both origins and objectives, between the plastic, Apollonian arts and the non-visual art of music inspired by Dionysos. The two creative tendencies developed alongside one another, usually in fierce opposition, each by its taunts forcing the other to more energetic production, both perpetuating in a discordant concord that agon[2] which the term *art* but feebly denominates: until at last, by the

---

[1]*Apollo and Dionysos (Dionysius)* Apollo is the god of music, healing, and archery, and, as Phoebus Apollo, is also regarded as the god of light. Dionysius is the god of wine and drunkenness.

[2]*agon* A contest or opposition of forces.

thaumaturgy[3] of an Hellenic art of will, the pair accepted the yoke of marriage and, in this condition, begot Attic tragedy,[4] which exhibits the salient features of both parents.

To reach a closer understanding of both these tendencies, let us   2 begin by viewing them as the separate art realms of *dream* and *intoxication*, two physiological phenomena standing toward one another in much the same relationship as the Apollonian and Dionysiac. It was in a dream, according to Lucretius,[5] that the marvelous gods and goddesses first presented themselves to the minds of men. That great healing sculptor, Phidias,[6] beheld in a dream the entrancing bodies of more-than-human beings, and likewise, if anyone had asked the Greek poets about the mystery of poetic creation, they too would have referred him to dreams and instructed him much as Hans Sachs[7] instructs us in *Die Meistersinger:*

> My friend, it is the poet's work
> Dreams to interpret and to mark.
> Believe me that man's true conceit
> In a dream becomes complete:
> All poetry we ever read
> Is but true dreams interpreted.

The fair illusion of the dream sphere, in the production of which   3 every man proves himself an accomplished artist, is a precondition not only of all plastic art, but even, as we shall see presently, of a wide range of poetry. Here we enjoy an immediate apprehension of form, all shapes speak to us directly, nothing seems indifferent or redundant. Despite, the high intensity with which these dream realities exist for us, we still have a residual sensation that they are illusions; at least such has been my experience—and the frequency, not to say normality, of the experience is borne out in many passages of the poets. Men of philosophical disposition are known for their constant premonition

---

[3]*thaumaturgy*   A magical change. Nietzsche means that a powerful transformation was needed for Apollo and Dionysius to be able to join together.

[4]*Attic tragedy*   Greek tragedy performed in Athens, in the Greek region of Attica, sixth century–fourth century B.C.

[5]*Lucretius (100?–55 B.C.)*   A Roman philosopher whose book on natural science was standard for more than a millennium.

[6]*Phidias (fl. 430 B.C.)*   Greek sculptor who carved the figures of the gods and goddesses on the Parthenon.

[7]*Hans Sachs*   The legendary singer-hero of Richard Wagner's opera, *The Master-Singer;* the lines quoted are from that opera.

that our everyday reality, too, is an illusion, hiding another, totally different kind of reality. It was Schopenhauer[8] who considered the ability to view at certain times all men and things as mere phantoms or dream images to be the true mark of philosophic talent. The person who is responsive to the stimuli of art behaves toward the reality of dream much the way the philosopher behaves toward the reality of existence: he observes exactly and enjoys his observations, for it is by these images that he interprets life, by these processes that he rehearses it. Nor is it by pleasant images only that such plausible connections are made: the whole divine comedy of life, including its somber aspects, its sudden balkings, impish accidents, anxious expectations, moves past him, not quite like a shadow play—for it is he himself, after all, who lives and suffers through these scenes—yet never without giving a fleeting sense of illusion; and I imagine that many persons have reassured themselves amidst the perils of dream by calling out, "It is a dream! I want it to go on." I have even heard of people spinning out the causality of one and the same dream over three or more successive nights. All these facts clearly bear witness that our innermost being, the common substratum of humanity, experiences dreams with deep delight and a sense of real necessity. This deep and happy sense of the necessity of dream experiences was expressed by the Greeks in the image of Apollo. Apollo is at once the god of all plastic powers and the soothsaying god. He who is etymologically the "lucent" one, the god of light, reigns also over the fair illusions of our inner world of fantasy. The perfection of these conditions in contrast to our imperfectly understood waking reality, as well as our profound awareness of nature's healing powers during the interval of sleep and dream, furnishes a symbolic analogue to the soothsaying faculty and quite generally to the arts, which make life possible and worth living. But the image of Apollo must incorporate that thin line which the dream image may not cross, under penalty of becoming pathological, of imposing itself on us as crass reality: a discreet limitation, a freedom from all extravagant urges, the sapient tranquillity of the plastic god. His eye must be sunlike, in keeping with his origin. Even at those moments when he is angry and ill-tempered there lies upon him the consecration of fair illusion. In an eccentric way one might say of Apollo what Schopenhauer says, in the first part of *The*

---

[8]***Arthur Schopenhauer (1788–1860)*** German philosopher who influenced Nietzsche. His books, *The World as Will and Idea* (1883–1886) and *On the Will in Nature* (1836; tr. 1889), emphasized the power of free will as a chief force in the world.

World as Will and Idea, of man caught in the veil of Maya:[9] "Even as on an immense, raging sea, assailed by huge wave crests, a man sits in a little rowboat trusting his frail craft, so, amidst the furious torments of this world, the individual sits tranquilly, supported by the *principium individuationis*[10] and relying on it." One might say that the unshakable confidence in that principle has received its most magnificent expression in Apollo, and that Apollo himself may be regarded as the marvelous divine image of the *principium individuationis,* whose looks and gestures radiate the full delight, wisdom, and beauty of "illusion."

In the same context Schopenhauer has described for us the tremendous awe which seizes man when he suddenly begins to doubt the cognitive modes of experience, in other words, when in a given instance the law of causation seems to suspend itself. If we add to this awe the glorious transport which arises in man, even from the very depths of nature, at the shattering of the *principium individuationis,* then we are in a position to apprehend the essence of Dionysiac rapture, whose closest analogy is furnished by physical intoxication. Dionysiac stirrings arise either through the influence of those narcotic potions of which all primitive races speak in their hymns, or through the powerful approach of spring, which penetrates with joy the whole frame of nature. So stirred, the individual forgets himself completely. It is the same Dionysiac power which in medieval Germany drove ever increasing crowds of people singing and dancing from place to place; we recognize in these St. John's and St. Vitus' dancers the bacchic choruses[11] of the Greeks, who had their precursors in Asia Minor and as far back as Babylon and the orgiastic Sacaea.[12] There are people who, either from lack of experience or out of sheer stupidity, turn away from such phenomena, and, strong in the sense of their own sanity, label them either mockingly or pityingly "endemic diseases." These benighted souls have no idea how cadaverous and ghostly their

4

---

[9]*Maya* A Hindu term for the material world of the senses. The veil of Maya is the illusion hiding the reality that lies beneath material surfaces.

[10]*principium individuationis* The principle of the individual, as apart from the crowd.

[11]*bacchic choruses* Bacchus was the god of wine (a variant of Dionysius); thus, this term means drunken choruses. The St. John's and St. Vitus' dancers were ecstatic Christian dancers of the Middle Ages. Their dance was a mania which spread to a number of major religious centers.

[12]*Sacaea* A Babylonian summer festival for the god Ishtar. The point is that such religious orgies are ancient.

"sanity" appears as the intense throng of Dionysiac revelers sweeps past them.

Not only does the bond between man and man come to be forged once more by the magic of the Dionysiac rite, but nature itself, long alienated or subjugated, rises again to celebrate the reconciliation with her prodigal son, man. The earth offers its gifts voluntarily, and the savage beasts of mountain and desert approach in peace. The chariot of Dionysos is bedecked with flowers and garlands; panthers and tigers stride beneath his yoke. If one were to convert Beethoven's "Paean to Joy"[13] into a painting and refuse to curb the imagination when that multitude prostrates itself reverently in the dust, one might form some apprehension of Dionysiac ritual. Now the slave emerges as a freeman; all the rigid, hostile walls which either necessity or despotism has erected between men are shattered. Now that the gospel or universal harmony is sounded, each individual becomes not only reconciled to his fellow but actually at one with him—as though the veil of Maya had been torn apart and there remained only shreds floating before the vision of mystical Oneness. Man now expresses himself through song and dance as the member of a higher community; he has forgotten how to walk, how to speak, and is on the brink of taking wing as he dances. Each of his gestures betokens enchantment; through him sounds a supernatural power, the same power which makes the animals speak and the earth render up milk and honey. He feels himself to be godlike and strides with the same elation and ecstasy as the gods he has seen in his dreams. No longer the *artist,* he has himself become a *work of art:* the productive power of the whole universe is now manifest in his transport, to the glorious satisfaction of the primordial One. The finest clay, the most precious marble—man—is here kneaded and hewn, and the chisel blows of the Dionysiac world artist are accompanied by the cry of the Eleusinian mystagogues:[14] "Do you fall on your knees, multitudes, do you divine your creator?"

So far we have examined the Apollonian and Dionysiac states as the product of formative forces arising directly from nature without the mediation of the human artist. At this stage artistic urges are satisfied directly, on the one hand through the imagery of dreams, whose perfection is quite independent of the intellectual rank, the artistic

---

[13]***Paean to Joy*** This is Friedrich von Schiller's (1759–1805) poem, *Ode to Joy,* which Ludwig van Beethoven (1770–1827) set to music in the last movement of his Symphony no. 9, the Choral symphony.

[14]***Eleusinian mystagogues*** Those who participate in the ancient Greek Eleusinian secret ceremonies celebrating life after death.

development of the individual; on the other hand, through an ecstatic reality which once again takes no account of the individual and may even destroy him, or else redeem him through a mystical experience of the collective. In relation to these immediate creative conditions of nature every artist must appear as "imitator," either as the Apollonian dream artist or the Dionysiac ecstatic artist, or, finally (as in Greek tragedy, for example) as dream and ecstatic artist in one. We might picture to ourselves how the last of these, in a state of Dionysiac intoxication and mystical self-abrogation,[15] wandering apart from the reveling throng, sinks upon the ground, and how there is then revealed to him his own condition—complete oneness with the essence of the universe—in a dream similitude.

Having set down these general premises and distinctions, we now turn to the Greeks in order to realize to what degree the formative forces of nature were developed in them. Such an inquiry will enable us to assess properly the relation of the Greek artist to his prototypes or, to use Aristotle's expression, his "imitation of nature."[16] Of the dreams the Greeks dreamed it is not possible to speak with any certainty, despite the extant dream literature and the large number of dream anecdotes. But considering the incredible accuracy of their eyes, their keen and unabashed delight in colors, one can hardly be wrong in assuming that their dreams too showed a strict consequence of lines and contours, hues and groupings, a progression of scenes similar to their best bas-reliefs.[17] The perfection of these dream scenes might almost tempt us to consider the dreaming Greek as a Homer and Homer as a dreaming Greek; which would be as though the modern man were to compare himself in his dreaming to Shakespeare.

Yet there is another point about which we do not have to conjecture at all: I mean the profound gap separating the Dionysiac Greeks from the Dionysiac barbarians. Throughout the range of ancient civilization (leaving the newer civilizations out of account for the moment) we find evidence of Dionysiac celebrations which stand to the Greek type in much the same relation as the bearded satyr,[18] whose

---

[15]*self-abrogation* The reveler "loses" his self, his sense of being an individual apart from the throng.

[16]*"imitation of nature"* A key term in Aristotle's theory of *mimesis*, the doctrine that art imitates nature and that the artist must observe nature carefully. Nietzsche emphasizes dreams as a part of nature and something to be closely observed by the artist.

[17]*bas-reliefs* Sculptures projecting only slightly from a flat surface; they usually tell a story in a series of scenes.

[18]*satyr* Greek god, half man, half goat; a symbol of lechery.

name and attributes are derived from the he-goat, stands to the god Dionysos. The central concern of such celebrations was, almost universally, a complete sexual promiscuity overriding every form of established tribal law; all the savage urges of the mind were unleashed on those occasions until they reached that paroxysm of lust and cruelty which has always struck me as the "witches' cauldron" *par excellence.* It would appear that the Greeks were for a while quite immune from these feverish excesses which must have reached them by every known land or sea route. What kept Greece safe was the proud, imposing image of Apollo, who in holding up the head of the Gorgon[19] to those brutal and grotesque Dionysiac forces subdued them. Doric art has immortalized Apollo's majestic rejection of all license. But resistance became difficult, even impossible, as soon as similar urges began to break forth from the deep substratum of Hellenism itself. Soon the function of the Delphic god[20] developed into something quite different and much more limited: all he could hope to accomplish now was to wrest the destructive weapon, by a timely gesture of pacification, from his opponent's hand. That act of pacification represents the most important event in the history of Greek ritual, every department of life now shows symptoms of a revolutionary change. The two great antagonists have been reconciled. Each feels obliged henceforth to keep to his bounds, each will honor the other by the bestowal of periodic gifts, while the cleavage remains fundamentally the same. And yet, if we examine what happened to the Dionysiac powers under the pressure of that treaty we notice a great difference: in the place of the Babylonian Sacaea, with their throwback of men to the condition of apes and tigers, we now see entirely new rites celebrated: rites of universal redemption, of glorious transfiguration. Only now has it become possible to speak of nature's celebrating an *esthetic* triumph; only now has the abrogation of the *principium individuationis* become an esthetic event. That terrible witches' brew concocted of lust and cruelty has lost all power under the new conditions. Yet the peculiar blending of emotions in the heart of the Dionysiac reveler—his ambiguity if you

---

[19]**Gorgon** Powerful monster in Greek mythology with serpents for hair. There were three Gorgons, all sisters, but only Medusa was not immortal. With the help of the goddess Athena, Perseus beheaded Medusa, whose very glance was supposed to turn men to stone. Later Perseus vanquished his enemies by exposing the head to them and turning them to stone.

[20]**Delphic god** Apollo. The oracle at the temple to Apollo at Delphi, in Greece, was for more than 1,000 years a source of prophecies of the future. It was among the most sacred places in Greece.

will—seems still to hark back (as the medicinal drug harks back to the deadly poison) to the days when the infliction of pain was experienced as joy while a sense of supreme triumph elicited cries of anguish from the heart. For now in every exuberant joy there is heard an undertone of terror, or else a wistful lament over an irrecoverable loss. It is as though in these Greek festivals a sentimental trait of nature were coming to the fore, as though nature were bemoaning the fact of her fragmentation, her decomposition into separate individuals. The chants and gestures of these revelers, so ambiguous in their motivation, represented an absolute *novum*[21] in the world of the Homeric Greeks; their Dionysiac music, in especial, spread abroad terror and a deep shudder. It is true: music had long been familiar to the Greeks as an Apollonian art, as a regular beat like that of waves lapping the shore, a plastic rhythm[22] expressly developed for the portrayal of Apollonian conditions. Apollo's music was a Doric architecture of sound—of barely hinted sounds such as are proper to the cithara.[23] Those very elements which characterize Dionysiac music and, after it, music quite generally: the heart-shaking power of tone, the uniform stream of melody, the incomparable resources of harmony—all those elements had been carefully kept at a distance as being inconsonant with the Apollonian norm. In the Dionysiac dithyramb[24] man is incited to strain his symbolic faculties to the utmost; something quite unheard of is now clamoring to be heard: the desire to tear asunder the veil of Maya, to sink back into the original oneness of nature; the desire to express the very essence of nature symbolically. Thus an entirely new set of symbols springs into being. First, all the symbols pertaining to physical features: mouth, face, the spoken word, the dance movement which coordinates the limbs and bends them to its rhythm. Then suddenly all the rest of the symbolic forces—music and rhythm as such, dynamics, harmony—assert themselves with great energy. In order to comprehend this total emancipation of all the symbolic powers one must have reached the same measure of inner freedom those powers themselves were making manifest; which is to say that the votary of

---

[21]*an absolute novum* A genuine novelty.

[22]*plastic rhythm* Plastic in this sense means capable of being shaped, responsive to slight changes—not rigid.

[23]*cithara* An ancient stringed instrument, the lyre, used to accompany songs and recitations.

[24]*Dionysiac dithyramb* A passionate hymn to Dionysius, usually delivered by a chorus.

Dionysos[25] could not be understood except by his own kind. It is not difficult to imagine the awed surprise with which the Apollonian Greek must have looked on him. And that surprise would be further increased as the latter realized, with a shudder, that all this was not so alien to him after all, that his Apollonian consciousness was but a thin veil hiding from him the whole Dionysiac realm.

In order to comprehend this we must take down the elaborate edifice of Apollonian culture stone by stone until we discover its foundations. At first the eye is struck by the marvelous shapes of the Olympian gods who stand upon its pediments, and whose exploits, in shining bas-relief, adorn its friezes. The fact that among them we find Apollo as one god among many, making no claim to a privileged position, should not mislead us. The same drive that found its most complete representation in Apollo generated the whole Olympian world, and in this sense we may consider Apollo the father of that world. But what was the radical need out of which that illustrious society of Olympian beings sprang?

Whoever approaches the Olympians with a different religion in his heart, seeking moral elevation, sanctity, spirituality, loving-kindness, will presently be forced to turn away from them in ill-humored disappointment. Nothing in these deities reminds us of asceticism, high intellect, or duty: we are confronted by luxuriant, triumphant *existence*, which defies the good and the bad indifferently. And the beholder may find himself dismayed in the presence of such overflowing life and ask himself what potion these heady people must have drunk in order to behold, in whatever direction they looked, Helen[26] laughing back at them, the beguiling image of their own existence. But we shall call out to this beholder, who has already turned his back: Don't go! Listen first to what the Greeks themselves have to say of this life, which spreads itself before you with such puzzling serenity. An old legend has it that King Midas[27] hunted a long time in the woods for the wise Silenus, companion of Dionysos, without being able to catch him. When he had finally caught him the king asked him what he

---

[25]***votary of Dionysos*** A follower of Dionysius; one devoted to Dionysian ecstasy.

[26]***Helen*** The runaway wife of Menelaus, immortalized in Homer's *Iliad* as the cause of the ten-year Trojan War. She was not "good" or ascetic, but her intensity of living secured her a permanent place in history and myth.

[27]***King Midas*** Midas was a foolish king who kidnapped Silenus, a satyr (half man, half goat) who was a companion of Dionysius. Silenus, a daemon or spirit, granted Midas his wish to have everything he touched turn to gold. Because his food turned to gold, he almost died. Dionysius eventually saved him by bathing him in a sacred river.

considered man's greatest good. The daemon remained sullen and un-communicative until finally, forced by the king, he broke into a shrill laugh and spoke: "Ephemeral wretch, begotten by accident and toil, why do you force me to tell you what it would be your greatest boon not to hear? What would be best for you is quite beyond your reach: not to have been born, not to *be,* to be *nothing.* But the second best is to die soon."

What is the relation of the Olympian gods to this popular wisdom?   11
It is that of the entranced vision of the martyr to his torment.

Now the Olympian magic mountain opens itself before us, show-   12
ing us its very roots. The Greeks were keenly aware of the terrors and horrors of existence; in order to be able to live at all they had to place before them the shining fantasy of the Olympians. Their tremendous distrust of the titanic forces of nature: *Moira,*[28] mercilessly enthroned beyond the knowable world; the vulture which fed upon the great phi-lanthropist Prometheus;[29] the terrible lot drawn by wise Oedipus; the curse on the house of Atreus which brought Orestes to the murder of his mother: that whole Panic philosophy,[30] in short, with its mythic examples, by which the gloomy Etruscans perished, the Greeks con-quered—or at least hid from view—again and again by means of this artificial Olympus. In order to live at all the Greeks had to construct these deities. The Apollonian need for beauty had to develop the Olympian hierarchy of joy by slow degrees from the original titanic hierarchy of terror, as roses are seen to break from a thorny thicket. How else could life have been borne by a race so hypersensitive, so emotionally intense, so equipped for suffering? The same drive which called art into being as a completion and consummation of existence, and as a guarantee of further existence, gave rise also to that Olympian realm which acted as a transfiguring mirror to the Hellenic will. The gods justified human life by living it themselves—the only satisfactory theodicy[31] ever invented. To exist in the clear sunlight of such deities was now felt to be the highest good, and the only real grief suffered by

---

[28]***Moira*** Fate personified; the figure who gives each person his fate.

[29]***Prometheus*** The god who gave men fire—thus, his generosity is philanthropy, the love of man. He was punished by the gods.

[30]***Panic philosophy*** Belief in fate. Oedipus's fate was to murder his father and marry his mother. He tried to escape it, but could not. Orestes murdered his mother, Clytemnestra, because she had murdered his father Agamemmon. All of these were mem-bers of the cursed house of Atreus and examples of how fate works.

[31]***theodicy*** Examination of the question whether the gods are just. Because the gods shared human life, they ennobled it; they suffered evil as well.

Homeric man was inspired by the thought of leaving that sunlight, especially when the departure seemed imminent. Now it became possible to stand the wisdom of Silenus on its head and proclaim that it was the worst evil for man to die soon, and second worst for him to die at all. Such laments as arise now arise over short-lived Achilles,[32] over the generations ephemeral as leaves, the decline of the heroic age. It is not unbecoming to even the greatest hero to yearn for an afterlife, though it be as a day laborer. So impetuously, during the Apollonian phase, does man's will desire to remain on earth, so identified does he become with existence, that even his lament turns to a song of praise.

It should have become apparent by now that the harmony with 13
nature which we late-comers regard with such nostalgia, and for which Schiller has coined the cant term *naïve*,[33] is by no means a simple and inevitable condition to be found at the gateway to every culture, a kind of paradise. Such a belief could have been endorsed only be a period for which Rousseau's Émile was an artist and Homer just such an artist nurtured in the bosom of nature. Whenever we encounter "naïveté" in art, we are face to face with the ripest fruit of Apollonian culture— which must always triumph first over titans, kill monsters, and overcome the somber contemplation of actuality, the intense susceptibility to suffering, by means of illusions strenuously and zestfully entertained. But how rare are the instances of true naïveté, of that complete identification with the beauty of appearance! It is this achievement which makes Homer so magnificent—Homer, who, as a single individual, stood to Apollonian popular culture in the same relation as the individual dream artist to the oneiric[34] capacity of a race and of nature generally. The naïveté of Homer must be viewed as a complete victory of Apollonian illusion. Nature often uses illusions of this sort in order to accomplish its secret purposes. The true goal is covered over by a phantasm. We stretch out our hands to the latter, while nature, aided by our deception, attains the former. In the case of the Greeks it was the will wishing to behold itself in the work of art, in the transcen-

---

[32]*short-lived Achilles*   Achilles' fate was to lead the Greeks to victory at Troy, but to die by an arrow shot by Paris, who had taken Helen to Troy. Apollo guided the arrow so that it hit Achilles in the heel, his one vulnerable spot. Achilles, like many heroes, lived a brief but intense life.

[33]*naïve*   Schiller's *On the Naïve and the Sentimental in Poetry* (1795–1796) contrasted the Classic (naïve) with the Romantic (sentimental) in art. It is not the same as Nietzsche's distinction, but it is similar. Nietzsche uses "naïve" to refer to a kind of classical purity and temper.

[34]*oneiric*   Pertaining to dreams.

dence of genius; but in order so to behold itself its creatures had first to view themselves as glorious, to transpose themselves to a higher sphere, without having that sphere of pure contemplation either challenge them or upbraid them with insufficiency. It was in that sphere of beauty that the Greeks saw the Olympians as their mirror images; it was by means of that esthetic mirror that the Greek will opposed suffering and the somber wisdom of suffering which always accompanies artistic talent. As a monument to its victory stands Homer, the naïve artist.

We can learn something about that naïve artist through the analogy of dream. We can imagine the dreamer as he calls out to himself, still caught in the illusion of his dream and without disturbing it, "This is a dream, and I want to go on dreaming," and we can infer, on the one hand, that he takes deep delight in the contemplation of his dream, and, on the other, that he must have forgotten the day, with its horrible importunity, so to enjoy his dream. Apollo, the interpreter of dreams, will furnish the clue to what is happening here. Although of the two halves of life—the waking and the dreaming—the former is generally considered not only the more important but the only one which is truly lived, I would, at the risk of sounding paradoxical, propose the opposite view. The more I have come to realize in nature those omnipotent formative tendencies and, with them, an intense longing for illusion, the more I feel inclined to the hypothesis that the original Oneness, the ground of Being, ever-suffering and contradictory, time and again has need of rapt vision and delightful illusion to redeem itself. Since we ourselves are the very stuff of such illusions, we must view ourselves as the truly non-existent, that is to say, as a perpetual unfolding in time, space, and causality—what we label "empiric reality."[35] But if, for the moment, we abstract from our own reality, viewing our empiric existence, as well as the existence of the world at large, as the *idea* of the original Oneness, produced anew each instant, then our dreams will appear to us as illusions of illusions, hence as a still higher form of satisfaction of the original desire for illusion. It is for this reason that the very core of nature takes such a deep delight in the naïve artist and the naïve work of art, which likewise is merely the illusion of an illusion. Raphael,[36] himself one of

14

---

[35] *"empiric reality"* The reality we can test by experience.

[36] *Raphael (1483–1520)* A Renaissance artist. Raphael was influenced by Classical forms, but his work became progressively more humanistic, in some cases tending to Schiller's "sentimental." *Transfiguration* (1517–1520), his last painting, points to the new age of Baroque painting: an intense, emotional, ecstatic style.

those immortal "naïve" artists, in a symbolic canvas has illustrated that reduction of illusion to further illusion which is the original act of the naïve artist and at the same time of all Apollonian culture. In the lower half of his "Transfiguration," through the figures of the possessed boy, the despairing bearers, the helpless, terrified disciplies, we see a reflection of original pain, the sole ground of being: "illusion" here is a reflection of eternal contradiction, begetter of all things. From this illusion there rises, like the fragrance of ambrosia, a new illusory world, invisible to those enmeshed in the first: a radiant vision of pure delight, a rapt seeing through wide-open eyes. Here we have, in a great symbol of art, both the fair world of Apollo and its substratum, the terrible wisdom of Silenus, and we can comprehend intuitively how they mutually require one another. But Apollo appears to us once again as the apotheosis[37] of the *principium individuationis*, in whom the eternal goal of the original Oneness, namely its redemption through illusion, accomplishes itself. With august gesture the god shows us how there is need for a whole world of torment in order for the individual to produce the redemptive vision and to sit quietly in his rocking rowboat in mid-sea, absorbed in contemplation.

If this apotheosis of individuation is to be read in normative terms, 15 we may infer that there is one norm only: the individual—or, more precisely, the observance of the limits of the individual: *sophrosyne*.[38] As a moral deity Apollo demands self-control from his people and, in order to observe such self-control, a knowledge of self. And so we find that the esthetic necessity of beauty is accompanied by the imperatives, "Know thyself," and "Nothing too much." Conversely, excess and *hubris*[39] come to be regarded as the hostile spirits of the non-Apollonian sphere, hence as properties of the pre-Apollonian era—the age of Titans[40]—and the extra-Apollonian world, that is to say the world of the barbarians. It was because of his Titanic love of man that Prometheus had to be devoured by vultures; it was because of his extravagant wisdom which succeeded in solving the riddle of the

---

[37]*apotheosis* Godlike embodiment. Nietzsche is saying that Apollo is the god in whom the concept of the individual is best expressed.

[38]*sophrosyne* Greek word for wisdom.

[39]*hubris* Greek word for pride, especially dangerous, defiant pride.

[40]*age of Titans* A reference to the gods who reigned before Zeus; an unenlightened age.

Sphinx[41] that Oedipus had to be cast into a whirlpool of crime: in this fashion does the Delphic god interpret the Greek past.

The effects of the Dionysiac spirit struck the Apollonian Greeks as 16 titanic and barbaric; yet they could not disguise from themselves the fact that they were essentially akin to those deposed Titans and heroes. They felt more than that: their whole existence, with its temperate beauty, rested upon a base of suffering and *knowledge* which had been hidden from them until the reinstatement of Dionysos uncovered it once more. And lo and behold! Apollo found it impossible to live without Dionysos. The elements of titanism and barbarism turned out to be quite as fundamental as the Apollonian element. And now let us imagine how the ecstatic sounds of the Dionysiac rites penetrated ever more enticingly into that artificially restrained and discreet world of illusion, how this clamor expressed the whole outrageous gamut of nature—delight, grief, knowledge—even to the most piercing cry; and then let us imagine how the Apollonian artist with his thin, monotonous harp music must have sounded beside the demoniac chant of the multitude! The muses presiding over the illusory arts paled before an art which enthusiastically told the truth, and the wisdom of Silenus cried "Woe!" against the serene Olympians. The individual, with his limits and moderations, forgot himself in the Dionysiac vortex and became oblivious to the laws of Apollo. Indiscreet extravagance revealed itself as truth, and contradiction, a delight born of pain, spoke out of the bosom of nature. Wherever the Dionysiac voice was heard, the Apollonian norm seemed suspended or destroyed. Yet it is equally true that, in those places where the first assault was withstood, the prestige and majesty of the Delphic god appeared more rigid and threatening than before. The only way I am able to view Doric art and the Doric[42] state is as a perpetual military encampment of the Apollonian forces. An art so defiantly austere, so ringed about with fortifications—an education so military and exacting—a polity so ruthlessly cruel—could endure only in a continual state of resistance against the titanic and barbaric menace of Dionysos.

---

[41]*riddle of the Sphinx* The sphinx, part woman and part beast, waited outside Thebes for years, killing all who passed by and could not solve its riddle. Oedipus (see note 30) answered the riddle: "What walks on four legs in the morning, two legs in the day, and three legs in the evening?" The answer: man, who crawls in infancy, walks upright in his prime, and uses a cane in old age. The solution freed Thebes from its bondage to the Sphinx, but it brought Oedipus closer to his awful fate.

[42]*Doric* The Doric styles were unadorned, clear, intellectual rather than sensual. They represent purity and uprightness.

Up to this point I have developed at some length a theme which   17
was sounded at the beginning of this essay: how the Dionysiac and
Apollonian elements, in a continuous chain of creations, each enhanc-
ing the other, dominated the Hellenic mind: how from the Iron Age,[43]
with its battles of Titans and its austere popular philosophy, there developed under the aegis of Apollo the Homeric world of beauty; how
this "naïve" splendor was then absorbed once more by the Dionysiac
torrent, and how, face to face with this new power, the Apollonian
code rigidified into the majesty of Doric art and contemplation. If the
earlier phase of Greek history may justly be broken down into four
major artistic epochs dramatizing the battle between the two hostile
principles, then we must inquire further (lest Doric art appear to us as
the acme and final goal of all these striving tendencies) what was the
true end toward which that evolution moved. And our eyes will come
to rest on the sublime and much lauded achievement of the dramatic
dithyramb and Attic tragedy, as the common goal of both urges; whose
mysterious marriage, after long discord, ennobled itself with such a
child, at once Antigone and Cassandra.[44]

---

[43]*Iron Age*   An earlier age, ruled by sterner, less humane gods, the Titans.

[44]*Antigone and Cassandra*   Children in Greek tragedies; Antigone, daughter of Oedipus, defied the authorities in *Antigone* by Sophocles (496?–406 B.C.), and suffered; Cassandra, daughter of Priam, king of Troy, appears in Homer's *Iliad* and several tragedies by
Aeschylus (525–456 B.C.) and Euripides (484?–406 B.C.). She had the gift of prophecy, but
was doomed never to be believed. She foresaw the destruction of Troy, and after its fall
she was taken prisoner by Agamemnon. She and Antigone were both heroic in their suffering.

QUESTIONS

1. Begin by defining "Apollonianism" and "Dionysianism." What kind of behavior does each word stand for?
2. What are the important distinctions between the self and the mob? Dream
   and illusion?
3. In paragraph 6, Nietzsche speaks of the "mystical experience of the collective." What does he mean by this phrase? Is there such a thing?
4. Which paragraphs in the selection are most obscure and difficult to understand? Do they seem to show Dionysian qualities?
5. Do you feel that any contemporary art unifies the Apollonian and the
   Dionysian? Would Nietzsche have thought a modern film could do so?

6. Do the distinctions Nietzsche makes give you useful insights into behavior?
7. What ethical issues might the Apollonian person interpret differently from the Dionysian person? Consider especially questions of law.
8. For which of these polarities of behavior is self-control more likely a virtue?

WRITING ASSIGNMENTS

1. Examine paragraph 6 carefully. How valid are Nietzsche's insights concerning the self and the "reveling throng"? Drawing on personal experience, contrast the behavior of yourself or a friend—first as an individual, then as a member of a large gathering of people. Are you (or your friend) "possessed" when a member of such an assemblage? Be as specific as possible in writing about this contrast.
2. Establish a principle of ethical behavior by which you feel the Apollonian can live. Establish the same for the Dionysian. Compare the two personalities to determine their differences and their similarities. What is it about the mental states represented by these polarities that makes their ethical systems different? On what would they agree? Is either of these polarities in danger of appearing unethical to people in general?
3. Music is the inspiration for this essay. Choose a piece of music that is very important to you. Consider it as an artifact and describe the qualities it has that you feel are Apollonian and those that are Dionysian. Is the range of the music—in terms of exciting or sustaining emotional response—narrow or great? Describe your emotional and intellectual reactions to the music and ask others about their responses to the same music. Is music an appropriate source for finding the conjunction of these two forces?
4. Examine aspects of our culture. Do they reveal our culture to be basically Apollonian or basically Dionysian? Be sure to consider political life; education; entertainment of various kinds, including literature, music, and sports; and any aspects of personal life in your immediate environment. In considering these features of our culture, you have an opportunity to use Nietzsche's technique of comparison and contrast. For instance, you may find the Apollonian and Dionysian sides of, say, football as interesting contrasts, just as you may wish to contrast the games of chess and rugby, rock music and Muzak, or any other related pairs.
5. Which of these two polarities of behavior most resembles your own behavior? Are you Apollonian or Dionysian? Define your behavior with reference to Nietzsche. Ask others who have read this selection to comment on your character in terms of the Apollonian–Dionysian distinction. Do you think that you achieve the kind of control that enables you to fully realize yourself in terms of these polarities, or do you feel that control is not an issue?

6. How would Marcus Aurelius or St. Augustine critique Nietzsche's proposals? Would either have been able to give credit to both positions as Nietzsche does? Would either feel that Apollonianism or Dionysianism threatened their ethical positions and their moral ideals? Decide which philosopher would more readily accept Nietzsche's views, but also establish what the limits of that acceptance would likely be.

SIMONE WEIL

Spiritual Autobiography

SIMONE WEIL *(1909–1943) was born in Paris and died in Kent, England. Weil (pronounced Vay) is a highly controversial figure in modern thought, ranking in some people's estimation as among the most important thinkers of her generation. She has been praised by Jean-Paul Sartre, Albert Camus, and T. S. Eliot for the spiritual intensity of her life and her writing. She has been described in terms that are usually reserved for saints. A remarkably contradictory person, Weil was born a Jew yet felt herself to be a Christian. She nevertheless resisted baptism into the Christian faith. Her struggles with Judaism paralleled her struggles with the authoritative aspects of the Roman Catholic church. Always, her sympathies were with the weak. The tenets and practices of institutional religions were often at odds with her thinking.*

She was an intellectual who demanded of herself that she bring her life into accord with her beliefs. She was influenced by Marxist thought when she was at the Sorbonne, and in 1931 she began teaching philosophy at a girls' school near Lyon. Her activities as a supporter of unemployed workers caused a scandal and cost her her job. It was not the last time such activism caused her to lose a teaching

Translated by Emma Craufurd. Originally appeared in *Waiting for God.*

post. In 1934 she began to feel that physical labor is an essential part of the spiritual life, and ultimately she stopped teaching to become a worker. She eventually worked at the Renault plant. It was after she left her factory job she began to think of herself a Christian.

During the Spanish civil war in 1936 she took part on the side of the anti-Fascist Republicans, posing as a journalist. Her health, which had always been frail, was dealt a serious blow when, early in her stay in Spain, she scalded her foot with a pot of boiling oil. She was invalided out of the war and returned to France after only two months. During her convalescence, she traveled to Portugal, then went to Italy where she found herself in the chapel of Santa Maria degli Angeli, where St. Francis of Assisi had often prayed. She found herself kneeling for the first time in her life—impressed, as she said, by a spiritual force that was greater than herself.

She was on extended sick leave from teaching in 1938 when the headaches that she had suffered from the age of twelve became almost unbearable. In the abbey of Solesmes that Easter she experienced a mystical revelation, as she informs us in her "Spiritual Autobiography." As she mentions, too, she became influenced by English metaphysical poetry of the seventeenth century, a spiritual, often mystical poetry that moved her deeply.

In 1939, at the beginning of World War II, she began writing extensively about religious matters and reading and studying Greek and Hindu philosophy. When France fell, she lived and worked on a farm in the unoccupied zone, called Vichy, and left some important writings with spiritual advisers. Among the most influential of the spiritual guides of this period was Father J.-M. Perrin, to whom the letter, "Spiritual Autobiography," is addressed.

In May 1942 Weil and her parents left France for the United States and eventually worked their way to New York. While she was in New York, she attended mass daily. After only a short time she decided that she had to help the French Resistance in England, and she managed to find passage to Liverpool. However, both her earlier pacifist views and the fact that she had fought for the Spanish Republicans—essentially supported by Communists—made the authorities suspicious of her.

Eventually, she attached herself to a Free French ministry, but in response to the fact that some French were dying of starvation in the German-occupied area of France, she began to cut her food to match the rations of her compatriots on the Continent. During this period, she wrote extensively about politics and philosophy. Eventually, she fell ill and refused to eat. In her final illness she also refused baptism *into the church, though she accepted the ministrations of a priest. She died in 1943 of starvation and tuberculosis at the age of thirty- four.*

"Spiritual Autobiography" tells Father Perrin a great deal about Weil's development as a Christian thinker. It also helps to explain why she felt herself to be Christian but refused to be baptized. She seems to have felt the need to remain an outsider, somewhat like Christ himself. Her religion was personal, mystical, outside the in- stitutional church. Her writings are subtle and complex, and they constantly probe the spiritual meaning of life.

Her "Spiritual Autobiography" reads more like a memoir of a sev- enteenth-century mystic than it does of a twentieth-century philoso- pher. Yet it is a document from the pen of a very unusual modern intellectual. It is unabashed, unashamed in describing events that are, to say the least, quite startling and, perhaps, difficult to be- lieve. But, we do not doubt that she believed what she said and that she expected Father Perrin to believe it too.

WEIL'S RHETORIC

This is a very straightforward work. Because it is a letter, it has a specific audience in mind, a priest who had been both her spiritual guide and her friend. Undoubtedly, Weil expected that the letter would be published, and therefore it is not typical of intimate corre- spondence. More like Martin Luther King, Jr.'s, "Letter from Birming- ham Jail," it is written in full awareness of the tradition of the epis- tles of the New Testament.

Interestingly, unlike King, she expected no reply, as she says im- mediately. She wrote the letter on May 15, and she left France forever on May 17. She implies that she and Father Perrin may have time for correspondence later, but her purposes are as explicit as are those stated in King's letter. She is trying to explain her indebtedness to Father Perrin and to convince him that she was not wrong to avoid baptism. Baptism would have brought her into the spiritual fold of Roman Catholicism—it would have made her officially a Christian.

Her letter is detailed, simple, and sometimes surprising. She ex- plains that, though she did not seek God, God found her. She tells us almost matter-of-factly that "Christ himself came down and took possession of me" (para. 21). Her reading had not prepared her for this event, and she is all the more grateful that this was so. It happened in a way that admitted no resistance; her experience was that of a mystic, of a modern St. Teresa of Avila (1515–1582), who described her visions of Christ in her journals, which constitute her autobiography.

When one reads this letter, it must be kept in mind that Weil was by no means an impressionable young woman. When she took a nationwide examination for college, she placed first in France; the great French intellectual Simone de Beauvoir was second. Weil's writings are deep, brilliant, and extensive in scope. They reveal a stunningly capacious mind. Thus, this record of a modern mystical experience cannot be simply dismissed. Rather, we must pay close attention to try to understand exactly what Weil experienced and to discover what that experience meant to her.

Spiritual Autobiography

P.S. TO BE READ FIRST

1 This letter is fearfully long—but as there is no question of an answer—especially as I shall doubtless have gone before it reaches you—you have years ahead of you in which to read it if you care to. Read it all the same, one day or another.

From Marseilles, about May 15

FATHER,

2 Before leaving I want to speak to you again, it may be the last time perhaps, for over there I shall probably send you only my news from time to time just so as to have yours.

3 I told you that I owed you an enormous debt. I want to try to tell you exactly what it consists of. I think that if you could really understand what my spiritual state is you would not be at all sorry that you did not lead me to baptism. But I do not know if it is possible for you to understand this.

4 You neither brought me the Christian inspiration nor did you bring me to Christ; for when I met you there was no longer any need; it had been done without the intervention of any human being. If it had been otherwise, if I had not already been won, not only implicitly but consciously, you would have given me nothing, because I should have

received nothing from you. My friendship for you would have been a reason for me to refuse your message, for I should have been afraid of the possibilities of error and illusion which human influence in the divine order is likely to involve.

I may say that never at any moment in my life have I "sought for God." For this reason, which is probably too subjective, I do not like this expression and it strikes me as false. As soon as I reached adolescence, I saw the problem of God as a problem the data of which could not be obtained here below, and I decided that the only way of being sure not to reach a wrong solution, which seemed to me the greatest possible evil, was to leave it alone. So I left it alone. I neither affirmed nor denied anything. It seemed to me useless to solve the problem, for I thought that, being in this world, our business was to adopt the best attitude with regard to the problems of this world, and that such an attitude did not depend upon the solution of the problem of God.

This held good as far as I was concerned at any rate, for I never hesitated in my choice of an attitude; I always adopted the Christian attitude as the only possible one. I might say that I was born, I grew up, and I always remained within the Christian inspiration. While the very name of God had no part in my thoughts, with regard to the problems of this world and this life I shared the Christian conception in an explicit and rigorous manner, with the most specific notions it involves. Some of these notions have been part of my outlook for as far back as I can remember. With others I know the time and manner of their coming and the form under which they imposed themselves upon me.

For instance I never allowed myself to think of a future state, but I always believed that the instant of death is the center and object of life. I used to think that, for those who live as they should, it is the instant when, for an infinitesimal fraction of time, pure truth, naked, certain, and eternal, enters the soul. I may say that I never desired any other good for myself. I thought that the life leading to this good is not only defined by a code of morals common to all, but that for each one it consists of a succession of acts and events strictly personal to him, and so essential that he who leaves them on one side never reaches the goal. The notion of vocation was like this for me. I saw that the carrying out of a vocation differed from the actions dictated by reason or inclination in that it was due to an impulse of an essentially and manifestly different order; and not to follow such an impulse when it made itself felt, even if it demanded impossibilities, seemed to me the greatest of all ills. Hence my conception of obedience; and I put this conception to the test when I entered the factory and stayed on there, even when I was in that state of intense and uninterrupted misery about which I recently told you. The most beautiful life possible has always seemed to me to be one where everything is determined, either by the pressure of circumstances or by impulses such as I have just mentioned and where there is never any room for choice.

At fourteen I fell into one of those fits of bottomless despair that come with adolescence, and I seriously thought of dying because of the mediocrity of my natural faculties. The exceptional gifts of my brother, who had a childhood and youth comparable to those of Pascal,[1] brought my own inferiority home to me. I did not mind having no visible successes, but what did grieve me was the idea of being excluded from that transcendent kingdom to which only the truly great have access and wherein truth abides. I preferred to die rather than live without that truth. After months of inward darkness, I suddenly had the everlasting conviction that any human being, even though practically devoid of natural faculties, can penetrate to the kingdom of truth reserved for genius, if only he longs for truth and perpetually concentrates all his attention upon its attainment. He thus becomes a genius too, even though for lack of talent his genius cannot be visible from outside. Later on, when the strain of headaches caused the feeble faculties I possess to be invaded by a paralysis, which I was quick to imagine as probably incurable, the same conviction led me to persevere for ten years in an effort of concentrated attention that was practically unsupported by any hope of results.

Under the name of truth I also included beauty, virtue, and every kind of goodness, so that for me it was a question of a conception of the relationship between grace and desire. The conviction that had come to me was that when one hungers for bread one does not receive stones. But at that time I had not read the Gospel.

Just as I was certain that desire has in itself an efficacy in the realm of spiritual goodness whatever its form, I thought it was also possible that it might not be effective in any other realm.

As for the spirit of poverty, I do not remember any moment when it was not in me, although only to that unhappily small extent compatible with my imperfection. I fell in love with Saint Francis of

---

[1] *Blaise Pascal (1623–1662)* French philosopher and mathematician whose most important work, *Pensées* (Thoughts), was published posthumously in 1670 in a version that was totally garbled. It was published again in 1844 in a restored version. He is famous for having pointed out that it is better to believe in God than not: there is everything to lose if God exists but nothing to lose if he does not exist. This has properly been condemned as a cynical and theologically useless argument.

Assisi[2] as soon as I came to know about him. I always believed and hoped that one day Fate would force upon me the condition of a vagabond and a Beggar which he embraced freely. Actually I felt the same way about prison.

From my earliest childhood I always had also the Christian idea of 12 love for one's neighbor, to which I gave the name of justice—a name it bears in many passages of the gospel and which is so beautiful. You know that on this point I have failed seriously several times.

The duty of acceptance in all that concerns the will of God, what- 13 ever it may be, was impressed upon my mind as the first and most necessary of all duties from the time when I found it set down in Marcus Aurelius[3] under the form of the *amor fati* of the Stoics. I saw it as a duty we cannot fail in without dishonoring ourselves.

The idea of purity, with all that this word can imply for a Chris- 14 tian, took possession of me at the age of sixteen, after a period of several months during which I had been going through the emotional unrest natural in adolescence. This idea came to me when I was contemplating a mountain landscape and little by little it was imposed upon me in an irresistible manner.

Of course I knew quite well that my conception of life was Chris- 15 tian. That is why it never occurred to me that I could enter the Christian community. I had the idea that I was born inside. But to add dogma[4] to this conception of life, without being forced to do so by indisputable evidence, would have seemed to me like a lack of honesty. I should even have thought I was lacking in honesty had I considered the question of the truth of dogma as a problem for myself or even had I simply desired to reach a conclusion on this subject. I have an extremely severe standard for intellectual honesty, so severe that I never met anyone who did not seem to fall short of it in more than one respect; and I am always afraid of failing in it myself.

Keeping away from dogma in this way, I was prevented by a sort of 16 shame from going into churches, though all the same I like being in

---

[2]*Saint Francis of Assisi (1182?–1226)* Founder of the Franciscan order of Roman Catholic monks. He committed himself to poverty and a simple life and was a model of pious devotion. In 1224 he fasted on a mountaintop for forty days and nights and experienced the stigmata, an appearance on his body of the wounds of Christ on the cross.

[3]*Marcus Aurelius (121–180)* Roman emperor and an important Stoic philosopher. Stoicism praised self-sacrifice to the state and praised one who could suffer his fate with dignity and in silence. His *Meditations* is his most important work; *amor fati* means love of (one's) fate or contentment with one's lot.

[4]*dogma* The tenets of the Roman Catholic faith.

them. Nevertheless, I had three contacts with Catholicism that really counted.

After my year in the factory, before going back to teaching, I had   17
been taken by my parents to Portugal, and while there I left them to go alone to a little village. I was, as it were, in pieces, soul and body. That contact with affliction had killed my youth. Until then I had not had any experience of affliction, unless we count my own, which, as it was my own, seemed to me, to have little importance, and which moreover was only a partial affliction, being biological and not social. I knew quite well that there was a great deal of affliction in the world, I was obsessed with the idea, but I had not had prolonged and first-hand experience of it. As I worked in the factory, indistinguishable to all eyes, including my own, from the anonymous mass, the affliction of others entered into my flesh and my soul. Nothing separated me from it, for I had really forgotten my past and I looked forward to no future, finding it difficult to imagine the possibility of surviving all the fatigue. What I went through there marked me in so lasting a man-ner that still today when any human being, whoever he may be and in whatever circumstances, speaks to me without brutality, I cannot help having the impression that there must be a mistake and that unfortu-nately the mistake will in all probability disappear. There I received forever the mark of a slave, like the branding of the red-hot iron the Romans put on the foreheads of their most despised slaves. Since then I have always regarded myself as a slave.

In this state of mind then, and in a wretched condition physically,   18
I entered the little Portuguese village, which, alas, was very wretched too, on the very day of the festival of its patron saint. I was alone. It was the evening and there was a full moon over the sea. The wives of the fishermen were, in procession, making a tour of all the ships, car-rying candles and singing what must certainly be very ancient hymns of a heart-rending sadness. Nothing can give any idea of it. I have never heard anything so poignant unless it were the song of the boatmen on the Volga. There the conviction was suddenly borne in upon me that Christianity is pre-eminently the religion of slaves, that slaves cannot help belonging to it, and I among others.

In 1937 I had two marvelous days at Assisi. There, alone in the   19
little twelfth-century Romanesque chapel of Santa Maria degli Angeli,[5] an incomparable marvel of purity where Saint Francis often used to

---

[5]***Santa Maria degli Angeli***   Saint Mary of the Angels, a church in which St. Francis prayed and received enlightenment.

pray, something stronger than I was compelled me for the first time in my life to go down on my knees.

In 1938 I spent ten days at Solesmes, from Palm Sunday to Easter 20 Tuesday, following all the liturgical services. I was suffering from splitting headaches; each sound hurt me like a blow; by an extreme effort of concentration I was able to rise above this wretched flesh, to leave it to suffer by itself, heaped up in a corner, and to find a pure and perfect joy in the unimaginable beauty of the chanting and the words. This experience enabled me by analogy to get a better understanding of the possibility of loving divine love in the midst of affliction. It goes without saying that in the course of these services the thought of the Passion of Christ entered into my being once and for all.

There was a young English Catholic there from whom I gained my 21 first idea of the supernatural power of the sacraments because of the truly angelic radiance with which he seemed to be clothed after going to communion. Chance—for I always prefer saying chance rather than Providence—made of him a messenger to me. For he told me of the existence of those English poets of the seventeenth century who are named metaphysical. In reading them later on, I discovered the poem of which I read you what is unfortunately a very inadequate translation. It is called "Love."[6] I learned it by heart. Often, at the culminating point of a violent headache, I make myself say it over, concentrating all my attention upon it and clinging with all my soul to the tenderness it enshrines. I used to think I was merely reciting it as a beautiful poem, but without my knowing it the recitation had the virtue of a prayer. It was during one of these recitations that, as I told you, Christ himself came down and took possession of me.

In my arguments about the insolubility of the problem of God. I 22 had never forseen the possibility of that, of a real contact, person to person, here below, between a human being and God. I had vaguely heard tell of things of this kind, but I had never believed in them. In the *Fioretti*[7] the accounts of apparitions rather put me off if anything, like the miracles in the Gospel. Moreover, in this sudden possession of me by Christ, neither my senses nor my imagination had any part; I only felt in the midst of my suffering the presence of a love, like that which one can read in the smile on a beloved face.

I had never read any mystical works because I had never felt any 23

---

[6] ***"Love"*** A poem by the English metaphysical poet George Herbert (1593–1633). He was a clergyman whose poems were often profoundly religious. His *The Temple* is a cycle of poems based on the architecture of the church.

[7] **Fioretti** Literally, little flowers. These were important writings of St. Francis.

call to read them. In reading as in other things I have always striven to practice obedience. There is nothing more favorable to intellectual progress, for as far as possible I only read what I am hungry for at the moment when I have an appetite for it, and then I do not read, I *eat*. God in his mercy had prevented me from reading the mystics, so that it should be evident to me that I had not invented this absolutely unexpected contact.

Yet I still half refused, not my love but my intelligence. For it 24 seemed to me certain, and I still think so today, that one can never wrestle enough with God if one does so out of pure regard for the truth. Christ likes us to prefer truth to him because, before being Christ, he is truth. If one turns aside from him to go toward the truth, one will not go far before falling into his arms.

After this I came to feel that Plato was a mystic, that all the *Iliad* 25 is bathed in Christian light, and that Dionysus and Osiris[8] are in a certain sense Christ himself; and my love was thereby redoubled.

I never wondered whether Jesus was or was not the Incarnation of 26 God; but in fact I was incapable of thinking of him without thinking of him as God.

In the spring of 1940 I read the *Bhagavad-Gita*.[9] Strange to say it 27 was in reading those marvelous words, words with such a Christian sound, put into the mouth of an incarnation of God, that I came to feel strongly that we owe an allegiance to religious truth which is quite different from the admiration we accord to a beautiful poem; it is something far more categorical.

Yet I did not believe it to be possible for me to consider the ques- 28 tion of baptism. I felt that I could not honestly give up my opinions concerning the non-Christian religions and concerning Israel—and as a matter of fact time and meditation have only served to strengthen them—and I thought that this constituted an absolute obstacle. I did not imagine it as possible that a priest could even dream of granting me baptism. If I had not met you, I should never have considered the problem of baptism as a practical problem.

During all this time of spiritual progress I had never prayed. I was 29

---

[8]*the Iliad . . . Dionysus . . . Osiris* Homer's epic *Iliad* tells the story of the destruction of Troy and establishes the role of the Greek gods in human affairs. Dionysus was, in ancient Greek religion, a god of fertility and was associated with ecstatic rites and rituals. Osiris was the center of an important early cult originating in Egypt and was associated with the god of the underworld.

[9]**Bhagavad-Gita** Song of the Blessed One; an Indian Sanskrit poem, part of the larger *Mahabbarata.* It is a sacred text explaining the relation of God to his loved one.

afraid of the power of suggestion that is in prayer—the very power for which Pascal recommends it. Pascal's method seems to me one of the worst for attaining faith.

Contact with you was not able to persuade me to pray. On the contrary I thought the danger was all the greater, since I also had to beware of the power of suggestion in my friendship with you. At the same time I found it very difficult not to pray and not to tell you so. Moreover I knew I could not tell you without completely misleading you about myself. At that time I should not have been able to make you understand.

Until last September I had never once prayed in all my life, at least not in the literal sense of the word. I had never said any words to God, either out loud or mentally. I had never pronounced a liturgical prayer. I had occasionally recited the *Salve Regina*,[10] but only as a beautiful poem.

Last summer, doing Greek with T——, I went through the Our Father word for word in Greek. We promised each other to learn it by heart. I do not think he ever did so, but some weeks later, as I was turning over the pages of the Gospel, I said to myself that since I had promised to do this thing and it was good, I ought to do it. I did it. The infinite sweetness of this Greek text so took hold of me that for several days I could not stop myself from saying it over all the time. A week afterward I began the vine harvest.[11] I recited the Our Father in Greek every day before work, and I repeated it very often in the vineyard.

Since that time I have made a practice of saying it through once each morning with absolute attention. If during the recitation my attention wanders or goes to sleep, in the minutest degree, I begin again until I have once succeeded in going through it with absolutely pure attention. Sometimes it comes about that I say it again out of sheer pleasure, but I only do it if I really feel the impulse.

The effect of this practice is extraordinary and surprises me every time, for, although I experience it each day, it exceeds my expectation at each repetition.

At times the very first words tear my thoughts from my body and transport it to a place outside space where there is neither perspective nor point of view. The infinity of the ordinary expanses of perception is replaced by an infinity to the second or sometimes the third degree.

---

[10]**Salve Regina** Hail Mary, a prayer or hymn to the Virgin Mary.

[11]***vine harvest*** At the time, Weil was working in the fields as a farm laborer in an effort to simplify her life and to get in closer touch with the soil.

At the same time, filling every part of this infinity of infinity, there is silence, a silence which is not an absence of sound but which is the object of a positive sensation, more positive than that of sound. Noises, if there are any, only reach me after crossing this silence.

Sometimes, also during this recitation or at other moments, Christ 36 is present with me in person, but his presence is infinitely more real, more moving, more clear than on that first occasion when he took possession of me.

I should never have been able to take it upon myself to tell you all 37 this had it not been for the fact that I am going away. And as I am going more or less with the idea of probable death, I do not believe that I have the right to keep it to myself. For after all, the whole of this matter is not a question concerning me myself. It concerns God. I am really nothing in it all. If one could imagine any possibility of error in God, I should think that it had all happened to me by mistake. But perhaps God likes to use castaway objects, waste, rejects. After all, should the bread of the host be moldy, it would become the Body of Christ[12] just the same after the priest had consecrated it. Only it cannot refuse, while we can disobey. It sometimes seems to me that when I am treated in so merciful a way, every sin on my part must be a mortal sin. And I am constantly committing them.

I have told you that you are like a father and brother at the same 38 time to me. But these words only express an analogy. Perhaps at bottom they only correspond to a feeling of affection, of gratitude and admiration. For as to the spiritual direction of my soul, I think that God himself has taken it in hand from the start and still looks after it.

That does not prevent me from owing you the greatest debt of grat- 39 itude that I could ever have incurred toward any human being. This is exactly what it consists of.

First you once said to me at the beginning of our relationship some 40 words that went to the bottom of my soul. You said: "Be very careful, because if you should pass over something important through your own fault it would be a pity."

That made me see intellectual honesty in a new light. Till then I 41 had only thought of it as opposed to faith; your words made me think that perhaps, without my knowing it, there were in me obstacles to the faith, impure obstacles, such as prejudices, habits. I felt that after having said to myself for so many years simply: "Perhaps all that is

---

[12]**bread of the host . . . Body of Christ**   The doctrine of transubstantiation, part of the sacrament of the mass, establishes that when the priest consecrates the bread (the host) it becomes the body of Christ, which is then partaken by the communicant.

not true,"I ought, without ceasing to say it—I still take care to say it very often now—to join it to the opposite formula, namely: "Perhaps all that is true," and to make them alternate.

At the same time, in making the problem of baptism a practical 42 problem for me, you have forced me to face the whole question of the faith, dogma, and the sacraments, obliging me to consider them closely and at length with the fullest possible attention, making me see them as things toward which I have obligations that I have to discern and perform. I should never have done this otherwise and it is indispensable for me to do it.

But the greatest blessing you have brought me is of another order. 43 In gaining my friendship by your charity (which I have never met anything to equal), you have provided me with a source of the most compelling and pure inspiration that is to be found among human things. For nothing among human things has such power to keep our gaze fixed ever more intensely upon God, than friendship for the friends of God.

Nothing better enables me to measure the breadth of your charity 44 than the fact that you bore with me for so long and with such gentleness. I may seem to be joking, but that is not the case. It is true that you have not the same motives as I have myself (those about which I wrote to you the other day), for feeling hatred and repulsion toward me. But all the same I feel that your patience with me can only spring from a supernatural generosity.

I have not been able to avoid causing you the greatest disappoint- 45 ment it was in my power to cause you. But up to now, although I have often asked myself the question during prayer, during Mass, or in the light of the radiancy that remains in the soul after Mass, I have never once had, even for a moment, the feeling that God wants me to be in the Church. I have never even once had a feeling of uncertainty. I think that at the present time we can finally conclude that he does not want me in the Church. Do not have any regrets about it.

He does not want it so far at least. But unless I am mistaken I 46 should say that it is his will that I should stay outside for the future too, except perhaps at the moment of death. Yet I am always ready to obey an order, whatever it may be. I should joyfully obey the order to go to the very center of hell and to remain there eternally. I do not mean, of course, that I have a preference for orders of this nature. I am not perverse like that.

Christianity should contain all vocations without exception since 47 it is catholic. In consequence the Church should also. But in my eyes

Christianity is catholic by right but not in fact. So many things are outside it, so many things that I love and do not want to give up, so many things that God loves, otherwise they would not be in existence. All the immense stretches of past centuries, except the last twenty are among them; all the countries inhabited by colored races; all secular life in the white peoples' countries; in the history of these countries, all the traditions banned as heretical, those of the Manicheans and Albigenses[13] for instance; all those things resulting from the Renaissance, too often degraded but not quite without value.

Christianity being catholic by right but not in fact, I regard it as   48
legitimate on my part to be a member of the Church by right but not in fact, not only for a time, but for my whole life if need be.

But it is not merely legitimate. So long as God does not give me   49
the certainty that he is ordering me to do anything else, I think it is my duty.

I think, and so do you, that our obligation for the next two or three   50
years, an obligation so strict that we can scarcely fail in it without treason, is to show the public the possibility of a truly incarnated Christianity. In all the history now known there has never been a period in which souls have been in such peril as they are today in every part of the globe. The bronze serpent must be lifted up again so that whoever raises his eyes to it may be saved.

But everything is so closely bound up together that Christianity   51
cannot be really incarnated unless it is catholic in the sense that I have just defined. How could it circulate through the flesh of all the nations of Europe if it did not contain absolutely everything in itself? Except of course falsehood. But in everything that exists there is most of the time more truth than falsehood.

Having so intense and so painful a sense of this urgency, I should   52
betray the truth, that is to say the aspect of truth that I see, if I left the point, where I have been since my birth, at the intersection of Christianity and everything that is not Christianity.

I have always remained at this exact point, on the threshold of the   53
Church, without moving, quite still, ἐν ὑπομονῇ[14] (it is so much more

---

[13]**Manicheans and Albigenses** The Manicheans were a third-century cult whose members believed that good and evil were in a constant struggle for the possession of the world and that the fate of the world was in doubt. This belief was declared heretical because it did not demonstrate faith in the providence of God. Albigensians were a thirteenth-century sect of Christians in southern France; they were Manicheans who believed that all matter was evil, and they practiced a form of birth control in order to prevent the soul—the human spirit—from being entrapped in a material fleshly body.

[14]ἐν ὑπομονῃ In patient endurance.

beautiful a word than *patientia!*); only now my heart has been transported, forever, I hope, into the Blessed Sacrament exposed on the alter.

You see that I am very far from the thoughts that H——, with the 54
best of intentions, attributed to me. I am far also from being worried
in any way.

If I am sad, it comes primarily from the permanent sadness that 55
destiny has imprinted forever upon my emotions, where the greatest
and purest joys can only be superimposed and that at the price of a
great effort of attention. It comes also from my miserable and continual sins; and from all the calamities of our time and of all those of all
the past centuries.

I think that you should understand why I have always resisted you, 56
if in spite of being a priest you can admit that a genuine vocation
might prevent anyone from entering the Church.

Otherwise a barrier of incomprehension will remain between us, 57
whether the error is on my part or on yours. This would grieve me
from the point of view of my friendship for you, because in that case
the result of all these efforts and desires, called forth by your charity
toward me, would be a disappointment for you. Moreover, although it
is not my fault, I should not be able to help feeling guilty of ingratitude. For, I repeat, my debt to you is beyond all measure.

I should like to draw your attention to one point. It is that there is 58
an absolutely insurmountable obstacle to the Incarnation of Christianity. It is the use of the two little words *anathema sit.*[15] It is not their
existence, but the way they have been employed up till now. It is that
also which prevents me from crossing the threshold of the Church. I
remain beside all those things that cannot enter the Church, the universal repository, on account of those two little words. I remain beside
them all the more because my own intelligence is numbered among
them.

The Incarnation of Christianity implies a harmonious solution 59
of the problem of the relations between the individual and the collective. Harmony in the Pythagorean[16] sense; the just balance of

---

[15]**anathema sit** "It is evil"—the church's powerful curse; it is pronounced during
excommunication. It was first pronounced during the excommunication of Martin Luther
in 1520.

[16]***Pythagorean*** This refers to Pythagoras (6th century B.C.), a Greek philosopher who
according to legend developed the tuned string and worked out the relationships between
the notes of the musical scale.

contraries. This solution is precisely what men are thirsting for today.

The position of the intelligence is the key to this harmony, because 60 the intelligence is a specifically and rigorously individual thing. This harmony exists wherever the intelligence, remaining in its place, can be exercised without hindrance and can reach the complete fulfillment of its function. That is what Saint Thomas[17] says admirably of all the parts of the soul of Christ, with reference to his sensitiveness to pain during the crucifixion.

The special function of the intelligence requires total liberty, im- 61 plying the right to deny everything, and allowing of no domination. Wherever it usurps control there is an excess of individualism. Wherever it is hampered or uneasy there is an oppressive collectivism, or several of them.

The Church and the State should punish it, each one in its own 62 way, when it advocates actions of which they disapprove. When it remains in the region of purely theoretical speculation they still have the duty, should occasion arise, to put the public on their guard, by every effective means, against the danger of the practical influence certain speculations might have upon the conduct of life. But whatever these theoretical speculations may be, the Church and the State have no right either to try to stifle them or to inflict any penalty material or moral upon their authors. Notably, they should not be deprived of the sacraments if they desire them. For, whatever they may have said, even if they have publicly denied the existence of God, they may not have committed any sin. In such a case the Church should declare that they are in error, but it should not demand of them anything whatever in the way of a disavowal of what they have said, nor should it deprive them of the Bread of Life.

A collective body is the guardian of dogma; and dogma is an object 63 of contemplation for love, faith, and intelligence, three strictly individual faculties. Hence, almost since the beginning, the individual has been ill at ease in Christianity, and this uneasiness has been notably one of the intelligence. This cannot be denied.

Christ himself who is Truth itself, when he was speaking before an 64 assembly such as a council, did not address it in the same language as he used in an intimate conversation with his well-beloved friend, and

---

[17]**St. Thomas**   St. Thomas Aquinas (1225?–1274) was among the most powerful philosophers of the Catholic Church. His *Summa Theologica* is still studied by modern theologians.

no doubt before the Pharisees[18] he might easily have been accused of contradiction and error. For by one of those laws of nature, which God himself respects, since he has willed them from all eternity, there are two languages that are quite distinct although made up of the same words; there is the collective language and there is the individual one. The Comforter whom Christ sends us, the Spirit of truth, speaks one or other of these languages, whichever circumstances demand, and by a necessity of their nature there is not agreement between them.

When genuine friends of God—such as was Eckhart[19] to my way of thinking—repeat words they have heard in secret amidst the silence of the union of love, and these words are in disagreement with the teaching of the Church, it is simply that the language of the market place is not that of the nuptial chamber. 65

Everybody knows that really intimate conversation is only possible between two or three. As soon as there are six or seven, collective language begins to dominate. That is why it is a complete misinterpretation to apply to the Church the words "Wheresoever two or three are gathered together in my name, there am I in the midst of them." Christ did not say two hundred, or fifty, or ten. He said two or three. He said precisely that he always forms the third in the intimacy of the tête-à-tête.[20] 65

Christ made promises to the Church, but none of these promises has the force of the expression "Thy Father who seeth in secret."[21] The word of God is the secret word. He who has not heard this word, even if he adheres to all the dogmas taught by the Church, has no contact with truth. 67

---

[18]***Pharisees*** Members of a Jewish group concerned with the law, both in its written and oral forms. Jesus spoke with them concerning the law and its interpretations. See Luke 7. Paul said, ". . . after the most straitest sect of our religion I lived a Pharisee," Acts 26:5.

[19]***Meister Johannes Eckhart (1260?–1327)*** An important early German mystic and theologian. The church found it difficult to accept some of his teachings, and some things he said were condemned after his death. He believed that God was everything— that everything had its own essence but that its existence was only in God. His ideas have sometimes been thought to be pantheistic—seeing God in everything.

[20]***tête-à-tête*** Literally, "head to head;" an intimate conversation.

[21]***"Thy Father who seeth in secret."*** Matthew 6:1–4: "Take heed that ye do not your alms before men, to be seen of them: otherwise ye have no reward of your Father which is in heaven. Therefore when thou doest thine alms, do not sound a trumpet before thee, as the hypocrites do in the synagogues and in the streets, that they may have glory of men. Verily I say unto you, They have their reward. But when thou doest alms, let not thy left hand know what thy right hand doeth: That thine alms may be in secret: and thy Father which seeth in secret himself shall reward thee openly."

The function of the Church as the collective keeper of dogma is 68 indispensable. She has the right and the duty to punish those who make a clear attack upon her within the specific range of this function, by depriving them of the sacraments.

Thus, although I know practically nothing of this business, I in- 69 cline to think provisionally that she was right to punish Luther.[22]

But she is guilty of an abuse of power when she claims to force 70 love and intelligence to model their language upon her own. This abuse of power is not of God. It comes from the natural tendency of every form of collectivism, without exception, to abuse power.

The image of the Mystical Body of Christ is very attractive. But I 71 consider the importance given to this image today as one of the most serious signs of our degeneration. For our true dignity is not to be parts of a body, even though it be a mystical one, even though it be that of Christ. It consists in this, that in the state of perfection, which is the vocation of each one of us, we no longer live in ourselves, but Christ lives in us; so that through our perfection Christ in his integrity and in his indivisible unity, becomes in a sense each one of us, as he is completely in each host. The hosts are not a *part* of his body.

This present-day importance of the image of the Mystical Body 72 shows how wretchedly susceptible Christians are to outside influences. Undoubtedly there is real intoxication in being a member of the Mystical Body of Christ. But today a great many other mystical bodies, which have not Christ for their head, produce an intoxication in their members that to my way of thinking is of the same order.

As long as it is through obedience, I find sweetness in my depriva- 73 tion of the joy of membership in the Mystical Body of Christ. For if God is willing to help me, I may thus bear witness that without this joy one can nevertheless be faithful to Christ unto death. Social enthusiasms have such power today, they raise people so effectively to the supreme degree of heroism in suffering and death, that I think it is as well that a few sheep should remain outside the fold in order to bear witness that the love of Christ is essentially something different.

The Church today defends the cause of the indefeasible rights[23] of 74

---

[22]**Martin Luther (1483–1546)** German theologian whose ninety-five theses in 1517 began the Protestant Reformation. He was excommunicated from the Roman Catholic church for refusing to change his stand on the question of whether good deeds contributed to salvation; he insisted that only faith mattered: doing good deeds was irrelevant to one's salvation.

[23]**indefeasible rights** Rights that cannot be made otherwise or cannot be repealed. They are absolute rights.

the individual against collective oppression, of liberty of thought against tyranny. But these are causes readily embraced by those who find themselves momentarily to be the least strong. It is their only way of perhaps one day becoming the strongest. That is well known.

You may perhaps be offended by this idea. You are not the Church. 75 During the periods of the most atrocious abuse of power committed by the Church, there must have been some priests like you among the others. Your good faith is not a guarantee, even were it shared by all your Order. You cannot foresee what turn things may take.

In order that the present attitude of the Church should be effective 76 and that she should really penetrate like a wedge into social existence, she would have to say openly that she had changed or wished to change. Otherwise who could take her seriously when they remembered the Inquisition?[24] My friendship for you, which I extend through you to all your Order, makes it very painful for me to bring this up. But it existed. After the fall of the Roman Empire, which had been totalitarian, it was the Church that was the first to establish a rough sort of totalitarianism in Europe in the thirteenth century, after the war with the Albigenses. This tree bore much fruit.

And the motive power of this totalitarianism was the use of those 77 two little words: *anathema sit.*

It was moreover by a judicious transposition of this use that all the 78 parties which in our own day have founded totalitarian régimes were shaped. This is a point of history I have specially studied.

I must give you the impression of a Luciferian pride is speaking 79 thus of a great many matters that are too high for me and about which I have no right to understand anything. It is not my fault. Ideas come and settle in my mind by mistake, then, realizing their mistake, they absolutely insist on coming out. I do not know where they come from, or what they are worth, but, whatever the risk, I do not think I have the right to prevent this operation.

Good-by, I wish you all possible good things except the cross; for I 80 do not love my neighbor as myself, you particularly, as you have noticed. But Christ granted to his well-beloved disciple, and probably to all that disciple's spiritual lineage, to come to him not through degradation, defilement, and distress, but in uninterrupted joy, purity, and

---

[24]***the Inquisition*** An organization founded by the church in the thirteenth century to root out heresy. It became a tyrannical court of inquiry which often tortured and executed its victims and expressed its power whimsically and viciously. It has become a symbol of the excesses that even benign powerful institutions such as the church sometimes can resort to.

sweetness. That is why I can allow myself to wish that even if one day you have the honor of dying a violent death for Our Lord, it may be with joy and without any anguish; also that only three of the beatitudes[25] (*mites, mundo corde, pacifici*) will apply to you. All the others involve more or less of suffering.

This wish is not due only to the frailty of human friendship. For, 81 with any human being taken individually, I always find reasons for concluding that sorrow and misfortune do not suit him, either because he seems too mediocre for anything so great or, on the contrary, too precious to be destroyed. One cannot fail more seriously in the second of the two essential commandments. And as to the first, I fail to observe that, in a still more horrible manner, for every time I think of the crucifixion of Christ I commit the sin of envy.

Believe more than ever and forever in my filial and tenderly grate- 82 ful friendship.

SIMONE WEIL

---

[25]***three of the beatitudes*** A reference to Christ's Sermon on the Mount, which begins, "Blessed are the poor in spirit." *Mites, mundo corde, pacifici* are the humble, the pure of heart, and the peacemakers.

QUESTIONS

1. Why does Weil tell Father Perrin that she was not brought to Christianity by means of human intervention? What does she mean by human intervention?
2. Does Weil seem aware that she was following a path to enlightenment? Which signs gave her that awareness?
3. What were the principal circumstances that helped Weil in her search for religious guidance?
4. Weil is deeply concerned with the nature of God. How does she imagine God? In any of her reflections on God's nature, is God a physical being?
5. What are Weil's feelings about her fellow humans? Is she concerned with the human condition or only with God and the divine condition?

WRITING ASSIGNMENTS

1. Write a letter to Simone Weil in which you present your version of a spiritual autobiography. Explore some of the same experiences as she does and explain the path that led you to your spiritual insights. Be sure to concentrate on your experiences and to describe them in detail.

2. Keeping in mind that Weil never formally joined the Catholic church, examine this selection for its statements concerning her religious views and opinions. Is Weil religious? How can someone be religious but still be reluctant to join a religion? Is there a difference in Weil's mind between being religious and being spiritual? Does joining a religion imperil one's spiritual development, according to Weil?

3. Compare Weil's statements about God with those of Mary Daly in the next selection. Daly is concerned that the Catholic church has put restrictions on itself by promoting symbols of religion that show God the Father as a man. Examine Weil's piece to determine just how she conceives the nature of God. Does her conception of God meet Mary Daly's need for change? Are you satisfied with Weil's conception of God, or do you feel that she is too conventional (or unconventional) in her thinking? Is God a spiritual concept to her?

4. What are the differences between Weil's path to enlightenment and the path to enlightenment suggested by the Buddha in his instructions for meditation? Are the religious ends the same or different? Could you say that Weil is seeking the same kind of "peace that passes understanding," or are her concerns quite different?

5. Ideally, what would Weil desire in a church? What could an institution that calls itself a religion ever give her that would support her spiritual needs? By what forces is she drawn to religion? Are they forces that emanate from a church? Why does she write her spiritual autobiography to a priest, an official member of the Catholic church whom she addresses in a formal way as "Father"? And how can the Catholic church, or any church, benefit from her spiritual insight?

6. Compare Simone Weil's views with those of people you know personally. Do you know people with a spiritual guest? How close to Weil's spiritual path is their path? Do you think that Weil would conduct herself differently if she were alive today and living in your society or immediate environment? Would she be tempted to be less or more spiritual?

7. Do you see evidence that Simone Weil had read Plato, Marcus Aurelius, St. Augustine, and Nietzsche? She was a fine scholar, and it is certain that she was familiar with these writers. Did their thinking affect hers? Did their thinking affect her spiritual mission or the direction of her quest?

8. What troubles Simone Weil about the Catholic church as an institution? She complains in several passages about the nature of the institution and why she is reluctant to become a member. Do you feel that her concerns are legitimate, or are they the result of a misunderstanding? Write an essay addressed to Weil in which you take a stand on whether or not the church as an institution is likely to further or inhibit her quest for a spiritually meaningful life.

MARY DALY

The Qualitative Leap
Beyond Patriarchal Religion

MARY DALY (b. 1928) is arguably the most prominent feminist
philosopher in America. She was educated in Roman Catholic schools
in the United States and later attended the University of Fribourg in
Switzerland, where she received an St.D. in theology in 1963 and a
Ph.D. in philosophy in 1965. (She holds a total of three doctorates.)
She currently teaches at Boston College where she is an associate professor in the Department of Theology. She describes herself as a
"PostChristian," a term designed to reflect her belief that the patriarchal underpinnings of all major religions have been damaging to all
women. Her reputation as a radical feminist has often caused her difficulty in her academic career, but she has persisted in discussing the
united goals of feminism, existentialism, and theology.

Her work is controversial and marked by a level of ethical seriousness that is second to none. As she tells us in "The Qualitative Leap
Beyond Patriarchal Religion," some of the great injustices in the
world have been supported by the church's patriarchal imagery and
symbolism. In general, patriarchy is a social structure that favors
men ("patriarchy" is derived from the Latin for "father"). The church

---

From *Quest: A Feminist Quarterly*, Vol. I, No. 4, Spring 1975.

patriarchs are the church fathers who have written virtually all of the documents that govern the church and that serve to interpret the laws of the religion.

Daly believes that patriarchy has so structured the church that women really have no voice in what is done or how it is done. Moreover, she feels that the primary symbols of the Christian church, such as the concept of the Trinity, are transparently gender based and designed to keep women second-class citizens. Some of her writings are among the most influential texts of modern religious social theory. Her works include Natural Knowledge of God in the Philosophy of Jacques Maritain *(1966);* The Church and the Second Sex *(1968), its title a clear allusion to Simone de Beauvoir;* Beyond God the Father: Toward a Philosophy of Women's Liberation *(1973);* Gyn/Ecology: The Metaethics of Radical Feminism *(1978);* Pure Lust: Elemental Feminist Philosophy *(1984); and* Websters' First New Intergalactic Wickedary of the English Language *(1987) [conjured in cahoots with Jane Caputi]. These works have placed her in the forefront of modern feminist theory.*

Her latest book incorporates many interesting discussions centering on words, and in doing so reminds us, as does the essay included here, that language can be either a tool of oppression or a tool of liberation. She calls her discussion of language a "Wickedary" because it supplies new meaning to words, such as "Witch," that standard dictionaries define in a negative way. Daly suggests that a Witch is a woman who is an advanced (read "radical") feminist in a society that will not tolerate her.

One of the most interesting sections of "The Qualitative Leap Beyond Patriarchal Religion" begins at paragraph 43 with her discussion of the word "androgyny," the combination of male and female qualities. She brings care and skill to her analysis of the word. At one point, she considers turning the word around and spelling it "gynandry," with the female part of the word appearing first. In part, this reworking reorients us to the concepts that underlie the term, but it also reminds us that in dealing with the term on any level, we are also dealing with male and female stereotypes that are socially structured rather than biologically given.

In another discussion of language, Daly discusses the words "God" and "Goddess." She regards the use of "God" language as a kind of intellectual prison from which both she and we need to break. For her, the concept of 'Be-ing' seems closer to what others mean when they use the word God in a sense that is not gender linked (if avoiding gender-based descriptions is at all possible).

For her, much of the problem lies in religious images such as the Trinity, which she describes as the "All Male Divine Family." Recognizing the problems that a religious image system involves and that women must always emerge a distant second, she recommends that the concept of the transcendent become something other than a physical man, such as Jesus, and become instead an ontological force that reaches far beyond our traditional concepts. Such thinking is not foreign to religion, or even to Christianity. One of the most important of contemporary Christian theologians, Paul Tillich (1886–1965), wrote extensively in his book Dynamics of Faith *(1957) about the effect of symbolism in religion. Daly agrees with his proposal that the idea of the transcendent be detached from the emblem of a specific human figure. She believes that such a choice will help to rid religion of its oppressiveness.*

Underlying much of her discussion of language is her conviction that radical feminism cannot settle for a simple redistribution of masculine power. Feminism must create something quite new: an order of thought that is free of gender-based illusions and gender-based privilege, for these always reduce the women in the world to subservience.

One of her demands (paras. 29–34) is a "remythologization" of male institutions, starting with the concept of the procession (academic, religious, military—cermonies of all kinds led by males). The idea of the procession was analyzed earlier by Virginia Woolf, the world-famous writer who was excluded from academic processions: specifically, the graduating class of a university. Because she was a woman, Woolf could not attend the university (she was overage when British universities finally admitted women) or even use the library of the university for her research. Because she was so excluded, Woolf began to question why she should support the professions that all depended on the procession of graduation. It was, as she said, a procession of the "sons of educated men." Woolf said, in Three Guineas, *"Nothing would induce the authorities encamped within the sacred gates to allow the women to enter. They said that God was on their side, Nature was on their side, Law was on their side, and Property was on their side. The college was founded for the benefit of men only; men only were entitled by law to benefit from its endowments." Daly interprets the male-controlled professions, "church, state, university, army," as gynocidal: death to women. But she also regards them as genocidal, implying death for men and women alike. Although she does not elaborate on this theme in this essay, she believes that the male stereotype of aggressive behavior is at the root of war and destruction.*

DALY'S RHETORIC

This essay was originally delivered as a paper at an international symposium to a primarily male audience of theologians and sociologists; later it appeared in this abridged form in Quest, *a feminist journal that is no longer published. Daly did not expect to change the minds of the conservative audience at the conference, nor to encounter serious resistance to her ideas from the readers of* Quest. *Thus, she does not employ a rhetorical strategy explicitly designed to "reason" the audience into agreement with her.*

In a manner reminiscent of Jefferson's Declaration of Independence, Daly begins by listing twenty-three items that must be addressed by women who are "becoming." This strategy is sometimes called enumeration and recalls not only Jefferson but also Francis Bacon, who enumerates four areas of discussion in "The Four Idols." The technique, useful for its clarity and its capacity to isolate issues for discussion, also possesses the quality of the pronunciamento, a tactic especially fitting for an essay on the oppression of a group of people because the items demand explication and expansion. For example, in item six Daly writes that the symbols of Christianity are essentially sexist and related to such godfathers as Vito Corleone, the fictional (and symbolic) head of the Mafia, a statement that requires further discussion.

Her rhetorical strategy is based on identifying a condition: the patriarchy of the church, as upheld by the patriarchal imagery and symbolism that have characterized the church from the beginning. Consequently, her definition of patriarchy and her representation of the symbolism remain critical to her position. For those who may not already agree with her position, her claims that the gender distinctions that exist in our society make it a "rapist society" may sound exaggerated. But, a few days spent listening to TV or radio news or reading the newspapers of any major city ought to help anyone to understand her point.

Another aspect of her rhetorical strategy consists of her realization that she is unlikely to convince anyone to whom her cause is not already important. Many men may feel that the existing imagery and symbolism of the church are appropriate and are also historically validated by the Bible. Therefore, Daly knows that her reasoning, no matter how effective, will not alter the male point of view. In her article, After the Death of God the Father, she holds out a specter for the church to consider: religion, if it does not rid itself of its oppressive tendencies, will "go out of business."

The Qualitative Leap
Beyond Patriarchal Religion

Prolegomena

1. There exists a planetary sexual caste system, essentially the same in Saudi Arabia and in New York, differing only in degree.
2. This system is masked by sex role segregation, by the dual identity of women, by ideologies and myths.
3. Among the primary loci of sexist conditioning is grammar.
4. The "methods" of the various "fields" are not adequate to express feminist thought. Methodolatry requires that women perform Methodicide, an act of intellectual bravery.
5. All of the major world religions function to legitimate patriarchy. This is true also of the popular cults such as the Krishna movement and the Jesus Freaks.
6. The myths and symbols of Christianity are essentially sexist. Since "God" is male, the male is God. God the Father legitimates all earthly Godfathers, including Vito Corleone,[1] Pope Paul, Pres-

---

[1] **Vito Corleone** The fictional Mafia character who founds the family "business" in Mario Puzo's novel, *The Godfather.*

ident Gerald Ford, the Godfathers of medicine (e.g., the American Medical Association), of science (e.g., NASA), of the media, of psychiatry; of education, and of all the -ologies.

7. The myth of feminine evil, expressed in the story of the Fall, is reinforced by the myth of salvation/redemption by a single human being of the male sex. The idea of a unique divine incarnation in a male, the God-man of the "hypostatic union,"[2] is inherently sexist and oppressive. Christolatry is idolatry.

8. A significant and growing cognitive minority of women, radical feminists, are breaking out from under the sacred shelter of patriarchal religious myths.

9. This breaking out, facing anomy when the meaning structures of patriarchy are seen through and rejected, is a communal, political event. It is a revelatory event, a creative, political ontophany.[3]

10. The bonding of the growing cognitive minority of women who are radical feminists, commonly called *sisterhood*, involves a process of new naming, in which words are wrenched out of their old semantic context and heard in a new semantic context. For example, the "sisterhoods" of patriarchy, such as religious congregations of women, were really mini-brotherhoods. *Sisterhood* heard with new ears is bonding for women's own liberation.

11. There is an inherent dynamic in the women's revolution in Judeo-Christian society which is Antichurch, whether or not feminists specifically concern ourselves with churches. This is so because the Judeo-Christian tradition legitimates patriarchy—the prevailing power structure and prevailing world view—which the women's revolution leaves behind.

12. The women's revolution is not only Antichurch. It is a postchristian spiritual revolution.

13. The ethos of Judeo-Christian culture is dominated by The Most Unholy Trinity: Rape, Genocide, and War. It is rapism which spawns racism. It is gynocide which spawns genocide, for sexism (rapism) is fundamental socialization to objectify "the other."

14. The women's revolution is concerned with transvaluation of values, beyond the ethics dominated by The Most Unholy Trinity.

15. The women's revolution is not merely about equality within a patriarchal society (a contradiction in terms). It is about *power* and redefining power.

16. Since Christian myths are inherently sexist, and since the wom-

---

[2]**hypostatic union**   The union of the divine and human aspects of Jesus Christ.
[3]**ontophany**   Manifestation of being.

en's revolution is not about "equality" but about power, there is an intrinsic dynamic in the feminist movement which goes beyond efforts to reform Christian churches. Such efforts eventually come to be recognized as comparable to a Black person's trying to reform the Ku Klux Klan.

17. Within patriarchy, power is generally understood as power *over* people, the environment, things. In the rising consciousness of women, power is experienced as *power of presence* to ourselves and to each other, as we affirm our own being against and beyond the alienated identity (non-being) bestowed upon us within patriarchy. This is experienced as *power of absence* by those who would objectify women as "the other," as magnifying mirrors.

18. The presence of women to ourselves which is *absence* to the oppressor is the essential dynamic opening up the women's revolution to human liberation. It is an invitation to men to confront non-being and hence affirm their be-ing.

19. It is unlikely that many men will accept this invitation willingly, or even be able to hear it, since they have profound vested (though self-destructive) interest in the present social arrangements.

20. The women's movement is a new mode of relating to the self, to each other, to men, to the environment—in a word—to the cosmos. It is self-affirming, refusing objectification of the self and the other.

21. Entrance into new feminist time/space, which is moving time/space located on the boundaries of patriarchal institutions, is active participation in ultimate reality, which is de-reified,[4] recognized as Verb, as intransitive Verb with no object to block its dynamism.

22. Entrance into radical feminist consciousness involves recognition that all male-dominated "revolutions," which do not reject the universally oppressive reality which is patriarchy, are in reality only reforms. They are "revolutions" only in the sense that they are spinnings of the wheels of the same senescent system.

23. Entrance into radical feminist consciousness implies an awareness that the women's revolution is the "final cause" (pun intended) in the radical sense that it is the cause which can move the other

---

[4]***de-reified*** Reify means to give a definite form to an abstraction; de-reify means to return that form to an abstraction. Thus, moving from the form of God as a man—reification of an abstraction—Daly wants to de-reify the concept God as a man and substitute for it the concept of Verb. She wants to remove the concept of a human body from the idea of God.

causes. It is the catalyst which can bring about real change, since it is the rising up of the universally and primordially objectified "Other," discrediting the myths which legitimate rapism. Rapism is by extension the objectification and destruction of all "others" and inherently tends to the destruction of the human species and of all life on this planet.

Radical feminism, the becoming of women, is very much an Other- 24
world Journey. It is both discovery and creation of a world other than patriarchy. Some observation reveals that patriarchy is "everywhere." Even outer space and the future have been colonized. As a rule, even the more imaginative science fiction writers (seemingly the most fore-telling futurists) cannot/will not create a space and time in which women get far beyond the role of space stewardess. Nor does this situation exist simply "outside" women's minds, securely fastened into institutions which we can physically leave behind. Rather, it is also internalized, festering inside women's heads, even feminist heads.

The journey of women *becoming*, then, involves exorcism of the 25
internalized Godfather, in his various manifestations (His name is legion). It involves dangerous encounters with these demons. Within the Christian tradition, particularly in medieval times, evil spirits have sometimes been associated with the Seven Deadly Sins, both as personifications and as causes.[5] A "standard" and prevalent listing of the Sins is, of course, the following: pride, avarice, anger, lust, gluttony, envy, and sloth.[6] I am contending that these have all been radically misnamed, that is, inadequately and even perversely "understood" within Christianity. These concepts have been used to victimize the oppressed, particularly women. They are particularized expressions of the overall use of "evil" to victimize women. The feminist journey involves confrontations with the demonic distortions of evil.

Why has it seemed "appropriate" in this culture that a popular 26
book and film *(The Exorcist)* center around a Jesuit who "exorcises" a girl-child who is "possessed"? Why is there no book or film about a woman who exorcises a Jesuit?[7] Within a culture possessed by the myth of feminine evil, the naming, describing, and theorizing about

---

[5]An elaborate historical study of the Sins is to be found in Morton W. Bloomfield, *The Seven Deadly Sins* (Michigan State University Press, 1952, 1967). [Daly's note]

[6]Bloomfield gives a variety of "listings" of Deadly Sins in different periods and cultures, with useful contextual information. [Daly's note]

[7]See Dolores Bargowski's review of the film in *Quest: A Feminist Quarterly* I, No. 1, (Summer, 1974), pp. 53–57. [Daly's note]

good and evil has constituted a web of deception, a Maya. The journey of women becoming is breaking through this web—a Fall into free space. It is reassuming the role of subject, as opposed to object, and naming good and evil on the basis of our own intuitive intellection.

Breaking through the web of the Male Maya is both exorcism and ecstasy. These are two aspects of the same journey. Since women have been prohibited from real journeying, that is, from encountering the strange, the unknown, the women's movement is movement into uncharted territory. The process involves removal of the veils which prevent confrontation with the unknown. Let it be noted that "journey" is a multidimensional word and that the various meanings and images conjured up by the word are not sharply distinguishable. One thinks of mystical journeys, quests, adventurous travel, advancement in skills, in sports, in intellectual probing, in psychological integration and transformation. So also the "veils," the insulations against the unknown imposed upon women by male mediators, are multidimensional and intertwined. The veils are woven of religious myths (for example, the myth of the "good woman," the Virgin Mother who has only a Son, not a Daughter), legal restrictions, social customs, medical and psychoanalytic ideologies and practices, academic restrictions (withholding of access to "higher" education, to certain professions), grammatical conditioning ("he" supposedly includes "she"), economic limitations. The very process of exorcism, of casting off the blinding veils, is movement outside the patriarchally imposed sense of reality and identity. This demystification process, standing/moving outside The Lie, *is* ecstasy. 27

The process of encountering the unknown, of overcoming the "protection" racket, also involves a continual conversion of the previously unknown into the familiar.[8] This requires the use of tools and instruments now in the possession of women's captors. Amazon expeditions into the male-controlled "fields" such as law, medicine, psychology, philosophy, theology, literature, history, sociology, biology, and physics are necessary in order to leave the Fathers' cave and live in the sun. A crucial problem has been to learn how to plunder righteously while avoiding being caught too long in the cave. In universities, and in virtually all of the professions, there are poisonous gases which are almost invisible and odorless, and which gradually stifle women's minds and spirits. Those who carry out the necessary expeditions run the risk 28

---

[8]This idea is developed in a remarkable article. See Peggy Allegro, "The Strange and the Familiar," *Amazon Quarterly*, I, 1, pp. 29–41. [Daly's note]

of shrinking into the mold of the mystified Athena,[9] the twice-born who forgets and denies her Mother and Sisters. "Reborn" from the Father, she becomes Daddy's Girl, the mutant who serves the master's purposes. The token woman, who in reality is enchained, possessed, "knows" that she is free. She is a useful tool of the patriarchs, particularly against her sister Artemis who knows better, respects her womanself, bonds with her sisters, and refuses to sell her freedom, her original birthright, for a mess of respectability.

Exorcism, Processions, and Remythologization

What clues can we find concerning the "nature" and direction of 29 the Other-world journey of radically feminist (i.e., conscious) women? Some important hints can be discovered in *Three Guineas*, an astonishing book published in the 1930s by a prophetic foremother. In that book Virginia Woolf links processions (e.g., academic, churchly, military, judicial) with professions and processions. She asks:

> What are these ceremonies and why should we take part in them? What are these professions and why should we make money out of them? Where, in short, is it leading us, the procession of the sons of educated men?[10]

Clearly, they are leading us to destruction of the human species 30 and of the planet. The rigid, stylized, hierarchical, gynocidal and genocidal processions of male-controlled professions—of church, state, university, army—are all intimately interconnected. These processions capture and reify process. They are deadly. It is important to understand them in order to understand what feminist process/journeying is *not*.

Patriarchal processions both generate and reflect the archetypal im- 31 age of "procession" from and return to God the Father. In Christian myth, this is a cyclic pattern: separation and return. Christians participate in the procession—they join the parade—through Baptism, which explicitly contains a rite of exorcism. This mythic symbolic proces-

---

[9]**Athena** Athena sprang full-grown and armed from the head of Zeus, the chief of Greek gods. She was born without the need of a mother and is therefore "Daddy's Girl," as Daly says.

[10]Virginia Woolf, *Three Guineas* (New York: Harcourt, Brace, and World, Inc., 1938, 1966), p. 63. [Daly's note]

sion toward "God," then, begins with belief in possession by evil forces ("possession" technically in a broad sense, of course), release from which requires captivity by the church. What is ultimately sought is reconciliation with the Father.

Clearly, the ultimate symbol of "procession" is the All Male Trin- 32 ity itself. In various abstruse ways theologians have elaborated upon the "mystery," or as some would say, the "symbol," of the Trinity. What is of great significance here is the fact that this is a myth of Father and Son (no Mother or Daughter involved) in total unity, so total that this "love" is expressed by the Third Person, the Holy Spirit. This is the epitome of male bonding, beyond the wildest dreams of Lionel Tiger.[11] It is (almost?) erotic male homosexual mythos, the perfect All Male Marriage, the All Male Divine Family. It is asymmetric patriarchy carried to the sublime absurdity of contradiction, christened "mystery." To the timid objections sometimes voiced by Christian women, the classic answer has been: "You're included. The Holy Spirit is feminine." The conclusion of this absurd logic arrives quickly if one asks: How then, did "he" impregnate the Virgin Mary?

Mere human males, of course, cannot fully identify with the divine 33 Son. Perfect consubstantiality[12] with the Father, therefore, cannot be achieved. The earthly processions of the sons of men have as their basic paradigm[13] an attempted identification with the Father. (God the Father, the Godfather, the Oedipal Father[14]). The junior statesman dreams of becoming The President. The academic junior scholar (disciple) dreams of becoming The Professor (Master). The acolyte dreams of becoming The Priest. And, as Woolf[15] recognized, the death-oriented military processions reveal the real direction of the whole scenario, which is a funeral procession of the human species. God the Father requires human sacrifice.

Women becoming must indeed recognize the fact of having been 34 possessed by the structures of evil. However, the solution is not "re-

---

[11]*Lionel Tiger (b. 1937)* At the time this piece was written, Tiger was regarded as a scholarly antagonist of the feminist movement. He wrote *Men in Groups* (1984).

[12]*consubstantiality* Having the same essence and substance.

[13]*paradigm* Model, example.

[14]*Oedipal Father* Each of the three examples Daly gives is a model or paradigm for the idea of father. The Oedipal Father is the figure that, according to Freud, the male child wants to kill in order to have the mother all to himself (see the selection from Freud in Part Three of this book).

[15]*Virginia Woolf (1882–1941)* British novelist and distinguished critic (see the selection by Woolf in Part Six of this book).

birth" or Baptism by the Father's surrogates, for it is this socialized "rebirth" which is the captivity from which we are trying to escape. Radical feminism is *not* reconciliation with the Father. It begins with saying "No" to the Father, who attempts to eradicate our Mother and to transform us into mutants by forcing "rebirth" (whether from the head of Zeus or from the rib of Adam or from baptismal "grace"). More than this: radical feminism means saying "Yes" to our original birth, the original movement-surge toward life. This is both a remembering and a rediscovering. Athena remembers and rediscovers her Mother. That which is generated between us is Sisterhood. We are then no longer confined by our identities as "Mother" or "Daughter." The Daughter is *not* obedient to the Mother "unto death." The Mother does not send her forth to be crucified for the sins of women or of men. Rather, they go forth as Sisters. Radical feminism releases the inherent dynamic in the Mother-Daughter relationship toward Sisterhood, which is thwarted within the Male-mastered system. The Mother does *not* demand self-sacrifice of the Daughter. Rather, both demand of each other affirmation of the self and of each other in an on-going personal/political process which is mythic in its depths—which is both an exorcising and a remythologizing process. The "sacrifice" that is required is not mutilation of the hands of men, but rather the discipline needed for action together, for self-defense and self-actualization on a planet dominated by the Reign of Terror which is the Reign of the Godfathers. It is important that we consider the actual conditions of this terrain through which we must make our journey.

The Land of the Fathers

As Phyllis Chesler[16] has pointed out, the story of the Virgin Mary, 35 impregnated by God to bring forth his only Son, is classic patriarchal rape-incest myth. The Madonna has no Divine Daughter. Moreover, as the same author perceptively says, she foregoes sexual pleasure, physical prowess, and economic and intellectual power in order to become a "mother" for her "divine" son.[17] And this is the primary role-model for women in our culture. This is the life that women are condemned

---

[16]**Phyllis Chesler** An author who writes on feminist issues. Her works include *Women and Madness* (1972).

[17]Phyllis Chesler, *Women and Madness*, (New York: Doubleday, 1972), pp. 24–26. [Daly's note]

to live out—an alienation which is personal, social, mythic—and which is all the deeper because unrecognized, unacknowledged.

In a society in which women are in fact *robbed* of physical prowess, of economic and intellectual power, we live in a State of Siege.[18] As Jeanne Lafferty and Evelyn Clark wrote: 36

> Every female person knows the humiliation of being constantly harassed and solicited by males. Having her person talked at, whistled at, yelled at, grunted at, hooted and howled at, visually dismembered or stared and winked at by males everywhere—on the street, at work, at school, at home—everywhere.[19]

This is the very real condition of women in a rapist society. Moreover, the dismemberment is not always only visual. Male fetishism concerning women's bodies, the cutting into objectified parts which is the prime material of advertising and pornography, has as its logical outcome the brutal rape murders and actual physical dismemberments which take place in such a society. In a world ruled by God the Father this is not considered a serious problem. A feminist author wrote: "Rape is too personal and too terrible a crime to be left to the punishment of indifferent male law."[20]

In a society possessed by the sexual caste system, that is, in a rapist   37 society, there is a deep struggle on the part of those designated "victims" to cast out the deception that warps the soul. The deception inflicted upon women is a kind of mindbinding comparable to the footbinding procedure which mutilated millions of Chinese women for a thousand years.[21] Just as footbinding destroyed the capacity for physical movement—walking, running, dancing—mindbinding damages the capacity for autonomous creativity, action, thinking, imaging, willing. Stripping away the mindbindings of lies that reduce women to the status of physical, mental, and spiritual rapes is the basic loving act in such a society.

---

[18]This expression was used by Emily Culpepper in an unpublished paper entitled "Reflections on Ethics and Self Defense: Establishing a Firm Stance." [Daly's note]

[19]"Self Defense and the Preservation of Females," in *The Female State: A Journal of Female Liberation*, Issue 4 (April, 1970), p. 96. [Daly's note]

[20]Elizabeth Gould Davis, author of *The First Sex* (New York: G.P. Putnam's Sons, 1971) wrote this in an article about her own devastating rape in *Prime Time*, June, 1974, p. 3. [Daly's note]

[21]The horrors of footbinding are recounted by Andrea Dworkin, *Woman Hating* (New York; Dutton, 1974), pp. 95–117. These "tiny feet" were malodorous, mutilated humps. Women fell from one to the other. These stumps were described in fantastically deceptive euphemistic language and were the objects of sadistic male fetishism. [Daly's note]

The Qualitative Leap

Creative, living, political hope for movement beyond the gynocidal 38
reign of the Fathers will be fulfilled only if women continue to make
qualitative leaps in living our transcendence. A short-circuited hope of
transcendence has caused many to remain inside churches, and patriarchal religion sometimes has seemed to satisfy the hunger for transcendence. The problem has been that both the hunger and the satisfaction generated within such religions have to a great extent alienated
women from our deepest aspirations. Spinning in vicious circles
of false needs and false consciousness, women caught on the patriarchal wheel have not been able to experience women's own experience.

I suggest that what is required is *ludic cerebration*, the free 39
play of intuition in our own space, giving rise to thinking that is
vigorous, informed, multi-dimensional, independent, creative, tough.
Ludic cerebration is thinking out of experience. I do not mean the
experience of dredging out All That Was Wrong with Mother, or of
instant intimacy in group encounters, or of waiting at the doctoral
dispensary, or of self-lobotomization in order to publish, perish, and
then be promoted. I mean the experience of being. *Be-ing* is the
verb that says the dimensions of depth in all verbs, such as intuit-
ing, reasoning, loving, imaging, making, acting, as well as the cour-
aging, hoping, and playing that are always there when one is really
living.

It may be that some new things happen within patriarchy, but one 40
thing essentially stays the same: women are always marginal beings.
From this vantage point of the margin it is possible to look at what is
between the margins with the lucidity of The Compleat Outsider. To
change metaphors: the systems within the System do not appear so
radically different from each other to those excluded by all. Hope for a
qualitative leap lies in *us* by reason of that deviance from the "norm"
which was first imposed but which can also be *chosen* on our own
terms. This means that there has to be a shift from "acceptable" female deviance (characterized by triviality, diffuseness, dependence
upon others for self-definition, low self-esteem, powerlessness) to deviance which may be unacceptable to others but which is acceptable
to the self and *is* self-acceptance.

For women concerned with philosophical/theological questions, 41
it seems to me, this implies the necessity of some sort of choice.
One either tries to avoid "acceptable" deviance ("normal" female

idiocy) by becoming accepted as a male-identified professional, or else one tries to make the qualitative leap toward self-acceptable deviance as ludic cerebrator, questioner of everything, madwoman, and witch.

I do mean witch. The heretic who rejects the idols of patriarchy is 42 the blasphemous creatrix of her own thoughts. She is finding her life and intends not to lose it. The witch that smolders within every woman who cared and dared enough to become a philosophically/spiritually questing feminist in the first place seems to be crying out these days: "Light my fire!" The qualitative leap, the light of those flames of spiritual imagination and cerebral fantasy can be a new dawn.

On "Androgyny"[22]

Feminists have searched for a word to express the concept-reality 43 of psychic wholeness, of integration, which we are just beginning to glimpse intuitively, experientially, as realizable. In this search for the right word we have experienced the poverty of the language bequeathed to us, and we have recognized the manner in which it constricts and even distorts our thought. In my book *Beyond God the Father*, I frequently use the word "androgyny" to express this intuition and incipient experience of wholeness, which transcends sex-role stereotyping—the societally imposed "eternal feminine" and "eternal masculine." Feminist ethicist Janice Raymond[23] has written perceptively of an "intuition of androgyny" as identical with the intuition of being.[24] Two young theologians, graduates of Harvard Divinity School, used the term to convey a feminist understanding of wholeness in a much discussed jointly published article.[25] Feminist poet Adrienne

---

[22]***Androgyny*** Possessing the qualities of both sexes.

[23]***Janice Raymond (b. 1943)*** Author of *A Passion for Friends: Toward a Philosophy of Female Affection*.

[24]"Beyond Male Morality," in *Women and Religion*, Revised Edition, edited by Judith Plaskow and Joan Romero, (Missoula, Montana: American Academy of Religion and The Scholars' Press, 1974), pp. 115–125. [Daly's note]

[25]Linda L. Barufaldi and Emily E. Culpepper, "Androgyny and the Myth of Masculine/Feminine," *Christianity and Crisis*, April 16, 1973, pp. 69–71. [Daly's note]

Rich[26] used the word in her poem *The Stranger,* which concludes with the following lines:

> I am the androgyne
> I am the living mind you fail to describe
> in your dead language
> the lost noun, the verb surviving
> only in the infinitive
> the letters of my name are written under the lids
> of the newborn child.[27]

All of these authors now experience some hesitancy about using the word "androgyny" to express our vision(s). This hesitancy is at least in part due to an increasing understanding of the political use and abuse of language. This increased sophistication has resulted from some distressing misinterpretations of the word.   44

In speaking to audiences, I have sometimes had the impression that people hearing this term vaguely envisage two distorted halves of a human being stuck together—something like John Wayne and Brigitte Bardot scotch-taped together—as if two distorted "halves" could make a whole. That is, there is a kind of reification of wholeness, instead of recognition that what is being described is continual process. This non-understanding of "androgyny," which feminists have used when attempting to describe the *process* of integration, is also reflected in the assumption on the part of some women (and men) that a woman who is successful in a career on male terms (for example, a successful business executive) and at the same time a model housewife has achieved "androgyny." In fact, this career housewife as described fails to criticize radically either the "masculine" or the "feminine" roles/worlds. She simply compartmentalizes her personality in order to function within both, instead of recognizing/rejecting/transcending the inherent oppressiveness of such institutions as big business and the nuclear family.   45

When one becomes conscious of the political usages of language, she recognizes also that the term "androgyny" is adaptable to such mystifying usage as the expression "human liberation" has been sub-   46

---

[26] ***Adrienne Rich (b. 1929)*** One of America's most distinguished poets.

[27] The lines from "Diving into the Wreck" from *Diving into the Wreck, Poems 1971–1972,* by Adrienne Rich, are reprinted by permission of the author and the publisher. Copyright © 1973 by W.W. Norton & Company, Inc.

jected to. That is, it can easily be used to deflect attention from the fact that women and men at this point in history cannot simply "get together and work it out," ignoring the profound differences in socialization and situation within the sexual caste system. Both "androgyny" and "human liberation" function frequently to encourage false transcendence, masking—even though unintentionally—the specific content of the oppression of women, and suggesting that wholeness depends upon identification with men. Some of us do still use the term "androgyny," of course, but less frequently, more circumspectly, and with some apprehension that we will be misunderstood.

Some feminists began to feel somewhat less comfortable with the 47 word "androgyny" when the implications of a small terse fact surfaced to consciousness. That fact is etymological: the first part of the word obviously is derived from the Greek *aner, andros* (man), while the second part is from *gyne* (woman). This, of course, carries its own message. A first reaction was to employ the word "gynandry," which, from the perspective of women's becoming, is more appropriate. But it soon became evident that the priority problem in the etymology of the word was really symptomatic of deeper problems.

In fact, the term "androgyny" comes to us heavily fraught with 48 traditional associations, that is, associations of male-centered tradition(s). The image conveyed by the word is that of a "feminized" male. This fact has been brought home to me in public discussions with male Christian theologians who, confronted with the problem of the inherent oppressiveness of Christolatry, have responded earnestly that there really is no problem since "Jesus was androgynous." Whatever this may mean, it has little relevance to the problem of women's becoming *now*, and in fact it distracts from the real issues confronting us. Dressing up old symbols just will not work for women who are conscious of sexist religiosity.

"Gynandry" helps to shift images away from the traditional biases, 49 but only to a limited degree. Placing the female part of the word first does not dissolve the inherent dependency of the word itself upon stereotypes in order that there be any meaningful content at all. To put it another way, in an "androgynous" or "gynandrous" society it would be senseless to speak of "androgyny" or "gynandry" since people would have no idea of the sex-stereotyped characteristics and/or roles referred to by the components of the terms. Use of these terms at this point in history is dysfunctional to the extent that it encourages on some level a perpetuation of stereotypes (as is the case with Jungian ideology of the "anima" and "animus"). "Gynandry" or "androgyny" *can* function in a liberating way if they are seen as "transitional" words, or, more precisely, as self-liquidating words. They should be understood as having a built-in planned obsolescence[28]

Wanted: "God" or "The Goddess"?

Feminist consciousness is experienced by a significant number of 50 women as ontological becoming, that is, be-ing. This process requires existential courage, courage to be and to *see*, which is both revolutionary and revelatory, revealing our participation in ultimate reality as Verb, as intransitive Verb.

The question obviously arises of the need for anthropomorphic 51 symbols for this reality. There is no inherent contradiction between speaking of ultimate reality as Verb and speaking of this as personal. The Verb is more personal than a mere static noun. However, if we choose to *image* the Verb in anthropomorphic symbols, we can run into a problematic phenomenon which sociologist Henri Desroche[29] calls "crossing." "Crossing" refers to a notable tendency among oppressed groups to attempt to change or adapt the ideological tools of the oppressor, so that they can be used *against* him and *for* the oppressed. The problem here is the fact that the functioning of "crossing" does not generally move far enough outside the ideological framework it seeks to undermine. In the "Black theology" of James Cone[30], for example, we find a Black God and a Black Messiah, but this pigmentation operation does not significantly alter the behavior of Jahweh & Son. Cone's Black God is as revengeful and sexist as his White prototype. For feminist eyes it is clear that this God is at least as oppressive as the old (for black women as well as for white women). The message in the alteration of symbol is simply about *which* male-ruled racial group will be on top and which will be on the bottom. The basic presupposition of *hierarchy* remains unaltered: that is, the presupposition

---

[28]In a speech delivered at the Modern Languages Association Forum, December, 1973, Cynthia Secor noted that there is no "Androgyne Quarterly"—most probably because there are no androgynes around to publish it. [Daly's note]

[29]**Henri Desroche**   Author of *Religious Inspiration and Temporal Structures* (1948).

[30]**James Cone (b. 1938)**   Theologian and author of *Black Theology and Black Power* (1969).

that there must be an "us" or a "them" on top, and a corresponding "them" or "us" on the bottom.

Some women religious leaders within Western culture in modern   52
times have performed something like a "crossing" operation, notably such figures as Mary Baker Eddy[31] and Ann Lee,[32] in stressing the "maternal" aspect of the divinity. The result has been mixed. Eddy's "Father-Mother God" is, after all, the Christian God. Nor does Ann Lee really move completely outside the Christian framework. It is interesting that their writings lack the thirst for vengeance that characterizes Cone's all too Christian Black theology, which is certainly in their favor. But it is also necessary to note that their theologies lack explicit relevance to the concrete problems of the oppression of women. Intellection and spirituality remain cut off from creative political movement. In earlier periods also there were women within the Christian tradition who tried to "cross" the Christian all-male God and Christ to some degree. An outstanding example was Juliana of Norwich,[33] an English recluse and mystic who lived in the last half of the fourteenth century. Juliana's "God" and "Jesus" were—if language conveys anything—hermaphroditic constructs, with the primary identity clearly male. While there are many levels on which I could analyze Juliana's words about "our beloved Mother, Jesus, (who) feeds us with himself,"[34] suffice it to say here that this hermaphroditic image is somewhat less than attractive. The "androgynous" God and Jesus present problems analogous to and related to those problems which occur in connection with the use of the term "androgyny" to describe the direction of women's becoming. There is something like a "liberation of the woman within" the (primarily male) God and Jesus.

Indeed, it is harder to perform a transsexual operation on the Judeo-   53
Christian divinity than a mere pigmentation operation. This is one reason, no doubt, why Cone is able to achieve a purely Black God and Black Messiah, rather than a Mulatto, whereas the Christian women

---

[31]***Mary Baker Eddy (1821–1910)*** Author of *Science and Health, with key to the Scriptures*. She is the founder of Christian Science.

[32]***Ann Lee (1736–1784)*** Religious leader known as "Mother Ann" who founded the Shaker communal religious sect in the American colonies. She preached celibacy and believed she embodied the female half of God's dual nature.

[33]***Juliana of Norwich (d. 1443)*** A mystic whose *Revelations of Divine Love* (c. 1393) is based on sixteen visions of Jesus Christ. She is often referred to as Julian of Norwich, which illustrates Daly's point.

[34]Juliana of Norwich, *Revelations of Divine Love*, edited by Clifton Walters (Baltimore, Maryland: 1966), Ch. 61. [Daly's note]

mentioned brought forth hermaphrodites, with emphasis upon male-ness. Indeed, they did something on the symbolic level which is anal-ogous to "liberating the woman within the man." Since they went only this far, they accomplished little or nothing, in social or mythic terms, toward the genuine liberation of women.

One fact that stands out here is that these were women whose imaginations were still partially controlled by Christian myth. My contention is that they were caught in a contradiction (which is not the case in the work of Black *male* theologians). I am saying that there is a profound contradiction between the inherent logic of radical fem-inism and the inherent logic of the Christian symbol system. I would not have said this ten years ago, at the time of writing the original edition of *The Church and the Second Sex*, which expressed hope for reform of Christianity in general and Roman Catholicism in particu-lar. Nor would some women today say this—women who still perceive their identity as both Christian and feminist. 54

Both the reformers and those who leave Judaism and Christianity behind are contributing and will contribute in different ways to the process of the becoming of women. The point here is not to place value judgments upon individual persons and their efforts—and there are heroic efforts at all points of the feminist spectrum. Rather, it is to disclose an inherent logic in feminism. The courage which some women have in affirming this logic comes in part from having been on the feminist journey for quite awhile. Encouragement comes also from knowing increasing numbers of women who have chosen the route of the logical conclusion. Some of these women have "graduated" from Christianity or religious Judaism, and some have never even been as-sociated closely with church or synagogue, but have discovered spiri-tual and mythic depths in the women's movement itself. What we share is a sense of becoming in cosmic process, which I prefer to call the Verb, Be-ing, and which some would still call "God." 55

For some feminists concerned with the spiritual depth of the move-ment, the word "God" is becoming increasingly problematic, however. This by no means indicates a movement in the direction of "atheism" or "agnosticism" or "secularism," as these terms are usually under-stood. Rather, the problem arises precisely because of the spiritual and mythic quality perceived in feminist process itself. Some use expres-sions such as "power of being." Some reluctantly still use the word "God" while earnestly trying to divest the term of its patriarchal as-sociations, attempting to think perhaps of the "God of the philoso-phers" rather than the overtly masculist and oppressive "God of the theologians." But the problem becomes increasingly troublesome, the 56 more the "God" of the various Western philosophers is subjected to feminist analysis. "He"—"Jahweh" still often hovers behind the abstractions, stunting our own thought, giving us a sense of contrived doublethink. The word "God" just may be inherently oppressive.

Indeed, the word "Goddess" has also been problematic, but for different reasons. Some have been worried about the problem of "crossing." However, that difficulty appears more and more as a pseudo-difficulty when it is recognized that "crossing" is likely to occur only when one is trying to work *within* a sexist tradition. For example, Christian women who in their "feminist liturgies" experiment with referring to "God" as "she" and to the Trinity as "The Mother, the Daughter, and the Holy Spirit," are still working within all the boundaries of the same symbolic framework and the same power structure. Significantly, their services are at the same place and time as "the usual," and are regarded by most of the constituency of the churches as occasional variations of "business as usual."

As women who are outside the Christian church inform ourselves of evidence supporting the existence of ancient matriarchy and of evidence indicating that the Gods of patriarchy are indeed contrived, pale derivatives and reversals of the Great Goddess of an earlier period, the fear of mere "crossing" appears less appropriate and perhaps even absurd. There is also less credibility allowable to the notion that "Goddess" would function like "God" in reverse, that is, to legitimate an oppressive "female-dominated" society, if one is inclined to look seriously at evidence that matriarchal society was not structured like patriarchy, that it was non-hierarchical.[35]

Would "Goddess" be likely to function oppressively, like "God"? Given the present situation of women, the danger is not imminent. "Would it function that way in the future?" My inclination is to think not, but it is not my intention to attempt to "prove" this point at this time. The question has a quality of "abstraction" and remoteness from the present social realities and it is, it seems to me, diversionary. When it is raised, and it is usually raised by men, one senses an "atmosphere" about the question, an aroma of masculine hysteria, a fear of invading hordes of "matriarchs" (read: female patriarchs) taking over the Man's world.

There are however, two points concerning the symbol "Goddess" which I think *are* relevant to the existing situation. First, it can at the

[35]See Robert Briffault, *The Mothers*, (New York: Macmillan, 1927), Vol. I. See also J.J. Bachofen, *Myth, Religion and Mother-Right*, trans. by Ralph Manheim (Princeton: Princeton University Press, 1967). [Daly's note]

very least be pointed out that whenever the pendulum has swung extremely in one direction (and it *has*—for millennia), it is psychologically/socially/ethically important to emphasize "the other side." The hemaphroditic[36] image hardly seems satisfactory for anyone. For an increasing minority of women—and even for some men[37]—"Goddess" is becoming more functional, meaningful, and loaded with healing associations. As this minority grows, Western society will be shaken by the presence of gynarchic symbolism in a new and potent way. It should be noted that women are inclined to speak and write of "The Goddess," whereas one seldom says "The God." In our culture it has been assumed that "goddesses" are many and trivial, whereas the "real" divinity *is* "God," who does not even require the definite article. The use of the expression, "The Goddess," is a way of confronting this trivialization, of exorcising the male "God," and of affirming a different myth/reality.

A second, and related, point has to do with the fact that the "self-transcending immanence," the sense of giving birth to ourselves, the sense of power of being within, which is being affirmed by many women, does not seem to be denoted, imaged, adequately pointed to, or perhaps even associated with the term "God." With her permission, I will relate a story told to me by a theologian for whose insights I have the greatest respect. This woman told me that in the past when riding in planes (and feeling fearful about the situation) she often conjured up images remembered from childhood of "God" as "having the whole world in his hands." Later, this image/prayer? became meaningless. When she was on a plane recently, the ride suddenly became extremely "bumpy" and rough. It occurred to her to "try on" the name/image "Goddess." The result, as she described it, was immediate, electrifying, consoling. She sensed a presence and had/heard? the thought: "Just let go. Just sit on the seat and sit on the air waves and ride." The ride, though as rough as before, became a joyful experience.[38]

Clearly, it would be inappropriate and arrogant to try to "explain" or "interpret" this experience of another person. I can only comment that many women I know are finding power of being within the self, rather than in "internalized" father images. As a philosopher, my pref-

---

[36]***Hermaphroditic***   The hermaphrodite possessed the sexual organs of both sexes and was therefore imaginary; however, the image persists.

[37]Kenneth Pitchford chooses Goddess imagery, which occurs frequently in his more recent poems. [Daly's note]

[38]The story was told by Professor Nelle Morton of Drew Theological Seminary and paraphrased by myself. [Daly's note]

erence has been for abstractions. Indeed I have always been annoyed and rather embarrassed by "anthropomorphic" symbols, preferring terms such as "ground and power of being" (Tillich), "beyond subjectivity and objectivity" (James), "the Encompassing" (Jaspers), or the commonly used "Ultimate Reality," or "cosmic process." More recently I have used the expression "Intransitive Verb." Despite this philosophical inclination, and also because of it, I find it impossible to ignore the realm of symbols, or to fail to recognize that many women are experiencing and participating in a remythologizing process, which is a new dawn.

It is necessary to add a few remarks about the functioning of the 63 confusing and complex "Mary" symbol within Christianity. Through it, the power of the Great Goddess symbol is enchained, captured, used, cannibalized, tokenized, domesticated, tranquilized. In spite of this, I think that many women and at least some men, when they have heard of or imaged the "Mother of God," have, by something like a selective perception process, screened out the standardized, lobotomized, dull, derivative and dwarfed Christian reflections of a more ancient symbol; they have perceived something that might more accurately be described as the Great Goddess, and which, in human terms, can be translated into "the strong woman who can relate because she can stand alone." A woman of Jewish background commented that "Mother of God" had always seemed strange and contradictory to her. Not having been programmed to "know" about the distinctions between the "divine" and the "human" nature of "Christ," or to "know" that the "Mother of God" is less than God, this woman had been able to hear the expression with the ears of an extraenvironmental listener. It sounded, she said, something like "infinite plus one."[39] When this symbolic nonsense is recognized, it is more plausible simply to *think* "infinite," and to *image* something like "Great Mother," or "Goddess."

It may appear that the suffix "-ess" presents a problem, when one 64 considers other usages of that suffix, for example, in "poetess," or in "authoress." In these cases, there is a tone of depreciation, a suggestion that women poets and authors are in a separate and "inferior" category to be judged by different standards than their male counterparts. However, the suffix does not always function in this "diminishing" way. For example, there appear to be no "diminuitive" overtones suggested by the word "actress." So also it seems that the term "Goddess"—or "The Goddess"—*is not only non-diminuitive*, but very strong. Indeed,

---

[39]Comment of Linda Franklin, Boston College student. [Daly's note]

it calls before the mind images of a powerful and ancient tradition before, behind, and beyond Christianity. These are multi-dimensional images of women's present and future becoming/be-ing.

"Priests" or "Priestesses"?

I would suggest that "priestess" has diminuitive connotations if it is applied within the framework of Christianity (Episcopalian priestesses?), since of course within the limitations of that framework the role "acted out" by women has to be seen as derivative. It is only when one considers the possibility that the Christian tradition is itself derivative from a far more ancient and woman-centered tradition, that one's perception of priesthood changes. For women to be priestesses then is no longer perceived simply as a derivative phenomenon, but as primary and authentic. But then neither is it a Christian phenomenon. The priesthood of women need not seek legitimation within Christian churches. Nor need it be seen as a title or office conferred upon certain officially designated women to the exclusion of others. **65**

Moreover, there are impossible contradictions in the idea of woman-identified Christian priests. While it may be possible for a twice-born Athena to "say Mass," or to commit baptism "in the name of the Father and of the Son and of the Holy Ghost," this sort of behavior presents incredible problems, that is, problems of credibility. Moreover, as I have said, it is inconsistent simply to try to fit a "feminine" symbolism into these sclerotic vessels. The "form" would still be the message, with some alterations in "content." **66**

Is it true, as Malcolm Boyd[40] has recently argued, that "when the (Christian) priest is a woman, even God is no longer a male?"[41] At one time, some years ago, I might have agreed with this. However, it is important to look at Protestant churches which have been ordaining women for years. Clearly, their God (and Gods) are still male. Large patriarchal institutions are still male. Large patriarchal institutions are still quite capable of absorbing a few tokens and in fact of profiting from this, appearing "liberal" while at the same time attracting women who are doubly devoted to the task of serving male Gods. I say "doubly devoted" because, as the cliche goes, a woman has to be twice as "good" as a man to get half as much recognition. **67**

---

[40]**Malcolm Boyd (b. 1923)** Author of *The Underground Church* (1968).
[41]*Ms.*, December, 1974. [Daly's note]

It is instructive to read the list of 110 Catholic signers who have   68
called for the ordination of women "to the priesthood of the universal
church."[42] Having read some writings of some of them, I question (1)
whether they can possibly understand what the logic of feminism is
all about (i.e., leaving behind and thus leaving to die the inherently
oppressive structures of patriarchal religions); (2) whether they *do* "understand" what the logic of feminism is about and see "containment"
as an important tactic for holding women in bondage as long as possible.

The women's movement *is* about refusal to be merely contained as   69
well as refusal to be mere containers. It is about saying "Yes" to ourselves, which is the deepest way of saying "Yes" to others. At some
point in her history a woman may sincerely see ordination to the
Christian priesthood as her way of saying this "Yes." It is my hope
that such women will *continue* their journey. Ambition to "ordination" perhaps reaches a respectable altitude for the jet age, but it does
not reach very far, I think, into feminist space/time. It is my hope that
these sisters will raise their ambitions and their self-respect higher,
immeasurably higher, that they will one day outgrow their books of
common prayer and dream less common dreams.

---

[42]Reported in *National Catholic Reporter*, November 8, 1974, p. 5. [Daly's note]

QUESTIONS

1. Is the imagery connected with the Trinity sexist in the way that Daly
   suggests?
2. Is it possible to approach Christianity in a nonsexist way and yet still adhere to its tenets? For example, is it possible to be Christian and still interpret the Trinity as Daly does?
3. According to Daly, what effects do patriarchal symbols have on the culture? Do you find yourself agreeing with her that ours is a rapist society?
4. What is the "myth of feminine evil"? Do you think it affects our society
   today?
5. Is there such a thing in our society as "The Most Unholy Trinity: Rape,
   Genocide, and War"?
6. Mary Daly believes that the women's movement is beginning to affect the
   fabric of society. Do you see evidence of such an influence?

WRITING ASSIGNMENTS

1. Describe the alternatives that religious people have to thinking about God as a man or as a woman. How could a religion renovate its symbolism and its beliefs in order to accommodate such a change in its position? In your opinion, would such a change make the religion more spiritual in character, or less spiritual?

2. In paragraph 16 Mary Daly writes, "Christian myths are inherently sexist." Is this statement true? How can its truth be demonstrated? How can its falseness be demonstrated? Examine our society for evidence that points in one direction or the other on this issue.

3. How do religious symbols function to promote a specific kind of belief? What religious symbols can you specifically point to that have had an effect on popular thought? What is it about symbols that make them powerful enough to affect the way people think? In what sense are they substitutions for ideas or for independent thought? Are the religious symbols with which you are familiar coherent in their meaning, or do they sometimes seem contradictory? Choose three or four symbols and examine them carefully.

4. Write a brief response to Daly concerning her concept of the androgyne. Begin by looking the word up in an unabridged dictionary. Then look up the term in an encyclopedia of myth. The term is used in Plato's *Republic*, in his narration of a myth explaining the origins of sexuality. He states that originally people were both male and female, androgynes, and that our troubles began when the androgyne split into separate beings. What is your reaction to the concept of the androgyne? Do you feel it is desirable for people to try to relinquish gender role distinctions and encompass the qualities of both genders?

5. What are the ethical issues in this essay? Daly talks about "a society possessed by the sexual caste system, that is, . . . a rapist society" (para. 37). Do you accept her views on the nature of our society, and if so, do you feel that we are fully aware of the ethical consequences of male dominance?

6. Compare Daly's concerns with those of some of the other philosophers in Part Four. Do any of the male philosophers discuss the relations between the sexes? Do any of them include feminist issues in their exhortations to ethical behavior? Does Simone Weil raise questions that might be described as feminist in nature? Is the feminist issue an ethical issue?

7. Is there an ethical issue at stake in the phenomenon that Daly describes as "crossing"? (The term is defined and discussed beginning in paragraph 51.) "Crossing" refers to adopting the position of the oppressor and practicing what amounts to self-oppression. Is this a genuine phenomenon? Do you think that women sometimes "cross" in the sense that Daly suggests? If so, do you think that there is an ethical question that should be raised regarding such women? Why should such a phenomenon concern us at all?

PART SIX

IDEAS IN THE WORLD OF THE ARTS

SHOULD OUR PROPER RESPONSE TO ART BE EMOTIONAL OR INTELLECTUAL?

———✦———

Aristotle
José Ortega y Gasset
Virginia Woolf
Susanne K. Langer
Susan Sontag

INTRODUCTION

THE RELATIONSHIP between art and human emotion is one that has interested commentators since the time of the Greeks. For many people, their interest in art lies in its stimulation of emotions that are then controlled and ordered by the artist in order to achieve aesthetic insight. For others, art is interesting because it remains detached from human emotion and life in order to be more completely and readily contemplated.

The first of these essays remains the most durable commentary on how we contemplate a work of art. In the *Poetics*, Aristotle gave us a language with which to discourse on dramatic literature and other arts. For him the basic questions about art were rooted in its imitative capacities. Art imitates nature, and the way in which it does so holds the mirror up to our human nature, thereby allowing us to understand ourselves better.

Emotions were certainly an important part of the aesthetic experience for Aristotle. In his discussion of tragedy, he explains that the tragic poet excites in his audience two primary emotions: pity and terror. On the one hand, the audience experiences pity for the tragic hero caught in the coils of fate. The hero is another human being, one with whom we can sympathize and whom we can understand on an immediate personal level. On the other hand, the audience is also made to feel terror, partly for the high-born tragic hero and partly for their own humble potential for tragedy.

For Aristotle, the emotions associated with laughter were inappropriate for tragedy but suitable for comedy. Ridicule and farcical humor were reserved for plays with less elevated subjects and vulgar characters. Combining laughter and pity and terror would have been unacceptable to the Greeks. It wasn't until the other great age of tragedy, the Elizabethan Age, that the drama of Shakespeare introduced comic relief in tragedies of almost unendurable pain.

The Spanish philospher José Ortega y Gasset saw modern art heading away from an expression of human emotion. Instead, he felt such art made special demands on us, demands for a response in emotional terms reserved entirely for aesthetic experiences. Indeed, he explained, the emotions of "lived" experience were rejected by the modern artists as a way of maintaining a separateness between art and life. Ortega described the modern style, the style of the nonobjective or surrealist artist or writer, as representing a new, dehumanizing approach that transforms us into spectators who must respond with special aesthetic emotions.

In "A Letter to a Young Poet," Virginia Woolf lamented the state of poetry and to some extent the profession itself—although in such a way as to encourage the young poet to whom she was writing. But in the course of discussing poetry, Woolf revealed how she is affected: "I find myself . . . hit, roused, scraped, bared, swung through the air, so that life seems to flash by. . . ." Feelings for her, have a definite place in poetry, and she explains how and why. To Woolf, poetry, far from encouraging a dehumanizing response, is the very stuff of humanity.

Susanne K. Langer's "Expressiveness" stands as a seminal essay, in which she asserted that art educates the emotional life. Art provides objects that are congruent with emotions and so yield insight into those emotions. Because we inevitably feel when in the presence of a work of art, art just as inevitably shapes and refines our emotions, as well as lends us perception into emotions of which we are only dimly aware. Far from accepting a separation between art and life, Langer believed that art is the vehicle by which sensitive people endow their lives with meaning.

In "Against Interpretation," Susan Sontag opposes interpretation because it relinquishes the emotional reactions that she assumes are integral to understanding and appreciating art. Searching for the meaning in a work of art may subordinate the feelings that the work of art arouses in us. Therefore, she demands an erotics of art instead of a dissection of art, elevating feeling to its proper place, in her estimation, in relation to the activities of the artist. Thinking, instead of feeling, about art is undesirable. For Sontag a proper act of criticism would consist of an examination of feeling—perhaps even a Langerian response.

Sontag's essay is characteristically brilliant. She struck at the heart of the act of interpretation as it has been practiced since its beginnings in her review of the nature of interpretation in the works of Plato and Aristotle, and of their theory of art as mimesis—art imitating life. Sontag's approach to the problem of how interpretation affects our understanding of the arts continues to sound both historical and philosophical, and her command of the major ideas that have contributed to the way we think about interpretation remains illuminating and thought-provoking.

These essays treat the problems of art with great thoughtfulness. Written by critics whose personal involvement with the arts is intense and fruitful, the essays explore how the arts excite emotions, the kinds of emotions they excite, and the ways we can approach the arts in order to respond more deeply and more responsibly.

ARISTOTLE

---❦---

Tragedy and the Emotions
of Pity and Fear

ARISTOTLE (384–322 B.C.) *is one of a succession of Greeks who changed the world of philosophy in ancient times. Socrates was Plato's teacher, and Plato was Aristotle's teacher, who in turn was Alexander the Great's teacher. Aristotle was a brilliant student in Plato's Academy; he remained there for twenty years and earned the nickname of the "Intellect" of the school. He later conducted his own school in Athens, called the Lyceum, in a spot sacred to Apollo. His views differed essentially from Plato's, although as long as Plato lived, Aristotle avoided direct conflict with his teacher.*

Plato's views were based on idealistic principles. He held that ideas are more important than things that could be perceived; hence, perception is not of great worth. Conversely, Aristotle believed that perception was the starting point for all thought. Beginning with sense perception, the thinker could then proceed to abstract thought, which Aristotle, like Plato, held to be the most desirable and most distinctive kind of thought.

Aristotle's methods can be seen at work in the selection from the Poetics, *his treatise on Greek drama. The* Poetics *is a discussion of the principles of comedy and tragedy as they were commonly understood by the Greeks at that time, and it is well rooted both in observation and in an understanding of the history of drama and of the* traditions of the Greek festivals. Aristotle's theories about drama, in other words, are related to both his observation and his capacity to make comparisons and examine practices. Based on his observation, he is able to establish what the nature of comedy and tragedy is and to theorize about what things are most significant and most effective in the construction of drama.

The tradition in ancient Greece was to hold an important series of contests between dramatists during the festival of Dionysus. The occasion was highly organized by the time Aristotle began to write about it; in fact, many of the greatest Greek dramatists had already done their work. Playwrights were chosen for the competition by experts. Prominent and wealthy citizens were awarded the honor of paying for the costs of the production of the plays, including the actors and the scaena (stage setting) and other equipment. The archons, or judges, would sit in a place of honor during the productions of the plays and, at the end, would award prizes. It was an immense honor to be awarded a prize, and all the greatest playwrights won several prizes during their lives.

The plays were public and popular events. The tragedies were usually produced in trilogies; afterward, very coarse comedies would be presented to change the mood. The tradition of social comedy—comedy that indirectly comments on society—was beginning to develop before Aristotle wrote, but it is clear that his chief focus is on the higher and nobler form of drama: tragedy. He tells us at the outset that comedy is drama about people who are low in estate. Naturally, he is speaking of his own time, and since he lived in an aristocratic world, in which some people were thought of as inherently noble and others as inherently common, he means that comedy is not about members of the nobility but about ordinary people.

Tragedy, on the other hand, is drama whose main characters are noble, and the chief point of tragedy is to show how a person's fortune can change because of circumstances that are—or may sometimes seem to be—beyond his or her control. It was essential for a tragic hero or heroine to be noble since he or she must fall from a great height (a commoner has no great height to fall from). The hero in a tragedy presents a model for all of us: if someone can fall from a great height, we can as well. Because the noble hero falls, his fate is inherently more moving and dramatic than the fall of an ordinary person; thus, it is naturally more suitable for tragedy.

Aristotle argued that tragedy should evoke two emotions: terror and pity. The terror results from our realization that the hero's fate might just as easily be ours; the pity results from our human sympathy with a fellow sufferer. Therefore, the fearful and pathetic represent significant emotions crucial to our witnessing of the drama.

Aristotle does not discuss fate, but the Greek view was that fate ruled the world and that the most noble thing a person could do was to face his or her fate with dignity, even when that fate might be grim. In this selection he talks at length about the requirements of tragedy and their relative importance. He notes important requirements for tragedy: plot, characters, verbal expression, thought, song-composition, and visual adornment (in order of importance). In part of his discussion, he takes each of these in turn and demonstrates its significance.

One of the most complex elements of Aristotle's thinking on drama is not readily apparent from this selection; it has to do with his theory of mimesis, or imitation. For him, art is "imitation of something else; in the case of plot, for example, it is the imitation of an action" (para. 8). This concept has been examined in detail in recent years, and it is important for us to understand that the matter of how a plot imitates an action is central to drama. Aristotle talks about the poet's job of representing "what is likely to happen" as opposed to the historian's job of representing "what has happened" (para. 16).

Among the more surprising aspects of his discussion may be the declaration that plot is more important than character (para. 4). He goes so far as to suggest that tragedy may exist without character but not without plot (para. 5). He also says that beginning dramatists are capable of creating characters but definitely not of creating plot. To us, this is surprising, because most modern theories of literature emphasize character. And when we think of great Shakespearian tragedies, we think of the characters whose names are the titles of the plays (e.g. Hamlet, King Lear, Macbeth, Othello, Julius Caesar, and Antony and Cleopatra).

Aristotle's concepts of peripety and recognition are central to any understanding of tragedy. Though he explains the terms in paragraph 22, they may well be discussed briefly here. "Peripety" derives from the Greek word meaning to walk; in other words, it means the progress of a character or action in a given direction—but with a sudden shift. For example, a character may appear to be heading toward a *personal victory, only to have his efforts suddenly end in his unex-pected defeat. Peripety—the sudden shift in the direction of events—is essential to tragedy. "Recognition" is the awareness of a significant truth that may, in fact, produce the peripety. As Aristotle says, the best recognition takes place at the same time as the peripety. Usu-ally, the recognition in tragedy is the chief character's awareness of a truth which that character would rather suppress. Oedipus, in Sophocles' Oedipus Rex, discovers several things, but the worst thing is that the person whom he seeks as the one who has brought a curse on the land is himself. He had long before heard the oracle tell him that he was fated to kill his father and marry his mother, and had left home as a result. But he did not know that he had been adopted and that when he was challenged at a crossroads by an older man— whom he fought with and killed—he had begun to carry out his fate. Only after he had married his mother and taken his father's place did he learn that he was the "criminal" he had set out to find. In Oedipus Rex, the recognition comes at the moment of the peripety, when Oed-ipus's fate "turned around."*

ARISTOTLE'S RHETORIC

One of the most interesting ironies about Aristotle is that the works he prepared for publication and by which he gained immense fame and influence were for the most part lost to the world by the end of the first century A.D. At that time, another group of works sur-faced that were edited in Rome and were produced in a scholarly edition. This group is peculiar for a clipped and notelike style that has led many modern Aristotle experts to conclude that these works were reconstructed from lectures.

The Poetics closely resembles a lecture that might have been given to students of drama. It has a number of the rhetorical "trademarks" of the lecture: it is on a single subject, along with related adjuncts, and it relies on a step-by-step procedure that always pauses to review what has already been said. In this selection Aristotle provides ade-quate definitions for all the key terms he introduces; he also takes care to refer his audience to elements that have been previously dis-cussed (a number of these are referred to but are not included in this passage).

Another Aristotelian trademark that may be a result of his writing for a student audience is his categorical structure. He constantly re-minds us that things have a specific number of categories that will be discussed. *Epic poetry has three qualities; tragedy has six elements; plot has two kinds—and so on. Whenever he can, Aristotle breaks things down into parts or categories and then examines each component separately on the assumption that such an examination will yield greater knowledge of the thing under discussion.*

The Poetics *is a discussion of several categories of poetic performance, beginning with the comedy, then the epic, and proceeding to the tragedy. First each category is discussed; then its subcategories are discussed. Of course, the chief category is tragedy, and considering the thought that Aristotle devoted to his treatment of it, he must have believed it to be the most noble, uplifting, serious, and important category of all.*

Today, this essay is the starting point for all those who wish to talk and think about literature seriously. Aristotle's approach was so thorough that there are still people who think that no critical statement has since penetrated as deeply into the heart of dramatic literature. The principles presented in this essay are relevant to contemporary discussion of literature. All of us who wish to deepen our thinking about the art of literature must begin with an understanding of Aristotle.

Tragedy and the Emotions of Pity and Fear

Tragedy and Its Six Constituent Elements. Our discussions of imitative poetry in hexameters,[1] and of comedy, will come later; at present let us deal with tragedy, recovering from what has been said so far the definition of its essential nature, as it was in development. Tragedy, then, is a process of imitating an action which has serious implications, is complete, and possesses magnitude; by means of language which has been made sensuously attractive, with each of its varieties

---

[1]*hexameters* The first known metrical form for classical verse. Each line had six metrical feet, some of which were prescribed in advance. It is the meter used for epic poetry and for poetry designed to teach a lesson. The form has sometimes been used in comparatively modern poetry but rarely with success except in French.

found separately in the parts; enacted by the persons themselves and not presented through narrative; through a course of pity and fear completing the purification of tragic acts which have those emotional characteristics. By "language made sensuously attractive" I mean language that has rhythm and melody, and by "its varieties found separately" I mean the fact that certain parts of the play are carried on through spoken verses alone and others the other way around, through song.

Now first of all, since they perform the imitation through action 2 (by acting it), the adornment of their visual appearance will perforce constitute some part of the making of tragedy; and song-composition and verbal expression also, for those are the media in which they perform the imitation. By "verbal expression" I mean the actual composition of the verses, and by "song-composition" something whose meaning is entirely clear.

Next, since it is an imitation of an action and is enacted by certain 3 people who are performing the action, and since those people must necessarily have certain traits both of character and thought (for it is thanks to these two factors that we speak of people's actions also as having a defined character, and it is in accordance with their actions that all either succeed or fail); and since the imitation of the action is the plot, for by "plot" I mean here the structuring of the events, and by the "characters" that in accordance with which we say that the persons who are acting have a defined moral character, and by "thought" all the passages in which they attempt to prove some thesis or set forth an opinion—it follows of necessity, then, that tragedy as a whole has just six constituent elements, in relation to the essence that makes it a distinct species; and they are plot, characters, verbal expression, thought, visual adornment, and song-composition. For the elements by which they imitate are two (i.e., verbal expression and song-composition), the manner in which they imitate is one (visual adornment), the things they imitate are three (plot, characters, thought), and there is nothing more beyond these. These then are the constituent forms they use.

The Relative Importance of the Six Elements. The greatest of these 4 elements is the structuring of the incidents. For tragedy is an imitation not of men but of a life, an action, and they have moral quality in accordance with their characters but are happy or unhappy in accordance with their actions; hence they are not active in order to imitate their characters, but they include the characters along with the actions for the sake of the latter. Thus the structure of events, the plot, is the goal of tragedy, and the goal is the greatest thing of all.

Again: a tragedy cannot exist without a plot, but it can without 5
characters: thus the tragedies of most of our modern poets are devoid
of character, and in general many poets are like that; so also with the
relationship between Zeuxis and Polygnotus,[2] among the painters:
Polygnotus is a good portrayer of character, while Zeuxis' painting has
no dimension of character at all.

Again: if one strings end to end speeches that are expressive of 6
character and carefully worked in thought and expression, he still will
not achieve the result which we said was the aim of tragedy; the job
will be done much better by a tragedy that is more deficient in these
other respects but has a plot, a structure of events. It is much the same
case as with painting: the most beautiful pigments smeared on at random will not give as much pleasure as a black-and-white outline picture. Besides, the most powerful means tragedy has for swaying our
feelings, namely the peripeties and recognitions,[3] are elements of plot.

Again: an indicative sign is that those who are beginning a poetic 7
career manage to hit the mark in verbal expression and character portrayal sooner than they do in plot construction; and the same is true
of practically all the earliest poets.

So plot is the basic principle, the heart and soul, as it were, of trag- 8
edy, and the characters come second: . . . it is the imitation of an
action and imitates the persons primarily for the sake of their action.

Third in rank is thought. This is the ability to state the issues and 9
appropriate points pertaining to a given topic, an ability which springs
from the arts of politics and rhetoric; in fact the earlier poets made
their characters talk "politically," the present-day poets rhetorically.
But "character" is that kind of utterance which clearly reveals the bent
of a man's moral choice (hence there is no character in that class of
utterances in which there is nothing at all that the speaker is choosing
or rejecting), while "thought" is the passages in which they try to
prove that something is so or not so, or state some general principle.

Fourth is the verbal expression of the speeches. I mean by this the 10
same thing that was said earlier, that the "verbal expression" is the

---

[2]*Zeuxis (fl. 420–390 B.C.) and Polygnotus (470?–440 B.C.)* Zeuxis developed a method of painting in which the figures were rounded and apparently three-di-
mensional. Thus, he was an illusionistic painter, imitating life in a realistic style. Polygnotus was famous as a painter, and his works were on the Acropolis as well as at Delphi.
His draftsmanship was especially praised.

[3]*peripeties and recognitions* The turning-about of fortune and the recognition on
the part of the tragic hero of the truth. This is, for Aristotle, a critical moment in the
drama, especially if both events happen simultaneously, as they do in *Oedipus Rex*. It is
quite possible for these moments to happen apart from one another.

conveyance of thought through language: a statement which has the same meaning whether one says "verses" or "speeches."

The song-composition of the remaining parts is the greatest of the   11
sensuous attractions, and the visual adornment of the dramatic persons can have a strong emotional effect but is the least artistic element, the least connected with the poetic art; in fact the force of tragedy can be felt even without benefit of public performance and actors, while for the production of the visual effect the property man's art is even more decisive than that of the poets.

General Principles of the Tragic Plot. With these distinctions out of   12
the way, let us next discuss what the structuring of the events should be like, since this is both the basic and the most important element in the tragic art. We have established, then, that tragedy is an imitation of an action which is complete and whole and has some magnitude (for there is also such a thing as a whole that has no magnitude). "Whole" is that which has beginning, middle, and end. "Beginning" is that which does not necessarily follow on something else, but after it something else naturally is or happens; "end," the other way around, is that which naturally follows on something else, either necessarily or for the most part, but nothing else after it; and "middle" that which naturally follows on something else and something else on it. So, then, well constructed plots should neither begin nor end at any chance point but follow the guidelines just laid down.

Furthermore, since the beautiful, whether a living creature or any-   13
thing that is composed of parts, should not only have these in a fixed order to one another but also possess a definite size which does not depend on chance—for beauty depends on size and order; hence neither can a very tiny creature turn out to be beautiful (since our perception of it grows blurred as it approaches the period of imperceptibility) nor an excessively huge one (for then it cannot all be perceived at once and so its unity and wholeness are lost), if for example there were a creature a thousand miles long—so, just as in the case of living creatures they must have some size, but one that can be taken in a single view, so with plots: they shoud have length, but such that they are easy to remember. As to a limit of the length, the one is determined by the tragic competitions and the ordinary span of attention. (If they had to compete with a hundred tragedies they would compete by the water clock, as they say used to be done [?].) But the limit fixed by the very nature of the case is: the longer the plot, up to the point of still being perspicuous as a whole, the finer it is so far as size is concerned; or to put it in general terms, the length in which, with things happen-

ing in unbroken sequence, a shift takes place either probably or necessarily from bad to good fortune or from good to bad—that is an acceptable norm of length.

But a plot is not unified, as some people think, simply because it 14 has to do with a single person. A large, indeed an indefinite number of things can happen to a given individual, some of which go to constitute no unified event; and in the same way there can be many acts of a given individual from which no single action emerges. Hence it seems clear that those poets are wrong who have composed *Heracleïds, Theseïds*, and the like. They think that since Heracles was a single person it follows that the plot will be single too. But Homer, superior as he is in all other respects, appears to have grasped this point well also, thanks either to art or nature, for in composing an *Odyssey* he did not incorporate into it everything that happened to the hero, for example how he was wounded on Mt. Parnassus[4] or how he feigned madness at the muster, neither of which events, by happening, made it at all necessary or probable that the other should happen. Instead, he composed the *Odyssey*—and the *Iliad* similarly—around a unified action of the kind we have been talking about.

A poetic imitation, then, ought to be unified in the same way as a 15 single imitation in any other mimetic field, by having a single object: since the plot is an imitation of an action, the latter ought to be both unified and complete, and the component events ought to be so firmly compacted that if any one of them is shifted to another place, or removed, the whole is loosened up and dislocated; for an element whose addition or subtraction makes no perceptible extra difference is not really a part of the whole.

From what has been said it is also clear that the poet's job is not 16 to report what has happened but what is likely to happen: that is, what is capable of happening according to the rule of probability or necessity. Thus the difference between the historian and the poet is not in their utterances being in verse or prose (it would be quite possible for Herodotus' work to be translated into verse, and it would not be any the less a history with verse than it is without it); the difference lies

---

[4]***Mt. Parnassus*** A mountain in central Greece traditionally sacred to Apollo. In legend, Odysseus was wounded there, but the point Aristotle is making is that the writer of epics need not include every detail of his hero's life in a given work. Homer, in writing the *Odyssey*, was working with a hero, Odysseus, whose story had been legendary long before he began writing.

in the fact that the historian speaks of what has happened, the poet of the kind of thing that *can* happen. Hence also poetry is a more philosophical and serious business than history; for poetry speaks more of universals, history of particulars. "Universal" in this case is what kind of person is likely to do or say certain kinds of things, according to probability or necessity; that is what poetry aims at, although it gives its persons particular names afterward; while the "particular" is what Alcibiades did or what happened to him.

In the field of comedy this point has been grasped: our comic poets 17 construct their plots on the basis of general probabilities and then assign names to the persons quite arbitrarily, instead of dealing with individuals as the old iambic poets[5] did. But in tragedy they still cling to the historically given names. The reason is that what is possible is persuasive; so what has not happened we are not yet ready to believe is possible, while what has happened is, we feel, obviously possible: for it would not have happened if it were impossible. Nevertheless, it is a fact that even in our tragedies, in some cases only one or two of the names are traditional, the rest being invented, and in some others none at all. It is so, for example, in Agathon's *Antheus*—the names in it are as fictional as the events—and it gives no less pleasure because of that. Hence the poets ought not to cling at all costs to the traditional plots, around which our tragedies are constructed. And in fact it is absurd to go searching for this kind of authentication, since even the familiar names are familiar to only a few in the audience and yet give the same kind of pleasure to all.

So from these considerations it is evident that the poet should be a 18 maker of his plots more than of his verses, insofar as he is a poet by virtue of his imitations and what he imitates is actions. Hence even if it happens that he puts something that has actually taken place into poetry, he is none the less a poet; for there is nothing to prevent some of the things that have happened from being the kind of things that can happen, and that is the sense in which he is their maker.

Simple and Complex Plots. Among simple plots and actions the epi- 19 sodic are the worst. By "episodic" plot I mean one in which there is no probability or necessity for the order in which the episodes follow one another. Such structures are composed by the bad poets because

---

[5] **old iambic poets** Aristotle may be referring to Archilochus (fl. 650 B.C.) and the iambic style he developed. The iambic is a metrical foot of two syllables, a short and a long stress, and was the most popular metrical style before the time of Aristotle. "Dealing with individuals" implies using figures already known to the audience rather than figures whose names can be arbitrarily assigned because no one knows who they are.

they are bad poets, but by the good poets because of the actors: in composing contest pieces for them, and stretching out the plot beyond its capacity, they are forced frequently to dislocate the sequence.

Furthermore, since the tragic imitation is not only of a complete 20 action but also of events that are fearful and pathetic, and these come about best when they come about contrary to one's expectation yet logically, one following from the other; that way they will be more productive of wonder than if they happen merely at random, by chance—because even among chance occurrences the ones people consider most marvelous are those that seem to have come about as if on purpose: for example the way the statue of Mitys at Argos killed the man who had been the cause of Mitys' death, by falling on him while he was attending the festival; it stands to reason, people think, that such things don't happen by chance—so plots of that sort cannot fail to be artistically superior.

Some plots are simple, others are complex; indeed the actions of 21 which the plots are imitations already fall into these two categories. By *"simple"* action I mean one the development of which being continuous and unified in the manner stated above, the reversal comes without peripety or recognition, and by "complex" action one in which the reversal is continuous but with recognition or peripety or both. And these developments must grow out of the very structure of the plot itself, in such a way that on the basis of what has happened previously this particular outcome follows either by necessity or in accordance with probability; for there is a great difference in whether these events happen because of those or merely after them.

"Peripety" is a shift of what is being undertaken to the opposite in 22 the way previously stated, and that in accordance with probability or necessity as we have just been saying; as for example in the *Oedipus* the man who has come, thinking that he will reassure Oedipus, that is, relieve him of his fear with respect to his mother, by revealing who he once was, brings about the opposite; and in the *Lynceus,* as he (Lynceus) is being led away with every prospect of being executed, and Danaus pursuing him with every prospect of doing the executing, it comes about as a result of the other things that have happened in the play that *he* is executed and Lynceus is saved. And "recognition" is, as indeed the name indicates, a shift from ignorance to awareness, pointing in the direction either of close blood ties or of hostility, of people who have previously been in a clearly marked state of happiness or unhappiness.

The finest recognition is one that happens at the same time as a 23
peripety, as is the case with the one in the *Oedipus*. Naturally, there
are also other kinds of recognition: it is possible for one to take place
in the prescribed manner in relation to inanimate objects and chance
occurrences, and it is possible to recognize whether a person has acted
or not acted. But the form that is most integrally a part of the plot, the
action, is the one aforesaid; for that kind of recognition combined with
peripety will excite either pity or fear (and these are the kinds of action
of which tragedy is an imitation according to our definition), because
both good and bad fortune will also be most likely to follow that kind
of event. Since, further, the recognition is a recognition of persons,
some are of one person by the other one only (when it is already
known who the "other one" is), but sometimes it is necessary for both
persons to go through a recognition, as for example Iphigenia is recognized by her brother through the sending of the letter, but of him by
Iphigenia another recognition is required.

These then are two elements of plot: peripety and recognition; 24
third is the *pathos*. Of these, peripety and recognition have been discussed; a *pathos* is a destructive or painful act, such as deaths on stage,
paroxysms of pain, woundings, and all that sort of thing.

The tragic side of tragedy: pity and fear and the patterns of the com- 25
plex plot. The "parts" of tragedy which should be used as constituent
elements were mentioned earlier; (. . .) but what one should aim at
and what one should avoid in composing one's plots, and whence the
effect of tragedy is to come, remains to be discussed now, following
immediately upon what has just been said.

Since, then, the construction of the finest tragedy should be not 26
simple but complex, and at the same time imitative of fearful and pitiable happenings (that being the special character of this kind of poetry), it is clear first of all that (1) neither should virtuous men appear
undergoing a change from good to bad fortune, for that is not fearful,
nor pitiable either, but morally repugnant; nor (2) the wicked from bad
fortune to good—that is the most untragic form of all, it has none of
the qualities that one wants: it is productive neither of ordinary sympathy nor of pity nor of fear—nor again (3) the really wicked man
changing from good fortune to bad, for that kind of structure will excite sympathy but neither pity nor fear, since the one (pity) is directed
towards the man who does not deserve his misfortune and the other
(fear) towards the one who is like the rest of mankind—what is left is
the man who falls between these extremes. Such is a man who is neither a paragon of virtue and justice nor undergoes the change to mis-

fortune through any real badness or wickedness but because of some mistake; one of those who stand in great repute and prosperity, like Oedipus and Thyestes: conspicuous men from families of that kind.

So, then, the artistically made plot must necessarily be single 27 rather than double, as some maintain, and involve a change not from bad fortune to good fortune but the other way round, from good fortune to bad, and not thanks to wickedness but because of some mistake of great weight and consequence, by a man such as we have described or else on the good rather than the bad side. An indication comes from what has been happening in tragedy: at the beginning the poets used to "tick off" whatever plots came their way, but nowadays the finest tragedies are composed about a few houses: they deal with Alcmeon, Oedipus, Orestes, Meleager, Thyestes, Telephus,[6] and whichever others have had the misfortune to do or undergo fearful things.

Thus the technically finest tragedy is based on this structure. 28 Hence those who bring charges against Euripides[7] for doing this in his tragedies are making the same mistake. His practice is correct in the way that has been shown. There is a very significant indication: on our stages and in the competitions, plays of this structure are accepted as the most tragic, *if* they are handled successfully, and Euripides, though he may not make his other arrangements effectively, still is felt by the audience to be the most tragic, at least, of the poets.

Second comes the kind which is rated first by certain people, hav- 29 ing its structure double like the *Odyssey*[8] and with opposite endings for the good and bad. Its being put first is due to the weakness of the audiences; for the poets follow along, catering to their wishes. But this particular pleasure is not the one that springs from tragedy but is more characteristic of comedy.

Pity and fear and the tragic act. Now it is possible for the fearful or 30 pathetic effect to come from the actors' appearance, but it is also possible for it to arise from the very structure of the events, and this is closer to the mark and characteristic of a better poet. Namely, the plot must be so structured, even without benefit of any visual effect, that

---

[6]*Alcmeon . . . Telephus* Mythical characters who have been the heroes of Greek tragedies.

[7]*Euripides (480?–?406 B.C.)* Tragic playwright, author of *Alcestis, Medea, Elektra,* and *The Bacchae.*

[8]*Odyssey* Greek epic poem by Homer (c.900 B.C.), many of whose characters, including Odysseus, appear in Greek tragedies.

the one who is hearing the events unroll shudders with fear and feels pity at what happens: which is what one would experience on hearing the plot of the *Oedipus*. To set out to achieve this by means of the masks and costumes is less artistic, and requires technical support in the staging. As for those who do not set out to achieve the fearful through the masks and costumes, but only the monstrous, they have nothing to do with tragedy at all; for one should not seek any and every pleasure from tragedy, but the one that is appropriate to it.

Since it is the pleasure derived from pity and fear by means of im- 31 itation that the poet should seek to produce, it is clear that these qualities must be built into the constituent events. Let us determine, then, which kinds of happening are felt by the spectator to be fearful, and which pitiable. Now such acts are necessarily the work of persons who are near and dear (close blood kin) to one another, or enemies, or neither. But when an enemy attacks an enemy there is nothing pathetic about either the intention or the deed, except in the actual pain suffered by the victim; nor when the act is done by "neutrals"; but when the tragic acts come within the limits of close blood relationship, as when brother kills or intends to kill brother or do something else of that kind to him, or son to father or mother to son or son to mother— those are the situations one should look for.

Now although it is not admissable to break up the transmitted 32 stories—I mean for instance that Clytemnestra was killed by Orestes, or Eriphyle by Alcmeon—one should be artistic both in inventing stories and in managing the ones that have been handed down. But what we mean by "artistic" requires some explanation.

It is possible, then (1) for the act to be performed as the older poets 33 presented it, knowingly and wittingly; Euripides did it that way also, in Medea's murder of her children. It is possible (2) to refrain from performing the deed, with knowledge. Or it is possible (3) to perform the fearful act, but unwittingly, then recognize the blood relationship later, as Sophocles' Oedipus does; in that case the act is outside the play, but it can be in the tragedy itself, as with Astydamas'[9] Alcmeon, or Telegonus in the *Wounding of Odysseus*.[10] A further mode, in addition to these, is (4) while intending because of ignorance to perform some black crime, to discover the relationship before one does it. And there is no other mode besides these; for one must necessarily either do the deed or not, and with or without knowledge of what it is.

---

[9]*Astydamas*   Greek poet of the fourth century B.C.
[10]**The Wounding of Odysseus**   A play about the hero of the *Odyssey* that has not survived.

Of these modes, to know what one is doing but hold off and not 34 perform the act (no. 2) is worst: it has the morally repulsive character and at the same time is not tragic; for there is no tragic act. Hence nobody composes that way, or only rarely, as, for example, Haemon threatens Creon in the *Antigone*.[11] Performing the act (with knowledge) (no. 1) is second (poorest). Better is to perform it in ignorance and recognize what one has done afterward (no. 3); for the repulsive quality does not attach to the act, and the recognition has a shattering emotional effect. But the best is the last (no. 4): I mean a case like the one in the *Cresphontes* where Merope is about to kill her son but does not do so because she recognizes him first; or in *Iphigenia in Tauris* the same happens with sister and brother; or in the *Helle*[12] the son recognizes his mother just as he is about to hand her over to the enemy.

The reason for what was mentioned a while ago, namely that our 35 tragedies have to do with only a few families, is this: It was because the poets, when they discovered how to produce this kind of effect in their plots, were conducting their search on the basis of chance, not art; hence they have been forced to focus upon those families which happen to have suffered tragic happenings of this kind.

Enough, then, concerning the structure of events and what traits 36 the tragic plots should have.

---

[11]***Antigone*** A Play by Sophocles (*c*496?–?406 B.C.).
[12]**Cresphontes . . . Iphigenia in Tauris . . . Helle** Tragedies by Euripides; the *Cresphontes* is lost.

QUESTIONS

1. What is epic poetry?
2. What are the six elements of tragedy?
3. Which element do you feel is most important? Explain.
4. What are the stages of development of the literature Aristotle describes?
5. What does Aristotle mean by "an imitation of an action"? What would be the relationship to actual life of a work that "imitates an action"?
6. Why are the emotions of pity and terror appropriate for tragedy?

WRITING ASSIGNMENTS

1. Using Aristotle's method of categorizing as well as his method of referring to a specific play (choose a Shakespearian or other "modern" tragedy), offer your own analysis of what tragedy is. Be sure to consider the purposes of

tragedy—what kinds of truths are revealed and what tragic seriousness is. Then establish the relationship of plot, character, verbal expression, and thought, as well as visual adornment (setting and production values) and music.

2. If you have recently read a tragedy, examine it for its peripety and recognition. When do such moments occur? Do they occur simultaneously? What brings them about, and what is their importance? Would the tragedy you read have retained its impact if the peripety had not occurred? If the recognition had not occurred? What is the emotional value of these moments? Would they have pleased Aristotle?

3. Do you agree with Aristotle that plot is more important than character in drama? You need not restrict yourself to tragedy. You may wish to analyze a film or a television production in your approach to this question. Do producers of television shows seem to be in accord with Aristotle's ideas? Do film producers? Do play producers take a different view? Do you think a good drama is possible without fully developed characters? Do you agree with Aristotle that there can be tragedy without characters but not without plot?

4. Aristotle ranks thought as less important than action and character (para. 9). By "thought" he seems to mean what we call the message of the drama. Do you agree that thought is third in importance? If possible, comment on this by reference to at least one play in a discussion of its thought. What happens to drama when thought is first in importance rather than third?

5. In paragraphs 16 and 17, Aristotle talks about the difference between poetry and history. Do you agree with what he says about the differences and with his evaluation of the two modes—that "poetry is a more philosophical and serious business than history; for poetry speaks more of universals, history of particulars" (para. 16)? Construct an argument that takes one side of this question and establish your position.

6. Read or view *Oedipus Rex* by Sophocles. Which scenes most clearly evoke the emotions of pity and terror? Are other emotions aroused by the play? In which scenes are these emotions depicted?

JOSÉ ORTEGA Y GASSET

Dehumanization in Modern Art

JOSÉ ORTEGA Y GASSET (1883–1955) was Spain's most important philosopher. He received his doctorate from the University of Madrid in 1904, when barely twenty-one, and from 1910 to 1936, he was professor of Metaphysics at the University of Madrid. His essays on two major writers of the twentieth century, Marcel Proust and James Joyce, established him as an international figure and one of the most influential humanists in Spain.

Ortega was more than an academic. He participated in the government of Spain in the early 1930s, but when the revolution took hold in Spain and the lines were clearly drawn between Bolshevik Communists and Fascists under Francisco Franco (1892–1975), Ortega refused to take sides. He left Spain and went into voluntary exile to protest the revolution and its outcome: the victory of the Fascist forces and the elevation of Franco as Spain's dictator.

Ortega settled in Portugal in 1945 when the war in Europe was over. Despite the oppressive rule of Franco, he returned to Madrid in 1948 and established the Institute of the Humanities, where he

From *The Dehumanization of Art and Other Essays on Art, Culture, and Literature.*

worked relatively unharassed by the authorities. His writings ranged from literature to sociology to aesthetics. One of his earliest works, Meditations on Quixote *(1914), examined the symbols of Spanish writing, linking them to the Spanish people. In* Invertebrate Spain *(1922), he challenged what he felt was spineless leadership in the period following World War I. He pleaded for the development of a United States of Europe—a development that only now is being planned for the 1990s.*

His best-known book, The Revolt of the Masses *(first published in 1929), contains a political theme. Ortega feared that democracy as it was developing in Europe had within it the seeds of tyranny by the masses. He saw such a threat in Russian communism and in the fascism of Italy. He also feared that rapid population growth and occupational specialization would rob people of a common cultural past and cultural identity. Such a condition made it easier for a tyranny of masses to take over and to tolerate or even execute modern horrors, such as the concentration camps and exterminating ovens of Nazi Germany.*

The Dehumanization of Art, *from which this piece is drawn, was first published in 1925, then revised in 1948. It is a discourse in aesthetics designed to explain the directions of the sometimes perplexing modern artists.*

In The Dehumanization of Art *Ortega defined the boundaries between twentieth-century painting and other arts and those of the nineteenth-century. He typified the nineteenth-century artist as one concerned primarily with realism whose goal was a faithful reproduction of life. In contrast, the twentieth-century artist focused more on art as separate from the life to which it refers. Twentieth-century artists have drawn a sharper line between that which is art and that which is life.*

Necessarily, then, Ortega explained that modern art appeals to a special aesthetic sensibility. It is not the same sensibility that we bring to a view out our window of a lovely mountain. It is not the same sensibility that we bring to our observation of people in our lives. In Ortega's words, the artist cultivates "specifically aesthetic sentiments" (para. 18). These feelings are different from those that a person might express in an everyday human situation. Therefore, the feelings that we understand as human emotions may be of great importance to us in daily life but of little importance to us in contemplating a work of art.

Such a position may seem contradictory to our experience of the arts, but to Ortega there existed a universal confusion of art and life.

For him, "art ought to be full clarity, high noon of the intellect," and not distorted by the "psychic contagion" of emotion. In this sense, Ortega stands in sharp contrast with the other writers on art represented in Part Six. But for him, such an outlook is crucial to comprehending the nature of modern art.

ORTEGA'S RHETORIC

Ortega writes for a wide audience. Among his readers are those who are obviously learned—we know that because of his willingness to quote from several languages. His readers are knowledgeable, or wish to be knowledgeable, about art as we know from his references to artists, musicians, and writers. But he also intends to communicate with those who are not specialists because he has used an extremely effective rhetorical technique in introducing his discussion with an analogy.

This opening analogy involves a story about a man who is dying. Several people gather about his bed: his wife, a doctor, a reporter, and a painter. Each is either deeply involved in the event or somewhat detached. The question is, Who among the witnesses is most likely to see things as they really are? Ortega decides that they all see things truly but that each witness's vision is qualified by a limited point of view. The painter, the most detached, sees things "inhumanly." The wife, closest to the dying man sees things "humanly."

The distinction between the human and inhuman is, by analogy, extended to art. When we are involved with the lived reality (what is represented in the work of art) we are being most human. When we detach the representation from what it represents, we are being inhuman.

The terms "human" and "inhuman" are problematic for most of us, and Ortega was aware of this problem. He attempts to demonstrate that modern art is less connected with the world that it represents than the art from previous eras. We cannot take the same comfort in recognizing objects as "real." Ortega, realizing that modern art is difficult for most people to appreciate, tries in this essay to show us, by analogy, the advantages of the detachment that allows us to evaluate art on its own terms rather than in terms of how like reality it can be.

Another rhetorical device Ortega uses is the aphorism. He writes many general statements that sound aphoristic, such as "From Beethoven to Wagner all music is melodrama" (para. 25). But this is a *limited statement. A true aphorism—because it is universal—appears later in "To insist on neat distinctions is a symptom of mental honesty." The passage ends with another aphorism: "Poetry has become the higher algebra of metaphors." Aphorisms have the advantage— especially in the hands of a philosopher such as Ortega—of encapsulating wisdom, often appearing in the work of summing up, of enforcing in the reader's mind the intent of the discussion.*

Dehumanization
in Modern Art

When we analyze the new style we find that it contains certain closely connected tendencies. It tends (1) to dehumanize art, (2) to avoid living forms, (3) to see to it that the work of art is nothing but a work of art, (4) to consider art as play and nothing else, (5) to be essentially ironical, (6) to beware of sham and hence to aspire to scrupulous realization, (7) to regard art as a thing of no transcending consequence. 1

In the following I shall say a few words about each of these features of modern art. 2

A Few Drops of
Phenomenology[1]

A great man is dying. His wife is by his bedside. A doctor takes the dying man's pulse. In the background two more persons are discovered: a reporter who is present for professional reasons, and a painter whom mere chance has brought here. Wife, doctor, reporter, and painter witness one and the same event. Nonetheless, this identical event—a man's death—impresses each of them in a different way. So 3

---

[1]**Phenomenology** The study of concrete events and phenomena apart from any preconceptions concerning their structure and with the intent to describe and understand their essential relationships.

different indeed that the several aspects have hardly anything in common. What this scene means to the wife who is all grief has so little to do with what it means to the painter who looks on impassively that it seems doubtful whether the two can be said to be present at the same event.

It thus becomes clear that one and the same reality may split up 4
into many diverse realities when it is beheld from different points of view. And we cannot help asking ourselves: Which of all these realities must then be regarded as the real and authentic one? The answer, no matter how we decide, cannot but be arbitrary. Any preference can be founded on caprice only. All these realities are equivalent, each being authentic for its corresponding point of view. All we can do is to classify the points of view and to determine which among them seems, in a practical way, most normal or most spontaneous. Thus we arrive at a conception of reality that is by no means absolute, but at least practical and normative.

As for the points of view of the four persons present at the death- 5
bed, the clearest means of distinguishing them is by measuring one of their dimensions, namely the emotional distance between each person and the event they all witness. For the wife of the dying man the distance shrinks to almost nothing. What is happening so tortures her soul and absorbs her mind that it becomes one with her person. Or to put it inversely, the wife is drawn into the scene, she is part of it. A thing can be seen, an event can be observed, only when we have separated it from ourselves and it has ceased to form a living part of our being. Thus the wife is not present at the scene, she is in it. She does not behold it, she "lives" it.

The doctor is several degrees removed. To him this is a professional 6
case. He is not drawn into the event with the frantic and blinding anxiety of the poor woman. However it is his bounden duty as a doctor to take a serious interest, he carries responsibility, perhaps his professional honor is at stake. Hence he too, albeit in a less integral and less intimate way, takes part in the event. He is involved in it not with his heart but with the professional portion of his self. He too "lives" the scene although with an agitation originating not in the emotional center, but in the professional surface, of his existence.

When we now put ourselves in the place of the reporter we realize 7
that we have traveled a long distance away from the tragic event. So far indeed that we have lost all emotional contact with it. The reporter, like the doctor, has been brought here for professional reasons and not out of a spontaneous human interest. But while the doctor's

profession requires him to interfere, the reporter's requires him precisely to stay aloof; he has to confine himself to observing. To him the
event is a mere scene, a pure spectacle on which he is expected to
report in his newspaper column. He takes no feeling part in what is
happening here, he is emotionally free, an outsider. He does not "live"
the scene, he observes it. Yet he observes it with a view to telling his
readers about it. He wants to interest them, to move them, and if possible to make them weep as though they each had been the dying
man's best friend. From his schooldays he remembers Horace's[2] recipe:
"*Si vis me flere dolendum est primum ipsi tibi*"—if you want me to
weep you must first grieve yourself.

Obedient to Horace the reporter is anxious to pretend emotion, 8
hoping that it will benefit his literary performance. If he does not
"live" the scene he at least pretends to "live" it.

The painter, in fine, completely unconcerned, does nothing but 9
keep his eyes open. What is happening here is none of his business; he
is, as it were, a hundred miles removed from it. His is a purely perceptive attitude; indeed, he fails to perceive the event in its entirety. The
tragic inner meaning escapes his attention which is directed exclusively toward the visual part—color values, lights, and shadows. In the
painter we find a maximum of distance and a minimum of feeling
intervention.

The inevitable dullness of this analysis will, I hope, be excused if 10
it now enables us to speak in a clear and precise way of a scale of
emotional distances between ourselves and reality. In this scale, the
degree of closeness is equivalent to the degree of feeling participation;
the degree of remoteness, on the other hand, marks the degree to
which we have freed ourselves from the real event, thus objectifying it
and turning it into a theme of pure observation. At one end of the scale
the world—persons, things, situations—is given to us in the aspect of
"lived" reality; at the other end we see everything in the aspect of
"observed" reality.

At this point we must make a remark that is essential in aesthetics 11
and without which neither old art nor new art can be satisfactorily
analyzed. Among the diverse aspects of reality we find one from which
all the others derive and which they all presuppose: "lived" reality. If
nobody had ever "lived" in pure and frantic abandonment a man's

---

[2]***Horace Quintus Horatius Flaccus (65–8 B.C.)*** A major Roman poet of the Augustan
Age. He was studied very closely in the traditional European education of Ortega's day.

death, the doctor would not bother, the readers would not understand the reporter's pathos, and the canvas on which the painter limned a person on a bed surrounded by mourning figures would be meaningless. The same holds for any object, be it a person, a thing, or a situation. The primal aspect of an apple is that in which I see it when I am about to eat it. All its other possible forms—when it appears, for instance, in a Baroque ornament, or on a still life of Cézanne's,[3] or in the eternal metaphor of a girl's apple cheeks—preserve more or less that original aspect. A painting or a poem without any vestiges of "lived" forms would be unintelligible, i.e., nothing—as a discourse is nothing whose every word is emptied of its customary meaning.

That is to say, in the scale of realities "lived" reality holds a peculiar primacy which compels us to regard it as "the" reality. Instead of "lived" reality we may say "human" reality. The painter who impassively witnesses the death scene appears "inhuman." In other words, the human point of view is that in which we "live" situations, persons, things. And, vice versa, realities—a woman, a countryside, an event— are human when they present the aspect in which they are usually "lived." 12

As an example, the importance of which will appear later, let us mention that among the realities which constitute the world are our ideas. We use our ideas in a "human" way when we employ them for thinking things. Thinking of Napoleon,[4] for example, we are normally concerned with the great man of that name. A psychologist, on the other hand, adopts an unusual, "inhuman" attitude when he forgets about Napoleon and, prying into his own mind, tries to analyze his idea of Napoleon as such idea. His perspective is the opposite of that prevailing in spontaneous life. The idea, instead of functioning as the means to think an object with, is itself made the object and the aim of thinking. We shall soon see the unexpected use which the new art has made of this "inhuman" inversion. 13

---

[3]**Paul Cézanne (1839–1906)** One of the most important French painters of his day. His style, sometimes called Postimpressionist, contributed to the development of cubism in the first two decades of the twentieth century.

[4]**Napoleon Bonaparte (1769–1821)** The first national military leader in modern times to conduct war on an almost global scale. Named emperor of France, he was in the minds of many a potential tyrant. This is something of what Ortega means when he says that people interpret the name in terms of an idea.

First Installment on the
Dehumanization of Art

With amazing swiftness modern art has split up into a multitude 14
of divergent directions. Nothing is easier than to stress the differences.
But such an emphasis on the distinguishing and specific features
would be pointless without a previous account of the common fund
that in a varying and sometimes contradictory manner asserts itself
throughout modern art. Did not Aristotle already observe that things
differ in what they have in common? Because all bodies are colored
we notice that they are differently colored. Species are nothing if not
modifications of a genus, and we cannot understand them unless we
realize that they draw, in their several ways, upon a common patrimony.

I am little interested in special directions of modern art and, but 15
for a few exceptions, even less in special works. Nor do I, for that
matter, expect anybody to be particularly interested in my valuation
of the new artistic produce. Writers who have nothing to convey but
their praise or dispraise of works of art had better abstain from writing.
They are unfit for this arduous task.

The important thing is that there unquestionably exists in the 16
world a new artistic sensibility.[5] Over against the multiplicity of special directions and individual works, the new sensibility represents the
generic fact and the source, as it were, from which the former spring.
This sensibility it is worth while to define. And when we seek to ascertain the most general and most characteristic feature of modern artistic production we come upon the tendency to dehumanize art. After
what we have said above, this formula now acquires a tolerably precise
meaning.

Let us compare a painting in the new style with one of, say, 1860. 17
The simplest procedure will be to begin by setting against one another
the objects they represent: a man perhaps, a house, or a mountain. It
then appears that the artist of 1860 wanted nothing so much as to give
to the objects in his picture the same looks and airs they possess outside it when they occur as parts of the "lived" or "human" reality.
Apart from this he may have been animated by other more intricate
aesthetic ambitions, but what interests us is that his first concern was

---

[5]This new sensibility is a gift not only of the artist proper but also of his audience.
When I said above that the new art is an art for artists I understood by "artists" not only
those who produce this art but also those who are capable of perceiving purely artistic
values. [Ortega's note]

with securing this likeness. Man, house, mountain are at once recognized, they are our good old friends; whereas on a modern painting we are at a loss to recognize them. It might be supposed that the modern painter has failed to achieve resemblance. But then some pictures of the 1860's are "poorly" painted, too, and the objects in them differ considerably from the corresponding objects outside them. And yet, whatever the differences, the very blunders of the traditional artist point toward the "human" object; they are downfalls on the way toward it and somehow equivalent to the orienting words "This is a cock" with which Cervantes[6] lets the painter Orbanejo enlighten his public. In modern paintings the opposite happens. It is not that the painter is bungling and fails to render the natural (natural = human) thing because he deviates from it, but that these deviations point in a direction opposite to that which would lead to reality.

Far from going more or less clumsily toward reality, the artist is 18 seen going against it. He is brazenly set on deforming reality, shattering its human aspect, dehumanizing it. With the things represented on traditional paintings we could have imaginary intercourse. Many a young Englishman has fallen in love with Gioconda.[7] With the objects of modern pictures no intercourse is possible. By divesting them of their aspect of "lived" reality the artist has blown up the bridges and burned the ships that could have taken us back to our daily world. He leaves us locked up in an abstruse universe, surrounded by objects with which human dealings are inconceivable, and thus compels us to improvise other forms of intercourse completely distinct from our ordinary ways with things. We must invent unheard-of gestures to fit those singular figures. This new way of life which presupposes the annulment of spontaneous life is precisely what we call understanding and enjoyment of art. Not that this life lacks sentiments and passions, but those sentiments and passions evidently belong to a flora other than that which covers the hills and dales of primary and human life. What those ultra-objects[8] evoke in our inner artist are secondary passions, specifically aesthetic sentiments.

It may be said that, to achieve this result, it would be simpler to 19 dismiss human forms—man, house, mountain—altogether and to con-

---

[6]***Miguel de Saavedra Cervantes (1547–1616)*** Author of the great Spanish novel *Don Quixote.*

[7]***La Gioconda*** The Italian name for Leonardo da Vinci's painting in the Louvre, usually known as "The Mona Lisa."

[8]"Ultraism" is one of the most appropriate names that have been coined to denote the new sensibility. [Ortega's note]

struct entirely original figures. But, in the first place, this is not feasible.[9] Even in the most abstract ornamental line a stubborn reminiscence lurks of certain "natural" forms. Secondly—and this is the crucial point—the art of which we speak is inhuman not only because it contains no things human, but also because it is an explicit act of dehumanization. In his escape from the human world the young artist cares less for the *"terminus ad quem,"* the startling fauna at which he arrives, than for the *"terminus a quo,"*[10] the human aspect which he destroys. The question is not to paint something altogether different from a man, a house, a mountain, but to paint a man who resembles a man as little as possible; a house that preserves of a house exactly what is needed to reveal the metamorphosis; a cone miraculously emerging—as the snake from his slough—from what used to be a mountain. For the modern artist, aesthetic pleasure derives from such a triumph over human matter. That is why he has to drive home the victory by presenting in each case the strangled victim.

It may be thought a simple affair to fight shy of reality, but it is by no means easy. There is no difficulty in painting or saying things which make no sense whatever, which are unintelligible and therefore nothing. One only needs to assemble unconnected words or to draw random lines.[11] But to construct something that is not a copy of "nature" and yet possesses substance of its own is a feat which presupposes nothing less than genius. 20

"Reality" constantly waylays the artist to prevent his flight. Much cunning is needed to effect the sublime escape. A reversed Odysseus,[12] he must free himself from his daily Penelope and sail through reefs and rocks to Circe's Faery. When, for a moment, he succeeds in escap- 21

---

[9]An attempt has been made in this extreme sense—in certain works by Picasso—but it has failed signally. [Ortega's note]

[10]*terminus . . . quo* Terminus ad quem means the starting point; *terminus a quo*, the end point.

[11]This was done by the dadaistic hoax. It is interesting to note again (see the above footnote) that the very vagaries and abortive experiments of the new art derive with a certain cogency from its organic principle, thereby giving ample proof that modern art is a unified and meaningful movement. [Ortega's note]

[12]*Odysseus* The reference is to the cunning hero of Homer's epic poem *The Odyssey.* Penelope is the faithful wife who waited for twenty years for Odysseus to return from the Trojan War. Circe was a sorceress who tried to enchant Odysseus and prevent him from continuing his journey. Ortega's reference reverses the story: here the beguiler Circe represents imagination and art, while the traditionally "real" Penelope represents a waylaying sorceress—a distraction from Odysseus's proper mission.

ing the perpetual ambush, let us not grudge him a gesture of arrogant triumph, a St. George gesture with the dragon prostrate at his feet.

Invitation to Understanding

The works of art that the nineteenth century favored invariably 22 contain a core of "lived" reality which furnishes the substance, as it were, of the aesthetic body. With this material the aesthetic process works, and its working consists in endowing the human nucleus with glamour and dignity. To the majority of people this is the most natural and the only possible setup of a work of art. Art is reflected life, nature seen through a temperament, representation of human destinies, and so on. But the fact is that our young artists, with no less conviction, maintain the opposite. Must the old always have the last word today while tomorrow infallibly the young win out? For one thing, let us not rant and rave. *"Dove si grida,"* Leonardo da Vinci warns us, *"no é vera scienza." "Neque lugere neque indignari sed intelligere,"* recommends Spinoza.[13] Our firmest convictions are apt to be the most suspect, they mark our limits and our bonds. Life is a petty thing unless it is moved by the indomitable urge to extend its boundaries. Only in proportion as we are desirous of living more do we really live. Obstinately to insist on carrying on within the same familiar horizon betrays weakness and a decline of vital energies. Our horizon is a biological line, a living part of our organism. In times of fullness of life it expands, elastically moving in unison almost with our breathing. When the horizon stiffens it is because it has become fossilized and we are growing old.

It is less obvious than academicians assume that a work of art must 23 consist of human stuff which the Muses comb and groom. Art cannot be reduced to cosmetics. Perception of "lived" reality and perception of artistic form, as I have said before, are essentially incompatible be-

---

[13]***Leonardo da Vinci (1452–1519)*** A great Renaissance artist of realistic paintings and an inventor. The Italian reads, "Where there is clamoring, there is no true knowledge." ***Benedict Spinoza (1632–1677)*** Philosopher born in Amsterdam of Portuguese-Jewish descent; of great importance to modern theology. His Latin phrase reads, "Neither to decry nor to become angry but to be aware." Both expressions recommend that we act not in rage against the changes of style but that we try to understand them instead. This is essentially Ortega's recommendation as well.

cause they call for a different adjustment of our perceptive apparatus. An art that requires such a double seeing is a squinting art. The nineteenth century was remarkably cross-eyed. That is why its products, far from representing a normal type of art, may be said to mark a maximum aberration in the history of taste. All great periods of art have been careful not to let the work revolve about human contents. The imperative of unmitigated realism that dominated the artistic sensibility of the last century must be put down as a freak in aesthetic evolution. It thus appears that the new inspiration, extravagant though it seems, is merely returning, at least in one point, to the royal road of art. For this road is called "will to style." But to stylize means to deform reality, to derealize; style involves dehumanization. And vice versa, there is no other means of stylizing except by dehumanizing. Whereas realism, exhorting the artist faithfully to follow reality, exhorts him to abandon style. A Zurbarán enthusiast, groping for the suggestive word, will declare that the works of this painter have "character." And character and not style is distinctive of the works of Lucas and Sorolla, of Dickens and Galdós.[14] The eighteenth century, on the other hand, which had so little character was a past master of style.

More about the Dehumanization of Art

The young set has declared taboo any infiltration of human con- 24 tents into art. Now, human contents, the component elements of our daily world, form a hierarchy of three ranks. There is first the realm of persons, second that of living beings, lastly there are the inorganic things. The veto of modern art is more or less apodictic[15] according to the rank the respective object holds in this hierarchy. The first stratum, as it is most human, is most carefully avoided.

This is clearly discernible in music and in poetry. From Beethoven 25

---

[14]*Zurbarán . . . Galdós* Francisco de Zurbarán (1598–?1664), a Spanish Baroque painter, whose style is realistic. Lucas van Leyden (1494–1533) was a famous printmaker much regarded for his astonishingly realistic technique. Joaquín Sorolla y Bastida (1863–1923) was a Spanish realist painter. Charles Dickens (1812–1870) and Benitez Pérez Galdós (1843–1920) were novelists known for their powerful depiction of characters. Galdós was especially known for his series of historical novels about Napoleonic Spain.

[15]*apodictic* What can be clearly shown by argument. Ortega tells us that the new young artists tend to avoid painting "the realm of persons" in favor of subject matter that is more easily dehumanized.

to Wagner[16] music was primarily concerned with expressing personal feelings. The composer erected great structures of sound in which to accommodate his autobiography. Art was, more or less, confession. There existed no way of aesthetic enjoyment except by contagion. "In music," Nietzsche declared, "the passions enjoy themselves." Wagner poured into *Tristan and Isolde* his adultery with Mathilde Wesendonck, and if we want to enjoy this work we must, for a few hours, turn vaguely adulterous ourselves. That darkly stirring music makes us weep and tremble and melt away voluptuously. From Beethoven to Wagner all music is melodrama.

And that is unfair, a young artist would say. It means taking advantage of a noble weakness inherent in man which exposes him to infection from his neighbor's joys and sorrows. Such an infection is no mental phenomenon; it works like a reflex in the same way as the grating of a knife upon glass sets the teeth on edge. It is an automatic effect, nothing else. We must distinguish between delight and titillation. Romanticism hunts with a decoy, it tampers with the bird's fervor in order to riddle him with the pellets of sounds. Art must not proceed by psychic contagion, for psychic contagion is an unconscious phenomenon, and art ought to be full clarity, high noon of the intellect. Tears and laughter are, aesthetically, frauds. The gesture of beauty never passes beyond smiles, melancholy or delighted. If it can do without them, better still. *"Toute maîtrise jette le froid"* (Mallarmé).[17]

There is, to my mind, a good deal of truth in the young artist's verdict. Aesthetic pleasure must be a seeing pleasure. For pleasures may be blind or seeing. The drunken man's happiness is blind. Like everything in the world it has a cause, the alcohol; but it has no motive. A man who has won at sweepstakes is happy too, but in a different manner; he is happy "about" something. The drunken man's merriment is hermetically enclosed in itself, he does not know why he is happy. Whereas the joy of the winner consists precisely in his being conscious of a definite fact that motivates and justifies his content-

26

27

---

[16]***Beethoven . . . Wagner*** Ludwig van Beethoven (1770–1827) and Richard Wagner (1813–1883), major German composers whose work is often discussed in terms of its relationship to their lives. Mathilde Wesendonck was Wagner's mistress whom he celebrated in his composition known as "The Wesendonck Songs." His relationship with her caused him great pain and forced him to separate from his wife and leave his home in Zurich for Venice, where he completed the opera *Tristan and Isolde.*

[17]***François-René-Auguste Mallarmé (1755–1835)*** The most important French poet of his time. The French expression means "All mastery springs from a coolness."

ment. He is glad because he is aware of an object that is in itself gladdening. His is a happiness with eyes and which feeds on its motive, flowing, as it were, from the object to the subject.[18]

Any phenomenon that aspires to being mental and not mechanical   28
must bear this luminous character of intelligibility, of motivation. But the pleasure aroused by romantic art has hardly any connection with its content. What has the beauty of music—something obviously located without and beyond myself in the realm of sound—what has the beauty of music to do with that melting mood it may produce in me? Is not this a thorough confusion? Instead of delighting in the artistic object people delight in their own emotions, the work being only the cause and the alcohol of their pleasure. And such a *quid pro quo* is bound to happen whenever art is made to consist essentially in an exposition of "lived" realities. "Lived" realities are too overpowering not to evoke a sympathy which prevents us from perceiving them in their objective purity.

Seeing requires distance. Each art operates a magic lantern that re-   29
moves and transfigures its objects. On its screen they stand aloof, inmates of an inaccessible world, in an absolute distance. When this de-realization is lacking, an awkward perplexity arises: we do not know whether to "live" the things or to observe them.

Madame Tussaud's[19] comes to mind and the peculiar uneasiness   30
aroused by dummies. The origin of this uneasiness lies in the provoking ambiguity with which wax figures defeat any attempt at adopting a clear and consistent attitude toward them. Treat them as living beings, and they will sniggeringly reveal their waxen secret. Take them for dolls, and they seem to breathe in irritated protest. They will not be reduced to mere objects. Looking at them we suddenly feel a misgiving: should it not be they who are looking at us? Till in the end we are sick and tired of those hired corpses. Wax figures are melodrama at its purest.

The new sensibility, it seems to me, is dominated by a distaste for   31
human elements in art very similar to the feelings cultured people have always experienced at Madame Tussaud's, while the mob has al-

---

[18]Causation and motivation are two completely different relations. The causes of our states of consciousness are not present in these states; science must ascertain them. But the motive of a feeling, of a volition, of a belief forms part of the art itself. Motivation is a conscious relation. [Ortega's note]

[19]***Madame Marie Tussaud (1760–1850)*** Swiss wax-modeler who moved to London and established a wax museum in which she displayed figures of important historical personages. The museum still exists.

ways been delighted by that gruesome waxen hoax. In passing we may here ask ourselves a few impertinent questions which we have no intention to answer now. What is behind this disgust at seeing art mixed up with life? Could it be disgust for the human sphere as such, for reality, for life? Or is it rather the opposite: respect for life and unwillingness to confuse it with art, so inferior a thing as art? But what do we mean by calling art an inferior function—divine art, glory of civilization, *fine fleur*[20] of culture, and so forth? As we were saying, these questions are impertinent; let us dismiss them.

In Wagner, melodrama comes to a peak. Now, an artistic form, on 32 reaching its maximum, is likely to topple over into its opposite. And thus we find that in Wagner the human voice has already ceased to be the protagonist and is drowned in the cosmic din of the orchestra. However, a more radical change was to follow. Music had to be relieved of private sentiments and purified in an exemplary objectification. This was the deed of Dubussy.[21] Owing to him, it has become possible to listen to music serenely, without swoons and tears. All the various developments in the art of music during these last decades move on the ground of the new ultraworldly world conquered by the genius of Debussy. So decisive is this conversion of the subjective attitude into the objective that any subsequent differentiations appear comparatively negligible.[22] Debussy dehumanized music, that is why he marks a new era in the art of music.

The same happened in poetry. Poetry had to be disencumbered. 33 Laden with human matter it was dragging along, skirting the ground and bumping into trees and house tops like a deflated balloon. Here Mallarmé was the liberator who restored to the lyrical poem its ethereal quality and ascending power. Perhaps he did not reach the goal himself. Yet it was he who gave the decisive order: shoot ballast.

For what was the theme of poetry in the romantic century? The 34 poet informed us prettily of his private upper-middle-class emotions, his major and minor sorrows, his yearnings, his religious or political preoccupations, and, in case he was English, his reveries behind his pipe. In one way or another, his ambition was to enhance his daily

---

[20]*fine fleur*   Translated, "delicate flower."

[21]*Claude Debussy (1862–1918)*   The first important Impressionist composer. Ortega feels that Debussy dehumanized music because he created musical descriptions of phenomena that did not depend on emotional reactions for their interpretation. One of his best-known compositions is *La Mer*, or *The Sea*.

[22]A more detailed analysis of Debussy's significance with respect to romantic music may be found in the author's above quoted essay "Musicalia." [Ortega's note]

existence. Thanks to personal genius, a halo of finer substance might occasionally surround the human core of the poem—as for instance in Baudelaire.[23] But this splendor was a by-product. All the poet wished was to be human.

"And that seems objectionable to a young man?" somebody who   35
has ceased to be one asks with suppressed indignation. "What does he want the poet to be? A bird, an ichthyosaurus,[24] a dodecahedron?"

I can't say. However, I believe that the young poet when writing   36
poetry simply wishes to be a poet. We shall yet see that all new art (like new science, new politics—new life, in sum) abhors nothing so much as blurred borderlines. To insist on neat distinctions is a symptom of mental honesty. Life is one thing, art is another—thus the young set think or at least feel—let us keep the two apart. The poet begins where the man ends. The man's lot is to live his human life, the poet's to invent what is nonexistent. Herein lies the justification of the poetical profession. The poet aggrandizes the world by adding to reality, which is there by itself, the continents of his imagination. Author derives from *auctor*, he who augments. It was the title Rome bestowed upon her generals when they had conquered new territory for the City.

Mallarmé was the first poet in the nineteenth century who wanted   37
to be nothing but a poet. He "eschewed"—as he said himself—"the materials offered by nature" and composed small lyrical objects distinct from the human fauna and flora. This poetry need not be "felt." As it contains nothing human, it contains no cue for emotion either. When a woman is mentioned it is "the woman no one"; when an hour strikes it is "the hour not marked on dials." Proceeding by negatives, Mallarmé's verse muffles all vital resonance and presents us with figures so extramundane that merely looking at them is delight. Among such creatures, what business has the poor face of the man who officiates as poet? None but to disappear, to vanish and to become a pure nameless voice breathing into the air the words—those true protagonists of the lyrical pursuit. This pure and nameless voice, the mere acoustic carrier of the verse, is the voice of the poet who has learned to extricate himself from the surrounding man.

---

[23]*Charles Baudelaire (1821–1867)* an important precursor of modernism in French poetry. In his volume *Flowers of Evil*, he investigated his own responses to emotional situations that were usually off-limits to the poet.

[24]*ichthyosaurus* A prehistoric fish. A dodecahedron is an object with twelve sides. Each of these represents a preposterous interpretation of poetic ambition.

Wherever we look we see the same thing: flight from the human 38
person. The methods of dehumanization are many. Those employed
today may differ vastly from Mallarmé's; in fact, I am well aware that
his pages are still reached by romantic palpitations. Yet just as modern
music belongs to a historical unity that begins with Debussy, all new
poetry moves in the direction in which Mallarmé pointed. The land-
marks of these two names seem to me essential for charting the main
line of the new style above the indentations produced by individual
inspirations.

It will not be easy to interest a person under thirty in a book that 39
under the pretext of art reports on the doings of some men and women.
To him, such a thing smacks of sociology or psychology. He would
accept it gladly if issues were not confused and those facts were told
him in sociological and psychological terms. But art means something
else to him.

Poetry has become the higher algebra of metaphors. 40

QUESTIONS

1. How is modern art dehumanized?
2. Is the dehumanization of art a good or a bad thing for art?
3. What is realistic art?
4. What does Ortega mean when he states (para. 37) that Mallarmé's "poetry
   need not be 'felt' "? He says it contains no emotion. Is this possible in
   poetry?
5. In paragraph 29, Ortega states that "Seeing requires distance." Explain
   what he means.
6. Explain Ortega's opinion of Madame Tussaud's wax museum.

WRITING ASSIGNMENTS

1. Which kinds of emotions are appropriate for us to feel in relation to a work
   of art? Choose a specific work of art and describe it in terms that Ortega
   might approve. Attempt to distance yourself from the work, using the
   analogy of the dying man in order to approach the art in the best way
   possible. Imagine yourself taking the position of the painter in that analogy.
2. Choose a representative painting by a painter working in the 1920s or
   1930s. Examine the painting for its relationship to life, as described by
   Ortega. Does it clearly represent a human moment or does it distort the

representation in such a way as to dehumanize its subject as Ortega thinks modern art does? Comment on the subject matter, the coloration, the perspective, and the figures that may be represented in the painting. Does Ortega's thesis about modern art hold up?

3. Ortega talks about "specifically aesthetic sentiments" in paragraph 18. Which emotions could be specifically focused on works of art, but not on life? Is there such a thing as a specifically aesthetic emotion? Ortega regards it as highly desirable, because it removes art out of everyday life and places it in a separate sphere. Is it possible for art to be so positioned? Examine Ortega's theory in relation to a work of art or a group of art works and decide whether he is correct or incorrect in his assumptions.

4. Ortega discusses realism in works of art at length. What is realism in painting? How is realism achieved, and once achieved, how does it affect you emotionally? What is the relationship between the excellence of a work of art and its ability to achieve realism? Why is realism a powerful concept in painting? Is it a concept that you specially value?

5. Ortega states flatly in paragraph 23 that "perception of 'lived' reality and perception of artistic form, as I have said before, are essentially incompatible because they call for a different adjustment of our perceptive apparatus." Explain what Ortega means and, by comparing two paintings that treat "lived" reality differently, demonstrate what Ortega's expectations are of painting and of our responses to painting.

VIRGINIA WOOLF

A Letter to a Young Poet

VIRGINIA WOOLF *(1882–1941), one of the most gifted of modern novelists, was part of a literary and artistic group that had formed when many of its members were at Cambridge University. When they graduated and took residence in London, they seemed to gravitate toward the area near Virginia Woolf's home in Gordon Square, in Bloomsbury. Before long they were known as the Bloomsbury group and were often humorously referred to as "Bloomsberries." The fact that Virginia, her husband Leonard Woolf, her sister Vanessa Bell, with her husband Clive Bell, and their friends Lytton Strachey, Duncan Grant, David Garnett, John Maynard Keynes (see Part Two), and Roger Fry—as well as others less famous—all gathered together to talk about their work is significant. It meant that they had a forum for their thinking. And it meant, as well, that they were generous with their ideas.*

"A Letter to a Young Poet" is symptomatic of the Bloomsbury ethic: it is strikingly generous when a highly successful and world-famous novelist takes time to write to an unknown poet to be encouraging. Woolf was like others in her group in that she felt that they were all part of an ongoing tradition of the arts. Anything she did to help those who were developing was an investment in the future of literature.

Woolf is best known for her adventurous and experimental novels, particularly Jacob's Room (1922), Mrs. Dalloway (1925), To the Lighthouse (1927), Orlando (1928), and The Waves (1931). She also constantly wrote critical essays for papers and journals, and many of her essays, such as this letter, have been assembled in collections such as The Common Reader, First Series (1925), and The Second Common Reader (1932).

Woolf was also noted for championing feminist causes. One of her most influential books, A Room of One's Own (1929), treats the problems that women face when entering professional life, including the arts. There is a celebrated discussion in that book of what would have happened had Shakespeare had a sister who was as gifted as he. Woolf's achievement as a novelist and a critic places her in the forefront of English writers, not only of her own time but of all time.

"A Letter to a Young Poet" is fascinating not only for its general advice but also for its general assessment of the nature of poetry at the time. Woolf repeatedly excuses herself on the grounds that she is a prose writer and not a poet. At one point she mentions that because she did not have formal university training, she knows none of the meters that are available to the poet. She explains that she had not gone to Cambridge, like the male members of the Bloomsbury group, but had been educated at home. Her father, Leslie Stephen, was a broadly educated man and a noted writer and editor, and his library among the most impressive she could have had access to. Her mother died when she was twelve years old, and Woolf's life was unusually bookish. Yet, as she tells her correspondent in this letter, there is more to literature than "book-learning"; one must pay attention to the sensory experience of everyday life.

She tells her young poet that much of what she reads in contemporary poetry is centered on the poet. She bases this on a reading of three contemporary poets whose work she excerpts. None of the excerpts is especially impressive; from them, one could conclude that contemporary poetry is not in good shape. Yet she is optimistic rather than pessimistic—as is the imaginary old gentleman she opens the essay with—the fellow who condemns all modern verse, saying it is dead.

She advises her poet to write about people who are unlike himself; in other words, she urges him not to focus on the poetic self but to use the poetic self to observe the world outside. She uses as her model William Shakespeare, whose characters, she insists, helped him create great poetry because they demanded that their lines be spoken as they had to be spoken—in their own voices rather than in Shake-

*speare's. She urges the young poet to observe other people and to ob-
serve them keenly.*

WOOLF'S RHETORIC

*Because this is a letter, it is relaxed in tone. Like many letters,
however, this one has all the earmarks of having been conceived as
a document that could be published, and in fact became the title
essay of* A Letter to a Young Poet *(1932). Indeed, Woolf mentions that
many letters are written for publication but that "authentic" letters
are filled with the scraps and details of real life and therefore burned.
She knows her letter will not be burned, and she adds the last, ironical lines saying that, in effect, the juicy parts are not included. She
also refers to bits of gossip and scandal that were included in the
letter to which she "responds," so that we have the feeling of an ongoing and lively correspondence between two people who know one
another well. In a sense, we have the delightfully guilty feeling that
we are eavesdropping.*

*Among Woolf's rhetorical resources is allusion. She is able to al-
lude to many literary greats because she is writing to a literary person. Those of us who are not "literary people" naturally need the foot-
notes, and Woolf knew that too; in a sense, she is taking this
opportunity to introduce us to names of writers she has enjoyed, and
because she is offhand about it, she does not seem to be an instructor
but, rather, an interested friend. Remember that two of her most
successful books are addressed to the "Common Reader," whom she
always had in mind when she wrote. She is generous in that she
wishes to share her enthusiasms and discoveries with everyone. Her
declaration of ignorance about the intricacies of poetic meter remind
us that she is not a know-it-all.*

*One of her most delightful rhetorical surprises is revealed in par-
agraph 4 where she decides to "be" the person she addresses. "Let me
try to imagine . . . what it feels like to be a young poet in the autumn
of 1931," she says, and then goes on to reveal her observations as if
from that perspective. Her correspondent has told her that he is anxious, that he fears modern poetry is dead, that he does not know
whether he can carry on. Her response respects his feelings but encourages him by commenting on poetry which is not altogether
successful. She offers critical comments on the poetry she quotes,*

and as she does so she reminds the poet that she is simply giving him a personal reaction, a "hasty analysis" (para. 7). But it is one that leads her to encourage her friend to write about the world around him.

Poetry, she reminds him, has gone through many phases, and it is in a new and encouraging phase now. Therefore, he can break out in new directions, perhaps even write a poetry that would make people laugh. She wants to relieve the poet's "inner gloom" and "fixity" and encourage him to look outside himself. Ultimately she wants him to write about the "actual, the colloquial." In a sense, her conclusion to the letter is an amusing reminder that the parts that we do not get to see—"the intimate, the indiscreet, and indeed, the only really interesting parts of this letter . . ."—would be actual and colloquial.

⟶⟵

A Letter to a Young Poet

MY DEAR JOHN,

Did you ever meet, or was he before your day, that old gentleman— 1 I forget his name—who used to enliven conversation, especially at breakfast when the post came in, by saying that the art of letter-writing is dead? The penny post, the old gentleman used to say, has killed the art of letter-writing. Nobody, he continued, examining an envelope through his eyeglasses, has the time even to cross their t's. We rush, he went on, spreading his toast with marmalade, to the telephone. We commit our half-formed thoughts in ungrammatical phrases to the post card. Gray is dead, he continued; Horace Walpole is dead; Madame de Sévigné[1]—she is dead too, I suppose he was about to add, but a fit of choking cut him short, and he had to leave the room before he

---

[1]***Thomas Gray (1716–1771); Horace Walpole (1717–1797); Madame de Sévigné (1626–1696)*** Thomas Gray is famous for his "Elegy in a Country Churchyard" (1751) and is an important preromantic poet. Walpole, an intimate of Gray's at Eton, wrote *The Castle of Otranto* (1764), one of the first romantic novels. Like Gray and Walpole, Madame de Sévigné was well known for her vibrant letters and was part of one of the most dazzling intellectual circles in the history of France. She was a brilliant writer and a dashing woman.

had time to condemn all the arts, as his pleasure was, to the cemetery. But when the post came in this morning and I opened your letter stuffed with little blue sheets written all over in a cramped but not illegible hand—I regret to say, however, that several t's were uncrossed and the grammar of one sentence seems to be dubious—I replied after all these years to that elderly necrophilist[2]—Nonsense. The art of letter-writing has only just come into existence. It is the child of the penny post. And there is some truth in that remark, I think. Naturally when a letter cost half a crown to send, it had to prove itself a document of some importance; it was read aloud; it was tied up with green silk; after a certain number of years it was published for the infinite delectation of posterity. But your letter, on the contrary, will have to be burnt. It only cost three-halfpence to send. Therefore you could afford to be intimate, irreticent, indiscreet in the extreme. What you tell me about poor dear C. and his adventure on the Channel boat is deadly private; your ribald jests at the expense of M. would certainly ruin your friendship if they got about; I doubt, too, that posterity, unless it is much quicker in the wit than I expect, could follow the line of your thought from the roof which leaks ("splash, splash, splash into the soap dish") past Mrs. Gape, the charwoman, whose retort to the greengrocer gives me the keenest pleasure, via Miss Curtis and her odd confidence on the steps of the omnibus; to Siamese cats ("Wrap their noses in an old stocking my Aunt says if they howl"); so to the value of criticism to a writer; so to Donne; so to Gerard Hopkins;[3] so to tombstones; so to goldfish; and so with a sudden alarming swoop to "Do write and tell me where poetry's going, or if it's dead?" No, your letter, because it is a true letter—one that can neither be read aloud now, nor printed in time to come—will have to be burnt. Posterity must live upon Walpole and Madame de Sévigné. The great age of letter-writing, which is, of course, the present, will leave no letters behind it. And in making my reply there is only one question that I can answer or attempt to answer in public; about poetry and its death.

But before I begin, I must own up to those defects, both natural and acquired, which, as you will find, distort and invalidate all that I have to say about poetry. The lack of a sound university training has always made it impossible for me to distinguish between an iambic and a

2

---

[2]*necrophilist* One who loves the dead (because the elderly gentleman believed that the arts were dead).

[3]*John Donne (1573–1631); Gerard Manley Hopkins (1844–1889)* Poets noted both for their intellectuality and for the complex wit of their poems. Both were clergymen: Donne was dean of St. Paul's, an Anglican cathedral; Hopkins was a Jesuit priest.

dactyl,[4] and if this were not enough to condemn one for ever, the practice of prose has bred in me, as in most prose writers, a foolish jealousy, a righteous indignation—anyhow, an emotion which the critic should be without. For how, we despised prose writers ask when we get together, could one say what one meant and observe the rules of poetry? Conceive dragging in "blade" because one had mentioned "maid"; and pairing "sorrow" with "borrow"? Rhyme is not only childish, but dishonest, we prose writers say. Then we go on to say, And look at their rules! How easy to be a poet! How strait the path is for them, and how strict! This you must do; this you must not. I would rather be a child and walk in a crocodile down a suburban path than write poetry, I have heard prose writers say. It must be like taking the veil and entering a religious order—observing the rites and rigors of meter. That explains why they repeat the same thing over and over again. Whereas we prose writers (I am only telling you the sort of nonsense prose writers talk when they are alone) are masters of language, not its slaves; nobody can teach us; nobody can coerce us; we say what we mean; we have the whole of life for our province. We are the creators, we are the explorers. . . . So we run on—nonsensically enough, I must admit.

Now that I have made a clean breast of these deficiencies, let us 3 proceed. From certain phrases in your letter I gather that you think that poetry is in a parlous way, and that your case as a poet in this particular autumn of 1931 is a great deal harder than Shakespeare's, Dryden's, Pope's or Tennyson's.[5] In fact it is the hardest case that has ever been known. Here you give me an opening, which I am prompt to seize, for a little lecture. Never think yourself singular, never think your own case much harder than other people's. I admit that the age we live in makes this difficult. For the first time in history there are readers—a large body of people, occupied in business, in sport, in nursing their grandfathers, in tying up parcels behind counters—they all read now; and they want to be told how to read and what to read; and their teachers—the reviewers, the lecturers, the broadcasters—must in all humanity make reading easy for them; assure them that literature

---

[4]*an iamb and a dactyl* Metrical feet: the iamb has an unaccented syllable followed by an accented syllable; the dactyl has an accented syllable followed by two unaccented syllables.

[5]*William Shakespeare (1564–1616); John Dryden (1631–1700); Alexander Pope (1688–1744); Alfred, Lord Tennyson (1809–1892)* Each of these poets was a giant in his own time. Shakespeare was the greatest Elizabethan poet, Dryden the most visible Restoration poet, Pope the most influential neoclassical poet, and Tennyson one of the greatest Victorian poets.

is violent and exciting, full of heroes and villains; of hostile forces perpetually in conflict; of fields strewn with bones; of solitary victors riding off on white horses wrapped in black cloaks to meet their death at the turn of the road. A pistol shot rings out. "The age of romance was over. The age of realism had begun"—you know the sort of thing. Now of course writers themselves know very well that there is not a word of truth in all this—there are no battles, and no murders and no defeats and no victories. But as it is of the utmost importance that readers should be amused, writers acquiesce. They dress themselves up. They act their parts. One leads; the other follows. One is romantic, the other realist. One is advanced, the other out of date. There is no harm in it, so long as you take it as a joke, but once you believe in it, once you begin to take yourself seriously as a leader or as a follower, as a modern or as a conservative, then you become a self-conscious, biting, and scratching little animal whose work is not of the slightest value or importance to anybody. Think of yourself rather as something much humbler and less spectacular, but to my mind far more interesting—a poet in whom live all the poets of the past, from whom all poets in time to come will spring. You have a touch of Chaucer[6] in you, and something of Shakespeare; Dryden, Pope, Tennyson—to mention only the respectable among your ancestors—stir in your blood and sometimes move your pen a little to the right or to the left. In short you are an immensely ancient, complex, and continuous character, for which reason please treat yourself with respect and think twice before you dress up as Guy Fawkes[7] and spring out upon timid old ladies at street corners, threatening death and demanding twopence-halfpenny.

However, as you say that you are in a fix ("it has never been so 4 hard to write poetry as it is today") and that poetry may be, you think, at its last gasp in England ("the novelists are doing all the interesting things now"), let me while away the time before the post goes in imagining your state and in hazarding one or two guesses which, since this is a letter, need not be taken too seriously or pressed too far. Let me try to put myself in your place; let me try to imagine, with your letter to help me, what it feels like to be a young poet in the autumn of 1931. (And taking my own advice, I shall treat you not as one poet in

---

[6]*Geoffrey Chaucer (1342?–1400)* The most important English poet of the Middle Ages. He is best known for *The Canterbury Tales* (1387?–1400).

[7]*Guy Fawkes (1570–1606)* A would-be revolutionary English Catholic who plotted to blow up the assembled gathering of the king, his court, the law justices, and the House of Commons during King James I's coronation. He was discovered; the plot was revealed; and Fawkes and his fellow conspiraters were tried, convicted, and executed.

particular, but as several poets in one.) On the floor of your mind, then—is it not this that makes you a poet?—rhythm keeps up its perpetual beat. Sometimes it seems to die down to nothing; it lets you eat, sleep, talk like other people. Then again it swells and rises and attempts to sweep all the contents of your mind into one dominant dance. Tonight is such an occasion. Although you are alone, and have taken one boot off and are about to undo the other, you cannot go on with the process of undressing, but must instantly write at the bidding of the dance. You snatch pen and paper; you hardly trouble to hold the one or to straighten the other. And while you write, while the first stanzas of the dance are being fastened down, I will withdraw a little and look out of the window. A woman passes, then a man; a car glides to a stop and then—but there is no need to say what I see out of the window, nor indeed is there time, for I am suddenly recalled from my observations by a cry of rage or despair. Your page is crumpled in a ball; your pen sticks upright by the nib in the carpet. If there were a cat to swing or a wife to murder now would be the time. So at least I infer from the ferocity of your expression. You are rasped, jarred, thoroughly out of temper. And if I am to guess the reason, it is, I should say, that the rhythm which was opening and shutting with a force that sent shocks of excitement from your head to your heels has encountered some hard and hostile object upon which it has smashed itself to pieces. Something has worked in which cannot be made into poetry; some foreign body, angular, sharp-edged, gritty, has refused to join in the dance. Obviously, suspicion attaches to Mrs. Gape; she has asked you to make a poem of her; then to Miss Curtis and her confidences on the omnibus; then to C., who has infected you with a wish to tell his story—and a very amusing one it was—in verse. But for some reason you cannot do their bidding. Chaucer could; Shakespeare could; so could Crabbe, Byron, and perhaps Robert Browning.[8] But it is October 1931, and for a long time now poetry has shirked contact with—what shall we call it?—Shall we shortly and no doubt inaccurately call it life? And will you come to my help by guessing what I mean? Well then, it has left all that to the novelist. Here you see how easy it would be for me to write two or three volumes in honor of prose and in mockery of verse; to say how wide and ample is the domain of the one, how starved and stunted the little grove of the other. But it would be simpler and perhaps fairer to check these theories by opening one

---

[8]*George Crabbe (1754–1832); George Gordon, Lord Byron (1788–1824); Robert Browning (1812–1889)* Crabbe and Byron were prominent romantic poets; Browning was one of the dominant poets of the later nineteenth century.

of the thin books of modern verse that lie on your table. I open and I find myself instantly confuted. Here are the common objects of daily prose—the bicycle and the omnibus. Obviously the poet is making his muse face facts. Listen:

> Which of you waking early and watching daybreak
> Will not hasten in heart, handsome, aware of wonder
> At light unleashed, advancing, a leader of movement,
> Breaking like surf on turf on road and roof,
> Or chasing shadow on downs like whippet racing,
> The stilled stone, halting at eyelash barrier,
> Enforcing in face a profile, marks of misuse,
> Beating impatient and importunate on boudoir shutters
> Where the old life is not up yet, with rays
> Exploring through rotting floor a dismantled mill—
> The old life never to be born again?

Yes, but how will he get through with it? I read on and find: 5

> Whistling as he shuts
> His door behind him, travelling to work by tube
> Or walking to the park to it to *ease the bowels*,

and read on and find again:

> As a boy lately come up from country to town
> Returns for the day to his village in *expensive shoes*—

and so on again to:

> Seeking a heaven on earth he chases his shadow,
> Loses his capital and his nerve in pursuing
> What yachtsmen, explorers, climbers and *buggers are after.*

These lines and the words I have emphasized are enough to con- 6
firm me in part of my guess at least. The poet is trying to include Mrs. Gape. He is honestly of opinion that she can be brought into poetry and will do very well there. Poetry, he feels, will be improved by the actual, the colloquial. But though I honor him for the attempt, I doubt that it is wholly successful. I feel a jar. I feel a shock. I feel as if I had stubbed my toe on the corner of the wardrobe.[9] Am I then, I go on to ask, shocked, prudishly and conventionally, by the words themselves? I think not. The shock is literally a shock. The poet as I guess has strained himself to include an emotion that is not domesticated and

---

[9]***wardrobe*** In an English house of the time, the closet would have been a freestanding structure—a wardrobe—in a bedroom. Thus, it would be easy to stub a toe on it.

acclimatized to poetry; the effort has thrown him off his balance; he rights himself, as I am sure I shall find if I turn the page, by a violent recourse to the poetical—he invokes the moon or the nightingale. Anyhow, the transition is sharp. The poem is cracked in the middle. Look, it comes apart in my hands: here is reality on one side, here is beauty on the other; and instead of acquiring a whole object rounded and entire, I am left with broken parts in my hands which, since my reason has been roused and my imagination has not been allowed to take entire possession of me, I contemplate coldly, critically, and with distaste.

Such at least is the hasty analysis I make of my own sensations as 7
a reader; but again I am interrupted. I see that you have overcome your difficulty, whatever it was; the pen is once more in action, and having torn up the first poem you are at work upon another. Now then if I want to understand your state of mind I must invent another explanation to account for this return of fluency. You have dismissed, as I suppose, all sorts of things that would come naturally to your pen if you had been writing prose—the charwoman, the omnibus, the incident on the Channel boat. Your range is restricted—I judge from your expression—concentrated and intensified. I hazard a guess that you are thinking now, not about things in general, but about yourself in particular. There is a fixity, a gloom, yet an inner glow that seem to hint that you are looking within and not without. But in order to consolidate these flimsy guesses about the meaning of an expression on a face, let me open another of the books on your table and check it by what I find there. Again I open at random and read this:

> To penetrate that room is my desire,
> The extreme attic of the mind, that lies
> Just beyond the last bend in the corridor.
> Writing I do it. Phrases, poems are keys.
> Loving's another way (but not so sure).
> A fire's in there, I think, there's truth at last
> Deep in a lumber chest. Sometimes I'm near
> But draughts puff out the matches, and I'm lost.
> Sometimes I'm lucky, find a key to turn,
> Open an inch or two—but always then
> A bell rings, someone calls, or cries of "fire"
> Arrest my hand when nothing's known or seen,
> And running down the stairs again I mourn.

and then this:

> There is a dark room,
> The locked and shuttered womb,

> Where negative's made positive.
> Another dark room,
> The blind and bolted tomb,
> Where positives change to negative.
> We may not undo that or escape this, who
> Have birth and death coiled in our bones,
> Nothing we can do
> Will sweeten the real rue,
> That we begin, and end, with groans.

And then this:

> Never being, but always at the edge of Being
> My head, like Death mask, is brought into the Sun.
> The shadow pointing finger across cheek,
> I move lips for tasting, I move hands for touching,
> But never am nearer than touching,
> Though the spirit leans outward for seeing.
> Observing rose, gold, eyes, an admired landscape,
> My senses record the act of wishing
> Wishing to be
> Rose, gold, landscape or another—
> Claiming fulfilment in the act of loving.

Since these quotations are chosen at random and I have yet found three different poets writing about nothing, if not about the poet himself, I hold that the chances are that you too are engaged in the same occupation. I conclude that self offers no impediment; self joins in the dance; self lends itself to the rhythm; it is apparently easier to write a poem about oneself than about any other subject. But what does one mean by "oneself"? Not the self that Wordsworth, Keats, and Shelley[10] have described—not the self that loves a woman, or that hates a tyrant, or that broods over the mystery of the world. No, the self that you are engaged in describing is shut out from all that. It is a self that sits alone in the room at night with the blinds drawn. In other words the poet is much less interested in what we have in common than in what he has apart. Hence I suppose the extreme difficulty of these poems—and I have to confess that it would floor me completely to say from one reading or even from two or three what these poems mean. The poet is trying honestly and exactly to describe a world that has perhaps no existence except for one particular person at one particular moment. And the more sincere he is in keeping to the precise outline

---

[10]*William Wordsworth (1770–1850); John Keats (1795–1821); Percy Bysshe Shelley (1792–1822)* All three are among the most important of the romantic poets.

of the roses and cabbages of his private universe, the more he puzzles us who have agreed in a lazy spirit of compromise to see roses and cabbages as they are seen, more or less, by the twenty-six passengers on the outside of an omnibus. He strains to describe; we strain to see; he flickers his torch; we catch a flying gleam. It is exciting; it is stimulating; but is that a tree, we ask, or is it perhaps an old woman tying up her shoe in the gutter?

Well, then, if there is any truth in what I am saying—if that is you   9 cannot write about the actual, the colloquial, Mrs. Gape or the Channel boat or Miss Curtis on the omnibus, without straining the machine of poetry, if, therefore, you are driven to contemplate landscapes and emotions within and must render visible to the world at large what you alone can see, then indeed yours is a hard case, and poetry, though still breathing—witness these little books—is drawing her breath in short, sharp gasps. Still, consider the symptoms. They are not the symptoms of death in the least. Death in literature, and I need not tell you how often literature has died in this country or in that, comes gracefully, smoothly, quietly. Lines slip easily down the accustomed grooves. The old designs are copied so glibly that we are half inclined to think them original, save for that very glibness. But here the very opposite is happening: here in my first quotation the poet breaks his machine because he will clog it with raw fact. In my second, he is unintelligible because of his desperate determination to tell the truth about himself. Thus I cannot help thinking that though you may be right in talking of the difficulty of the time, you are wrong to despair.

Is there not, alas, good reason to hope? I say "alas" because then I   10 must give my reasons, which are bound to be foolish and certain also to cause pain to the large and highly respectable society of necrophiles—Mr. Peabody, and his like—who much prefer death to life and are even now intoning the sacred and comfortable words, Keats is dead, Shelley is dead, Byron is dead. But it is late: necrophily induces slumber; the old gentlemen have fallen asleep over their classics, and if what I am about to say takes a sanguine tone—and for my part I do not believe in poets dying; Keats, Shelley, Byron are alive here in this room in you and you and you—I can take comfort from the thought that my hoping will not disturb their snoring. So to continue—why should not poetry, now that it has so honestly scraped itself free from certain falsities, the wreckage of the great Victorian age,[11] now that it

---

[11]**great Victorian age** A historical era, dating essentially from 1837, the accession of Queen Victoria to the throne of England, to 1901, the year of her death. It was an age

has so sincerely gone down into the mind of the poet and verified its outlines—a work of renovation that has to be done from time to time and was certainly needed, for bad poetry is almost always the result of forgetting oneself—all becomes distorted and impure if you lose sight of that central reality—now, I say, that poetry has done all this, why should it not once more open its eyes, look out of the window and write about other people? Two or three hundred years ago you were always writing about other people. Your pages were crammed with characters of the most opposite and various kinds—Hamlet, Cleopatra, Falstaff.[12] Not only did we go to you for drama, and for the subtleties of human character, but we also went to you, incredible though this now seems, for laughter. You made us roar with laughter. Then later, not more than a hundred years ago, you were lashing our follies, trouncing our hypocrisies, and dashing off the most brilliant of satires. You were Byron, remember; you wrote *Don Juan*.[13] You were Crabbe also; you took the most sordid details of the lives of peasants for your theme. Clearly therefore you have it in you to deal with a vast variety of subjects; it is only a temporary necessity that has shut you up in one room, alone, by yourself.

But how are you going to get out, into the world of other people? That is your problem now, if I may hazard a guess—to find the right relationship, now that you know yourself, between the self that you know and the world outside. It is a difficult problem. No living poet has, I think, altogether solved it. And there are a thousand voices prophesying despair. Science, they say, has made poetry impossible; there is no poetry in motor cars and wireless. And we have no religion. All is tumultuous and transitional. Therefore, so people say, there can be no relation between the poet and the present age. But surely that is nonsense. These accidents are superficial; they do not go nearly deep enough to destroy the most profound and primitive of instincts, the instinct of rhythm. All you need now is to stand at the window and let your rhythmical sense open and shut, open and shut, boldly and freely, until one thing melts in another, until the taxis are dancing

11

---

of great industrial expansion, colonialization, and imperial design. It also was marked by a straitlaced social surface influenced by the manners of Victoria that produced "certain falsities" we now refer to as hypocrisies.

[12]***Hamlet, Cleopatra, Falstaff*** Characters in plays of Shakespeare. Falstaff appears in several plays, most notably *Henry IV, Part I* (1598), and *The Merry Wives of Windsor* (1602).

[13]**Don Juan** A long poem by Lord Byron centering on the romantic escapades of the legendary lover.

with the daffodils, until a whole has been made from all these separate fragments. I am talking nonsense, I know. What I mean is, summon all your courage, exert all your vigilance, invoke all the gifts that Nature has been induced to bestow. Then let your rhythmical sense wind itself in and out among men and women, omnibuses, sparrows—whatever comes along the street—until it has strung them together in one harmonious whole. That perhaps is your task—to find the relation between things that seem incompatible yet have a mysterious affinity, to absorb every experience that comes your way fearlessly and saturate it completely so that your poem is a whole, not a fragment; to rethink human life into poetry and so give us tragedy again and comedy by means of characters not spun out at length in the novelist's way, but condensed and synthesized in the poet's way—that is what we look to you to do now. But as I do not know what I mean by rhythm nor what I mean by life, and as most certainly I cannot tell you which objects can properly be combined together in a poem—that is entirely your affair—and as I cannot tell a dactyl from an iambic, and am therefore unable to say how you must modify and expand the rites and ceremonies of your ancient and mysterious art—I will move on to safer ground and turn again to these little books themselves.

When, then, I return to them I am, as I have admitted, filled, not with forebodings of death, but with hopes for the future. But one does not always want to be thinking of the future, if, as sometimes happens, one is living in the present. When I read these poems, now, at the present moment, I find myself—reading, you know, is rather like opening the door to a horde of rebels who swarm out attacking one in twenty places at once—hit, roused, scraped, bared, swung through the air, so that life seems to flash by; then again blinded, knocked on the head—all of which are agreeable sensations for a reader (since nothing is more dismal than to open the door and get no response), and all I believe certain proof that this poet is alive and kicking. And yet mingling with these cries of delight, of jubilation, I record also, as I read, the repetition in the bass of one word intoned over and over again by some malcontent. At last then, silencing the others, I say to this malcontent, "Well, and what do *you* want?" Whereupon he bursts out, rather to my discomfort, "Beauty." Let me repeat, I take no responsibility for what my senses say when I read; I merely record the fact that there is a malcontent in me who complains that it seems to him odd, considering that English is a mixed language, a rich language; a language unmatched for its sound and color, for its power of imagery and suggestion—it seems to him odd that these modern poets should write as if they had neither ears nor eyes, neither soles to their feet nor

12

palms to their hands, but only honest enterprising book-fed brains, unisexual bodies and—but here I interrupted him. For when it comes to saying that a poet should be bisexual, and that I think is what he was about to say, even I, who have had no scientific training whatsoever, draw the line and tell that voice to be silent.

But how far, if we discount these obvious absurdities, do you think   13 there is truth in this complaint? For my own part now that I have stopped reading, and can see the poems more or less as a whole, I think it is true that the eye and ear are starved of their rights. There is no sense of riches held in reserve behind the admirable exactitude of the lines I have quoted, as there is, for example, behind the exactitude of Mr. Yeats.[14] The poet clings to his one word, his only word, as a drowning man to a spar. And if this is so, I am ready to hazard a reason for it all the more readily because I think it bears out what I have just been saying. The art of writing, and that is perhaps what my malcontent means by "beauty," the art of having at one's beck and call every word in the language, of knowing their weights, colors, sounds, associations, and thus making them, as is so necessary in English, suggest more than they can state, can be learnt of course to some extent by reading—it is impossible to read too much; but much more drastically and effectively by imagining that one is not oneself but somebody different. How can you learn to write if you write only about one single person? To take the obvious example. Can you doubt that the reason why Shakespeare knew every sound and syllable in the language and could do precisely what he liked with grammar and syntax, was that Hamlet, Falstaff and Cleopatra rushed him into this knowledge; that the lords, officers, dependents, murderers and common soldiers of the plays insisted that he should say exactly what they felt in the words expressing their feelings? It was they who taught him to write, not the begetter of the Sonnets. So that if you want to satisfy all those senses that rise in a swarm whenever we drop a poem among them—the reason, the imagination, the eyes, the ears, the palms of the hands and the soles of the feet, not to mention a million more that the psychologists have yet to name, you will do well to embark upon a long poem in which people as unlike yourself as possible talk at the tops of their voices. And for heaven's sake, publish nothing before you are thirty.

That, I am sure, is of very great importance. Most of the faults in   14

---

[14]**William Butler Yeats (1865–1939)**   Yeats called himself the last romantic. He is considered one of the most influential modern poets writing in English.

the poems I have been reading can be explained, I think, by the fact that they have been exposed to the fierce light of publicity while they were still too young to stand the strain. It has shriveled them into a skeleton austerity, both emotional and verbal, which should not be characteristic of youth. The poet writes very well; he writes for the eye of a severe and intelligent public; but how much better he would have written if for ten years he had written for no eye but his own! After all, the years from twenty to thirty are years (let me refer to your letter again) of emotional excitement. The rain dripping, a wing flashing, someone passing—the commonest sounds and sights have power to fling one, as I seem to remember, from the heights of rapture to the depths of despair. And if the actual life is thus extreme, the visionary life should be free to follow. Write then, now that you are young, nonsense by the ream. Be silly, be sentimental, imitate Shelley, imitate Samuel Smiles;[15] give the rein to every impulse; commit every fault of style, grammar, taste, and syntax; pour out; tumble over; loose anger, love, satire, in whatever words you can catch, coerce or create, in whatever meter, prose, poetry, or gibberish that comes to hand. Thus you will learn to write. But if you publish, your freedom will be checked; you will be thinking what people will say; you will write for others when you ought only to be writing for yourself. And what point can there be in curbing the wild torrent of spontaneous nonsense which is now, for a few years only, your divine gift in order to publish prim little books of experimental verses? To make money? That, we both know, is out of the question. To get criticism? But your friends will pepper your manuscripts with far more serious and searching criticism than any you will get from the reviewers. As for fame, look I implore you at famous people; see how the waters of dullness spread around them as they enter; observe their pomposity, their prophetic airs; reflect that the greatest poets were anonymous; think how Shakespeare cared nothing for fame; how Donne tossed his poems into the wastepaper basket; write an essay giving a single instance of any modern English writer who has survived the disciples and the admirers, the autograph hunters and the interviewers, the dinners and the luncheons, the celebrations and the commemorations with which English society so effectively stops the mouths of its singers and silences their songs.

---

[15]*Samuel Smiles (1812–1904)* A Scots author and journalist, best known for numerous volumes of popular biography. He also wrote the widely read *Self-Help* (1859).

But enough. I, at any rate, refuse to be necrophilous. So long as you 15
and you and you, venerable and ancient representatives of Sappho,[16]
Shakespeare, and Shelley, are aged precisely twenty-three and propose—O enviable lot!—to spend the next fifty years of your lives in
writing poetry, I refuse to think that the art is dead. And if ever the
temptation to necrophilize comes over you, be warned by the fate of
that old gentleman whose name I forget, but I think that it was Peabody. In the very act of consigning all the arts to the grave he choked
over a large piece of hot buttered toast and the consolation then offered
him that he was about to join the elder Pliny in the shades gave him,
I am told, no sort of satisfaction whatsoever.

And now for the intimate, the indiscreet, and indeed, the only 16
really interesting parts of this letter. . . .

---

[16]*Sappho (fl. c. 610–580 B.C.)* A Greek lyric poet of the island of Lesbos. Her
work exists only in fragments, but she had a great reputation among the ancients.

QUESTIONS

1. What state of mind was the young poet in when he wrote his letter to
   Woolf? What questions did he ask her?
2. What is the emotional significance of the shock Woolf records having felt
   in paragraph 6? Is her shock an emotion connected with poetry as an art
   or an emotion connected with the life she leads apart from poetry and art?
3. What do the poetry excerpts tell you about the then current situation in
   poetry? Do you think these were good poems? What were their strengths?
   What were their weaknesses?
4. Examine paragraph 12 and later paragraphs. Find the references that Woolf
   makes to the varieties of emotion she associates with poetry. Does Woolf
   share any of Ortega's views on the inappropriateness of emotions in responding to poetry?
5. What does Woolf expect poetry to do? Does the young poet seem to expect
   the same things of poetry?
6. How useful do you think Woolf's advice might have been to this poet?

WRITING ASSIGNMENTS

1. Open a book of modern poetry or a current poetry magazine, or read some
   poetry from student publications and choose at random three selections
   from poems that can be considered contemporary. Offer your commentary
   on them in the same manner that Woolf comments on the poems she examines. She calls her examination a "hasty analysis," which alludes to its

brevity. Aim to give your reader a sense of what your perception of contemporary poetry is based on the samples you choose. Do you find the same kinds of things to be true of poetry today as Woolf found in 1932?

2. Early in her essay, Woolf comments on the art of letter writing. She links the letter with the cost of sending it, referring at one point to the penny-post—a long-lost phenomenon. What is your assessment of the current state of the art of letter writing? Woolf says that her era is the great age of letter writing. Do you think she would say that today? Examine a variety of letters in the course of constructing your essay, including letters you have written and letters written to you (both personal and business). Then turn to the pages of the *New York Times*, your local or regional newspaper, a campus publication, *Time* magazine, the *Christian Science Monitor*, *TV Guide*, *Ebony*, and at least three other published sources. What is the state of the art of letter writing today?

3. How is evaluating a poem affected by the emotions that it arouses? Is emotion in poetry important enough for Woolf to reflect on its proper place relative to the evaluation of poetry? For Woolf, what role does emotion play in modern poetry.

4. In paragraph 8, Woolf says, "it is apparently easier to write a poem about oneself than about any other subject." Determine whether this is true by writing a poem about yourself and by commenting on the ease or difficulty of the task. Give some thought to whether you felt it would be easy or difficult before you began, whether your expectations were fulfilled, and whether you think that other poets would be likely to have similar experiences.

5. In paragraph 12, Woolf gives the poet very detailed advice on what to do about his work. She urges him to listen to rhythms in language and to respond by observing life closely: "What I mean is, summon all your courage, exert all your vigilance, invoke all the gifts that Nature has been induced to bestow. Then let your rhythmical sense wind itself in and out among men and women, omnibuses, sparrows—whatever comes along the street—until it has strung them together in one harmonious whole. That perhaps is your task—to find the relation between things that seem incompatible yet have a mysterious affinity, to absorb every experience that comes your way fearlessly and saturate it completely so that your poem is a whole, not a fragment; to rethink human life into poetry and so give us tragedy again and comedy by means of characters not spun out at length in the novelist's way, but condensed and synthesized in the poet's way— that is what we look to you to do now." Try to take her advice by observing life around you. Write a poem that includes the speech patterns of people you know and of people you hear from any source at all (including radio and television), and create characters who make demands on you. Capture their speech and their attitudes toward life. Make your poem reflect the living experience that is yours each day.

SUSANNE K. LANGER

Expressiveness

*S*USANNE K. *LANGER (1895–1985) developed a youthful interest in philosophy. She was born in New York City and attended Radcliffe College where she studied with Alfred North Whitehead and a number of other distinguished philosophers. She stayed on as a tutor at Harvard University from 1927 to 1942. Thereafter, she taught at the University of Delaware, Columbia University, and from 1954 to the end of her teaching career at Connecticut College. Her career as a teacher was distinguished, and her influence as a philosopher in the area of the arts has been widespread. Her* Philosophy in a New Key: A Study in the Symbolism of Reason, Rite, and Art *(1942) is probably her most widely read book. It explores certain implications of language and other kinds of symbols by which we shape our lives.*

In Problems of Art *(1957), from which the following selection is taken, she continues her interest in symbolism but concerns herself, too, with questions of creativity, abstraction, and the relation of emotion to the arts. "Expressiveness" is important because it at-*

From *Problems of Art*.

695

tempts to establish the ways in which a work of art will express emotion. Her major assertion is, as it is in Philosophy in a New Key, that the arts are somehow congruent with our emotions, that they express those emotions. This view is extraordinarily complex, but it has also been unusually influential. Her idea is that works of art are by nature ineffable, that is, they cannot be reduced to language or discourse. They simply are. Emotions are also not reducible to language: Who can "translate" disappointment into words? In music, as Langer has shown in another essay, we have become accustomed to a composer using a specific musical passage to suggest a specific range of emotions. Agitated strings and horns will suggest emotional agitation to a listener. All that is rather oversimple, perhaps, but for many aestheticians, her view has the seeds of truth.

Essentially, Langer is interested in the ways in which the arts extend our capacities of understanding beyond language. She tells us that "it is by virtue of language that we can think, remember, imagine" (para. 19). But she also tells us that language has limits (para. 20) and that many human experiences are beyond the reach of language to describe. The arts reach into these areas because they are areas dominated by feeling.

One of the points she has made in her work in aesthetics is that it is by virtue of studying and responding to works of art that we educate our feelings. Most of us spend a good deal of time mastering facts, learning processes, and performing rational exercises. But we spend little time developing our emotional capacities. These are best "educated" by the arts because the arts are products of emotional understanding—they are, she says, congruent with feeling—and they are therefore capable of extending our feelings. Thus, they can educate our emotions. The subject of "Expressiveness" is the issue of art's capacity to express and interpret emotion.

LANGER'S RHETORIC

This work is, like most philosophical essays, a closely reasoned one. Langer has an argument which takes a complex form. The process of presenting the argument that the arts express emotion and that we can learn from that expressiveness demands careful analysis of a variety of implications. Analysis, taking the argument point by point, is the principle that guides her rhetorical strategy.

Definition is the most important device she uses in her argument, since she must make clear precisely what she is talking about to enable us to grasp the importance of her position. The most difficult of all definitions in a work of this sort is the definition of art. But Langer aims directly at providing a definition that will work within her theory regarding expressiveness: "A work of art is an expressive form created for our perception through sense or imagination, and what it expresses is human feeling" (para. 5). This definition, like most definitions, presents problems.

Langer recognizes these problems and organizes the remainder of the work around the simplest approach to solving them. She tells us at the end of paragraph 5, "In stating what a work of art is, I have just used the words 'form,' 'expressive,' and 'created'; these are key words. One at a time, they will keep us engaged." The rest of this piece considers the implications of each of these terms in order. Paragraphs 6–17 treat of the questions relating to form, offering a complex definition of the term. Paragraphs 18–25 clarify the nature of expressiveness. The remainder of the piece examines the term "created," although this concept receives vastly less emphasis than do the first two.

In conducting her argument and in making the points she wishes to make about the relationship of the arts to expression, Langer's most reliable rhetorical strategy is that of attempting definitions. Once the terms of her definition of art are defined, we are in a position to accept or reject it. If we accept it, then we accept, too, her basic contention that the arts have in common one thing—the fact that they express emotions and feelings.

Expressiveness

When we talk about "Art" with a capital "A"—that is, about any or all of the arts: painting, sculpture, architecture, the potter's and goldsmith's and other designers' arts, music, dance, poetry, and prose fiction, drama and film—it is a constant temptation to say things about "Art" in this general sense that are true only in one special domain, or to assume that what holds for one art must hold for another.

For instance, the fact that music is made for performance, for presentation to the ear, and is simply not the same thing when it is given only to the tonal imagination of a reader silently perusing the score, has made some estheticians pass straight to the conclusion that literature, too, must be physically heard to be fully experienced, because words are originally spoken, not written; an obvious parallel, but a careless and, I think, invalid one. It is dangerous to set up principles by analogy, and generalize from a single consideration.

But it is natural, and safe enough, to ask analogous questions: "What is the function of sound in music? What is the function of sound in poetry? What is the function of sound in prose composition? What is the function of sound in drama?" The answers may be quite heterogeneous; and that is itself an important fact, a guide to something more than a simple and sweeping theory. Such findings guide us to exact relations and abstract, variously exemplified basic principles. 2

At present, however, we are dealing with principles that have proven to be the same in all the arts, when each kind of art—plastic, musical, balletic, poetic, and each major mode, such as literary and dramatic writing, or painting, sculpturing, building plastic shapes—has been studied in its own terms. Such candid study is more rewarding than the usual passionate declaration that all the arts are alike, only their materials differ, their principles are all the same, their techniques all analogous, etc. That is not only unsafe, but untrue. It is in pursuing the differences among them that one arrives, finally, at a point where no more differences appear; then one has found, not postulated, their unity. At that deep level there is only one concept exemplified in all the different arts, and that is the concept of Art. 3

The principles that obtain wholly and fundamentally in every kind of art are few, but decisive; they determine what is art, and what is not. Expressiveness, in one definite and appropriate sense, is the same in all art works of any kind. What is created is not the same in any two distinct arts—this is, in fact, what makes them distinct—but the principle of creation is the same. And "living form" means the same in all of them. 4

A work of art is an expressive form created for our perception through sense or imagination, and what it expresses is human feeling. The word "feeling" must be taken here in its broadest sense, meaning *everything that can be felt*, from physical sensation, pain and comfort, excitement and repose, to the most complex emotions, intellectual tensions, or the steady feeling-tones of a conscious human life. In stating what a work of art is, I have just used the words "form," "ex- 5 pressive," and "created", these are key words. One at a time, they will keep us engaged.

Let us consider first what is meant, in this context, by a *form*. The word has many meanings, all equally legitimate for various purposes; even in connection with art it has several. It may, for instance—and often does—denote the familiar, characteristic structures known as the sonnet form, the sestina, or the ballad form in poetry, the sonata form, the madrigal, or the symphony in music, the contre-dance[1] or the classical ballet in choreography, and so on. This is not what I mean; or rather, it is only a very small part of what I mean. There is another sense in which artists speak of "form" when they say, for instance, "form follows function," or declare that the one quality shared by all good works of art is "significant form," or entitle a book *The Problem of Form in Painting and Sculpture* or *The Life of Forms in Art*, or *Search for Form*. They are using "form" in a wider sense, which on the one hand is close to the commonest, popular meaning, namely just the *shape* of a thing, and on the other hand to the quite unpopular meaning it has in science and philosophy, where it designates something more abstract; "form" in its most abstract sense means structure, articulation, a whole resulting from the relation of mutually dependent factors, or more precisely, the way that whole is put together.   6

The abstract sense, which is sometimes called "logical form," is involved in the notion of expression, at least the kind of expression that characterizes art. That is why artists, when they speak of achieving "form," use the word with something of an abstract connotation, even when they are talking about a visible and tangible art object in which that form is embodied.   7

The more recondite[2] concept of form is derived, of course, from the naive one, that is, material shape. Perhaps the easiest way to grasp the idea of "logical form" is to trace its derivation.   8

Let us consider the most obvious sort of form, the shape of an object, say a lampshade. In any department store you will find a wide choice of lampshades, mostly monstrosities, and what is monstrous is usually their shape. You select the least offensive one, maybe even a good one, but realize that the color, say violet, will not fit into your room; so you look about for another shade of the same shape but a   9

---

[1]***contre–dance*** A formal, composed dance involving two lines of dancers; originally an English country dance.

[2]***recondite*** Learned and obscure.

different color, perhaps green. In recognizing this same shape in another object, possibly of another material as well as another color, you have quite naturally and easily abstracted the concept of this shape from your actual impression of the first lampshade. Presently it may occur to you that this shade is too big for your lamp; you ask whether they have *this same shade* (meaning another one of this shape) in a smaller size. The clerk understands you.

But what is *the same* in the big violet shade and the little green 10
one? Nothing but the interrelations among their respective various dimensions. They are not "the same" even in their spatial properties, for none of their actual measures are alike; but their shapes are congruent. Their respective spatial factors are put together in the same way, so they exemplify the same form.

It is really astounding what complicated abstractions we make in 11
our ordinary dealing with forms—that is to say, through what twists and transformations we recognize the same logical form. Consider the similarity of your two hands. Put one on the table, palm down, superimpose the other, palm down, as you may have superimposed cut-out geometric shapes in school—they are not alike at all. But their shapes are *exact opposites*. Their respective shapes fit the same description, provided that the description is modified by a principle of application whereby the measures are read one way for one hand and the other way for the other—like a timetable in which the list of stations is marked: "Eastbound, read down; Westbound, read up."

As the two hands exemplify the same form with a principle of re- 12
versal understood, so the list of stations describes two ways of moving, indicated by the advice to "read down" for one and "read up" for the other. We can all abstract the common element in these two respective trips, which is called the *route*. With a return ticket we may return only by the same route. The same principle relates a mold to the form of the thing that is cast in it, and establishes their formal correspondence, or common logical form.

So far we have considered only objects—lampshades, hands, or re- 13
gions of the earth—as having forms. These have fixed shapes; their parts remain in fairly stable relations to each other. But there are also substances that have no definite shapes, such as gases, mists, and water, which take the shape of any bounded space that contains them. The interesting thing about such amorphous fluids[3] is that when they

---

[3]*amorphous fluids* Fluids without a shape of their own.

arc put into violcnt motion thcy do cxhibit visiblc forms, not boundcd by any container. Think of the momentary efflorescence of a bursting rocket, the mushroom cloud of an atomic bomb, the funnel of water or dust screwing upward in a whirlwind. The instant the motion stops, or even slows beyond a certain degree, those shapes collapse and the apparent "thing" disappears. They are not shapes of things at all, but forms of motions, or dynamic forms.

Some dynamic forms, however, have more permanent manifesta-   14
tions, because the stuff that moves and makes them visible is constantly replenished. A waterfall seems to hang from the cliff, waving
streamers of foam. Actually, of course, nothing stays there in midair;
the water is always passing; but there is more and more water taking
the same paths, so we have a lasting shape made and maintained by
its passage—a permanent dynamic form. A quiet river, too, has dynamic form; if it stopped flowing it would either go dry or become a
lake. Some twenty-five hundred years ago, Heracleitos[4] was struck by
the fact that you cannot step twice into the same river at the same
place—at least, if the river means the water, not its dynamic form, the
flow.

When a river ceases to flow because the water is deflected or dried   15
up, there remains the river bed, sometimes cut deeply in solid stone.
That bed is shaped by the flow, and records as graven lines the currents
that have ceased to exist. Its shape is static, but it *expresses* the dynamic form of the river. Again, we have two congruent forms, like a
cast and its mold, but this time the congruence is more remarkable
because it holds between a dynamic form and a static one. That relation is important; we shall be dealing with it again when we come to
consider the meaning of "living form" in art.

The congruence of two given perceptible forms is not always evi-   16
dent upon simple inspection. The common *logical* form they both exhibit may become apparent only when you know the principle
whereby to relate them, as you compare the shapes of your hands not
by direct correspondence, but by correspondence of opposite parts.
Where the two exemplifications of the single logical form are unlike
in most other respects one needs a rule for matching up the relevant
factors of one with the relevant factors of the other; that is to say, a

---

[4]*Heracleitos (540?–475 B.C.)* A Greek philosopher who believed that the basis of
all matter was fire. He also believed that everything was a result of the clash of opposite
forces.

rule of translation, whereby one instance of the logical form is shown to correspond formally to the other.

The logical form itself is not another thing, but an abstract con- 17 cept, or better an *abstractable* concept. We usually don't abstract it deliberately, but only use it, as we use our vocal cords in speech without first learning all about their operation and then applying our knowledge. Most people perceive intuitively the similarity of their two hands without thinking of them as conversely related; they can guess at the shape of the hollow inside a wooden shoe from the shape of a human foot, without any abstract study of topology.[5] But the first time they see a map in the Mercator projection[6]—with parallel lines of longitude, not meeting at the poles—they find it hard to believe that this corresponds logically to the circular map they used in school, where the meridians bulged apart toward the equator and met at both poles. The visible shapes of the continents are different on the two maps, and it takes abstract thinking to match up the two representations of the same earth. If, however, they have grown up with both maps, they will probably see the geographical relationships either way with equal ease, because these relationships are not *copied* by either map, but *expressed,* and expressed equally well by both; for the two maps are different *projections* of the same logical form, which the spherical earth exhibits in still another—that is, a spherical—projection.

An expressive form is any perceptible or imaginable whole that ex- 18 hibits relationships of parts, or points, or even qualities or aspects within the whole, so that it may be taken to represent some other whole whose elements have analogous relations. The reason for using such a form as a symbol is usually that the thing it represents is not perceivable or readily imaginable. We cannot see the earth as an object. We let a map or a little globe express the relationships of places on the earth, and think about the earth by means of it. The understanding of one thing through another seems to be a deeply intuitive process in the human brain; it is so natural that we often have difficulty in distinguishing the symbolic expressive form from what it conveys. The symbol seems to be the thing itself, or contain it, or be contained in it. A child interested in a globe will not say, "This means the earth,"

---

[5]*topology* The study or mapping of surfaces.

[6]*Mercator projection* A flattened map of the earth. Gerardus Mercator (1512–1594), Flemish mapmaker, published his first Mercator projection in 1568, with longitudes and latitudes at right angles.

but "Look, this is the earth." A similar identification of symbol and meaning underlies the widespread conception of holy names, of the physical efficacy of rites, and many other primitive but culturally persistent phenomena. It has a bearing on our perception of artistic import; that is why I mention it here.

The most astounding and developed symbolic device humanity has 19 evolved is language. By means of language we can conceive the intangible, incorporeal things we call our *ideas*, and the equally inostensible[7] elements of our perceptual world that we call *facts*. It is by virtue of language that we can think, remember, imagine, and finally conceive a universe of facts. We can describe things and represent their relations, express rules of their interactions, speculate and predict and carry on a long symbolizing process known as reasoning. And above all, we can communicate, by producing a serried array of audible or visible words, in a pattern commonly known, and readily understood to reflect our multifarious concepts and percepts and their interconnections. This use of language is *discourse*; and the pattern of discourse is known as *discursive form*. It is a highly versatile, amazingly powerful pattern. It has impressed itself on our tacit thinking, so that we call all systematic reflection "discursive thought." It has made, far more than most people know, the very frame of our sensory experience—the frame of objective facts in which we carry on the practical business of life.

Yet even the discursive pattern has its limits of usefulness. An ex- 20 pressive form can express any complex of conceptions that, via some rule of projection, appears congruent with it, that is, appears to be of that form. Whatever there is in experience that will not take the impress—directly or indirectly—of discursive form, is not discursively communicable or, in the strictest sense, logically thinkable. It is unspeakable, ineffable;[8] according to practically all serious philosophical theories today, it is unknowable.

Yet there is a great deal of experience that is knowable, not only as 21 immediate, formless, meaningless impact, but as one aspect of the intricate web of life, yet defies discursive formulation, and therefore ver-

---

[7]*inostensible* Not apparent or evident. Langer implies here that the world of perceived "facts" is no more tangible than the world of ideas because all perceptions are filtered through the mind, which creates ideas of things.

[8]*ineffable* Literally, unspeakable; thus unknowable, because anything that cannot be expressed through language cannot be known.

bal expression: that is what we sometimes call the *subjective aspect* of experience, the direct feeling of it—what it is like to be waking and moving, to be drowsy, slowing down, or to be sociable, or to feel self-sufficient but alone; what it feels like to pursue an elusive thought or to have a big idea. All such directly felt experiences usually have no names—they are named, if at all, for the outward conditions that normally accompany their occurrence. Only the most striking ones have names like "anger," "hate," "love," "fear," and are collectively called "emotion." But we feel many things that never develop into any designable emotion. The ways we are moved are as various as the lights in a forest; and they may intersect, sometimes without cancelling each other, take shape and dissolve, conflict, explode into passion, or be transfigured. All these inseparable elements of subjective reality compose what we call the "inward life" of human beings. The usual factoring of that life-stream into mental, emotional, and sensory units is an arbitrary scheme of simplification that makes scientific treatment possible to a considerable extent; but we may already be close to the limit of its usefulness, that is, close to the point where its simplicity becomes an obstacle to further questioning and discovery instead of the revealing, ever-suitable logical projection it was expected to be.

Whatever resists projection into the discursive form of language is, indeed, hard to hold in conception, and perhaps impossible to communicate, in the proper and strict sense of the word "communicate." But fortunately our logical intuition, or form-perception, is really much more powerful than we commonly believe, and our knowledge—genuine knowledge, understanding—is considerably wider than our discourse. Even in the use of language, if we want to name something that is too new to have a name (for example, a newly invented gadget or a newly discovered creature), or want to express a relationship for which there is no verb or other connective word, we resort to metaphor; we mention it or describe it as something else, something analogous. The principle of metaphor is simply the principle of saying one thing and meaning another, and expecting to be understood to mean the other. A metaphor is not language, it is an idea expressed by language, an idea that in its turn functions as a symbol to express something. It is not discursive and therefore does not really make a statement of the idea it conveys; but it formulates a new conception for our direct imaginative grasp. 22

Sometimes our comprehension of a total experience is mediated by a metaphorical symbol because the experience is new, and language has words and phrases only for familiar notions. Then an extension of 23 language will gradually follow the wordless insight, and discursive expression will supersede the nondiscursive pristine symbol. This is, I think, the normal advance of human thought and language in that whole realm of knowledge where discourse is possible at all.

But the symbolic presentation of subjective reality for contempla- 24 tion is not only tentatively beyond the reach of language—that is, not merely beyond the words we have; it is impossible in the essential frame of language. That is why those semanticists[9] who recognize only discourse as a symbolic form must regard the whole life of feeling as formless, chaotic, capable only of symptomatic expression, typified in exclamations like "Ah!" "Ouch!" "My sainted aunt!" They usually do believe that art is an expression of feeling, but that "expression" in art is of this sort, indicating that the speaker has an emotion, a pain, or other personal experience, perhaps also giving us a clue to the general kind of experience it is—pleasant or unpleasant, violent or mild—but not setting that piece of inward life objectively before us so we may understand its intricacy, its rhythms and shifts of total appearance. The differences in feeling-tones or other elements of subjective experience are regarded as differences in quality, which must be felt to be appreciated. Furthermore, since we have no intellectual access to pure subjectivity, the only way to study it is to study the symptoms of the person who is having subjective experiences. This leads to physiological psychology—a very important and interesting field. But it tells us nothing about the phenomena of subjective life, and sometimes simplifies the problem by saying they don't exist.

Now, I believe the expression of feeling in a work of art—the func- 25 tion that makes the work an expressive form—is not symptomatic at all. An artist working on a tragedy need not be in personal despair or violent upheaval; nobody, indeed, could work in such a state of mind. His mind would be occupied with the causes of his emotional upset. Self-expression does not require composition and lucidity; a screaming baby gives his feeling far more release than any musician, but we don't go into a concert hall to hear a baby scream; in fact, if that baby is brought in we are likely to go out. We don't want self-expression.

A work of art presents feeling (in the broad sense I mentioned be- 26 fore, as everything that can be felt) for our contemplation, making it visible or audible or in some way perceivable through a symbol, not

---

[9]*semanticists* Those concerned with the meaning of words; in this case, Langer refers to those who treat words as coherent symbols of meaning and think of feelings as simply reactions to (symptoms of) a stimulus.

inferable from[10] a symptom. Artistic form is congruent with the dynamic forms of our direct sensuous, mental, and emotional life; works of art are projections of "felt life," as Henry James[11] called it, into spatial, temporal, and poetic structures. They are images of feeling, that formulate it for our cognition. What is artistically good is whatever articulates and presents feeling to our understanding.

Artistic forms are more complex than any other symbolic forms we 27 know. They are, indeed, not abstractable from the works that exhibit them. We may abstract a shape from an object that has this shape, by disregarding color, weight and texture, even size; but to the total effect that is an artistic form, the color matters, the thickness of lines matters, and the appearance of texture and weight. A given triangle is the same in any position, but to an artistic form its location, balance, and surroundings are not indifferent. Form, in the sense in which we artists speak of "significant form" or "expressive form," is not an abstracted structure, but an apparition; and the vital processes of sense and emotion that a good work of art expresses seem to the beholder to be directly contained in it, not symbolized but really presented. The congruence is so striking that symbol and meaning appear as one reality. Actually, as one psychologist who is also a musician has written, "Music sounds as feelings feel." And likewise, in good painting, sculpture, or building, balanced shapes and colors, lines and masses look as emotions, vital tensions and their resolutions feel.

An artist, then, expresses feeling, but not in the way a politician 28 blows off steam or a baby laughs and cries. He formulates that elusive aspect of reality that is commonly taken to be amorphous and chaotic; that is, he objectifies the subjective realm. What he expresses is, therefore, not his own actual feelings, but what he knows about human feeling. Once he is in possession of a rich symbolism, that knowledge may actually exceed his entire personal experience. A work of art expresses a conception of life, emotion, inward reality. But it is neither a confessional nor a frozen tantrum; it is a developed metaphor, a nondiscursive symbol that articulates what is verbally ineffable—the logic of consciousness itself.

---

[10]*inferable from*   Able to be rendered understandable from.
[11]*Henry James (1843–1916).*   One of America's greatest novelists; brother of the philosopher William James. "Felt life" was James's term for a deeply understood experience, particularly of the sort that developed into his own works.

QUESTIONS

1. What is Susanne Langer's definition of "art"?
2. Why does Langer tell us that it is "dangerous to set up principles by analogy" (para. 1)?
3. What does Langer mean by "feeling" (para. 5), and what is the relationship of human feeling to emotions?
4. Is Langer's use of the analogy of the lampshade "dangerous" (paras. 9–10)? Is it effective in her argument?
5. What does it mean to say that "Music sounds as feelings feel" (para. 27)?
6. What role does Langer feel emotion should play in a work of art? How do emotions function in the process of resonding to art?

WRITING ASSIGNMENTS

1. In paragraph 25, Langer says, "Now, I believe the expression of feeling in a work of art—the function that makes the work an expressive form—is not symptomatic at all." Clarify precisely what she means by this statement. Use her rhetorical method of relying on definition. The key terms to define are "expression of feeling," "expressive form," and "symptomatic." You may wish to quote from statements Langer makes on the question.
2. At one point Langer asserts that things which are not discursive, that is, not susceptible to discursive treatment, are not knowable. In essence, she is saying that language is essential for thinking and for knowing things. Is this assertion true? Is it possible for someone to know something that is not determined by language? If it is not possible, what are the implications for someone who is deficient in mastering language? To what extent is knowledge dependent on a mastery of language and discourse? Construct an essay that answers these questions.
3. One of the important points Langer makes at the end of this piece has to do with what feelings an artist expresses in a work of art. She discusses the question of whether a work of art is symptomatic; by that she means whether a given work expresses a feeling that the artist happens to have while he or she is creating. Her opinion is that the artist does not express feeling in this way. She says that the artist expresses what is serious about feelings, not his own feelings (para. 28). Do you feel that this assertion is true? Argue for this position using what you know about your own efforts to create works of art. But be sure, too, that you consult other people who make works of art for their views. It would help to ask anyone who is seriously interested in art what they think about this question. See paragraph 24.

4. In essence, this piece is an extended definition of art with separate definitions of several key terms. If possible, construct your own definition of art and use the technique Langer uses to develop a complete essay that clarifies the nature of that definition. If you find it impossible to construct your own definition, use someone else's definition. You may select one of the following definitions to work from:

> Art is the exercise of objectifying the depth of understanding of the human condition.

> A work of art is the most natural response the artist can give to the circumstances of his life.

> The work of art is by nature a symbolic interpretation of an artist's experience.

5. In paragraph 25, Langer asserts that we do not want self-expression in art. This statement may seem to be a contradiction in terms, since art is often represented to us as a useful means of self-expression. Is Langer's assertion correct? Analyze her statements on this subject, using her rhetorical strategies of definition. What exactly is self-expression, and how might it relate to art?

6. To what extent does Langer account for Ortega's apprehension concerning the confusion of "lived" experience with the representations of reality we confront in works of art? Does she hold the same view—that our emotions in response to works of art are or should consist of special aesthetic emotions?

SUSAN SONTAG

Against Interpretation

SUSAN SONTAG *(b. 1933) is a probing critic whose commentaries on art, high and low, have earned her a place as a sharp, perceptive interpreter of aesthetic experience. But she is not an observer of art to the exclusion of other human concerns. Her political sensibilities were aroused, like those of many of her generation, because of the upheavals of the 1960s brought on by the Vietnam War and by civil disturbances at home. Much of her work has been published in intellectual journals aimed at an aware political audience.*

*Yet Sontag is a product of the academy, with degrees from the University of Chicago and Harvard University, and with experience as a faculty member at several colleges teaching both English and philosophy. She has been involved with film criticism and filmmaking since the late 1960s and has written and directed her own films, both feature films and documentaries. Some of her work has centered on the goals of feminism, but she has not always pleased feminists, who have often criticized her essay, "The Third World of Women" (*Partisan Review, *1973). Her political activities were such that she journeyed to Hanoi, capital of North Vietnam, in 1968, during the worst period of the Vietnam War. Her book,* Trip to Hanoi *(1968), expresses her anguish at the nature of this painful war.*

Sontag is also a novelist and short-story writer, with several inter-

esting books to her credit—The Benefactor *(1963),* Death Kit *(1967),* and I, etcetera *(1978)—though her creative efforts has been somewhat slighted in contrast to the generally credited brilliance of her critical writings on the arts.* Against Interpretation and Other Essays *(1966) established her as among the most interesting and surprising of contemporary commentators on the arts. Her stance has always been surprising and provocative, as it is, for instance, in "Against Interpretation," which, in a book of criticism, seems to argue against the very process that makes criticism what it is.* Styles of Radical Will *(1969) continued a discussion of the modern sensibility and explored the issue of how we approach unusual and unexpected modern art forms.*

Three other books, Illness as Metaphor *(1978),* On Photography *(1977), and* AIDS and Its Metaphors *(1988) have had much impact. Her experience with cancer served as the impetus for the first book, which treated the ways in which society reacts to illness and the ways individuals sometimes exploit their illness. It is a book remarkable for its refusal to submit to the temptation to exploit the metaphor of illness in an autobiographical way. As a filmmaker and a relentless photographer, she wrote a book on photography that often condemned the way the camera appropriates everything visually without regard to the feelings or concerns of those who are photographed. Yet it is a book that stands as one of the most provocative and interesting statements on the art of photography.*

"Against Interpretation" is an essay that, in many ways, is a reaction to an age in which all art must submit to commentary and interpretation. Sontag makes an effort to assess exactly what interpretation is: "The task of interpretation is virtually one of translation. The interpreter says, Look, don't you see that X is really—or, really means—A? That Y is really B? That Z is really C?" (para. 11). She believes that interpretation is not only an intermediary for works of art but that it substitutes for them and tames them. As she says, "one tames the work of art. Interpretation makes art manageable, comfortable" (para. 18). She is quick to admit that during some ages interpretation is a positive force, but she believes that in other ages—such as the present one—it is not.

Early in the essay Sontag distinguishes between two aspects of the work of art: the form and the content. She focuses on literature and films, though she is obviously referring to all mimetic arts. As Aristotle tells us (see the first essay in this part), art imitates life and is therefore mimetic. Sontag explains that if art is mimetic it therefore has a content that relates it to life and that is interpretable. Her com-

plaint is not just that commentators separate the form of a work of art from its content but that the act of interpretation concentrates on content to the exclusion of form—or virtually so.

Content is meaning, and interpretation aims to explain the meaning of a work of art. As a result of an overemphasis on content, interpretation has helped to distort art: "Most American novelists and playwrights are really either journalists or gentlemen sociologists and psychologists. They are writing the literary equivalent of program music" (para. 30). The only art forms that escape this fate are those which are not mimetic: abstract and decorative arts. To these categories, she adds Pop Art, which is, like Andy Warhol's Campbell soup cans, uninterpretable as art because it is not only mimetic of life, it replicates life.

Ultimately, Sontag urges us to discontinue our emphasis on content and to restore attention to form. She believes that film is the most vital current art, and she reminds us that modern films—and she is thinking of those by artistic filmmakers, not those by commercial entertainers—are interesting largely by virtue of their visual form, by those elements which transcend content.

She ends her essay by making an appeal for a new approach to the arts, one that does not interpret but that examines and reports back on the facts, the perceptual elements of the work of art. She calls this "an erotics of art" because it emphasizes a growing awareness of sensory experience. She feels that sensory experience is important because the act of interpretation emphasizes intellectualization at the expense of experience. Thus, she says, "We must learn to see more, to hear more, to feel more" (para. 40).

S O N T A G ' S   R H E T O R I C

Because this essay is an argument, Sontag depends on definition and on logical presentation. Ordinarily, she might have relied on sample interpretations or on concrete examples of works of art, but doing so is not possible in a general essay of this kind. Therefore, she depends upon establishing her definition of interpretation, commenting on how it affects works of art and their audience, and then making a recommendation based on her understanding. Naturally, she expects that we will share her understanding by the end of the essay.

Prominent in her rhetorical approach is a reliance on the historical survey. Since part of her argument is that interpretation can be good in some ages and not so good in other ages—and especially that it is not good in this age—the historical survey takes on significance. She begins with Plato and Aristotle, reminding us of Plato's view that everything we see on earth is an imitation of the ideal, which is in "heaven." As a result of that view, art is of little interest to Plato, since it can only be an imitation of an imitation. Aristotle developed the more acceptable view of art as mimetic—imitating life in order to reveal it more fully to us—and was, therefore, able to comment incisively on Greek drama in his Poetics.

Sontag goes on to discuss those who interpreted the Bible in the first centuries after Christ. She points out that the tradition of biblical hermeneutics—examining the Bible for its hidden meaning—derives from an era in which the text itself was unacceptable. She points out the example of the Song of Solomon, which is an explicit, elaborate love song. The Song of Solomon was interpreted to be a model of the wooing of the church by God—and therefore it was retained among the books of the Bible.

In more modern times, the doctrines of Karl Marx and Sigmund Freud demanded that we look behind art to their economic and psychological significance, respectively. Freud postulated that the dreams his patients discussed with him had a manifest content (what the dream seemed to be saying) and a more important latent content (what the dream was really saying). Psychoanalysis had among its tasks the job of determining the latent content and meaning of dreams, but it was not long before modern interpreters adopted the method and assumed that all art also had subtexts, hidden meanings that needed to be revealed through the process of interpretation.

Finally, in commenting on contemporary circumstances, Sontag reminds us that generations of commentary have begun to obscure the work of art and that commentary has become a substitute for it. If we accept this argument, we should agree with her that it is time to restore the work of art by putting interpretation aside so that we can approach the arts with a new, sensory freshness.

Against Interpretation

Content is a glimpse of something, an encounter like a flash. It's very tiny—very tiny, content.

WILLEM DE KOONING,
in an interview

It is only shallow people who do not judge by appearances. The mystery of the world is the visible, not the invisible.

OSCAR WILDE,
in a letter

The earliest experience of art must have been that it was incanta- 1
tory, magical; art was an instrument of ritual. (Cf. the paintings in the caves at Lascaux, Altamira, Niaux, La Pasiega,[1] etc.) The earliest *theory* of art, that of the Greek philosophers, proposed that art was mimesis, imitation of reality.[2]

It is at this point that the peculiar question of the value of art 2
arose. For the mimetic theory, by its very terms, challenges art to justify itself.

Plato,[3] who proposed the theory, seems to have done so in order to 3
rule that the value of art is dubious. Since he considered ordinary material things as themselves mimetic objects, imitations of transcendent forms or structures, even the best painting of a bed would be only an "imitation of an imitation." For Plato, art is neither particularly useful (the painting of a bed is no good to sleep on) nor, in the strict sense, true. And Aristotle's arguments in defense of art do not really challenge Plato's view that all art is an elaborate *trompe l'oeil*,[4] and there-

---

[1] *Lascaux, Altamira, Niaux, La Pasiega* Limestone caves in France and Spain on the walls of which are magnificent prehistoric paintings dating possibly to 15,000 B.C. The subjects of the paintings are animals, and the paintings are thought to have been part of magic rituals designed to gain control over the animals.

[2] *mimesis, imitation of reality* See Aristotle's *Poetics* (first selection, this part): Aristotle suggests that art, whether painting or drama, imitates life.

[3] *Plato (c. 428–348 B.C.)* In "The Allegory of the Cave" (see Part Five), he demonstrates that reality is in "heaven" and that what we see on earth is only an imitation of the divine ideal.

[4] *trompe l'oeil* French, "fool the eye"; an optical illusion; a style of painting that gives the illusion of actual objects or a photograph.

fore a lie. But he does dispute Plato's idea that art is useless. Lie or no, art has a certain value according to Aristotle because it is a form of therapy. Art is useful, after all, Aristotle counters, medicinally useful in that it arouses and purges dangerous emotions.

In Plato and Aristotle, the mimetic theory of art goes hand in hand 4 with assumption that art is always figurative. But advocates of the mimetic theory need not close their eyes to decorative and abstract art. The fallacy that art is necessarily a "realism" can be modified or scrapped without over moving outside the problems delimited by the mimetic theory.

The fact is, all Western consciousness of and reflection upon art 5 have remained within the confines staked out by the Greek theory of art as mimesis or representation. It is through this theory that art as such —above and beyond given works of art—becomes problematic, in need of defense. And it is the defense of art which gives birth to the odd vision by which something we have learned to call "form" is separated off from something we have learned to call "content," and to the well-intentioned move which makes content essential and form accessory.

Even in modern times, when most artists and critics have discarded 6 the theory of art as representation of an outer reality in favor of the theory of art as subjective expression, the main feature of the mimetic theory persists. Whether we conceive of the work of art on the model of a picture (art as a picture of reality) or on the model of a statement (art as the statement of the artist), content still comes first. The content may have changed. It may now be less figurative, less lucidly realistic. But it is still assumed that a work of art *is* its content. Or, as it's usually put today, that a work of art by definition says something. ("What X is saying is . . ." "What X is trying to say is . . ." "What X said is . . ." etc., etc.)

None of us can ever retrieve that innocence before all theory when 7 art knew no need to justify itself, when one did not ask of a work of art what it said because one knew (or thought one knew) what it did. From now to the end of consciousness, we are stuck with the task of defending art. We can only quarrel with one or another means of defense. Indeed, we have an obligation to overthrow any means of defending and justifying art which becomes particularly obtuse or onerous or insensitive to contemporary needs and practice.

This is the case, today, with the very idea of content itself. What- 8 ever it may have been in the past, the idea of content is today mainly a hindrance, a nuisance, a subtle or not so subtle philistinism.[5]

---

[5]*philistinism* A smugly uncultured or anticultural position.

Though the actual developments in many arts may seem to be   9
leading us away from the idea that a work of art is primarily its content, the idea still exerts an extraordinary hegemony. I want to suggest
that this is because the idea is now perpetuated in the guise of a certain way of encountering works of art thoroughly ingrained among
most people who take any of the arts seriously. What the overemphasis on the idea of content entails is the perennial, never-con-
summated project of *interpretation*. And, conversely, it is the habit
of approaching works of art in order to *interpret* them that sustains
the fancy that there really is such a thing as the content of a work
of art.

Of course, I don't mean interpretation in the broadest sense, the   10
sense in which Nietzsche[6] (rightly) says, "There are no facts, only
interpretations." By interpretation, I mean here a conscious act of the
mind which illustrates a certain code, certain "rules" of interpretation.

Directed to art, interpretation means plucking a set of elements   11
(the X, the Y, the Z, and so forth) from the whole work. The task of
interpretation is virtually one of translation. The interpreter says,
Look, don't you see that X is really—or, really means—A? That Y is
really B? That Z is really C?

What situation could prompt this curious project for transforming   12
a text? History gives us the materials for an answer. Interpretation first
appears in the culture of late classical antiquity, when the power and
credibility of myth had been broken by the "realistic" view of the
world introduced by scientific enlightenment. Once the question that
haunts post-mythic consciousness—that of the *seemliness* of religious
symbols—had been asked, the ancient texts were, in their pristine
form, no longer acceptable. Then interpretation was summoned, to
reconcile the ancient texts to "modern" demands. Thus, the Stoics,[7] to
accord with their view that the gods had to be moral, allegorized away
the rude features of Zeus and his boisterous clan in Homer's epics.
What Homer really designated by the adultery of Zeus with Leto, they
explained, was the union between power and wisdom. In the same

---

[6]***Friedrich Nietzsche (1844–1900)*** One of the most important nineteenth-century German philosophers (see Part Five). His theory of the superman asserts that certain
individuals are above conventional wisdom and should be permitted to live and act as
they wish.

[7]***the Stoics . . . Homer's epics*** The Stoic philosophers in ancient Greece interpreted the Greek myths in accordance with their views of a morality of self-sacrifice and
public welfare. Homer (9th–8th centuries B.C.), who preceded the Stoics, could retell the
adulterous myths of Zeus without having to interpret them to fit a "higher" public morality.

vein, Philo of Alexandria[8] interpreted the literal historical narratives of the Hebrew Bible as spiritual paradigms. The story of the exodus from Egypt, the wandering in the desert for forty years, and the entry into the promised land, said Philo, was really an allegory of the individual soul's emancipation, tribulations, and final deliverance. Interpretation thus presupposes a discrepancy between the clear meaning of the text and the demands of (later) readers. It seeks to resolve that discrepancy. The situation is that for some reason a text has become unacceptable; yet it cannot be discarded. Interpretation is a radical strategy for conserving an old text, which is thought too precious to repudiate, by revamping it. The interpreter, without actually erasing or rewriting the text, *is* altering it. But he can't admit to doing this. He claims to be only making it intelligible, by disclosing its true meaning. However far the interpreters alter the text (another notorious example is the rabbinic and Christian "spiritual" interpretations of the clearly erotic Song of Songs[9]), they must claim to be reading off a sense that is already there.

Interpretation in our own time, however, is even more complex. 13 For the contemporary zeal for the project of interpretation is often prompted not by piety toward the troublesome text (which may conceal an aggression) but by an open aggressiveness, an overt contempt for appearances. The old style of interpretation was insistent, but respectful; it erected another meaning on top of the literal one. The modern style of interpretation excavates, and as it excavates, destroys; it digs "behind" the text, to find a sub-text which is the true one. The most celebrated and influential modern doctrines, those of Marx and Freud,[10] actually amount to elaborate systems of hermeneutics,[11] aggressive and impious theories of interpretation. All observable phenomena are bracketed, in Freud's phrase, as *manifest content*. This

---

[8]***Philo of Alexandria (30*** B.C.–A.D. ***45)*** A Jewish philosopher of importance to our knowledge of Jewish thought in the first century A.D. His theories were closely aligned with Stoicism (see note 7). His most important work is a commentary on Genesis in which he sees all the characters as allegorical representations of states of the soul.

[9]***Song of Songs*** This is the Song of Solomon in the Bible, referred to in the headnote. The inclusion of the Song of Solomon in the Bible was marked by much dispute because it is an erotic, and very beautiful, piece of literature. The dispute was settled when agreement was reached in its interpretation: it was seen as a metaphor of the love of God for his creation.

[10]***Marx and Freud*** See the introductions for each of these authors in Parts Two and Three, respectively.

[11]***hermeneutics*** A system of critical analysis that examines texts for their deeper meanings.

manifest content must be probed and pushed aside to find the true meaning—the *latent content*—beneath. For Marx, social events like revolutions and wars; for Freud, the events of individual lives (like neurotic symptoms and slips of the tongue) as well as texts (like a dream or a work of art)—all are treated as occasions for interpretation. According to Marx and Freud, these events only *seem* to be intelligible. Actually, they have no meaning without interpretation. To understand *is* to interpret. And to interpret is to restate the phenomenon, in effect to find an equivalent for it.

14 Thus, interpretation is not (as most people assume) an absolute value, a gesture of mind situated in some timeless realm of capabilities. Interpretation must itself be evaluated, within a historical view of human consciousness. In some cultural contexts, interpretation is a liberating act. It is a means of revising, of transvaluing[12] of escaping the dead past. In other cultural contexts, it is reactionary, impertinent, cowardly, stifling.

15 Today is such a time, when the project of interpretation is largely reactionary, stifling. Like the fumes of the automobile and of heavy industry which befoul the urban atmosphere, the effusion of interpretations of art today poisons our sensibilities. In a culture whose already classical dilemma is the hypertrophy[13] of the intellect at the expense of energy and sensual capability, interpretation is the revenge of the intellect upon art.

16 Even more. It is the revenge of the intellect upon the world. To interpret is to impoverish, to deplete the world—in order to set up a shadow world of "meanings." It is to turn *the* world into *this* world. ("This world"! As if there were any other.)

17 The world, our world, is depleted, impoverished enough. Away with all duplicates of it, until we again experience more immediately what we have.

18 In most modern instances, interpretation amounts to the philistine refusal to leave the work of art alone. Real art has the capacity to make us nervous. By reducing the work of art to its content and then interpreting *that*, one tames the work of art. Interpretation makes art manageable, conformable.

19 This philistinism of interpretation is more rife in literature than in

---

[12]**transvaluing** The act of evaluating by a new principle, such as interpreting a sonnet of Shakespeare by means of Freudian principles.
[13]**hypertrophy** overdevelopment.

any other art. For decades now, literary critics have understood it to be their task to translate the elements of the poem or play or novel or story into something else. Sometimes a writer will be so uneasy before the naked power of his art that he will install within the work itself—albeit with a little shyness, a touch of the good taste of irony—the clear and explicit interpretation of it. Thomas Mann[14] is an example of such an overcooperative author. In the case of more stubborn authors, the critic is only too happy to perform the job.

The work of Kafka,[15] for example, has been subjected to a mass 20 ravishment by no less than three armies of interpreters. Those who read Kafka as a social allegory see case studies of the frustrations and insanity of modern bureaucracy and its ultimate issuance in the totalitarian state. Those who read Kafka as a psychoanalytic allegory see desperate revelations of Kafka's fear of his father, his castration anxieties, his sense of his own impotence, his thralldom to his dreams. Those who read Kafka as a religious allegory explain that K. in *The Castle* is trying to gain access to heaven, that Joseph K. in *The Trial* is being judged by the inexorable and mysterious justice of God. . . . Another body of work that has attracted interpreters like leeches is that of Samuel Beckett,[16] Beckett's delicate dramas of the withdrawn consciousness—pared down to essentials, cut off, often represented as physically immobilized—are read as a statement about modern man's alienation from meaning or from God, or as an allegory of psychopathology.

Proust, Joyce, Faulkner, Rilke, Lawrence, Gide[17] . . . one could go 21 on citing author after author; the list is endless of those around whom thick encrustations of interpretation have taken hold. But it should be noted that interpretation is not simply the compliment that mediocrity pays to genius. It is, indeed, the modern way of understanding something, and is applied to works of every quality. Thus, in the notes

---

[14]*Thomas Mann (1875–1955)* A major modern German novelist. Sontag may be referring to his most important novel, *The Magic Mountain* (1924).

[15]*Franz Kafka (1883–1924)* A largely surrealist writer whose dreamworlds are often close to the nightmare. The novels referred to, *The Castle* and *The Trial*, both published in 1937, concentrate on the struggles of the individual against institutions whose nature is baffling and intimidating.

[16]*Samuel Beckett (b. 1906)* Irish writer whose work is enigmatic. He is best known for his play *Waiting for Godot* (1956).

[17]*Marcel Proust (1871–1922); James Joyce (1882–1941); William Faulkner (1897–1962); Rainer Maria Rilke (1875–1926); D. H. Lawrence (1885–1930); André Gide (1869–1951)* Important modern writers whose work has attracted considerable interpretive attention.

that Elia Kazan[18] published on his production of *A Streetcar Named Desire*, it becomes clear that, in order to direct the play, Kazan had to discover that Stanley Kowalski represented the sensual and vengeful barbarism that was engulfing our culture, while Blanche DuBois was Western civilization, poetry, delicate apparel, dim lighting, refined feelings and all, though a little the worse for wear, to be sure. Tennessee Williams's forceful psychological melodrama now became intelligible: it was about something, about the decline of Western civilization. Apparently, were it to go on being a play about a handsome brute named Stanley Kowalski and a faded mangy belle named Blanche DuBois, it would not be manageable.

It doesn't matter whether artists intend, or don't intend, for their works to be interpreted. Perhaps Tennessee Williams thinks *Streetcar* is about what Kazan thinks it to be about. It may be that Cocteau[19] in *The Blood of a Poet* and in *Orpheus* wanted the elaborate readings which have been given these films, in terms of Freudian symbolism and social critique. But the merit of these works certainly lies elsewhere than in their "meanings." Indeed, it is precisely to the extent that Williams's plays and Cocteau's films do suggest these portentous meanings[20] that they are defective, false, contrived, lacking in conviction.

From interviews, it appears that Resnais and Robbe-Grillet[21] consciously designed *Last Year at Marienbad* to accommodate a multiplicity of equally plausible interpretations. But the temptation to interpret *Marienbad* should be resisted. What matters in *Marienbad* is the pure, untranslatable, sensuous immediacy of some of its images, and its rigorous if narrow solutions to certain problems of cinematic form.

Again, Ingmar Bergman[22] may have meant the tank rumbling down

<small>22</small>
<small>23</small>
<small>24</small>

---

[18]***Elia Kazan (b. 1909)*** American theatrical director who championed the early productions of Tennessee Williams (1914–1984), particularly *A Streetcar Named Desire* (1947).

[19]***Jean Cocteau (1889–1963)*** French writer, painter, filmmaker. His *Orpheus* (1924) reinterpreted the Greek myth for modern times.

[20]***portentous meanings*** Meanings that imply great significance or seriousness and that may imply ominous developments. Sontag implies that the meanings suggested for the works are overblown and unlikely.

[21]***Alain Resnais (b. 1922) and Alain Robbe-Grillet (b. 1922)*** The filmmaker and screenwriter, respectively, for a very "arty" and experimental film, *Last Year at Marienbad* (1961).

[22]***Ingmar Bergman (b. 1918)*** Swedish film director, one of the most influential of modern filmmakers.

the empty night street in *The Silence* as a phallic symbol. But if he did, it was a foolish thought. ("Never trust the teller, trust the tale," said Lawrence.) Taken as a brute object, as an immediate sensory equivalent for the mysterious abrupt armored happenings going on inside the hotel, that sequence with the tank is the most striking moment in the film. Those who reach for a Freudian interpretation of the tank are only expressing their lack of response to what is there on the screen.

It is always the case that interpretation of this type indicates a dissatisfaction (conscious or unconscious) with the work, a wish to replace it by something else. 25

Interpretation, based on the highly dubious theory that a work of art is composed of items of content, violates art. It makes art into an article for use, for arrangement into a mental scheme of categories. 26

Interpretation does not, of course, always prevail. In fact, a great deal of today's art may be understood as motivated by a flight from interpretation. To avoid interpretation, art may become parody. Or it may become abstract. Or it may become ("merely") decorative. Or it may become non-art. 27

The flight from interpretation seems particularly a feature of modern painting. Abstract painting is the attempt to have, in the ordinary sense, no content; since there is no content, there can be no interpretation. Pop Art[23] works by the opposite means to the same result; using a content so blatant, so "what it is," it, too, ends by being uninterpretable. 28

A great deal of modern poetry as well, starting from the great experiments of French poetry (including the movement that is misleadingly called Symbolism)[24] to put silence into poems and to reinstate the *magic* of the word, has escaped from the rough grip of interpretation. The most recent revolution in contemporary taste in poetry—the 29

---

[23]**Pop Art**   A form of art that in the later 1950s and the 1960s reacted against the high seriousness of abstract expressionism and other movements of the 1940s and 1950s. Instead of stressing deep content, it stressed no content; instead of profound meaning, no meaning other than what was observable.

[24]**Symbolism**   A movement in poetry begun in France in the later part of the nineteenth century and popularized in England by Arthur Symons. It sought expression through the symbol rather than through discursive language. By silencing the discourse, the symbolists hoped to put magic back into poetry—the magic representing what was inexpressible in words but could be felt in symbol.

revolution that has deposed Eliot and elevated Pound[25]—represents a turning away from content in poetry in the old sense, an impatience with what made modern poetry prey to the zeal of interpreters.

I am speaking mainly of the situation in America, of course. Interpretation runs rampant here in those arts with a feeble and negligible avant-garde:[26] fiction and the drama. Most American novelists and playwrights are really either journalists or gentlemen sociologists and psychologists. They are writing the literary equivalent of program music. And so rudimentary, uninspired, and stagnant has been the sense of what might be done with form in fiction and drama that even when the content isn't simply information, news, it is still peculiarly visible, handier, more exposed. To the extent that novels and plays (in America), unlike poetry and painting and music, don't reflect any interesting concern with changes in their form, these arts remain prone to assault by interpretation.

But programmatic avant-gardism—which has meant, mostly, experiments with form at the expense of content—is not the only defense against the infestation of art by interpretations. At least, I hope not. For this would be to commit art to being perpetually on the run. (It also perpetuates the very distinction between form and content which is, ultimately, an illusion.) Ideally, it is possible to elude the interpreters in another way, by making works of art whose surface is so unified and clean, whose momentum is so rapid, whose address is so direct that the work can be . . . just what it is. Is this possible now? It does happen in films, I believe. This is why cinema is the most alive, the most exciting, the most important of all art forms right now. Perhaps the way one tells how alive a particular art form is is by the latitude it gives for making mistakes in it and still being good. For example, a few of the films of Bergman—though crammed with lame messages about the modern spirit, thereby inviting interpretations— still triumph over the pretentious intentions of their director. In *Winter Light* and *The Silence,* the beauty and visual sophistication of the images subvert before our eyes the callow pseudo-intellectuality of the story and some of the dialogue. (The most remarkable instance of this sort of discrepancy is the work of D. W. Griffith).[27] In good films, there

---

[25]**T. S. Eliot (1888–1965) and Ezra Pound (1885–1972)** Two of America's most important modern poets.

[26]**avante-garde** Art that is ahead of its time; literally, in the advance guard of a movement forward.

[27]**D. W. Griffith (1875–1948)** The first world-class American film director.

is always a directness that entirely frees us from the itch to interpret. Many old Hollywood films, like those of Cukor, Walsh, Hawks,[28] and countless other directors, have this liberating antisymbolic quality, no less than the best work of the new European directors, like Truffaut's *Shoot the Piano Player* and *Jules and Jim*, Godard's *Breathless* and *Vivre sa Vie*, Antonioni's *L'Avventura*, and Olmi's[29] *The Fiancés*.

The fact that films have not been overrun by interpreters is in part 32 due simply to the newness of cinema as an art. It also owes to the happy accident that films for such a long time were just movies; in other words, that they were understood to be part of mass, as opposed to high, culture, and were left alone by most people with minds. Then, too, there is always something other than content in the cinema to grab hold of, for those who want to analyze. For the cinema, unlike the novel, possesses a vocabulary of forms—the explicit, complex, and discussable technology of camera movements, cutting, and composition of the frame that goes into the making of a film.

What kind of criticism, of commentary on the arts, is desirable to- 33 day? For I am not saying that works of art are ineffable, that they cannot be described or paraphrased. They can be. The question is how. What would criticism look like that would serve the work of art, not usurp its place?

What is needed, first, is more attention to form in art. If excessive 34 stress on *content* provokes the arrogance of interpretation, more extended and more thorough descriptions of *form* would silence. What is needed is a vocabulary—a descriptive, rather than prescriptive,[30] vocabulary—for forms.[31] The best criticism, and it is uncommon, is of

---

[28]*George Cukor (1899–1983); Raoul Walsh (1887–1980); Howard Hawks (1896–1977)* American filmmakers who were important before 1950.

[29]*François Truffaut (1932–1984); Jean-Luc Godard (b. 1930); Michelangelo Antonioni (b. 1912); Ermanno Olmi (b. 1931)* Important modern influences in the film.

[30]*descriptive, rather than prescriptive, vocabulary* A prescriptive vocabulary in criticism aims to establish what a work of art ought to be; a descriptive vocabulary concentrates on what is. Sontag encourages a criticism that tells us what has happened, not one that tells us what ought to happen.

[31]One of the difficulties is that our idea of form is spatial (the Greek metaphors for form are all derived from notions of space). This is why we have a more ready vocabulary of forms for the spatial than for the temporal arts. The exception among the temporal arts, of course, is the drama; perhaps this is because the drama is a narrative (i.e., temporal) form that extends itself visually and pictorially, upon a stage. What we don't have yet is a poetics of the novel, any clear notion of the forms of narration. Perhaps film criticism will be the occasion of a breakthrough here, since films are primarily a visual form yet they are also a subdivision of literature. [Sontag's note]

this sort that dissolves considerations of content into those of form. On film, drama, and painting respectively, I can think of Erwin Panofsky's essay "Style and Medium in the Motion Pictures," Northrop Frye's essay "A Conspectus of Dramatic Genres," Pierre Francastel's essay "The Destruction of a Plastic Space." Roland Barthes's book *On Racine* and his two essays on Robbe-Grillet are examples of formal analysis applied to the work of a single author. (The best essays in Erich Auerbach's *Mimesis*, like "The Scar of Odysseus," are also of this type.) An example of formal analysis applied simultaneously to genre and author is Walter Benjamin's essay "The Storyteller: Reflections on the Works of Nicolai Leskov."[32]

Equally valuable would be acts of criticism which would supply a   35
really accurate, sharp, loving description of the appearance of a work of art. This seems even harder to do than formal analysis. Some of Manny Farber's[33] film criticism, Dorothy Van Ghent's essay "The Dickens World: A View from Todgers'," Randall Jarrell's essay on Walt Whitman are among the rare examples of what I mean. These are essays which reveal the sensuous surface of art without mucking about in it.

Transparence is the highest, most liberating value in art—and in   36
criticism—today. Transparence means experiencing the luminousness of the thing in itself, of things being what they are. This is the greatness of, for example, the films of Bresson and Ozu and Renoir's[34] *The Rules of the Game.*

Once upon a time (say, for Dante),[35] it must have been a revolu-   37
tionary and creative move to design works of art so that they might be experienced on several levels. Now it is not. It reinforces the principle of redundancy that is the principal affliction of modern life.

Once upon a time (a time when high art was scarce), it must have   38
been a revolutionary and creative move to interpret works of art. Now it is not. What we decidedly do not need now is further to assimilate Art into Thought, or (worse yet) Art into Culture.

Interpretation takes the sensory experience of the work of art for   39

---

[32]***Panofsky and others***   These are all works by modern critics; they are the kind that Sontag feels will help to reinstate formal analysis.

[33]***Manny Farber and others***   These are examples of critics whose purpose is to describe accurately the surfaces of works of art.

[34]***Robert Bresson (b. 1907); Yasujiro Ozu (1903–1963); Alain Renoir (1894–1979)***   Directors who are or were significant influences on contemporary filmmakers.

[35]***Dante Alighieri (1265–1321)***   Italian poet and scholar. His most important work was *The Divine Comedy.*

granted, and proceeds from there. This cannot be taken for granted now. Think of the sheer multiplication of works of art available to every one of us, super-added to the conflicting tastes and odors and sights of the urban environment that bombard our senses. Ours is a culture based on excess, on overproduction; the result is a steady loss of sharpness in our sensory experience. All the conditions of modern life—its material plenitude, its sheer crowdedness—conjoin to dull our sensory faculties. And it is in the light of the condition of our senses, our capacities (rather than those of another age), that the task of the critic must be assessed.

What is important now is to recover our senses. We must learn to *see* more, to *hear* more, to *feel* more.   40

Our task is not to find the maximum amount of content in a work of art, much less to squeeze more content out of the work than is already there. Our task is to cut back content so that we can see the thing at all.   41

The aim of all commentary on art now should be to make works of art—and, by analogy, our own experience—more, rather than less, real to us. The function of criticism should be to show *how it is what it is*, even *that it is what it is*, rather than to show *what it means*.   42

In place of a hermeneutics we need an erotics of art.   43

QUESTIONS

1. What does Sontag say about Plato's valuation of works of art? Does Plato's attitude toward art seem to derive naturally from his attitude toward mimesis? What is mimesis?
2. Sontag mentions two approaches to art: art as a statement of reality and art as a statement of the artist. Which of these is in agreement with your views of art?
3. What is Sontag's definition of interpretation? Is it satisfactory? Does her definition limit the nature of her argument?
4. Why would the Freudian idea of dreams having a manifest content and a latent content be of value to interpretation?
5. The term "hermeneutics" is used to describe a form of interpretation. What does Sontag seem to mean by this term?
6. What does Sontag mean by "an erotics of art"? Is it a useful term, or is it simply confusing?

WRITING ASSIGNMENTS

1. Sontag explains that works of art have a content and a form. She also explains that the terminology for formal elements in literary works is not as fully developed as it is for visual works. Therefore, it is difficult to talk about the form of a work of literature. If you were to comment on a work of literary art—of poetry, drama, or fiction—what formal elements would you have to discuss? Could you discuss them without performing an act of interpretation? Choose a specific work for your commentary. Root your discussion in an examination of one work.

2. Do you agree with Sontag about the artistic vitality of contemporary film? Using examples from films you have seen recently (whether on television or in a theater), defend or attack her judgment regarding the preeminence of the film among contemporary arts.

3. Refer to Ortega's essay, "The Dehumanization of Art." Would Sontag agree with his views about the role of feelings and emotions in art? To what extent does her commentary on "subjective expression" suggest an emotional content in works of art? What kinds of emotions would she admit into art? Which emotions would she wish to omit from art or from discussions of art?

4. Sontag says in paragraph 6 that "most artists and critics have discarded the theory of art as representation of an outer reality in favor of the theory of art as subjective expression" and that "it is still assumed that a work of art *is* its content." To what extent do you think these statements are true? Refer to your experience in reading, in viewing paintings, or in experiencing other works of art. Is there any special problem in examining the form of a work of art if we assume that art is subjective expression—in other words, the expression of the artist's feelings or of his or her understanding of things? Would subjective expression be more likely to affect the content or the form of a work of art?

5. Take Sontag's advice and approach a favorite poem by doing as she says: create an erotics of art instead of a hermeneutics. In other words, follow up on what she says in her final words of advice in paragraph 42: "The aim of all commentary on art now should be to make the works of art—and, by analogy, our own experience—more, rather than less, real to us. The function of criticism should be to show *how it is what it is*, even *that it is what it is*, rather than to show *what it means*."

6. Offer a counterargument to Sontag's views. Write an essay called "In Defense of Interpretation" and try to establish clearly what interpretation is, how it functions, and why it is defensible. Why is it good? Why is it desirable? In the process, you may comment on any of Sontag's arguments and counter them in turn. Decide whether her distinction between form and content is acceptable and whether it is necessary to your argument. Use specific examples of your interpretation (or the interpretations of others) of works of art to defend your position.

WRITING ABOUT IDEAS

———⦿———

An Introduction to Rhetoric

Wᴿɪᴛɪɴɢ ᴀʙᴏᴜᴛ ɪᴅᴇᴀѕ performs several functions. First, it helps make our thinking available to others for examination. Naturally, the writers whose works are presented in this book benefited from the reactions of their first readers, at times revising their work considerably as a result of criticism. Writing about ideas also helps us to refine what we think—even without criticism from others. Writing is a self-instructional experience. We learn by writing in part because writing clarifies our thinking. When we think silently, we construct phrases and then reflect on them. When we speak, we both utter these phrases and sort them out in order to give our audience a tidier version of our thoughts. But spoken thought is difficult to sustain because we cannot review or revise what we said an hour earlier. Writing has the advantage of permitting us to expand our ideas, work them through completely, and possibly revise in the light of later discoveries. It is by writing that we truly gain control over our ideas.

GENERATING TOPICS FOR WRITING

Filled with sophisticated discussions of important ideas, the selections in this volume endlessly stimulate our responses and our writing. Reading the works of great thinkers can also be chastening to the point of making us feel sometimes that they have said it all and there is no room for our own thoughts. However, the suggestions that follow will assist you to write in response to the ideas of an important thinker.

The Technique of the Question. One of the most reliable ways to start is to ask a question and then to answer it. In many ways, that is what the writers in this book have done again and again. Karen Horney asked whether what Freud said about female psychology was true. Loren Eiseley, after observing a woman whose skeletal structure resembled that of the Neanderthal, asked himself whether it might be possible for the Neanderthal to have survived and be living among us. As he begins to answer that question, he demonstrates the magnitude of the question and its implications for our attitudes toward human development. John Kenneth Galbraith asked questions about why poverty still existed in a prosperous economy. B. F. Skinner's "What Is Man?" poses questions about our deeper motivations. Even Aristotle asked himself what constituted tragedy. Such questioning is at the center of all inquiry.

As a writer stimulated by other thinkers, you can use the same technique. For example, turn back to the Machiavelli exerpt annotated in "Evaluating Ideas: An introduction to Critical Reading" (p. 1). All of the annotations can be easily turned into questions. Any of the following questions, based on the annotations and our brief summary of the passage, could be the basis of an essay.

Should a leader be armed?

Is it true that an unarmed leader is despised?

Will those leaders who are always good come to ruin among those who are not good?

To remain in power, must a leader learn how not to be good?

One technique is to structure an essay around the answer to such a question. Another is to develop a series of questions and to answer each of them in various parts of an essay. Yet another technique is to use the question indirectly—by answering it, but not obviously. Virginia Woolf, in "A Letter to a Young Poet," is actually responding to his question about whether there is any future in writing poetry. She does not come out and say, "Here is my answer." Instead, she explores the circumstances of modern poetry and, in the process, offers her answer to his question. You can do the same kind of thing.

Many kinds of questions can be asked of a passage even as brief as the sample from Machiavelli. For one thing, we can limit ourselves to our annotations and go no further. But we can also reflect on the larger issues and ask a series of questions that would constitute a fuller inquiry. Out of that inquiry we can also generate ideas for our own writing.

Two important ideas were isolated in our annotations. The first was that the prince must devote himself to war. In modern times, this implies that a president or other national leader must put matters of defense first—that all a leader's knowledge, training, and concerns must revolve around warfare. Taking that idea in general, we can develop other questions that, stimulated by Machiavelli's selection, can be used to generate essays.

Which modern leaders would Machiavelli approve?

Would Machiavelli approve of our current president?

Do military personnel make the best leaders?

Should our president have a military background?

Could a modern state survive with no army or military weapons?

What kind of a nation would we be if we did not stockpile nuclear weapons?

These questions derive from the first idea that we isolated in the annotations. The next group of questions comes from the second idea, the issue of whether a leader can afford to be moral.

Which virtues might cause a leader to lose power?

Is Machiavelli being cynical about morality, or is he being realistic (as he claims he is)? (We might also ask if Machiavelli uses the word "realistic" as a synonym for "cynical.")

Do most American leaders behave morally?

Do most leaders believe that they should behave morally?

Should our leaders be moral all the time?

Which vices can we permit our leaders to have?

Are there any vices we want our leaders to have?

Which world leaders behave most morally? Are they the ones we most respect?

Could a modern government govern well or at all if it were to behave morally in the face of immoral adversaries?

One of the reasons for reading Machiavelli is to help us confront large and serious questions. One of the reasons for writing about these ideas is to help clarify our own positions on such important issues.

Using Suggestions for Writing. Every selection in this book is followed by a number of questions and a number of writing assignments. The questions are designed to help clarify the most important issues raised in the piece. Unlike the questions derived from annotation, their purpose is to stimulate a classroom discussion so that you can benefit from hearing others' thoughts on these issues. Naturally, subjects for essays can arise from such discussion, but the discussion is most important for refining and focusing your ideas. The writing assignments, on the other hand, are explicitly meant to provide a useful starting point for producing an essay of 700 to 1,000 words.

A sample suggestion for writing about Machiavelli follows:

> Machiavelli advises the prince to study history and reflect on the actions of great men. Would you support such advice? Machiavelli mentions a number of great leaders in his essay. Which leaders would you recommend a prince should study? Do you think Machiavelli would agree?

Like most of the suggestions for writing, this one could be worked with in any one of several ways. It can be broken down into three parts. The first is the question of whether it is useful to study, as Machiavelli does, the performance of past leaders. If you agree, then the second part of the question asks you to name some leaders whose behavior you would recommend studying. If you do not agree, you can point to the performance of some past leaders and explain why their study would be pointless today. Finally, the third part of the question asks whether you think Machiavelli would agree with your choices.

To deal successfully with this suggestion for writing, you could begin by giving your reasons for recommending that a political leader study "the actions of great men." George Santayana once said, "Those who cannot remember the past are condemned to repeat it." That is, we study history in order not to have to live it over again. If you believe that a study of the past is important, the first part of an essay can answer the question of why such study could make a politician more successful.

The second part of the suggestion focuses on examples. In the sample from Machiavelli above, we omitted the examples, but in the complete essay they are very important for bringing Machiavelli's point home. Few things can convince as completely as examples, so the first thing to do is to choose several leaders to work with. If you have studied a world leader, such as Indira Gandhi, Winston Churchill, Franklin Delano Roosevelt, or Joseph Stalin, you could use that figure as one of your examples. If you have not done so, then the most appropriate procedure is to use the research library and—in the sections on history and politics—find books or articles on one or two leaders and read them with an eye to establishing their usefulness for your argument. The central question you would seek to answer is how a specific world leader could benefit from studying the behavior and conduct of a modern leader.

The third part of the suggestion for writing—whether Machiavelli would agree with you—is very speculative. It invites you to look through the selection to find quotes or comments that indicate probable agreement or disagreement on Machiavelli's part. You can base your argument only on what Machiavelli says or implies, and this means that you will have to reread his essay to find evidence that will support your view.

In a sense, this part of the suggestion establishes a procedure for working with the writing assignments. Once you have clarified the parts of the assignment and have some useful questions to guide you, and once you have determined what research, if any, is necessary, the next step is to reread the selection with an eye to finding the most appropriate information to help you in writing your own essay. One of the most important activities in learning how to write from these selections is rereading, while you pay close attention to the annotations that you've made in the margins of the essays. It is one of the most important ways in which reading about significant ideas differs from reading for entertainment. Important ideas demand reflection and reconsideration. Rereading provides both.

SOME USEFUL RHETORICAL TECHNIQUES

Every one of the selections, whether by Francis Bacon or Susan Sontag, Frederick Douglass or B. F. Skinner, is marked by the use of specific rhetorical techniques that help the author communicate complex ideas. Some of the more important rhetorical achievements are identified in the introduction to each selection so that you can observe them and possibly learn how to use them in your own writing.

"Rhetoric" is a general term used to discuss special writing techniques. For example, one of the interesting rhetorical techniques

Machiavelli uses is that of illustration by example, usually to prove his points. Francis Bacon uses the technique of enumeration—partitioning his essay into four sections. Enumeration is especially useful when one wishes to be very clear or when one wishes to cover a subject point by point, using each point to accumulate more authority in the discussion. Martin Luther King, Jr., uses the technique of allusion, reminding his readers from the clergy that St. Paul also wrote similar letters to try to help early Christians better understand the nature of their faith. By alluding to the Bible and St. Paul, King effectively reminded his audience that they were all serving God.

A great many more rhetorical techniques may be found in these readings. Some of the techniques are familiar because many of us already use them naturally, but we study them to become aware of their value and to remind us to use them. After all, without using rhetorical techniques it is impossible to communicate the significance of even the most important ideas. Many of the authors in this book would surely admit that the effect of their ideas actually depends upon the way they are expressed, which is a way of saying that they depend upon the rhetorical methods used to express them.

Methods of Development

Most of the more specific rhetorical methods are discussed in the introductions to the individual selections. Several represent exceptionally useful general techniques. These are methods of development. They represent approaches to working up material; that is, developing ideas that contribute to the fullness and completeness of an essay. You may think of them as techniques that can be applied to any idea in almost any situation. They can enlarge upon the idea, clarify it, express it, and demonstrate its truth or effectiveness. Sometimes a technique may be direct, sometimes indirect. Sometimes it will call attention to itself; sometimes it will work behind the scenes. Sometimes it will be used alone, sometimes in conjunction with other methods. The most important techniques will be explained and then illustrated with examples from the selections in the book.

Development by Definition. Definition is essential for two purposes: the first is to make certain that you have a clear grasp of your concepts; the second is to make certain that you communicate a clear understanding to your reader. Many of the selections are devoted almost entirely to the act of definition. For example, in "The Position of

Poverty," John Kenneth Galbraith begins by defining the two kinds of poverty that he feels characterize the economic situation of the poor: case poverty and insular poverty. He defines case poverty in this paragraph:

> Case poverty is commonly and properly related to some characteristic of the individuals so afflicted. Nearly everyone else has mastered his environment; this proves that it is not intractable. But some quality peculiar to the individual or family involved—mental deficiency, bad health, inability to adapt to the discipline of industrial life, uncontrollable procreation, alcohol, discrimination involving a very limited minority, some educational handicap unrelated to community shortcoming, or perhaps a combination of several of these handicaps—has kept these individuals from participating in the general well-being. (para. 9)

When he begins defining insular poverty, however, he is unable to produce a neat single-paragraph definition. He establishes that insular poverty describes a group of people alienated from the majority for any of many reasons. So, next he spends five paragraphs discussing what can produce such poverty—migration, racial prejudice, and lack of education. When working at the level of seriousness that characterizes his work, Galbraith shows us that definition works best when it avoids simple dictionary-style glosses in favor of full description and complex, detailed discussion.

Were we to write an essay on the annotated selection from Machiavelli we might want to define a number of key ideas. For example, if we suspect that Machiavelli might be cynical in suggesting that his prince would not hold power for long if he were to act morally, we would need to define what it means to be cynical. We might also need to define "moral behavior" in political terms. When we argue any point, it is very important to spend time defining key ideas.

Martin Luther King, Jr., in "Letter from Birmingham Jail," takes time to establish some key definitions so that he can speak forcefully to his audience:

> Let us consider a more concrete example of just and unjust laws. An unjust law is a code that a numerical or power majority group compels a minority group to obey but does not make binding on itself. This is a *difference* made legal. By the same token, a just law is a code that a majority compels a minority to follow and that it is willing to follow itself. This is *sameness* made legal. (para. 17)

This is an adequate definition as far as it goes, but most serious ideas need more extensive definition than this passage gives us. And King does go further, providing what Machiavelli does in his essay: examples and explanations. Every full definition will profit from the extension of understanding that an explanation and example will provide. Consider this paragraph from King:

> Let me give another explanation. A law is unjust if it is inflicted on a minority that, as a result of being denied the right to vote, had no part in enacting or devising the law. Who can say that the legislature of Alabama which set up that state's segregation laws was democratically elected? Throughout Alabama all sorts of devious methods are used to prevent Negroes from becoming registered voters, and there are some counties in which, even though Negroes constitute a majority of the population, not a single Negro is registered. Can any law enacted under such circumstances be considered democratically structured? (para. 18)

King makes us aware of the fact that definition is complex and capable of great subtlety. It is an approach that can be used to develop a paragraph or an essay. Since some of the suggestions for writing that follow the selections ask you to use definition as a means of writing about ideas, some of the following tips should be kept in mind:

Definition can be used to develop a paragraph, a section, or an entire essay.

It considers questions of function, purpose, circumstance, origin, and implications for different groups.

Explanations and examples make all definitions more complete and effective.

Development by Comparison. Comparison is a natural operation of the mind. We rarely talk for long about any topic without resorting to a comparison with something else. We are always fascinated with comparisons between ourselves and others, and we realize that we come to know ourselves better as a result of such comparisons. Machiavelli compares the armed with the unarmed prince and shows us, by means of examples, the results of being unarmed.

Thomas Kuhn, in "The Essential Tension: Tradition and Innovation in Scientific Research," deals with two approaches to doing science. One is the rather romantic, renegade theory which suggests that great findings were made by those who sought their own course; who could not fit themselves into the patterns of things as they were; and who, because of their individuality, found dramatic solutions to sticky problems. Kuhn calls such people divergent thinkers. Then there are the traditionalists who find it comfortable to accept current thinking and to work within established patterns. Surprisingly, when Kuhn compares the two, he finds that it is the latter scientists who make the real breakthroughs. He comes to the conclusion that science thrives best when there is a tension between the two approaches. Notice how Kuhn sets up his comparison:

> I do not at all doubt that this description of "divergent thinking" and the concomitant search for those able to do it are entirely proper. Some divergence characterizes all scientific work, and gigantic divergences lie at the core of the most significant episodes in scientific development. But both my own experience in scientific research and my reading of the history of sciences lead me to wonder whether flexibility and open-mindedness have not been too exclusively emphasized as the characteristics requisite for basic research. I shall therefore suggest below that something like "convergent thinking" is just as essential to scientific advance as is divergent. Since these two modes of thought are inevitably in conflict, it will follow that the ability to support a tension that can occasionally become almost unbearable is one of the prime requisites for the very best sort of scientific research. (para. 3)

Kuhn has not only made the comparison between these two ways of thinking central to his discussion but has also shown that their opposition produces a necessary condition for progress in science. The tension between these modes of thought is expressed in the title of his essay, and the essay naturally goes on to clarify the differences and the similarities between them.

Comparison usually includes the following:

A definition of two or more elements to be compared.

Definition may be by example, explanation, description, or any combination of these.

Discussion of the qualities the elements have in common.

Discussion of the qualities the elements have in distinction from one another.

A clear reason for making the comparison.

Development by Example. Examples make abstract ideas concrete. When Virginia Woolf discusses the state of modern poetry, she does not continue for long before she begins to quote lines and cite specific examples. When she does so, she is able to make what she has to say vital and relevant. When Machiavelli talks about looking at history to learn political lessons, he actually cites specific cases and brings them to the attention of his audience, the prince. Every selection in this book offers examples as a way of convincing us of the truth of a proposition or as a way of deepening our understanding of a statement.

In some selections, such as Charles Darwin's discussion of natural selection, the argument hinges entirely on examples, and we find Darwin citing one example after another. Stephen Jay Gould shows how a particular example, that of the ichneumon fly, causes certain philosophical difficulties to theologians studying biology, and therefore to anyone who wishes to look closely at nature. The problem with the ichneumon is that it attacks caterpillars, which have earned sympathy from people, whereas the ichneumon is ugly and seems evil. As he tells us, one result is that we dislike the parasite and approve of its victim. But there is another side to this, a second theme.

> The second theme, ruthless efficiency of the parasites, leads to the opposite conclusion—grudging admiration for the victors. We learn of their skills in capturing dangerous hosts often many times larger than themselves. Caterpillars may be easy game, but the psammocharid wasps prefer spiders. They must insert their ovipositors in a safe and precise spot. Some leave a paralyzed spider in its own burrow. *Planiceps hirsutus*, for example, parasitizes a California trapdoor spider. It searches for spider tubes on sand dunes, then digs into nearby sand to disturb the spider's home and drive it out. When the spider emerges, the wasp attacks, paralyzes its victim, drags it back into its own tube, shuts and fastens the trapdoor, and deposits a single egg upon the spider's abdomen. Other psammocharids will drag a heavy spider back to a previously prepared cluster of clay or mud cells. Some amputate a spider's legs to make the passage easier. Others fly back over water, skimming a buoyant spider along the surface. (para. 13)

Examples need to be chosen carefully because the burden, not only of proof but of explanation and clarity, often depends on them. The sample suggestion given earlier for writing on Machiavelli's essay obviously implies the use of carefully chosen examples when it asks who among world leaders Machiavelli might have approved. For that reason, when doing research for an essay, it is very important to be sure that the example or examples you settle on really suit your purposes.

Examples can be used in several ways. One is to do as Darwin does and present a large number of examples that force one to a given conclusion. This is a somewhat indirect method and is sometimes time-consuming. However, the very weight of numerous examples will be unusually effective. A second method, such as Machiavelli's, can also be effective. One makes a statement that is controversial or questionable and that can be tested by example. If you provide the right example, then your audience must draw a reasonable conclusion.

When using examples, keep these points in mind:

Choose a few strong examples that support your point.

Be concrete and specific, naming names, citing events, giving details where necessary.

Develop each example as fully as possible, being sure to point out its relevance to your position.

Development by Analysis of Cause and Effect. People usually express an interest in causes. If something happens, we often ask what causes it, as if understanding the cause or causes could somehow help us accept the results. Yet dealing with cause and effect is rather subtle. In the case of definition, comparison, and examples, we can point to something specific and feel that the connections between it and our main points are reasonable. In the case of cause and effect, we must recognize that the cause of something has to be reasoned out. After an event has already occurred, it may only be possible to offer a hypothesis of a theory for its cause. In the same sense, if no effect has yet been obtained, it may only be possible to speculate on what it will be if a given plan of action is followed. In both cases, reasoning and imagination must be employed to establish the relationship of cause and effect.

And, subtle though this method of development is, it is quite natural to our general way of thinking. We can see the method in action in the following portion of paragraph 11 of the selection from Frederick Douglass's autobiography:

> I was quite disappointed at the general appearance of things in New Bedford. The impression which I had received respecting the character and condition of the people of the north, I found to be singularly erroneous. I had very strangely supposed, while in slavery, that few of the comforts, and scarcely any of the luxuries, of life were enjoyed at the north, compared with what were enjoyed by the slaveholders of the south. I probably came to this conclusion from the fact that northern people owned no slaves. I supposed that they were about upon a level with the non-slaveholding population of the south. I knew *they* were exceedingly poor, and I had been accustomed to regard their poverty as the necessary consequences of their being non-slaveholders. I had somehow imbibed the opinion that, in the absence of slaves, there could be no wealth, and very little refinement.

Douglass's conclusions were drawn from an analysis based on his experience in the South: people with slaves had wealth; those without had none. The cause (possessing slaves) naturally led in his mind to the effect (being wealthy). Notice that Douglass is pointing out that his initial conclusion was wrong. We should all be warned that the use of cause and effect must be conducted with real attention to the terms and situations we write about. It is easy to be wrong about causes and effects. Their relationship must be worked on thoughtfully.

As has been indicated, in "The Essential Tension" Thomas Kuhn examines the question of creativity in the sciences. He knows that his audience assumes that independent thinking—"divergent thinking"— is essential to making creative discoveries in science. But Kuhn demonstrates through careful argument—examining numerous instances of cause and effect—that it is most often traditional thinking that produces discoveries. His whole essay is built around the relationship of traditional thought and divergent thought in science. He uses as well the methods of definition and comparison, demonstrating that writers use a battery of methods of development in order to make their thinking full and convincing.

Everywhere in this collection authors rely on cause and effect to develop their thoughts. Thomas Jefferson establishes the relationship between the abuses of the English and the need for America to sever its colonial ties. Karl Marx establishes the capitalist economic system as the cause of the oppression of the workers who produce the wealth that the rich enjoy. The Buddha regards spiritual fulfillment as the result of the practice of meditation. John Kenneth Galbraith is concerned with the causes of poverty, which he feels is an anomaly in modern society. Henry David Thoreau establishes what causes demand the effect of civil disobedience. Even Simone Weil's "Spiritual Autobiography" is an examination of the causes of her becoming a Christian mystic.

The power of the rhetorical method of development through cause and effect is such that you will find it in every section of this book, in the work of virtually every author. Some suggestions to keep in mind when using it to develop your own thinking are:

Clearly establish in your own mind the cause and the effect you wish to discuss.

Develop a good line of reasoning that will demonstrate the relationship between the cause and the effect.

Be sure that the cause-effect relationship is real and not merely apparent.

Development by Analysis of Circumstances. Everything we want to discuss exists as certain circumstances. Traditionally, the discussion of circumstances has had two parts. The first is an examination of what is possible or impossible in a given situation. Whenever you are trying to convince your audience that a specific course of action should be taken, it is helpful to show that, given the circumstances, no other course is possible. On the other hand, people may intend to follow a specific course of action because none other seems possible. If you disagree with that course of action, you may have to demonstrate that another is indeed possible.

The second part of this method of development is the analysis of what has been done in the past. If something has been done in the past, then it may be possible to do it again in the future. Therefore, it is often true that a historical survey of a situation is a form of examination of circumstances.

In "The Qualitative Leap Beyond Patriarchal Religion" Mary Daly investigates the nature of the institution of the church, looking back to its early structure. She sees that the church is based on a patriarchy that in some instances has had very negative effects on women. Even the symbols and imagery of the church are masculine. Daly claims that the patriarchal bias injures not only women but everyone. The male-controlled professions, she asserts, are in a complex way genocidal and must change. She reminds us that it is possible for institutions such as the church to alter its imagery and its stance, and when it does so it will be the better for it.

Machiavelli is also interested in the question of possibility, since he is trying to encourage his ideal prince to follow a prescribed pattern of behavior. As he constantly reminds us, if the prince does not do so it is possible that he will be deposed or killed. Taken as a whole, "The Qualities of the Prince" is a recitation of the circumstances that are necessary to guarantee success in politics. Machiavelli establishes this in a single paragraph.

> Therefore, it is not necessary for a prince to have all of the above-mentioned qualities, but it is very necessary for him to appear to have them. Furthermore, I shall be so bold as to assert this: that having them and practicing them at all times is harmful; and appearing to have them is useful; for instance, to seem merciful, faithful, humane, forthright, religious, and to be so; but his mind should be disposed in such a way that should it become necessary not to be so, he will be able and know how to change to the contrary. And it is essential to understand this: that a prince, and especially a new prince, cannot observe all those things by which men are considered good, for in order to maintain the state he is often obliged to act against his promise, against charity, against humanity, and against religion. And therefore, it is necessary that he have a mind ready to turn itself according to the way the winds

of Fortune and the changeability of affairs require him; and, as I said above, as long as it is possible, he should not stray from the good, but he should know how to enter into evil when necessity commands. (para. 23)

This is the essential Machiavelli, the Machiavelli who is often thought of as a cynic. He advises his prince to be virtuous but says that it is not always possible to be so. Therefore, the prince must learn how not to be good when "necessity commands." The circumstances, he tells us, always determine whether it is possible to be virtuous. The most charitable reading of this passage can only conclude that his advice is amoral.

Many of the essays in this collection rely on an analysis of circumstances. Frederick Douglass examines the circumstances of slavery and freedom. Charlotte Perkins Gilman examines the circumstances of women in her society and concludes that the economic dependency of women is an intentional result of a society that differentiated people by gender instead of by ability or talent.

When Jean Jacques Rousseau begins his selection with "Man is born free, and everywhere he is in chains," he begins an examination of the circumstances that have led to that fact. He examines the past— even alluding to social structures of prehistory in an effort to establish the origins of society. By doing so, he hopes to cast light on the present and to explain his sad opening salvo.

When using the method of examination of circumstances to develop an idea, keep in mind the following tips:

Clarify the question of possibility and impossibility.

Review past circumstances so that future ones can be determined.

Suggest a course of action based on an analysis of possibility and past circumstances.

Establish the present circumstances, listing them if necessary. Be detailed; concentrate on facts.

Development by Analysis of Quotations. Not every essay in this collection refers to or quotes other writers, but a good many of them do. And often they point to writers who are held in esteem by their audience. Sometimes the authors do not quote directly but allude to texts that support their views. This is what Martin Luther King, Jr., does when he reminds his audience of certain important passages in the Bible. Similarly, Simone Weil alludes to events in the life of St. Francis. She also refers to the Indian poem, the *Bhagavad-Gita*, to Homer's *Iliad*, and to other works. But she does not quote them at length in order to comment on them.

Virginia Woolf, however, is careful to quote modern poets in order to cast some light on the conditions of modern poetry. In the course of her letter she alludes to dozens of important writers—all of whom she presumes her poet would have known and read. But when she quotes a few lines of modern poetry, she pauses to comment on them (para. 6). She does not analyze the lines themselves. Instead, she analyzes her reactions and compares them to what she suspects the poet imagined they would be. She says:

> "I feel a jar. I feel a shock. I feel as if I had stubbed my toe on the corner of the wardrobe. Am I then, I go on to ask, shocked, prudishly and conventionally, by the words themselves? I think not. The shock is literally a shock. The poet as I guess has strained himself to include an emotion that is not domesticated and acclimatized to poetry; the effort has thrown him off his balance; he rights himself, as I am sure I shall find if I turn the page, by a violent recourse to the poetical—he invokes the moon or the nightingale."

Woolf is being slightly amusing here, particularly in her description of what the "poetical" might be. But she is also interested in her own feelings and why she has had them in response to the poetry.

In your own writing you will find plenty of opportunity to cite passages from an author whose ideas have engaged your attention. In writing an essay in response to Machiavelli, B. F. Skinner, Susan Sontag, or any of the authors in the book, you may find yourself quoting and commenting in some detail on specific lines or passages. This is especially true if you find yourself in disagreement with a point. Your first job, then, is to establish what you disagree with—and usually it helps to quote, which is essentially a way of producing evidence.

The uses of quotation can be rich and various. The most obvious technique is to place a large chunk of quotation into the discussion, setting it off much as I have done above and will do again below. But there are other ways. For example, B. F. Skinner, in "What Is Man?" sometimes invokes a flurry of quotations as a means of explaining. Examine the following paragraph for its gathering of relevant comments from writers whose primary fame comes from their concerns for humanistic values.

> The picture which emerges from a scientific analysis *is* not of a body with a person inside, but of a body which *is* a person in the sense that it displays a complex repertoire of behavior. The picture is, of course, unfamiliar. The man thus portrayed is a stranger, and from the

traditional point of view he may not seem to be a man at all. "For at least one hundred years," said Joseph Wood Krutch, "we have been prejudiced in every theory, including economic determinism, mechanistic behaviorism, and relativism, that reduces the stature of man until he ceases to be man at all in any sense that the humanists of an earlier generation would recognize." Matson has argued that "the empirical behavioral scientist . . . denies, if only by implication, that a unique being, called Man, exists." "What is now under attack," said Maslow, "is the 'being' of man." C. S. Lewis put it quite bluntly: Man is being abolished. (para. 34)

Skinner has almost no time to comment on these quotes. There are a great many of them in one paragraph—for some people's taste, too many. But each of the quotes amasses an argument. Skinner includes them because he is arguing against them, and he wants us to feel that he recognizes the seriousness of his argument and the weight of opinion that is against him. In this sense, the paragraph is successful. Skinner is the first to admit that he must account for the opinions of such worthies as Krutch, Maslow, and Lewis if he is to convince us that his new view of the nature of man is accurate.

Skinner comments on these quotes (and indirectly on many more as well) in subsequent paragraphs. He is arguing for a new view of man throughout the essay, and by quoting judiciously he can accommodate many positions that he well knows are opposed to his.

When you use quotations some pointers to remember are:

Quote accurately and do not distort the context of the original source.

Choose quotations that are most representative of your author.

Unless the quotation is absolutely self-evident in importance, offer your own clarifying comments and analysis.

Make your audience understand why you chose to quote your author: establish clearly the function of the quote.

Finally, it must be admitted that only a few important points concerning the rhetorical methods used by the authors in this book have been discussed here. Rhetoric is a complex art that needs fuller study. But the points raised above are important because they are illustrated in many of the texts you will read, and by watching them at work you can begin to learn to use them yourself. By using them you will be able to achieve in your writing the fullness and purposiveness that mark mature prose.

A SAMPLE ESSAY

The following sample essay is based on the first several paragraphs of Machiavelli's "The Qualities of the Prince" that were annotated in "Evaluating Ideas: An Introduction to Critical Reading." The essay is based on the annotations and the questions that were developed from them:

Should a leader be armed?

Is it true that an unarmed leader is despised?

Will those leaders who are always good come to ruin among those who are not good?

To remain in power, must a leader learn how not to be good?

Not all these questions are dealt with in the essay, but they serve as a starting point and a focus. The methods of development that are discussed above form the primary rhetorical techniques of the essay. Marginal notes identify each method as it is used simply to show in detail its effectiveness. The sample essay does two things simultaneously: it attempts to clarify the meaning of Machiavelli's advice, and then it attempts to apply that advice to a contemporary circumstance. Naturally, the essay could have chosen to discuss only the Renaissance situation that Machiavelli described, but to do so would have required unusual knowledge of that period. The assumption in this sample essay is simply that the questions prompted by the annotations serve as the basis of the discussion.

The Qualities of the President

Intro-
duction   Machiavelli's essay, "The Qualities of the Prince," has a

number of very worrisome points. The ones that worry me most

have to do with the question of whether it is reasonable to

expect a leader to behave virtuously. I think this is connected

to the question of whether the leader should be armed. Machiavelli

emphasizes that the prince must be armed or else face the possi-

bility that someone will take over the government. When I think

about how that advice applies to modern times, particularly in

terms of how our president should behave, I find Machiavelli's
position very different from my own.

Circum-stance   First, I want to discuss the question of being armed. That
is where Machiavelli starts, and it is an important concern. In
Machiavelli's time, the late fifteenth and early sixteenth
centuries, it was common for men to walk in the streets of
Florence wearing a rapier for protection. The possibility of
robbery or even attack by rival political groups was great in
those days. Even if he had a bodyguard, it was still important
for a prince to know how to fight and to be able to defend himself.
Machiavelli seems to be talking only about self-defense when he
recommends that the prince be armed. In our time, sadly, it too
is important to think about protecting the president and other
leaders.

Examples   In recent years there have been many assassination attempts
on world leaders, and our president, John F. Kennedy, was killed
in Dallas in 1963. His brother Robert was killed when he was
campaigning for the presidency in 1968. Also in 1968 Martin
Luther King, Jr., was killed in Memphis because of his beliefs
in racial equality. In the 1980s Pope John Paul II was shot by
a would-be assassin, as was President Ronald Reagan. They both
lived, but Indira Gandhi, the leader of India, was shot and killed
in 1984. This is a frightening record. Probably even Machiavelli
would have been appalled. But would his solution--being armed--
have helped? I do not think so.

Cause/ effect   For one thing, I cannot believe that if the pope had a gun he
would have shot his would-be assassin, Ali Acga. The thought of
it is almost silly. Martin Luther King, Jr., who constantly
preached the value of nonviolence, logically could not have shot
at an assailant. How could John F. Kennedy have returned fire at

a sniper? Robert Kennedy had bodyguards, and both President Reagan and Indira Gandhi were protected by armed guards. The presence of arms obviously does not produce the desired effect: security. The only thing that can produce that is to reduce the visibility of a leader. The president could speak on television or, when he must appear in public, use a bulletproof screen. The opportunities for would-be assassins can be reduced. But the thought of an American president carrying arms is unacceptable.

Com-
parison

The question of whether a president should be armed is to some extent symbolic. Our president stands for America, and if he were to appear in press conferences or state meetings wearing a gun, he would give a symbolic message to the world: look out, we're dangerous. Cuba's Fidel Castro usually appears in a military uniform with a gun, and when he spoke at the United Nations, he was the first, and I think the only, world leader to wear a pistol there. I have seen pictures of Benito Mussolini and Adolf Hitler appearing in public in military uniform, but never in a business suit. The same is true of Libyan leader Muammar al-Qaddafi. Today when a president or a head of state is armed there is often reason to worry. The current leaders of Russia usually wear suits, but Joseph Stalin always wore a military uniform. His rule in Russia was marked by the extermination of whole groups of people and the imprisonment of many more. We do not want an armed president.

Use of
quotations

Yet, Machiavelli plainly says, "among the other bad effects it causes, being disarmed makes you despised . . . for between an armed and an unarmed man there is no comparison whatsoever"

also

Com-
parison

(para. 2). The problem with this statement is that it is more relevant to the sixteenth century than the twentieth. In our time the threat of assassination is so great that being armed would be no sure protection, as we have seen in the case of the

assassination of President Sadat of Egypt, winner of the Nobel
Peace Prize. On the other hand, the pope, like Martin Luther
King, Jr., would never have appeared with a weapon, and yet it
can hardly be said they were despised. If anything, the world's
respect for them is enormous. President Reagan also commands the
world's respect, as does Margaret Thatcher, prime minister of
Great Britain. Yet neither would ever think of being armed. If
what Machiavelli said was true in the early 1500s, it is pretty
clear that it is not true today.

Defini-
tion

All this basically translates into a question of whether
a leader should be virtuous. I suppose the definition of
<u>virtuous</u> would differ with different people, but I think of it
as holding a moral philosophy that you try to live by. No one
is ever completely virtuous, but I think a president ought to
try to be so. That means the president ought to tell the truth,
since that is one of the basic virtues. The cardinal virtues--
which were the same in Machiavelli's time as in ours--are justice,
prudence, fortitude, and temperance. In a president, the virtue
of justice is absolutely a must, or else what America stands for
is lost. We definitely want our president to be prudent, to use
good judgment, particularly in this nuclear age, when acts of
imprudence could get us blown up. Fortitude, the ability to
stand up for what is right, is a must for our president. Temperance is also important; we do not want a drunk for a president,
nor do we want anyone with excessive bad habits.

Conclu-
sion

It seems to me that a president who was armed or who emphasized arms in the way Machiavelli appears to mean would be
threatening injustice (the way Stalin did) and implying intemperance, like many armed world leaders. When I consider this
issue, I cannot think of any vice that our president ought to

possess at any time. Injustice, imprudence, cowardice, and
intemperance are, for me, unacceptable. Maybe Machiavelli was
thinking of deception and lying as necessary evils, but they
are a form of injustice, and no competent president--no president
who was truly virtuous--would need them. Prudence and fortitude
are the two virtues most essential for diplomacy. The president
who has those virtues will govern well and uphold our basic values.

The range of this essay is controlled and expresses a viewpoint that is focused and coherent. This is a brief essay, about 1,000 words. It illustrates each of the methods of development discussed in the text and shows how it helps further the argument. The writer takes issue with an aspect of Machiavelli and presents an argument based on personal opinion, but it is bolstered by reference to example and to an analysis of current political conditions as they compare with those of Machiavelli's time. A longer essay could have gone more deeply into any of the issues raised in any single paragraph, and it could have studied more closely the views of a specific president, such as Ronald Reagan, who opposed stricter gun control laws even after he had been shot.

The range of the selections in this volume is great. They represent a considerable breadth and constitute a significant introduction to thought in many areas. They are especially useful for stimulating our own thought and ideas. Obviously, there are no absolute rules for how to do this. But observing how serious writers work and how they apply rhetorical methods in their writing is one of the ways to begin our own development as writers. The suggestions for essays following each selection provide guides that can be useful for learning from these writers, who encourage our learning and reward our study.

Acknowledgments (continued from page iv)

Simone de Beauvoir. "The Psychoanalytic Point of View." From *The Second Sex* by Simone de Beauvoir, translated and edited by H. M. Parshley. Copyright 1952 by Alfred A. Knopf, Inc. Reprinted by permission of the publisher.

Mary Daly. "The Qualitative Leap Beyond Patriarchal Religion." Originally appeared in *Quest* magazine, Vol. I, No. 4, Spring 1975. Reprinted by permission of the author.

Loren Eiseley. "The Last Neanderthal." From *The Unexpected Universe.* Copyright © 1969 by Loren Eiseley. Reprinted by permission of Harcourt Brace Jovanovich, Inc.

Sigmund Freud. "Infantile Sexuality." From *The Basic Writings of Sigmund Freud,* translated and edited by Dr. A. A. Brill. Copyright 1938, copyright © renewed 1965 by Gioia B. Bernheim and Edmund R. Brill. Reprinted by permission. Originally from *Three Essays on the Theory of Sexuality* (1905).

John Kenneth Galbraith. "The Position of Poverty." From *The Affluent Society,* Fourth Edition, by John Kenneth Galbraith. Copyright © 1958, 1969, 1976, 1984 by John Kenneth Galbraith. Reprinted by permission of Houghton Mifflin Company.

Stephen Jay Gould. "Nonmoral Nature." With permission from *Natural History,* Vol. 91, No. 2. Copyright by the American Museum of Natural History, 1982.

Karen Horney. "The Distrust Between the Sexes." Speech read before the Berlin-Brandenburg Branch of the German Women's Medical Association on November 20, 1930 as "Das Misstrauen zwischen den Geschlechtern." *Die Ärztin,* VII (1931), pp. 5–12. Reprinted in translation with the permission of the Karen Horney Estate.

Carl Jung. "Anima and Animus." From *Aspects of the Feminine,* translated by R. F. C. Hull. Bollingen Series 20, Vol. 27. Copyright © 1982 by Princeton University Press. Excerpt, pp. 85–100, reprinted with permission of Princeton University Press.

John Maynard Keynes. "The End of Laissez-Faire." Extract from Vol. 9, *Essays in Persuasion* in *Collected Writings* by John Maynard Keynes. Reprinted by permission of the Royal Economic Society and Macmillan, London and Basingstoke.

Martin Luther King, Jr. "Letter from Birmingham Jail" (April 16, 1963). From *Why We Can't Wait* by Martin Luther King, Jr. Copyright © 1963, 1964 by Martin Luther King, Jr. Reprinted by permission of Harper & Row, Publishers, Inc.

Thomas Kuhn. "The Essential Tension: Tradition and Innovation in Scientific Research." From *The Third (1959) University of Utah Research Conference on the Identification of Scientific Talent (1959).* Permission granted by the University of Utah Press.

Susanne K. Langer. "Expressiveness." Originally titled "Expressiveness and Symbolism." Reprinted with permission of Macmillan Publishing Company from *Problems of Art* by Susanne K. Langer. Copyright © 1957 by Susanne K. Langer; copyright renewed 1985 by Leonard Langer.

Lao-Tzu. "Thoughts from the *Tao Te Ching.*" Excerpted from *Tao Te Ching,* translated by D. C. Lao. Viking Penguin, London, 1978. Reprinted by permission of Viking Penguin Ltd.

Lucretius. "Matter and Space." From *On the Nature of the Universe,* translated by R. E. Latham. Penguin Classics, London, 1951. Copyright © R. E. Latham 1951. Reprinted by the permission of Viking Penguin Ltd., London.

Niccolò Machiavelli. "The Qualities of the Prince." From *The Portable Machiavelli,* translated by Mark Musa and Peter Bondanella. Copyright © 1979 by Viking Penguin Inc. All rights reserved. Reprinted by permission of Viking Penguin, a division of Penguin Books USA, Inc.

Friedrich Nietzsche. "Apollonianism and Dionysianism." From *The Birth of Tragedy and the Genealogy of Morals* by Friedrich Nietzsche, translated by Francis Golffing. Copyright © 1956 by Doubleday, a division of Bantam Doubleday Dell Publishing Group, Inc.

José Ortega y Gasset. "Dehumanization in Modern Art." From *The Dehumanization of Art and Other Essays on Art, Culture, and Literature,* translated by Helen Weyl. Copyright 1948, © 1968, 1976 renewed by Princeton University Press. Excerpt, pp. 14–32, reprinted by permission of Princeton University Press.

Jean Jacques Rousseau. "The Origin of Civil Society." From *Social Contract: Essays by Locke, Hume, and Rousseau,* edited by Sir Ernest Baker, translated by Gerald Hopkins (1947). Reprinted by permission of Oxford University Press.

Siddhārtha Gautama, the Buddha. "Meditation: Path to Enlightenment." Excerpted from *Buddhist Scriptures*, translated by Edward Conze (Penguin Classics, 1959). Reprinted by the permission of Viking Penguin Ltd., London. Copyright © 1959 by Edward Conze.

B. F. Skinner. "What Is Man?" From *Beyond Freedom and Dignity* by B. F. Skinner. Copyright © 1971 by B. F. Skinner. Reprinted by permission of Alfred A. Knopf, Inc.

Susan Sontag. "Against Interpretation." From *Against Interpretation* by Susan Sontag. Copyright © 1961, 1962, 1963, 1964, 1965, 1966 by Susan Sontag. Reprinted with permission of Farrar, Straus & Giroux, Inc.

Simone Weil. "Spiritual Autobiography." Reprinted by permission of the Putnam Publishing Group from *Waiting for God* by Simone Weil. Copyright © 1959, 1979 by G.P. Putnam's Sons.

Virginia Woolf. "A Letter to a Young Poet." From *The Death of the Moth and Other Essays* by Virginia Woolf. Copyright 1942 by Harcourt Brace Jovanovich, Inc.; renewed 1970 by Marjorie T. Parsons, Executrix. Reprinted by permission of Harcourt Brace Jovanovich, Inc., the Virginia Woolf Estate, and the Hogarth Press.

INDEX OF
RHETORICAL TERMS

To the Student

We regularly revise the books we publish in order to make them better. To do this well we need to know what instructors and students think of the previous edition. At some point your instructor will be asked to comment on *A World of Ideas,* Third Edition; now we would like to hear from you.

Please take a few minutes to rate the selections and complete this questionnaire. Send it to Bedford Books of St. Martin's Press, 29 Winchester Street, Boston, Massachusetts 02116. We promise to listen to what you have to say. Thanks.

School _____

School Location (city, state) _____

Course title _____

Instructor's name _____

	Definitely Keep	Probably Keep	Uncertain	Drop	Not Assigned
Part One					
Lao-Tzu	___	___	___	___	___
Machiavelli	___	___	___	___	___
Rousseau	___	___	___	___	___
Jefferson	___	___	___	___	___
Wollstonecraft	___	___	___	___	___
Douglass	___	___	___	___	___
Thoreau	___	___	___	___	___
King	___	___	___	___	___
Part Two					
Marx	___	___	___	___	___
Gilman	___	___	___	___	___
Veblen	___	___	___	___	___
Keynes	___	___	___	___	___
Galbraith	___	___	___	___	___
Part Three					
Freud	___	___	___	___	___
Jung	___	___	___	___	___
Horney	___	___	___	___	___
Skinner	___	___	___	___	___
Beauvoir	___	___	___	___	___

	Definitely Keep	Probably Keep	Uncertain	Drop	Not Assigned
Part Four					
Lucretius	—	—	—	—	—
Bacon	—	—	—	—	—
Darwin	—	—	—	—	—
Kuhn	—	—	—	—	—
Eiseley	—	—	—	—	—
Gould	—	—	—	—	—
Part Five					
Buddha	—	—	—	—	—
Plato	—	—	—	—	—
Marcus Aurelius	—	—	—	—	—
St. Augustine	—	—	—	—	—
Nietzsche	—	—	—	—	—
Weil	—	—	—	—	—
Daly	—	—	—	—	—
Part Six					
Aristotle	—	—	—	—	—
Ortega y Gasset	—	—	—	—	—
Woolf	—	—	—	—	—
Langer	—	—	—	—	—
Sontag	—	—	—	—	—

Did you find the introductions to each selection helpful? How can we improve them? (Please use additional paper if necessary.)

_____

_____

Did your instructor assign the general introduction to the text? If so, did you find it useful?

_____

_____

Any general comments?

_____

_____

Name _____ Date _____

Address _____